The Sydney Morning Herald

good food guide 2010

Simon Thomsen & Joanna Savill

PENGUIN BOOKS

The editors offer silver-plated thanks to the extraordinary people who make this book possible: our wise and tasty reviewing team, especially regional editor Angie Schiavone; the smart, sharp and ever reliable Paul McLean; Caroline Lowry, Yemee Fernandes and Simon Bates; Scott Bolles and Helen Greenwood; our Melbourne colleague Janne Apelgren; Shane Brady for spit and polish; Richard Birch for photography; Jocelyn Hungerford, Megan Pigott, Ingrid Ohlsson and the Penguinettes; Les Schirato and the Vittoria Coffee team. Simon especially sends his love and gratitude to the amazingly supportive and understanding Sally Webb for six years of waving her husband off to dinner most evenings. Big hugs to Archie and Lulu, who have excellent table manners and love restaurants. Thanks also to Oma and Opa for their untiring love and pride. Lily Rose and Milena earn Joanna's applause for (finally) learning to cook, clean and wash up properly in what has been a far too busy year for their mum. And to Giuliano, steadfast arbiter of taste, wine nerd and unfailingly excellent master of the stove, un bacione grosso.

• •

PENGUIN BOOKS

Published by the Penguin Group
Penguin Group (Australia)
250 Camberwell Road, Camberwell, Victoria 3124, Australia
(a division of Pearson Australia Group Pty Ltd)

Penguin Books Ltd, Registered Offices: 80 Strand, London WC2R 0RL, England

First published by Penguin Group (Australia), 2009

1 3 5 7 9 10 8 6 4 2

Copyright © Fairfax Media Publications Pty Ltd, 2009
1 Darling Island Road, Pyrmont NSW 2009
The Sydney Morning Herald is a registered trademark of Fairfax Media Publications Pty Ltd
The Sydney Morning Herald Good Food Guide is a registered trademark of Fairfax Media Publications Pty Ltd
Internal photographs copyright © Richard Birch, 2009

The moral right of the authors has been asserted

All rights reserved. Without limiting the rights under copyright reserved above, no part of this publication may be reproduced, stored in or introduced into a retrieval system, or transmitted, in any form or by any means (electronic, mechanical, photocopying, recording or otherwise), without the prior written permission of both the copyright owner and the above publisher of this book.

Cover design by Megan Pigott © Penguin Group (Australia)
Text design by Ann Loveday, The Sydney Morning Herald, and Megan Pigott, Penguin Group (Australia)
Internal photographs by Richard Birch, except page 300 by Dean Cambray
Photographs taken at Ash St Cellar, bills, Braza, Cafe Giulia, Churrascaria, Delicado Foods, Deus Cafe, Ju-Rin, Lucio's, Margan, Morpeth Sourdough, Palace Chinese, Plan B, Roberts, Rockpool Bar & Grill, Time to Vino, Wall Cafe
Artwork on page xiv–xv from Wall Cafe by Greg Paton and Keith Shreeve and used with permission of artists

Maps by Country Cartographics
Hat logo design by David Band. The Hat logo is a registered trademark of Fairfax Media Publications Pty Limited
Typeset in Frutiger Light by Post Pre-press Group, Brisbane, Queensland
Colour reproduction by Splitting Image, Clayton, Victoria
Printed and bound in Australia by BPA Print Group Pty Ltd

Production Editor, Sydney – Paul McLean
Publisher, Commercial – Caroline Lowry

For advertising enquiries for *The Sydney Morning Herald Good Food Guide 2011*,
please contact Fairfax Books on (02) 9282 2514.

ISBN 9780143011552

penguin.com.au

Contents

Meet the Editors	vi	Hunter Valley	214
Introduction	vii	Central Coast & Newcastle	230
About the Book	x	South Coast	242
Stayers	xii	Southern Highlands	256
Awards	xiv	North Coast	265
Stop Press	xvi	The West	284

City + Suburbs 1

Bars & Cafes 155

Global Gems 165

10 of the Best 175
Breakfasts 176
Guilty Pleasures 178
Sushi 180
Yum Cha 182
Green Eateries 184

Regional 186
Blue Mountains 187
Canberra & Snow Regions 197

Interstate 300

Index 310
Alphabetical 311
Cuisine 315
BYO 317
Dine and Stay 318
Late-night Dining 318
New Entries 318
Private Rooms 319
Vegetarian 319
Wheelchair Access 320

Maps 324

Meet the Editors

Simon Thomsen, co-editor
Simon was restaurant critic for *The Sydney Morning Herald* for almost four years. This is his sixth edition as co-editor of *The Sydney Morning Herald Good Food Guide*. He used to cook professionally before turning his hand to writing, and has spent the past 14 years as a *Good Food Guide* reviewer. He thinks the conversation across a table is the best and most important part of any meal, which is why he'll always have a soft spot for Fratelli Paradiso, because he met his wife over the calamari Sant' Andrea. Simon now plans to cook at home a little bit more, but still loves it when others do the washing up.

Joanna Savill, co-editor
Joanna Savill has been travelling, eating and writing about it for rather longer than she'll admit. In the course of her travels – first as a trainee translator and later as a TV reporter – she has tasted everything from Macedonian kebabs to witjuti grub risotto. Focussing on Sydney's amazing food scene, especially over the last three years as co-editor of this guide, has been a particular joy. Her next big task is to show it off to the world, as director of the inaugural Sydney International Food Festival (October 2009 and annually thereafter, www.siff.com.au).

Angie Schiavone, regional editor
Angie's life has revolved around food even more than usual this year. In between scouring regional New South Wales for the best dining on offer, she's spent hours in the kitchen with her nonni, compiling a family recipe book. She wishes her Italian was better, but usually the food does the talking. This is Angie's second year as regional editor, but she's been part of the team since 2005.

Other reviewers
City Jeanine Bribosia, Anthony Dennis, Hugh Fitzhardinge, Molly Foskett, Guy Griffin, Amanda Hooton, Anthony Huckstep, Fouad Kassab, Catherine Keenan, Sally Lewis, Les Luxford, Sarah Macdonald, Paul McLean, Lyndey Milan, Akiko Mori Ganivet, Roberta Muir, Lynne Mullins, Sarah Nicholson, Danielle Oppermann, Sunita Patradoon-Ho, Philip Putnam, Lauren Quaintance, John Saxby, Angie Schiavone, Barbara Sweeney, Paul van Reyk, Pui Sing Wong, Stephanie Wood

Regional Jeanine Bribosia, Victoria Cosford, Bruce Elder, Hugh Fitzhardinge, Molly Foskett, Adelaide Harris, Amanda Hooton, Belinda Jeffery, Fouad Kassab, Catherine Keenan, Sally Lewis, Liz Love, Sarah MacDonald, Paul McLean, James Mayson, Danielle Oppermann, Sunita Patradoon-Ho, Philip Putnam, Joanna Savill, Angie Schiavone, Rosemary Stanton, Barbara Sweeney, Simon Thomsen, Paul van Reyk

Wine list judges Stuart Gregor, Huon Hooke, Chris Morrison, Simon Thomsen

Introduction

The Sydney Morning Herald Good Food Guide is celebrating its silver anniversary. That's 25 years of great eating, and 25 years of editors dedicated to the cause of celebrating the best of Sydney's food.

We thought it was time to reminisce.

Simon Thomsen & Joanna Savill
July 2009

Leo Schofield (1984–93)

I blame it on Anne O'Donovan. As publisher of *The Age Good Food Guide* (yes, for once Melbourne beat Sydney to the punch) she was keen to reach out to the less enlightened Sydney dining public. For eight years she wheedled, coaxed, cajoled, bludgeoned or beat copy out of me while still managing to remain a treasured friend, even to this day. Her trusty lieutenant, Margaret Barrett, reinforced the notion instilled in me by one of my *Herald* subs that everyone needs a good editor. I did the first eight editions and got off the restaurant roundabout before boredom set in. Not to mention obesity.

I'm proud of the publication and its subsequent success under a string of eminent colleagues who continue to chronicle the splendours and miseries but mostly the mighty advance of our food culture.

Jenna Price (1984–85)

If the chic Melbourne publisher Anne O'Donovan hadn't cornered the *Herald*'s editor-in-chief Vic Carroll, there would be no *Good Food Guide* today. She told him that it had worked in Melbourne, would work in Sydney and would hardly cost a cent. At least two of those things were true. The other thing I remember was riotous disagreements about which cuisine ruled: French (Leo) or Italian (David Dale and me).

My most vivid memory was campaigning over two years to get Steve Manfredi's first gig, The Restaurant, a hat. He was the closest thing we had to Alice Waters, who remains my favourite chef. And then, of course, I hit the babymaking years and discovered what Edmund Capon meant when he recommended McDonald's: "The first tumultuous bite into a Big Mac is eternally a moment of ecstasy."

We should also commemorate the people who checked every tiny little thing in the *Guide*: Margaret Barrett, the editor and forensic investigator supreme. Long may her standards live. And to Eric Beecher, whose enthusiasm for the task, all tasks really, funnelled everyone's energy into the product.

David Dale (1984)

The first *Good Food Guide* came out as Sydney was approaching the peak of the Greed is Good decade, when businessmen needed to prove they had money to burn, and restaurateurs were eager to help them. As I wrote in one review: "Nothing succeeds like excess."

The fad was France: 67 restaurants were described as French in that first *Guide* (compared to 36 in the 2009 edition). Pretentious chefs had not yet discovered foam or truffle oil, but they'd read about "nouvelle cuisine" and most of them thought it meant replicating a Matisse on the plate.

Slices of tamarillo and kiwifruit were helpful for colour effects. Menu language such as "mousseline", "noisettes", "feuillete", "sabayon", "quenelles" and "en croute" convinced the expense-account showoffs your place was worth the investment. As further reassurance, the *Guide* ended each review with the names of VIPs who frequented the restaurant – Alan Bond liked Berowra Waters Inn, Daryl Somers liked the Manor House in Balmain, Carla Zampatti liked Our Pleasure in the city, John Laws liked Darcy's in Paddington.

John Amy (1986–1988)

The truly long lunch was a very blokey thing but it was great fun. In the 1980s we went to lunch every day without fail. Blokes used to fight to get the bill because it was tax deductible. That all changed in September 1985. Dire predictions were made that FBT would kill the restaurant trade, but places like Oasis Seros and Tre Scalini still opened – and went gangbusters. But workplaces became so boring! In 1984 Montana sauvignon blanc was the only Kiwi wine on any restaurant list. Now you can't move for sav blancs and pinot noirs from Marlborough, Hawkes Bay and Central Otago. When the 1986 edition went to press, I looked and felt like Robert de Niro in *Raging Bull*, punch-drunk from too much eating out. Tightening copy to a 120-word limit was tough. Surf 'n' turf eateries were a doddle but more creative menus ("medallions of pork encrusted with sesame seeds in aniseed-flavoured juices with fruit chutney") meant that after three dishes you were almost out of space.

Michael Dowe (1988–1993)

Looking back, there is much that we trumpeted that I still feel positive about today. First, some comfort stations: Buon Ricordo, Lucio's and Marigold. Secondly, a meteor: Prasit Prateeprasen. He revolutionised our notions of Thai cuisine. His mainstays were chunky herbs, vegetables and chillies that initially seemed like a touch of napalm. His signature ingredient was sour tamarind. These incredibly vibrant flavours were a far cry from the culture of coconut cream and sugar.

Then there was the diamond – Tetsuya Wakuda. At the start of our watch, he was in Ultimo, known only among the cognoscenti for meticulously crafted creme brulee. By the time we handed over the baton, he was in Rozelle, astonishing clients with a masterful, inspired salmon confit.

Today you will find that dish all over the world as confit of ocean trout. And internationally, Tetsuya Wakuda is Australia's best known chef.

Helen Greenwood (1994–95)

In 1995, the *Guide* celebrated a decade. Restaurants were booming, Kings Cross and Darlinghurst were new grazing zones and Sydney dining was so complex we introduced maps.

A recession had bitten hard (nothing new) and the next generation of chefs needed cheap ways to launch a career. The cafe-bistro became the place where the customers could be casual but the food never was. (Sean Moran, take a bow.)

A memorable moment was giving the Josephine Pignolet Award to a quiet, impressive young apprentice called Mark Best. Also memorable was the way Janni Kyritsis could turn a pig's ear into a heavenly purse of crisp strips. (We miss you, Janni.) Both men, by the way, were former electricians.

Hotel dining was hot. Asian was cool. Food was stacked high. Chefs were leaving cramped quarters for designer dining rooms. But bars were a long way off.

We said hello to balsamic vinegar, sourdough bread, wood-fired pizza and Mid-East-meets-Med cooking. We waved goodbye to kumera chips, fusion food and char-grilled everything. The words "regional" and "seasonal" became part of everyday language. And the *Good Food Guide* convinced the dining public that there was such a thing as modern Australian cuisine.

William Fraser (1994–95)

Co-editor Helen Greenwood and I juggled budgets, schedules and more-than-full-time jobs, and recruited colleagues, friends and family to cover the territory. My lasting memory was marvelling that the *Guide* appeared at all, given the minuscule budgets and scant support. It was a labour of love and Anne O'Donovan was a gracious presence throughout.

My most memorable episode was deciding which of two finalists would win the Newcomer of the Year award. One was a worthy possibility

and the other the much-hyped current talk-of-the-town that prided itself on not taking bookings. We tried to get a table (as usual without divulging who we were) and a staff member dismissively told us we didn't have a hope. The other restaurant won the award.

Neither lasted long.

Jill Dupleix and Terry Durack (1996–2001)

If you graphed Sydney dining for the last six years of the twentieth century, it would run a straight line to the top right-hand corner. In that time, we saw the restaurant industry turn from Am to Pro. A motley bunch of young chefs and restaurateurs got serious about food, wine, interior design and marketing. They started doing television, writing cookbooks and creating brands. Both the industry and the *Guide* prospered. In a way, we all grew up together, surviving the introduction of GST, smoking bans, the 2000 Olympic Games and a little hiccup that became known as the "Chefs' Letter", calling for the dismissal of the editors following the removal of Rockpool's third hat in the 2000 edition.

The high points: the end of the North Shore restaurant famine, Circular Quay and Finger Wharf, then-Premier Bob Carr's *Good Food Guide* launch speeches, the 1999 Josephine Pignolet Award won by Brett Graham, Pond's basil-infused tuna, Claude's beetroot-cured salmon, Mario's wood-fired pizza, Golden Century's XO chilli clams, BBQ King's duck, Rockpool's date tart, bills' scrambled eggs, Longrain's eggnets, Sailors Thai's pad Thai, Banc's basil and sweetcorn soup, De Beers' (Peter Gilmore's) five textures of Valrhona chocolate cake, Infinity bread, unoaked chardonnay, Illabo lamb, Yamba prawns, Wallis Lake oysters, and the first ever cultivated Australian truffles from Tasmania.

The low points: rancid butter, over-filled wine glasses, bland background music, wine lists without vintages, new restaurant names ripped off from overseas, gratuitous garnishing, food (other than soup) in deep bowls, fluffy bread, fluffy coffee, fish knives, sports cars in dining rooms, the inability of waiters to pronounce bruschetta or spell Caesar salad, having to ask for a glass of water, pasteurised cheeses, and sticky toffee pudding and oxtail in 40-degree heat.

Lisa Hudson (2002–04)

In post-Olympics Sydney, restaurants were at last gaining recognition as being among the world's best. The modern French bistro was booming and panna cotta had become the new sticky date pud. We celebrated Guillaume's arrival at Bennelong and the opening of Becasse, est. and Icebergs. Sommeliers were at last lauded for their expertise. There was talk of an economic slowdown (but we hadn't seen anything yet) and we reeled in the aftermath of 9/11. And a waiter told me, as I pored over a menu wondering what to order for a *Good Food Guide* review, that I must be hungry as I'd already started on my fingernails.

So many experiences, friendships, fun… and fear as launch night approached. Condensing three years of The *Good Food Guide* into a couple of paragraphs is as tough as the gig itself. Perhaps it's best to say simply that to have been involved in Sydney's restaurant culture – one that still makes me immensely proud – was a huge pleasure and an honour indeed.

Matthew Evans (2002–06)

Who'd want to be a restaurant reviewer anywhere else? Brilliant French, amazing Italian, wonderful Vietnamese, Chinese, Turkish and Indian? Dining in Sydney could never be called boring with such a melting pot and the sublime local creations that come out of it. If anything, my time was marked by quite of lot of daring in top-end kitchens, one hallmark of truly world-class dining. This culinary brinkmanship has its inherent risks, but also carries with it the possibility of perfection.

Low points included a lack of affordable, personal restaurants springing from the owner's imagination. Where were the intimate expressions of Sydney style rather than formulaic restaurants boasting hard surfaces, carbon-copy menus and over-handled food? And at times Sydney seemed more hung up on celebrity chefs than the quality of their restaurants' cooking. Oh – and defamation laws that treat the public like idiots.

Simon Thomsen (2005–10)

Technology is changing our meals. A decade after Ferran Adria moved on from foams, Sydney chefs fell under the Spaniard's thrall and spherification became the rage. Kitchens now look like NASA labs with vacuum sealers for sous vide cooking, a Pacojet for ice cream, a Thermomix, dehydrators and liquid hydrogen. But it hasn't stopped a simple, classic steak and chips remaining a top seller.

Meanwhile, restaurants became internet-savvy, with websites and email lists and daily specials appearing on Twitter. Every diner with a blog and digital camera became a critic.

The *Guide* went online too, but continued to be a best seller in print. The regional section grew and more restaurants scored 12/20 than we could fit in the book. Just as $50 entrees arrived, restaurants got cheaper. The recession revived meal deals. Sub-$30 mains and BYO made comebacks. We abandoned three-course meals to graze, or went the whole hog with degustations.

We became sophisticated about beef, cheese, wine and other ingredients. Mineral water turned into bling. Dinner conversations were interrupted by waiters delivering a thesis on each dish.

Sustainability came to the fore. Kitchen gardens, organics and recycling became part of the recipe. Thankfully, small producers are usurping factory-farmed animals grown for convenience rather than flavour. The biggest of bogeymen, GM food, still battles for a place at the table. That fight isn't over.

Cath Keenan (2007)

In 2007, Sydney caught Italian fever. New ristoranti popped up everywhere. Surry Hills, especially, was awash in house-made pasta and ragu. The most successful arrivals were not big or glitzy. Like our favourite Mediterranean restaurant that year, Vini, they were small and affordable, with short menus of fresh, home-style food. Many loved them; many imitated them. Viva Italia!

Meanwhile, there is nothing wrong with salt and pepper squid or caramelised pork belly. Both can be fine dishes. But our hearts sank as they turned up on every menu, alongside the mandatory chicken, confit duck leg and steak. Sure, give diners what they like. But coax us to discover new things to like too.

Joanna Savill (2008–10)

Bringing up the rear on 25 years' worth of words has been a mammoth challenge (and a lot of dinners). 2008 was the shock of the same: pork belly, panna cotta, veloutes, purees and foams on almost every plate. With chocolate brown the restaurant hue du jour, there were times when even the decor became interchangeable. Everyone became a reviewer (in print, online and even on telly) but the Us and Them chasm – between diner plebs and prominent food celebs – grew wider.

Many have since lifted their service game. They're also sourcing better produce, stocking more NSW wines and serving excellent cheese. Our Asian expertise has reached new highs, with great Korean and even better Japanese. We went tapas, pizza and bakery mad. And everyone still loves Italian. We introduced Global Gems to celebrate the more casual eateries everyone loves to discover, and *Guide* sales were at an all-time high. Thanks for dining with us.

About the Book

How we review
Every scored restaurant in the *Good Food Guide* has been visited anonymously in the past 12 months by at least one reviewer. We pay for our meal in full and sample at least four dishes, if not five or six. Each three-hat candidate is visited numerous times, likewise many of the two-hatters. We visit many more restaurants than will fit into this book. If we wouldn't feel comfortable recommending a restaurant to a friend, we won't include it. In total we visit more than 500 restaurants throughout New South Wales to publish more than 420 reviews.

Feedback
We welcome your recommendations and comments. Email goodfoodguide@smh.com.au. Send us a Tweet at www.twitter.com/goodfoodguide or write to The Sydney Morning Herald Good Food Guide, GPO Box 506, Sydney or Sydney NSW 2000.

Bill
We want to let you know how much eating out will cost, so we've listed the range of prices for entree (**E**), main (**M**) and dessert (**D**). Some places have set prices, higher prices (or minimum spends) on weekends or degustation menus, so we've tried to include those too. Remember, though, that this is only an indication, typically based on dinner, and we don't include share plates, oysters by the dozen, live seafood or cheese plates, as they tend to skew the results. Meanwhile, credit card surcharges are becoming commonplace, so this year we've listed them to give you some advance warning.

Wine
Wine is a very important part of dining out, so we've given you a user-friendly description of the wine list for each restaurant as well as the cost of BYO. Corkage is either per person (e.g. $2 pp) or per bottle. Most of the restaurants in this *Guide* are BYO for bottled wine only – no beer, spirits or casks. Restaurants are listed in the index as BYO only if they allow BYO all the time. A wineglass symbol indicates a particularly good wine list.

Wheelchair access
Using information supplied to us by the restaurants, we cite wheelchair access only if accessible toilets are also provided. If in doubt, call ahead.

Child friendly
Most restaurants welcome (well-behaved) children. Some go to an extra effort with kids' menus, high chairs and things to entertain, so we list them as 'child friendly'. If we don't mention it, that doesn't necessarily mean they don't welcome kids, but best ring and check.

Bookings
Bookings are recommended for all restaurants that take them. We mention it only if a restaurant regards it as essential or if they are not accepted at all.

Vegetarian
Not everyone wants to eat meat, so we've singled out places that go to extra effort to cater for plant eaters, but that doesn't mean the others don't serve vegetarian food. Most restaurants offer at least one meat-free entree and main. Best call ahead of time if you have any issues or dietary restrictions.

Late-night dining
Everyone has a different definition of 'late'; we have listed restaurants as open late in the index only if the kitchen is open after 10.30pm.

And…
Because we want to provide as much information as we can, this is to let you know something incidental, interesting and hopefully useful, but not necessarily essential.

Accuracy
We check the information in the *Guide* numerous times, but things still come unstuck if a restaurant closes suddenly or changes its pricing, chef or opening times. This is, unfortunately, beyond our control.

The scores
Apart from our chef's-hat ratings, we score restaurants out of 20 to give you a more useful sense of their merits. The score comprises 10 points for food, 5 for service, 3 for ambience, with an extra 2 points possible for a sprinkling of magic, whether it's a great location, stunning service or food that is sublime beyond belief. Places scoring less than 12/20 are not included.

12	Reasonable
13	Some respectable highlights
14	A solid, enjoyable experience
15	♟ Reliably good
16	♟♟ A bit of that WOW factor
17	♟♟ Amazingly good
18	♟♟♟ World class
19	♟♟♟ Truly spectacular
20	♟♟♟ Perfection on a plate

Awards

Besides the chef's hats, we have other awards designed to recognise greatness. Some awards are self-explanatory, the others are listed below.

Vittoria Coffee Restaurant of the Year – a place that has shown remarkable energy and consistency and sets a standard others should aspire to.

Chef of the Year – for a talented individual in the kitchen, and not necessarily the head chef of an award-winning restaurant, whom we believe to be on the rise.

Best Regional Restaurant – the best in the bush or on a beach, but certainly beyond Sydney.

Editors' Picks – these are restaurants we love to eat at when we're spending our own money, for the simple joy of dining out.

Sydney Fish Markets Best Seafood Restaurant – for a restaurant that demonstrates a commitment to quality seafood, showcasing it in inventive ways.

Star City Award for Professional Excellence – for long-term contribution to the restaurant industry.

Brown Brothers Wine List of the Year – it's not about size, but how well a wine list fits with a restaurant's setting and food. It offers diners accessible excitement and adventure.

Small Wine List of the Year – new award for a list of fewer than 100 bins (different wines), suited to the food and style of restaurant.

Regional Wine List of the Year – as above, outside of Sydney.

Sommelier of the Year Award – recognises an individual wine waiter whose knowledge and service style make drinking a pleasure.

Good Food Guide Sustainability Award – a new award, recognising the extra effort restaurants are going to in serving clean, green food and reducing their carbon footprint.

The Josephine Pignolet Best Young Chef – chosen by some of Sydney's leading chefs in memory of a great chef, it's the ultimate accolade for a passionate, talented young cook.

Silver Anniversary Stayer Award – To the restaurant and/or restaurateur who has rated a listing consistently over the last 25 years – a sign of great culinary fortitude.

Vittoria Legend Award – chosen by Les Schirato of Vittoria Coffee for an individual's outstanding contribution to the industry.

Symbols

★	An award-winning restaurant
♀	A particularly good wine list
	A new restaurant
	A restaurant featured previously, but not in the 2009 edition
🛏	Places where you can dine and stay the night afterwards
AE	American Express
DC	Diners Club
MC	MasterCard
V	Visa

good food guide xi

Stayers

It's not just our anniversary in 2010. There are a number of restaurants that have stayed the distance too. Some, like Claude's, have done so in style. Under a succession of owners, the tiny Woollahra landmark has consistently ranked highly – three hats for most of its history.

Beppi Polese is foremost among those who have been with us since the start, and then some. Beppi clocks up 54 years in business in 2010. A veritable institution and a worthy recipient of our Silver Anniversary Stayer Award.

Other big names dotted throughout the years include Bilson's, Bennelong and, returning to its former glory last year, Berowra Waters. And where would casual Sydney dining be without the Bayz?

Here's our list of those who were with us at the start, and who still make the grade in the 2010 edition.

25+

Art Gallery Restaurant, The Domain
Bennelong (now Guillaume at Bennelong), Sydney
Beppi's, East Sydney
Claude's, Paddington
Barrenjoey House, Palm Beach
Bayswater Brasserie, Kings Cross
Berowra Waters Inn, Berowra
Clareville Kiosk, Clareville
Courtney's Brasserie, Parramatta
Jaspers, Hunters Hill
Jonah's, Palm Beach
Kable's, Sydney
La Botte d'Oro, Leichhardt
La Grillade, Crows Nest
La Perla, Gladesville
Malaya, Sydney (then on George Street)
Marigold, Haymarket
Milsons, Kirribilli
Royal Bar & Grill, Paddington
Sails on Lavender Bay, McMahons Point
Summit, Sydney
The Wharf, Walsh Bay
Old George & Dragon, Maitland

20+

The Bathers' Pavilion, Balmoral
Bellevue Hotel, Paddington
Buon Ricordo, Paddington
Four in Hand, Paddington
Golden Century, Sydney
Il Perugino, Mosman
Lucio's, Paddington
Machiavelli, Sydney
Macleay Street Bistro, Potts Point
Quay (then Bilson's), Circular Quay
Riverview Hotel, Balmain
Rockpool, The Rocks
Szechaun Garden, St Leonards
Tetsuya's (then in Rozelle), Sydney
Lorenzo's Diner, Wollongong

15+

Arun Thai, Potts Point
Bistro Moncur, Paddington
Cottage Point Inn, Cottage Point
Dov at Delectica, Potts Point
Fook Yuen, Chatswood
Forty One, Sydney
Galileo, Millers Point
Neptune Palace, Circular Quay
Perama, Petersham
Pier, Rose Bay
Ratu Sari, Kingsford
Regal, Sydney
Sean's Panaroma, Bondi
Sea Treasure, Crows Nest
Roberts, Hunter Valley
Ottoman Cuisine, Canberra
Darley's, Katoomba

Awards

Vittoria Coffee Restaurant of the Year
Quay, Circular Quay

Chef of the Year
Mark Best of Marque, Surry Hills

Best New Restaurant
Rockpool Bar & Grill, Sydney

Best Regional Restaurant
Darley's, Katoomba

The Star City Award for Professional Excellence
Peter Bowyer of Sailors Thai

***The Sydney Morning Herald* Silver Service Award**
Rachel McNabb of Restaurant Como, Blaxland

Silver Anniversary Stayer Award
Beppi's, East Sydney

Sommelier of the Year
Franck Moreau of Merivale

Brown Brothers Wine List of the Year
Pilu at Freshwater

Small Wine List of the Year
Bistrode, Surry Hills

Regional Wine List of the Year
Union Bank, Orange

The Josephine Pignolet Best Young Chef
Mitchell Orr of Sepia

Vittoria Legend Award
Mr John (John Hemmes) of Merivale

Sydney Fish Markets Best Seafood Restaurant
Pier, Rose Bay

Good Food Guide Sustainability Award
Billy Kwong, Surry Hills

Editors' Picks
Favourite Wine Bar – Ash St Cellar
Favourite Global Menu – Universal
Favourite Asian – Ju-Rin
Favourite Global Gem – Din Tai Fung
Favourite Bargain – Friday lunch at Marque
Favourite Extravagance – anything from Adriano Zumbo's Cafe Chocolat (and patisserie)
Favourite Cafe – Deus Cafe
Favourite Sushi - Yoshii

City

Bilson's, est., Marque, Pier, Quay, Tetsuya's

Aria, Assiette, Becasse, Bentley Restaurant & Bar, Berowra Waters Inn, Bistro Ortolan, Buon Ricordo, Claude's, Guillaume at Bennelong, Icebergs Dining Room and Bar, Lucio's, Pilu at Freshwater, Restaurant Balzac, Rockpool, Rockpool Bar & Grill, Sean's Panaroma, Universal

Altitude, Astral, Azuma, The Bathers' Pavilion Restaurant, Bird Cow Fish, Bistro Moncur, Bistrode, Blancharu, The Boathouse on Blackwattle Bay, Fish Face, Flying Fish, Forty One, Four in Hand Dining Room, Foveaux Restaurant + Bar, Galileo, Jonah's, L'étoile, Longrain, Oscillate Wildly, Otto Ristorante, Pendolino, Restaurant Arras, Sailors Thai Restaurant, Sepia, Yoshii

Regional

Darley's (Katoomba), Rock (Pokolbin)

Bacchus (Newcastle), Bamboo (Casuarina Beach), Bells at Killcare (Killcare Heights), Bistro Molines (Mount View), Caveau (Wollongong), Fins (South Kingscliff), Journeyman (Bowral), Katers (Sutton Forest), Lochiel House (Kurrajong Heights), Lolli Redini (Orange), Neila (Cowra), No. 2 Oak Street (Bellingen), The Old George & Dragon (East Maitland), Ottoman Cuisine (Barton), Pacific Dining Room (Byron Bay), Restaurant Como (Blaxland), Restaurant II (Newcastle), Satiate (Bangalow), sourcedining (Albury), Tonic (Millthorpe), Vulcans (Blackheath), Waters Edge (Parkes), Zest (Nelson Bay)

We would like to thank Vittoria Coffee for their generous support of The Sydney Morning Herald Good Food Guide *launch.*

Stop Press

Changes due as we go to press.

Carrington Place
132 Young Street, Carrington
Tel 4961 1116
The former Oriental Hotel in Newcastle has been reborn as a 14-bed boutique guesthouse with a bar, a cafe serving tapas-style fare and a dining room serving popular old favourites, including caesar salad, prawn cocktail, pizza and pasta, but the highlight is beef cooked in the stone hearth oven.

Eleven Kitchen & Cellar
11 Lime Street, King St Wharf
Tel 9290 3500
Some remember Jeff Schroeter for Eat City, others for his more recent residency at Bayswater Brasserie. This new venture is a two-in-one mix of laidback European dining space with food to share upstairs and a downstairs waterside wine bar. Due September 2009.

Grand National
161 Underwood Street, Paddington
Tel 9363 3096
We love this classy pub bistro, year in and year out, and think chef Ian Oakes is a genius, but the Grand Nash is missing this year because renovation plans are afoot, meaning a long closure. The dates aren't set in concrete as we go to press, so call. You never know your luck.

Mai House
Imperial Gardens, 18 Myoora Road, Terrey Hills
This French colonial bistro by Berowra Waters' Dietmar Sawyere is set in three antique Sumatran teak "houses" around a traditional Oriental garden with koi ponds and water features. Mid-priced French bistro fare will be updated with Indochine flavours. Scheduled for late 2009.

Omerta
235 Victoria Road, Darlinghurst
Tel 9360 1011
A Tavola's Eugenio Maiale has turned the former Pellagio site opposite into an Italian-style enoteca (wine bar) with a relaxed range of Italian nibbles, from prosciutto to salt-cod fritters, meatballs, grilled eggplant with scamorza and tomato, and cotechino with peas. There's plenty to please on the wine list so join the omerta (Mafia term for code of silence) gang.

Poteno
358 Cleveland Street, Surry Hills
The Bodega boys are working on an Agentinian grill and barbecue restaurant at the old Dimitri's site (between Elizabeth and Crown streets) come February 2010.

Sake Restaurant & Bar
Argyle Precinct, 12 Argyle Street, The Rocks
Tel 9259 5600
Sushi guru Shaun Presland (ex Sushi e, Teppanyaki and Nobu) will head a modern Japanese venture in the Argyle heritage precinct from November 2009. Expect a blend of new-style sushi and classic Japanese dishes in a funky space with a sushi bar, low tables and communal dining, then choose from among 50 different sakes.

City + Suburbs

····· city + suburbs ·········•

a tavola

348 Victoria Street, Darlinghurst
Tel 9331 7871   Map 2

Italian

Score 14/20

The concept is simple: a huge family table, a simple spread of antipasti, bowls of pasta, lots of salads and buzz and ambience to burn. And did we mention the pasta? House-made strands of dough hang like quirky curtains around the spotlit front room with its dark corners and sexy ochre and white-crazed marble table. Daily fresh pasta specials are chalked on a blackboard. Out back in the always crowded courtyard, things are more raucous still. No wonder the kitchen sometimes struggles to keep pace and standards seem to have slipped. Braised swiss brown mushrooms and peas with a hint of mint and grated ricotta salata are family-style cosy; a salad of buffalo mozzarella, tomato, prosciutto and rocket classic yet contemporary. Fat eggplant and provola-stuffed tortellini shows the pasta maker's able hand, although uneven cooking spoiled the effect. Too much cooking did little for house-made stracci (rag pasta) tossed with calamari tubes, sultanas and chilli. But with fluffy zabaglione over fresh fruit, topped with acid-sweet vincotto, it's all happy families again.

Hours Lunch Fri noon–3pm; Dinner Mon–Thurs 6–10pm, Fri–Sat 6–11pm; bookings essential
Bill E $15–$19 **M** $22–$39 **D** $13–$15
Cards AE (+2.5%) V MC Eftpos
Wine All Italian, as concise and simple as the menu, 6 by the glass; BYO (corkage $15 a bottle)
Chef/owner Eugenio Maiale
Seats 65; private room; bar
Child friendly Small pasta portions available
www.atavola.com.au
And...a tavola is Italian for "come to the table"

Abhi's

163 Concord Road, North Strathfield
Tel 9743 3061   Map 6

Indian

Score 13.5/20

Turn your back on the Concord Road traffic, and on any prejudices you might have about a typical neighbourhood Indian. Abhi's has been breaking stereotypes for almost 20 years with its imaginative, regionally diverse menu served by affable, well-informed waiters. The chic interior has been renovated to keep up with Aki's, the trendier brother eatery down at Woolloomooloo Wharf. The two places have other things in common, too, such as the wonderfully crunchy palak patta chat – spinach leaves in lentil batter, covered with creamy yoghurt and dates, or chatpata squid – a spicy play on the salt-and-pepper classic, magically soft, lifted by tamarind and ginger. The delicacy of prawns and scallops is allowed to shine in Cochin curry, fragrant with mustard seeds and curry leaves, and perhaps India's answer to bouillabaisse. The light touch extends to desserts such as double ka meetha, a Moghul-influenced bread pudding doused with sugar syrup and served with rose petal ice-cream. This is a neighbourhood Indian worth travelling for.

Hours Lunch Sun–Fri noon–3pm; Dinner daily 6–10pm
Bill E $10.80–$18.80 **M** $16.80–$24.80 **D** $9.80–$10.80
Cards AE V MC
Wine Brief but well-chosen list of Australians; 8 by the glass; BYO (corkage $2.50pp)
Chefs Kumar Mahadevan & Ranjan Choudhury
Owners Kumar & Suba Mahadevan
Seats 180; private room; wheelchair access
Child friendly Highchairs
Vegetarian A third of the menu
www.abhisindian.com.au
And...knowledgeable waiters explain dish origins and offer wine-matching advice

city + suburbs

Aki's

1/6 Cowper Wharf Road, Woolloomooloo
Tel 9332 4600   Map 2

Indian
Score 13.5/20

Sydney awaits an Indian restaurant that can stand shoulder-to-slow-braised-shoulder with upmarket Thai, Italian or French, but Aki's aims high. The wharfside location with city skyline views is just right for vindaloo with a view. Take an outside table, with a Kingfisher beer and a shot glass full of crisp chickpea-battered okra – presentation here is well above what we've come to expect from Indian restaurants – and you'll wonder why you haven't been before. Sometimes consistency, on the plate and on the floor, can be found wanting. Aki's signature dish is a case in point: shredded blue swimmer crab meat tossed with black mustard seeds, fresh tomato and ginger, and served on string hoppers (discs of vermicelli), but with only the accompanying coconut broth providing a much needed flavour and aroma hit. Whole baby eggplant and banana chillies simmered in a peanut and browned coconut sauce demonstrate that spicing and sophistication can coexist happily. In a city more accustomed to butter chicken, Aki's exceeds expectations.

Hours Lunch Sun–Fri noon–3pm; Dinner daily 6–10pm
Bill E $10–$23 **M** $19–$29 **D** $13
Cards AE V MC
Wine Good range of New and Old World, well priced; some half-bottles; 13 by the glass
Chefs Kumar Mahadevan, Vikram Arumugam & Vijayan Ramasamy
Owners Kumar & Suba Mahadevan
Seats 150; outdoor seating; bar
Child friendly Highchairs
Vegetarian Plenty of options
www.akisindian.com.au
And…there's chocolate naan for dessert

Alio

5 Baptist Street, Redfern
Tel 8394 9368   Map 3b

Italian
Score 13/20

Alio performs one of the more interesting sleight-of-hand tricks of restaurant dining: the look doesn't match the food. The look is an inclined-to-be-echoey modernist room with big blocks of wall colour and a sharply right-angled bar. The food? The old-fashioned, warm, rounded flavours of Italy. Go on a busy night and enjoy stracciatella – Roman chicken broth soup with cheese ravioli – which is shimmeringly good and full of comfort food flavours. From among several entree dishes, the daily risotto, made to order, might feature a pungent and more-ish combination of gorgonzola and fresh sorrel. Alas, roasted barramundi with green asparagus and sauce vierge (a French dressing of herbs and tomatoes that's Italian at heart) was a little bland. Pappardelle with dark braised duck leg restores the faith, enlivened by fresh thyme and enriched by chestnuts. Vanilla bean panna cotta was slightly too firm and unyielding. But this is food made and served with care and enthusiasm by an assured brother–sister team.

Hours Dinner Mon–Sat 6–10pm; bookings essential
Bill E $18–$19 **M** $28–$32 **D** $14
Cards AE DC V MC Eftpos
Wine Brief, well-priced list; 15 by the glass; BYO (corkage $8 a bottle)
Chef Ashley Hughes
Owners Tracey & Ashley Hughes
Seats 90; private room; wheelchair access; bar
Vegetarian 4–6 options daily
www.alio.com.au
And…try the chef's tasting menu

····· city + suburbs ·········•

Almond Bar

379 Liverpool Street, Darlinghurst
Tel 9380 5318   Map 2

Middle Eastern

Score 13.5/20

Enter the Syrian–Australian sister act. At their cool Darlinghurst den, adorned with carved wooden panels and sparkling tealights, Carol and Sharon Salloum have created a warm, inviting space, which lends itself equally to cocktails and mezze or a lingering Middle Eastern feast. After tucking into a neat quartet of flavoured almonds (maybe chilli, cinnamon, smoked and natural), create your own banquet of Sharon's honest, home-style tastes. A zippy salad of tomato, chickpeas and dense, salty baladeh cheese gets its punch from a pomegranate molasses dressing, while earthy fried cauliflower arr'nabit charms with a silky lemon tahini sauce. It's easy to see why mukloubi was the chef's childhood fave: pillowy, cinnamon-laced rice layered with chicken, eggplant and a thick blanket of yoghurt is pure comfort. Dessert might bring out your inner child, too, as you duel it out for the last scoop of divine rosewater ice-cream or a delightfully chewy chocolate and pistachio version.

Hours Lunch Fri noon–3pm; Dinner Tues–Sun 5.30–10.30pm
Bill Mezza plates $6–$25; 10% surcharge on Sundays & public holidays
Cards AE DC V MC Eftpos
Wine Well-chosen, Australian-focused list; 13 by the glass; exotic cocktails
Chef Sharon Salloum
Owner Carol Salloum
Seats 50; bar
Vegetarian Banquet menu, plus excellent choice of mezze, dips and salads
www.almondbar.com.au
And...buy bags of your favourite almonds to go

Altitude

Level 36, Shangri-La Hotel,
176 Cumberland Street, The Rocks
Tel 9250 6123   Map 1

Contemporary

Score 15/20

At this altitude, with the city below, plus the glowing Opera House and velvety harbour, even the most cynical would be impressed. While the breathtaking views from the upper floors of the Shangri-La may come as no surprise, the revelation that one of Sydney's top hotels is serving food to match its views might. A well-balanced menu, an exciting wine list and finely tuned service take Altitude to great culinary heights. An example of chef Steven Krasicki's terrific execution is the not-to-be-missed entree, rabbit pithivier. Rich and gamey, it's paired with fine morel mushrooms and celeriac. Scallops with a glossy Jerusalem artichoke puree and mushroom duxelle is another tempting partnership. Rare roast venison with black pepper gnocchi and earthy cavolo nero reveals a talent for game, while white onion tarte tatin is satisfying enough to stand up against meatier mains. Poached peaches with mascarpone semifreddo has a simplicity and purity that will leave you on a high.

Hours Dinner Mon–Sat 6–10.30pm; bookings essential
Bill E $24–$28 **M** $30–$42 **D** $18; 7-course degustation $135pp; 10% surcharge on public holidays
Cards AE DC V MC Eftpos
Wine Excellent compilation of local and imported benchmarks with quirky boutiques; 22 by the glass
Chef Steven Krasicki
Owner Shangri-La Hotel
Seats 80; private room; wheelchair access; bar
Child friendly Kids' menu; highchairs
Vegetarian Outstanding vego menu
www.altitudesydney.com
And...the cocktail bar shares the amazing views

MARINATED EGG YOLKS
FROM CHEF CARLO CRACCO.
ACQUA PANNA FROM TUSCANY.

From Tuscany, for the love of food.

The story of the egg is as old as the world itself. Chef Carlo Cracco has simply changed the ending, showing that those who think it has reached its last chapter are indeed mistaken. And those who think it makes no difference which water is used to accompany the intense flavour of his marinated egg yolk are just as mistaken. To enhance the pleasures of the palate and bring out the unique savour of his recipes, Carlo Cracco chooses the perfectly balanced, velvety-smooth taste of Acqua Panna, from a beautiful nature reserve in the hills of Tuscany. The water you will find on the world's leading tables.

Trade Enquiries: 1800 660 189
www.acquapanna.com

Harvey Norman
THE COOKING APPLIANCE SPECIALIST!

"At Harvey Norman, we have the **best brands**, **best prices** and the **best advice** to cater for all your cooking needs."

Whether you need a new fridge, dishwasher or complete kitchen overhaul, **Harvey Norman** have what you're looking for. Our specialist staff can help you choose the right appliances and give you the best prices.

WE OFFER ALL THE LEADING BRANDS IN:
- OVENS • FREESTANDING COOKERS
- COOKTOPS • RANGEHOODS
- SINKS • TAPS • DISHWASHERS
- REFRIGERATORS & MORE!

  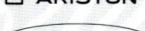   

Harvey Norman
THE COOKING APPLIANCE SPECIALIST

FOR YOUR NEAREST STORE CALL
1300 GO HARVEY
(1300 46 4278)
www.harveynorman.com.au

Harvey Norman® stores are operated by independent franchisees.

157832_NSM

city + suburbs

a'Mews

99 Glebe Point Road, Glebe
Tel 9660 4999 Map 5b

French/English

Score 13.5/20

Blink and you'll miss the entrance, but you'll be glad you didn't once you enter this quirky little bistro on Glebe's busiest stretch. Affable and beaming waiters keep busy scaling the stairs of this intimate four-level diner with private nooks where locals can relax, enjoy a tipple then tip their hats to the French-inspired nosh. Chef Richard Moyser's food is flamboyantly pretty in one breath and scrumptious the next. Citrus-cured tuna rests on an apple and radish salad held to ransom by dollops of avocado and beetroot. Orange, fennel and hazelnut combine with a splash of sherry vinegar to help cut through slivers of roast duck breast. Moyser's mains really warm the cockles. A crepinette of braised lamb titillates the tongue, served with a raunchy ratatouille plus chorizo and olive tapenade for good measure. Slowly braised shoulder of pork bathes in apple broth – haricot beans and buttered savoy cabbage give the dish depth. Indulge with a trio of chocolate treats in white, milk and dark.

Hours Lunch Fri noon–2.30pm (bookings only); Dinner Tues–Sat 6.30–9.30pm; bookings essential
Bill E $21–$24 **M** $28–$35 **D** $15; 6-course degustation $78pp
Cards AE DC (+2%) V MC Eftpos
Wine Quirky and good value mix to suit any budget; 25 by the glass; BYO Tues–Thurs only (corkage $10 a bottle)
Chef Richard Moyser
Owners Richard, Dani & Ian Moyser
Seats 50; private room; outdoor seating
www.amews.com.au
And… save room for the cracking cheese selection

Amici

465 Miller Street, Cammeray
Tel 9922 2222 Map 5a

Italian/Pizza

Score 13/20

Forget the mushy pea and pie floater. Rigatoni with peas and pecorino beats it hands down – the ridged pasta an ideal snag for half whole/half mashed peas, nuggets of pecorino, and cubes of juicy chicken, dressed with leaves of parmesan. It's a simple dish carried off well, and characteristic of this very neighbourly, handkerchief-sized pizzeria and ristorante. The polpi brasat is baby octopus slow cooked to an almost cheesy pulpiness, with fat Sicilian green olives and blazing red sauteed chillies. Fiori di zucca (zucchini flowers), generously full of goat's cheese, are lightly battered and complemented with a delicate saute of diced eggplant, capsicum and tomato. An insalata of beans, garlic and almonds slivers is simplicity itself, the beans pliant but crunchy, and the dressing not dominant. A dessert of affogato is refreshingly unfussed, just a couple of scoops of vanilla ice-cream, strong black coffee, and a shot of Frangelico. Amici is light and cheerful, with a constant stream of local diners late into the night. It's just how friends should be.

Hours Dinner daily 6–10pm
Bill E $15.50–$20.50 **M** $15.50–$30.50 **D** $8.50–$12.50
Cards AE V MC Eftpos
Wine Small range suited to the simple dishes; 10 by the glass; BYO (corkage $3pp)
Chef El Mostafa Solaihan
Owners Marco Pietrobon, Antonio Castelnuovo & Jac Sogomonian
Seats 90; private room; wheelchair access; outdoor seating; bar
Child friendly Kids' menu
Vegetarian Good choices across the menu
And… monthly Italian regional specials

city + suburbs

Aperitif

7 Kellett Street, Potts Point
Tel 9357 4729 Map 2

French/Mediterranean

Score 14/20

A place, a mood, an attitude. Bookended by two Kellett Street nightspots where the trashionistas sometimes get boisterous, this long, narrow wine bar/bistro with a Moroccan vibe and leafy courtyard is an oasis of charm. The owners are hospitality veterans who think the city should have more wine bars. They also reckon they should serve good food. No surprise, Aperitif ticks both boxes. A smart wine list offers interesting European and local drops in tasting size (70ml) glasses. Sample several different styles throughout your meal. The menu choice is pleasantly confusing (amuse bouche, hors d'oeuvres, small plates, large plates, plates for two), so allow your hosts to assist. You'll like meaty vintage anchovies on toast; then four perfectly cooked wild sea scallops with an avocado mousse (an aromatic gruner veltliner to accompany?). Roast bone marrow and a gutsy grilled onglet steak (perhaps a mid-weight savoury lirac rouge?) is serious soul food. Finish with house-made yoghurt and figs, escorted by a luscious monbazillac.

Hours Dinner Mon & Wed–Sat 6pm–3am, Sun 6pm–midnight
Bill E $7–$18 **M** $25–$29 **D** $14
Cards AE DC V MC Eftpos
Wine Never boring; smaller European (chiefly French) producers well represented; 22 by the glass
Chef Laurent Curvat
Owners Elie Griplas & Charles Leong
Seats 80; wheelchair access; outdoor seating; bar
www.aperitif.net.au
And…keep this up your sleeve for a late-night drink and dine after clubbing

Aqua Dining

Cnr Paul & Northcliff streets, Milsons Point
Tel 9964 9998 Map 5a

Contemporary

Score 13/20

Need to impress a visitor with stunning harbour views and a crash-course in the city's contemporary fare? Then try this arresting elongated fish tank overlooking North Sydney Olympic pool, the Coathanger and Opera House. Chef Jeff Turnbull professes French and Italian influences in a pleasing balance of surf or turf options, such as pan-fried barramundi served with basil gnocchi, champagne sauce and asparagus, or alternatively King Island tenderloin beef. However, there are Middle Eastern cameos as well, with ras el hanout-spiced soft shell crab with baby spinach salad and pine nuts. Service can be hectic on busy Saturday nights, and we'd prefer to get to know just one or two members of the team rather than meeting everyone. An Eton mess-style dessert of an "orgy" of summer berries, mascarpone, champagne mousse, meringue and raspberry sorbet brightens our mood considerably. Aqua Dining shows you can have your cake and enjoy the view too.

Hours Lunch daily noon–2.30pm; Dinner daily 6.30–10pm
Bill E $25–$28 **M** $36–$39 **D** $18–$21; 3-course menu $69pp, Sat–Sun lunch & Sun dinner only
Cards AE DC V MC
Wine An impressive, if exhaustive, list of interesting New and Old World wines; 14 by the glass; BYO Sat–Sun lunch & Sun dinner only (corkage $10 a bottle)
Chef Jeff Turnbull
Owner Bill Drakopoulos
Seats 140; wheelchair access; outdoor seating
Child friendly Special kids' meals for $18
www.aquadining.com.au
And…take the ferry, which stops at the adjacent Milsons Point Wharf

city + suburbs

Aria

1 Macquarie Street, East Circular Quay
Tel 9252 2555   Map 1

Contemporary

Score 17/20

No matter how high celebrity chef Matt Moran's star rises, he'll never be the biggest Sydney attraction here, not when the Opera House and Harbour Bridge loom right outside the restaurant's floor-to-ceiling windows. Still, Moran and maitre d' Peter Sullivan put on a show as good as anything you'd see under those iconic sails, starting perhaps with swordfish sashimi – a trio of fresh fish discs with tart yuzu (Japanese citrus) puree and pickled radish. Scallops, expertly cooked, were let down by not-so-crisp prawn crisps, but are well matched with shaved fennel and arty swirls of fennel puree and tamarind and date dressing. Of the mains, succulent slow-cooked quail breast is irresistible with almond dressing, vibrant crushed mint peas, and zucchini flowers plump with ricotta. Lamb is served three ways, including a tender roast cutlet and a petite lamb pastia (or bastilla) – shredded meat encased in crisp pastry. Polished, pleasant service keeps diners at ease in the glorious semicircular room, while warm pear tart with vanilla ice-cream and caramel will certainly please.

Hours Lunch Mon–Fri noon–2.30pm; Dinner daily 5.30–10.30pm; bookings essential
Bill E $36–$46 **M** $44–$56 **D** $24–$28; lunch & pre-theatre menus $68–$85pp; 10% surcharge on Sundays & public holidays
Cards AE DC V MC
Wine Epic Australian and European list with great advice on hand; 20 by the glass
Chefs Matt Moran & Ben Turner
Owners Matt Moran & Peter Sullivan
Seats 180; private rooms; wheelchair access; bar
www.ariarestaurant.com
And... book "the kitchen table" for eight and watch the cooks at work

Arun Thai

28 Macleay Street, Potts Point
Tel 9326 9132   Map 2

Thai

Score 13/20

Arun Thai's charm lies in its consistency. Here, among the aged teak furniture, silks and well-versed staff, dishes from all parts of Thailand feature on an extensive menu. With so much choice, start with the basics: tod mun (fishcakes) come light and fluffy with peanut, cucumber and sweet chilli dipping sauce; marinated chicken wrapped in fragrant pandan leaves is addictive, so too fresh spring rolls topped with sticky plum and tamarind sauce. Northern and southern styles go together nicely – a larb of chicken with ground rice, mint, chilli and lime will have you reaching for more water. Roast duck curry arrives studded with cherry tomatoes and pineapple to tame the fire. A steamed seafood patty (hor mok) lacked spice and was too watery, and khao yum, rice traditionally made with prawn paste, could have used some. Klua kling, a dry curry of chilli paste and kaffir lime is a standout: try it with beef. For dessert, do as Thais do, and spoon up coconut ice-cream with sticky rice.

Hours Lunch Thurs–Fri & Sun noon–3pm; Dinner daily 6–10.30pm
Bill E $14–$22.50 **M** $18.50–$30 **D** $11–$14; $3pp surcharge on public holidays
Cards AE DC V MC Eftpos
Wine Epic wine list; 18 by the glass
Chef Supot Rattanakolmon & Kham Signavong
Owner Kham and Tess Signavong
Seats 150; private room; bar
Vegetarian Separate menu
www.arunthai.com.au
And... there's a takeaway service, too

good food guide

city + suburbs

Ash St Cellar ★

The Ivy, 1 Ash Street, Sydney
Tel 9240 3000   Map 1

Mediterranean

Score 14/20

FAVOURITE WINE BAR

This buzzing little wine bar is more demure than the rest of the glitzy Ivy complex: think Parisian bistro meets Melbourne laneway dining, with the majority of the patrons relaxing on rattan chairs at outdoor tables. The smaller inside area has a smart, dark-wood interior, a cluster of marble-topped tables and impressive carved chandeliers over the bar and open kitchen. Grab a seat and flag down a busy waiter to help choose a wine from the incredible list. Bruschetta topped with succulent mushrooms and wonderfully salty, crisp and oily guanciale (cured pig's cheek) is a standout. Full-throttle flavours star in a salad of tangy white anchovies, sharp caperberries, sweet red onions and parsley; and there's a good charcuterie selection, including quality jamon and prosciutto. It's mostly small nibbles to share, with the wine in mind, including a fine cheese plate. Lamb cutlets topped with spiced yoghurt came on a bland chickpea salad, but a warm chocolate and hazelnut tart, one of the two desserts on offer, is light and airy, rich and indulgent all at once.

Hours Mon–Fri noon–10.30pm; no bookings
Bill Shared plates $12–$28; **D** $14
Cards AE DC (+3%) V MC
Wine Remarkable international list; 18 by the glass, taste or carafe
Chef Lauren Murdoch
Owner Merivale Group
Seats 80; wheelchair access; outdoor seating; bar
www.merivale.com
And...match a few tasting glasses to the food

Assiette

48 Albion Street, Surry Hills
Tel 9212 7979   Map 3b

Contemporary

Score 16/20

The name tells all: assiette (French for plate) as several riffs on one ingredient theme. French technique underpins Warren Turnbull's picture-pretty food, along with a few contemporary Asian moments. A white asparagus barigoule features spanner crab in both a spring roll and quenelle with lemon mayo, delicate on a thin saffron jelly ribbon with baby leeks, golden beets, potatoes, shaved carrot, and saffron and beet sorbet. Textures of carrot with crisp skinned barramundi includes Vichy carrots in parsley, carrot ribbons, chips and roasted puree beneath a Maltaise (orange) sauce. Maybe the tiny accompanying prawn beignet was overkill but the intricately assembled food avoids any fussiness. Here is balance, care, thought, great technique, flavour and even a little humour. Mango and passionfruit nestle inside a raviolo of agar jelly, with mango sorbet and a whisper of coconut foam in a rolled coconut tuile. There's attention to detail too, with informed, friendly staff and an immaculate interior with engaging black and white artwork, recurring cutlery motifs on menus and doors and screens.

Hours Lunch Fri noon–3pm; Dinner Tues–Sat 6–10pm; bookings essential
Bill E $24 **M** $35 **D** $16; 3-course lunch $30pp
Cards AE DC V MC Eftpos
Wine Well-chosen list with diverse, well-priced Australian and French wines; 12 by the glass
Chefs Warren Turnbull & Soren Lascelles
Owner Warren Turnbull
Seats 54
www.restaurantassiette.com.au
And...there's a 10-course degustation menu for $90 or with matching wines for $150

Astral

Level 17, Hotel Tower, Star City Casino,
80 Pyrmont Street, Pyrmont
Tel 9657 8687   Map 5b

Modern European

Score 15/20

Here's a sign of the times. The much-debated $1000 degustation is gone, and Yorkshire-born chef Sean Connolly has returned to his roots. This is still unmistakeably high-end dining, though: 17th-floor views, stiff-backed upholstered chairs, formal serving trolleys and an almost reverential atmosphere. The menu is divided into hot, warm, cold and sweet, with everything designed for sharing. The richness of ham hock terrine with a strip of foie gras is balanced by light brioche and the sharpness of tiny pickled vegetables. King prawn cannelloni with foamed treacle beurre blanc and sprinkled with roe and chives is a contrast of sweet and briny. The delicate flavour of buffalo mozzarella is overtaken by a feisty white anchovy, speck and radicchio salad. Lancashire lamb hotpot concealed under a potato lid is meltingly good, although a side of greens is needed. Apple and blackberry souffle with a crumble top served in a copper pot is another reworked classic appropriate for more ascetic times.

Hours Breakfast Mon–Fri 6–10.30am, Sat–Sun 7–11am; Dinner Tues–Sat 6–10pm; bookings essential
Bill Share menu **E** from $22 **M** from $36 **D** from $14; 10% surcharge on public holidays
Cards AE DC V MC Eftpos
Wine An impressive international list with some hard-to-find back vintages; 20 by the glass
Chefs Sean Connolly & Sebastien Lutaud
Owner Star City/Tabcorp
Seats 60; private room; wheelchair access; bar
www.astralrestaurant.com.au
And...bring your camera for postcard-worthy shots from the terrace

Azuma

Level 1, Chifley Plaza, 2 Chifley Square, Sydney
Tel 9222 9960   Map 1

Japanese

Score 15/20

Flavours can be both subtle and striking at this long-standing CBD favourite. Sake-steamed alfonsino (a tropical, deep-sea fish) is most notable for its delicate moistness, while a lip-smackingly tender special of tempura baby octopus reinforces Azuma-san's reputation as the tempura king. Sushi and sashimi come in many forms, traditional nigiri is glisteningly fresh while Azuma's "unique nigiri" menu offers memorable treats, such as seared salmon belly spiked with lemon juice and salt. Unagi fans will love warm, slightly smoky, vaguely sweet grilled eel with cucumber and ponzu (citrus soy), while ramen devotees can drown in a big, steaming, murky bowl of salty, sesame-flavoured broth with slices of tender pork, boiled egg and long, thin egg noodles for slurping. Some parts of the "corporate neutral" decor are looking a little frayed around the edges, and desserts aren't a strong suit, but polite staff keep the green tea coming and Mitsuo Shoji's beautiful ceramics make every table a work of art.

Hours Lunch Mon–Fri noon–2.30pm; Dinner Mon–Sat 6–10pm; bookings essential
Bill Set lunch $36–$42, degustation lunch $70pp; Dinner sushi bar set $88 or $120pp, degustation $110pp, a la carte $15–$66; **D** $14.50–$20
Cards AE DC V MC Eftpos
Wine Well-priced Old and New World selection, plus big-ticket items; 8 by the glass; shochu list
Chef Kimitaka Azuma
Owners Kimitaka & Yuki Azuma
Seats 85; private rooms
Vegetarian Set-course menu; sushi, tempura
www.azuma.com.au
And...bento box lunches, plus free evening parking from 5.30pm

city + suburbs

Azuma Kushiyaki

NEW ENTRY

Ground Floor, Regent Place,
501 George Street, Sydney
Tel 9267 7775   Map 1

Japanese

Score 14/20

One of Sydney's finest Japanese chefs, Kimitaka Azuma, has opened this excellent offshoot of his eponymous Chifley Tower Japanese, to specialise in grilled skewers (kushiyaki) and sake-friendly snacks (otsumami). The three-page menu leaves you spoilt for choice, and bristles with authentic flavours, whether it's the acquired taste of shiokara – salty, sweet, spicy and pungent fermented squid – or divine sushi, sashimi and tempura. There are lunchtime set menus, too. The service, while polite, can be tardy, but there's plenty of sake to see you through until the skewers arrive, impaling everything from delicious shiitake mushrooms stuffed with minced prawns, to crisp chicken skin or gelatinous beef tongue. Tofu nimono, a comforting, gingery bowl of prawns, silken tofu and seaweed with crystal clear flavours, shouldn't be missed before the fun of wagashi – decorative cakes made from red bean paste and glutinous rice. That's if the French patisserie staples, from Mont Blanc to opera cake, don't appeal.

Hours Lunch Mon–Fri noon–2.30pm;
Dinner daily 6–10pm
Bill Set lunch $33–$39; a la carte $10.50–$35; Dinner kushiyaki $2.50–$$6.50; Tasting plates $14.50–$19.50; Dinner otsumami $8–$$18; Tasting plate $30; a la carte $7–$35 **D** $7.50–$13
Cards AE V MC
Wine Small, idiosyncratic yet clever international list, plus 20 sake; 13 by the glass
Chef Kimitaka Azuma
Owner Kimitaka & Yuki Azuma
Seats 82; wheelchair access
And… also try the Ton Ton ramen bar opposite

Bai Yok

Shop 2A, 122 Edinburgh Road, Castlecrag
Tel 9967 3433   Map 7

Thai

Score 13/20

The yum hua plee (prawn and banana blossom salad) arrives as a Thai royal purple crown of blossom leaves cupping firm prawns. They sit atop sauteed blossom stamens (with no trace of bitterness) dressed with red onion, kaffir lime leaf, mint and a delicate, turmeric-highlighted sauce. The flavours are beautifully balanced, sharp, sweet and with a chilli tingle. The pleasure here is reflected in a thoughtful menu, taking well-considered deviations away from a predictable Thai path. Scallop miang achieves a lot with scallop, roasted coconut, palm sugar, lime and onion on a betel leaf. Yang chicken brings thin lemongrass-infused grilled fillets together with chilli sauce. Black sesame ice-cream doesn't need strawberries, but that small false note is excusable. A narrow, deep space simply and elegantly decorated, at the quieter, tree-lined residential end of the Castlecrag village shops, attentive waiters and a terrace for summer evenings make dining here very pleasurable indeed.

Hours Lunch Fri noon–3pm;
Dinner Tues–Sat 6–10pm, Sun 5.30–9.30pm
Bill E $8–$14 **M** $13–$28 **D** $5–$10;
$2pp surcharge on public holidays
Cards AE V MC Eftpos
Wine Short list of familiar Australian names; 4 by the glass; BYO wine only (corkage $3pp)
Chef Warangkana Lui
Owner Michael Lui
Seats 75; wheelchair access; outdoor seating
Child friendly Highchairs; kids' cutlery and bowls; milder dishes
Vegetarian A good range of options
And… the servings are more than generous, so take your appetite along

12 good food guide

city + suburbs

Bambini Trust Cafe
185 Elizabeth Street, Sydney
Tel 9283 7098   Map 1

Modern European
Score 14/20

Things don't change often here – and no one wants them to. For 12 years this atmospheric little piece of Europe – think dark timber, cosy booths, soft lighting and waiters long on charm – has been packed from breakfast to dinner with magazine mavens and media moguls. All have their favourites on a menu of classics and comfort dishes, with daily specials to keep things interesting. Ravioli of caramelised pumpkin and Persian fetta is delectable, drenched in brown butter, sage and capers. Just as smooth is chicken liver and black truffle paté, with toasted brioche and the acid kick of apple and ginger chutney. Milk-fed veal Milanese was a tad dull in its breadcrumb case, but a special of snapper al cartoccio (in a bag) is meltingly magnificent, thanks to nothing more than lemon and white wine. The cheese list is as tempting as desserts, such as raspberry, strawberry and vanilla semifreddo, with mint-spiked berries alongside. Bambini is much imitated but rarely matched. It's a restaurant that deserves its swagger.

Hours Breakfast Mon–Fri 7–11am;
Lunch Mon–Fri noon–3pm;
Dinner Mon–Sat 5.30–10.30pm; bookings essential
Bill E $20–$28 **M** $30–$38 **D** $16.50
Cards AE DC V MC
Wine Tempting cocktails and an excellent wine list, strong on local, Italian and French drops; 20 by the glass
Chef Oliver Carruthers
Owners Michael & Angela Potts
Seats 76; wine room; wheelchair access; outdoor seating; bar
www.bambinitrust.com.au
And...excellent breakfasts, too. Porridge in winter is heavenly

Banana Blossom   RE-ENTRY
318a Military Road, Cremorne
Tel 9908 1588   Map 5a

Modern Asian
Score 13/20

If you were eating out in Bangkok, this is the kind of modern Thai you'd be enjoying – essential ingredients reshuffled into something new. Chef Ben Thomas's restaurant is smart and spacious. Start with the signature turmeric wafer – a crisp rice flour taco packed with spicy chicken, fresh longan berries, chilli jam and basil. Crunchy soft-shell crab is served with a lemony chilli dipping sauce. Miang kham, betel leaf-wrapped caramelised coconut, peanuts and lime comes three ways – traditionally with salted dried shrimp, chicken and even smoked trout. Southern style orange snapper curry topped with kaffir lime leaves needed less sweetness and more fire, while beef cheeks and pickled ginger braised in an orange peel-infused low dang (wine-based) sauce, might be a tad rich for some. To finish, there's house-made ice-cream, albeit a little pricey, to share: toasted black sesame, coconut and the cool fusion of mango and red tea all soothing the palate.

Hours Dinner Mon–Sat 6–10pm
Bill E $16–$20 **M** $28–$32 **D** $10
Cards AE V MC Eftpos
Wine Limited list; 8 by the glass; BYO (corkage $3.50pp)
Chef Ben Thomas
Owners Natchanan & Ben Thomas
Seats 116
Child friendly Kids' menu; drawing materials
Vegetarian Separate menu
www.bananablossom.com.au
And...start with a pre-dinner cocktail

good food guide   13

city + suburbs

Barrenjoey House

RE-ENTRY

1108 Barrenjoey Road, Palm Beach
Tel 9974 4001   Map 7

Modern Italian/Mediterranean
                          Score 14/20

Darren Simpson, the garrulous Irish bloke with an Italian passion, has shifted his easygoing, relaxed style to this equally laidback, northern peninsula boutique guesthouse, bar and restaurant, giving it new life and energy. The old favourites are back, including The River Cafe's chocolate nemesis (he worked there) and a pretty entree of tangy buffalo mozzarella with fresh black figs, red basil, rocket and mint. The fresh-faced room and open terrace, gazing through the pines to Pittwater, is like a beach house, with bare tables, scrubbed timber furniture and candy-striped napkins, while the cheery service can be a little too relaxed. The menu's simple baker's dozen Italian dishes is supplemented by a few daily specials, such as a platter of Pino Tomini Foresti's excellent salumi. Flathead fish and chips is as bright as the sunshine, while half a wonderfully moist roast organic chicken is stuffed with sultanas, pine nuts, lemon and oregano and splashed with pesto. It feels like paradise here and tastes like it, too.

Hours Daily 11.30am–10pm; bookings essential
Bill E $16–$22 **M** $24.50–$39 **D** $12–$14; 10% surcharge on Sundays & public holidays
Cards AE DC V MC Eftpos
Wine Small, modestly priced and mostly domestic; 20 by the glass
Chef Darren Simpson
Owners Brendon Barry & Darren Simpson
Seats 140; private room; outdoor seating; bar
Child friendly Kids' menu; highchairs; toys; books
www.barrenjoeyhouse.com.au
And... express bus stop out the front, so you don't have to drive

The Bathers' Pavilion Restaurant

4 The Esplanade, Balmoral
Tel 9969 5050   Map 7

Contemporary
                          Score 15/20

Blue of bay and dark tan of evening beach leach in through the wall of glass doors that lead to the terrace, colouring the dining room furnishings. The shot silk mauve of the waiters' shirts is the colour of the sunset sky out through the Heads. Throughout the meal resonances of beachcombing surface. Sourdough rolls made on the premises look like huge fish lips eager for a gloss of creamy, house-made butter. Slivers of tomato and whole basil leaves float in a terrine translucent as a rock pool and as cool. Accompanying yabbies, capsicum, smoked cheese and jamon beignets look for all the world like those little sand balls rolled by crabs, and deliver a burst of intense, complex flavours. Beef tenderloin with brisket is draped with potatoes, artichokes, roast shallot and a wash of porcini sauce, a study of driftwood, the flavours subtle, balanced, clean. An assiette of star fruit plays with the textures of sea foam – whipped, frothed, creamed. This is dining refreshing to palate and eye.

Hours Lunch daily noon–2pm; Dinner daily 6.30–8.30pm
Bill 2-course dinner & weekend lunch menu $95pp, 3 courses $115; weekday lunch 2 courses $75pp, 3 courses $90
Cards AE DC V MC
Wine Excellent global and local range; 15 by the glass; BYO Monday dinner only (corkage $10pp)
Chefs Serge Dansereau & Alan Compton
Owner Serge Dansereau
Seats 80; private rooms; wheelchair access; bar
Child friendly Kids' menu; highchairs
Vegetarian a la carte and degustation menus
www.batherspavilion.com.au
And... amble along the beach afterwards

city + suburbs

Bayleaf Brasserie

Shops 12–14, 103–111 Willoughby Road, Crows Nest
Tel 9906 6080   Map 5a

Indian

Score 14/20

There might just be a special something about the venue which launched Nilgiri's and then Bayleaf, now with a new owner-chef. So, it's a very ordinary location in a tired shopping centre. But here is a wonderful oasis of outstanding authentic regional Indian food, with sunny service that's as professional yet as relaxed as you might ever find. Pappadams arrive, broken shards in a tower on a completely greaseless paper-lined plate. Beetroot and kumera patties are piping hot, soft and spicy inside, dusted with a crisp coat of semolina, balanced by coriander chutney. Achari goat is a generous mound of diced goat, succulent with slow cooking and spiked with fennel, nigella and whole pickling spices. Goan prawns are firm and plump in a sea of coconut milk spiced with mustard seeds, curry leaves and red chillies. Kulfi comes in five guises, including pistachio and saffron, beautifully accompanied by rose syrup. While it's already great value for money, daily specials make it easy for you to become a regular.

Hours Lunch Sun–Fri noon–3pm; Dinner daily 6–10pm
Bill E $10–$13 **M** $15–$19 **D** $6; set-price menus $19.50–$39.50
Cards AE DC V MC Eftpos
Wine BYO (corkage $2pp)
Chef/owner Gaurav Sakhuja
Seats 70; private room; wheelchair access
Child friendly Kids' platter; highchairs
Vegetarian Several options and vegetarian thali on Sundays as well as Mon–Fri lunches
www.bayleafindian.com
And...monthly cooking classes, curry club and regional degustation dinners (last Sunday of every month)

Bayswater Brasserie

32 Bayswater Road, Kings Cross
Tel 9357 2177   Map 2

Contemporary

Score 14/20

Little wonder the "Bayz" keeps on keeping on. It's a well-oiled machine with some of Sydney's best service; solicitous, helpful and professional. As smooth and instinctual as the best Parisian bistro it could easily be, with tiled floor, dark wood chairs, papered linen tables and low table lamps. The bread, French-style of course, is house-made and fabulous. Seafood sings, from the ever-changing choice of freshly shucked regional oysters to a light and lovely special of Bermagui garfish, the delicate fillets contrasted with a deftly balanced classic olive, caper and parsley salad. Seared scallops rest on a bed of petits pois a la francaise, which are a touch firm. Risotto of sweet pea, carrot and celeriac was a touch too subtle, although the accompanying parmesan crisp was not. Boned lemon spatchcock nests on a delightfully light bed of julienned jicama. A glorious fig is splayed and splashed with honey beside vanilla bean-flecked panna cotta. It makes you wonder why you're not here every week.

Hours Dinner Mon–Sat 6–10.30pm
Bill E $15–$19 **M** $27–$39 **D** $14–$14.50
Cards AE DC V MC
Wine Australasian-dominated but global list; 10 by the glass
Chef Jeff Schroeter
Owners Nigel Lacy & Robert Smallbone
Seats 140; private rooms; bar
Child friendly Kids' meals; highchairs
www.bayswaterbrasserie.com.au
And...try the bar for a huge range of drinks served with knowledge and panache

good food guide

Becasse

204 Clarence Street, Sydney
Tel 9283 3440 Map 1

Modern European

Score 17/20

In keeping with the times, Justin North has opened a budget-conscious spin-off, Etch, but continues to keep finer diners happy here. And who wouldn't be content, ensconced in one of the CBD's most handsome, and recently redecorated, dining rooms – we'll never tire of the Swarovski crystal-studded chandeliers – being waited on by some of its finest floor staff, while poring over North's produce-driven menu and surprisingly affordable wine list? Confit belly of Cornish black pork is paired with king prawns rolled in crackling, the richness cut by fresh apple. Elsewhere citrus-marinated ocean trout is slow-cooked in aromatic olive oil, and heirloom tomatoes are matched with olive oil sorbet. Slow-cooked Victorian lamb saddle with semi-dried tomatoes is classy comfort food. Milk-fed veal is baked in coffee and clay, providing fine and revelatory flavours. Banana creme brulee matched with salted peanut brittle also raises a smile, along with the list of a dozen cheeses. This is stylish dining with all the trimmings, and the talent to match.

Hours Lunch Mon–Fri noon–2.30pm; Dinner Mon–Sat 6–10.30pm

Bill E $27 **M** $45 **D** $20; degustation menu $130pp

Cards AE DC V MC

Wine Length, breadth and value, a good number of half-bottles; 16 by the glass

Chefs Justin North & Monty Koludrovic

Owners Georgia & Justin North

Seats 85; bar

Vegetarian Degustation menu available $120pp

www.becasse.com.au

And…ask about regular producers' lunches

bel mondo

Gloucester Walk, The Rocks
Tel 9241 3700 Map 1

Contemporary/Italian

Score 13.5/20

Climb the stone steps from the Argyle Cut to this lovely, well-appointed space under a warehouse roof, make your way through the long bar and settle back under high timber beams softened with sheer, languid drapes. Watch, spoon poised, the molten core from a chocolate fondant ooze across the smear of cardamom and orange sauce. The room is flanked on one side by the kitchen and on the other by an atmospheric view over Dickensian chimney pots with the Harbour Bridge an imposing backdrop. The highly approachable menu is well executed, and the service charming. While some flavours – an insipid parsnip puree – could have been more assertive, there are cheeky touches. Mop-the-plate elderflower sauce lifts a warm salad of plump quail with witlof spikes, cauliflower and peeled grapes; Earl Grey jus splashes a tender roast duck breast; and the sweet earthiness of beetroot adds complexity to the fondant. Happily sated, you can roll back down to the Cut.

Hours Lunch Fri noon–3pm; Dinner Mon–Sat 6–10pm

Bill 2-course plat du jour lunch $35pp, 3 courses $47pp; 2-course a la carte $49pp, extra 3rd course $15pp; degustation $85pp

Cards AE DC V MC Eftpos

Wine Solid, wide-ranging list of locals and Europeans; 10 by the glass

Chef Andy Ball

Owner Mealand Holdings

Seats 150; wheelchair access; outdoor seating; bar

www.belmondo.com.au

And…an aperitif and/or digestif on the balcony

city + suburbs

Bellevue Hotel Dining Room

159 Hargrave Street, Paddington
Tel 9363 2293   Map 4a

Contemporary

Score 14/20

Retro Paddington pub at the front; cool, rustic French *bouchon* out the back. Well insulated from the bustle of the bar and the purring of pokies, the damask-topped tables overlaid with paper are overlooked by the semi-open kitchen. This smart space is decorated with tasteful prints and large cream sails to deflect the sun from the glass ceiling. Service is switched on, pleasant and proficient. Offal lovers will be delighted with perfectly seared chicken livers, crisp bacon, sweet onions and grilled sourdough. You'll find mains a difficult and tantalising choice. They range from full-flavoured corned wagyu silverside, nuzzled by melt-in-the-mouth bechamel alongside verjuice-braised cabbage, to the ultimate comfort food – crumbed lamb cutlets with minted peas and a mountain of creamy, buttery mash. A voluptuously gooey frozen nougat mousse with mellifluous roasted peaches zings on the tongue, and rounds this out to an utterly memorable experience.

Hours Lunch Tues–Fri noon–2.30pm, Sat–Sun 12.30–3pm; Dinner Mon–Sat 6–10pm
Bill E $17–$19 **M** $20.50–$36.50 **D** $15
Cards AE DC V MC Eftpos
Wine Well constructed and suited to the menu, glimpses of French and Italian; 14 by the glass
Chef Hamish Ingham
Owners Damien Pignolet & Ron White
Seats 110; private rooms; bar
Child friendly Kids' portions
www.bellevuehotel.com.au
And…enjoy a nightcap at the heritage bar on the way out

Bentley Restaurant & Bar

320 Crown Street, Surry Hills
Tel 9332 2344   Map 2

Contemporary

Score 16/20

The Bentley is like a pair of designer jeans – dressed down and comfortable but with the hallmarks of haute couture. The interior is more off-the-peg than custom-fit, but the makeover of what was a down-at-heel corner pub is clever. The warm, muted cast of the red table lamps makes it difficult to see what's on the plate, which is a shame, as food this engaging deserves a spotlight. Standouts, both from the tapas menu, include almond gazpacho in a trio of the Spanish soup; and kingfish ceviche with pickled watermelon and coriander paste. Roasted duck with smoked leek, black funghi and kohlrabi is a fabulous combination. Wafer-thin shards of black sesame with a sphere of pea green fondant, snow peas and goat's curd is a great example of Brent Savage's efforts to bring art and science to the table. Right through to the elaborate desserts, this constant interplay of colour, shape and texture never conforms to expectations, so go with it: it's a great show.

Hours Lunch Tues–Sat noon–5pm; Dinner Tues–Sat 6–11pm
Bill E $19–$25 **M** $29–$40 **D** $3–$16; tapas menu $5–$16; 8-course tasting menu $105; tapas tasting lunch $50pp
Cards AE DC V MC Eftpos
Wine Rewards the adventurous and nurtures the novice; 25 by the glass
Chef Brent Savage
Owners Brent Savage & Nick Hildebrandt
Seats 80; outdoor seating; bar
Child friendly Highchairs
Vegetarian Good choices; 8-course tasting menu
www.thebentley.com.au
And…the wine list is as enticing as the food

city + suburbs

Beppi's ★

21 Yurong Street, East Sydney
Tel 9360 4558   Map 2

Regional Italian

Score 13.5/20

SILVER ANNIVERSARY STAYER AWARD

Beppi's introduced Sydneysiders to Italian cuisine in 1956, and while the eponymous octogenarian is still on the floor, greeting old mates and charming new chums, son Marc now plies the family trade with equal panache. Service is traditional and friendly, and each table in this rustic room with its grotto-like nooks scores a selection of four breads, along with olive paste and crostini of creamy whipped baccala (salt cod). Classics such as frittelle di annate (whitebait fritters) and seafood pasta still feature, and since chef Joe Camilleri's move from Mezzaluna, they seem lighter and fresher. There's even a far-from-traditional vitello tonnato of medium-rare veal fillet topped with tuna sauce and enriched by the roasting juices. Zucchini flowers, stuffed with a nicely balanced ricotta and porcini mix, are satisfyingly crisp. Ravioloni of lobster and crab, served on a rich prawn-meat salsa, is beautifully crafted. Mixed berries with Grand Marnier cream is a simple and simply delicious excuse to linger in this lovely, timeless space.

Hours Lunch Mon–Fri noon–3pm; Dinner Mon–Sat 6–11pm
Bill E $19–$32 **M** $28–$49 **D** $16–$19
Cards AE DC V MC
Wine Good list of quality Australians with some modern Italian choices and a remarkable Australian "museum collection"; 21 by the glass
Chefs Joe Camilleri & Di Duady
Owners Beppi, Norma & Marc Polese
Seats 120; private rooms
Vegetarian A good choice
www.beppis.com.au
And… Beppi's homemade grappa is as good as the old country's

The Beresford Hotel

NEW ENTRY

354 Bourke Street, Darlinghurst
Tel 9357 1111   Map 2

Italian

Score 14/20

Danny Russo has made a long-awaited return to Sydney dining in this revamped pub, via a trattoria nodding as much to Manhattan as it does to its art deco heritage. It's noisy, dark and moody with dark timber floors, and glass cabinets full of wine and dining collectables. Menus are wittily laid out with old photographs and vintage typefaces. Attentive floor staff speak Italian as easily as English. House-made bread emerges from the wood-fired oven and all starts well with crisp, tender baby calamari fritti. Russo's deftness with pasta dough shows in lovely open lasagne, interleaved with crisp artichokes, porcini mushrooms and hazelnuts, and flecked with herbs. The cauliflower panna cotta beside a disc of chunky ocean trout tartare was a touch cloying, and there's an odd juxtaposition in raw marinated tuna resting on risotto sprinkled with bottarga and peas. But lamb rump with pine mushrooms and celeriac puree is pure comfort. And Russo's fabulous zuppa inglese is a meringue-swathed take on the classic Italian trifle.

Hours Lunch Wed–Sun noon–3pm; Dinner daily 6–10pm except Sun; bookings essential
Bill E $19–$35 **M** $35–$42 **D** $15; 10% surcharge on public holidays
Cards AE V MC
Wine Italian varietals from Italy and Australia in 3 sections: cheap ($35), decent ($45) and good ($55); 28 by the glass
Chef Danny Russo
Owner Ashod Nassibian
Seats 110; wheelchair access; outdoor seating; bar
www.theberesford.com.au
And… a set-price Sunday "family feast" in the courtyard

city + suburbs

Berowra Waters Inn
Via public wharf, Berowra Waters
Tel 9456 1027   Map 6

French/Contemporary

Score 17/20

Sydney has no shortage of dapper waterside dining, yet this iconic sandstone, timber and louvred-glass setting, tucked into bushland, is in a league of its own. City worries fade as the boatman ferries you to chef Dietmar Sawyere's "weekender". After 17 high-flying years at Forty One, Sawyere's energies now seem firmly focused on this sophisticated make-your-own degustation. Choose between four and six dishes. A luscious chilled vichyssoise with oscietra and salmon caviars and oyster beignets is a regular star. Sawyere's virtuoso French-styled cooking creates perfect harmonies of imagination, playfulness and opulence. Murray cod with Israeli couscous (a jumbo version of the North African variety) revels in the perfume of rosemary veloute. Roast marron is a robust match for a porky cassolette of belly, trotters and cured cheek. While seafood is strong, there's a fine Rossini-inspired wagyu minute steak. We're not convinced Bailey's is the right "wine" match for a floating island with nicely bitter chocolate, but nonetheless, this gorgeous space deserves its high position in Australia's restaurant pantheon.

Hours Lunch Fri–Sun noon–2pm;
Dinner Fri–Sat 7–10pm; bookings essential
Bill 4/5/6 courses, $125pp/$135pp/$150pp
Cards AE DC V MC
Wine Classy international list with great boutique Australians and benchmark wines; 20-plus by the glass
Chef/owner Dietmar Sawyere
Seats 75; private room; outdoor seating
Child friendly Kids' meals; highchairs; toys; books; fishing
Vegetarian Numerous dishes available
www.berowrawatersinn.com
And...the deck is an ideal spot for a cocktail party

Big Mama's
51 Moncur Street, Woollahra
Tel 9328 7629   Map 4a

Italian

Score 13/20

Sure, it's an institution for the well-heeled Woollahra set, but for anyone hailing from outside the elite east, the name Big Mama's conjures up just another run-of-the-mill pizza joint or worse, an Eddie Murphy movie. Don't let the name deceive you. Big Mama's is the friendly, quality, reliable local restaurant we wish was around the corner from home. It's all boisterous greetings and knowing smiles on arrival – it seems everyone knows everyone here in this double-fronted terrace. The menu has more classics than Gold FM, and each is executed well. A salad of tomato, buffalo mozzarella and prosciutto is decent produce served simply. So too calamari fritti, all brittle batter and soft squid. Pale pink veal comes as escalopes with a squeeze of lemon, osso buco falls off the bone, while a textbook tiramisu could represent Italy at the culinary Olympics. The wine list has some big names but also some undiscovered gems and the prices are fair. Bravo Big Mama's.

Hours Dinner Tues–Sun 6–10pm
Bill E $18–$22 **M** $28–$37 **D** $10–$12
Cards AE V MC
Wine A commendable list of mainly Australian labels and varieties with about 10 representing Italy; 10 by the glass
Chef Carlo Lombardo
Owners Carlo Lombardo & Michael Currenti
Seats 140; private room; outdoor seating; bar
Child friendly Kids' menu; highchairs; activity books
And...beware the house-made limoncello that might arrive post-dessert

good food guide

.... city + suburbs ....•

Billy Kwong ★

3/355 Crown Street, Surry Hills
Tel 9332 3300   Map 3b

Chinese

Score 14.5/20

SUSTAINABILITY AWARD

A steaming, sizzling, clanking kitchen, hungry diners plonked on black laminate stools, packed into a dimly lit room – this is a world of its own. Kylie Kwong takes you into her universe in this perennially popular "teahouse". The menu is seasonal and predominantly organic (see page 184). Staff slide quickly through the crowded room, getting the job done but lacking some warmth. A salad of Asian herbs and sweet calamari is true freshness on a plate. Sang choi bau is pleasingly sweet and salty in its lettuce casing. While white steamed chicken with coriander and chilli dressing failed to excite, the generous portion can't be faulted. Prawns with deep-fried tofu livens things up, both melting and soft, and crunchy. For dessert, one choice – a plate of sweet tropical fruit with pieces of organic dark chocolate. Out into Crown Street, the glass door closes, and this bustling little world is once more just a dream.

Hours Dinner Mon–Thurs 6–10pm, Fri–Sat 6–11pm, Sun 6–9pm; no bookings except 1 table for 6–8 people

Bill E $14–$32 **M** $26–$49 **D** $15; banquet $95pp; $3pp surcharge on weekends

Cards AE V MC

Wine Selection of domestic biodynamic & organic producers; 6 by the glass; BYO (corkage $12 a bottle)

Chefs Mathew Lindsay & Kylie Kwong

Owner Kylie Kwong

Seats 50

Vegetarian Plenty of options

www.kyliekwong.org

And…arrive early or prepare to wait in The Dolphin across the road

Bilson's

Radisson Plaza Sydney Hotel,
27 O'Connell Street, Sydney
Tel 8214 0496   Map 1

Contemporary/French

Score 18/20

Former head chef Manu Feildel (now at L'etoile) was such an integral part of this hotel fine diner's success, we wondered what next for bow-tied Tony Bilson. We shouldn't have worried, since the Francophile Bilson has enlisted Spanish-born Alfonso Ales to maintain his restaurant's tradition of exploratory cuisine. Bold flavours, striking combinations and pretty arrangements are the hallmark of this new regime, in a long room that's rather low-key inoffensive, except for the patron's art collection. Begin with the remarkable contrasts of a pomegranate-bejewelled Crystal Bay prawn carpaccio escorted by plinths of braised pork neck – a confronting, utterly delicious mix of raw and cooked, sweet and savoury, hot and cold, land and sea. Cured ocean trout "cannelloni" is filled with spanner crab and celeriac remoulade, presented three ways, including a crown of oscietra caviar. Grimaud duck hints at a French classic with orange confit witlof and hazelnut. Yes, desserts are outrageously expensive, but the witty play on mont blanc with milk sorbet is followed by complimentary coffee and wicked petits fours.

Hours Lunch Friday noon–3pm; Dinner Tues–Sat 6–10pm; bookings essential

Bill E $35 **M** $50 **D** $35

Cards AE DC V MC

Wine Impressive, albeit expensive array of top-flight Australian, plus strong French focus; 17 by the glass

Chefs Tony Bilson, Alfonso Ales & Jeremie Martelin

Owner Tony Bilson

Seats 80; private rooms; wheelchair access

www.bilsons.com.au

And…a fabulous cheese tray of Europe and Australia's finest

THE HOTEL SCHOOL SYDNEY

A DEGREE A JOB A FUTURE

The Hotel School Sydney is a unique partnership between Southern Cross University and Mulpha Australia's hotel portfolio including InterContinental Sydney, Hayman Great Barrier Reef, Sanctuary Cove, Hyatt at Sanctuary Cove, Hilton Melbourne and Bimbadgen Estate Wines.

Our aim is to prepare well-rounded graduates for employment in hotel and tourism management positions in Australia and internationally. Candidates are selected on the basis of academic performance, achievements and an interview.

YEAR 1
Diploma - six months study and six months paid internship at one of our partner hotels

YEAR 2
Associate Degree

YEAR 3
Bachelor of Business

FEE-HELP SCHEME AVAILABLE

FOR FURTHER INFORMATION PLEASE CONTACT THE HOTEL SCHOOL SYDNEY
117 Macquarie Street Sydney NSW Australia 2000 Phone 02 9240 1280 Fax 02 9240 1338
e-mail hotel@scu.edu.au www.hotelschool.scu.edu.au
SCU CRICOS Number 01241G Course Code 024239A

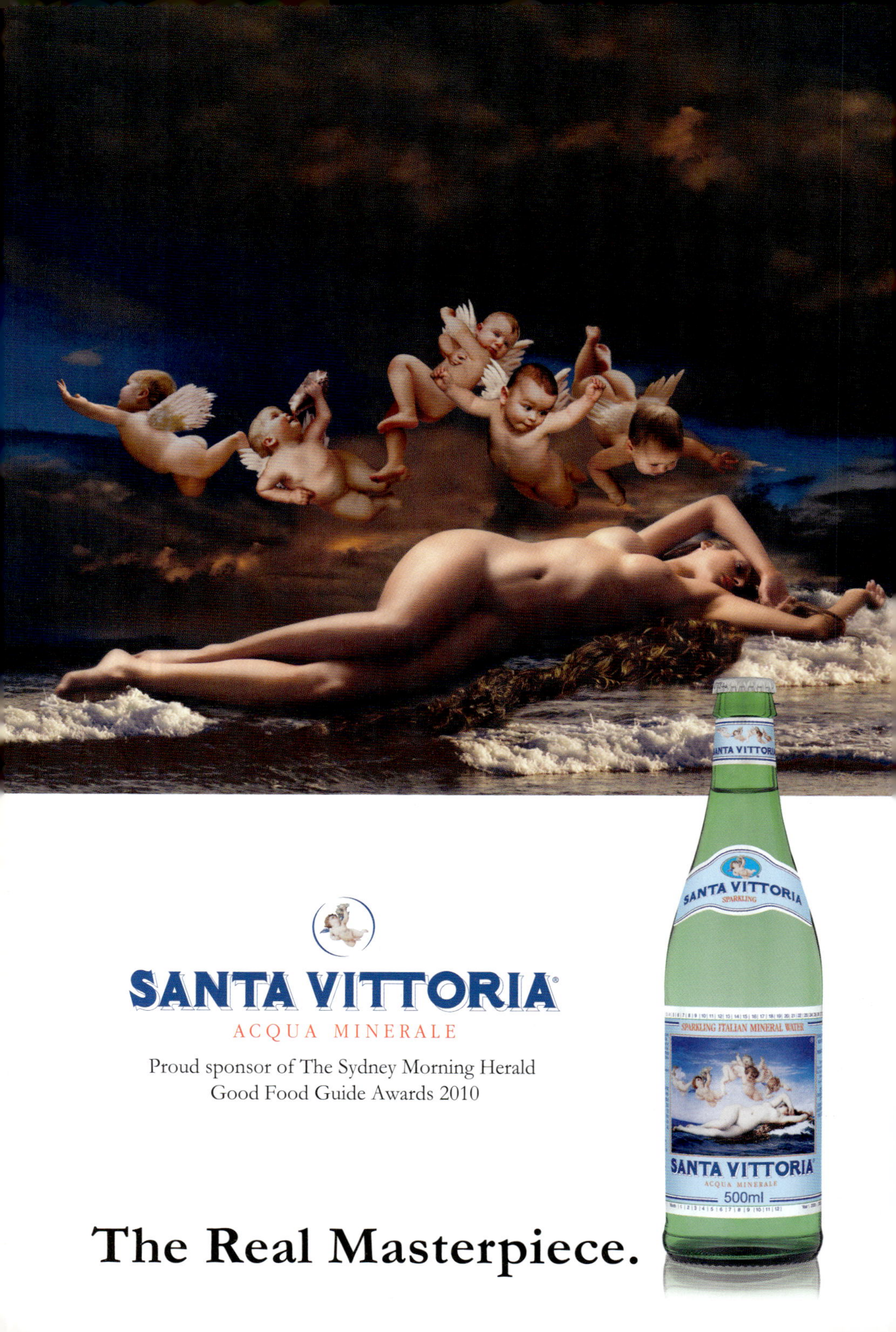

SANTA VITTORIA
ACQUA MINERALE

Proud sponsor of The Sydney Morning Herald
Good Food Guide Awards 2010

The Real Masterpiece.

city + suburbs

Bin24 Wine Bar & Wood Fire Eatery

The Bakehouse Quarter, 3–24 George Street, North Strathfield
Tel 9764 5084   Map 6

Contemporary/Mediterranean

Score 13/20

The contemporary design of the Bakehouse Quarter cleverly incorporates nostalgic remnants of its predecessor, the old Arnott's biscuit factory. Converted into cobblestone streets, it houses offices, shops, cafes and the fashionable Bin24, boasting British-trained chef Derek Baker (formerly of Alchemy 731). The long room has a bar at one end, leading to a dining space of white leather chairs, timber tables and banquettes, plus a large outdoor area popular with families tucking into wood-fired pizza. The newly enlivened menu delivers a stunning entree of beetroot-cured salmon delicately textured with celeriac remoulade and citrus fruit. Cassoulet of confit chicken and toulouse sausage comes in its own earthenware pot, albeit restrained in flavour. Braised lamb shoulder rewards handsomely, with tender meat slices topped with a robust medley of olives, lentils and mint gremolata. Service is friendly but needs a polish to match the well-executed kitchen offerings. Dark chocolate and pear tart with orange mascarpone is a luscious finish.

Hours Lunch Tues–Sun 11.30am–3pm; Dinner Tues–Sun 6–11pm; bookings essential
Bill E $14–$22 **M** $24–$32 **D** $10–$14
Cards AE V MC Eftpos; surcharge on Sundays & public holidays
Wine 25 by the glass
Chef Derek Baker
Owner Bin 24 Restaurants Pty Ltd
Seats 220; wheelchair access; outdoor seating; bar
Child friendly Kids' meals; highchairs
Vegetarian Number of options
www.bin24.com.au
And…great wood-fired pizzas to take away

Bird Cow Fish

Shops 4 & 5, 500 Crown Street, Surry Hills
Tel 9380 4090   Map 3b

Contemporary

Score 15/20

Bentwood chairs, creamy tealights and chocolate tones create a warm atmosphere, while the sounds of relaxed Surry Hills denizens fill the often noisy room. The same warmth and down-to-earth charm are integral to Alex Herbert's bistro menu, which displays flair with each of its namesake forms of protein. A snappy frisee and witlof salad topped with crisp prosciutto and a soft-poached egg is a good start, yet outshone by fresh pasta sheets with oxtail and caramelised eschalots, the heavenly, slow-braised sauce permeated with fragrant orange zest. Layers of autumn colours and flavours build in pancetta-wrapped roast Barossa chicken stuffed with porcini risotto and served on a bed of radicchio. Celeriac remoulade ably cuts through rich, crisp-skinned salmon. Buttermilk panna cotta completes the picture, lifted beyond its ubiquity on Sydney menus by a velvety texture, sticky sangiovese verjuice syrup and grilled figs. It confirms BCF's status as one of the city's Best in Show.

Hours Breakfast Sat–Sun 8am–2.30pm; Lunch daily noon–2.30pm; Dinner Mon–Thurs 6–9.30pm, Fri–Sat 6–10pm
Bill E $18.50 **M** $32.50–$38.50 **D** $15; 10% surcharge on Sundays & public holidays
Cards AE V MC Eftpos
Wine Interesting list of boutique Australians joined by French and Italian; 30 by the glass; BYO Mon–Thurs (corkage $15 a bottle)
Chef Alex Herbert
Owners Alex Herbert & Howard Gardner
Seats 85; wheelchair access; outdoor seating
Child friendly Highchairs; kids' meals; crayons
www.birdcowfish.com.au
And…buy their panforte, jams and sauces to take home

city + suburbs

Bistro CBD

Level 1, 52 King Street
(cnr York Street), Sydney
Tel 8297 7010   Map 1

Contemporary

Score 14/20

At the top of a precipitous staircase, above this popular George Street bar, Bistro CBD is not what you'd expect of a typical business-lunch venue. In fact, the high-ceilinged, arch-windowed, blessedly soundproof space has become a byword for elegant city dining, serving (albeit sometimes slowly) everyone from bankers to weary shoppers. Among the entrees, plump fresh figs stuffed with St Agur and swaddled with pancetta are luscious, although Sydney Rock oysters with golden shallot champagne dressing were a little lacklustre. A complimentary shot of velvety potato soup is a generous touch before mains, which range from a pleasing tarte tartin with roast pumpkin and tangy goat's cheese to a first-class angus fillet: smoky, juicy, and paired with sauteed kipflers, field mushrooms and cepe butter. Dessert is even better – the most creamy, come-hither duo of hand-made ice-creams, with lemon sorbet to boot. It's cuisine worth the climb.

Hours Lunch Mon–Fri noon–3pm; Dinner Mon–Fri 6–10pm
Bill E $19 **M** $36–$39 **D** $14; bookings essential
Cards AE DC V MC
Wine Short Australian list with a French and Kiwi twist; 12 by the glass; BYO Mon–Wed dinner only (corkage $10pp)
Chef Simun Dragicevich
Owner Merivale Group
Seats 80; wheelchair access; bar
www.merivale.com
And...try a '96 Sauternes for $30 and a dessert souffle is free

Bistro-Fax

Radisson Plaza Hotel, Cnr Pitt, Hunter
& O'Connell streets, Sydney
Tel 8214 0400   Map 1

Contemporary

Score 14/20

Happy tourist groups are nourished on the lower level with its open kitchen while business meetings and ladies who lunch occupy the second tier of this light, airy respite from the city bustle. Inside a beautiful heritage building, cloths cover the white tables at night, and there are additional meat offerings from the grill. Service is friendly and capable as warm bread rolls accompany a complimentary cup of prawn bisque. Begin with a beautifully presented salad of ruby beetroot discs beneath ripe figs, scrolls of ham and mesclun. Flavours are fresh and pristine in plump seared scallops between two open squares of saffron ravioli with shards of asparagus and a foamy sauce. Crisp-skinned barramundi nestles on cauliflower puree with snowpeas, green onions and shiitake mushrooms. While a lunchtime summer salad of squid and chickpeas might lack clarity, it's great value for money. The knockout dessert is a cone of peach jelly encircled by poached peaches, four seasonal sorbets, fresh raspberries and mint chiffonade.

Hours Breakfast Mon–Fri 6.30–10.30am, Sat–Sun 7–11am; Lunch Mon–Fri noon–2pm; Dinner daily 6–10pm
Bill E $14–$19.50 **M** $21–$38 **D** $14–$15
Cards AE DC V MC Eftpos
Wine Interesting list focusing on Australasian; 28 by the glass; BYO (corkage $8 a bottle)
Chef Jeremy Clark
Owner Radisson Plaza Hotel Sydney
Seats 100; wheelchair access
Child friendly Kids' menu; highchairs
www.radisson.com/sydneyau_plaza
And...relax in the adjacent ABX bar before or after

city + suburbs

Bistro Moncur

The Woollahra Hotel,
116 Queen Street, Woollahra
Tel 9327 9713 Map 4a

French

Score 15/20

While the rest of the world is in GFC meltdown, Bistro Moncur rattles along, sure in its intent. By 8.30pm, the blondwood chairs and tables are crammed, and the room, with its signature black-and-white mural, is rocking. Little has changed in the past decade except the prices (upwards), and owner Damien Pignolet would face a revolt if he rocked the boat. So still they come for the vine-ripened tomato salad, French onion souffle, blue swimmer crab omelette followed by a medium-rare steak (fillet, minute, sirloin, flank), house-made pork sausages and perhaps a special of NZ dory with rocket sauce. Occasionally, things in the kitchen don't quite go to plan: the fish was overpowered with truffle butter, while a broad bean and bug salad came sans broad beans. However, the bread and butter are top notch, a trio of ices (maybe lemon, raspberry rockmelon) terrific, as is the high-octane coffee. A Woollahra institution, and long may it reign.

Hours Lunch Tues–Sun noon–3pm; Dinner Mon–Sat 6–10.30pm, Sun 6–9pm; no bookings
Bill E $17.90–$32.50 **M** $29.50–$43 **D** $17.50–$18
Cards AE DC V MC Eftpos
Wine A large-ish list with a French accent, that could be better off with some more classic varieties and labels; 40 by the glass
Chefs Damien Pignolet & Tom Walton
Owners Damien Pignolet & Ron White
Seats 108; wheelchair access; outdoor seating; bar
Child friendly Kids' menu; crayons
Vegetarian Several options
www.bistromoncur.com.au
And…head upstairs to Moncur Terrace for a mini-me version

Bistro Ortolan

134 Marion Street, Leichhardt
Tel 9568 4610 Map 5b

French

Score 16.5/20

An ortolan is a small, migratory bird. Having landed in this unlikely inner-west habitat, Bistro Ortolan is a rare bird indeed. Irish-born chef Paul McGrath flew his homeland coop more than a decade ago, and now perches near the top of Sydney dining. His cooking, backed by impeccable service, shines in dishes such as ceviche of cuttlefish, cured ocean trout and prawn with grapefruit and baby summer purslane, creating a near-perfect work of art. Poached milk-fed veal tenderloin and its casserole with smoked potato puree, savoy cabbage and pearl onions is just one in a range of exquisite dishes. Roasted, line-caught barra fillet arrives with white asparagus, shiitake mushrooms and smoked eel brandade. French cuisine of this contemporary and accomplished tone reveals a consummate talent. An irresistible raspberry and white bombe alaska with fresh raspberries tops the first-class desserts. Bistro Ortolan is a stellar reminder that fine dining holds its place in Sydney's eating-out pantheon.

Hours Dinner Tues–Sat 6–10pm
Bill E $19–$28 **M** $29–$42 **D** $16–$18; 10% surcharge on public holidays
Cards AE (+2.5%) DC (+2.5%) V MC
Wine Small, sophisticated list with a balance of French and Australasian drops; 12 by the glass; BYO Tues–Thurs (corkage $10 a bottle)
Chef Paul McGrath
Owners Paul & Jenny McGrath
Seats 60; private rooms; wheelchair access; outdoor seating
www.bistroortolan.com.au
And…set aside time, and funds, for the spectacular degustation menu

good food guide

city + suburbs

Bistrode ★

478 Bourke Street, Surry Hills
Tel 9380 7333   Map 3b

European

Score 15/20

SMALL WINE LIST OF THE YEAR

The combined talents of Jane and Jeremy Strode continue to shimmer in their fondly recalled bistro. Dining in the converted butcher's shop is something easily enjoyed every week, and many do just that. The softly lit room has a warm, rustic feel that carries through to real bistro food crafted with premium produce. Service is attentive and well informed. An entree of ocean trout, twirled into a vibrant disc, sits on top of a potato pancake dressed with beetroot and sour cream. Whole roast quail is filled with pork and veal mince, pistachios and sourdough stuffing and presented on English spinach. It's scrumptious, with a thoughtful finger bowl to savour every morsel. Ox tongue is unadorned, full of flavour and texture alongside green herb sauce and potato salad. Crisp blue-eye is luscious with a zesty blend of prawns, salami and chilli. Seasonal peaches and berries are elegant in pink champagne jelly or there's the all-time favourite honey tart with peanut butter ice-cream.

Hours Lunch Fri noon–2pm;
Dinner Tues–Sat 6–10pm
Bill E $16.50–$19.50 **M** $32.50–$39.50
D $15–$17.50
Cards AE DC V MC
Wine Balanced, thoughtful list of locals with strong global interest; 12 by the glass; BYO Tues–Thurs only (corkage $10 a bottle)
Chefs/owners Jane & Jeremy Strode
Seats 40; outdoor seating
Child friendly Highchairs; smaller portions
www.bistrode.com
And…a great place for offal lovers

Blackwater

1/8 Water Street, Sans Souci
Tel 9529 4893   Map 8

Contemporary Italian

Score 13/20

It's no wonder these Sans Souci locals are so carefree. With its backlit onyx counter, clothed tables and bentwood chairs, this sleek Italian dining room has brought a splash of style to the south. Chef Riccardo Roberti's ingredients and techniques may be anchored in tradition, yet his nuanced, modern menu tacks happily from light, seafood-focused starters, such as fried baby calamari or bug and broad bean salad, to house-made pasta and meaty mains. Tagliatelle carbonara, decked out with strips of crisp guanciale (cured pig's cheek) and the smooth richness of truffled duck egg, is so good you'll want to drag your bread through the sauce. It's not all smooth sailing, though – the seafood in a generous misto di mare stew was overwhelmed by a buttery sauce, and lamb cutlets with pancetta and balsamic were a tad overdone. Dessert shows a return to form, as an ethereal white chocolate budino (pudding) narrowly edges out profiteroles with buffalo-milk ice cream for line honours.

Hours Lunch Wed–Fri & Sun noon–2.30pm; Dinner Tues–Sat 6–9.30pm; bookings essential
Bill E $15.80–$25.80 **M** $26.80–$42.80
D $14–$15.80; 10% surcharge on public holidays
Cards AE V MC
Wine Good spread of Australian and Italian drops; 14 by the glass; BYO except Fri–Sat dinner (corkage $3.50pp)
Chefs Riccardo Roberti & John O'Riordan
Owners Riccardo Roberti & Natasha Battikha
Seats 100; wheelchair access; bar
Child friendly Highchairs
www.blackwaterrestaurant.com.au
And…finish with a sgroppino: lemon sorbet, champagne and vodka

city + suburbs

Blancharu

Shop 1, 21 Elizabeth Bay Road, Elizabeth Bay
Tel 9360 3555   Map 2

French/Japanese

Score 15/20

Who'd have guessed that after wowing hotel diners at Galileo with culinary fireworks, chef Haru Inukai would renounce it all to open a bistro? But here's the thing: this is a pleasing mix of well-priced, comforting, assured flavours and clever innovation. Haru-san's time with Joel Robuchon in Japan results in refined and remarkable bistro dishes such as tempura zucchini flowers filled with an ethereal Shinjo-style (no cream) cuttlefish mousse, and a main of perfectly seared, buttery and lush Tajima wagyu scotch fillet with layered potato cake and gingery ponzu sauce. Sometimes it gets a little too experimental and confused, such as Japanese-style fettuccine with coq-au-vin. But with the genial chef enthusiastically patrolling the floor of this neat and homely room, and its casual bar space and sunken, alfresco dining area, it's hard to resist Blancharu's many charms. Poached white peach with peach jelly and peach sorbet sings an elegant song of summer, before Haru-san appears offering complimentary green tea madeleines as a final thank you.

Hours Lunch Fri–Sat noon–2.30pm; Dinner Mon–Sat 6–10pm
Bill E $12–$22 **M** $18–$39 **D** $12–$16; 4-course degustation $65pp, 8 courses $75
Cards AE V MC Eftpos
Wine Small, affordably priced and interesting international list; 14 by the glass; BYO (corkage $10 a bottle)
Chef/owner Haru Inukai
Seats 55; wheelchair access; outdoor seating
www.blancharu.com.au
And…look out for ama ebi, a Japanese raw prawn classic

Blancmange

1 Station Street (cnr West Street), Petersham
Tel 9568 4644   Map 8

European

Score 14/20

Now here's a restaurant for the times. This stylish yet homey corner bistro (love the nanna-style crockery and artworks) offers echoes of your favourite Parisian bistro plus a view of Petersham Park. Combined with super-attentive service led by owner Ian Meggitt, and honest, contemporary, mostly European fare, it feels like a special treat – but three courses are only $50. It's terrific value for a deeply satisfying potato, onion and chorizo gratin with radish and frisee salad, or the feathery ricotta and spinach twice-cooked souffle. Calamari on fennel and parsley with lemon and chive beurre blanc was less successful – as was a slightly chewy steak and fries – but mulloway with peperonata on baby spinach showcases the kitchen's talent. Desserts are particularly comforting. Try stone fruit crumble with surprisingly spiky ginger ice-cream, or the "bread" and butter pud, made with brioche and served with heavenly vanilla anglaise. A local to return to time and again.

Hours Dinner Tues–Sat 6–9.30pm
Bill E $16 **M** $28 **D** $12; 3-course menu $50pp
Cards V MC Eftpos
Wine Plenty of French choices, and Australian, at price points to match the menu; 14 by the glass; BYO Tues–Thurs (corkage $3.50pp)
Chefs Nigel Douglas & Brian Martinez
Owner Ian Meggitt
Seats 66; private room; wheelchair access
Child friendly Highchairs; crayons; toys; sense of humour; parental empathy; bespoke meals
www.restaurantblancmange.com.au
And…check out the changing array of artworks. Ben Quilty lent a piece for a while

city + suburbs

Blue Eye Dragon

Shop 2, 42 Harris Street, Pyrmont
Tel 9518 9955   Map 5b

Taiwanese

Score 13/20

In a city where Cantonese food dominates Chinese cuisine, it's refreshing to discover Blue Eye Dragon and its take on modern Taiwanese. Characterised by subtle spiciness, abundant seafood, sauces and stews – here's the place to try non-standard Sino fare. A concise menu balances staples with new twists, and the service is swift, amiable and knowledgeable. For something new, calamari rolls with salted duck egg and seaweed is a creative clash of flavour and delicious texture. Water chestnuts, shallots and celery feature in the tasty prawn dumplings served with a fine vinegar dipping sauce. Salt-and-pepper soft-shell crab could do with a lighter batter, while slow-cooked pork belly in soy, aniseed and light chilli gets it just right. Steamed barramundi in fish sauce, topped with ginger and shallots, was a touch overcooked, while pork mince and prawn stuffed tofu in oyster sauce is real comfort food. For dessert, try the selection of ice-creams and sticky rice cakes.

Hours Lunch Tues–Fri noon–2.30pm; Dinner Tues–Sat 6–9.30pm; bookings essential
Bill E $10–$24 **M** $20–$36 **D** $10–$14; tasting menu $60pp
Cards AE (+2%) V MC Eftpos
Wine Small, reasonable list; 3 by the glass; BYO (corkage $5pp)
Chef Jade Chen
Owner Muriel Chen
Seats 60
Child friendly Highchairs
www.blueeyedragon.com.au
And...love the food? Buy the cookbook, on sale in the restaurant

The Boathouse on Blackwattle Bay

End of Ferry Road, Glebe
Tel 9518 9011   Map 5b

Seafood

Score 15/20

If there really are plenty of fish in the sea, you can eat most of them here. The Boathouse menu features a terrific variety of fish dishes, all expertly cooked, plus a plethora of fresh Sydney rock oysters from various NSW locations. A panoramic view of the Anzac Bridge and the city lights sparkling on the water will impress. So too will a delicate entree of Tasmanian Gould's squid involtini, stuffed with capers, breadcrumbs and parsley and sliced ever so thinly. The famous snapper pie is as popular as ever, but pan-fried mahi mahi also entrances, served with smoky eggplant puree and piquant preserved lemon salsa. Etuvee of ocean trout is delectable, the fish moist and flaky with crisp skin, accompanied by mussels and refreshing cucumber. Polite and focused floor staff ensure it's smooth sailing all the way, while apple and gingerbread souffle in a small copper saucepan with cinnamon ice-cream on the side, should really float your boat.

Hours Lunch Tues–Sun noon–2.30pm; Dinner Tues–Sun 6–9.30pm; Bar menu Tues–Sun noon–9.30pm
Bill E $27 **M** $36–$48 **D** $18
Cards AE DC V MC
Wine An extensive list with a few half-bottles and plenty of menu-friendly appropriate choices; 13 by the glass
Chef Perry Hill
Owners Tony Papas & Robert Smallbone
Seats 110; wheelchair access; bar
www.boathouse.net.au
And...have a pre- or post-dinner drink in the small bar area

city + suburbs

Bodega

216 Commonwealth Street, Surry Hills
Tel 9212 7766   Map 3b

Spanish/Latin
Score 14.5/20

More than three years after Bodega surfed the Sydney tapas new wave, it's still riding as high as the rockabilly hairdos of the boys in the open kitchen. The service is in the same groove, flitting confidently among the cool crowd, and the Spanish-meets-South-American fare is a balance of style and substance. Pumpkin empanadas, spiked with cumin and swiped through garlicky yoghurt, speak of homey comfort, while spiced fried school prawns – guest stars on the menu in season – are impossible to resist. Balance things out with a salad of tender, smoky charred octopus and kipflers, or the piggy take on a caesar – rich, livery-tasting kurobuta white sausage and crispy pork skin (chicharrones) nestled on lettuce beneath an as-promised "perfect" fried egg. Dessert demonstrates the plus side of a communal table, as word of the famed "banana split" – cream flan, dulce de leche ice-cream on banana puree, and toasted banana marshmallow on the side – travels down its length like a Mexican wave, and each group orders it in turn.

Hours Lunch Thurs–Fri noon–2.30pm; Dinner Mon–Sat 6–10pm; no bookings
Bill Tapas menu $6–$26; **D** $12–$14
Cards AE V MC
Wine Interesting choices from Spain and South America; 16 by the glass (plus 10 sherries)
Chefs Elvis Abrahamowicz & Ben Milgate
Owners Joseph Valore, Elvis Abrahamowicz & Ben Milgate
Seats 60; wheelchair access; outdoor seating; bar
Vegetarian 8 dishes
www.bocegatapas.com
And...next door is the cafe-style Bodega Cocina by day, and bar (with separate menu) at night

The Book Kitchen

255 Devonshire Street, Surry Hills
Tel 9310 1003   Map 3b

Contemporary
Score 13/20

The Book Kitchen is the kind of neighbourhood joint you'd be happy to drop in to every week, whether for their trademark soft-boiled biodynamic eggs with Vegemite soldiers and restorative coffee, or a casual weekend dinner. With its rough-edged industrial space, open kitchen and shelves stocked with cookbooks old and new, there's a relaxed ambience that belies the quality of the food. Chef David Campbell lets the produce shine in ocean trout salad with kipfler potatoes, crunchy asparagus and sharp black olives, topped with a divinely runny poached egg. Moist blue swimmer crab cakes are served simply on a bed of rocket, topped with fresh avocado and shaved tomato. Olive oil is drizzled over spaghettini with chunks of artichoke, green and black olives and lemon peel. Date and fig pikelets with poached pear, roasted rhubarb and ricotta were, however, too fat and doughy so the intended flavour was lost. Overall, though, this is a cafe you'd love to see at the end of your street.

Hours Breakfast daily 8am–3pm; Lunch daily noon–3pm; Dinner Fri–Sat 6.30–11pm
Bill E $10–$22 **M** $22–$30 **D** $12; 10% surcharge on Sundays & public holidays
Cards AE (+3%) V MC Eftpos
Wine A small list of mostly Australian wines; 16 by the glass; BYO (corkage $5pp)
Chef David Campbell
Owners David & Nicole Campbell
Seats 50; wheelchair access; outdoor seating
Child friendly Highchairs
www.thebookkitchen.com.au
And...the Hungry Duck in Berry (see South Coast) is also run by David Campbell

good food guide   29

city + suburbs

Botanic Gardens Restaurant

Royal Botanic Gardens,
Mrs Macquarie's Road, Sydney
Tel 9241 2419   Map 2

Contemporary

Score 13/20

Flying foxes, hanging wisteria and a pond full of water lilies below – there's something magical about lunch in the middle of the Botanic Gardens. Gallery visitors, CBD workers and the occasional well-dressed tourist enjoy light food in a bright and lovely room. Entrees were underwhelming – a duck bistilla (pastry triangle) lacked flavour and moisture, and cucumber soup with crab meat and avocado was refreshing but a little watery. Mains are far more successful, such as perfectly cooked blue-eye served with green masala sauce and coconut rice. A generously sized lamb loin sits on an eggplant and tomato salad with a beautiful cumin fragrance. As you sit under a green canopy and watching lunchtime joggers pass by, it really feels like there is no need to return to work. So stay for a mango and ginger brulee, tea, coffee or whatever will keep you a little longer in this garden wonderland.

Hours Breakfast Sat–Sun 9.30–11.30am; Lunch daily noon–3pm; bookings essential
Bill E $17–$21 **M** $26–$34 **D** $16–$18; 10% surcharge on Sundays & public holidays
Cards AE V MC
Wine Predominantly local list with a good range of small to large wineries; 10 by the glass
Chef Janet Kirkwood
Owner AIH Group
Seats 130; private rooms; wheelchair access; balcony seating
Child friendly Kids' menu; highchairs
www.trippaswhite.com.au
And… take the Henry Lawson Gate for quickest access through the Gardens

Bronte Road Bistro

282 Bronte Road, Waverley
Tel 9389 3028   Map

European

Score 13.5/20

Like any bistro worth its frites, on the brown paper menu there's a fine steak – onglet, where flavour triumphs over tenderness – with cafe de paris butter. Chef Dave Pegrum (formerly of Forbes & Burton) has opted for a light, simple yet scrumptious approach to French and Mediterranean combinations. Smoked eel, grated apple and rocket salad is delicate and light, dressed with the sweet, peppery and smoky flavours of an apple, grain mustard and verjuice dressing. The main dining space is an outdoorsy, paver-floored sunroom with timber tables and a cushion-strewn banquette, although the lighting can be too low to read the menu. At least then you'd spot the sweet dates, which didn't do much to help the otherwise delightful seared ocean trout with horseradish cream, salmon roe and a cucumber and walnut salad. Fanned fresh mango slices drizzled with vanilla syrup beside scoops of Serendipity coconut-macaroon ice-cream and toasted coconut shavings is as delightful as ducking down the hill for a dip.

Hours Lunch Thurs–Sat noon–3pm; Dinner Tues–Sat 6–10pm
Bill E $16 **M** $28 **D** $11
Cards V MC Eftpos
Wine Affordable local and French, plus impressive reserve list of back vintages; 10 by the glass
Chef Dave Pegrum
Owners Stewart & Jessica Parsons
Seats 55; outdoor seating; bar
Child friendly Kids' menu; highchairs
www.bronteroadbistro.com
And… organic coffee and good herbal teas

city + suburbs

Brown Sugar

106 Curlewis Street, Bondi
Tel 9130 1566   **Map** 4b

Mediterranean

Score 13/20

Ah, good old Bondi, home of the all-day breakfast. Arriving for the renowned Sunday lunch, it is obvious that the majority is generation Y, still tucking in to cholesterol-sustaining breakfast-meets-brunch-meets-lunch. This quaint shopfront restaurant, a decent stroll from the famous beach, is Bondi casual at its boldest, featuring packed tables and relaxed but effective service. Brown sugar caramelised walnuts add sparkle to a stylish beetroot, spinach, pear and goat's cheese salad with a generous splash of balsamic vinegar for further complexity. South Australian mussels in an aromatic pool of tomato, chilli and white wine broth are succulent and tender and adorned with ample grilled sourdough for mopping up the savoury juices. A delicate palette in cream and pink – two thick slices of silky Pedro Ximenez semifreddo studded with pomegranate sequins and surrounded by wedges of rosy figs – is as pretty as a Bondi sunset.

Hours Breakfast Fri–Sun 8.30am–2.30pm;
Lunch Fri–Sun noon–2.30pm;
Dinner Tues–Sun 6.30–10.30pm

Bill E $12–$17 **M** $25–$32 **D** $10–$14;
$1pp surcharge on Sundays, 10% surcharge on public holidays

Cards AE (+3%) V MC Eftpos

Wine Short and practical list; 9 by the glass; BYO (corkage $8 a bottle)

Chef Neil Gottheiner

Owners Neil & Lianne Gottheiner

Seats 48; wheelchair access; outdoor seating

Child friendly Highchairs

Vegetarian Huge range of options for breakfast, lunch & dinner

www.brownsugarbondi.com.au

And…return for dinner from the large blackboard

Buon Ricordo

108 Boundary Street, Paddington
Tel 9360 6729   **Map** 2

Italian

Score 16.5/20

Theatre is a major part of a visit to Buon Ricordo. The backdrop is a room lined with flamboyant art, the audience is very Sydney establishment, and the director is larger-than-life chef Armando Percuoco, a consummate host who ensures everyone enjoys the show. The star, of course, is the food – a refined take on the peasant fare of, predominantly, his native southern Italy. Ricotta has never tasted as indulgent as when teamed with provola and salami in a small, neat, fried calzone, Naples style. Vegetable antipasto treats eggplant, zucchini and capsicum with individual care. A main of snapper baked in pizza dough is broken open at the table, the waiter filleting its perfectly steamed flesh with a consummate flourish – although a salty tomato, thyme and lemon zest salsa slightly overpowered. Dainty boned quail, on the other hand, is stacked on a harmonious jumble of witlof, pear and vincotto. Baked peach halves filled with amaretti biscuits are a memorable finale, almost trumped by a petit four encore of tiny, orange-blossom-water-scented cannoli.

Hours Lunch Fri–Sat noon–3pm;
Dinner Tues–Sat 6–10.45pm

Bill E $23.50–$33.50 **M** $39.50–$57.50 **D** $21

Cards AE DC V MC Eftpos

Wine Large Italian/Australasian selection backed by a formidable cellar; 15 by the glass

Chefs Armando Percuoco & Darren Taylor

Owners Armando Percuoco & Gemma Cunningham

Seats 100; private room

Vegetarian Separate menu and degustation

www.buonricordo.com.au

And…look out for Armando's cookbook celebrating 30 years in the business

city + suburbs

The Burlington Bar and Dining
6 Burlington Street, Crows Nest
Tel 9439 7888   Map 5a

Modern European

Score 14.5/20

The northside has warmly embraced this sparkling bistro from the team behind Randwick's Restaurant Balzac. Since it offers generous wining and dining versatility at prices to please, it's no surprise. Most dishes are offered in entree and main sizes, with wines available by the glass, carafes in two sizes or bottle. Now that's clever, rather like a terrine of smoked ham hock and pork cheek; the flavour and texture superb alongside beignets of pig's ear and celeriac remoulade. A square pastry tart, crowned with bright crimson marinated peppers, fresh goat's cheese, olives and basil, is gorgeous. The careful casualness from friendly, focused staff suits this bistro with its warm tones, banquettes and timber tables. Crisp, pan-seared mahi mahi rests on risotto richly flavoured with fennel, calamari and dried chilli. Under a flaky pastry lid are lushly generous slices of poached free-range chicken, baby leek and creme fraiche. The final triumph is a heavenly summer pudding trifle.

Hours Lunch Mon–Fri noon–3pm; Dinner Mon–Sat 6–10pm; bookings essential
Bill E $10–$18 **M** $18–$28 **D** $12
Cards AE DC V MC Eftpos
Wine Concise, impressive global list offered in 150ml, 250ml, 375ml and full bottle serves; 21 by the glass
Chefs Matthew Kemp & Chad Muir
Owners Matthew Kemp & Lela Radojkovic
Seats 95; private room; bar
Child friendly Kids' menu; highchairs; toys
www.burlingtonbardining.com.au
And…ask about express lunch specials

Busshari
119 Macleay Street, Potts Point
Tel 9357 4555   Map 2

Japanese

Score 14/20

Potts Point is proving a real haven for foodies who know a good thing when they see it. Busshari knows the beat of this city with its dark and moody decor enlivened by a row of kitsch paper lanterns and vivacious staff ensuring you have a good time. As the crowd buzzes, grab a stool at the tall Tasmanian oak tables or, if you're lucky, pull up a pew in pole position and watch the sushi chef ply his trade. Chef Nobu Ito delivers contemporary and consistent Japanese staples. Start with a stellar sashimi plate where snapper, scampi, scallops, tuna, kingfish and bonito show their true colours and shine. Fresh, slippery little sea urchin sushi satisfies, while the fat marbling of toro, bluefin tuna belly, lives up to its tag as the wagyu of the sea. If it doesn't make you moo then a sizzling pot of wagyu beef will get you by the horns. Ice-cream and sorbet in Japanese flavours covers the pretty dessert platter.

Hours Dinner Mon–Sat 6–10.45pm
Bill E $5–$17 **M** $12–$39 **D** $6.50–$20
Cards AE DC V MC Eftpos JCB
Wine Decent list, even better sake range; 13 by the glass; BYO (corkage $7 a bottle)
Chef Nobu Ito
Owner Busshari Pty Ltd
Seats 36; wheelchair access
Child friendly Highchairs
www.busshari.com.au
And…the sake list is huge and lots of fun

city + suburbs

buzo trattoria
3 Jersey Road, Woollahra
Tel 9328 1600   Map 4a

Italian
Score 13.5/20

Buzo fits seamlessly into the Woollahra restaurant mould. Tucked into two floors of a refurbished terrace – embossed wallpaper, polished wood, green tones – it's well-groomed and effortlessly smart. Just like the customers, really. The food is carefully conceived along Italian lines and the staff are whip-swift and courteous, flitting tirelessly up and down stairs. Whet the appetite with a neatly vinegared cucumber salad and white anchovy antipasto or head straight for soft gnocchi, hiding under a gentle sausage and tomato-laden sauce. Orecchiette (ear-shaped) pasta was bathed in too much tomato sauce, however, with too few slivers of baccala (salt cod) and crouton, rather than crumb-sized pangrattato. Slender slices of seared liver appear in a trice, good fluffy-crunchy fried potatoes and lemon-dressed green beans on the side. Fresh fruit for dessert, in the Italian way, is an elegant touch but torta di verona – a finely textured, almond, amaretti and mascarpone dessert – is far more alluring, along with the extensive grappa list.

Hours Dinner Mon–Sat 6–11pm; bookings essential
Bill E $17–$19.50 **M** $27–$32 **D** $9.50–$16.50
Cards AE DC V MC
Wine Wide-ranging bottle (and grappa) choice with plenty of Italian; 20 by the glass
Chefs James Hird & Todd Garratt
Owners James Hird, Todd Garratt & Traci Trinder
Seats 80
Vegetarian Always options on menu, including pasta, antipasto & risotto
www.buzorestaurant.com.au
And... menu changes frequently to allow for regular dining

Cafe Sopra
7 Danks Street, Waterloo
Tel 9699 3174   Map 9
Also at 81 Macleay Street, Fotts Point
Tel 9368 6666   Map 2

Italian
Score 14.5/20

There's something wonderfully infectious about this place, from the downstairs produce market to the anticipation of climbing warehouse stairs and finding an expansive, light-filled room with one half devoted to Italian larder food. Eat at the bar or at communal or individual tables. Service is friendly and quick, while out the back Andy Bunn is making deceptively simple, well-priced food. Plump chunks of buffalo mozzarella sit on sweet, vine-ripe tomatoes with freshly plucked baby basil taken from punnets in the kitchen. Classic penne al ragu comes with a fragrant veal mince sauce laced with hints of onion, garlic, dried chilli and fresh mint. Fresh deep sea bream is delicately pan-fried with green beans while lemon and anchovies add a further dimension. A simple rocket salad sings with imported Italian parmesan and lemon vinaigrette. For dessert, banoffee pie comes with a crunchy biscuit base layered with caramel, fresh banana and whipped cream.

Hours Sun–Fri 10am–3pm, Sat 8am–3pm; no bookings
Bill E $9.50–$22 **M** $16–$22 **D** $6.50–$14
Cards AE V MC Eftpos
Wine Varied and vast Italian list; 19 by the glass
Chefs Andy Bunn (Waterloo); Sean Corkery (Potts Point)
Owner Fratelli Fresh
Seats 80; private room
Child friendly Highchairs
Vegetarian Many options
www.fratellifresh.com.au
And... arrive early to get a table or expect to wait

good food guide

city + suburbs

Cafe Sydney

Level 5, Customs House,
31 Alfred Street, Circular Quay
Tel 9251 8683   Map 1

Contemporary

Score 13/20

You know you're on the tourist trail when the waiter greets you with, "Hello. Where are you from?" Er, Sydney, actually. From the top of the gracious, historic Customs House there are captivating views from the expansive terrace to the bridge, the Opera House and beyond. If the weather is unkind, there's ample accommodation within the large, energetic space under the imposing gantry. Grilled squid and pork belly works a treat with a clean, light-tasting fennel, watercress and citrus salad. Cavolo nero, goat's cheese and green peas are soothed by scrumptious butternut pumpkin and sage gnocchi. A dance of ingredients waltzes beautifully on a plate of roasted jewfish, seared scallops and salsa verde spiked with lemon vinaigrette. A finale of lusciously textured vanilla cheesecake with poached lychee, mango and lychee syrup topped with an elegant brandy snap cigar is a killer combo. Service is turbocharged and spot-on.

Hours Mon–Fri noon–11pm; Sat 5–11pm; Sun noon–4pm; bookings essential
Bill E $22–$27 **M** $32–$39 **D** $16
Cards AE DC V MC
Wine Extensive and expensive, sommelier's suggestions; 48 by the glass
Chef Matt Bates
Owners Customs House Cafe Pty Ltd
Seats 290; private room; wheelchair access; outdoor seating; bar
Child friendly Healthy kids' menu; highchairs; pencils; portable DVD
Vegetarian Separate vegan menu, plus numerous vego options
www.cafesydney.com
And... a great place to show the city off to visitors

Catalina

Lyne Park, Rose Bay
Tel 9371 0555   Map 9

Contemporary

Score 14/20

Someone had to score pole position beside the moored boats, right on the water's edge looking onto the harbour's fairy lights. The McMahon family have occupied their little piece of prime real estate for 16 years. In a way, it shows just a little, in the bluff, bland concrete exterior and plain, pimple-plaster interior of their large, noisy eatery. Catalina is something of an upscale cafeteria for the eastern suburbs set, reflected in the crowd-pleasing menu of everything from sushi and sashimi to Italian and French-inspired contemporary dishes, as well as the ebb and flow of practised staff. Hand-rolls of tuna and California-style avocado and prawn are made to order, but the sushi rice was just a tad too sticky. Seared squid with tiny, crumbed duck's tongues seemed strangely conceived, ditto the acid overtones of confit tuna with avocado puree. Large, smooth gnocchi in red wine sauce with braised beef is delicious, and a caramel-striped slice of honeycomb parfait is as decadent as this stalwart's location.

Hours Lunch daily noon–5pm; Dinner Mon–Sat 5–10pm; bookings essential
Bill E $22–$37 **M** $42–$47 **D** $19–$22; 10% surcharge on Sundays & public holidays
Cards AE DC V MC Eftpos
Wine A terrific selection with knowledgeable wine service; 35 by the glass
Chef Paul McMahon
Owners Michael, Judy & Paul McMahon
Seats 160; outdoor seating; bar
www.catalinarosebay.com.au
And... ask about special set-menu deals

city + suburbs

Catalonia

Shop 2, 31a Fitzroy Street, Kirribilli
Tel 9922 4215   Map 5a

Spanish
                                    Score 13.5/20

Sydneysiders like to share. At least that's what the lively crowds here suggest, as they tuck into some, if not all, of the 19 tapas on offer (plus sides). Despite covering two floors and spilling outdoors, this tapas restaurant is cosy with warm timber tones and vibrant red wallpaper. Service is intelligent and relaxed – and almost as endearing as a glass of tempranillo – while the menu includes unexpected combinations such as salty, smoked duck breast, draped over chargrilled watermelon, shredded radicchio and parsley, drizzled with sweet vincotto. Aged manchego (sheep's milk cheese) croquetas are gooey in the centre and golden crisp outside, served with patatas a lo pobre (poor man's potatoes). Pork belly is as tender as it comes with super-crunchy crackling. Peppers de Padron, sweet green chillies fried with coarse salt, attract a warning: one in 10 may be eye-poppingly hot. If you take a hit, dessert will salve your palate. Try rich brie de Meaux with truffle honey ice-cream.

Hours Brunch Sat–Sun 11am-1pm; Lunch Wed–Sun noon–3pm; Dinner Tues–Sat 6–10pm, Sun 6–9pm
Bill Tapas $4–$19.50; **D** $12–$12.50
Cards AE (+2.5%) V MC Eftpos
Wine A fitting list from Spain and its neighbours; 11 by the glass
Chefs Brian Villahermosa & Daniel Masters
Owners Brian Villahermosa & Thomas Hoff
Seats 90; private room; wheelchair access; outdoor seating
Child friendly Drawing materials
Vegetarian Six tapas options, plus cheese & snacks
www.catalonia.com.au
And…outside eating ends at 9pm to appease local residents, so an early dinner is a good idea

Centennial Parklands Restaurant

Cnr Grand Drive & Banksia Way, Centennial Park
Tel 9380 9350   Map 4b

Contemporary
                                    Score 13/20

Take a relaxed tree-lined setting, add Mark Best as consultant chef, stir in a smart revamp, then bake for a few hours in dazzling sunshine. The result is a lovely, if pricey, daytime setting for clever modern fare. While the three-hat chef's name creates high expectations, David Whitting's kitchen is mostly up to the task, whether it's the sultry textures of hickory-smoked blue mackerel with braised and raw beetroot, plus sweet, crunchy hazelnut praline, or an amusing wagyu carpaccio with fried capers, Ortiz anchovies and chopped parsley. The room is crisp and clean, the service smartly polite. Mains include a delightful potato "risotto" – diced to resemble rice – bejewelled with asparagus and peas and laced with nutty parsnip puree, as well as the protein hit of kurobuta pork neck with boar sausage and apple puree. Watermelon panna cotta is a harmonious duet, the accompanying macadamia praline sandwich of lychee sorbet making it two desserts in one.

Hours Lunch Wed–Sun noon–3pm
Bill E $18–$24 **M** $28–$36 **D** $13; 3-course lunch Wed–Sat $45pp; 10% surcharge on Sundays, 15% on public holidays
Cards AE V MC Eftpos
Wine 16 by the glass
Chef David Whitting
Owner Trippas White Catering
Seats 110; wheelchair access
Child friendly Kids' menu; highchairs
Vegetarian Entree & main options available
www.cpdining.com.au
And…walk off lunch in the park

city + suburbs

Chequers

Shop 220, Level 2, Mandarin Centre,
65 Albert Avenue, Chatswood
Tel 9904 8388   Map 7

Chinese (Cantonese)

Score 13.5/20

They call it Chinatown Northside but some say Chatswood is more interesting than Haymarket. There's an impressive and ever-increasing range of Asian dining options along the Victoria Avenue mall and its periphery. Still, Cantonese stalwarts such as this, tucked away on the food court level of the busy Mandarin Centre, haven't lost their appeal. Yum cha is always a drawcard here but take the opportunity to venture off-piste to the a la carte menu. The quality of seafood at Chequers is a hallmark. Steamed scallops come direct from the bubbling tanks, so the freshness is exemplary, requiring nothing more than a subtle ginger and shallot dressing. Whole parrotfish, steamed, with a light soy sauce, is memorable for its sweet, moist flesh. Another highlight is traditional pigeon, roasted pinkly, carved and served with Sichuan salt. Service is friendly, if occasionally bemused by inquiries about the wine list.

Hours Lunch Mon–Fri 11am–3pm, Sat–Sun 10am–3pm; Dinner daily 5.30–11pm
Bill E $6.80–$24.80 **M** $16.80–$108
D $4.50–$9; $2.50 per adult & $1 per child surcharge on public holidays
Cards AE DC V MC
Wine Commercial, predictable but graciously priced; 5 by the glass; BYO (corkage $5pp)
Chef Shen Jia Hua
Owner Airfoal Pty Ltd
Seats 200; private rooms; wheelchair access; bar
Child friendly Highchairs
Vegetarian Plenty of options
And... good Asian food shopping, too, at the supermarket downstairs

Chinta Ria... Temple of Love

The Roof Terrace, Level 2, Cockle Bay Wharf, Darling Park, 201 Sussex Street, Sydney
Tel 9264 3211   Map 1

Malaysian

Score 12.5/20

It's not until you're faced with colossal wooden doors, a huge, smiling Buddha and offerings of incense that the name, Temple of Love, begins to make sense. Its position ensures a well-dressed, buzzing crowd intent on having a good night out. Hawker-style food (read quick and affordable), served in Chinta Ria's temple-like interior and outdoor garden – as well as funky live jazz – are a fine way to kick-start a fast-paced evening. The waiters know this all too well, and their mission is speedy and efficient delivery of the food, but little else in between, to the point of occasional brusqueness. Plump chicken wonton broth with water chestnut and black fungus, plus falling-apart beef rendang, cooked slowly in coconut milk and spices, race out of the kitchen. Intensely dark Sassy's duck special, wok-tossed with spinach and Chinese wine and spices, was overly sweet, but you'll be ready to join the party again after creamy sago pudding.

Hours Lunch daily noon–2.30pm; Dinner Mon–Sat 6–11pm, Sun 6–10.30pm; bookings lunch only
Bill E $13.50–$28.50 **M** $16–$28.50 **D** $7.50; 10% surcharge on public holidays
Cards AE DC V MC
Wine Suitable, affordable, Australian list; 21 by the glass; BYO (limited bottles in December, corkage $10 a bottle)
Chef Donny Pang
Owner Simon Goh
Seats 160; wheelchair access; outdoor seating
Child friendly Kids' menu; highchairs; drawing materials
www.chintaria.com
And... no dinner reservations, so expect to queue

Break down the boundaries of fine dining

SHARE MENU BY SEAN CONNOLLY

There is only one thing better than enjoying a beautifully balanced dish in a magnificent restaurant, and that's enjoying two... or three. Fulfill your culinary dream with the Astral shared dining experience. Sean Connolly's new menu offers not only the opportunity to taste a range of the kitchen's best, but also to experience dining as a social creature. So share the experience, pass a selection of dishes amongst the table, relax & enjoy.

Astral Awards
2007, 2008 & 2009 CHEF'S HAT, GOOD FOOD GUIDE
2009 ONE STAR, AUSTRALIAN GOURMET TRAVELLER AWARDS

Sean Connolly
2008 CHEF OF THE YEAR, GOOD FOOD GUIDE
2008 CHEF OF THE YEAR, GQ MAN OF THE YEAR
2009 CHEF OF THE YEAR, AUSTRALIAN HOTELS ASSOCIATION

ASTRAL RESTAURANT
LEVEL 17 80 PYRMONT STREET, PYRMONT NSW 2009 WWW.ASTRALRESTAURANT.COM.AU
STAR CITY PRACTISES THE RESPONSIBLE SERVICE OF ALCOHOL

Nothing but the wine.

Brown Brothers a proud sponsor of

If only choosing a restaurant was as easy.

Brown Brothers Pinot Grigio. The obvious choice for a fresh, crisp, dry, lighter style and easy drinking white wine.

www.brownbrothers.com.au

city + suburbs

Civic Dining

Level 1, Civic Hotel, 388 Pitt Street
(cnr Goulburn Street), Sydney
Tel 8080 7040   Map 3a

Modern Greek

Score 14.5/20

Throughout his culinary odyssey – from Eleni's to Omega and now this art deco pub – Peter Conistis has feverishly and imaginatively reworked Greek classics. It's been more than a civil service. His signature moussaka is like no other: a marvel of texture with two discs of lacquered eggplant and scallops sandwiched together by viscid, salty taramasalata. Less audacious is the blue swimmer crab and haloumi tartlet, topped with an elegant salad of pale green witlof and needles of cucumber. Lightness reigns in the slippery cheese and spinach filled manti – Conistis's Hellenic version of ravioli. Lamb shoulder, braised with rosemary and olive oil, is grounded in tradition and made universal paired with fetta-enriched polenta. The dance with tradition continues and it's sweet – the fig and nut tart an artful complement of texture and flavour. The recently rejuvenated setting is as nourishing as the food: a tan banquette and dark timber give the impression of a chocolate box.

Hours Lunch Thurs–Fri noon–3pm; Dinner Thurs–Sat 6–10pm
Bill E $19–$25 **M** $28–$36 **D** $10–$16
Cards AE DC V MC
Wine A thoughtful list of Australian and Greek wines designed to suit the food; 14 by the glass
Chef Peter Conistis
Owners James and John Kospetas
Seats 50–60; private room; cocktail bar
Vegetarian Several dishes available
www.civichotel.com.au
And… a daily mezze plate on offer at the bar

Clareville Kiosk

27 Delecta Avenue, Clareville Beach
Tel 9918 2727   Map 7

Contemporary

Score 14/20

When a restaurateur is as graciously passionate about her establishment and wine as Padie Starr, you know you'll be well catered for. Warm light beckons from this corner cottage of fresh flowers, colourful art, crisp tablecloths and sparkling glasses. Inventive touches characterise the nicely concise menu. Three chubby scallops carry the vivid tastes of caponata surprisingly well, albeit tempered by blander swirls of broccoli and sweet corn purees. There's a fine contrast in flavour between beef cheek and fillet with spinach, reduced Madeira sauce, and too-subtly truffled polenta batons. Dessert brings a smile: a tumbler of light, creamed mascarpone, caramelised walnuts, chopped fig, and yoghurt sorbet is topped with a delicate disc of chocolate. A jug of warm, orange-infused olive oil is poured on and the chocolate melts into the delightful jumble below. Delecta Avenue is aptly named, as this "kiosk" endures as a reliable outpost of fine, relaxed dining.

Hours Lunch Sat–Sun noon–4pm; Dinner Wed–Sun 6–10.30pm
Bill E $20–$25 **M** $37–$40 **D** $16.50; 10% surcharge on public holidays
Cards AE (+2.5%) DC (+2.5%) V MC
Wine A short, well-priced, predominantly Australian list, with some lesser-known gems among popular labels; 10 by the glass
Chef Leander Gstrein
Owner Padie Starr
Seats 40
Child friendly Healthy kids' menu; highchairs; toys; drawing materials
www.clarevillekiosk.com.au
And… drive down Hudson Parade and look for the restaurant sign at the Delecta Avenue turn

good food guide   39

city + suburbs

Claude's

10 Oxford Street, Woollahra
Tel 9331 2325   Map 4a

Modern French

Score 17/20

A mere 30-plus years young, Claude's remains charming, tiny and immensely inviting. It's one of the city's most exclusive, elegant and recently restyled dining rooms with seating for just 45 privileged diners in a hushed, linen-set space. It's now five years since Chui Lee Luk became just the fourth custodian of this culinary temple, patiently blending continuity with innovation. Inspired by French kitchen technique in some standout sauces, her really innovative moments have often been Asian-influenced: a superb "drunken" freshwater crayfish, the best green papaya salad you've tasted, and a soft-shell crab in fermented lentil batter that's a mini masterpiece of textures. Unfortunately, some details have disappointed of late. On recent visits, quail galette was rather dry and subtle, if not for pork dumplings, a play on xiao long bao, while angus sirloin with cabernet sauce and mini yorkshire pudding lacked the boldness and complexity of other dishes. Thankfully, the new combination of lobster, liver and ginger shows Luk's thoughtful imagination at its finest and the service remains flawless.

Hours Dinner Tues–Sat 7.30–9.30pm; bookings essential
Bill 3-course menu $135pp; degustation menu $165pp
Cards AE DC V MC
Wine A small but perfectly tailored list of quality domestic and European wines; 8 by the glass; BYO (corkage $20 per bottle)
Chef/owner Chui Lee Luk
Seats 45; private room
www.claudes.com.au
And…a lovely upstairs room for private parties or wine tastings

Coast

The Roof Terrace, Cockle Bay Wharf, Darling Harbour, Sydney
Tel 9267 6700   Map 1

Italian

Score 14.5/20

They don't coast at Coast. Friendly floor staff bustle, and dedication shows in the cooking. Simply dressed, simply delicious pearl-white calamari is dotted with dinky cubes of fresh tomato, plated with a dark smear of squid ink dressing and crisp wafers of eggplant. An impeccable splay of sliced duck breast sides with cherry halves and saba – a cinnamon-tinged, sweet balsamic vinegar and quince dressing. John dory fillet needs no more than fresh peas, slivers of preserved lemon and delicate strips of basil. Peach panna cotta wasn't peachy enough, but a (large) single serve of ossau-iraty – the Pyrenees sheep's milk cheese – more than compensates. Tourists and city types relax as summer sun glares and shadecloths slide over the wide, glass-roofed, timber verandah. They still enjoy this reliable waterside haven when winter nips in and glass panels close along the long, oblong dining room, cheered by a cheeky citrus frieze and black op-art print chairs.

Hours Lunch Mon–Fri noon–2.30pm; Dinner Mon–Sat 6–10pm
Bill E $17–$32 **M** $32–$44 **D** $9–$16; 2-course lunch plus glass of wine $39pp, 3 courses $50; 4-course dinner $59pp, 6-course tasting menu $85pp; 10% surcharge on public holidays
Cards AE DC V MC
Wine Comprehensive, Italian–Australian list of good names; 17 by the glass
Chef Jonathan Barthelmess
Owners Tim Connell & Michael McCann
Seats 250; private room; wheelchair access; outdoor seating; bar
Child friendly Under-14s half-price; books; pencils
Vegetarian Tasting menu changes regularly
www.coastrestaurant.com.au
And…a quiet retreat from the nearby nightlife

40   good food guide

city + suburbs

The Codfather

83 Percival Road, Stanmore
Tel 9568 3355   Map 8

Seafood

Score 12.5/20

You know you're in Sydney's leafy inner-west: service comes with a smile, parking's a breeze, the menu screams value, and there's a dog bowl at the entrance. The Codfather, a one-time corner shop, promotes itself as a "seafood bistro", and has all the hallmarks — oysters (Tassie's St Helens, perhaps) are opened to order, there's a catch of the day and the chips are chunky and truly delicious. There were, however, some hitches. Saucy sides that accompany entrees were out of sorts — an insipid galangal aioli did nothing to win over chargrilled cuttlefish, and the XO sauce with orange blossom teamed with crispy crab wontons just tasted odd. Mains, though, reel us in. Crisp-skinned ocean trout is showered with steamed clams and meaty speck, and morwong wears a truss of tomatoes and strips of white anchovies. Curious desserts include sticky pavlova with poached plums and spicy long-pepper cream. The crazy fish street art adorning the wall, fishy placemats and tentacle-like light fitting all add to The Codfather's charm.

Hours Lunch Sun noon–4pm;
Dinner Tues–Sat 5.30–10pm
Bill E $15 **M** $25 **D** $10
Cards AE V MC Eftpos
Wine Fully licensed; BYO wine only (corkage $3pp)
Chef Javier Carmona
Owners Javier Carmona, Chris Sharpe & Ross Godfrey
Seats 50; private room; outdoor seating
Child friendly Kids' menu; highchairs; drawing materials
And... try the $45 three-course menu

Cottage Point Inn

2 Anderson Place, Cottage Point
Tel 9456 1011   Map 7

Contemporary

Score 13.5/20

If you are in need of respite from the stresses of city life, there's no finer cure than an afternoon spent at this tranquil spot in the Kur-ring-gai Chase National Park. An elegant former boatshed, Cottage Point Inn offers diners a front-row view of seaplanes swooping in and pleasure boats gliding by. Whether you're visiting for lunch or dinner, expect to spend a few hours — service can be leisurely, but that's part of the appeal. To start, Queensland scallops surrounded by cauliflower puree are anchored by the earthiness of black pudding. Buffalo mozzarella with tomatoes and prosciutto would benefit from a splash of vinegar acidity. Risotto with porcini mushrooms, crisp asparagus and melted mozzarella and basil is a good combination of textures and flavours. However, the intriguing "hot mussel popcorn" (deep-fried, spicy mussels) was inexplicably missing from an otherwise sound blue-eye trevalla with open saffron ravioli. No need to rush off when you can linger over vanilla and raspberry roulade with grape and riesling jelly and tarragon cream.

Hours Lunch daily noon–3pm;
Dinner Fri–Sat 6.30–9.30pm; bookings essential
Bill E $22.50–$29.50 **M** $41–$46 **D** $19–$23
Cards AE DC V MC
Wine A well-thought-out list with independents alongside name drops; 10 by the glass
Chef Kevin Kendall
Owners Daniel McKinnon & Amanda Cameron
Seats 70; outdoor seating
Child friendly Kids' menu
Vegetarian Separate menu of three dishes
www.cottagepointinn.com.au
And... work up an appetite by hiring a kayak from the nearby kiosk

good food guide

city + suburbs

Courtney's Brasserie
70 Phillip Street, Parramatta
Tel 9635 3288   Map 6

Modern European
Score 12/20

The signs are encouraging: a mighty blackboard on one wall features a simple chalked map drawing the boundaries within which the chef endeavours to source his produce. Beside the map, a list of the sources: plums, peaches, figs and lemons from Southern Highlands orchards; organic lamb from near Bathurst; olives, oil and olive blossom honey from Silverdale south of Penrith. Thus, in a pleasant, timber-floored room with period detailing, excellent produce arrives in dishes that, on paper, have great appeal. But quality produce can't overcome occasional slips in technique. Baked figs are lovely, wrapped in prosciutto with blue cheese, truffle and honey sauce. A clever Willowbrae goat's curd and beetroot tasting plate was let down by a heavy raviolo filled with goat's curd. Fine roasted organic duck with cauliflower puree is paired with caramelised apple. Dessert sticks to safe options, including steamed blueberry and Cointreau pudding – with divine strawberries – and vanilla bean panna cotta.

Hours Lunch Tues–Fri noon–3pm; Dinner Tues–Sat 6–10pm
Bill E $14–$24 **M** $26–$33 **D** $15; starters from $3.50–$9.50
Cards AE DC V MC Eftpos
Wine A reasonable range; 8 by the glass
Chefs Paul Kuipers & Federico Rekowski
Owner Paul Kuipers
Seats 50; private room; outdoor seating
Child friendly Kids' menu; highchairs
Vegetarian Separate menu, offering 7–8 dishes
www.courtneysbrasserie.com.au
And... Courtney's turned 25 in September '09

da Gianni trattoria
127 Booth Street, Annandale
Tel 9660 6652   Map 5b

Italian
Score 13.5/20

What a lovely room. With vintage posters, a high bar, red backlighting, who wouldn't want to hang at Gianni's place? Or should that be Gianni and Cinzia's? This husband (in the kitchen) and wife (on the floor) team has the retro Italian vibe sorted, right down to the often cheesy soundtrack, raided from Cinzia's parents' record collection. She makes a joyful, efficient and hospitable host, offering fat crumbed olives (but no, they're not complimentary) while you wait for Gianni's well-cooked, mostly classic, Italian food. House-made pasta is masterful, twisted into caramelle (lollies) with a sweet amaretti and pumpkin filling, tossed with nutty brown butter and fried sage. A ragu of hare, porcini and olives adorns excellent gnocchi. Whole baby barra in acqua pazza is cooked just right, a little monotone however with bursting cherry tomatoes and the bitterness of baked lemon. Seared lamb on fat braised borlottis is happy and hearty. Marvellous whipped-to-order zabaglione with mandarin liqueur is worth the extra wait.

Hours Dinner Mon–Sat 6–10pm; bookings essential
Bill E $15.50–$21.50 **M** $28.50–$33.50 **D** $15; 6-course tasting menu $85pp; 10% surcharge on public holidays
Cards V MC
Wine Easy Italian list with lots of greatest hits; 16 by the glass; BYO (corkage $9.50 a bottle)
Chef Giovanni Spinazzola
Owners Cinzia & Giovanni Spinazzola
Seats 70; private room; bar
Child friendly Kids' options; highchairs; books
Vegetarian Separate menu with five options
www.dagianni.com.au
And... family-hour menu available for kids

city + suburbs

Danks Street Depot

1/2 Danks Street, Waterloo
Tel 9698 2201   Map 9

Contemporary

Score 14.5/20

Jared Ingersoll's local eatery keeps getting better. Founded on Slow Food principles with an emphasis on seasonal and sustainable ingredients, this understated warehouse dining hall consistently dazzles its faithful clientele. A daily changing menu reads like a foodie's checklist: grain-fed, hand-cut, line-caught and truffled, yet the food is simple, bold, wholesome and unpretentious. Locally sourced produce is used creatively, dishes are texturally complex and portions generous. Kingfish carpaccio arrives on a tantalising bed of crisp apple, cucumber, radish and coriander. Warm duck confit is lifted by bursts of pink grapefruit, crunchy walnuts and rocket. For vegetarians and cheese lovers, polenta and fromager d'affinois is a triple brie-style cheese sandwiched by fried polenta cakes, and served with truffled shiitake, oyster and field mushrooms plus tomato fondue. Biodynamic roast duck breast with bacon sauerkraut and boulangere potatoes is a heart starter. Chocolate fondant and chantilly cream with liqueur strawberries wraps the adventure up nicely. Great produce, seasonal matchings … this is why you want to eat out in the first place!

Hours Breakfast Mon–Fri 7.30–11am, Sat 8–11am, Sun 9–11am; Lunch daily 11am–3pm; Dinner Thurs–Sat 6–10pm
Bill E $18.50–$23 **M** $22–$36 **D** $18.50; 10% surcharge on Sundays & public holidays
Cards AE V MC Eftpos
Wine Australian and New Zealand wines only; 20 by the glass
Chef/owner Jared Ingersoll
Seats 100; bar
Child friendly Highchairs; better for breakfast/lunch
www.danksstreetdepot.com.au
And…there's a gallery next door

Dome

First Floor, Arthouse Hotel,
275 Pitt Street, Sydney
Tel 9284 1230   Map 1

Contemporary

Score 13/20

High, domed ceilings, 19th century plasterwork and heritage architectural features set the stage for a quiet bistro experience above a busy bar. The spacious dining room is lined with French cafe chairs and white-clothed tables, with original artworks adorning the padded mauve walls. Upon arrival, wood-fired Italian bread is promptly served with extra virgin olive oil and balsamic vinegar. Chicken liver paté satisfies with its rich velvety texture, spread over thinly sliced crostini and topped with caramelised orange peel. Gin-cured kingfish with wasabi creme fraiche leaned more towards vinegar than gin, and could have done with more restraint. Pan-fried scallops were let down by the lack of lightness in the accompanying ricotta and spinach gnocchi. Roast beef sirloin is well executed, with an interesting twist – a knob of cafe de Paris butter, crumbed and deep-fried, oozing with richness when cut against the steak. Coconut panna cotta with the tartness of passionfruit provides a light finish to an enjoyable meal.

Hours Lunch Mon–Fri noon–3pm; Dinner Tues–Sat 6–10pm
Bill E $17–$20 **M** $26–$30 **D** $13
Cards AE DC V MC
Wine All Australian list; 19 by the glass
Chefs Liz Willis-Smith & Franca Manfredi
Owner Liz Willis-Smith
Seats 120; wheelchair access; bar
www.thearthousehotel.com.au
And…a Wednesday Cinem-Attic offer ($25 for a main and movie)

good food guide   43

city + suburbs

Dukes Lane

79 Darling Street, East Balmain
Tel 9555 9764   Map 5b

European

Score 14.5/20

No more foams, no more smears, the fine dining of Sojourn has morphed effortlessly into the casual Dukes Lane. But if Paul Camilleri has opted to relax, it doesn't show. His food's even more attractive, flavours clearly defined in lovely, slinky pappardelle with Macleay Valley rabbit, chestnuts, pine mushrooms and sweet shavings of brussels sprout. Under-appreciated skate wing is crusted, nestled on a fine celeriac puree, tickled with garlic-infused olive oil, and suffused with ham hock broth. It's all deliciously robust, but not lacking in finesse. Salt sparks quail salad, a tennis ball of Gruyere and Roquefort souffle is slivered with olives. Panna cotta is layered in a glass with crushed meringue and mint leaves. This is assured cooking, prettily presented in a cosy terrace with raw sandstone walls, one featuring the website photo blown up cheekily big. The tablecloths might have gone but service and glasses sparkle, ensuring we'll sojourn again in Dukes Lane.

Hours Lunch Fri–Sat noon–2.30pm; Dinner Mon–Fri 6–10.30pm; bookings essential
Bill E $20–$23 **M** $28–$32 **D** $14–$16; 10% surcharge on public holidays
Cards AE (+2%) V MC
Wine Concise, snappy, international list; 18 by the glass or 375ml carafe
Chefs Paul Camilleri & David Wright
Owners Paul & Kim Camilleri
Seats 60; private room; wheelchair access; bar
Child friendly Yes, but no specific kids' menu
Vegetarian Please advise when you book
www.dukeslane.com
And... come by ferry to check out the Friday set lunch, $30 for three courses

Efendy

79 Elliott Street (cnr Darling Street), Balmain
Tel 9810 5466   Map 5b

Turkish

Score 13.5/20

This handsome house with its large front courtyard and dark brown architraves captures the Balmain vibe. Light streaming through leadlight windows colours the walls decorated with old photographs of Turkish scenes. Meanwhile the anise tones of raki – Turkey's answer to ouzo – tint a cream sauce with five king-sized prawns. An eggplant puree, authentically smoky, is deliciously laced with kasar – Anatolian sheep's milk cheese. The menu intrigues and the food is generous in flavour and size while the service is as warm as the pide (Turkish bread). The mezze menu changes regularly, so consider seriously how many dips, bright salads and plump, battered mussels you can handle before hoeing into spoon-soft beef cheek on a rich, cheesy mash. Pedro Ximenez-macerated berries are topped with fairy floss and sprinkled with rosewater atop a tile of "milk pudding" – cousin to panna cotta. Salep, Turkey's orchid-based natural thickener, adds a pleasing elasticity to ice-cream. If this is modern Turkish, more please.

Hours Breakfast Sat–Sun 9am–2pm; Lunch Sat–Sun noon–5pm; Dinner Tues–Sun 6pm–midnight
Bill 5 mezze for $15 **M** $24–$29 **D** $10–$12
Cards AE V MC Eftpos
Wine Concise, exciting list, priced fairly, a few foreigners; 16 by the glass; BYO Tues–Fri & Sun (corkage $5pp)
Chefs Somer Sivrioglu & Serhan & Serhat Pazar
Owners Somer & Asli Sivrioglu
Seats 130; private rooms; outdoor seating; bar
Child friendly Kids' menu; highchairs; play table
Vegetarian Many delightful, unusual choices
www.efendy.com.au
And... upstairs casual, cushioned mezze bar; downstairs basement bar

city + suburbs

Element Bistro

163 King Street, Sydney
Tel 9231 0013   Map 1

French

Score 14/20

The moment you enter this tiny, below-stairs bistro you feel you've been let in on a big secret. It's a slender, intimate, homely space of timber tables, dark brown carpet and cream walls in the belly of the CBD. Friendly, fun service doesn't miss a beat, and chef Matt Barnett is in his element dishing up the kind of French-accented comfort food you wish for at home every night. A wild bunch of Clarence River school prawns are brought into line, beautifully pan-fried and served with spicy rouille. Glistening egg yolk lathers a finely cut steak tartare, served with cornichons and crunchy toast slices. Tiny cubes of potato, sauteed Brussels sprouts and pine nuts accentuate a scrumptious confit duck that slides off the bone, while slow braised strips of veal shin splash about with casareccia pasta in a rich ragout zesty with gremolata. Leave room for a devious and bittersweet chocolate and honeycomb mousse. You'll be in your element, too.

Hours Lunch Mon–Fri 11.45am–3pm; Dinner Mon–Fri 5.45–9pm
Bill E $16–$18 **M** $27–$34 **D** $14
Cards AE V MC Eftpos
Wine Small but spot-on list at a good price; 10 by the glass; BYO (corkage $9 a bottle)
Chef/owner Matt Barnett
Seats 40; outdoor seating
www.elementbistro.com.au
And... you might need hiking boots and a GPS to find the toilets

Elio

159 Norton Street, Leichhardt
Tel 9560 9129   Map 5b

Italian

Score 14/20

The room has a hard-edged, spartan gleam: white walls, plate glass front and a marble bar with rows of multi-coloured grappa bottles twinkling on the shelf behind. However, the food traverses Italy with a generosity and creative amplitude that belies such austerity. Start, for instance, with the salty crunch of a whitebait fritter softened with the creamy sweetness of Balmain bug meat, artichoke hearts and lemon aioli dressing. Cinnamon vinaigrette adds interest to a superbly subtle salad of baby witlof, apple, taleggio and roast walnuts. Potato and ricotta gnocchi with rabbit ragu, artichoke and Calabrese olives is bounteous in size and flavour. Even better is pan-fried lamb rump, crusted with green peppercorns, served with portobello mushroom rusticone (mushies in a pastry case) and Mediterranean yoghurt dressing. Ownership may have changed, yet the amiable service, along with long-term chef Daniele Giannuzzi's light touch, complete a package that has long been a highlight on this little strip of Italy.

Hours Lunch Fri noon–3pm; Dinner Tues–Sun 6–10pm
Bill E $18–$22 **M** $27–$28 **D** $3–$14.90
Cards AE V MC Eftpos
Wine A page each of reds and whites, with Italian choices among the locals; also a reserve list; 9 by the glass; BYO (corkage $8 a bottle)
Chef Daniele Giannuzzi
Owner Tommy Duris
Seats 130; private rooms; outdoor seating; bar
Child friendly Kids' menu; highchairs
www.elio.com.au
And... they're adding a degustation menu

city + suburbs

Elysium

133 Avoca Street, Randwick
Tel 9398 7766   Map 9

Contemporary

Score 13/20

NEW ENTRY

Emma's on Liberty

59 Liberty Street, Enmore
Tel 9550 3458   Map 8

Lebanese

Score 12.5/20

Everyone deserves a well-priced and reliable bistro like Elysium in the 'hood. From an affable menu of French–Italian pop hits to an enjoyably loud, homely room of paper-on-cloth tables – the walls decorated with antique French aperitif posters – and pleasantly upbeat service, its appeal is obvious. Settle in to a soothing roast pumpkin soup sprinkled with salty goat's fetta, invigorated by chilli oil. (Perhaps it didn't need sweet, crushed amaretti biscuits.) Lightly battered calamari with smoky sweet paprika mayonnaise is refreshed by a tomato, mint and cucumber salad. Mains are just as comfortable, from a Macleay Valley rabbit "cacciatore" pie capped with puff pastry escorted by chunky, hand-cut chips and mashed peas; to delightfully light potato gnocchi with prawns, pumpkin, peas and basil, contrasted by a rich prawn bisque sauce. Desserts continue the good times, whether it's a lush passionfruit creme brulee with a mixed-berry sorbet, or a hot apple tart with caramel. It's a great addition to this sleeper strip of Randwick eating.

Hours Dinner Mon–Sun 6–10pm
Bill E $17–$19 **M** $25–$29 **D** $8–$14
Cards AE DC V MC
Wine Small, excellent value & mostly local; 11 by the glass; BYO Mon–Fri (corkage $3pp)
Chef Micah Rodgers
Owners Sarina & Micah Rodgers
Seats 55; private room
www.elysiumrestaurant.com
And...midweek $20 deal of a main course and glass of wine

The Arabic script decorating the walls brings a touch of the Middle East to this small, open, modern venue that dishes out Lebanese fare in a casual style. Translated, the writing is simply a list of Lebanese specialities, and this is Emma's raison d'etre. Don't be discouraged by the two-sittings system, or the rushed and slightly impersonal service. Instead grab a seat or bench at the communal table and count on the kitchen to deliver the goods. Babaghanoush is delicately smoky, and hummus is creamy and expertly balanced. Arak prawns are packed with garlicky goodness, but missed the aniseed hit of the Lebanese spirit. Sujuk, a semi-dry, dense and spicy Armenian sausage is deliciously authentic as are thin pan-fried strips of home-style, wine-marinated veal shawarma, drizzled with a light lemony tahini. For dessert, though, the textures of thick sesame halva were at odds with overly sweet vanilla ice-cream. But delicately perfumed orange blossom tea more than makes amends.

Hours Dinner Tues–Sat 6–9.30pm
Bill Mezze dishes $11–$19 **D** $3–$8.50; 7-course banquet $39–$44pp
Cards Cash only
Wine BYO (corkage $2.50pp)
Chef/owner Anthony Sofy
Seats 70
Vegetarian More than half the menu
And...the two sittings means you're out early or in late

46   good food guide

city + suburbs

est.

1/252 George Street, Sydney
Tel 9240 3000   Map 1

Contemporary

Score 18/20

There are hints of Mediterranean and Asian influences, but in reality the cuisine can only be described as Peter Doyle's. He's a chef who brings a sense of poetry to the plate, along with beautiful balance and complex flavours. Four fat, juicy prawns are gently grilled and served on a bed of diced chorizo, pimento, goat's fetta and green olives to create an eclectic wave of tastes. The gamey flesh of rare pigeon is masterfully paired with a picada of pomegranate, cherry and almond cream. Lamb rib eye with roast garlic revels in its quality. Desserts include picture-perfect souffles and an incredibly light, deconstructed black forest cake, with contrasting layers of sweetness. The cheese plate is a showcase of prime European and Australian creativity. Order a coffee, not least for the beautifully crafted petits fours. An encyclopedic wine list, a glossily gorgeous heritage-style room, friendly, faultless service and incredible attention to detail add up to fine dining that's truly fine.

Hours Lunch Mon–Fri noon–2.30pm;
Dinner Mon–Sat 6–10pm; bookings essential
Bill E $28–$39 **M** $45–$53 **D** $22–$28; degustation lunch $110pp; dinner tasting menu $155; 2-course credit crunch lunch $50pp, 3 courses $60
Cards AE DC (+3%) V MC
Wine Sensational list of heavy hitters and little-known international gems; 29 by the glass
Chef Peter Doyle
Owner Merivale Group
Seats 104; private room; wheelchair access; bar
Vegetarian Separate menu
www.merivale.com
And...trust group sommelier Franck Moreau's advice

Etch

62 Bridge Street, Sydney
Tel 9247 4777   Map 1

European

Score 14.5/20

It's not quite baby Becasse, but Justin North's casual all-day diner is an affordably clever take on bistro style, underpinned by carefully sourced produce. Dark timber tables and fabric-padded chairs fill the long, smartly lit European-styled room with its cathedral windows, adjacent to the Intercontinental Hotel. Service is approachably relaxed, if occasionally lax. The menu explores Basque, Italian and French influences in sometimes simple, sometimes complex pairings, beginning with snappy nibbles such as a cone of beer-battered skate "knobs" with caper aioli, and sardines on toast with green apple and a shot glass of green tomato gazpacho. After an elegantly reworked prawn cocktail, a daily special of roast suckling pig wasn't quite special enough, however smoky saltbush lamb leg with provencal vegetables and lemony crushed potatoes is easy to love. For dessert, jubes, gels and sorbets is whimsically textural and a cunning twist on a fruit platter, while caramel date tart with wicked burnt butter ice-cream and Earl Grey tea syrup is downright luscious.

Hours Mon–Fri noon–11pm, Sat 5–11pm
Bill E $16–$23 **M** $22–$38 **D** $15
Cards AE DC V MC
Wine Petite, clever global wine list with pro rata prices for 150ml glass, 375ml carafe and bottle; 26 by the glass
Chefs James Metcalfe & Tristan Robertson
Owners Justin & Georgia North
Seats 120; private rooms; wheelchair access
Child friendly Highchairs
www.etchdining.com
And...try the grass-fed wagyu burger

city + suburbs

Eurolounge

Shop 21, The Piazza, Castle Towers,
Castle Street, Castle Hill
Tel 8850 7077   Map 6

European

Score 13/20

They do great crisp skin at Eurolounge. It's nicely salty on a melting block of pork belly partnered by a delicate pear puree, and again on a perfectly presented barramundi fillet. This assured technique is confirmed by glorious, properly rested, medium-rare venison, partnered by mushroom risotto. If the batter on zucchini flowers was a tad heavy, at least green beans are crisp, and pan-wilted mint lifts robust lamb ravioli. In a gleefully retro touch, bombe alaska is flamed at the table, meringue browning, orange sauce caramelising, choc hazelnut ice-cream interior remaining sweetly intact. Service is attentive in this comfortable, relaxed room, neatly segmented by blinds, and fronting a mod mall complex of shops, cinemas and restaurants. Now if only they'd replace those clunky wine glasses. It's a tough call pleasing everyone from families to groups, loving couples and business diners, yet Eurolounge does so admirably, from high tea to degustation.

Hours High tea daily 10am–4pm; Lunch daily 11.30am–3.30pm; Dinner daily 5.30–10pm
Bill E $17.90–$27.90 **M** $24.90–$59
D $10.90–$17.90; 2-course lunch $24.50pp; Sun–Thurs 2-course dinner plus drink $39pp; 10% surcharge on public holidays
Cards AE DC V MC Eftpos
Wine A good, wide-ranging list with sommelier's suggestions and notes; 23 by the glass
Chef Alex Hau
Owners Peter & Karlene Dimbrowsky
Seats 160; private rooms; wheelchair access; outdoor seating; bar
Child friendly Kids' menu; highchairs
www.eurolounge.com.au
And…a long beer and spirits list, too

Fare Nosh

117 Smith Street, Summer Hill
Tel 9716 6300   Map 8

Contemporary

Score 12.5/20

Like a glass of wine or two with dinner? This spot should appeal – home and away by train, with the station just around the corner. The wooden fit-out creates an atmospheric French bistro experience accented by charcoal contemporary art, softly illuminated. Service is unassuming with no fuss and never skips a beat. A high-rise stack of crunchy tempura vegetables comes in a kaleidoscope of colours with punchy dipping pots of wasabi mayo and chilli jam. The standout is pan-fried snapper enlivened by a lime-spiked mango, cucumber and chilli salsa. Beef eye fillet with a roasted sweet potato timbale is bold and satisfying, surrounded by a pool of rich red wine sauce. To finish, order the popular piglet's plate – the chef's selection of petite desserts. You're supposed to share this pretty palette, but it's so good you might want to order your own.

Hours Dinner Tues–Sat 6–10pm
Bill E $19.50–$24 **M** $29.50–$31.50 **D** $12
Cards AE V MC
Wine Short and sharp list; 6 by the glass; BYO (corkage $3pp)
Chef/owner Peter Meijer
Seats 30; wheelchair access
And…ample parking in the neighbourhood

city + suburbs

Fico Ristorante
342 Darling Street, Balmain
Tel 9818 3868   Map 5b

Italian

Score 13/20

This newish sibling to Cucinetta in Woolwich is doing all the family work while the latter is closed for renovations. Maybe youth is the reason for some lack of focus in the fit-out, wine list and service. But there's potential in this two-storey terrace. That potential is already being realised in the food, if again, sometimes with a lack of focus. There's no faulting schiacciatella, a buoyantly bubbled and out-of-shape flat-crust pizza, crunchy, tomatoey and herby, and served with a dollop each of goat's cheese and olive tapenade. Crudo di pesce, on the other hand, didn't get its tuna, bottarga and mayonnaise balance right. More successful is a special of caramelle – three long lozenges of pasta wrapped around a mixed seafood mince, dished up with a delicate eggplant cream. Roast duck with cannellini beans, cherries and spinach is mostly successful, the broth strong, thin and with a not-too-sweet palate. Drown in an affogato dessert – coffee and gelato, of course.

Hours Mon–Sun 6–10pm
Bill E $15–$25 **M** $30–$34 **D** $14–$16
Cards AE V MC
Wine Some average locals, more interesting Italian, 20 by the glass.
Chef Vincenzo Mazotta
Owners Vincenzo Mazotta & Giovanni Finocchiaro
Child friendly Kids' menu, highchairs
Seats 120; outdoor seating
And...it's Darling Street, so parking is at a premium

finefish
75 Grosvenor Lane, Neutral Bay
Tel 9908 4448   Map 5a

Seafood

Score 13.5/20

Downstairs it looks like a fish 'n' chipper, albeit a very good one from one of Sydney's leading restaurant suppliers, Martin's Seafoods, but press on and climb the rear stairs to a breezy, cheerful fish bistro where the welcome is warm and the produce first rate, from fine sourdough bread with Little General olive oil to an eclectic menu of things aquatic. For such a casual setting and bare tables, what appears on the plate is remarkably ambitious and complex, whether it's the extravagance of Nova Scotia lobster claw on truffled scrambled eggs with king brown mushrooms and inconsequential summer truffle shavings, or lightly crumbed whiting fillets with gently spiced lentil puree and brinjal pickle. Mains span other nations, from the Mediterranean glory of john dory with beetroot, ruby grapefruit and a shaved fennel salad, to buttery steamed toothfish with a pungent soy and ginger dressing, wilted lettuce and salted black beans. Peach melba's not quite as Escoffier planned, but it's still yummy.

Hours Lunch Tues–Fri noon–3pm; Dinner Mon–Sat 5.30–9pm; bookings essential
Bill E $18–$25 **M** $30–$35 **D** $13.50; 2-course lunch $35pp, 3 courses $45; 10% surcharge on public holidays
Cards AE (+2.75%) V MC
Wine Modest, quirky, mostly domestic list with 375ml carafe options; 10 by the glass; BYO Mon–Thurs (corkage $5pp)
Chef Paul Pereira
Owner Andrew Boyd
Seats 50; wheelchair access; outdoor seating
Child friendly Kids' menu; highchairs
www.finefish.com.au
And...fresh fish downstairs to take home & cook

good food guide 49

city + suburbs

Fiorenzoni
Shop 1, 809 Pacific Highway, Chatswood
Tel 9419 6411   Map 7

Modern Italian

Score 14/20

Here's a little touch of Italian class amid Chatswood's concrete jungle. There are tiles on the floor and photos on the wall, but this isn't your average ristorante: the space and the food presentation are more Aussie nouvelle than classic Roman. Think semolina gnocchi cut into squares, with deeply flavoured lamb ragu piled in one corner and a rich reggiano sauce in the other; and tuna tartare is surprisingly sweet. The freshness and quality of the produce, and the care with which it is handled – breads, pasta, grissini and gelato are all made daily on the premises – remind you that this is Italian cooking done with love. Juicy fresh wedges of rockmelon draped with imported prosciutto and goat's cheese are simple and delicious; and eye fillet steak with crispy speck and baked potato stack is timelessly good. A close-to-perfect panna cotta, delicately scented with lemon, is a flourishing finish. Fiorenzoni makes the jungle swing.

Hours Lunch Mon–Fri noon–2.30pm;
Dinner Mon–Sat 6–9.30pm; bookings essential
Bill E $14.90–$19.50 **M** $25.90–$34.90 **D** $14.90
Cards AE DC V MC Eftpos
Wine One-pager of well-priced Australasian options with the odd Italian drop; 8 by the glass; BYO up to 6 people only (corkage $8 a bottle)
Chefs Mario Nogarotto, Anita Nogarotto & Andrea Rossi
Owner Mario Nogarotto
Seats 50; wheelchair access; outdoor seating
www.fiorenzoni.com.au
And…think about their home catering for your next party

Fish Face
132 Darlinghurst Road, Darlinghurst
Tel 9332 4803   Map 2

Seafood

Score 15/20

Face it, this seafood cafe is a Sydney gem(fish). It's also a veritable marvel in the use of ridiculously limited space. In a room populated by high tables and stools, barely big enough to swing a cat(fish), chef Stephen Hodges shows he's serious about proteins marine, letting their freshness shine with a clean, simple approach. He even squeezes in a sushi bar, for goodness sake, with seriously skilled hands at work. If you come here, however, looking for anything other than fish served in myriad styles, you're a meathead. Those styles include classics such nicoise salad and fish and chips, or more creative options such as kingfish – extremely rare in the middle – with spiced beetroot relish and crisp pancetta. No-nonsense waiters don't encourage discussion. The oversized omelette of the day is a triumph, stuffed with spanner crab and served with Asian greens and oyster sauce. This is one fish eatery that keeps us feeling perpetually chipper.

Hours Dinner Mon–Sat 6–10pm, Sun 6–9pm
Bill E $19–$22 **M** $33–$39 **D** $15
Cards V Eftpos
Wine Tiny but terrific list, with a bias towards whites; 24 by the glass; BYO wine only (corkage $5 a bottle)
Chefs Stephen Hodges, Leif Ibrahim & Joshua Niland
Owner Stephen Hodges
Seats 48
www.fishface.com.au
And…bookings are taken for 6–7pm only, otherwise you might have to queue

city + suburbs

Fix St James

111 Elizabeth Street, Sydney
Tel 9232 2767   Map 1

Mediterranean

Score 14/20

Whether you're an oenophile, office worker, or both, this unassuming city diner ticks the boxes. The wine list by owner–sommelier Stuart Knox stretches to 100 bottles, and those by the glass – and there are plenty – are available in both a 75ml tasting pour and a 150ml "thank God it's Friday" measure. There's joy, too, in sitting down to Sam Bennett's (formerly of Glebe Point Diner) menu, which might feature an heirloom tomato salad, Robert Marchetti's salumi, roasted bone marrow, whole yellowbelly flounder and rabbit and sausage carbonara. A grass-fed scotch fillet from Tasmania's Cape Grim comes with lovely roast chats but the huge nuggets of parmesan in the accompanying rocket salad raise eyebrows. Wagyu flank with eschalot sauce, spinach and chips, meanwhile, is pure corporate comfort food, and spatchcock with tarragon and peas is earmarked for a return visit. The dessert list is brief, but the six cheeses hold promise as you wait for that wonderful wine list to be brought back to the table.

Hours Lunch Mon noon–3pm, Tues–Fri noon–3.30pm; Dinner Tues–Wed 5.30–9pm, Thurs–Fri 5.30–10pm
Bill E $9–$22 **M** $20–$42 **D** $10–$14
Cards AE DC V MC Eftpos
Wine Interesting, wide-ranging list of Old and New World; 30 by the glass; BYO evenings only (corkage $15 a bottle)
Chef Sam Bennett
Owner Stuart Knox
Seats 60; outdoor seating; bar
Vegetarian Several options
www.fixstjames.com.au
And…free BYO every night if you spend more than $50pp

Flavour of India

120–128 New South Head Road, Edgecliff
Tel 9326 2659   Map 9

Indian

Score 13/20

On a busy road, mostly taking you elsewhere in the east, is one of our more elegant Indian restaurants, featuring mushroom-coloured walls, chandeliers and white linen tablecloths. Friendly staff deliver an unusual starter of "elephant ears" – layers of spinach leaves and chickpea meal, rolled up, deep-fried and sliced, resulting in almost kumara-like swirls that are slightly stodgy yet hum with chilli. Thin shells of potato are piled high with a more-ish mixture of shredded crab and coconut, lifted with a squeeze of lemon. Delicious pumpkin curry, or spice-infused tomato-lush aloo gobi with cauliflower, peas and potato, can be ordered as small portions, so you'll have room for the "best chicken butter masala". We won't argue. It's pretty good, especially with warm naan. Although fresh-tasting tandoori fish fillets were a tad dry, and the accompanying preserved-lemon achar (relish) very sweet, the pleasingly salty marinade is nicely tempered with soothing raita. For sweet tooths, date and pistachio kulfi with orange syrup will seal the deal.

Hours Dinner daily 6–11pm
Bill E $8.50–$15.15 **M** $14.50–$24 **D** $9.50–$12.50
Cards AE DC V MC Eftpos
Wine Succinct, appropriate list 10 by the glass; BYO (corkage $5 a bottle)
Chef Mahammod Hayat
Owner Lola Crossingham
Seats 100; bar
Child friendly Highchairs; drawing materials
Vegetarian Plenty of options
www.flavourofindiaedgecliff.com.au
And…street parking out front after 7pm weekdays and weekends

city + suburbs

Flavours of Peking

7/100 Edinburgh Road, Castlecrag
Tel 9958 3288   Map 7

Chinese (Northern)

Score 13/20

To some Sydneysiders, the Harbour Bridge is as much an obstacle to dining as the Great Wall of China was to invaders. So perhaps it's fitting that this northside diner is a stronghold of northern Chinese cuisine. Try to pick those specialities from the menu. Otherwise you're at risk of meal envy as dishes are brought to other groups gathered in the unassuming, grey-on-grey room that would appreciate a polish. Service isn't particularly helpful, but start with fluffy pork and prawn buns topped with a contrasting sail of crisped rice paper, or what look like DIY sausage rolls – sesame pockets ready to be packed with mince and vegie filling. Peking noodles with pork and cucumber were disappointing, smothered in sweet, gluggy sauce, but sizzling, spicy prawns are perfectly cooked, their crunch equalling that of the accompanying bamboo and cloud-ear fungus. Peking duck is a highlight, naturally, but there are other ways to get your pancake fix – aromatic shredded duck or lamb with shallot will also have you twirling the lazy susan for more.

Hours Lunch daily noon–3pm; Dinner Sun–Thurs 5.30–10pm, Fri–Sat 5.30–11.30pm; bookings essential
Bill E $8.80–$18.80 **M** $19.80–$53.80 **D** $6.80–$12.80; $2.50pp surcharge on public holidays
Cards AE DC V MC
Wine Basic Australasian list; 2 by the glass; BYO (corkage $2.50pp)
Chef/owner Zhi Feng Chen
Seats 170; private room; bar
Child friendly Highchairs
Vegetarian Separate banquet
And…plan ahead – some special dumplings and main dishes need to be ordered in advance

Flinders Inn

160a Flinders Street, Paddington
Tel 9331 0208   Map 3b

French

Score 13.5/20

Who wouldn't love an intimate little bistro like this in their 'hood? White linen tables, warm and helpful service, a small wine list with some cracker half bottles, a menu of French classics at reasonable prices – plus, scribbled in red lipstick on the mirrors, a list of specials such as duck confit and oysters. Chef Morgan McGlone might look a little tough in the open kitchen, but he cooks like an angel, giving plenty of oomph to standards ranging from an intensely garlicky bouillabaisse to ethereal gnocchi with sweetly braised beef. Mains are just as passionately prepared, although the roasted cauliflower puree with confit pork belly and caramelised apples was a little too mustard-brown and bland to appeal. Daube of beef with parsnip and turnip is full of flavour, braised to such flaky softness that it would fall apart in a light breeze. While tart citron is textbook-sharp, aided by creme fraiche, steamed chocolate pudding with honey ice-cream and candied orange peel is simply jolly good fun.

Hours Lunch Fri noon–3pm; dinner Mon-Sat 6–10pm; bookings essential
Bill E $16–$18 **M** $29 **D** $12
Cards AE V MC
Wine Small, clever Australasian & French list; 11 by the glass
Chef/owner Morgan McGlone
Seats 50
Child friendly
www.flindersinn.com
And…parking's not easy around here, especially if there's a game at the SCG

Good Nude Guide

THE SYDNEY MORNING HERALD GOOD FOOD GUIDE AWARDS 2010

Congratulations to the award winning restaurants that choose to serve Santa Vittoria.

♛♛♛ THREE HAT WINNERS
BILSON'S, SYDNEY
PIER, ROSE BAY
TETSUYA'S, SYDNEY

♛♛ TWO HAT WINNERS
GUILLAUME AT BENNELONG, BENNELONG POINT
ICEBERGS DINING ROOM AND BAR, BONDI BEACH
ROCKPOOL, THE ROCKS
ROCKPOOL BAR & GRILL, SYDNEY

♛ ONE HAT WINNERS
ALTITUDE, THE ROCKS
AZUMA, SYDNEY
BISTRO MONCUR, WOOLLAHRA
FISH FACE, DARLINGHURST
FLYING FISH, PYRMONT
FORTY ONE, SYDNEY

GALILEO, SYDNEY
NO 2 OAK STREET, SYDNEY
OTTOMAN CUISINE, CANBERRA
RESTAURANT II, NEWCASTLE
SEPIA, SYDNEY
ZEST, NELSON BAY

SANTA VITTORIA
ACQUA MINERALE
ITALIAN MINERAL WATER BOTTLED AT THE SOURCE

Proud sponsor of The Sydney Morning Herald Good Food Guide Awards 2010

YOU BE THE JUDGE!

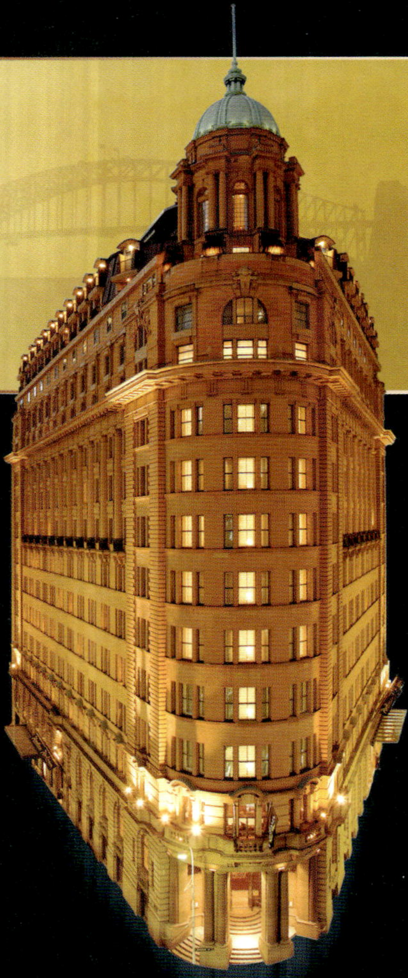

For the discerning guest, Radisson Plaza Hotel Sydney is a taste of relaxed elegance – come stay with us and judge for yourself.

Choose from 362 guest rooms, dine in two award winning restaurants; Bilson's and Bistro-Fax, unwind in the Health Club and select from eight meeting rooms all at Sydney's most valued five star address.

To book your delicious experience call direct on 02 8214 0000 or toll free 1800 333 333 or visit www.radisson.com/sydneyau_plaza

Radisson Plaza Hotel Sydney 27 O'Connell Street, Sydney

city + suburbs

Flying Fish

Jones Bay Wharf, 19–21 Pirrama Road, Pyrmont
Tel 9518 6677   Map 5b

Seafood

Score 15.5/20

Tap along the cobblestone passage through the Dickensian darkness of the wharf or the boardwalk alongside. Either leads to one of Sydney's most glorious restaurant settings. Flying Fish is a neat reimagining of a wharfside chop shop and tavern, all dark wood and amber glow, with a marvellous golden resin chandelier. It's a fitting venue for Peter Kuruvita's thoroughly modern handling of seafood. Mousse-like poached Coffin Bay oysters loll in a champagne emulsion, its foam breaking on firm king crab tortellini. A massive Tasmanian crayfish, flash fried and golden crusted, cracks to surrender chunky, sweet flesh to dredge in black pepper, curry leaf and pan juices – a nod to the chef's Sri Lankan heritage. A red witlof and frisee salad with Persian fetta and pistachios has just the right sharpness. Dessert is almost redundant, however raspberry souffle with coulis and clotted cream is airy and just tart enough. Please sir, I want some more.

Hours Lunch Tues–Fri noon–2.30pm, Sun noon–3.30pm; Dinner Tues–Sat 6–10.30pm; bookings essential
Bill E $28–$32 **M** $39–$45 **D** $18; main plus glass of wine $35pp; 8% surcharge on public holidays
Cards AE DC V MC (+1.5% on all cards) Eftpos
Wine Excellent global range with some intriguing surprises; 21 by the glass
Chefs Peter Kuruvita & Jodie Wallace
Owners Peter Kuruvita & Con Dedes
Seats 198; private rooms; wheelchair access; outdoor seating; bar
Child friendly Highchairs; drawing materials
Vegetarian Vegan degustation menu
www.flyingfish.com.au
And…sit upstairs for a view of the sushi prep area, it's dining as theatre

Fook Yuen

Level 1, 7 Help Street, Chatswood
Tel 9413 2688   Map 7

Chinese

Score 13/20

A wonderfully large, kitsch neon light directs you upstairs to this vast and bustling first-floor restaurant. Catering to a strong local Chinese community, the Fookie also plays host to office workers for lunch and yum cha. The interior features white linen tablecloths and red velvet curtains, while two huge plasma screens showcase the specials. Ultra-efficient floor managers direct you to your seat, and ordering is swift. Daily dim sum include an array of dumplings, congee and salt-and-pepper squid. Sichuan chicken ordered off the menu is laced with red peppers and a fiery chilli sauce. Best splash out on the vast array of seafood, perhaps live pipis, presented for inspection before they return minutes later swimming in spicy XO sauce. Coral trout is delicately steamed with ginger, shallots and soy sauce. If the budget allows, move on to mud crab, abalone or lobster. Twenty years on, Fook Yuen remains a reliable old faithful.

Hours Lunch Mon–Fri 10.30am–3pm, Sat–Sun 10am–3pm; Dinner daily 5.30–11pm; open Christmas Day & Boxing Day
Bill E $7.50–$19 **M** $19–$45 **D** $7–$8; $2.50pp surcharge on public holidays
Cards AE DC V MC
Wine Some famous Australian names; 2 by the glass
Chef Kai Chiu Leung
Owner ALLFX Pty Ltd
Seats 320; private rooms
Child friendly Highchairs
Vegetarian Wide variety of dishes
And…booking is recommended

good food guide

city + suburbs

Forty One

Chifley Tower, 2 Chifley Square, Sydney
Tel 9221 2500   Map 1

Contemporary

Score 15/20

On a clear evening, you'll see to the Heads and beyond through Forty One's mighty glass windows. Even on a stormy night it might be difficult to turn away from the lightning show to focus on the menu, a European-accented document that also speaks the culinary language of our age. Jamon Iberico might share a plate with divine duck liver parfait, while marinated kingfish and a fat oyster form a striking team with Vietnamese-dressed green tea noodles. A salty blue swimmer crab croquette is boldly matched with grilled chorizo and Jerusalem artichoke. But there were some missteps, including a curious calamari "schnitzel" with an anchovy and truffle-infused green bean salad; and we longed for more assertiveness in pasta parcels of Yamba prawn meat claiming Thai influence in a "spiced broth" foam. Deferential service, the complimentary amuse bouche, and a blue-hued, five-star-hotel decor might make you nostalgic for the headier days of generous corporate expense accounts. Yet that view remains as timeless as it is priceless.

Hours Lunch Tues–Fri noon–2.30pm; Dinner Mon–Sat 6–9.30pm; bookings essential
Bill Lunch 2 courses $65pp, 3 courses $80, 4 courses $95; Dinner 8 courses $150pp
Cards AE DC V MC
Wine An impressive, lengthy list, take the plunge rather than rely on set matches; 14 by the glass
Chef Rainer Korobacz
Owner Dietmar Sawyere
Seats 135; private rooms; wheelchair access; bar
Child friendly Kids' menu; highchairs; drawing materials
Vegetarian Eight-course degustation menu
www.forty-one.com.au
And...take an early booking so you see the view at dusk; ask for a window seat

Four in Hand Dining Room

105 Sutherland Street
(cnr Elizabeth Street), Paddington
Tel 9362 1999   Map 4a

French

Score 15/20

It's good to see that little changes at this likeable local. The dark, handsome eating space is full of character, refined by the large Luke Sciberras watercolour of a squid above the long banquette. The exceptional wine list, smooth service and flawless technique of chef Colin Fassnidge maintain its enviable reputation. The menu is a daring balance of creativity: an entree of grilled scallops immersed in creamy, richly flavoured brandade soup is topped with crisp chorizo and zucchini flowers. It's a knockout. Grilled lamb's tongue is skilfully offset with eggplant puree, and calzone is plump with lamb shoulder. Mains deliver more triumphs: veal fillet with mustard, horseradish and herb crust is a perfect harmony of texture and flavour, resting in a dashi bouillon dotted with ox and sage dumplings. Mahi mahi is sweet but firm on a vibrant sea of pea and ham puree, scattered with strips of salt-and-pepper squid. Hoegaarden beer ice-cream has a mellow hint of Belgian brew that's scrumptious with roast peach and lemon curd.

Hours Lunch Tues–Sun noon–2.30pm; Dinner Tues–Sat 6.30–9.30pm, Sun 6.30–8.30pm
Bill E $24 **M** $34 **D** $16; 3-course menu $75pp (functions only)
Cards AE DC V MC
Wine Plenty of local gems and an interesting international list; 13 by the glass
Chef Colin Fassnidge
Owners Joseph Saleh & Paul Bard
Seats 50; private room; bar
Child friendly Kids' menu; highchair
www.fourinhand.com.au
And...choose a cheese from the impressive board

city + suburbs

Foveaux Restaurant + Bar

65–67 Foveaux Street, Surry Hills
Tel 9211 0664   Map 3b

Modern European

Score 15/20

Soft lights wash up the worn brick walls of this narrow room. With no view and minimal adornment, it feels more New York than Sydney, and the creams, purees and smears place the menu firmly in contemporary 21st century territory, with challenging combinations. Crab ice-cream adds an extra dimension to ceviche of diced kingfish with cucumber and crunchy croutons, while a smear of carrot paint enlivens tangy goat's curd sandwiched between two translucent taro chips. First-rate produce finds harmonious matches; a tile of just-set baked rainbow trout with morels, clams and purslane nestles into a thin pillow of sweet corn puree. Warm, lightly smoked duck with two thin twigs of crisp, cured liver is enhanced by subtle licorice cream. Cherry beignet looks and tastes like a grown-up jam doughnut, caramel milk sorbet, chicory cream and almond puree adding contrasting textures and flavours. Service is polite and informed, and the sultry, Moroccan-inspired downstairs bar is the perfect place to relax before or after dinner.

Hours Lunch Fri noon–3pm; Dinner Tues–Sat 6–10pm; bookings essential
Bill E $22 **M** $34 **D** $15; 6-course tasting menu $75pp
Cards AE DC V MC Eftpos
Wine A serious list with good choice of vintages, Old and New World and plenty of big-ticket items, but also a fair selection under $60; 18 by the glass
Chef/owner Darrell Felstead
Seats 46; bar
Vegetarian Six-course tasting menu
www.foveaux.com.au
And… good snacky bar menu downstairs

Fratelli Paradiso

12–16 Challis Avenue, Potts Point
Tel 9357 1744   Map 2

Italian

Score 14/20

This sexy trattoria, the quintessential bustling Potts Point eatery, is as Melbourne as you can get. Regulars on a "ciao" basis with the charming fratelli are not deterred by the no-booking policy, nor by the menu scribbled on the blackboard, all in Italian. The staff are eager to elaborate on the gamberi, risotto and puttanesca, but be prepared to battle for their attention. You could also resort to pointing to the next table because everybody's ordering the signature flash-fried calamari in all its tender glory, spiked with the sweet-acidic injection of balsamic vinegar. Tagliatelle is adorned with hearty beef ragu, while melting cheese adds oomph to invitingly salmon-coloured risotto pomodoro. Of course, there's nothing like washing it down with fine prosecco. The excellent espresso is a surefire way to finish off a lingering meal, accompanied by the creamy, nutty richness of zuccotto (dome-shaped layered cake) or a perfectly shaped palmier from the adjoining pasticceria.

Hours Mon–Fri 7am–11pm, Sat–Sun 7am–5pm; no bookings
Bill E $16–$21 **M** $20–$30 **D** $10–$12; 10% surcharge on public holidays
Cards AE DC V MC
Wine Well thought-out Italian wines; 25 by the glass
Chefs Teofilo Nobrega & Tosh Nakayasu
Owners Enrico & Giovanni Paradiso & Marco Ambrosino
Seats 64; private room; wheelchair access; outdoor seating
And… don't forget it's closed Saturday and Sunday nights

city + suburbs

fu manchu

249 Victoria Street, Darlinghurst
Tel 9360 9424   Map 2

Chinese (South-East Asian)

Score 12.5/20

This funky hole in the wall has been feeding Darlo regulars for more than a decade, many of its dishes inspired by owner Annie Lee's Nonya heritage. The little red plastic stools remain, as do the sit-up tables attached to the side wall. It can be a little cramped when crowded, but friendly and knowledgeable service more than makes up. Daily specials written on a neon light board include basa fillet with black bean sauce and shallots. Seafood gow gees are plump and bursting with flavour although the vegetarian dumplings were a little doughy. A standout is Huangdi chicken, tender and spicy, with dried chillis, cashews and green beans thrown in. Stir-fried Shanghai bok choy and shiitake mushrooms easily satisfies the vegetarian in us. A request for a half serve of the house favourite, Peking duck wraps, is happily met. As you trip out into buzzy, funky Victoria Street afterwards, be glad fu manchu is still part of the scenery.

Hours Lunch Mon–Fri noon–2.30pm; Dinner daily 5.30–10.30pm
Bill E $5–$18 **M** $8–$20 **D** $5; 10% surcharge on public holidays
Cards AE V MC Eftpos
Wine Tiny wine list with Asian beers; 3 by the glass; BYO (corkage $2pp)
Chefs Tony Huang & Annie Lee
Owner Annie Lee
Seats 80; private rooms; outdoor seating
Child friendly Kids' menu
Vegetarian Separate menu
www.fumanchu.com.au
And…catering also available

Galileo

The Observatory Hotel,
89–113 Kent Street, Sydney
Tel 9256 2215   Map 1

French

Score 15/20

A new chef and lower prices have re-energised this stately hotel fine diner, so everyone can afford a little luxury. The room retains its old-fashioned opulence with heavy drapes, chandeliers and generous tables. Chef Masahiko Yomoda's cleverly spiced French fare inclines more towards India than his native Japan, but unfailingly dazzles with its beautiful presentation and evocative combinations. These include a luxurious "millefeuille" of avocado and crab in a sunset-red pool of vinegary tomato. Truffle tart with confit tomato, lemony leek, crisp onion, crunchy kataifi pastry and clove-scented foie gras sauce was a little too ambitious, downplaying the star of the show, but hazelnut and coriander seed-crusted roast lamb rack with carrots and minted peas is superb. Curry-spiced crayfish in fennel bisque is pleasurably heady and lush. Desserts are expensive, but the pungently alcoholic Grand Marnier souffle with passionfruit sauce is as satisfying and refined as the smartly attired, polite waiters.

Hours Breakfast daily 6.30–10.30am; Dinner Tues–Sat 6.30–10.30pm
Bill E $16–$22 **M** $22–$36 **D** $19; 5-course degustation $98pp
Cards AE DC V MC Eftpos
Wine Delightful international list, with great half-glass and half-bottle options; 25 by the glass
Chef Masahiko Yomoda
Owner The Observatory Hotel
Seats 65; wheelchair access; bar
Child friendly Kids' menu
www.observatoryhotel.com.au
And…let Christian Baeppler, one of Sydney's finest sommeliers, guide you

city + suburbs

Garfish

1/39 East Esplanade, Manly
Tel 9977 0707   Map 7
Also at 2/21 Broughton Street, Kirribilli
Tel 9922 4322   Map 5a
Also at 6/29 Holtermann Street, Crows Nest
Tel 9966 0445   Map 5a

Seafood

Score 13.5/20

If seafood is your thing and a water view makes you happy, Garfish Manly ticks all the boxes. There's seafood cooked every which way, although the extensive menu and daily fresh catches make it hard to choose. Seafood tapas is the easiest decision, with good salt-and-pepper calamari and creamy scallops among other morsels. Watch the chefs at work on television screens linked to the kitchen, which alternate with explanations on fish varieties. You may need these to help you mix and match from the daily specials and accompaniments. Depending on the day, you could combine roasted blue-eye with smoked eggplant salad, or grilled silver dory with sticky rice and papaya salad. Mussels are one of several dishes prepared in the wood-fired oven. Watch tourists pour onto the wharf from the ferries, and linger over roasted black figs with baklava.

Hours Breakfast Sat 8–11am, Sun 9–11am; Lunch daily noon–3pm; Dinner Mon–Sat 5.30–10pm, Sundays and public holidays 5.30–9pm
Bill E $16–$20 **M** $22–$32 **D** $10–$12; 5% surcharge on Sundays, 10% public holidays
Cards AE DC V MC
Wine Decent, seafood-friendly, mainly Australian list; 30 by the glass; BYO (corkage $3.30pp)
Chefs Stewart Wallace & Michael Nash
Owners Mark Dickey & Mark Scanlan
Seats 140; private room; wheelchair access; bar
Child friendly Kids' menu; booster seats
Vegetarian Good selection of entrees & mains
www.garfish.com.au
And...a couple of meat dishes for carnivores

Ginger & Spice

240 Military Road, Neutral Bay
Tel 9908 2552   Map 5a

Malaysian/Singaporean

Score 13.5/20

Diehard fans rave about this North Shore favourite, popular among Singaporean and Malaysian groups and even chef Tetsuya Wakuda. Overlook its retro sandstone walls, blue tablecloths and brisk service and settle in for serious street fare. Bite into ngoh hiang – light, fluffy bean curd rolls with juicy chunks of five spice minced pork, prawns and water chestnut. Chew on sweet, sticky deep-fried kecap manis squid, which is great with ice-cold beer. Smoked hor fun arrives with an aromatic waft of wok charring, the flat rice noodles smothered with egg sauce. The piece de resistance is the signature Singapore chilli crab (to be ordered in advance), generously coated in a fiery garlic and chilli sauce and waiting to be dipped with flaky roti prata for a lip-smacking indulgence. Refresh with a cendol dessert: an ice-cold coconut milk and palm sugar confection, swirling with green tapioca strips and red beans, and topped with shaved ice.

Hours Lunch Tues–Sun noon–3pm; Dinner daily 5.30–10pm; bookings essential
Bill E $7–$12 **M** $15–$23 **D** $5–$6; $2.50pp surcharge on public holidays
Cards Cash only
Wine Predominantly Australasian; 2 by the glass; BYO (corkage $3pp)
Chef/owner Alex Lee
Seats 75
Child friendly Highchairs
And...hard-to-find weekend specials include cuttlefish kang kong, popiah (crepe-like rolls) and mee siam (noodles in spiced gravy)

good food guide

city + suburbs

Glass Brasserie

Level 2, Hilton Sydney,
488 George Street, Sydney
Tel 9265 6068 Map 1

French/Australian

Score 14.5/20

Hotel brasserie? Fine diner? Casual after-drinking fuel stop? Hard to be all things to all people but Glass has a pretty fair crack at it. The room is a fine start: huge mirrored ceiling, gossamer curtains, long, convivial tables for big groups, nooks and crannies for avoiding the crowds. Swivel your gaze from the wall of wine racks, and the phonebook-sized wine list and turn to the please-everyone menu, divided easily for all tastes and appetites. Pork belly with cuttlefish, papaya, pork crackling and a lush, brown, sweetly tangy sauce is a knockout start, unless you go classic with steak tartare, mixed at the table with all the trimmings. Meaty mains – from the grill – include excellent steak. Or you might prefer spiced scallops and bug meat with a lovely corn puree, and pea and coriander stuffed pasta. Dessert could be glorious sheep's yoghurt with rhubarb and dried raspberries, or yummy banana souffle in a little copper pot. Or have the lot.

Hours Lunch Mon–Fri noon–3pm; Dinner daily 6–10pm
Bill E $21–$30 **M** $35.50–$52 **D** $14.50–$21; 2-course lunch with glass of wine $45pp; 10% surcharge on Sundays & public holidays
Cards AE DC V MC
Wine What a list. It covers the globe: 30 by the glass, and helpful wine service, too
Chefs Luke Mangan & Joe Pavlovich
Owners Luke Mangan & Hilton Hotels
Seats 200; private dining area and chef's table; wheelchair access; bar
Child friendly Kids' menu; highchairs
www.glassbrasserie.com.au
And…the cheese selection is excellent, too

Glebe Point Diner

407–409 Glebe Point Road, Glebe
Tel 9660 2646 Map 5b

Contemporary

Score 14.5/20

There's much to love about Glebe Point Diner: the buzzy, high-ceilinged space; the big blackboard menus (helpfully reproduced on paper); the prized outdoor tables; the cheerfully efficient waiters. Here is a restaurant really hitting its straps, and everyone – patrons and staff alike – is enjoying the moment. The food is great, too, as chef Alex Kearns continues his success with strong, unapologetically earthy flavours that pull both punters and serious foodies in droves. Fresh yellow-eyed mullet stuffed with fennel and herbs goes nicely with nutty bread and hand-churned butter, both made on-site. A special of crisp roast Melanda Park pork with lentils is indulgent autumn fare, although vegetarian lasagne lacked pizzazz. Desserts, however, are perfect: a creamy floating island on aromatic bay leaf custard and piquant blackberry sauce, and a wonderfully wobbly, smooth-as-silk panna cotta with vivid baked quince. Long may the moment last.

Hours Lunch Thurs–Sun noon–2.30pm; Dinner Wed–Sat 6–9pm; bookings essential
Bill E $18 **M** $26–$36 **D** $14
Cards V MC
Wine Engaging, well-priced list of Old and New World; 20 by the glass and plenty of one-third and half-bottles; BYO (corkage $15 a bottle)
Chef Alex Kearns
Owners Charles Plumridge & Steven Tracey
Seats 45; wheelchair access; outdoor seating
Child friendly Some half-portions; drawing materials
And…despite the crowds, last-minute early dinner bookings are often possible

city + suburbs

Golden Century

393–399 Sussex Street, Sydney
Tel 9212 3901   Map 3a

Chinese
Score 14/20

There's a rumour doing Sydney's culinary carousel about Golden Century's weekly turnover. We're talking kilos of king crabs, abalone and first growth Bordeaux waltzing out the door. And well done Eric Wong and Kevin Kam, Golden Century's owners, who have run this all-day and all-night posh Cantonese canteen for nearly 25 years. They've certainly nailed the formula to success: take close to a tonne of live seafood and add an army of snappy waiters, a roll call of Cantonese favourites cooked admirably and a better-than-your-average-Asian-restaurant wine list. Luckily we all love Cantonese staples, Sydney's produce is as fresh as you can get, and most will forgive service that's brusque, as long as it's brisk. Order simply – steamed fish with ginger and shallots, XO pipis, salt-and-pepper mud crab, barbecued duck and pork, and steamed vegetables and seafood congee after 9pm – or badger the waiters for seasonal and house specials. After midnight, of course, the chefs of Sydney roll in and the live seafood tanks are plundered afresh.

Hours Daily noon–4am
Bill E $6–$12 **M** from $16 **D** $2.50–$6; $3pp surcharge on public holidays
Cards AE DC V MC Eftpos, Union Pay
Wine Big list with plenty of big names from here and abroad; 15 by the glass; BYO (corkage $5pp)
Chef Lee Ho
Owners Eric Wong & Kevin Kam
Seats 600; private rooms
Child friendly Highchairs; booster seats
Vegetarian Lots of options
www.goldencentury.com.au
And… go in a large group to order up big and share the cost of live seafood

Golden Sichuan

NEW ENTRY

17–19 Goulburn Street, Sydney
Tel 9212 1868   Map 3a

Chinese (Sichuanese)
Score 13/20

You wouldn't choose this feisty, chilli-laced Chinese for its looks: utilitarian yet gaudy decor over three floors with pale yellow walls, dark carpets, a splash of red and paper-on-cloth tables. The windows are filled with pictures of food, and there's some entertainment in reading the Chinglish sign out front as well as the menu's dozen illustrated pages, where dishes are given a one- to three-chilli rating. Pick the pungently fiery entree of brown-skinned cold duck and fabulous chilli-flecked, fish-flavoured braised eggplant. Dry-fried, crunchy, shell-on king prawns with hot pepper, capsicum, shallots and ginger shards have a two-chilli rating and addictive heat. It's all lively, authentic Sichuanese with great textures and complexity. While the rice flour-coated steamed beef was a bit too gluggy, you can feel the black-skinned mountain chicken soup with American ginseng doing you good. Alas, service seemed a little bored and distracted, so best signal rather than hope. Skip desserts such as glutinous rice with brown sugar sauce and have an extra main instead, such as the sweet, smoky, sharp and searing chilli hit of tofu with pork mince and peanuts.

Hours Daily noon–11pm
Bill E $4–$6 **M** $12.80–$36 **D** $4.50–$6
Cards AE (+3%) DC (+3%) V MC Eftpos; 3% surcharge on orders under $30 paid by card
Wine Workable, cheap, commercial list; 10 by the glass; BYO (corkage $3pp)
Chefs Doug Xie & Qiang Yuan
Owners Hua Li Song & Chao Wen Zhong
Seats 300; private rooms; wheelchair access
Child friendly Highchairs
And… live tanks for parrotfish, barra and crabs

good food guide

city + suburbs

Grappa

Shop 1, 267–277 Norton Street, Leichhardt
Tel 9560 6090   Map 5b

Italian

Score 14/20

Grappa welcomes you to Little Italy with true gusto. Couples canoodle at the bar, families share large, thin-crust pizzas. There's something reassuring in the giant portions of deft, familiar dishes. Four prosciutto-wrapped figs are slathered in melted gorgonzola, sweetened by balsamic, with hazelnuts adding texture. There's finesse in a fine carpaccio of tuna, dressing restrained. Crisp-skinned duck breast (let's call it half a duck), succulently cooked through, is sticky with brandy and orange sauce. Two john dory fillets are simply chargrilled, with blistered tomatoes and a dark, earthy dollop of tapenade. It's a well-honed operation in a big, clean, well-glassed room, with terrace tables for smokers and lovers, the service friendly and efficient, the food well paced. After a generous chunk of testun al barolo, effusively described in the cheese list, and an affogato with a crumble of house-made honeycomb, give the fascinating grappa list a workout and choose a shot of something smooth and strong.

Hours Lunch Tues–Fri & Sun noon–3pm; Dinner Tues–Sat 6–10pm, Sun 6–9.30pm
Bill E $17–$27 **M** $17–$39 **D** $10.50–$35
Cards AE DC V MC Eftpos
Wine Varied Italian list with museum selections; 14 by the glass; BYO (corkage $4.50pp)
Chef Wade Revell
Owners Charlie & Antonio Colosi
Seats 160; wheelchair access; outdoor seating; bar
Child friendly Kids' menu; highchairs; drawing materials
Vegetarian Good selection
www.grappa.com.au
And…immediately off the freeway into the free underground car park

Green Gourmet

538 Pacific Highway, St Leonards
Tel 9439 6533   Map 5a
Also at 115–117 King Street, Newtown
Tel 9519 5330   Map 8

Asian Vegan

Score 12.5/20

Asia has a long vegetarian history: strict Buddhists don't eat animal flesh, and Taoists prefer vegetables for health reasons. But that hasn't stopped numerous vegetable dishes being prepared to resemble their meaty counterparts. This casual, no-meat, no-alcohol diner is a case in point. Take the amazing Peking not duck: a perfect Beijing duck pancake complete with hoi sin sauce and cucumber, served with a slice of soy protein "duck" with the texture of the real thing. Lion king's claypot is a vegetarian version of the famous Shanghainese lion's head pork meatballs – with taro, mushroom and water chestnut providing deep and almost pork-like overtones. Less imaginatively named dishes are just as good: spring rolls are beautifully crunchy, while salt-and-pepper bean curd is nicely crisp and dry outside and bursting with silky-soft tofu within. Big mushroom caps are filled with taro and sticky rice to surprisingly complex effect. There's even tofu ice-cream, best sampled with a crispy lotus seed cake.

Hours Lunch Tues–Sat 11.30am–2.30pm; Dinner Tues–Thurs & Sun 5.30–9.30pm, Fri–Sat 5.30–10pm
Bill E $3.20–$8.80 **M** $10.80–$19.80 **D** $5.80–$9.80
Cards V MC
Wine No alcohol allowed
Chef Mr Ho
Owners Peter & Doris Wong
Seats 80; private room
Vegetarian The lot
And…no onion or garlic are used – apparently it leads to lust

good food guide

city + suburbs

Guillaume at Bennelong

Sydney Opera House, Bennelong Point, Sydney
Tel 9241 1999   Map 1

Contemporary/French

Score 17/20

A sense of occasion surrounds every visit to the Sydney Opera House, and stepping inside Guillaume Brahimi's fine diner, tucked beneath its southernmost shell, serves only to heighten expectations. The views are grand, the greetings warm and the wow factor all around, including on the plate. It's there in a deceptively simple starter of seasonal vegetables and goat's curd dusted with a confetti of micro-herbs; in deftly handled scallops served with a zucchini veloute, or basil-wrapped yellowfin tuna infused with a soy and mustard seed vinaigrette. White River veal rack makes a suitably dramatic entrance, brought to the table in the roasting pan it shares with a caramelised head of garlic, before returning, plated for two, with speck, peas, sweetbread croutons and the same garlic cloves as a puree. While service can slacken, the legendary paris mash is whipped decadence, a theme that carries through to dessert, where nougat with roasted peanuts, caramel ice-cream and banana is guaranteed to bring the crowd to its feet.

Hours Lunch Thurs–Fri noon–3pm; Dinner Mon–Sat 5.30–11pm; bookings essential
Bill E $30–$50 **M** $38–$75 **D** $25; 2-course pre-theatre menu $63pp, 3 courses $75; 10% surcharge on public holidays
Cards AE DC V MC
Wine World-class list of chiefly Australian and French marques; 19 by the glass
Chefs Guillaume Brahimi & Jose Silva
Owner Guillaume Brahimi
Seats 168; private rooms; wheelchair access; bar
Child friendly Kids' menu
www.guillaumeatbennelong.com.au
And... tapas in the Bennelong Bar

harbourkitchen&bar

Park Hyatt Sydney, 7 Hickson Road, The Rocks
Tel 9256 1465   Map 1

Contemporary/Italian

Score 14/20

This is more than a harbour kitchen. This is extreme waterside dining, in the classiest of ringside seats. Add immaculate, Italian-inspired cooking plus savvy wine service, and who could fault it? Well, it's a shame about the bland decor, occasionally fumbling waiters and low ambience quotient. Simply wallow instead in the luxury of a grainy-creamy risotto, dabbed with aged balsamic and reggiano. Nibble on a crunchy salt cod fritter with a sweet-sharp tomato-basil sauce, or the discreet elegance of baked buffalo ricotta with shaved fennel, radish slivers and zucchini petals. Nut-brown spaghetti alla chitarra (from the unique, guitar-strung pasta machine) is chewy with chestnut flour and slippery with duck ragout. The wood-fired oven plays a part – in gorgeous pork involtini with the tang of mustard fruits, for example, while dessert is a thing of beauty: a "millefeuille" of chocolate shards with Amedei ganache and sorbet, or a quartet of strawberry textures, from sorbet to gooey jam.

Hours Breakfast Mon–Sat 6.30–10.30am, Sun 6.30–11am; Lunch daily noon–2.30pm; Dinner daily 6–10.30pm
Bill E $12–$25 **M** $28–$48 **D** $16–$20; 10% surcharge on Sundays & public holidays
Cards AE DC V MC
Wine A wide-ranging global list with some excellent choices by the glass: 18 by the glass
Chef Alessandro Pavoni
Owner Park Hyatt Sydney
Seats 150; private rooms; wheelchair access; bar
Child friendly Kids' menu; highchairs
Vegetarian Separate menu
www.harbourkitchen.com.au
And... the degustation menu reflects chef Pavoni's northern Italian heritage

good food guide   63

city + suburbs

Hotel Saravana Bhavan

NEW ENTRY

15 The Strand, Croydon
Tel 9747 8779   Map 8

Indian/Sri Lankan

Score 12.5/20

Look for the colourful umbrellas hanging upside down in the window, and with them you'll find terrific Indian and Sri Lankan fare. A long menu features the usual suspects, including malai kofta: lusciously soft cottage cheese balls with a creamy cashew and butter masala sauce. But, along with courteous staff and carefully presented dishes, it's chef Deepak Kumar's specials that make visiting truly worthwhile. Start with Sri Lankan spicy crab – shredded crabmeat cooked with cumin seeds, ginger, garlic and chilli, served in a hollowed-out half potato with sweet tamarind chutney to drizzle on top. Drawing everyone's attention as it travels, sizzling, from kitchen to table, is chicken hotpot. It's a must-have, with on-the-bone chicken pieces full of flavour from a wonderfully aromatic tomato and onion-based sauce, a squeeze from a wedge of lemon adding tang. Mop up the extra sauce with tandoori roti and move straight on to dessert: house-made pistachio ice-cream.

Hours Lunch Sat–Sun noon–3pm; Dinner daily 5.30–10.30pm
Bill E $7.50–$12.90 **M** $12.90–$21.90 **D** $5.50
Cards V MC Eftpos
Wine BYO (corkage $1pp); licence pending
Chefs Deepak Kumar, Jit Bhadur Gurung, Sashi Bista & Nitin Shrestha
Owners Deepak Kumar & Raj Kumar Dixit
Seats 80; private rooms; wheelchair access; outdoor seating
Child friendly Highchairs
Vegetarian Almost half the menu
And...there's a good bottle shop across the road

Hugo's Bar Pizza

33 Bayswater Road, Kings Cross
Tel 9332 1227   Map 2

Italian

Score 14/20

Bar dining is a fashion statement at this chic watering hole. This is Friday night grazing at its best, with a serious cocktail bible laid out as entree (aperitif), main (in between) and dessert (digestif). The menu is all antipasti, gourmet pizza, new wave pasta dishes and a few meatier mains. Start with a refreshing apple and riberry cocktail, vodka or gins from around the globe. To nibble, pizzas are good, with crisp, pull-apart crusts and unusual toppings, such as pork belly with sour onions and radicchio, or asparagus with truffled oil. Alternatively, there's wagyu sirloin with earthy porcini, rocket salad and kipfler potatoes. Kingfish pasta is a refreshing take on tradition, but could do with more sauce and less rocket. Desserts are as artfully prepared as the cocktails. A decadent caramel opera slice has a sprinkling of salt over its crunchy peanut brittle garnish. Service is extremely attentive, and the pleasant vibe remains, even when it's crowded.

Hours Tues–Wed 5pm–midnight, Thurs–Sat 5pm–1am, Sun 3pm–midnight; no bookings after 7pm
Bill E $18–$24 **M** $22–$38 **D** $10–$14; 10% surcharge on Sundays & public holidays
Cards AE DC V MC
Wine A truly global wine list; 16 by the glass; but the cocktails are the real stars
Chefs Pete Evans & Gerard D'Ombrille
Owners Pete & David Evans & David Corsi
Seats 70; wheelchair access; outdoor seating; bar
www.hugos.com.au
And...half-price cocktails and pizza from 3–5pm on Sundays

city + suburbs

Hugo's Manly

NEW ENTRY

Shop 1, Manly Wharf, East Esplanade, Manly
Tel 8116 8555   Map 7

Italian/Pizza

Score 14/20

If you've ever fancied dining alfresco on your own catamaran, this comes close. Hugo's Manly is for grown-ups: dark wood, earthy jazz tunes and candlelight, overlooking the harbour as the ferry glides in. This is relaxed glamour for the northern beaches, but more of a bar with a restaurant than vice versa, while the service can be flighty. The view is best shared, and so is the food. A tasting plate of warm fig salad, Sydney rock oysters and ocean trout carpaccio was let down by tough fried calamari. Pan-roasted barramundi on fennel salad with saffron dressing brings Mod Oz to the mostly Italian menu, while a traditional favourite – roast chicken with lemon, rosemary and cavolo nero, plated with a single red pepper – is simple and inviting. Don't get distracted by the fanciful pizzas, such as caramelised pineapple and ham. Best stick to classics: margherita or pepperoni with buffalo mozzarella. Grilled Bethonga pineapple with coconut ice-cream sweetens the scene, while tiramisu is a perfect excuse to linger a little longer.

Hours Daily noon–11pm
Bill E $18–$27 **M** $22–$38 **D** $12–$15; 10% surcharge Sundays, 10% public holidays
Cards AE V MC
Wine Solid list of local and Italian wines; 18 by the glass
Chef Pete Evans
Owner Dave Evans, Pete Evans & David Corsi
Seats 300; wheelchair access; bar
Child friendly Kids' meals; drawing materials
Vegetarian Various pizzas & pasta dishes
www.hugos.com.au
And…try for a seat outside where you can hear the waves, smell the sea and bask in the romance

Icebergs Dining Room and Bar

Level 3, 1 Notts Avenue, Bondi Beach
Tel 9365 9000   Map 4b

Mediterranean

Score 17/20

Just entering this glamorous room makes you feel something special might happen. There's that Bondi Beach and Icebergs pool view of course – magical at any time of day. The long room in aqua tones is both soothing and sexy. The crowd ranges from hip locals to attractive families, with the occasional visiting celebrity. Amid all of this, Robert Marchetti casts his own spell. From the simplicity of fried gamberetti (tiny school prawns) with aioli, to an Italian flag of shredded rocket, boiled egg and basil arranged on the finest carpaccio of Petuna ocean trout, Marchetti's Italian fare is as satisfying as it is beautiful. Ingredients such as berkshire pork shine, served with the finest of panzanella salads. Coral trout adds to the richness of a tomato risotto. With the ever-changing ocean vista laid out beyond the white linen tablecloths, there's no push to tackle dessert, but share the signature zabaglione with a loved one and see the beauty of Sydney through a visitor's eyes.

Hours Lunch Tues–Sun noon–3pm; Dinner Tues–Sun 6.30–10pm
Bill E $22–$28 **M** $36–$54 **D** $18; 10% surcharge on Sundays & public holidays
Cards AE DC V MC Eftpos
Wine Globetrotting, luxurious, iconic; superb champagne content; 21 by the glass
Chefs Robert Marchetti, Ben Horne & Damien McCleery
Owners Robert Marchetti, Maurice Terzini, Kimme Shaw & Tony Zaccagnini
Seats 105; wheelchair access; bar
www.idrb.com
And…have a bellini in the bar beforehand to really capture that holiday feeling

good food guide

city + suburbs

Il Perugino
171 Avenue Road, Mosman
Tel 9969 9756   Map 7

Italian (Central)

Score 14/20

After more than 20 years at the helm, veteran Maurizio Mencio has officially handed over the reins to his next of kin. Thankfully, the special family feeling remains at this much-loved Mosman institution. Locals keep coming back, special bottles of wine in hand, to this elegant room with terracotta tiled floor, simple wooden seats and linen tablecloths. It's more sedate at lunch where there's a common antipasto spread on offer. At night it's boisterous as ever with waiters reciting what's available (there's no written menu as it changes daily). Zucchini flowers are delicately fried, stuffed with a sensuous filling of ricotta cheese and mixed herbs. A seafood risotto with vongole, crab meat, prawns and peas was ultra-fresh and flavoursome, yet just a bit dry. Duck maryland is better, delicately braised on the bone with simple chat potatoes and marinated zucchini. To finish, a well-textured cheesecake with a walnut butter base comes with a topping of sweet berry sauce.

Hours Lunch Wed–Fri noon–2.30pm; Dinner Mon–Sat 6–10pm; bookings essential
Bill E $17–$19.50 **M** $25–$30 **D** $12
Cards V MC
Wine BYO (no corkage)
Chefs Melinda Hagan & Phil Licciardo
Owners Mencio-Hagan family
Seats 60; private rooms
And… book the large upstairs rooms for 10 to 32 people

il piave
639 Darling Street, Rozelle
Tel 9810 6204   Map 5b

Italian

Score 14.5/20

This terrific neighbourhood trattoria is certainly worth a trip from wherever you call home. Il piave (named for a river in north-eastern Italy) presents a northern Italian menu, without tomato sauce cliches, in a bright, modern atmosphere. Eel salad is an example of the unusual dishes from the daily specials – the fishy smokiness pervading yet never overpowering the salad leaves. Plump tortelloni al fagiano is stuffed with finely minced pheasant, served with a braised mushroom sauce. Pumpkin lasagne, layered with spinach and fontina cheese, is topped with sage-infused burnt butter. The quality of produce is seen in a rack of lamb: a double rib served with shredded and pressed lamb shoulder for an intriguing contrast in textures, nicely paired with pickled eggplant. Twice-cooked duck is huge, crisp on the outside and meltingly flaky within. Desserts include trusted northern staples such as a good vanilla panna cotta and seasonal delights such as a highly flavoured fig and honey tart.

Hours Dinner Tues–Sat 6.30–10pm; bookings essential
Bill E $18.90–$21.90 **M** $24.90–$34.90 **D** $11.90–$13.90
Cards AE V MC Eftpos
Wine A small, smart list with a sprinkling of good Italians, strong in the mid-price range; 8 by the glass; BYO Tues–Thurs (corkage $8 a bottle)
Chefs Vanessa Martin & Amber Doig
Owners Robert & Vanessa Martin
Seats 60; outdoor seating
Child friendly Kids' menu
Vegetarian Separate menu
And… go for the small front room if you want intimacy

city + suburbs

Il Punto
387 Hume Highway, Liverpool
Tel 9822 2005   Map 6

Italian
Score 12.5/20

With cars roaring past on the highway outside, big noisy tables of families tucking into platefuls of pasta, and Frank Sinatra crooning on the stereo, this is an Italian trattoria that wouldn't be out of place in Tony Soprano's New Jersey. If you can resist the intoxicating aromas from the wood-fired pizza oven, start with fat figs wrapped in prosciutto in a puddle of gorgonzola sauce. Chef Giuseppe Defrancesco serves simple, homely Italian food that's as generous as it is well priced. Two tender chicken involtini, stuffed with spinach and mozzarella, are served with a red capsicum sauce on potato gratin. Sometimes, however, the kitchen needs a lighter touch: spinach-flecked ricotta gnocchi with a creamy porcini sauce was unnecessarily salty, as was the red wine and tomato sauce surrounding beef osso buco. Desserts tick all the boxes; warm, amaretti-filled peaches would bring a smile to the most hardened mobster's face.

Hours Dinner Tues–Sun 6–10.30pm
Bill E $7–$22 **M** $16–$34 **D** $10–$16; 10% surcharge on public holidays
Cards AE (+3%) DC (+3%) V MC Eftpos
Wine Compact, extremely affordable list of Australian and Italian wines; 13 by the glass; BYO (corkage $3pp)
Chef Giuseppe Defrancesco
Owners Giuseppe & Alison Defrancesco
Seats 74; bar
Child friendly Kids' menu; highchairs; drawing materials
Vegetarian Several options plus pizza
And… 14 different types of wood-fired pizza available to take away

Infusion @ 333
Mezzanine Level, 333 George Street, Sydney
Tel 9290 3333   Map 1

Modern Asian
Score 13/20

If voting with your feet is any indication of a good thing, Infusion@333 wins by a landslide. On the floor above the monolithic Bar 333, young and efficient waiters weave through a modern space dominated by bright lights, banquette seating and vivid red pillars. The largely open room is packed to the rafters with boisterous inner-city workers waxing lyrical over a liquid-fuelled lunch. The food is infusion without confusion – a clutch of simple Asian-inspired dishes designed to share and compare. Nori-wrapped yellowfin tuna is seared and served on a sharp cucumber and pickled ginger salad. Meaty Peking duck pancakes perhaps needed a little less fresh chilli, however. New Zealand king salmon served medium rare demands the accompanying wasabi soy, while boiled then wok-fried eggs add a whole new dimension. Silky snapper and plump prawns swim in a light green curry that could rival any in the city – you'll lick the bowl while no one's watching. There's just one dessert – a pleasing selection of cheese.

Hours Lunch Mon–Fri noon–3pm
Bill E $16–$22 **M** $24–$35 **D** $14–$17
Cards AE DC V MC Eftpos
Wine Very reasonably priced mix of Australasian and French; 10 by the glass
Chef Darrien Potaka
Owners John & Sally Ryan
Seats 90; wheelchair access; bar
Child friendly Kids' menu; drawing materials
And… will open at dinner for groups of 10 or more

city + suburbs

Intermezzo Ristorante
Ground Floor, GPO Building,
1 Martin Place, Sydney
Tel 9229 7788   Map 1

Italian (Neapolitan)
Score 14/20

The grand old GPO is a maze of eating opportunities, including this attractive Italian fine-diner. Take a table outside under the renaissance-style colonnades or pick a spot in the cordoned-off glass atrium, with its soaring glass ceiling. Lunchtime is for civilised banker types, while evenings draw the pre-theatre crowd. No wonder, Intermezzo is all elegance with white tablecloths and hovering waiters clad in jackets and bow ties. The food is Italian, simple and classic. Calamari is delicately fried, dressed only with lemon and pungent chilli oil. Carpaccio sealed with lemon juice hits a high note with the added bite of rocket and parmigiano. A hearty linguine dish combines scampi, cherry tomatoes and plenty of fresh parsley. Even more successful is fresh snapper with a glorious accompaniment of pea puree and porcini mushrooms. Generous house-made Sicilian cannoli stuffed with ricotta and candied peel bring this very pleasant interlude to an end.

Hours Lunch Mon–Fri noon–3pm;
Dinner Mon–Sat 6–10pm
Bill E $16–$23 **M** $31–$39 **D** $15.50;
8% surcharge for parties of 10 or more
Cards AE DC V MC Eftpos
Wine Exceptional, large Australian and European list; 18 by the glass
Chef Mario Percuoco
Owner Peter Petroulas
Seats 80–100; wheelchair access; outdoor seating; bar
Child friendly Highchairs
www.gposydney.com
And...look for the massive wine tower in the atrium

Iron Chef
84 Broomfield Street, Cabramatta
Tel 9723 6228   Map 6

NEW ENTRY

Chinese (Cantonese)
Score 14/20

There are no fierce battles in this kitchen stadium. The sprawling dining room is a picture of calm during dinner service. Tiered seafood tanks, occasional alcoves of bamboo trees and dark wood chairs, smarter decor and sleeker service set this restaurant apart from the din of the Chinatown clan. Among chef Jack Ng's many unusual specialities are spice-baked lamb chops and wok-seared kangaroo fillet marinated with Shanghai herbs. Traditional fare is more successful though. Peking-style roasted duck offers great value, and appears, true to form, as two courses – the first as wafer-thin meat slices for wrapping in thin pancakes with cucumber, shallots and hoi sin, the second stir-fried, perhaps, into sang choi bau. Diced beef fillets dry-fried with a hint of wasabi (another chef's secret recipe) bursts with the smokiness of the wok without losing tenderness. Desserts are generous – with a choice of the ubiquitous fruit platter, deep-fried ice-cream and warming red bean soup.

Hours Lunch Mon–Fri 10am–3pm, Sat–Sun 9am–3.30pm; Dinner Mon–Fri 5.30–10.30pm, Sat–Sun 5.30–11pm
Bill E $6.80–$24.80 **M** $16.80–$38.80 **D** $6–$8
Cards AE (+3.4%) V MC
Wine Small, Australian-dominated list;
12 by the glass; BYO (corkage $8 a bottle)
Chef Jack Ng
Owner Phillip Visalli
Seats 500; private rooms; wheelchair access; outdoor seating; bar
Child friendly Highchairs
Vegetarian Vegetable and tofu sections on menu
www.ironchef.com.au
And...watch out for monthly promotions

All-Clad
METALCRAFTERS LLC

Cookware
The Professionals Use.

All-Clad cookware was originally created for professionals and that legacy continues today. What makes All-Clad the preferred choice of renowned chefs? Superior cooking performance and a dedication to the most rigorous standards in design and manufacturing. All-Clad cookware will meet your needs and inspire creativity.

www.allclad.com.au

Win a piece of All-Clad from the Stainless Collection (valued from $199) by entering the monthly All-Clad Good Food Guide promotion.

To enter, send your full name, address and phone number and an answer to the following question in 25 words or less. "Why would you like to receive a piece of All-Clad cookware?" Send your entry to allclad@au.groupeseb.com

Conditions apply, see www.allclad.com.au. Limit 1 entry permitted per person per month. Entries close each month at 11:59pm AEST/AEDST as follows: 29/09/09, 28/10/09, 29/11/09, 31/12/09, 28/01/10, 25/02/10, 30/03/10, 29/04/10, 30/05/10, 29/06/10, 29/07/10 and 30/08/10.

city + suburbs

Japaz

165 Wycombe Road, Neutral Bay
Tel 9904 0688   Map 5a

Contemporary/Tapas

Score 14/20

It's tapas meets izakaya – the small-plate tradition of Spain merged with Japanese bar food. Curious as it may sound, you'll soon relax into this casual, cafe-like space, thanks to a personable, busy but professional waiter, a seductive wine list and appealing morsels of well-crafted food from a chef with Robuchon and Tetsuya's on his CV. Check the blackboard for specials such as sliced, fried morcilla (black pudding) on sourdough and piquillo peppers paired with a herbed crab filling. The tone may be Spanish but the ceramic serving plates channel Japanese aesthetics. Umami (the Japanese "fifth taste") comes to the fore in fat scallops on the shell with sweet soy and onion butter, tiny shreds of fresh leek and baby spinach leaves, and soft slices of baked eggplant with a crust of pine nuts and cured mullet roe. A cornichon, seeded mustard and red wine vinaigrette cuts through melt-in-the-mouth, twice-cooked beef tongue. Peach sorbet refreshes on apple cider jelly with vanilla-infused olive oil. It's all about balance. And it works.

Hours Lunch Thurs–Fri noon–3pm;
Dinner Mon–Sat 6–10pm
Bill Tapas $6–$19 **D** $7–$9; tasting menu $68pp
Cards AE V MC
Wine Appealing, well-priced global list including sake, beers and a reserve list; 12 by the glass; BYO lunch & Mon–Wed dinner only (corkage $6 a bottle)
Chef/owner Hiro Takagi
Seats 40; outdoor seating
Vegetarian Numerous tapas options
www.japaz.com.au
And…come again and again to try the 30-plus dishes

Jaspers

54 Alexandra Street, Hunters Hill
Tel 9879 3200   Map 7

Contemporary

Score 14/20

It's quite the Hunters Hill institution – a pretty sandstone cottage nestled under leafy green trees on the main drag down to the peninsula. Ownership has changed over the years but the culinary skills of Luke Mangan-trained Martin Stacey have clearly struck a chord with Jaspers' loyal clientele. Decor is brown on brown, but a lush Sichuan-glazed duck breast, creatively presented with baby beets, baby mache and a mellifluous almond and fig dressing, raises sparks. An unusual combo of twice-cooked kurobuta pork belly and palm hearts with tamarind and star anise sauce is a popular menu player, while melt-in-the-mouth blue-eye trevalla fillet and garlic confit is adorned with tomatoes, eschalots and piquant capers. Cosy pillows of pan-fried porcini gnocchi with a melange of crisp, al dente vegies displays high-end technique with its elegant truffle dressing. Stacey's imprint is also on the knockout caramel panna cotta surrounded by delicately poached nectarines and spiked with ruby grapefruit. Institution status is maintained.

Hours Lunch Tues–Fri noon–3pm;
Dinner Mon–Sat 6–10pm
Bill E $20–$22 **M** $28–$38 **D** $14–$18;
10% surcharge on public holidays and Sundays
Cards AE DC V MC Eftpos
Wine Smattering of European reds, no aged wines; 15 by the glass; BYO (corkage $7pp)
Chef Martin Stacey
Owners Lisa Steuerwald & Graeme Laycock
Seats 85; private rooms
Child friendly Kids' menu; highchairs
www.jaspersrestaurant.com.au
And…Jaspers' lunch special, plate of the day $25

city + suburbs

jimmy liks
186–188 Victoria Street, Potts Point
Tel 8354 1400   Map 2

South-East Asian
Score 14.5/20

The long, dark room brings a sense of mystery and adventure, enhanced by the aroma of Asian spices and herbs. Ease onto a communal table among the eclectic crowd and let the procession begin. Oysters in nahm jim dressing set the pace. Betel leaf with smoked eel, shrimp and galangal merges a touch of the West with a traditional Thai snack. Steamed pork and prawn dumplings are sexed up with a heady Chinese black vinegar dressing. Vietnamese braised wagyu beef is simply sensational, with big, meltingly flaky beef slices infused with a beautifully balanced, aromatic broth. Whole fish of the day is served crisp in a slightly oversweet chilli sauce. Desserts complete this South-East Asian tour de force, with coconut ice-cream and popular cassia bark and coconut banana fritters. This is a spice trip with all the perfumes and flavours of the East, without the chilli burn. Jimmy liks keeps things very cool.

Hours Dinner daily 6–11pm; bookings for 6–7pm only
Bill E $3.80–$19 **M** $22–$33 **D** $14–$32; 9-course banquet menu $55pp; 10% surcharge on Sundays & public holidays
Cards AE DC V MC Eftpos
Wine Small but well-chosen for the spicy cuisine; 23 by the glass
Chef Ali Carter
Owner Joe Elcham
Seats 100; outdoor seating; bar
www.jimmyliks.com
And... Asian-inspired cocktails in the bar

Jonah's
69 Bynya Road, Whale Beach
Tel 9974 5599   Map 7

Contemporary
Score 15/20

The plush, muted greys of the dining room fade away as you gaze out the panoramic windows – with the jaws of first-time visitors likely to drop as quickly as the escarpment falls away to Whale Beach below. When your attention returns to the table, you'll find quietly attentive staff flitting among well-heeled diners, and a bright, sophisticated menu with a sprinkling of fun – such as a Jenga stack of toast soldiers, sandwiched with fontina cheese and black truffle slivers, ready to be dipped in a soft-boiled truffled egg. Deep-fried oysters, while creamy and well-matched with a spicy Cajun remoulade, disappeared somewhat in their thick semolina crust. Different cuisines mingle sociably in a main of blue-eye on squid-ink fettuccine with jamon, clams and slender salt-and-pepper calamari curls; like-minded diners, meanwhile, can share a classic aged entrecote of beef. A lush, juicy peach Melba tea ice-cream sundae, swirled with raspberry, adds a glorious twist to a luxe day by the beach.

Hours Breakfast daily 8–9.45am; Lunch daily noon–3 pm; Dinner daily 6.30–9pm (Wed–Sun only March–Oct); bookings essential
Bill E $29–$31 **M** $41–$51 **D** $16–$18; 10% surcharge on Sundays & public holidays
Cards AE DC V MC Eftpos
Wine Extensive list, mostly Australian; 25 by the glass
Chef George Francisco
Owner Jonah's Restaurant Pty Ltd
Seats 100; private room; wheelchair access; outdoor seating; bar
Child friendly Kids' menu; highchairs; drawing materials
www.jonahs.com.au
And... soak up the view for less with an antipasto plate or burgers on the terrace (until 9pm)

city + suburbs

Jugemu & Shimbashi
246 Military Road, Neutral Bay
Tel 9904 3011   Map 5a

Japanese

Score 14.5/20

Japanese artisan chefs take their specialities seriously. With its two separate entrances, this is a showcase for two authentic forms of Japanese dining craft. One door leads to a soba (buckwheat) noodle house, and another to a teppanyaki bar. Once inside, though, you can enjoy both. In the dimly lit Shimbashi, soba expert Tojo-san carefully grinds and kneads Tasmanian buckwheat flour before service. His legendary soba is silky smooth but easy to grasp, and marvellous in a sweet, smoky duck and mushroom broth. While the teppan (open griddle) is all about grills, the modern, red-walled Jugemu side also turns out winning okonomiyaki – a filling, savoury pancake that's pure home food. Try it topped with pork, an excellent match for the yolky mayonnaise and fruity worcestershire sauce drizzled over the dense, steaming package. An assortment of teppan-fired mushrooms – firm, earthy and gloriously buttery – is presented like a fan on a ceramic dish. Service can be shaky but there's no doubting the treasures behind these two doors.

Hours Lunch Tues–Sat noon–2pm; Dinner Tues–Sat 6–9.30pm, Sun 6–9pm; bookings essential
Bill E $5–$18 **M** $13–$38 **D** $6–$12
Cards AE DC V MC Eftpos
Wine Smart list of Japanese-friendly Australian wines plus good sake and shochu; 9 by the glass
Chefs Masahiko Tojo & Koji Sano
Owner VWC International Pty Ltd
Seats 86; private room; wheelchair access
Child friendly Highchairs
And... granita-style frozen plum wine is a pleasantly sweet aperitif

Ju-Rin
316 Pacific Highway, Crows Nest
Tel 9966 5811   Map 5a

Japanese

Score 14/20

FAVOURITE ASIAN
There's Sydney Japanese and there's Sydney Japanese. At its most banal, it's factory sushi and instant-broth ramen. At its best, it's skilled, authentic and as fresh as it gets. Enter Ju-rin, with its expert sushi master, genial host, a top Japanese seafood supplier and a strong expat following. The key, in this long red-and-grey room with its corner counter, are the daily specials, inspired by what's come in from the sea. Start with appetisers: baby abalone, perhaps, with just a hint of chew, sanma (a sardine-like Japanese fish) in dark soy, Pacific oysters in a light dashi jelly, prawns with a soft egg filling. Sushi and sashimi depend on the day – maybe negi (shallot) and toro (tuna belly) in tiny nori rolls. Unmissable are wakame salad – slimy seaweed squares with mesclun leaves and a sesame-oil dressing – grilled mackerel or eggplant with black miso. Giant bowls of udon, soba or donburi (one-bowl rice dishes) fill the gaps, then lick up a scoop of grassy green tea ice-cream with red beans.

Hours Lunch Tues–Fri noon–2pm; Dinner Tues–Sun 6–9.30pm
Bill Dishes from $4.80–$29.50 **D** $6.50–$7; sushi course $50pp
Cards AE V MC Eftpos
Wine Some wine, but best check the sake list or ask host Terry for a suggestion; 4 by the glass
Chef Naoki Fakushima
Owner Terry Nishiura
Seats 45
Vegetarian Plenty of choice
www.jurin.com.au
And... sit at the sushi counter for the best view of your meal

city + suburbs

Kable's

Four Seasons Hotel,
199 George Street, Sydney
Tel 9250 3226 Map 1

Contemporary

Score 14.5/20

Yes, Kable's is still a discreet, comfortable, high-ceilinged room in soothing browns on the hotel's mezzanine level, where waiters hover solicitously, and the sommelier is gently helpful (believe it or not, choose from 25 different waters). Under chef Carl Middleton this one-time star is fast recapturing its reputation as a grand hotel dining room. If the menu reads rather hotel-ish, fear not, the food's terrific. Rondels of foie gras and rabbit are superb. A beautifully composed salad balances subtly smoked lamb loin with slivers of carrot, zucchini and radish, plus goat's cheese. Broad beans, asparagus, tomatoes and shimeji mushrooms are scattered amid cute black tie pasta (squid ink farfalle), while a shimmering, poached organic hen's egg balances on top. It's a vivacious, seductive dish, as is an unusually light risotto, well laced with spanner crab. A trifle, prettily presented in a martini glass, bursts with blueberries and a hit of Grand Marnier. We'll be back, and we're glad Kable's is too.

Hours Lunch Tues–Fri noon–2.30pm;
Dinner Tues–Sat 6–11pm
Bill E $24–$28 **M** $34–$110 **D** $12–$16;
2-course set lunch with glass of wine $39pp
Cards AE DC V MC
Wine A long, well-constructed international list, with lots of fine locals; 31 by the glass
Chef Carl Middleton
Owner Four Seasons Hotels & Resorts
Seats 80; private rooms; wheelchair access
Child friendly Kids' menu
Vegetarian Separate menu
www.fourseasons.com/sydney/dining/kable_s.html
And... a water menu of 25 international H2Os

Kam Fook

Level 6, Westfield Shopping Centre,
Bondi Junction
Tel 9386 9889 Map 9
Also at Level 6, Westfield Shopping Centre,
Chatswood
Tel 9413 9388 Map 7

Chinese (Cantonese)

Score 13.5/20

Children are a good litmus test for restaurants, and here the results come in after only two courses. Rudely plump prawn gow gees disappear in a trice. Quiet reigns as Peking duck, carved at the table for pancakes and then served as decadent fried rice, is shovelled down. A cavalcade of waiters bustles about like ants in a colony, and the space, naturally lit through the day via soaring windows, is pure theatre. Dishes arrive with brisk efficiency. Steamed scallops hidden under a thatch of shallot and ginger julienne seemed rather small and mean, and the crabmeat in soft egg – a cumulus cloud of scrambled egg generously flecked with crab – was a tad too salty. The fish in the salt-and-pepper seafood, along with prawns and squid, flakes as only perfectly cooked fish can. From the tank, barramundi with ginger and shallot, and bok choy with soy and oyster sauce up the ante for adult diners.

Hours Lunch daily 10am–3pm;
Dinner Mon–Wed 5.30–10.30pm, Thurs–Sat 5.30–11pm, Sun 5–10pm; bookings essential
Bill E $6–$16 **M** $18–$36 **D** $6–$12; $3.20pp surcharge on public holidays
Cards AE DC V MC Eftpos
Wine An intelligent, extensive list with some highlights; 20 by the glass
Chef Lam Ping
Owner Rosetta Lee
Seats 200 (Bondi Junction); wheelchair access
Child friendly Highchairs
Vegetarian Several options
www.kamfook.com.au
And... grab a lolly from the golden cow

city + suburbs

Kazbah on Darling

379 Darling Street, Balmain
Tel 9555 7067   Map 5b

Middle Eastern

Score 13.5/20

Who says the Sharif don't like it? Everybody else reckons the Kazbah on Darling rocks, with a menu that reads like a travel journal, drawing and blending inspirations from the Levantine sunrise to the North African sunset. It's modern fusion in an ornamental interior, borrowing from the spectrum with za'atar from Lebanon, muhammara from Syria, dukkah from Egypt and preserved lemons from Morocco. The picture is complete with white-clad staff dishing out fragrant delights to an adoring crowd. Not everything works, and service can be clumsy. But artichoke hearts stuffed with labna and wrapped in kataifi pastry is a textural triumph, and the ever-changing Kazbah tagine, in this case a smoky, moist spatchcock accompanied by light, fluffy couscous, is delectably wholesome. Another winner is dukkah-spiced lamb fillet taken to new heights by full-flavoured ratatouille – similar to Tunisian chakchouka with the addition of eggplant. Berries and nuts, mixed with cold, creamy salep – a traditional drink made with ground orchid – ensure a Turkish-influenced finale.

Hours Breakfast Tues–Fri 8am–3pm; Sat–Sun 9am–3pm; Lunch Sat–Sun noon–3pm; Dinner Tues–Sat 6 30–10pm
Bill E $5.50–$18 **M** $35–$37 **D** $14–$28; 2 courses & glass of wine $40pp
Cards AE DC V MC
Wine Small, well-priced list of safe crowd-pleasers; 16 by the glass; BYO (corkage $3.50pp)
Chefs Zahi Azzi & Aaron Callander
Owners Zahi & Penny Azzi
Seats 110; wheelchair access; outdoor seating
Child friendly Kids' meals on request; crayons
www.kazbah.com.au
And... convince the maitre d' to let you buy some of the beautiful Moroccan dinner plates

Kensington Peking

172 Anzac Parade, Kensington
Tel 9313 7100   Map 9

Chinese (Northern Peking)

Score 13/20

What hits you first is that it's startlingly bright – white walls with a couple of silk embroidered scenes on one side and a dozen A4 sheets with hand- and typewritten specials matted on the other. What you realise next is that it's crowded with families, business types and students alike, most of them obviously regulars. And finally, you cotton on. This is something good. While the focus may be on northern fare, there's a lot to come from the tanks, Cantonese style, such as fat scallops, pert in their shell, tressed with shavings of shallots and ginger. Smokey, tan, handmade noodle laces are tossed with strips of pork and shredded Chinese cabbage. Crisp-fried blocks of creamy tofu flecked with coriander sit on lettuce leaves doused in a light prawn sauce. A hotpot of mushy eggplant and pork mince is thick, slightly sweet, enlivened with thin chilli rings. A plate of fruit to end the meal is just the refresher you're after.

Hours Lunch Thurs–Tues 11am–3pm; Dinner Thurs–Tues 5–10.30pm; bookings essential
Bill E $5.80–$15.80 **M** $10.80–$42.80 **D** $6.80–$16; $2pp surcharge on public holidays
Cards V MC Eftpos
Wine BYO (corkage $2pp)
Chef/owner Peter Lo
Seats 200; private rooms; wheelchair access
Child friendly Kids will love the place, and it clearly loves them; highchair; booster seat
Vegetarian Lots of non-meat options from tofu to greens
And... don't hesitate to pump staff for suggestions

good food guide

city + suburbs

Koi

102 Woolwich Road, Woolwich
Tel 9817 6030   Map 7

NEW ENTRY

Japanese
Score 14/20

Let's start at the sushi bar. Pull up a stool and watch maestro Kenji Nishinakagawa (formerly of Unkai at the ANA Hotel) make seafood sing with precision and elegance. Sashimi, both traditional and modern, includes five types of salmon toro (belly). Seared scallop carpaccio is sensual and superb, the sweet, shimmering, thinly sliced flesh bathing in rich, salty soy butter. Tuna tartare is a luscious concoction of coddled egg, the faintest scent of truffle oil and smoky avruga. This stylish, low-key suburban Japanese is a polished gem, with lavishly Asian-styled decor and honey-coloured timbers. Service is warm and efficient, while the wide-ranging menu blends tradition with adventure. Sometimes the modern approach goes awry, such as glorious veal with edamame salad and yuzu dressing with toffee popcorn, but hinadori – teriyaki-roasted Thirlmere spatchcock – with quail egg yolks, toasted pine nuts and creamy miso sauce delights. Desserts go global: cheesecake, chocolate tart, souffle or cheese, but the extensive sake list should keep you entertained.

Hours Lunch Thurs–Sun noon–2.30pm; Dinner Tue–Thurs 6–10pm, Fri–Sat 6–10.30pm, Sun 6–9.30pm
Bill Share dishes $5.50–$58; **D** $15.50–$18; 3-course lunch and a beverage $40pp
Cards AE DC V MC Eftpos
Wine Extensive, clever international list, plus strong sake selection; 18 by the glass
Chef Kenji Nishinakagawa
Owner Robert Frost
Seats 50; private room
Child friendly Highchairs
www.koi-dining.com.au
And…serving plates are works of art

Kuali

Level 1, 115 Longueville Road, Lane Cove
Tel 9418 6878   Map 7

Malaysian
Score 13/20

The decor is more canteen than dining haven, but if you crave hawker flavours, this is the place to be. Kuali favourites are stir-fried mamak mee – noodles and prawns, quickly tossed in curry powder and tomato sauce, plus gently poached Hainanese chicken rice served with ginger and chilli. Service is attentive, if occasionally pushy. The star is the signature curry mud crab, redolent with chef John Poh's aromatic sauce, and sprinkled with deep fried curry leaves. Mop it up with a serving of flaky roti canai, and you're in spice heaven. Bring friends to enjoy it as the price can be hefty (and make sure staff give you costs first to avoid a shock at bill time). A more frugal main is sambal prawns, coated with a spicy coconut chilli sauce and served in banana leaves – a good complement to stir-fried kang kong in pungent belachan. If your mouth's on fire by now, cool down with a refreshing sago pudding drizzled in coconut cream and palm sugar syrup.

Hours Dinner Tues–Sun 5.30–10pm
Bill E $4.60–$11 **M** $13–$27 **D** $7–$10; 10% surcharge on public holidays
Cards AE V MC Eftpos; 2.5% surcharge on all cards for bills under $50
Wine Predominantly Australian; 6 by the glass; BYO (corkage $2.50pp)
Chef/owner John Poh
Seats 120; bar
Child friendly Highchairs
Vegetarian Separate menu
www.kuali.com.au
And…signature dishes served at Chinese New Year and Malaysian national day in August

city + suburbs

La Grande Bouffe

758 Darling Street, Rozelle
Tel 9818 4333   Map 5b

French

Score 13.5/20

Glimpses of la belle epoque can be seen in the decor of this small corner restaurant, albeit a pared-back, modern version. Black Perspex chandeliers hang from the ceiling and bevelled mirrors from the exuberant wallpapered wall. It may not be Maxim's, but La Grande Bouffe exudes a certain Gallic charm. There are small, nuggety, very French escargots to start. Ballotine of ocean trout seduces with a smooth, citrus-infused texture. Twice-baked goat's cheese souffle with cream and zucchini is more comfort food than lustrous but Escoffier would not have scoffed at well-seasoned calf's liver, cooked pink as requested, served with crisp mushrooms and witlof on a puddle of mash. Pan-fried pork fillet with celeriac puree, confit garlic and earthy lentils also hits the mark with its contrasts in texture and colour. A rich, glossy chocolate tart, skilfully partnered with suitably sharp marmalade syrup and ice-cream, is a gourmand's dream.

Hours Breakfast & lunch daily 7.30am–2.30pm; Dinner Tues–Sat 6.30–9.30pm
Bill E $18.50 **M** $29 **D** $12–$18; 2-course lunch $35pp, 3-course dinner $60pp; 10% surcharge on public holidays
Cards AE DC V MC Eftpos
Wine An easy-drinking, mid-priced list of French and Australian wines; 13 by the glass; BYO Mon–Thurs only (corkage $10 a bottle)
Chef Robert Hodgson
Owners David & Meredith Poirier
Seats 50; wheelchair access; outdoor seating
Child friendly Kid-friendly menu; toys
www.lagrandebouffe.com.au
And...there's a menu for dogs, too

La Grillade

118 Alexander Street (cnr Albany Street), Crows Nest
Tel 9439 3707   Map 5a

French/Steakhouse

Score 13/20

La Grillade, French for "the grill", has pleased punters for almost three decades, particularly those who like a fine steak with all the trimmings. Sure, it's caught in an 80s time capsule and looks a little dated, particularly with the main room's classic French homestead feel, but happily, the back dining room is a touch more refreshing. Service can be scatty, but James Dorton's reliable take on French fare sates seriously hungry bellies and the silverbacks who see this steakhouse as their natural habitat. Start with a dozen snails, buttered-up with garlic, or a classic hand-cut eye fillet steak tartare, a soft-boiled quail egg yolk running over. Roast Barbury duck breast and confit leg splashes in a puddle of armagnac jus that was a little too rich. A 200-day grain-fed Black Angus sirloin is cooked, rested and delivered at its optimum to slice like butter. A towering passionfruit meringue partnered with a sour cream ice-cream takes two to conquer, but you'll eat it till the cows come home.

Hours Lunch Mon–Fri noon–3pm; Dinner Mon–Sat 6–10.30pm
Bill E $14.50–$22 **M** $25–$78 **D** $16
Cards AE DC V MC Eftpos
Wine Huge but pricey list with drops from all over the globe; 20 by the glass
Chef James Dorton
Owner AIH Group
Seats 140; private rooms; outdoor seating; bar
www.lagrillade.com.au
And...hit the bar early for an aperitif or end the evening with a nightcap

city + suburbs

La Locanda
65B Macpherson Street, Bronte
Tel 9389 3666   Map 9

Italian
Score 13/20

Here's some good news if you're sick of getting industrial deafness in Sydney restaurants. Despite the small, closely packed wooden tables in this narrow black and white-tiled room, the acoustics are good. And the short blackboard menu of antipasti, pasta, secondi, contorni and dolci – four of each – provides plenty of choice. Two just warmed-through figs with a gorgonzola heart and sweet, rich caramelised onion puree is an excellent start. Although calamari ripieni was a little tough with lacklustre stuffing, the accompanying fresh tomato sauce shows what the kitchen is capable of. Big, fat pillows of light gnocchi have a simple sauce of roasted cherry tomatoes and diced eggplant. Succulent, crisp-skinned barramundi is drizzled with a sweet-sour, sultana-studded sauce. The Italian mantra of fresh, quality produce simply prepared is followed here, although a little more flavour might lift some dishes from good to great. Service is friendly, if busy, and the creamy plum semifreddo on a crunchy hazelnut praline base sends everyone away with a smile.

Hours Dinner Tues–Sun 6–10pm
Bill E $15–$17 **M** $22–$28 **D** $13–$15
Cards AE V MC Eftpos
Wine Small, appropriate, good value, almost half Italian; 10 by the glass; BYO Tues–Thurs & Sun only (corkage $5pp)
Chef Andrea Vagge
Owners Andrea Vagge & Fiona Bloomer
Seats 55; outdoor seating
Child friendly Kids' menu; highchair
www.lalocanda.com.au
And…pasta is made in-house daily

La Perla
255 Victoria Road, Gladesville
Tel 9816 1161   Map 7

Italian (Southern)/Seafood
Score 13.5/20

Aquamarine walls, glass doors and pine chairs transport you to a seaside Italian trattoria. Or is it the chatty, energetic owner Giorgio Colosi, who makes his customers overlook the busy, nondescript strip of Victoria Road outside? Honest, straightforward seafood fare is chef Dominic Bertuccio's mission in life, and it shows in the long list of "fish of the day" specials, grilled or fried to perfection. Delicately moist garfish, nabbed at the markets by Giorgio and painstakingly cleaned that morning, is a standout, along with crunchy, deep-fried calamari sitting over tomato-sweet, pleasantly firm linguine. Portions are well-sized, even for a grande famiglia, so go easy on the Brasserie bread and enticing flash-fried entree options, such as whitebait and stuffed zucchini flowers. Traditional Italian desserts and a good espresso are a must. A heavenly, Galliano-spiked crepe oozes with luscious mascarpone and chocolate, and again, is more than enough to share. What a pearler.

Hours Lunch Tues–Fri noon–3pm; Dinner Tues–Sun 6–10pm; bookings essential
Bill E $16–$22 **M** $24–$45 **D** $10–$14
Cards AE DC V MC Eftpos
Wine Affordable list of mainly Aussie wines plus some Italian; 17 by the glass; BYO (corkage $4pp)
Chef Dominic Bertuccio
Owner Giorgio Colosi
Seats 130; private room; wheelchair access
Child friendly Absolutely – it's Italian and there's fish & chips
www.laperla.com.au
And…there are a few meat options, too

city + suburbs

La Tratt
Fairfield RSL, 14 Anzac Avenue, Fairfield
Tel 9727 5000   Map 6

Italian

Score 13.5/20

Las Vegas meets Asian-styled resort, all in a suburban club. This ain't your average "rissole", especially not when the pokies part to reveal a glamorous mod-Asian pho shop, with spice display and vermilion walls, as well as an intimately lit, mood-music enhanced, Italian restaurant. Then add a Greek Australian chef to the mix, and the sweetest, most efficient waitresses. Endearingly attributed to a selection of Italian cookbooks, the menu is well conceived, prettily presented and cleverly avoids over-ambitious combinations. A salad of pickled beetroot with San Daniele prosciutto and goat's curd is just as promised. Three cheese ravioli is flying-saucer-sized al dente discs, overlaid with pan-fried sage leaves and nut-brown butter. The light sweetness of pan-fried blue-eye sits comfortably with wilted treviso, creamed polenta and teensy caper and tomato dice. Take in the chandeliers, black-and-white Florence Broadhurst-like wallpaper, bronze walls and bamboo basket lighting as you spoon up caramelly brown butter ice-cream and puff pastry pear tart and marvel at the magnificence of multicultural Sydney.

Hours Dinner Wed–Sat 6–9.30pm
Bill E $12.90–$18.90 **M** $22–$35 **D** $12.50–$16.90
Cards DC V MC Eftpos
Wine An easy, mostly Australian list, with good prices; 13 by the glass
Chef Jason Joannou
Owner Fairfield RSL Club
Seats 60; wheelchair access; bar
Child friendly Kids' menu; highchairs
www.fairfieldrsl.com.au
And…explore and check out the decor throughout

Le Bukhara
Level 1, 55 Bay Street (cnr Cross Street), Double Bay
Tel 9363 5510   Map 9

Mauritian/Indian

Score 13/20

An upstairs corner in schnitzel and strudel territory is an unusual place to find a Mauritian restaurant, but Le Bukhara endures. It does so through an interesting range of dishes, and charming, if occasionally wayward, service. Regulars relax in a large, neatly furnished room with a black flagged floor, ochre tones and wraparound windows. The menu shows characteristic French-Creole influences while demonstrating how Mauritius has plundered the Indian subcontinent for spices, herbs and influences. Highlights include juicy gingered lamb chops from the tandoor with spiced mustard oil; naan slathered with garlic; a plain lassi that's anything but; dry yet tender okra; and a rich tomato sauce on a fine Mad-as-styled fish curry, fillets firm under their coating of spices. And do stay for dessert. A side of spicy chai ice-cream with warm gulab jamun – dense dumplings of cottage cheese touched with cinnamon syrup – could have you regularly climbing the Bukhara stairs, too.

Hours Dinner Sun–Thurs 5.30–10.30pm, Fri–Sat 5.30–11pm
Bill E $7.90–$15 **M** $13.90–$25 **D** $7–$12
Cards AE DC V MC Eftpos
Wine Short list of reliable Australian names; 13 by the glass; BYO (corkage $3pp)
Chef Vijay Baboo
Owners Vijay Baboo, Heman Pullut & Jean-Noel Seetaloo
Seats 100; bar
Vegetarian Separate menu: great okra and eggplant
www.bukhararestaurant.com.au
And…a surprising cocktail list: try one with Mauritian rum

good food guide   79

Le Pelican

411 Bourke Street, Darlinghurst
Tel 9380 2622   Map 2

French/Basque

Score 14/20

Leave the tat and tumble of Taylor Square behind and take a trip to the Basque country, in this quaint, heritage-listed 1850s cottage. Sandstone walls, polished wooden floorboards, white tablecloths and menus of renowned French and Basque chefs adorn walls. It's a fine, if not homely, setting for passionate service and magic morsels from the tiny kitchen. Every dish tilts its hat to chef Jean-Francois Salet's Michelin-starred French education. Duck and foie gras terrine is light – apple and walnut chutney cuts through the richness. Seared scallops and baby beets nestle up to a salubrious asparagus bavarois, while a bold parmesan-crusted kingfish rests on olives, cherry tomato and chorizo in a luscious truffle jus. Duck two ways – confit thigh and pan-fried breast – will get your heart racing as the carrot and fennel puree streaks across the plate. Baked desserts with excellent ice-cream may tempt, or end with an homage to fromage – a trio of white mould, aged and blue cheeses.

Hours Lunch Wed–Fri noon–3pm; Dinner Tues–Sun 6–10.30pm; bookings essential
Bill E $15–$19 **M** $27–$35 **D** $14–$15
Cards AE V MC Eftpos
Wine Small, joyous list of winners of mainly Australasian and French wines; 14 by the glass; BYO Tues–Thurs only (corkage $10 a bottle)
Chef/owner Jean-Francois Salet
Owners Jean-Francois & Ally Salet
Seats 48; private room; outdoor seating
Child friendly Kids' menu
www.lepelican.com.au
And…all entrees can be made as a main course for an extra $10

L'étoile

211 Glenmore Road, Paddington
Tel 9332 1577   Map 4a

French

Score 15/20

With the world getting back to basics, it's not surprising a chef of Manu Feildel's calibre would downsize from the highwire dining of Bilson's (where he was head chef for four years) to this humbler, yet equally satisfying, French brasserie. In a stylish terrace of warm timbers with a narrow bar for classy cocktails and a smart rear courtyard for alfresco dining, Feidel produces the classics with Gallic panache. A sweetly sharp French onion soup with gruyere crouton is packed with dark, mysterious depths of flavour. Beautiful, textured scallop boudin (sausage) with shellfish bisque is bejewelled with salmon roe. For mains, an opulent bouillabaisse was let down by undercooked, crunchy boiled potatoes, but rest assured the duck fat-sauteed potatoes with lushly salty duck confit are spot-on. With service that's personable and chatty, a wine list littered with French gems, and excellent cheeses, this is Paris Paddo-style, with a pear tarte tatin as dreamy as your first visit to the City of Love.

Hours Lunch Fri–Sun noon–3pm; Dinner daily 6–11pm; bookings essential
Bill E $18 **M** $32 **D** $15; 10% surcharge on public holidays
Cards AE DC V MC
Wine Petite, classy, French-garnished list with a few splurges; 18 by the glass
Chef Manu Feildel
Owners Michele & Yannick Besnard & Manu Feildel
Seats 100; outdoor seating; bar
Child friendly Highchairs
www.letoilerestaurant.com.au
And…set lunch menu, with omelettes, too

city + suburbs

Libertine

1 Kellett Street, Kings Cross
Tel 9368 7507   Map 2

French/Vietnamese

Score 13/20

Offer a dish called "best-ever wok-fried eggplant", and you'd better deliver. This ode to Indochine comes pretty close, with gleaming squishy rings of eggplant tossed with tofu, asparagus, red chilli slices and basil leaves, in a deft balance of flavours and textures. Deftness carries through Libertine's street snacks, such as spiced, red curried corn cakes – a confection of golden kernels just held together by light batter – to a series of Asian-inspired mains. Whole, fried barramundi with crisp, crumbed skin over firm, moist flesh is set off by a quartet of flavourings: cucumber and galangal salsa, peanut and tamarind sauce, red chilli and salt, and grilled lime. Desserts are equally well conceived: a trio of sorbets is as fresh and cleansing as their fruit bases. Restraint and subtlety is abandoned in the decor, however, thanks to gaudy red and gold walls, blatantly faux chandeliers, waitresses in tight black cocktail frocks, and red lanterns raised in the courtyard – a cheeky take on its location in Sydney's premier red light district.

Hours Dinner Tues–Thurs 6–10pm, Fri–Sat 6–11pm
Bill E $7–$16 **M** $18–$29 **D** $9–$12
Cards AE V MC
Wine A good selection of local, New Zealand and European suited to the food; 10 by the glass
Chef Apple Khorthon
Owners Andrew Baturo, Jamie Webb & Axel Arnott
Seats 120; outdoor seating; bar; wheelchair access
Vegetarian Good choice in the street snacks and the mains
www.libertine.net.au
And...street snacks in the lounge nook with a beer or cocktail

The Light Brigade Bistro

2a Oxford Street, Woollahra
Tel 9331 2930   Map 4a

French

Score 14/20

The Light Brigade has had more facelifts than Joan Rivers and more name changes than Prince. It has been a rugby pub and a preppy pub. Now it's an art deco drinking pub with a TAB. In the past, this identity crisis downstairs has worked its way to the restaurant upstairs, which has been everything from Thai to a cocktail bar. It has now settled into mod French bistro led by captain James Privett (formerly of Hotel CBD). The ambition remains, but the execution can vary. Crisp ocean trout with a cucumber sorbet comes with a hit of green curry sauce. Juicy scallops pair with an interesting combo of smoky eel and cumin honey. But a breast of braised veal arrived, surprisingly, rolled, crumbed and fried, and a dry-aged sirloin steak was overcooked. Desserts, including wobbly coconut panna cotta, easily pass muster as does the terrific wine list (although make sure your choice is in stock). Long may the Light Brigade lead the charge.

Hours Dinner Tues–Sat 6–10pm
Bill E $18–$22 **M** $29–$39 **D** $12–$14
Cards AE DC V MC Eftpos
Wine A lovely, long list of benchmark varietals and styles across the globe with something to please everyone; 27 by the glass
Chef James Privett
Owner Haritos Hotels
Seats 80; bar
www.lightbrigade.com.au
And...the Sports Bar delivers plasmas, pies and pasta, along with sporting memorabilia

good food guide   81

city + suburbs

Longrain

85 Commonwealth Street, Surry Hills
Tel 9280 2888   Map 3a

Thai

Score 15/20

It's been years since Longrain introduced Sydney's hip set to the joys of aromatic betel leaves with smoked trout; lacy eggnet encasing a sweet tumble of pork, prawn, peanuts and sprouts; and gloriously sticky caramelised pork hock. Then, of course, there are the stick drinks in the ultra-cool bar that make the wait for a table bearable. These perennial faves still please fans lining the communal tables, along with hits such as twice-cooked suckling pig – the slices crowned with shaved cuttlefish, coriander and ginger slivers – a blissful balance of flavour and texture. Generous pieces of flavoursome mud crab and slightly spongy prawns drift in a sour orange curry that's light and soupy; and although Barossa chicken with sweet-and-sour blood-plum sauce wasn't fried crisp, as promised, it's tender, and given a spicy lift with sichuan pepper. The dessert platter, featuring silky coconut caramel custard with grilled banana, is a star in its own right. Long live Longrain.

Hours Lunch Mon–Fri noon–2.30pm; Dinner Mon–Sat 6–11pm, Sun 5.30–10pm; no dinner bookings
Bill Dishes range from $5.50–$49; 10% surcharge on Sundays & public holidays
Cards AE DC V MC
Wine Well-chosen, broad list; 15 by the glass; plus a smart cocktail menu
Chef Martin Boetz
Owners Sam Christie, John Sample & Martin Boetz
Seats 96; private room; wheelchair access; bar
Child friendly Some kid-friendly dishes; highchairs; drawing materials
Vegetarian Separate menu
www.longrain.com
And... banquet menus and a smart private room

Lotus

22 Challis Avenue, Potts Point
Tel 9326 9000   Map 2

Contemporary

Score 14.5/20

The lotus eaters of Potts Point must be very content with their lot. There's a new dining vitality in the neighbourhood and the 2007 Josephine Pignolet Award-winner, Daniel Hong, at the helm. Hong dares diners to think about familiar European and South-East Asian flavours in a different way. Spaetzle with shiitake mushrooms? Check. A sweet and spicy kicker of chilli jam and squid ink in a Catalan-style dish of cuttlefish, chorizo and romesco sauce? Check. Jalapeno peppers, crab and ginger dressing a sous-vide blue-eye that flakes beautifully on the fork? Wow. Hong has chutzpah in spades, achieving unexpected flavour effects through unexpected means. Some ideas didn't work, such as a perplexing pork belly, goat curd and watermelon dish; but you want to thank the chef for trying. There's pure fun in his signature hot fudge sundae with raspberries and honeycomb. This simple bistro with its footpath dining and slightly worn interior elegance has plenty of life in it yet.

Hours Dinner Tues–Sat 6–11pm; bookings essential
Bill E $18–$22 **M** $32–$38 **D** $14–$16; 3-course set menu $39pp from 6–7pm
Cards AE DC V MC
Wine Very good European and domestic list; impressive champagne selection; 14 by the glass
Chef Daniel Hong
Owner Merivale Group
Seats 60; wheelchair access; outdoor seating; bar
www.merivale.com
And... bring in your own cocktail from the sexy back bar

Lucio's

47 Windsor Street, Paddington
Tel 9380 5996   Map 4a

Italian (Northern)

Score 16/20

It's the perfect triptych: an Italian menu with both a classical bent and contemporary vim; walls covered in paintings by Australia's finest artists; and an eponymous host exuding old-school charm. Lucio's has a refined yet typically relaxed Italian sensibility. It's a celebration of *la dolce vita*, made all the more vivid for Lucio Galletto's presence on the tiled floor of this colourful terrace. The menu's hearty, rustic approach nods to Galletto's childhood in the Ligurian hills, but first and foremost, the focus is on clean, lively flavours. There are cute nibbles to tempt: perhaps spice-coated quail eggs or salami. House-made pasta is always sublime. Fazzoletti neri translates as glossy black "handkerchief"-shaped pasta, contrasted against a zippy jumble of cuttlefish, mussels, prawns and chilli. Whole roast quail, stuffed with tomato and nutty fregola (toasted Sardinian "couscous") is sweetened by sultana relish. Sheep's milk yoghurt panna cotta with watermelon and hazelnut wafer is as dreamy and refreshing as time spent in these glorious surrounds.

Hours Lunch Mon–Sat 12.30–3pm; Dinner Mon–Sat 6.30–10.45pm
Bill E $28–$34 **M** $39–$45 **D** $17.50
Cards AE (+2.5%) DC (+2.5%) V MC Eftpos
Wine 16 by the glass
Chef Logan Campbell
Owners Lucio & Sally Galletto
Seats 75; private rooms
www.lucios.com.au
And… you might spot one of the artists dining here

Machiavelli

123 Clarence Street, Sydney
Tel 9299 3748   Map 1

Italian

Score 13/20

When you lunch at Machiavelli, you go for the classics: the traditional Italian menu, the old-fashioned waiters in their black waistcoats, and the power crowds who've been coming for years. The Machiavelli signatures are perennial too – prosciutto sliced on the central antipasto table, calamari fritti, and light but indulgent gnocchi with gorgonzola sauce. A fleshy piece of snapper is perfectly cooked. Steak diane is moist and theatrically served direct from the gueridon. There are no surprises with the accompaniments either: creamed spinach, sliced carrots and a slightly al dente gratin dauphinoise. Suited men, and the occasional suited woman, hold court around white-clothed tables, sussing who else is in the room and what networking can be done on the way out. Perhaps the only thing that's changed is this crowd's bonus payments, but despite the economic times, giants of industry still beam from their wall photos, from Rupert to Richo. Make sure you finish with the tiramisu, as always.

Hours Lunch Mon–Fri 12–2.30pm; Dinner Mon–Fri 6–9.30pm
Bill E $18 **M** $28 **D** $14–$13
Cards AE DC V MC
Wine A solid and satisfying collection of Australian and Italian classics; 21 by the glass
Chef Laurent Cambon
Owners Giovanna Toppi & Caterina Tarchi
Seats 180
Vegetarian Plenty of pasta options
www.machiavelli.com.au
And… steak tartare prepared tableside by a waiter who's been making it since opening

city + suburbs

Macleay Street Bistro

73A Macleay Street, Potts Point
Tel 9358 4891   Map 2

Contemporary

Score 14/20

Depending on your mood, nestle in a cosy nook inside or take a streetside perch to observe the ever-colourful Potts Point nightlife parading by. This neighbourhood constant hits all the right notes. Chatty waiters offer warmth and generosity to regulars and newcomers alike to set the tone for a relaxed dining experience. Chunky slices of skinless duck and pistachio sausage with sourdough toast meld beautifully with the sweetness of cumberland sauce for a superbly rustic opener. Tender eye fillet of beef finds a perfect bedfellow in a decadently rich port and red wine onion marmalade, snuggled together on a horseradish-smeared watercress salad. A classic steak tartare is right on the money. Finish with the meringue sugar rush of Eton mess with blueberries and a well-executed creme brulee. While other Macleay Street eateries come and go with changing fads and fashions, this grand old dame knows her audience, delivering exactly the right blend of comfort and class year after year.

Hours Dinner daily 6–11pm
Bill E $17.50–$18.50 **M** $24.50–$36.50 **D** $13.50; 10% surcharge on public holidays and groups of 7-plus
Cards AE V MC
Wine Compact, quality list of mainly Australasian drops with a sprinkling of Europeans; 12 by the glass; BYO (corkage $7 a bottle)
Chef Mark Flaherty
Owner Carole Becka
Seats 46; outdoor seating
And...snag one of the outdoor tables, and you can bring your pooch to dinner, too

Mad Cow

Ivy, Level 1, 320–330 George Street, Sydney
Tel 9240 3000   Map 1

Steakhouse

Score 14/20

Sydney steakhouses are often more about quantity than quality. That's all changed with this tongue-in-cheek, yellow and white, light-filled venue at Ivy, with its Peter Doyle (est.) devised menu. Staples, such as well-seasoned steak tartare topped with a raw egg yolk, sometimes get a slight twist – as with a prawn cocktail of three fat, juicy prawns, a wedge of iceberg and a dollop of chilli jam and clear tomato jelly. The menu's an exciting read for carnivores, from wagyu to black angus, grain-fed to grass, a 200-gram minute steak to an 800-gram on-the-bone rib-eye. Add a choice of sauces including uplifting chimichurri and a less-than-fiery horseradish cream. Non-meat dishes pack less punch, but who's here for fish? Finish in the style in which you began, with a retro-chic mini pavlova topped with strawberries and passionfruit. Upbeat staff walk the line between friendly and professional and the relaxed atmosphere lends itself to the revival of the long lunch.

Hours Lunch Mon–Fri noon–3pm; Dinner Mon–Sat 6–11pm; bookings essential
Bill E $21–$29 **M** $29–$70 **D** $14–$19; 2-course lunch $35pp; 2-course dinner $35pp before 7pm
Cards AE DC (+3%) V MC
Wine A broad selection of countries, vintages, varietals and prices; 18 by the glass
Chef Christopher Whitehead
Owner Merivale Group
Seats 80; wheelchair access; outdoor seating; bar
www.merivale.com
And...linger on in the Ivy bar for more drinkie-poos

84 good food guide

NEW Tastes

There are so many delights to discover in Gabriel Gaté's Gourmet Trail of Nouméa

Bonjour! You don't have to go all the way to France to enjoy some of the finest French cuisine, because cosmopolitan Nouméa is only 2 hours from Brisbane and less than 3 hours from Sydney. While there are many excellent French restaurants in New Caledonia, one of the true delights is to create a 'do it yourself' à la carte menu. I like to start at the market, where you will discover wonderful fresh produce, and it's a colourful place to enjoy a French-style breakfast. At the nearby supermarket you will find many easy meal ideas, including wonderful French cheeses and wines. Nouméa also offers many specialised gourmet stores including a choice of boulangeries and patisseries, master chocolatiers and much more. There are also some other enjoyable ways to explore the delights of Nouméa including a choice of great value tours, such as the 'Taste of France' Tour and 'Explorer Bus Pass'. Find out more in the free copy of my Gourmet Guide to New Caledonia - visit the website or call 1800 673 745. Bon Appétit!

Gabriel Gaté

NEW Caledonia

www.newcaledonia.com.au

city + suburbs

Mahjong Room
312 Crown Street, Surry Hills
Tel 9361 3985   Map 2

Chinese
Score 12.5/20

Although the raucous yum cha dens and lazy susans of Chinatown are only a few clicks west, this neat-as-a-pin Chinese beauty feels worlds away. It's not just set apart by the cool locale or chic decor of lacquered tables, primary colour-bright Maoist curios and mismatched ceramics; the menu also meanders off the Cantonese route to explore the lesser-plied byways of northern China. House-cured pickles and hot, salty fans of sliced shallot pancake make perfect beer food, while delicate half-moon crab gow gees are exalted by a splash of red vinegar sauce. In xiao long bao – the hearty soup dumplings of Shanghai – the rich pork filling rings true, even if our batch was let down by gluey wrappers. We're back on track, though, with a simple dish of silky steamed eggplant and tofu. And as the tiny warren of rooms quickly fills, the restaurant takes on the infectious buzz of Haymarket's finest; perhaps it's not so far off after all.

Hours Dinner Mon–Sat 6–10.30pm
Bill E $9–$24 **M** $14.50–$29 **D** $9–$14.50
Cards AE V MC Eftpos
Wine Well-suited, succinct list; 10 by the glass; BYO Mon–Thurs only (corkage $3pp)
Chef/owner William Hui
Seats 60; private rooms
Vegetarian Wide range of vegetarian dishes
www.mahjongroom.com.au
And…a summer tea of jasmine, peony and chrysanthemum is a real treat

Maitre Karl
197 High Street, Willoughby
Tel 9958 1110   Map 7

Alsatian (Franco–German)
Score 13.5/20

Master Karl makes no secret of his inclinations. From Swiss mineral water to the easy-drinking Austrian reds on his wine list, the accent at his convivial suburban eatery is resolutely Germanic. A genteel-y rowdy, murkily lit modern space at the village end of High Street, this local has no trouble pulling them in. Regulars flock for tarte flambee – a wafer-crunchy variation on pizza, brought north of its roots with a smear of fromage frais and the traditional Alsatian onion and speck, or perhaps flakes of smoked trout and teensy capers. A pumpkin and caramelised red onion salad is a sweet foil to just-pink lamb back strap with a milky lamb-brain croquette. Confit duck falls off the bone under lacquered skin. Sweet-sour red cabbage and good slippery spaetzle work the edicts of texture and taste to excellent effect. Dessert is crackly meringue, with eggy lemon curd, ice-cream and a fluff of Persian pashmak. With Master Karl in a black waistcoat and white shirt playing jovial mine host, it's a jolly way to dine.

Hours Lunch Tues–Sat noon–2.30pm; Dinner Tues–Thurs 6–9pm, Fri–Sat 6–10pm; bookings essential
Bill E $16.50–$19.50 **M** $17.50–$30.50 **D** $12
Cards AE DC V MC Eftpos
Wine Solid choices including some lesser-known Germans: 15 by the glass; BYO (corkage $8 a bottle)
Chef Joel Baur
Owners Karl & Paivi Geissler
Seats 70; wheelchair access; outdoor seating
Child friendly Kids' menu; highchairs
www.maitrekarl.com.au
And…ask about the annual Oktoberfest festivities

good food guide

city + suburbs

Malabar

6/274 Victoria Street, Darlinghurst
Tel 9332 1755   Map 2
Also at 334 Pacific Highway, Crows Nest
Tel 9906 7343   Map 5a

Indian (Southern)

Score 12.5/20

Picture a wall map of Sydney's Indian restaurants. The number of pushpins for those offering northern Indian stereotypes (bad decor, boring samosas, bain-maries and butter chicken) would vastly outnumber their southern counterparts. When you do go south, pay heed to the dosai. It's your best clue to how much you are going to enjoy the rest of your meal. At the eastern suburbs outpost of this North Shore stalwart, the masala dosai (a large, rolled, crispy-edged crepe filled with potato, onions and a southern-inspired masala) is one of the city's best. Mellagu prawns (tiger prawns spiced with peppercorns and tossed in a red onion relish) show real subtlety. A Goan fish curry was too bland to rock our world but the authentically sour vindaloo is compulsory. Heat and spice make some concessions to Western palates, but there is a lot to like, particularly the friendly service, above-boring decor and a 19th century Rajasthan mural featuring a life-size maharajah and his family.

Hours Lunch Wed–Sun noon–3pm; Dinner Fri–Sat 5.30–11.30pm, Sun–Thurs 5.30–10.30pm
Bill E $5–$13 **M** $15–$21 **D** $2.90–$5; 3-course menu $35pp
Cards AE DC V MC
Wine Small, commercial list; 6 by the glass; BYO (corkage $3pp)
Chef Mohammed Sali
Owner Wilson Varghese
Seats 70; wheelchair access
Child friendly Highchairs; kid-friendly options
Vegetarian Thali banquet-style selection
www.malabarcuisine.com.au
And... stick with Kingfisher beer for dinner

The Malaya

39 Lime Street, King Street Wharf, Sydney
Tel 9279 1170   Map 1

Malaysian

Score 13/20

So this is where corporate-types linger over a long lunch. The wines keep flowing as waiters shuffle tirelessly between big groups in this tall, slick eatery overlooking King Street Wharf. The portions are designed to share, and "medium hot" can at times mean more like "hot", so chilli fiends rejoice. Smooth otak otak (grilled white fish mince wrapped in banana leaf) shines as a prime entree, its piquant richness marrying well with a refreshing berry cocktail. Ayam perchick (barbecued chicken curry) exudes charcoal-tender goodness, and is lifted by a zingy blend of coconut milk and lemongrass. The gravy is also impossibly flavoursome in a tender beef rendang. Sichuan eggplant stir-fry was sickly sweet and made us clamour for the deep, spicy freshness of a hot and sour assam fish curry, singing with the tart sweetness of pineapple and tomato. Desserts are notional only but the business lunchers seem too happy to care.

Hours Lunch Mon–Sat noon–2.30pm; Dinner daily 6–10pm; bookings essential
Bill E $13–$22 **M** $18–$32; set menus $46–$52; 10% surcharge on Sundays
Cards AE DC V MC
Wine Medium-sized moderately priced list, plus half-bottles; 7 by the glass
Chef Mustapa Jaffar
Owners Lance & Givie Wong
Seats 300; private rooms; wheelchair access; outdoor seating; bar
Child friendly Highchairs
Vegetarian Set menu, plus plenty of a la carte options
www.themalaya.com.au
And... it first opened in 1963

good food guide

city + suburbs

Manta

6 Cowper Wharf Road, Woolloomooloo
Tel 9332 3822   Map 2

Contemporary

Score 14/20

There are few places as quintessentially Sydney. City lights flicker, boats bob on their moorings and well-groomed couples promenade along the restaurant strip. It's no surprise to find plenty of seafood on the menu although Manta is also very serious about steak. While the main dining room can lack atmosphere and the service bordered on neglectful, the kitchen is almost fanatical about the quality and provenance of its produce. An open lasagne features a lightly creamy, chive-flecked sauce with the freshest seafood and peas that are firm to the bite. Lightly battered fingers of john dory sit on a watercress, parsley, caper and kipfler potato salad that doesn't overwhelm the sweet fish. Crisp-skinned New Zealand snapper fillet is artfully arranged with translucent slices of golden beetroot, baby chard and asparagus, encircled by fennel puree. Although chocolate fondant with raspberries, mango puree, chocolate praline brittle and vanilla ice-cream was not totally cohesive, an outdoor table on a mild evening will set everything right.

Hours Lunch daily noon–3pm;
Dinner daily 6–10pm; bookings essential
Bill E $25–$28 **M** $38–$48 **D** $12–$18;
10% surcharge on Sundays & public holidays
Cards AE DC V MC Eftpos
Wine Extensive, mostly local list with some interesting European varietals; 17 by the glass
Chef Daniel Hughes
Owners Rob Rubis & Chris James
Seats 220; outdoor seating; bar
Child friendly Kids' menu; highchairs
Vegetarian Separate menu
www.mantarestaurant.com.au
And… hand-cut "angel" chips with truffle oil and grated parmesan are among the city's best

Marigold

Levels 4 & 5, 683 George Street, Sydney
Tel 9281 3388   Map 3a

Chinese (Cantonese)

Score 13.5/20

The lunch and dinner crowds at Marigold make Central Station seem deserted. Pouring from the lifts in this Haymarket high-rise, they flock to this slightly shabby, 700-seat Chinatown institution for the frenzied yum cha that has given Marigold its greatest claim to fame. It's almost as hectic at night, however, when live seafood takes centre stage. Waiters zoom by, yanking whole fish from tanks then delivering them to your table, fragrant with ginger and shallot. Alternatively, they're bearing sweet, fist-sized prawns in chilli, and mud crab so fresh it might pinch you. Peipa duck, roasted to a juicy yet earthy crispness, is another cracker. Tofu has a creamy sweetness you rarely find (try it with ginger-tinged sugar syrup for dessert). Service is perfunctory, some dishes a little below par (avoid the gelatinous, insipid soups), but there's enough good stuff here to have kept trade roaring for 18 years and counting.

Hours Lunch daily 10am–3pm;
Dinner daily 5.30–11pm
Bill E $6.50–$17.80 **M** $18–$36 **D** $5–$8;
$2 pp surcharge on public holidays
Cards AE DC V MC
Wine Better than most in Chinatown, plenty of Australian choices; 2 (house only) by the glass
Chef Chan Bing Chung
Owner Nedosu Pty Ltd
Seats 700; private rooms
Child friendly Booster seats
Vegetarian Many vegetable and tofu dishes
www.marigold.com.au
And… free parking below after 6pm

good food guide

city + suburbs

Marque ★
4/5 355 Crown Street, Surry Hills
Tel 9332 2225   Map 3b

French Contemporary

Score 18/20

CHEF OF THE YEAR
Is Mark Best Sydney's very own Willy Wonka and the ultra-chic, recently remodelled Marque his factory of culinary creativity? Even Best's band of loyal workers dishes out advice with a wink. The cheeky sommelier, Peter Healy, convinces diners to order Austrian red wine from the European-focused, eclectic wine list. Now that's pure magic. Some might find Best's take on contemporary French a little wacky, but it's mostly pure wizardry. Contemplate, for example, a "risotto" of calamari – tiny grains of calamari with prawn foam; or a dessert of caramelised tomato stuffed with 12 flavours reminiscent of Christmas pudding. Roast Muscovy duck is more old school, sitting in a pond of rich jus, while fruit salad with honey and yoghurt is anything but, arriving "deconstructed" – the seasonal fruit blasted with liquid nitrogen and dusted with honey powder. Best is an innovative master intent on pushing the envelope. And Sydney's all the richer for it.

Hours Lunch Fri noon–2.30pm;
Dinner Mon–Sat 6.30–10pm; bookings essential
Bill Degustation menu $145pp; 3-course a la carte menu $95pp; 2-course a la carte lunch menu $75pp, prix fixe 3-course lunch menu $45pp
Cards AE DC V MC
Wine Lots of unusual labels and varieties, and a European bent; 18 by the glass; BYO one bottle per table only (corkage $35 a bottle); plus choice aperitifs
Chefs Mark Best & Pasi Petanen
Owners Mark & Valerie Best
Seats 50; private room; wheelchair access
www.marquerestaurant.com.au
And…Friday's set three-course lunch menu – our favourite bargain pick (see page xiv) – changes weekly

MCA Cafe
140 George Street,
Circular Quay West, The Rocks
Tel 9241 4253   Map 1

Contemporary

Score 12.5/20

There might be captivating modern art inside the gallery, but the view from the MCA Cafe terrace, across the water towards the Sydney Opera House, is just as mesmerising. To start, golden-brown squares of crackling-crisp pork belly sit among celery heart, crisp apple slices and dark-red chunks of cherry and cherry tapenade, although the layers of fat weren't as melting as they could be. Pan-fried ocean trout with nicely cooked Asian greens sits in a delicate tomato and lemongrass broth with delightful, silky prawn ravioli. Friendly, if not always attentive, waiters deliver desserts that are pretty as a picture. A textbook white chocolate brulee is flanked by warm raspberry financier and zingy raspberry sorbet; and sweet honey parfait paired with a delicious sablé biscuit and a dainty salad of diced strawberry and fig is a master stroke.

Hours Daily 10am–4pm
Bill E $18–$19 **M** $25–$32 **D** $14;
10% surcharge Sundays, 15% public holidays
Cards AE V MC
Wine Effective and well-priced; 13 by the glass
Chef Jason Faulconbridge
Owners Charles Wilkins & Simon Fox
Seats 100; private room; wheelchair access; outdoor seating
Child friendly Kids' fish and chips; highchairs
www.culinaryedge.com.au
And…ask about lunchtime specials

city + suburbs

Medusa Greek Taverna

2 Market Street (cnr Kent Street), Sydney
Tel 9267 0799 Map 1

Greek

Score 13.5/20

A giant Greek island wall poster in sparkling Santorini blue and white offers an idyllic taverna image: pity about the office towers alongside. Despite its challenging Darling Harbour-side location, Medusa scores numerous hits, and only minor misses, on the authentic Greek eating scale. Thanks to veteran Greek restaurateur Peter Koutsopoulos and several assured hands in the kitchen and on the floor, this is exuberant Hellenic dining with lots to love. A vast mezze spread lays out the usual dips and salads as well as floppy home-style dolmades with runny yoghurt sauce, crisp-crusted, herb-dusted eggplant rounds with liquid skordalia (garlic potato sauce) and seriously more-ish calamari with yoghurt and fresh dill. No quibbles about main course: arni (baked lamb) encapsulates "fall-off-the-bone", in a light, lemony sauce with a daggy but delicious side serve of spuds and carrots. Waiters exude old-style Greek hospitality and know-how. And if you do succumb to a dessert special of loukoumades (Cypriot honey donuts), just waddle home.

Hours Lunch Mon–Fri noon–3pm; Dinner Mon–Sat 6–9.30pm; bookings essential
Bill E $7–$18 **M** $18–$32 **D** $10–$14
Cards AE V MC
Wine Affordable, easy-drinking Greek options; 10 by the glass
Chef Greg Akridas
Owner Peter Koutsopoulos
Seats 90; wheelchair access; outdoor seating
Vegetarian Plenty, plus weekly specials
www.medusagreektaverna.com.au
And...it's hidden just next to the Monorail

Mezzaluna

123 Victoria Street, Potts Point
Tel 9357 1988 Map 2

Italian

Score 13.5/20

Since a change of owners in 2008, a new team has revitalised this attractive Potts Point stalwart with Italian style and charm. Expect to be greeted like a long-lost relative. The prosciutto is San Daniele, Italy's sweetest. There's plenty of flavour and texture in a salad of crab and scampi with shoestring-sliced celeriac. Trio di mare combines the freshness of raw kingfish, tuna and ocean trout, served in hand-cut piles, with olive oil and capers. Mains can seem predictable but black linguine is beautifully crafted and full of rich iodine sea-sweetness – the pasta is infused with squid ink and tossed in a thick scampi and prawn bisque. A crisp insalata di radicchio, a Friulian speciality, revels in a finely balanced dressing. The influence of the far north travels through to desserts, with the unusual ravioli di papavero – sweet pasta parcels filled with chocolate and poppy seeds.

Hours Lunch Fri noon–3pm; Dinner Mon–Sat 6–11pm
Bill E $20–$35 **M** $36–$45 **D** $17; 3-course menu $85pp
Cards AE DC V MC
Wine A good, small list with some unusual Italian labels; 12 by the glass; good choice of grappa and digestivi
Chef Joe Cavallo
Owners Angelo Italiani & Aldo Bertoli
Seats 120; private room; outdoor seating; bar
Child friendly Kids' menu
www.mezzaluna.com.au
And...the city skyline view and classic Italian service make this a great romantic choice

city + suburbs

Milsons

17 Willoughby Street, Kirribilli
Tel 9955 7075   Map 5a

Contemporary

Score 14/20

The northside business district offers few options for the adventurous eater, but suits who want to impress clients with top-notch contemporary fare – and an impressive wine list – need only cross the highway to this genteel fine diner. The kitchen keeps the corporate types happy with posh steak and chips, but it's much more accomplished than that. Three quail ballotines, dressed with a foie gras mousse, on a bed of morels are transformed by the addition of port-soaked currants. Crab raviolo ringed by sweet Queensland scallops, artichoke veloute and asparagus spears, is subtly flavoured. The appealing Asian flavour of kingfish on a togarashi-spiced fish cake with coriander aioli and bok choy was undermined by dry, overcooked fish, while a slab of potato and onion "terrine" weighed down a vegetarian main of goat's cheese cannelloni and ratatouille. Still, it's hard to beat dessert: a soft meringue roulade with orange and cardamom cream, drizzled in passionfruit and accompanied by macerated strawberries, should seal the deal.

Hours Lunch Mon–Fri noon–3pm; Dinner Mon–Sat 6–10pm
Bill E $24–$29 **M** $32–$40 **D** $17
Cards AE DC V MC
Wine Intelligent, global list; 14 by the glass; BYO (corkage $12 a bottle Mon–Fri; Sat $20)
Chef Lee Kwiez
Owner Ben Pollock
Seats 78; private room
www.milsonsrestaurant.com.au
And…plenty of gluten-free options on the menu

Mino

521 Military Road, Mosman
Tel 9960 3351   Map 7

Japanese

Score 13/20

Kaiseki has become much more than the simple food of the tea ceremony, having evolved for over four centuries. This local version is quite a Mosman institution. Although less elaborate than the ritualised art form of the superlative, 14-course kaiseki tradition, Mino pours much thought and care into the content, order and presentation of its six courses, and slightly less into the design of its simple interior. The menu starts with a sakizuke course, a surprising amuse bouche of tomato and mozzarella tempura, and follows, to set the seasonal theme, with steamed king prawns and plum dressing. Sushi and sashimi is delicate and pretty, preceding the more substantial bento-style assorted entrees with standouts of beautifully moist grilled kingfish with fragrant ginger and soy sauce mayonnaise and an East-meets-West scallop salad with onion and olive oil vinaigrette. Choose from a variety of typical mains, such as free-range pork tonkatsu or equally good grilled salmon with walnut teriyaki, before a light dessert selection and Japanese tea.

Hours Dinner Tues–Sun 6–10pm; bookings essential
Bill E $6–$14 **M** $18–$24 **D** $5–$8; 6-course banquet $43–$59pp
Cards AE V MC Eftpos
Wine Concise list of Australians, shochu and sake; 2 by the glass; BYO (corkage $2pp)
Chef/owner Yoshikazu Honda
Seats 35–40
And…a pared-back (and cheaper) menu available weeknights

city + suburbs

Mission

3 Little Queen Street, Chippendale
Tel 9318 0815   Map 5b

Contemporary

Score 13.5/20

It's a stylish conversion from a 19th century church, once occupied by the Sydney City Mission, to a vibrant eatery and upstairs gallery. Its friendly and relaxed enough for a cocktail or snack and yet sufficiently special for an elegant dinner. Graze, surrounded by artwork, on whitebait fritters with lime aioli, and bruschetta topped with braised mushrooms, parmesan and rocket. Green pea and asparagus risotto, tangy with lemon, is topped with taleggio. Fresh produce shines in beetroot and goat's curd salad, resting on leaves laced with cumin, orange slices and toasted walnuts. Smashed peas, yes please, especially alongside nourishing house-made Mediterranean lamb pie and tomato relish. Lashings of smoked trout are superbly matched in a salad of kipfler potatoes, capers, preserved lemon and horseradish cream. Be led into final temptation with pistachio-sprinkled, caramelised peaches and vanilla bean ice-cream. And then venture upstairs to peruse the latest exhibition.

Hours Breakfast Sat 9am–1pm; Lunch Tues–Sat 11am–5.30pm; Dinner Tues–Sat 5.30–10pm
Bill E $7–$17 **M** $18–$27 **D** $12–$16
Cards V MC Eftpos
Wine Compact, thoughtful list; 20 by the glass; BYO (corkage $4 a bottle)
Chef Piera Potter
Owners Piera Potter & Nicky Ginsberg
Seats 40; private room; wheelchair access; bar
Child friendly Kids' menu
Vegetarian Plenty of choices
www.missonbar.com.au
And... great breakfasts on Saturdays

Moncur Terrace

Level 1, Woollahra Hotel, 115 Queen Street, Woollahra
Tel 9327 9777   Map 4a

Contemporary/Pizza

Score 13/20

Upstairs from restaurateur Damien Pignolet's grown-up Bistro Moncur, the Terrace is all about size – from the lofty walls that punctuate the space skywards to the robust golden orbs that are the prawn and dill cakes. It's big on bonhomie, too. Weaving through tables of well-shod and coiffed guests, insouciant waiters lend proceedings a casual air. Top-notch ingredients lift pub-grub staples up a notch. Zucchini flowers stuffed with brandade and dipped in spicy red pepper sauce give the accompanying Australian soft-shell crab a run for its money. Saskia Beer's Barossa chicken is so tasty it barely needs the addition of harissa, preserved lemon, or cannellini bean, tomato and olive salad. The semolina-sprinkled pizza of baked mushroom, ham and melted mozzarella and taleggio cheeses on a pita-like base is fine and tasty, but bears little resemblance to its Italian counterpart. From the specials menu, pavlova with strawberry compote and cream is big enough for two. The nicest thing about the bill is how small(ish) it is.

Hours Lunch Sat–Sun noon–4pm; Dinner Tues–Sat 6–10.30pm, Sun 6–9pm; no bookings
Bill E $8.50–$19.50 **M** $29 **D** $15
Cards AE DC V MC Eftpos
Wine Enticing list with plenty of variety and varietals; 31 by the glass
Chefs Damien Pignolet & Ben Hall
Owners Damien Pignolet & Ron White
Seats 160; wheelchair access; outdoor seating; bar
Child friendly Kids' menu
www.woollahrahotel.com.au
And... go early or be prepared to wait

good food guide

city + suburbs

MoS Cafe
37 Phillip Street (cnr Bridge Street), Sydney
Tel 9241 3636 Map 1

Contemporary

Score 13.5/20

Business is alive and kicking at this buzzy subterranean cafe beneath the Museum of Sydney. Right on cue at 12.30pm the hordes descend, laden with folders and laptops, to eat, drink, plan and negotiate. By 2pm it's all done and dusted, with only a few stragglers remaining. The drawcard is a smart cafe menu that belies the functional surrounds and rises above somewhat uninterested service. A swirling mix of caramelised garlic, intensely flavoured slow-roasted field mushrooms, crisp crostini and crumbled Bulgarian fetta borders on addictive. Then there's succulent chargrilled beef fillet, nestled on a bed of sweet onion puree. A few branches of crisp broccolini with a knob of crumbed marrow and shallot add to the savoury complexity. The star turn is a delicate brick of wobbly apple jelly stacked with blueberries, strawberries, kiwifruit and orange with vanilla bean gelato. It's a fun place whether you're here to work or play.

Hours Mon–Fri 7am–9pm, Sat–Sun 8.30am–5pm; bookings essential
Bill E $9.50–$22 **M** $27–$37 **D** $13.50–$14; 15% surcharge on Sundays & public holidays
Cards AE DC V MC
Wine Decent small list, mostly Australasian; 38 by the glass
Chef Nick Clarke
Owners Paul Lockrey & Ramy Shelhot
Seats 150; wheelchair access; outdoor seating
Child friendly Kids' menu
www.moscafe.com.au
And… spot the odd (or very odd) politician

Mumu Grill
70–76 Alexander Street, Crows Nest
Tel 9460 6777 Map 5a

Steakhouse/Tapas

Score 13/20

There's much to like about Mumu Grill – from warm, welcoming and efficient service to a relaxed village square feeling and commitment to sustainability. Prop up the long bar and nibble tapas, or sit inside – or out – and try something from the wood-fired oven, which also serves up takeaway pizza next door. Although stuffed zucchini flowers lacked finesse, with overly thick and indifferent batter, prosciutto-wrapped figs filled with Spanish cabra (goat's) cheese allow each element to be tasted separately, combining well with caramelised balsamic vinegar as the finishing touch. For mains it's hard to go past the neatly cooked and rested beef although organic chicken, saltbush lamb, duck and pork are contenders. The house favourite – grass-fed prime rib crusted in sichuan pepper – shows admirable restraint, balanced by a medley of greens and real chips served in a separate pot. Brown sugar pavlova is all it should be – not too sweet, crunchy yet refreshing with the tang of fresh pineapple and passionfruit.

Hours Lunch Wed–Sun noon–3pm; Dinner daily 6–10pm
Bill E $6.50–$12 **M** $16–$39 **D** $12–$16
Cards AE V MC Eftpos
Wine Varied, interesting and well-priced, plus good beers; 20 by the glass; BYO (corkage $8 a bottle)
Chef/owner Craig Macindoe
Seats 140; outdoor seating; bar
Child friendly Kids' menu; highchairs; drawing materials
Vegetarian Surprisingly varied options
www.mumugrill.com.au
And… look out for regular wine dinners and lunchtime specials

Nelson's Brasserie

Lord Nelson Brewery Hotel,
19 Kent Street, The Rocks
Tel 9251 4044   Map 1

Contemporary

Score 13/20

Built when Brittania ruled the waves and named after one of its greatest seafarers, Horatio Nelson, this is one of Sydney's oldest, most popular pubs. It oozes atmosphere in the lively downstairs bar where exposed sandstone walls are lined with naval history. The ales from the on-site microbrewery pair brilliantly with a pork pie or ploughman's lunch. Upstairs, calm prevails in the elegant, heritage-filled dining room with its white-clothed tables. Service is slick and the short menu offers an eclectic mix. Steamed prawn and seafood dumplings needed the zing of tomato and coriander, while roasted quail is fragrant with tarragon and sage. Chargrilled, grass-fed Tasmanian scotch fillet, topped with cafe de paris butter, comes with shiitake mushrooms and a pile of pommes frites. Crisp-crowned pork belly is hearty, textured with thyme-infused bean ragout. Finish with fresh mango, strawberries and Cointreau cream. It's just as refreshing as the Lord Nelson Brewery beers.

Hours Lunch Thurs–Fri noon–3pm; Dinner Tues–Sat 6–10pm
Bill E $13–$17 **M** $29–$30 **D** $10–$13
Cards AE DC V MC
Wine Interesting and diverse list, an impressive selection of premiums; 10 by the glass
Chef Lama Ang-Tendi
Owners Blair R. Hayden & Partners
Seats 70; bar
Child friendly Highchairs
www.lordnelson.com.au
And... try Three Sheets pale ale or Nelson's Blood, the chocolatey porter

Neptune Palace

Level 1, Gateway Building,
cnr Pitt & Alfred streets, Circular Quay
Tel 9241 3338   Map 1

Chinese/Malaysian

Score 13/20

Neptune might want to reconsider his interior decorator. Not every Roman god needs a palace of mirrored "columns", a powder-blue ceiling, teal carpet and the odd statue. However, upholstered chairs and white tablecloths make things comfortable, as do constantly patrolling staff, who guide you through the enormous menu at this upscale Chinese–Malaysian stalwart. The classic Penang kapitan chicken curry has a sweet creamy sauce with a hum of chilli and topping of crunchy, deep-fried pastry curls; but a dry, hard roti canai disappointed. Buttermilk prawns – a more unusual dish – has large, fresh prawns, curry leaves and chilli scattered with salty, fried buttermilk crumbs. In steak stir-fried with pungent XO sauce, the fishy flavour threatened to overpower the soft, thin pieces of steak, but a fluorescent-green pandanus pancake – filled with a palm sugar and coconut mixture and served with ice-cream and palm sugar syrup – pays fitting tribute to its South-East Asian origins.

Hours Lunch daily noon–3pm; Dinner daily 5–10.30pm; bookings essential
Bill E $11.80–$28.80 **M** $21.80–$46 **D** $7.80–$9.80
Cards AE DC V MC Eftpos
Wine Very comprehensive, with big-ticket Australian and French wines; 12 by the glass
Chefs Kim Fai Lam & Fom Sau Tan
Owners Lee Ngann Ly & Derek Lim
Seats 200; private room; bar
Child friendly Highchairs
Vegetarian Numerous options
www.neptunepalace.com.au
And... banquets from $48

city + suburbs

Nilgiri's

81–83 Christie Street, St Leonards
Tel 9966 0636 Map 5a

Indian

Score 14.5/20

Outside is a world of dull, grey office blocks, so make your way upstairs to Nilgiri's colourful dining room for a journey to India, through the many flavours and cooking styles of its multiple regions. Each month you'll end up in a different place, as the menu cycles through India's countless cuisines. Solicitous waiters are eager to guide you. Pappadams with house-made condiments – perhaps a sweet-and-sour date and tamarind chutney, carrot pickle and lemon pickle – are a taste of expertly spiced dishes to come. On a voyage through the southern states, baked chickpea-filled dumplings soak up a curry-leaf flavoured tomato rasam poured on at the table, while the open kitchen turns out a steady flow of signature mini dosai (crisp lentil and riceflour pancakes). Chicken chettinad is next, red and flavoursome yet not creamy, offset by vankai korma – lengths of fried baby eggplant in an equally rich sesame sauce. Date and honey kulfi is one of six iced desserts on offer, a lively stopping point on this exciting culinary excursion.

Hours Lunch Mon–Fri & Sun noon–3pm; Dinner daily 6–10pm

Bill E $15–$17 **M** $22–$27 **D** $10–$15; banquet menus $39.50–$47.50pp

Cards AE DC V MC Eftpos

Wine Decent Australasian selection of 19, with 10 half-bottles; 6 by the glass; BYO (corkage $6 a bottle)

Chef Ajoy Joshi

Owners Ajoy & Meera Joshi

Seats 180; private rooms; bar

Vegetarian Plenty, plus a separate banquet menu

www.nilgiris.com.au

And...join one of Ajoy's regular cooking classes

North Bondi Italian Food

118–120 Ramsgate Avenue, North Bondi
Tel 9300 4400 Map 4b

Italian

Score 14/20

Come for the setting: vibrant splashes of red and green on walls and placemat menus; waiters decked out in idiosyncratic combos of blue denim and white tees; a room of wall-to-wall chatter that spills out and across the great curve of Bondi Beach, sun a-shimmer in the day, moon-washed at night. Stay for the food, as close to rustic Italian fare as St Peter's to your parish church. Sure, the elements and presentation are simple, but there's deliberation in the way the kitchen achieves its subtle veneer of rusticity while being noticeably sophisticated. Carpaccio of pepper-crusted ox fillet and salsa erbe is pulpy soft, cool, zesty. Opening a browned bag of cartoccio – a whole snapper baked in paper – releases steam scented from its fennel and onion compote. Diced zucchini, asparagus, peas and waxy potatoes are dusted with mint and air-dried ricotta. Servings are not so ample that there isn't room for a dessert of strawberry moscato jelly, plump, spiced strawberries and vanilla custard.

Hours Lunch Fri–Sun noon–4pm; Dinner daily 6–10.30pm; no bookings

Bill Dishes range from $15–$29 **D** $9–$17; 10% surcharge on Sundays & public holidays

Cards AE DC V MC Eftpos

Wine Wide range across local and Mediterranean; 24 by the glass

Chefs Robert Marchetti, Ben Horne & Marjorie Robertson

Owners Robert Marchetti, Maurice Terzini, Kimme Shaw & Tony Zaccagnini

Seats 120; wheelchair access; outdoor seating; bar

Child friendly Futuristic black plastic highchairs

www.idrb.com

And...amble along the beach afterwards

city + suburbs

Nostos

121 Norton Street, Leichhardt
Tel 9550 0144   Map 5b

Greek

Score 13/20

When in Leichhardt, do as Italians do, unless you're at Nostos, where a Greek Australian team has established a small yet welcome foothold in the suburb's culinary landscape. Weekends feature live Greek music or opt for the more subdued weeknight atmosphere in this split-level, family-friendly eatery where rustic fare dominates. Salt-and-pepper calamari with lashings of lemon juice is simple and more-ish. Dreamy baked fetta isn't fancy, just good clean, honest flavours. Mosharak is prime comfort food – tender veal cutlet on a bed of manestra (Greece's risoni) with a tangy tomato and shallot sauce. And the signature dish of arni – falling-off-the-bone, oven-baked lamb shoulder, served with a roast head of garlic – is so good you'll be checking flights to Santorini. A tasting plate of decadent dessert treats – the custard and filo slice or galaktoboureko, sticky baklava and karithoelo, a mouthwatering sweetened yoghurt topped with walnuts and honey – round off this Greek odyssey.

Hours Lunch Sun 12–3pm;
Dinner Wed–Sun 6–10pm
Bill E $13–$17 **M** $17–$25 **D** $7.50
Cards V MC
Wine Wallet-friendly short list, with couple of Greek drops for good measure; 8 by the glass; BYO wine only (corkage $2pp)
Chef Antonios Sevvastidis
Owners Antonios Sevvastidis, Kosta Theodassopoulos, Nick Kapeleris
Seats 120; private room; outdoor seating
Vegetarian Lots of options; one speciality main dish
www.nostos.com.au
And…complimentary crunchy, lemony garlic potatoes and green beans with main courses

Number One Wine Bar

Shop 1, Goldfields House,
1 Alfred Street, Sydney
Tel 8252 9296   Map 1

Mediterranean

Unscored

You have to wonder whether veteran restaurateur Tony Bilson has described his latest venture as a wine bar to deflect the expectations of his clientele from his eponymous fine diner. After all, he is not in the kitchen here and a wine bar invites a more spontaneous approach. But this is mostly a classic bistro with white tablecloths, buttoned-down, if occasionally off-hand, staff and a conventional three-course menu. It's a slightly uninspiring space, dressed up with artwork. After an initial flurry of Spanish influences, a change of chef will see the menu return to Bilson's first love, France, with a focus on rustic regional cooking and seafood. Expect dishes such as mackerel in white wine and no doubt the excellent bouillabaisse marseillaise will continue, along with the Number One hamburger, snails in garlic butter and duck salad landaise, washed down so some fine French wines, if not great Australian ones. Regrettably, this shift happened as the *Guide* went to press, so while we don't doubt the wine bar will remain delicious, for now we must leave it unscored.

Hours Lunch Mon–Fri noon–5pm;
Dinner Mon–Fri 5pm–midnight
Bill E $12–$25 **M** $18–$31 **D** $15–$18
Cards AE DC V MC Eftpos
Wine New and Old World and impressive specials such as glasses of Penfolds Grange; 35 by the glass
Owner Tony Bilson
Seats 120; wheelchair access; outdoor seating; bar
Child friendly Highchairs
www.numberonewinebar.com
And…traditional French dishes on Fridays, such as bouillabaisse

good food guide

city + suburbs

Nu's

178 Blues Point Road, McMahons Point
Tel 9954 1780   Map 5a

Modern Thai

Score 13/20

With its whitewashed walls, chandeliers, paper-over-linen-covered tables and decorative baskets of butternut pumpkins, you'd be forgiven for thinking you'd stumbled into a posh trattoria instead of an upscale Thai. The confusion continues with the menu, which includes the traditional (tom yum goong, pad thai, a roast duck larb) but swerves towards fusion. Snapper, for instance, might be served with spiced turmeric and cumin potatoes and a salad of fresh figs, cucumber and crisp-fried eggs, while zucchini flowers arrive wrapped in prawn mince, like a play on Vietnamese sugarcane prawns. Nu's version of miang – the Thai snack on a betel leaf – is a showstopper: a jumble of smoked trout, kaffir lime leaf shreds, shallot and trout roe. But many dishes were jumbled, or relied on the curious addition of Japanese mayonnaise. If tempted by dessert, proceed carefully: quantities are more than generous. Sweetly sticky rice with mango and ice-cream will have you waving the white flag.

Hours Lunch Tues–Fri noon–3pm; Dinner Tues–Sun 6–11pm
Bill E $9–$25 **M** $25–$45 **D** $12–$18
Cards AE V MC Eftpos
Wine A serviceable list that could be more clearly arranged; 15 by the glass; BYO (corkage $10 a bottle)
Chefs Nu Suandokmai, Paul Webster & Peter Westfield
Owners Nu & Jane Suandokmai
Seats 120; private rooms; outdoor seating; bar
Child friendly Kids' menu; highchairs; painting kit
Vegetarian A plentiful range
www.nusrestaurant.com.au
And… a quirky "Thai tapas" list

Ocean Room

Bay 4, Ground Level, Overseas Passenger Terminal, Circular Quay West, The Rocks
Tel 9252 9585   Map 1

Modern Japanese/Seafood

Score 14/20

The vast aquarium wall brims with treasures from the sea, captivating diners with its variety of fish, crustaceans and shellfish. Handpicked daily by Japanese chef Raita Noda, the seafood complements the spectacular harbour setting (renovations are planned as the Guide goes to press) before being deftly prepared to your liking. Chargrilled, steamed with ginger and soy, chilli wok-fried and more, it can be mixed and matched to your preference. Service is friendly and polished. The occasional docked liner is an obstacle to the view but nothing detracts from the striking Asian-inspired room and exemplary dishes. It's easy to overindulge on feathery salt-and-pepper calamari pops or the sparkling fresh sushi and sashimi indulgence platter. Crisply fried prawns are kicked along by wasabi aioli. Steamed cod fillets marinated in sweet miso are teamed with ginger scented koshihikari (sushi rice) risotto. There's an excellent wagyu cheek meat pie for those seeking terrestrial produce. Japanese petits fours deliver an intriguing sweet finish.

Hours Lunch Tues–Fri noon–3pm; Dinner Mon–Sat 6–11pm; bookings essential
Bill E $15.50–$29 **M** $29–$42 **D** $12–$17; tasting menus $68–$90pp; 10% surcharge Sundays and public holidays
Cards AE DC V MC
Wine Impressive, well chosen list of mostly Australian wines; 15 by the glass
Chef Raita Noda
Owner Zetton Ocean Room Pty Ltd
Seats 200; private room; wheelchair access; outdoor seating; bar
Child friendly Kids' menu; highchairs
www.oceanroomsydney.com
And… great cocktails and small eats in the bar

city + suburbs

Oceanic Thai
309 Clovelly Road, Clovelly
Tel 9665 8942   Map 9

Thai
Score 13.5/20

There's a lychee and ginger vodka caprioska written up on the mirrored wall menu, hints of exposed brick and dark wooden tables – this pretty, compact space isn't your average suburban Thai. We set sail with a delicious relish of chicken with threads of lemongrass and ginger. Reminiscent of a rich red curry it arrives with cloud-like, moreish rice crackers. Other palate kick-starters include favoursome prawn cakes and chilli-laced miang – betel leaves topped with dried shrimp, coconut, pomelo and peanuts. Semi-dried strips of beef, stir-fried with gai lan and crunchy garlic shoots, are aromatic with spice, and a sour orange curry of rich salmon with the crunch of cabbage and snake beans is hot and light. On the side, spoon into deep-fried son-in-law eggs and let the yolks mingle with sticky tamarind sauce. The dessert platter is a sensation: caramelised pineapple atop tapioca, and pandanus dumplings filled with oozy warm chocolate and coconut ensure it's all smooth sailing.

Hours Dinner Tues–Sat 6–10pm
Bill E $14–$16 **M** $20–$24 **D** $16 (plate for 2); 4-course banquet $55pp
Cards V MC
Wine Compact list suited to the cuisine; 11 by the glass; BYO Tues–Thurs (corkage $5pp)
Chef Max Mullins
Owners Max Mullins & Sally Lynch
Seats 40; wheelchair access
Vegetarian Separate menus
www.oceanicthai.com.au
And... there's a great takeaway menu, too

Oliveto
Brays Bay Reserve, 443 Concord Road, Rhodes
Tel 8765 0006   Map 6

Italian
Score 13/20

Named for an olive grove, Oliveto is a welcome respite from busy Concord Road, with its serene outlook taking in green parkland by a secluded section of the Parramatta River. The interior radiates brightness, particularly at lunch, with floor-to-ceiling windows creating an atrium feel. Service is industrious and efficient but warm at the same time. The aroma of the open wood-fired oven pumping out thin-crust pizzas is an initial temptation. A starter of stringy king prawns in a hot sauce of tomato, chilli and garlic disappointed but things improve with delicately cooked grilled scampi with lemon, chilli and garlic on top. Spatchcock from the wood-fired oven is also a winner – flavoursome and moist with a caponata of chopped zucchini, celery, red onion and tomatoes. A refreshing espresso granita comes with mascarpone and delicate, house-made brioche.

Hours Lunch Mon–Fri & Sun noon–3pm; Dinner Tues–Sat 6–10pm
Bill E $13.50–$26 **M** $23–$38 **D** $14.50
Cards AE DC V MC Eftpos
Wine Classy, extensive Italian/Australian list; 17 by the glass; BYO (corkage $4.50pp)
Chef Chris Georgakopolous
Owners Tony Colosi, Charlie Colosi, Alessandro & Carmen Milozzi
Seats 140; wheelchair access; outdoor seating; bar
Child friendly Kids' menu; highchairs
Vegetarian Several dishes, specials & pizzas
www.oliveto.com.au
And... can be booked for Saturday lunch or Sunday night functions

city + suburbs

Onde

346 Liverpool Street, Darlinghurst
Tel 9331 8749   Map 2

French

Score 13/20

Thirteen years ago, this modern, open-space room was considered the chic, new wave place to be. (And yes, Onde does mean wave.) For many it still is *le dernier cri*, especially if you score a table by the big streetside window and watch the inner-city parade. Not much has changed; there's still a blackboard menu with simple French-style dishes that keep the crowds coming back. Perfectly crisp, battered zucchini flowers are enlivened by a dusting of parmesan. A traditional salt-cod brandade sits on intriguingly textured potato bread. Calf's liver comes with a traditional rich cabernet wine sauce. A big T-bone steak came with what appeared to be dull commercial chips, rather than French pommes frites. Snapper is served very simply, on beans and potato with a good tomato aioli. Typically French desserts – such as meringue with strawberries and cream or a chocolate terrine – are a highlight. Caramelised figs are a simple, seasonal pleasure.

Hours Dinner Mon–Fri 5.30–10.30pm, Sat–Sun 5.30–11pm
Bill E $15–$16 **M** $19–$28 **D** $10
Cards AE DC V MC
Wine Interesting, well-matched, from Australia, France and Italy; from $25 with a good selection under $50; 25 by the glass
Chef Laif Etournaud
Owners Laif Etournaud & Simone Lai
Seats 35
Vegetarian Reasonable choice from the menu
And...arrive early to be sure of a table

Oscillate Wildly

275 Australia Street, Newtown
Tel 9517 4700   Map 8

Contemporary

Score 15/20

After lifting the ambitions of this quirky restaurant several notches, chef Daniel Puskas has moved on, but the thrill is that his replacement, Karl Firla (formerly of est.), adds new lustre to this adventurous degustation. This small shopfront, with a simple bistro decor, maintains a cultish presence, while carefully laidback service keeps the groove going. A roller-coaster ride of flavours starts slowly, with a too-sweet jumble of walnuts, chestnuts and honey followed by yellowfin sashimi with pickled cucumber, pomelo and wasabi foam. Potato gnocchi with pepitas has the added intrigue of coffee, while buttery Glenloth corn-fed chicken breast shines on nutty, crunchy puffed buckwheat and braised celeriac. Venison is matched with beetroot and chocolate in a showcase of the contemporary techniques scattered through this thoroughly modern meal. The second of two desserts is a clever contrast of star anise-poached pear with celery sorbet and bitter chocolate notes. While your views might oscillate, at least your pulse will be racing wildly.

Hours Dinner Tues–Sat 6–10pm; bookings essential
Bill 8-course degustation $95pp
Cards AE V MC Eftpos
Wine Sophisticated & classy small list with serious Europeans; 9 by the glass; BYO (corkage $3pp)
Chefs Karl & Mark Firla
Owner Ross Godfrey
Seats 28
Vegetarian Separate degustation
And...check the menu to match your BYO with it

Make it a night to remember.

The Perfect Night

- ✓ Select your restaurant.
- ✓ Send her flowers on the day or to the restaurant.
- ✓ The rest is easy.

Score 20/20

Send her long-stemmed roses and take her to one of Sydney's premier restaurants. **You'll sweep her off her feet.**

rosesonly.com.au
1300 767 376

city + suburbs

Osvaldo Polletti
148 Norton Street, Leichhardt
Tel 9560 4525   Map 5b

Southern Italian
                                   Score 13.5/20

This likeable little place defies the cliches and stodge that too often appear to be the hallmarks of Norton Street's restaurant strip. In a renovated terrace with upstairs and downstairs dining rooms plus pavement tables, the kitchen produces loosely southern-style food to a frequently packed and noisy house. Pasta might include a version of pasta Norma, named for the heroine in Bellini's opera of the same name, with spiral pasta and herby little meatballs good enough to make a fat lady sing, or rotolini (pasta rolls), filled with pumpkin and ricotta, with pecorino and sage butter. Savvy regulars know to plunder the menu for its fish dishes: snapper on lemony caponata is impeccably cooked, as is a whole flounder, despite its inauthentic version of the classic Sicilian salmoriglio. Amusing T-shirt-clad waiters complete this no-frills package, although lumberjacks might complain about the portion sizes. A faultless tiramisu is a sweet star.

Hours Dinner Mon–Sat 6–10pm
Bill E $10–$16 **M** $25–$28 **D** $6–$11
Cards V MC Eftpos
Wine A short and sweet little Italian-only list; 9 by the glass; BYO (corkage $3.50pp)
Chefs Franco Napoliello & Luca de Martin
Owners Joe & Franco Napoliello
Seats 60
Child friendly Kids' menu; highchairs
Vegetarian Many options available
And… take a tour of Italy's wine regions via the list

Otto Ristorante
Area 8/6 Cowper Wharf Road, Woolloomooloo
Tel 9368 7488   Map 2

Italian
                                   Score 15/20

Is it too soon to call Otto a Sydney institution? After all the narcissistic tabloid fluff over the years, it's easy to forget how much this ever-cool evergreen has lifted the bar for harbourside dining. Popular with ordinary punters, as well as fashionista scenesters, it proves that we're all happy to pay for simple things done well – a pink sunset over the marina, a plate of just-shucked oysters, and the perfect gin martini with a twist of city skyline. Chef James Kidman's food has the good looks that a linen-set table demands but without gimmicks. Grilled whole barramundi is served simply with olive oil, sea salt and cheeks of lemon; grilled zucchini flowers filled with brandade sit alongside sublime wild-harvest Spencer Gulf prawns. A bowl of pappardelle in a husky pork ragu with Sicilian olives, followed by tiramisu, might be all you require for complete happiness. Service is whip-smart and friendly.

Hours Lunch daily noon–3.30pm; Dinner daily 6–10.30pm; bookings essential
Bill E $27–$29 **M** $36–$42 **D** $18–$20; 10% surcharge on Sundays & public holidays
Cards AE DC V MC
Wine Impressive, wide-ranging local and international selection by sommelier Patrick White; 26 by the glass
Chef James Kidman
Owner Leon Fink
Seats 250; private rooms; outdoor seating; bar
Child friendly Kids' menu; highchairs; drawing materials; space for prams
Vegetarian Vegan menu & vegetarian options
www.otto.net.au
And… a taxi rank at wharf end ensures speedy delivery and exit

good food guide   103

city + suburbs

Ottoman Cuisine

Pier 2, 13 Hickson Road, Walsh Bay
Tel 9252 0054   Map 1

Contemporary Turkish

Score 14/20

The location is extraordinary – just beyond the underbelly of the bridge's southern span. Service – after early hiccups – is polished, courteous and attentive. The food is sublime. Pick out a mezze spread, Turkish style, and relax. Ensure, however, that you're not booked in when a large group has taken over the dining room – function frivolities will ruin even the most upbeat evening. Etli borek, gorgeous crunchy filo rolls stuffed with slow-braised veal shank, currants and pine nuts, form a mouth-watering combination with sweet pomegranate and yoghurt sauce. King George whiting fillets with semolina crust are a delicate delight on thinly shaved fennel salad. Yahni is a beautifully succulent goat dish, braised with spinach and lentils. Traditional minced lamb kofte form a great textural contrast with white beans, red onion and rocket, and are superb in their simplicity. For a finale, indulge in creamy, burnt (in a good way) custard dessert, sticky with mastica extract, and topped with glistening sour cherries.

Hours Lunch Wed–Fri & Sun noon–3pm; Dinner Tues–Sat 6–10pm
Bill E $18–$21 **M** $30–$33 **D** $6–$14; 10% surcharge on Sundays
Cards AE DC V MC Eftpos
Wine Terrific globetrotting list, surprisingly affordable; 16 by the glass
Chef Serif Kaya
Owners Serif & Gucci Kaya
Seats 160; private rooms; wheelchair access; outdoor seating; bar
Vegetarian Plenty to choose from
www.ottomancuisine.com.au
And…waiters will happily choose dishes for you

Palace Chinese

Shop 38, Level 1, Piccadilly Tower, 133–145 Castlereagh Street, Sydney
Tel 9283 6288   Map 1

Chinese (Cantonese)

Score 13/20

There's no need to leave the CBD's smarter retail precincts to find this stylish Cantonese, tucked above a shiny arcade between Castlereagh and Pitt. It's just the thing for serious shoppers with weary wallets. Chewy chicken feet, glistening har gow and other dim sum specialities even come at a discount if you're out before 12.30pm. Evenings in these plush, carpeted surrounds are a less budget-friendly experience. Lobster straight from the tank is excellent stir-fried with garlic, ginger and shallots but can do more damage to your plastic than some of the designer stores below. Crisp-skinned desert chicken sits enticingly on deep-fried Chinese mustard greens, although it's curiously sprinkled with peanuts and sugar. Red-braised tofu with sugar snap peas, carrot and mushrooms is comforting, although it was a little cornstarch-heavy. For greater pleasure, and more satisfying prices, try classic Peking duck done two ways; and sweetly sticky pork ribs, Peking style.

Hours Lunch Mon–Fri 11am–3pm, weekends and public holidays 10.30am–3pm; Dinner daily 5–10.30pm; no bookings for yum cha
Bill E $6–$25.80 **M** $20.80–$68 **D** $6.80–$10.80; $2pp surcharge on public holidays
Cards AE DC V MC
Wine Australian-dominated list; 14 by the glass
Chefs Sung Ma & Ming Li
Owner Lee Ngann Ly
Seats 250; private rooms; wheelchair access
Child friendly Highchairs
Vegetarian Many options
www.palacechinese.com.au
And…$7 parking voucher available at night on weekends and public holidays only

city + suburbs

Pendolino

Shop 100, Level 2, The Strand Arcade,
412–414 George Street, Sydney
Tel 9231 6117   Map 1

Italian

Score 15/20

High in the heritage splendour of the city's finest Victorian arcade, Pendolino (literally "pendulum", but also an olive variety) swings several ways. Outside, it's an all-day cafe and evening wine bar. Inside, it's a beautifully intimate dining space with a bright, open kitchen and knowledgeable staff. Then there's the adjacent olioteca with its shelves of premium olive oils and vinegars. The olive theme continues in oil tastings for every table and several oil-matched dishes on the inventive regional Italian menu. Plump three-cheese and spinach ravioli in burnt butter and sage makes a fine entree, preceding sea-sweet Port Lincoln prawns and baby calamari paired with a fruttato allegro extra virgin oil, plus garlicky crushed potatoes speckled with anchovies and Sicilian green olives. Tender pork belly with perfect crackling and blood-orange infused oil needed a better foil than an overly sweet orange and fennel salad. Nonetheless, a double ristretto, and the creamy crunch of Ligurian honey and almond milk semifreddo with candied almonds, will have you swinging by here again and again.

Hours Breakfast Mon–Sat 9–11.30am;
Lunch Mon–Fri noon–3pm;
Dinner Mon–Sat 6–9.30pm; bookings essential
Bill E $19–$26 **M** $29–$39 **D** $12–$17
Cards AE V MC Eftpos
Wine Clever, medium-sized list with an Australian and Italian focus; 17 by the glass
Chef Nino Zoccali
Owners Nino Zoccali & SG Foodservice Pty Ltd
Seats 150; private room; bar
Vegetarian Ideal with great variety
www.pendolino.com.au
And…drop by for lunch at the cafe out front

Perama

88 Audley Street, Petersham
Tel 9569 7534   Map 8

Greek

Score 14/20

David Tsirekas shows a healthy respect for his ancestors, but he's not rule-bound. In his popular suburban taverna he serves traditional favourites, such as his mum's legendary pittes (savoury, homemade filo parcels) and slow-braised lamb skaras, as well as creative interpretations of familiar fare, and an intriguing mix of dishes from the ancient world. Excellent thria – little fig-leaf parcels of creamy manouri (salty sheep's milk cheese) – have a wonderfully smoky note from a quick grilling, but a Persian salad of chicken, dried apricots and cloying yoghurt was less successful. Mod options might include the signature pork-belly baklava, a refreshing watermelon, mint and buffalo-milk fetta salad and fried calamari with black sea salt and mild ouzo mayonnaise. While service is warm, best intentions appear to unravel when it's busy. Ingenuity pays off in flaky, citrus-laced baklava studded with sweet-savoury nubs of kalamata olive – tradition tweaked to great effect.

Hours Dinner Tues–Sat 6–10.30pm;
bookings essential
Bill E $4–$19.50 **M** $25–$35 **D** $5–$13.50;
8-course mezze banquet $50pp;
10% surcharge on public holidays
Cards V MC Eftpos
Wine Excellent Greek choices plus local and New Zealand drops; 16 by the glass; BYO (corkage $6 a bottle)
Chef David Tsirekas
Owners David & Belinda Tsirekas
Seats 120; private room; outdoor seating
Child friendly Home-style kids' menu
Vegetarian Good entree range, but only one main
www.perama.com.au
And…upstairs is great for group banquets

good food guide

city + suburbs

Pier
594 New South Head Road, Rose Bay
Tel 9327 6561   Map 9

Contemporary/Seafood

Score 18/20

BEST SEAFOOD RESTAURANT
As Canute reminded his acolytes, you can't hold back the tide. This long glass jetty has gone with the flow. The casual tasting room evaporated (alas), while the fine dining room's menu has been pared back to make room for a degustation. Of late, the service has opted for cool efficiency over its previous vibrant personality, but remains smooth. The decor goes for sleek, cool minimalism in white and blue, and the dozen-dish menu presents seafood in elaborate, nuanced and gorgeous ways, such as jewel-like coral trout carpaccio, carefully adorned with tomato and herb leaves. Spanner crab tian on scallop ceviche with a moat of green jus and tangle of pea shoots was more a triumph of texture than taste. Tuna, seared only on one side, is a translucent base for a crisp filigree of fennel, slivers of Sicilian olive and seared calamari, while Katrina Kanetani's desserts reveal a vivid imagination, especially whimsical, tangy blueberry cheesecake ice-cream with goat's curd and chestnut crumble.

Hours Lunch daily noon–3pm;
Dinner daily 6–10pm
Bill E $32–$45 **M** $49–$65 **D** $28; $10pp surcharge on Sundays, $12.50pp on public holidays
Cards AE DC V MC Eftpos
Wine 15 by the glass
Chefs Grant King, Katrina Kanetani & Greg Doyle
Owners Greg & Jenny Doyle
Seats 120; private room; bar
Child friendly Kids' menu
Vegetarian Separate menu
www.pierrestaurant.com.au
And...five- and eight-course degustations ($139pp and $179pp)

Pilu at Freshwater
End of Moore Road, Freshwater
Tel 9938 3331   Map 7

Italian (Sardinian)
Score 17/20

WINE LIST OF THE YEAR
So brightly does Giovanni Pilu's star shine that the surf views from this heritage timber cottage aren't the only thing to dazzle. Like sirens, Pilu's Sardinian specialities lure diners into this grown-up version of a beachside shack. We dare you not to suck clean each tiny vongole shell in a pile of malloreddus (saffron shell pasta), hoping vainly they will yield more of the salty, golden saffron and bottarga sauce. Fat calamari, stuffed with olives, herbs, pine nuts and grainy Sardinian fregola, loll on a rich tomato sauce that speaks of summer sunshine. The signature suckling pig – sweet and moist with a foamy layer of crackling – is sublime, surpassed only by whole baby snapper baked with green olives, garlic and vernaccia (an Italian white wine). The flavours of Pilu's island homeland continue with dolci. Warm zabaglione is spiked with vermentino (another white wine), while saffron donuts are doused with grappa-infused cherries. The service, like the food, is polished to a brilliant sheen.

Hours Lunch Wed–Sun noon–2.30pm;
Dinner Tues–Sat 6–10pm
Bill E $25–$29 **M** $37–$44 **D** $17; Sardinian tasting menu $100pp
Cards AE (+2.5%) DC (+2.5%) V MC
Wine Impressive 400-plus list with a Sardinian and southern Italian accent; 27 by the glass
Chef Giovanni Pilu
Owners Giovanni Pilu & Marilyn Annecchini
Seats 110; private rooms; outdoor seating
Child friendly Kids' menu; highchairs; drawing materials
Vegetarian A handful of options
www.piluatfreshwater.com.au
And...pack your togs for a swim

Pizza e Birra

Shop 1, 500 Crown Street, Surry Hills
Tel 9332 2510   Map 3b

Southern Italian/Pizza

Score 13.5/20

It's no longer the newest kid on the block but Pizza e Birra still enjoys the kind of queue-forming popularity that defies Sydney's fickle fashionistas. Regulars know that to nab a seat in this chic warehouse space, you have two choices: arrive early and join a host of hip parents with kids in tow, or come late and sit out the wait in a nearby bar. Options for differing dining experiences don't enc there: take the traditional route with a fine margherita – the crust chewy and charred just so – or choose a gutsier speck version strewn with salty cured pork, provola and earthy truffle paste. Still undecided? Hedge your bets with the mezzaluna (meaning "half-moon") – the only half-and-half you're likely to find here: an oozing ricotta and salami calzone on one side, a simple prosciutto pizza on the other. Round things out with a sharp radicchio and buffalo mozzarella salad, or live la dolce vita with smooth tiramisu, espresso and a grappa.

Hours Mon–Wed 6–10pm, Thurs–Sat noon–11pm, Sun noon–10pm; no dinner bookings
Bill E $7–$24 **M** $19–$32 **D** $14–$16
Cards AE DC V MC
Wine 50 fab local and Italian drops; 45 by the glass
Chefs Vishal Rummin & Gianni Cristiano
Owners Khali Khouri, Mauro Marcucci & Sabina Buoncompagni
Seats 100; wheelchair access; outdoor seating; bar
Child friendly Booster seats; kids' pasta & pizza; crayons
Vegetarian Several pizzas, plus antipasti & salads
And… as well as the house-label beer, there's a neat range of Italian liqueurs

Pomegranate Thai

191 Darling Street, Balmain
Tel 9555 5693   Map 5b

Thai

Score 13/20

Bench seats and exposed brick walls are hardly original, but the vibrant twists on old favourites at this creative Thai eatery certainly are. If you've had a yearning for miang kham since visiting Bangkok, here's the upmarket version, pla grob (caramelised whitebait in chilli jam), garnished with lime and toasted coconut, to wrap in a betel leaf and enjoy the punchy flavours. Chinese-influenced Balmain rolls of pork and prawn mince are fried in paper-fine tofu skin and served with sweet-sour plum sauce. Butter-soft lamb massaman and banana flower salad suffered from a little too much sweetness but crisp whole baby barramundi is divine, topped with a salsa of spiced green mango and crumbly fish flakes. Khai luk koei (son-in-law eggs) are Thai-style scotch eggs encased in prawn mince and bathed in a tart tamarind and ginger sauce. While the service can be slow, Pomegranate's contemporary Thai, including coconut ice-cream and a wedge of sticky rice on dried longans, is too good to ignore.

Hours Lunch Fri–Sat noon–3pm; Dinner Tues–Sun 5.30–10pm
Bill E $10.50–$12.50 **M** $18.50–$29.50 **D** $8–$10
Cards AE V MC Eftpos
Wine Small wine list; 9 by the glass, plus Thai beer; BYO (corkage $3pp)
Chef/owner Eric Sudardja
Seats 60; wheelchair access
Vegetarian A few, but most mains can be substituted with tofu and seasonal vegetables
And… waiting for a table is a breeze with The London nearby

...... city + suburbs ....•

Pompei's

Cnr Roscoe and Gould streets, Bondi Beach
Tel 9365 1233   Map 4b

Italian

Score 14/20

Out of apparent chaos comes order. And some of the most reliably good pizza and regional (north Italian) inspired pasta in town. In the midst of large family groups, kids on booster seats, local teens eyeing off the gelato of the day and George Pompei chatting with his regulars, a team of mostly European waiters manages to deliver slender, beautifully toasted pizza and fun Italian wine by the glass or frosty bottles of limonata. Pompei takes his business seriously, through to daily blackboard specials featuring freshly arrived buffalo mozzarella, San Daniele prosciutto-topped pizza, steamed organic vegetables or a wintry dish of squishy, gnocchi-like spinach spaetzle in a creamy provolone and ham-laced sauce. It's a struggle not to go straight to the pizza menu, although the longtime house specialty of casunzei — beetroot and poppyseed filled pasta crescents — can be a worthy distraction. A salad of bresaola with vibrant greens and sweet apple works with either. And Pompei's Amadei chocolate gelato, or the best-ever pistachio, is paradise in a chilly stainless steel cup.

Hours Tues–Thurs 3–11pm, Fri–Sun 11am–11.30pm
Bill E $7.50–$17.50 **M** $19.50–$32.50 **D** $6.20–$10.50
Cards AE V MC Eftpos
Wine A simple but interesting Italo-Oz list; 20 by the glass; BYO wine only (corkage $6/bottle)
Chefs George Pompei and Naimul Islam
Owners George and Adisa Pompei
Seats 100
Child-friendly Kids' menu; highchairs
www.pompeis.com.au

And...gelato in cones, cups or styropacks available for takeaway

Pony Lounge & Dining

Shops 14–15 The Rocks Centre,
Cnr Kendall Lane & Argyle streets, The Rocks
Tel 9252 7797   Map 1

Contemporary

Score 13.5/20

The cobblestone lane location just adds to the charm of this atmospheric, popular diner. Designer Michael McCann has given the former bond store a dramatic makeover: rope wall hangings, goatskin lights and, of course, plenty of pony hide. Diners are seated side by side in the narrow main room — or at a communal outside table — making for an intimate, if cramped, dining experience. The tapas menu has Asiatic leanings: shaved fennel scattered over citrus-cured salmon on a bed of sliced orange and rocket is a delicate starter, but thinly sliced seared sirloin was swamped by soy, lime, chilli and ginger sauce. Perfectly pink lamb tenderloin from the wood-fired grill is well matched with olive tapenade, although a soggy tomato tartlet disappointed. Scallop tortellini sits in a just-rich-enough puddle of citrus butter with a herb and leek "salad" garnish. Summer trifle is fun despite no wicked, alcoholic pay-off. Sassy and confident, Pony is a distinctively Sydney take on laneway dining.

Hours Lunch daily noon–3pm; Dinner Sun–Thurs 6–10pm, Fri–Sat 6–10.30pm
Bill E $4–$24 **M** $28–$58 **D** $12–$16; small share plates $4–$14
Cards AE DC (+2.5%) V MC Eftpos
Wine 20 by the glass
Chefs Damian Heads & Neil Nolan
Owners Nick & George Kyprianou
Seats 70; wheelchair access; outdoor seating; bar
Vegetarian Small plates; separate menu for main courses on request
www.ponydining.com.au

And...a tasting plate on the superb deck is a great pre-theatre option

city + suburbs

Postales Restaurante & Tapas Bar

NEW ENTRY

Lower Ground Floor, GPO Building,
1 Martin Place, Sydney
Tel 9229 7744 Map 1

Spanish

Score 13/20

The former Post seafood brasserie has joined Sydney's tapas infatuation, converting to Postales. At the front of this cavernous, subterranean space is a small tapas bar, with softly lit, red-hued restaurant booths and leather banquettes tucked behind curtains. As a jazzy flamenco soundtrack pounds and the rioja flows, graze on some of more than 20 tapas, plus several main course-sized, Spanish-style dishes. Top of the pops are albondigas, earthy meatballs using hare, in a spicy tomato sauce. A sticky nugget of braised oxtail with creamy cauliflower puree will have you stamping your feet and clicking your fingers. Service can be as sweet as the jamon de bellota, yet occasionally scatty. It matters not when a main of pan-fried salt cod, using blue-eye, is crusted with olive and tomato crust and paired with saffron aioli. Churros with caramel and chocolate dipping sauces may beckon but flan de nata gives creme caramel a run for its money.

Hours Lunch Mon–Fri noon–3pm;
Dinner Mon–Sat 6–10pm
Bill M $29–$34 **D** $9.50–$12;
tapas dishes $9.50–$19.50; 8% surcharge for groups of 10 or more
Cards AE DC V MC Eftpos
Wine Enjoyably Spanish, divided into regions, plus Australian varietals; 19 by the glass
Chefs Ben Pichon & Iwao Yamanishi
Owner Peter Petroulas
Seats 120; wheelchair access; bar
Child friendly Highchairs
www.gposydney.com
And...paella for two, dinner only

Prime

GPO Building, Lower Ground Floor,
1 Martin Place, Sydney
Tel 9229 7777 Map 1

Steakhouse/French/Japanese

Score 13/20

If your idea of cloud nine is a dozen Sydney rocks, meat and mash, and a gutsy red, take the stairway down to heaven, beneath the venerable GPO. While the bottom level of this 19th century building can feel like a glammed-up food hall, Prime is mostly about things of stone, wood and leather, plus great glasses and a mainly meaty menu. Stick to the grill and you can't go wrong. Pick a cut – fillet, sirloin or wagyu, perhaps – and it returns 30 minutes later (they're big on resting) with a sauce – perhaps bearnaise or red wine jus – plus spuds, puree or gratine. If that's a touch too formulaic, or you lean towards more aquatic cuisine, opt for a plump barra fillet in a soy-infused pond swimming with Asian greens. Service might sometimes need prompting (no scallop entree as advertised, beans arrived as sugar snaps) but all is forgotten as a gooey chocolate fondant literally oozes with charm.

Hours Lunch Mon–Fri noon–3pm;
Dinner Mon–Sat 6–10pm
Bill E $22–$26 **M** $30–$68 **D** $15.50–$16.50;
8% surcharge for groups of 10 or more
Cards AE DC V MC Eftpos
Wine A broadsheet full of New World reds (particularly SA shiraz) and Old World cognacs; 19 by the glass
Chef Iwao Yamanishi
Owner Peter Petroulas
Seats 130; private room; wheelchair access; bar
Child friendly Highchairs
www.gposydney.com
And...try the express lunch menu, or if you have more time, chateaubriand for two

good food guide

city + suburbs

Qmin

5/207B Pacific Highway, St Leonards
Tel 9966 5557   Map 5a

Indian

Score 13/20

There's more than rogan josh and tandoori lamb at this classily contemporary Indian eatery, set back from the highway on a somewhat soulless office plaza. Roaming the regions of the world's most populous democracy is something of a mission for Anil Ashokan. And his lababdaar tikke (butter chicken) and malt-vinegar braised pork vin d'alho (vindaloo) are as unlike their bain-marie counterparts at Indian takeaways around town as the spelling of his restaurant name and the spice to which it refers. Qmin is an attractive but spartan space with efficient service and pleasantly plated, carefully spiced food. Marinated prawns with carom seeds are creamy and sweet, although outclassed by tiny spinach-leaf fritters patta chaat tossed with toasted cashews and chickpeas. Baked flathead on mashed rice and lentils (macchi ne kitchri) and vinegary Hyderabad-style eggplant are intriguing but a vegetable biryani (spiced pilaf) lacked perfumed fluffiness and, at $20, seemed too expensive. Just-charred naan and roti make lovely sauce-soppers. And a spread of pretty desserts – nutmeggy bebinca or Goan layer cake, buttery carrot halva and melting saffron kulfi – stops the show.

Hours Breakfast Mon–Fri 8–11am; Lunch Mon–Fri noon–3pm; Dinner Mon–Sat 6–10pm
Bill E $14–$17 **M** $21–$28 **D** $11–$12
Cards AE DC V MC Eftpos
Wine A basic but functional list; 12 by the glass; BYO (corkage $7 a bottle)
Chef/owner Anil Ashokan
Seats 80; wheelchair access; outdoor seating
Vegetarian Extensive selection of dishes
www.qmin.com.au
And...check out Ashokan's sumptuous cookbook

Quay

Upper Level, Overseas Passenger Terminal, The Rocks
Tel 9251 5600   Map 1

Contemporary

Score 18/20

RESTAURANT OF THE YEAR

In his backyard vegetable patch, Farmer Gilmore experiments lovingly with rare and unusual edibles. In his kitchen, Chef Gilmore's communion with produce – teensy baby vegetables and flowering herbs, abalone, pearl meat, marron and morels – culminates in heavenly, transcendent textures and flavours. This is a restaurant as monumental as the ocean liners that moor alongside it. In a glassed-in, curvaceous space, a company of engaging, impeccable waiters delivers Gilmore's finest over four courses. You might choose the signature "sea pearl" dish – four precious little balls of fishy brilliance, including sashimi tuna subtly flavoured with bonito oil and white soy. Or intoxicating little tiles of confit pig belly with braised abalone and cuttlefish and handmade tofu silkier than any Chinese emperor's gown. Masterful desserts, such as a white peach snow egg, wrap up this spiritual dining experience, which is among the world's finest.

Hours Lunch Tues–Fri noon–2.30pm; Dinner daily 6–10pm; bookings essential
Bill 4-course a la carte dinner menu $145pp; 2-course lunch $75pp, 3 courses $95pp; 10% surcharge on public holidays
Cards AE DC V MC, JCB
Wine A thrilling global list and excellent selection by the glass and steep mark-ups; 20 by the glass
Chef Peter Gilmore
Owners John & Leon Fink
Seats 200; private rooms; wheelchair access; outdoor seating; bar
Child friendly Kids' menu
www.quay.com.au
And...sometimes the view is an ocean liner instead

city + suburbs

Rambutan
96 Oxford Street, Darlinghurst
Tel 9360 7772   Map 2

Thai (Southern)

Score 13.5/20

This moody Thai adds a touch of sleek class to Oxford Street's hustler end. A theatrical open kitchen shares space with the dimly lit dining room while the downstairs bar is as sultry as they come. It's all about host Joe Natale, busy on the floor, and a Thai-accented contemporary menu, with a communal table to add to the hip quotient. Bites of pla dip (kingfish sashimi) with grated apple and lemongrass tune the tastebuds nicely, and fried, salt-cured beef served with chilli dipping sauce is a great beer snack. Pla lath plik, crisp whole barramundi dressed with chillies, ginger and kaffir lime is a textural treat, while the fiery goodness of stir-fried pork belly with glossy green beans and red curry paste will give you cravings for days. Coconut jelly – Thai-style agar agar – topped with passionfruit might be a refreshing dessert. But the party crowd might prefer an Asian-inspired cocktail – a tart apple martini or the signature coconut and kaffir lime-infused daiquiri caravale.

Hours Dinner Tues–Sun 6–11pm
Bill E $4–$16 **M** $18–$32 **D** $6–$12; 10% surcharge on Sundays & public holidays
Cards AE V MC Eftpos
Wine Short, suitable, well-priced mainly Australian list, with a smattering of Europeans; 11 by the glass
Chefs Richard Wennerbom & Adam Lane
Owners Joe & Milena Natale
Seats 120; private room; bar
Vegetarian Numerous options
www.rambutan.com.au
And… most entrees are available as snacks at the dimly lit downstairs bar

Ratu Sari
470 Anzac Parade, Kingsford
Tel 9662 8788   Map 9

Indonesian

Score 12/20

Ratu Sari stands out amid the neon-lit noodle bars and late-night mini marts on this stretch of Anzac Parade. Pitched a notch above, it's decorated with stone tiles, timber-framed batik prints and greenery. The effect is one of order and rhythmic industry especially in the kitchen where Rohana Halim and her team of female assistants toil, all clad in bright red batik aprons. North Sumatran food, with its nonya influence, predominates. Beef rendang, more tender than it looks, suffered from too much salt in an otherwise aromatic sauce. Whole snapper, rubbed with red chilli paste and wrapped in mint and banana leaves and steamed, falls open with the merest nudge, the flesh succulent and moist. Stir-fried water spinach with shrimp paste and sambal belachan is suitably fiery. A salty note is struck again, this time in the warm black sticky rice with coconut milk, but it works, accentuating the earthy quality of the pudding and inviting one more spoonful.

Hours Lunch Tues–Sun noon–3pm; Dinner Tues–Sun 5.30–9.30pm
Bill E $6.50–$10.50 **M** $13.90–$21 **D** $6.50–$9.50
Cards AE DC V MC Eftpos
Wine BYO (no corkage)
Chef Rohana Halim
Owners Michael & Rohana Halim
Seats 70; wheelchair access
Child friendly Kids' banquet; highchairs
Vegetarian Several dishes but check they don't contain shrimp paste
And… visit Rohana's wall of fame, filled with framed awards and career highlights

city + suburbs

Red Chilli

Shop 3, 51 Dixon Street, Haymarket
Tel 9211 8122 Map 3a
Also at Red Chilli 2
Shop 108/25 Harbour Street, Haymarket
Tel 9211 8130 Map 3a

Chinese (Sichuan)

Score 13/20

Sichuan food is hot and numbing, warns signage in the takeaway lounge. Hot – that'll be chillies, flung with initially frightening abandon but tempered in each dish with either a cooling ingredient, such as the thin curls of cucumber accompanying the sliced chicken in chilli sesame sauce, or roasted and sweet, used as a bed for fat, crisp stir-fried prawns in their shells. At times their presence is subtle, like the thin rings of fresh red chilli in a cold green soybean salad, vibrant with emerald steamed beans, silky diced capsicum, and pale yellow slivers of garlic. Then there's the numbing part: sichuan peppercorns bobbing among pale green wedges of skinned, steamed eggplant in a bath of pickled chilli. Take heart, climb the worn red carpet to the ample dining area with its casual nod to decor and immerse yourself in a meal where texture, colour and flavour make pain a pleasure.

Hours Lunch daily 11.30am–2.30pm; Dinner daily 5–10.30pm
Bill E $3.30–$11.80 **M** $10.80–$58.80 **D** $3.20–$16.80; 10% surcharge on public holidays
Cards AE DC V MC Eftpos
Wine Skip wine for the 10 beers on offer; 2 wines by the glass; BYO (corkage $3pp)
Chefs Ping Zhou & Zheng Luo
Owners Teresa Dai, David Zhang & Jian Cheng
Seats 100; private room
Child friendly Highchairs
Vegetarian A very good range beyond stir-fries
www.redchillirestaurant.com.au
And...check upstairs for steamboats and the newer Red Chilli around the corner

Red Lantern

545 Crown Street, Surry Hills
Tel 9698 4355 Map 3b

Vietnamese

Score 13/20

If you think authentic Vietnamese needs a Cabramatta or Bankstown address, you'll be pleasantly surprised at this chic terrace at the gritty end of Crown Street. There's a brooding black and red interior (not a formica tabletop in sight) and the menu's reassuringly traditional approach, high-quality ingredients and clear, clean flavours remain true to owner Luke Nguyen's Cabramatta roots. Goi cuon (soft rice paper rolls with prawns, pork, vermicelli, shiso and garlic) are so popular they're an almost compulsory starter. The menu proudly advertises its green credentials, and organic eggplant and pasture-fed Peking duck play a starring role in cari vit (duck curry). Chuoi chien – fat, deep-fried banana fritters rolled in coconut rice – are a feelgood finale. Meanwhile, on the floor the service is brisk and accomplished whether you're inquiring about the origins of a dish, or the well-curated wine list, which includes some interesting European drops.

Hours Lunch Tues–Fri 12.30–3pm; Dinner daily 6–10pm; bookings essential
Bill E $15–$22 **M** $16–$35 **D** $14; tasting menus $55pp and $65pp; degustation menu $130pp; 10% surcharge on Sundays & public holidays
Cards AE DC V MC
Wine Well-matched wines from Europe and Australasia; 14 by the glass
Chefs Mark Jensen & Luke Nguyen
Owner Luke Nguyen
Seats 50; outdoor seating
Vegetarian A separate menu of 7 mains
www.redlantern.com.au
And... Vietnamese liqueur coffee made with brandy and condensed milk

city + suburbs

Rengaya

73 Miller Street, North Sydney
Tel 9929 6169   Map 5a

Japanese

Score 14/20

Welcome to DIY marbled beef heaven. This is where Japanese expats pining for a jovial but classy yakiniku (table barbecue) meal get their fix. This 16-year-old stalwart, with its politely conservative decor and oversupply of waiters, offers F1 wagyu (crossed with angus) in every cut imaginable and illustrated in the inviting menu. Sip an Asahi beer while firing up the barbie, then dive for the wagyu outside skirt and short rib. Give each glistening pink beauty a quick sear on both sides, season as required then slide it onto your tongue and let the melting fat fill your mouth with flavour. Salted ox tongue topped with shallots and garlic refreshes the palate. Spinach and almond salad with fragrant sesame oil dressing is a nice diversion, as is the rich heat of kimchi. There are other options, including decent seafood if you're not feeling beefy, but the hearty and spicy oxtail rice porridge should solve any lingering hunger pangs.

Hours Lunch Tues–Fri noon–2.30pm; Dinner daily 6–9.30pm
Bill E $4.80–$39.90 **M** $3.80–$39.80 **D** $9–$18.90; set menus from $69–$190pp; 10% surcharge Christmas & New Year holidays
Cards AE V MC Eftpos
Wine Simple list; 5 by the glass; BYO (corkage $20 a bottle)
Chef Munenori Saitou
Owner Yoshiro Inoue
Seats 100; private rooms; outdoor seating
www.yakiriku.com.au
And…free on-street parking after 6pm

Republic Dining

Republic Hotel,
cnr Bridge & Pitt streets, Sydney
Tel 9252 6522   Map 1

European

Score 13.5/20

While financial quarter suits haven't had much to cheer about in the past year, they'll be pleased to know there's still somewhere to invest that offers a good return. Perched atop the Republic Hotel, this masculine nosh pit is a no-fuss homage to European fare at stellar prices. Affable and attentive service pleases the burly business crowd in a long room of brown tones, mirrored walls and white paper-topped tables. The menu gets right to the point with simple but satisfying combinations. Salmon, smoked in-house, lies under a runny soft-boiled egg while succulent prawns sauteed in chilli and garlic share the plate with crisp sugar snaps. An honest slice of pork rack combines pretty-in-pink flesh with crisp crackling, while a dollop of romesco sauce – tomato, capsicum and almonds – adds a sharp twist. Slide into a scrumptious lemon tart before returning to the office humdrum.

Hours Lunch Mon–Fri noon–3pm; bookings essential
Bill E $19 **M** $33–$39 **D** $12.50
Cards AE DC V MC
Wine Big reds, mainly Australian wines with a few Old World; 20 by the glass
Chef Chris Coolahan
Owner Patrick Ryan
Seats 80; private room; wheelchair access; bar
www.republichotel.com
And…private dinner bookings are available by appointment

good food guide

city + suburbs

Restaurant Arras

Ground Floor, 24 Hickson Road, Walsh Bay
Tel 9252 6285   Map 1

Modern British

Score 15/20

A remodelled bond store — sandstone, timber beams and distressed brick — meets double-clothed tables, fine cutlery, Riedel glassware and deferential, intelligent service. For a moment, it seems far too earnest. Then the menu arrives and the fun begins. Forget quips about British food, Yorkshire-born chef Adam Humphrey will upstage you any time. Nostalgics after a gammon, egg and chip Brit brekkie will be suitably tickled with his ham, runny egg, super-long, fluffy "chip", and tomato ketchup sorbet. A riff on beef includes rich beefy "faggots" and real beef tea in a pot. Emerald-green nasturtium soup with potatoes is peppery, creamy and smoky with eel. Diced spuds star in a Raj-inspired "curry" of sweet, white-fleshed mulloway and masala broth. There's more hilarity with desserts: a liquorice allsorts platter of liquorice fluff, allsorts ice-cream (sadly, a little weary), glass-like toffee sticks and more; or crumbly gingerbread nuggets buried in a divine ginger souffle. The finale is a Wonka-esque petits fours tray — rows of mini British confectionery replicas.

Hours Lunch Tues–Fri noon–2.30pm; Dinner Tues–Sat 6–10pm; bookings essential
Bill E $23–$31 **M** $30–$45 **D** $16.50–$17.50
Cards AE DC V MC Eftpos
Wine A thoughtful, careful global list with great NSW regional highlights; 21 by the glass
Chefs/owners Adam Humphrey & Lovaine Allen
Seats 60; private room; wheelchair access
Child friendly Highchairs; drawing materials; food can be adapted for kids
Vegetarian Two options in each course
www.restaurant-arras.com.au
And... a fabulous cheese trolley, too

The Restaurant @ Art Gallery of NSW

Art Gallery Road, The Domain, Sydney
Tel 9225 1819   Map 2

Contemporary

Score 13/20

When fauvist fatigue sets in or the surrealists start messing with your mind, retreat to the relative calm of this modernist glass box floating above Woolloomooloo Bay. Savour sweeping views, from Finger Wharf and the harbour to the architectural hotch-potch of the Potts Point ridgeline, as friendly, informed staff breeze around the room, happy to guide diners through the simple, contemporary menu. Kick off with a hearty and heavenly portion of crisp pork belly, enlivened with thin smears of black pudding and a sweet aside of spiced apple. The delicate citrusy zing of gremolata scallops, however, got a little lost amid a sea of creamed corn. Chicken saltimbocca with madeira sauce — cooked too long for our liking — packs a flavoursome punch with creamy leek dauphinoise while tender pistou (herb paste) — crusted lamb rump duets superbly with a fine ratatouille. Perfectly textured honey yoghurt panna cotta, served with decadent port-poached plums, proves to be a fitting work of art to finish.

Hours Brunch Sat–Sun 10–11.30am; Lunch daily noon–3pm; High tea daily 2–4pm
Bill E $18–$21 **M** $28–$32 **D** $15–$16; 2 courses plus a glass of wine $45pp, 3 courses $55
Cards AE V MC
Wine Decently priced, mainly Australasian selection of well-known drops; 14 by the glass
Chef John McFadden
Owner Trippas White Catering
Seats 120; private room; wheelchair access
Child friendly $18 kids' menu; highchairs
www.trippaswhite.com.au
And... visit the Botanic Gardens later

city + suburbs

The Restaurant at 3 Weeds

197 Evans Street, Rozelle
Tel 9818 2788   Map 5b

Modern European

Score 14/20

Full-length glass panes separate the trendy pub area from its restaurant, a spacious, elegant room run smoothly by a group of young, sharp staff. New chef Leigh McDivitt is no stranger to the scene, having spent the past two years working under his predecessor John Evans. Unsurprisingly, given its previous success, there's no departure from that style on a short, hearty menu that begins with Tassie Pacific oysters with a red wine and eschalot dressing. An entree of delicious morcilla, Spain's black pudding, complements both the sweetness of a seared scallop and the earthiness of truffled white bean puree. The briny goodness of crisp-skinned kingfish fillet is amplified by a fat, crab-filled squid ink ravioli. Dessert didn't quite measure up, however. Quince tart was let down by layers of poorly cored poached fruit and seemingly indestructible pastry, yet the flavours are on track, and the accompanying honeycomb ice-cream is alone worth the trip.

Hours Dinner Tues–Sun 6–10pm
Bill E $18–$23 **M** $28–$36 **D** $15–$17
Cards AE DC V MC Eftpos
Wine Impressive, exceptionally well-priced list of hand-picked internationals and locals; 13 by the glass
Chef Leigh McDivitt
Owner Rylely Pty Ltd
Seats 75; wheelchair access; bar
www.3weeds.com.au
And... 7-course tasting menu ($85pp), available Tues–Thurs, plus a fantastic pub menu next door as well

Restaurant Atelier

22 Glebe Point Road, Glebe
Tel 9566 2112   Map 5b

Modern European

Score 14.5/20

Atelier makes a statement in a precinct where dining quality can be patchy. It begins with a sense of occasion as you step off Glebe Point Road into a low, elegant sandstone cottage. There's a mood of formality in the exposed brick walls, polished floors and claret-red interior, but host Bernadette Templeman and her friendly, professional team put you at ease with warm smiles and a lovely amuse bouche, perhaps an exquisite, tiny seafood ravioli with chickpea puree. Darren Templeman carries impressive British kitchen credentials, and it shows in a European-style menu that is technically clever without being too overwrought or gimmicky. Wow moments include gorgeous king salmon crowned with beetroot sorbet; fresh WA marron tail with foie gras mousse; and boned rabbit with baby carrot, dried pear and ginger. It's everything Thumper should be and usually isn't. Did we mention the great old-fashioned peach souffle with apricot sorbet?

Hours Dinner Tues–Sat 6–10pm
Bill E $20–$25 **M** $28–$34 **D** $15; degustation menu $80pp, $130 with matching wines; 3-course menu $59pp (Tues–Thurs only; maximum 8 people)
Cards AE V MC Eftpos
Wine An excellent, short, hand-picked list of unusual local and European wines; 14 by the glass; BYO Tues–Fri only (corkage $12 a bottle)
Chef Darren Templeman
Owners Darren & Bernadette Templeman
Seats 75; private room; wheelchair access; outdoor seating
www.restaurantatelier.com.au
And... dine outside in the courtyard on a windless summer evening

city + suburbs

Restaurant Balzac
141 Belmore Road, Randwick
Tel 9399 9660   Map 9

French/British

Score 16/20

This is the real deal in an unexpected location – for those who aren't regulars, that is. But judging by the Balzac crowds, the secret has spread far and wide, and snagging a table can be a battle. A stylish colonial sandstone building in a dominant position at the apex of a suburban shopping strip coalesces with an elegant modern space and professional service to deliver boldly confident fare. Matthew Kemp's talent is using immaculate technique to elevate humble ingredients beyond their reputation. A pan-seared sardine with earthy beetroot ravioli and peppery rocket studded with capers is a brilliant entree. Crisp-skinned ocean trout with confit fennel and olives offers complementary contrasts. Slow-cooked pork loin with soft pillows of sage gnocchi, and pumpkin and cider jus features a witty asterisk of crunchy pig's ear. Desserts are another strength, especially the heavenly tarte tatin of tangy caramelised apricot and mellow almond ice-cream.

Hours Lunch Fri noon–3pm; Dinner Tues–Sat 6–10pm; bookings essential
Bill E $20–$25 **M** $32–$37 **D** $14–$17; degustation menu $85pp
Cards AE DC V MC
Wine A stimulus package of enticing international wines; 16 by the glass; BYO Tues–Thurs only (corkage $14 a bottle)
Chefs Matthew Kemp & Matthew Hollingsworth
Owners Matthew Kemp & Lela Radojkovic
Seats 110; private rooms; wheelchair access; bar
Child friendly Booster seats
www.restaurantbalzac.com.au
And… $50 Friday lunch deal

Ripples at Chowder Bay
Deck C, Building 7, Chowder Bay Road, Mosman
Tel 9960 3000   Map 7

Contemporary

Score 12.5/20

Although the interior of this heritage-listed building is shady and elegant with high ceilings and gauzy curtains, it's really all about sitting on the deck for Harbour views as scuba trainees paddle around Chowder Bay. Service is friendly and professional, if a bit uncertain and occasionally tardy, and the servings from the Italian-leaning menu are generous. Three knobs of deep-fried gorgonzola with dollops of date and lemon chutney are rich and creamy. Thin grilled asparagus with crisp guanciale, soft-boiled egg and balsamic reduction offers a great sweet, sour, salty balance to get the tastebuds tuned for battered flathead fillets with tarragon-scented tartare sauce. Grilled WA lamb loin on a bed of nutty pearl barley soaked in green onion salsa is almost enough for two. Fruit zuppa – slivers of peach, melon and apple in fruit syrup topped with crunchy blood orange granita – is almost as refreshing as a dip in the sparkling bay.

Hours Breakfast Sat–Sun 8–10.30am; Lunch Mon–Fri noon–3pm, Sat–Sun noon–4pm; Dinner daily 6–9.30pm
Bill E $16–$19 **M** $24–$29 **D** $14; 15% surcharge on public holidays
Cards AE DC V MC
Wine Extensive, well-priced, largely Australian list; 26 by the glass; BYO (corkage $8 a bottle)
Chef Vaclav Dvorsky
Owner Bill Drakopoulos
Seats 100; private rooms; outdoor seating; bar
Child friendly Kids' menu; highchairs; drawing materials
www.ripplescafe.com.au
And… a newer Ripples at Pyrmont and Whale Beach

YOU ARE HERE

to taste it all

Cafés & Restaurants
Adria Rybar & Grill	9283 3393
Baia San Marco	9283 3434
Blackbird Café	9283 7385
Chinta Ria	9264 3211
Coast	9267 6700
I'm Angus Steak House	9264 5822
Lindt Chocolat Café	9267 8064
Nick's Seafood Restaurant	9264 1212
Nick's 103	9267 4404

Bars
Pontoon Bar	9267 7099
Tokio Hotel	9266 0600

Nightclub
Home	9266 0600

Function Centres
Dockside	9261 3777
L'Aqua	9261 3777

COCKLE BAY WHARF
www.cocklebaywharf.com

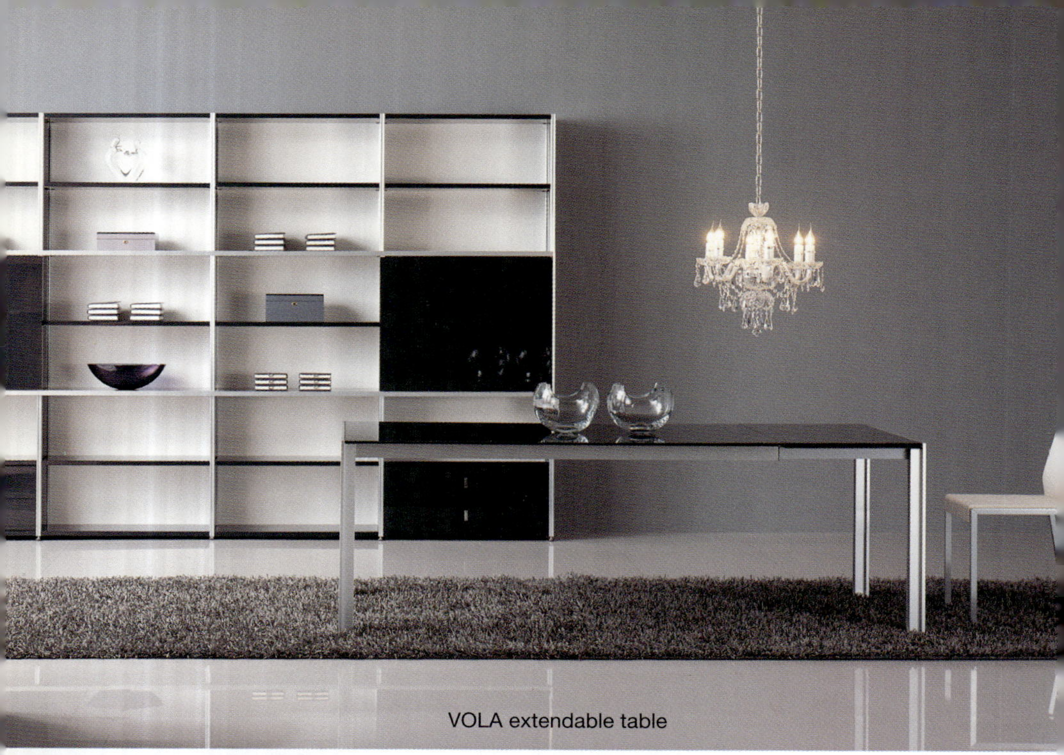

VOLA extendable table

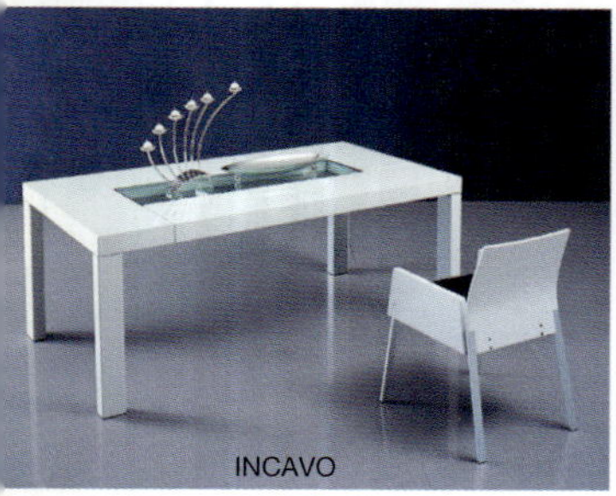

INCAVO

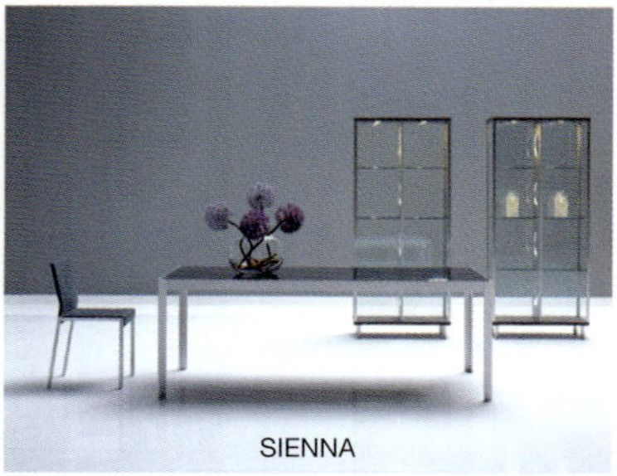

SIENNA

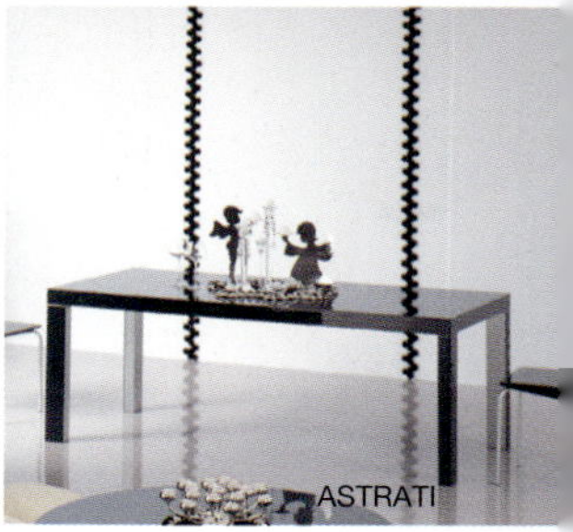

ASTRATI

To enjoy fine foods you need a stylish table.

www.beyondfurniture.com.au

BEYOND furniture

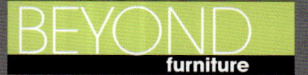

306 Pacific Highway, Crows Nest NSW 2065. Call 1300 11 22 33

Alexandria: (02) 9700 758
Belrose: (02) 9986 2639

city + suburbs

Riverview Hotel & Dining

RE-ENTRY

29 Birchgrove Road, Balmain
Tel 9810 1151   Map 5b

Modern British

Score 12.5/20

Our Dawn's old watering hole is back, with gastro pub aspirations. Climb the stairs of this 1880s pub to the carpeted first floor dining room with its comfy, modern decor in olive green and white, filled by dark timber tables and padded bistro chairs. The service seems a little matronly, and the comforting menu trawls the Old Country, with a few stopovers en route, thanks to chef James Watson's British background. It kicks off with several Italian-styled "tapas" before a short a la carte menu kicks in. Snapper chowder is pretty, with whole pan-fried fish amid a chive-speckled pool of broth sharpened by creme fraiche. Duck lasagne, punchy with pecorino, was let down by dry, minced meat. Veal scallopine with gremolata gets a little fancy with bacon gnocchi and osso buco sauce, while farmed kingfish with sweetcorn puree and peas pushes the lemon butter button hard. A martini glass of panna cotta with mandarin jelly and bitter chocolate mousse is classy.

Hours Lunch Fri–Sun noon–3pm; Dinner Wed–Sat 6–10pm
Bill E $17 **M** $28 **D** $13
Cards AE V MC Eftpos
Wine Long and strong boutique Australian with some overseas gems; 16 by the glass
Chef James Watson
Owner Brict Star Pty Ltd
Seats 60; private room; bar
Child friendly Kids' menu; highchairs
www.theriverviewhotel.com.au
And…four-course $65 "Trust The Chef" menu and $45 Sunday roast

Rocket

1–5 Railway Street (cnr Help Street), Chatswood
Tel 9411 8233   Map 7

Contemporary

Score 14/20

Who would've thought a bustling, throbbing train station could hide such a smart restaurant in its midst? At least the noise outside is not your tummy rumbling. Rocket is a sleek showpiece for Richard Allsop's highly tuned fare. Sure the outlook's not great (flourishing planter boxes of chillies, celery and kaffir limes soften the neon glow), but the food's fantastic, the service is switched-on, and the gentle hum from the open kitchen provides a pleasant distraction. When the meals arrive, it's all eyes on the plates, which are pretty as can be. Tomato chiboust is feather-light and deeply flavoured, the delicate mousse lounging between sharp parmesan wafers and a vibrant mix of tomatoes, olives and bocconcini. Excellent pan-fried snapper comes with a mop of sauteed chorizo, squid and iceberg lettuce, an apple-sweet tarragon dressing providing a neat counterpoint. Even the night's only misstep, an underdone apricot souffle, is soon forgotten, thanks to a platter of divine caramelised figs and lush honeycomb parfait.

Hours Lunch Tues–Fri noon–3pm; Dinner Tues–Sat 6–9.30pm
Bill E $18–$22 **M** $29–$37 **D** $15–$17
Cards AE DC V MC Eftpos
Wine Accessible, well-chosen list from the Old and New World; 11 by the glass; BYO (corkage $10 a bottle Tues–Fri; Sat $11)
Chef Richard Allsop
Owner Peter Fletcher
Seats 80; private rooms; wheelchair access; outdoor seating; bar
Child friendly Highchairs
www.rocketrestaurant.com.au
And…with transport downstairs, try the fine range of digestifs and dessert wines

city + suburbs

Rockpool

107–109 George Street, The Rocks
Tel 9252 1888   Map 1

Contemporary

Score 17/20

Rockpool turned 20 this year, and fittingly, after a flirtation as Rockpool (fish), has returned to the fine dining ethic that distinguished it for most of that time. Despite the opening of two new restaurants, Neil Perry's flagship remains in good form, due perhaps to new head chef (and former Josephine Pignolet award winner) Phil Wood. A return to a set four-course menu shows an eclectic, masterful use of spices, produce and technique. Overwhelming delicacy is the leitmotif of a beetroot platter – "raw, roast and jelly" – with a rich Roquefort millefeuille, while abalone with drunken chicken, seafood and vermicelli-like noodles is a subtle play on Asian flavours. These become more gutsy in melting, red-braised short ribs with gluey tendon and meaty shiitakes, or lacquered roast pigeon in sweet-tangy black vinegar. The signature date tart, oozing creme anglaise, is hard to resist but passionfruit souffle with passionfruit icecream provides serious competition. What else to say but here's to another 20 years?

Hours Dinner Tues–Sat 6–11pm
Bill 4 courses $120pp; 9 courses $195pp
Cards AE DC V MC
Wine Exceptional and expansive list; 32 by the glass
Chefs Neil Perry & Phil Wood
Owners Neil Perry & Trish Richards
Seats 120; private room; wheelchair access; bar
Child friendly Highchairs
www.rockpool.com
And... try the sleek, slightly more casual streetfront Oyster Bar on George Street

Rockpool Bar and Grill

66 Hunter Street, Sydney
Tel 8078 1900   Map 1

Modern Steakhouse

Score 16.5/20

BEST NEW RESTAURANT

The soaring, green marble art deco room is every bit as beautiful and breathtaking as the wine list, which boasts Sydney's most expensive drop (a '45 Romanee-Conti for $90 000, with a little change). The king of modern Sydney dining, Neil Perry, has brought his Melbourne steakhouse home in a final dramatic statement of his philosophy. The beef is aged on site, then cooked on the wood grill, which fills the cleverly lit open kitchen with smoky atmosphere. The extensive menu offers childhood reassurance in macaroni and cheese, creamed corn and succulent rotisserie chook with Tuscan bread salad. It's all about keeping great produce simple to speak for itself, from a hearty rubble of clams with serrano ham, flageolet beans and white wine, to a rich duck ragu with slightly flabby pappardelle noodles. From 11 steaks, listed by provenance, Cape Grim grass-fed on-the-bone rib-eye wins for both taste and price. Apple galette with brown butter ice-cream is the pleasure a dessert should promise.

Hours Lunch Mon–Fri noon–3pm; Dinner Mon–Sat 6–11pm
Bill E $15–$30 **M** $26–$110 **D** $6–$19; 15% surcharge on public holidays
Cards AE DC V MC
Wine An unbelievable array of the world's great wines, in varying vintages; 25 by the glass
Chefs Neil Perry & Khan Danis
Owners Neil Perry, Trish Richards & David Doyle
Seats 250; private rooms; wheelchair access; bar
www.rockpool.com.au
And... have a wagyu burger in the bar

city + suburbs

Royal Bar & Grill
Royal Hotel, 237 Glenmore Road, Paddington
Tel 9331 5055   Map 4a

Contemporary

Score 12/20

The Five Ways roundabout wouldn't be the same without the sight of diners enjoying sunset on the first floor balcony of this iconic pub. While the ground floor is a testosterone zone of punters watching sport, upstairs is more refined. At night it can be noisy but daytime is more relaxed in the old-school interior with wooden floorboards, chairs and tables. For starters, salt and chilli squid is nicely spiced with the lively addition of cucumber relish in marinated lime. Mains can be slow in coming but a complimentary drink and smile are welcome compensation. Spaghettini with cured salmon, rocket and lemon oil is a lovely collision of flavours. Alas, rib-eye steak was overdosed with bacon and peppercorn sauce, making the signature filet with bearnaise seem a better choice. On the sweet side of things, a generous serve of fig and brandy cheesecake is made to share. The setting and the tradition are the Royal's greatest assets.

Hours Lunch Mon–Fri noon–3pm; Dinner Mon–Fri 6–10pm; Sat noon–10pm; Sun noon–9pm
Bill E $12.50–$17.50 **M** $18.50–$29.50
D $8.50–$9.50; 10% surcharge on public holidays
Cards AE V MC Eftpos
Wine Solid Australian list with some premium names; 24 by the glass
Chef Keith O'Leary
Owner Foodsmith Pty Ltd
Seats 100; outdoor seating; bar
Child friendly Kids' menu (under $10); highchairs
www.royalhotel.com.au
And... open burgers with chips for $16.50

Safi
55 Ridge Street, North Sydney
Tel 9954 6146   Map 5a

Middle Eastern (Lebanese/Syrian)

Score 13/20

Wide stone walkways lead you through North Sydney's tree-lined back streets, past historic buildings and into a snug, friendly restaurant that brings authentic Middle Eastern cuisine to where it's well appreciated. There is restraint and a comfortable elegance to the decor. Simple square tables, white walls with matching designer chairs and a charming display of traditional objets d'art result in a clean, uncluttered space, fitting the literal translation of Safi: pure. This purity and simplicity still manages to translate to full-flavoured food – muhammara, a fragrant walnut and chilli paste, would make its Syrian homeland proud, and babaghanoush, the omnipresent eggplant dip, is strikingly creamy and smoky. Citrus-heavy fattoush lacked the essential onion but well-balanced tabbouleh scores one for the salads. Meats feature as well, especially skewers of grilled, marinated chicken shish taouk, and addictive makanek, spiced Lebanese sausages with lemon juice. To finish, ask the young, friendly waiters for ahweh (Lebanese coffee) and house-made baklava.

Hours Lunch Tues–Fri noon–2pm; Dinner Tues–Sat 6–9pm
Bill Shared plates $9.50–$17 **D** $2–$3; banquet menus $25–$35pp
Cards AE (+3%) V MC Eftpos
Wine BYO (corkage $3pp)
Chef Vic Philipossian
Owner Ani Philipossian
Seats 60; private room; outdoor seating
Child friendly Highchairs; booster seats
Vegetarian More than half the menu
www.safidining.com
And... the banquet is a great way to sample the variety of dishes on offer

good food guide   121

city + suburbs

Sahra by the River

2/76 Phillip Street, Parramatta
Tel 9635 6615   Map 6

Lebanese

Score 13.5/20

NEW ENTRY

Big white plates, table linen and an elegant space decorated with Arabic motifs and art – this is modern Lebanese with views of the Parramatta River. Add authentic food, friendly service, good music and belly dancing (on some nights), and the scene is set for fun times. Its cushioned outdoor space is also ideal for a quieter meal. Although familiar, the menu has influences from the broader Arab world. Lamb mansaf shows its Bedouin origins in purposely overcooked rice pilaf and tender lamb shanks. A salad of shankleesh, the Middle East's only mould-ripened cheese, is nicely pungent and salty, balanced by sweet red onions and peppery rocket. Steamed vegetables didn't do justice to Moroccan chicken and pistachio couscous, delightfully presented in a decorative tagine. However, crumbly, buttery parcels of spiced lamb sambousek bring an old favourite to new heights. While dessert choices are limited, an almond Turkish delight and cardamom coffee will have you happily drifting away.

Hours Lunch Tues–Fri noon–3pm, Sun noon–9pm; Dinner Tues–Fri 6–10pm, Sat 6–11pm
Bill E $7–$19 **M** $25–$39 **D** $8–$12; 11-course tasting menu $43pp, 15 courses $55pp
Cards AE DC V MC Eftpos
Wine A small, adequate, mainly Australian list; 10 by the glass
Chef Anthony Hasna
Owners Talal & Hanied Alamein
Seats 250; wheelchair access; outdoor seating; bar
Child friendly kids' menu; highchairs
Vegetarian A vast array of choices
www.sahrabytheriver.com.au
And... book in to see the gypsy fortune teller

Sailors Thai Restaurant

Lower Level, 106 George Street, The Rocks
Tel 9251 2466   Map 1

Thai

Score 15/20

In a city replete with pale imitations, this is not Thai for the timid. Sailors Thai stand outs amidst the historic sandstone and tourist traps of the Rocks with its boldly colourful, neatly modern rooms and sharp service. The flavours are big – a dramatic statement of the five cornerstones of Thai cooking: sweet, sour, savoury, bitter and spicy, which occasionally rises to a cacophony, yet mostly delivers perfect harmonies. Crisp rice cakes with chicken and prawn start things off with a big chilli bang, while the richness of roast duck salad is tempered by pickled-lime astringency. A special of lightly fried soft-shell crab is a tingling contrast of chewiness and crunch. Shiitake and oyster mushrooms are a garlicky, velvety counterpart to a rich and dense beef massaman curry. Desserts, unlike so many Asian offerings, are sublime, such as startling smoked coconut ice cream, paired with a sweet and sour pineapple and ginger sorbet.

Hours Lunch Mon–Fri noon–2.30pm; Dinner Mon–Sat 6–10pm
Bill E $24–$29 **M** $26–$39.50 **D** $12–$15; tasting menu $90pp
Cards AE DC V MC
Wine Brief and mostly Australian yet sympathetic to the food; 12 by the glass
Chef Ty Bellingham
Owner Peter Bowyer
Seats 90; outdoor seating
www.sailorsthai.com.au
And... try for an outside table and magical harbour views

city + suburbs

Sailors Thai Canteen

Street Level, 106 George Street, The Rocks
Tel 9251 2466 Map 1
Also at Sailors Thai Potts Point
71A Macleay Street, Potts Point
Tel 9361 4498 Map 2

Thai

Score 14/20

This little corker is a timely reminder of just how terrific Thai cuisine can be. Unafraid to explore the sour as well as the sweet, Sailors Thai Canteen serves up a veritable triple treat – vibrant fresh flavours, great value and a setting that still delights, 13 years on. Escape the bustle of The Rocks and pull up a bentwood chair at the long zinc communal table, slap bang in front of the buzzing kitchen, or snag a more restful balcony seat. Sure, the queues for a seat still form, but this is lively Thai that's worth the wait, and busting service keeps everything on the move. The stir-fried rice noodles with peanuts, dried prawns, bean curd, egg and bean sprouts is one of Sydney's benchmark versions of pad thai; deep-fried whole trout dressed with mint, shallots, lime and chilli is a zingy delight, the fish perfectly crunchy outside, juicy inside. And the Chiang Mai-style warm salad of minced duck and vegetables is like upmarket sang choi bau with a chilli kick. Sticky rice dessert soothes the palate before you reluctantly pitch back into the tourist throng outside.

Hours Mon–Sat noon–10pm; no bookings
Bill E $14 **M** $16–$28 **D** $12
Cards AE DC V MC
Wine Concise, very affordable, spice-friendly list; 12 by the glass
Chef Pacharin Jantrakool
Owner Peter Bowyer
Seats 54; outdoor seating
www.sailorsthai.com.au
And...try Sailors Thai in Potts Point, where it's not communal and you can book

Sails on Lavender Bay

2 Henry Lawson Avenue, McMahons Point
Tel 9955 5998 Map 5a

Contemporary

Score 13.5/20

It's long and skinny with maximum views. Luna Park and the bridge dominate. Ferries churn alongside the wharf just metres away. Sydney diners, eat your heart out. This is special occasion dining and the ultra-dim lighting (it fades with the light outside) only adds to the thrall. Food and service can fall short of the glamour location, however. A pretty entree of john dory was oversalted, the accompanying broccoli a little too soft, but preserved lemon puree is a neat twist. Strips of chorizo and capsicum cuddle up to seared squid curls, topped with almond crumbs. Crisp mulloway is delicately elegant with jamon and fresh peas, jumbled on the plate like an edible still life. Duck with swede puree, baby turnips and a sweet-spiced red wine sauce is all it should be. The triumph is melon salad for dessert – watermelon compressed until translucent, sparkling with pomegranate seeds alongside shiny watermelon jelly and ginger sorbet. Or perhaps vanilla crema catalana – a rich buttery swirl with hazelnuts and prune.

Hours Lunch Tues–Fri and Sun noon–3pm; Dinner Mon–Sat 6–10pm; bookings essential
Bill E $26–$31 **M** $35–$43 **D** $16–$17; 10% surcharge on Sundays & public holidays
Cards AE DC V MC Eftpos
Wine A serious global list; 25 by the glass
Chef Steven Skelly
Owners Greg Anderson & Patricia Nunes
Seats 100; private room; wheel chair access; bar
www.sailsrestaurant.com.au
And...follow the road right to the wharf and you're there

city + suburbs

Sakana-Ya

336 Pacific Highway, Crows Nest
Tel 9438 1468   Map 5a

Japanese

Score 13.5/20

This small shopfront has all the charm and style of a fish and chip shop, which is pretty much what the name means in Japanese. Fish reigns supreme, at affordable prices. As well as the standard sushi and sashimi there are some unusual, classy creations, plus basic home-style dishes. Usuzukuri, razor-thin sashimi cut from the fish of the day, is a delicate demonstration of great knife work. Grilled kingfish shows Japanese cuisine's gutsy side, with a whole fish head marooned on the plate so you can dig into the cheeks for gloriously gelatinous flesh. Rudderfish is served nimono style, simmered in a sweetish sake and soy-based sauce for perfect balance. Staples such as agedashi tofu and tempura are well executed, and there are interesting sides, such as sesame spinach and grilled beef tongue. Desserts are pretty limited: there's green tea ice-cream or a home-style sesame pudding. Better to finish Japanese style with soba noodles in soup.

Hours Lunch Mon–Sat noon–2.30pm; Dinner Mon–Sat 6–10pm
Bill E $5.50–$29 **M** $13.50–$39 **D** $7.50–$8; 7-course menu $66pp
Cards AE DC V MC
Wine Very basic wine list, but good sake range; 2 by the glass; BYO wine only (corkage $6 a bottle)
Chef Toshi Goto
Owner Yasu Yasuoka
Seats 75; private rooms
Child friendly Kids' menu
Vegetarian Six-course menu for $39pp
And… try the chef's tasting menu

Sanders Waterfront Restaurant

D'Albora Marina, 138 Cabarita Road, Cabarita
Tel 9736 2468   Map 6

Contemporary

Score 12.5/20

Let your worries drift away with the current while dining in this pavilion at the end of a jetty on Parramatta River. This airy spot is best enjoyed by day, as come nightfall, hot-pink lighting and a bright TV fish tank take away some of the magic. The fish-focused menu, though, will please any time. Start with a subtly flavoured ocean trout tartare hidden beneath salty potato crisps, with baby herb salad and beetroot jelly alongside. In a vegetarian dish, creamy Woodside goat's curd plays the starring role, served with warm brioche, half a black fig and drizzled with vincotto. For mains, a perfectly cooked crispy-skinned salmon fillet with salmon roe rests on creamy potato and celeriac gratin. Grain-fed beef tenderloin is chargrilled and lusciously tender, with sweet red wine onion jam, sauteed button mushrooms and sauce financiere (dark and truffle-infused). End with a refreshing affogato or indulge in choc creme brulee.

Hours Lunch Wed–Sun noon–4pm; Dinner Wed–Sat 6–9pm
Bill D $15; 2 courses $49pp; 10% surcharge Sundays & public holidays
Cards AE (+3%) V MC Eftpos
Wine Basic, affordable, mostly Australian list; 9 by the glass; BYO Wed–Fri only (corkage $5pp)
Chefs Belinda Geary & Lorenzo Crollini
Owners Grant Scott Philipp, Belinda Geary & Lorenzo Crollini
Seats 100; private room; wheelchair access; outdoor seating; bar
Child friendly Kids' menu; highchairs; drawing materials; kids' DVDs
www.sandersrestaurant.com.au
And… if driving, bring coins for the parking meters

city + suburbs

Sea Treasure

46 Willoughby Road, Crows Nest
Tel 9906 6388   Map 5a

Chinese (Cantonese)

Score 14/20

This stalwart Chinese is back with a vengeance, thanks to updated table settings, better food and friendlier service. What we appreciate most is the transparency in the live seafood prices, which can be elusive elsewhere. Live fish tanks along the glass frontage beckon you into this large, bright and breezy room. Both day and night dining are equally enjoyable. By day, salt-and-pepper prawns and spanner crabs offer luxurious variations to the usual yum cha menu. By night, the live seafood signatures dazzle. Stir-fried pipis, tossed in spicy XO sauce, are served on a bed of crisp, wok-seared noodles and blossom with flavour. The signature wagyu beef cubes in butter juices are smoky outside and still pink in the centre. Meanwhile, stir-fried Chinese mustard greens provide some balance and sensibility, just in case you're tempted into another round of the perfectly executed steamed scallops with soy, ginger and shallots.

Hours Lunch Mon–Fri 11am–3pm, Sat–Sun 10am–3pm; Dinner daily 5.30–11pm
Bill E $4.80–$36.80 **M** $12.80–$128
D $5–$24.30; $2.50pp surcharge (children $1) on public holidays
Cards AE DC V MC
Wine Familiar Australian range and plenty of reds; 7 by the glass; BYO (corkage $5pp)
Chef Lau Yui Wah
Owner Sea Treasure Pty Ltd
Seats 180; private rooms; wheelchair access; bar
Child friendly Highchairs
Vegetarian Numerous tofu and vegetable dishes
And... ask for a private dining room upstairs if you're a group

Sean's Kitchen

NEW ENTRY

Level 2, Hotel Tower, Star City Casino, 80 Pyrmont Street, Pyrmont
Tel 9657 9264   Map 5b

International

Score 14.5/20

An imposing bull statue invites you to step into the ring, marking the transition from the casino to this expansive dining room and bar. It's also the first of many Spanish accents running through the decor and menu, each section of which beckons with its own open kitchen station or display cabinet. Start with slices of imported jamon from the dedicated display case, silken Pambula oysters from the Ocean Shelf section, or try pigeon and rabbit terrine with high-rolling foie gras and truffle slivers. The less glitzy addition of a molten-yolked egg croquette steals the show. The grill turns out aged steaks with copper pots of bearnaise. A perfect pie crust releases a hearty tumble of tender rabbit and root veg. John dory, slightly overdone, is ably supported by clams with capsicum, tomato and jamon. Desserts range from the sublime – tangy milk sorbet with berries and elderflower jelly, to the ridiculously indulgent duck egg crema catalana.

Hours A la carte: Lunch daily 12–3pm; Dinner Sun–Thurs 6–10.30pm, Fri–Sat 6–11pm; tapas: Tues–Thurs noon–10pm, Fri–Sat noon–12am; bookings essential for restaurant, no bookings for tapas
Bill E $18–$40 **M** $24–$160 **D** $12; 10% surcharge on public holidays
Cards AE DC V MC Eftpos
Wine 300 Old and New World wines, as broad-ranging as the menu, 6 sherries; 18 by the glass
Chefs Sean Connolly & Tony Gibson
Owner Star City/Tabcorp
Seats 180; private room; wheelchair access; bar
Child friendly Highchairs
www.seanskitchen.com.au
And... on weekends, tapas in the bar till late

city + suburbs

Sean's Panaroma

270 Campbell Parade, Bondi Beach
Tel 9365 4924   Map 4b

Contemporary

Score 16/20

Despite a few changes in direction over the past year, this, beachside institution has sprung back as delightful as ever, reasserting its deeply soulful approach to food. Sean's is deceptively smart yet relaxed, aided by the view and tactile service effortlessly marrying casual charm and professionalism. Yes, it's cramped, loud and perhaps expensive, but the short menu on blackboard tiles raises comfort food to the Platonic ideal. Wrestle the sweetly briny flesh of blue swimmer crab from its fried shell to dip in finger-lime studded aioli or pick at a pretty salad playing on goat's cheese and hazelnuts with varied beetroot textures, both crisp and braised. A shallow bowl of pippis sings of the seaside, while wide green ribbons of nettle pappardelle with artichoke and thistle delivers wholesome satisfaction. A complimentary side dish of corn, roast potatoes and greens is both hospitable and delicious. Baked custard ringed by mandarin is typical of the seductive magic that always wins us over.

Hours Lunch Fri–Sun noon–3pm; Dinner Wed–Sat 6–10pm; bookings essential
Bill E $25–$45 **M** $33–$43 **D** $7–$19; 4-course chef's choice menu $95pp, 2-course lunch (Fri–Sat only) $65pp; $7pp surcharge on Sundays
Cards V MC
Wine Well-judged list with plenty of interest, and some excellent, modestly priced choices; 12 by the glass; BYO ($20 corkage a bottle)
Chefs Sean Moran & Lisa Rutherford
Owners Sean Moran & Michael Robertson
Seats 74; outdoor seating; bar
Vegetarian Good options
www.seanspanaroma.com.au
And…take home the delicious nougat

Selah

12 Loftus Street, Circular Quay
Tel 9247 0097   Map 1

Contemporary

Score 14/20

There's something to be said about small spaces serving impressive yet affordable fare with integrity among Circular Quay's flashier rivals. So don't dismiss the nondescript entrance and Selah itself (meaning "pause" in Hebrew). Culinary gems are served up by the friendly, efficient staff inside the milk chocolate walls of this cosy, recently refurbished dining room with colourful gingko leaf artworks. Seared scallops arrive piled high with finely shredded green papaya and duck, its sweetness lifted by a mint, chilli and lime dressing. House-made orecchiette pasta is tossed with king prawns in a flavour-packed garlic, chilli, lemon and parsley sauce. Cape Grim beef scotch fillet is chargrilled to perfection, with crisp potato and leek pie and roasted cherry tomatoes. Roast lamb rump, rich with Middle Eastern spicing, well-balanced by mint yoghurt sauce and eggplant relish, is equally satisfying. For dessert, a crisp, spiced mango filo tart hits the spot with creamy custard topped with roasted pistachio and mango sorbet.

Hours Lunch Mon–Fri noon–3pm; Dinner Mon–Sat 5.30–9.30pm
Bill E $17–$18 **M** $24–$32 **D** $15
Cards AE (+2.5%) DC (+3.5%) V MC Eftpos
Wine Small but steady Australian-dominated list; 15 by the glass
Chef Gavin Foster
Owner Sam Pask
Seats 55
www.selah.com.au
And…stylish, pocket-friendly, pre-theatre dining

Sepia

Darling Park, 201 Sussex Street, Sydney
Tel 9283 1990   Map 1

Contemporary

Score 15/20

This is a moment we've waited for: Martin Benn, Tetsuya's former head chef, with his own restaurant. It's a smart, clubby space of dark timbers with art deco touches, curving around the base of an office block. The menu's strong seafood focus is understandable with leading fishmonger, George Costi, as backer. Benn, like his previous mentor, blends an intelligent French approach with Japanese accents. Sweetly smoky barbecue eel reclines on vinegary sushi rice with additional interest from liquorice powder and leek confit. Creamy buckwheat "risotto" with spanner crab and mustard butter is covered in foamy shellfish essence, and shimmers with clever flavours. Alas, ocean trout confit was inexplicably short on flavour and seasoning, despite the accompanying bone marrow, braised mushies and roasted buckwheat. Butter-soft lamb loin and crisp belly with jerusalem artichokes, braised daikon and a mushroom broth is on surer ground, however, and service is smooth and wise. Citrus marshmallows with pineapple sorbet, mint whip and intriguingly, coriander sprouts, is like the best-ever take on a Splice.

Hours Lunch Mon–Fri noon–3pm; Dinner Mon–Sat 6–10pm; bookings essential
Bill E $22–$28 **M** $32–$42 **D** $16–$20
Cards AE DC V MC Eftpos
Wine A distinguished, well-priced global list; 24 by the class
Chef Martin Benn
Owners George & Andrea Costi, Martin Benn & Vicki Wild
Seats 80; private room; wheelchair access; bar
www.sepiarestaurant.com.au
And...it's a wine bar too, so drop by for a glass

Sevardi Cucina Italiana

1/12 Hannah Street, Beecroft
Tel 9980 1150   Map 6

Italian

Score 13/20

Antonio Abassi is king of the hill in leafy Beecroft, with this restaurant, the pizzeria next door and a cute cafe in the former post office at the top of the steep main street. Here is the flagship, enjoying longstanding loyalty from locals. There's warm hospitality in the greeting at the front door, and an appealing simplicity imbues the dining room with its wooden floorboards and photographic tributes to Roberto Sevardi, the famed photographer from Reggio Emilia in Italy's north. Much of the menu will please: good ravioli with pumpkin, walnut, brown butter and sage; an excellent veal scaloppine with prosciutto and white wine; memorable house-made gelato. Less satisfying was a sorely under-seasoned risotto and a john dory fillet short on excitement. The decibels can rise in this small room when there's a local crowd in and lots of laughter – and that's most nights. Service is smoothly professional and courteous.

Hours Dinner Tues–Sat 5.30–10pm
Bill E $6.50–$22 **M** $22–$30 **D** $8–$12; 15% surcharge on public holidays
Cards AE V MC Eftpos
Wine BYO (corkage $3 pp)
Chef/owner Antonio Abassi
Seats 30; wheelchair access
Child friendly Kids' menu; high chairs; crayons & books
Vegetarian Separate menu
www.sevardi.com.au
And...take a stroll up to the cafe at the top of the hill for a nightcap and a little local jazz

city + suburbs

Silvas

Shop 1, 82 New Canterbury Road, Petersham
Tel 9572 9911   Map 8

Portuguese

Score 12.5/20

Welcome to Little Portugal. Next stop, Silvas. Enter this informal neighbourhood favourite with the bustling takeaway section and, as your stomach starts grumbling, your eyes will be drawn across a busy, clean space to a large mural of a seaside town. This is Madeira, the former island home of chef Osvaldo Da Silva, and make no mistake, this is the source of the magic. Fresh prawns sizzle in garlic and oil, and a special of rich, citrussy pipis is worth fighting over. Both the barbecued octopus and grilled cuttlefish come in the same addictive sauce, but the latter wins the tenderness prize. Bacalhau a bras – salted cod with onions, potatoes and eggs – is hearty, but heavy with oil. Instead, try an espetada, a vertical skewer of charcoal-grilled aged rump served with grilled polenta. Of course, Portuguese chicken with chilli and garlic is failsafe fabulous. Desserts are on tempting display, so indulge in sweetly burnt creme caramel, if not the Portuguese tart. Or both.

Hours Tues–Thurs and Sun 11am–9pm, Fri–Sat 11am–9.30pm; bookings essential
Bill E $9.50–$16 **M** $19.50–$25 **D** $5–$7.50
Cards V MC Eftpos
Wine Small, suitable list with some interesting Portuguese; 14 by the glass; BYO wine only (corkage $2.50pp)
Chef Osvaldo Da Silva
Owners Osvaldo & Guida Da Silva
Seats 60; wheelchair access
Child friendly Highchairs
www.silvas.com.au
And...small and popular so make sure you book or you'll be queueing up for takeaway

Spice I Am

90 Wentworth Avenue, Surry Hills
Tel 9280 0928   Map 3a

Thai

Score 13/20

Five years on, the original Spice I Am is still a simple, convivial, hole-in-the-wall at the ho-hum edge of Surry Hills, with wooden tables and stools crowded under the pavement awning. Smiling staff stop running briefly to phone diners in nearby pubs waiting for a table. The menu is more than 80 items long, plus daily specials: and still no desserts. There's a joyous jangle and jostle of sweet, sour, salt and tangy flavours, chilli sneaking in the odd uppercut. Don't miss the special roast duck, finished in a slight batter, in tamarind sauce, or the textural triumph of superb soft-shell crab perched on julienned "green" mango salad, with its alluring citrus tones. Or har mok – the smoothest fish mousse, wrapped in a banana leaf, and ka nom jeen – fermented rice noodles with a gentle fish curry. This food is fast, with substance and subtlety. The punny name might still invite groans, but Spice I Am is always thai-riffic.

Hours Lunch Thurs–Sun 11.30am–3.30pm; Dinner daily 5.45–10pm
Bill E $7.90 **M** $13.90–$25.90
Cards Cash only
Wine BYO (no corkage)
Chef Sujet Saenkham
Owners Sujet Saenkham & Padet Nagsalab
Seats 40; outdoor seating
www.spiceiam.com
And...old standbys such as pork satay never fail

city + suburbs

Spice Temple
10 Bligh Street, Sydney
Tel 8078 1888   Map 1

NEW ENTRY

Modern Asian
Score 14.5/20

Neil Perry turns the chilli volume up to 11 to focus on evocative and feisty regional Chinese flavours. This low-lit basement room, surrounded by vertical venetian blinds that look like the lovechild of a paling fence and a Brett Whiteley match, is reminiscent of an opium den. The menu's 50-odd dishes range from stir-fried lobster to humble yet delicious ginger-and-garlic cucumber as a starting nibble. Preserved eggs with cool, silken tofu and a gingery soy, chilli and coriander dressing offers creamy, contrasting textures, while the lushly hot, sweet-and-sour "numbing" pork lives up to its name. The bubbling, interactive three-shot chicken is Perry's take on the Jiangxi province classic san beiji. Chocolate biscuits with caramel ice-cream and coffee granita is a just-in-case dessert, but the sweetly refreshing watermelon granita is a better bet. With generous portions, switched-on service and a pumping soundtrack (a bit too loud at times), Spice Temple rescues Sydney Sinophiles from the Cantonese doldrums.

Hours Lunch Mon–Fri noon–3pm; Dinner Mon–Fri 6–10pm, Sat 6–11pm
Bill E $8–$35 **M** $19–$120 **D** $10–$16; banquet menu $69 pp
Cards AE DC V MC
Wine 100 interesting, global wines at reasonable prices; 19 by the glass
Chefs Neil Perry & Andy Evans
Owners Neil Perry, Trish Richards & David Doyle
Seats 120; private room; wheelchair access; bar
Child friendly Highchairs
Vegetarian Numerous excellent options
www.spicetemple.com.au
And…check out the creative cocktails and fascinating tea menu

Starfish Avalon
23 Avalon Parade, Avalon
Tel 9918 2077   Map 7

Contemporary
Score 13/20

Starfish packs them in during the day with an appealing breakfast menu that gently rises a notch for lunch. Come evening, and despite softening touches, it's still a beachy cafe with noisy wooden floors, unclothed tables and ceiling fans languidly fighting the heat. The concise menu, however, is much more enticing; strongly Asian influenced with a slight nod to the Med. Flavours and textures sing in ocean trout tartare, with diced avocado, crisp cucumber discs, ginger vinaigrette and trout roe. However, fish sauce dominates wok-seared chilli squid salad in an otherwise delightful medley of Asian slaw, peanuts and crisp shallots. Sydney's favourite, crisp pork belly, has its richness cut with green apple and ginger salad while sumac-spiced lamb cutlets are deftly matched with smoky eggplant puree, pomegranate molasses, herb and goat's cheese salad. Apple, rhubarb and pistachio crumble was disappointingly thick and dry, but friendly, informed service and great presentation keep the locals coming back.

Hours Breakfast Sat–Sun 8.30–11.30am; Lunch Tues–Fri 11am–3pm, Sat–Sun noon–3pm; Dinner Tues–Sat 6–9.30pm
Bill E $15–$20 **M** $25–$35 **D** $6–$14; 10% surcharge on Sundays & public holidays
Cards V MC Eftpos
Wine Contemporary, affordable mostly Australasian list with a couple of standouts; 11 by the glass; BYO (corkage $7 a bottle)
Chefs Joji Shikama & Phillip Martin
Owners Shinny An, Phillip Martin & Joji Shikama
Seats 60; outdoor seating
Child friendly Kids' menu; highchair
Vegetarian Several lunch and breakfast options
And…sit outside and watch the world go by

good food guide

Steel Bar and Grill

60 Carrington Street, Sydney
Tel 9299 9997   Map 1

Steakhouse

Score 13/20

Urbanites fed up with waiting for the plethora of small bars promised under Macquarie Street's new licensing rules could do worse than bide their time in this glam space. Inside, pull up a leather upholstered chair amid slick industrial styling for a serious restaurant experience. The brigade in the luminous open kitchen presides over a menu of modern standards, from Asian-inspired salads and Middle Eastern mezze to Italian pasta, but takes particular pride in its ironbark-fired grill. A behemoth of a veal cutlet might land nicely charred with a rich jus and a layered potato cake, while a fine marinated spatchcock is doused with salsa verde. Outside, pretty young things at communal tables sip quirky cocktails and nibble from "small plates" – perhaps grilled fig with buffalo mozzarella, or platters of cured meats. Steel's service can be scatty, but one mouthful of the soft-centred pavlova and it matters not.

Hours Lunch Mon–Fri noon–3pm; Dinner Mon–Sat 6–10pm
Bill E $19–$24 **M** $26–$42 **D** $12–$18; small plates $4–$14
Cards AE DC V MC Eftpos
Wine The 3000-bottle wine cellar is a giveaway; a long and interesting list of locals and imports; 22 by the glass
Chefs Damian Heads & Charles DiMarco
Owners Nick & George Kyprianou & Damian Heads
Seats 140; private room; wheelchair access; outdoor seating; bar
Vegetarian Plenty of main menu options, plus small plates
www.steelbarandgrill.com
And... in winter, warm your hands and feet at the pit fireplace on the deck

Strangers with Candy

96 Kepos Street (cnr Phillip Street), East Redfern
Tel 9698 6000   Map 3b

Contemporary

Score 13/20

Strangers with Candy feels like the grown-up version of a uni share house: a little terrace of warm wood floors, where friendly strangers get stuck into the vino. The food fits too: eclectic, sometimes overly ambitious, but always enthusiastic. Tasty mussels with coriander and lemon start things off with a bang, as does a creamy, crispy, pork belly with spiced green papaya. Spaghettini with crab was disappointing – the crab lost in a waterlogged wilderness of pasta – but a special of handmade ravioli filled with parmesan and ricotta and lashed with burnt sage butter is scrumptious. The surprise standout is a wonderfully crunchy savoy cabbage and pine nut salad, while vanilla creme brulee with rhubarb is sour, sweet and stylish. There are good options for vegetarians, the service and servings are generous, and you bring your own wine. So channel your carefree student side, and enjoy the nostalgic ride.

Hours Breakfast & lunch Sat–Sun 9.30am–3.30pm; Dinner Wed–Sat 6–9.30pm; bookings essential
Bill E $16.50–$18.50 **M** $29.50 **D** $14.50
Cards Cash only
Wine BYO (corkage $3.50 pp)
Chef Veronica Stute
Owners Justin Wells & Veronica Stute
Seats 40; private rooms; outdoor seating
Vegetarian A good selection
www.strangerswithcandy.com.au
And... try brekky – great coffee – in the courtyard

city + suburbs

Subsolo
161 King Street
(cnr Castlereagh Street), Sydney
Tel 9223 7000   Map 1

Spanish/Portuguese

Score 14/20

In Sydney dining folklore, the better the view, the worse the food, so a windowless restaurant that's also below ground should be a safe bet. Subsolo (Portuguese for basement) delivers. What's more, it suits all comers – from those seeking a post-work cocktail to something more formal. The interior is all earthy brick and plush reds – the banquettes are very luxe – while modern tapas share menu space with more substantial dishes such as espetadas – attention-grabbing Portuguese skewers of meat, seafood or vegetables. Barbecued lamb cutlets with minted fig salsa and chickpea puree are a great start, along with garlic prawns in a wickedly creamy sauce – mopped up with extra bread. Crumbed meatballs ooze manchego. Paella with seafood, chorizo and chicken (there's a vego version) holds its own against an espetada of rump steak but the real culinary theatre is reserved for dessert and crema catalana, the toffee top made with a blowtorch at the table. Crepes with quince, while less dramatic, are also worth it.

Hours Lunch Tues–Fri 11.30am–2.30pm; Dinner Tues–Sat 6pm–midnight
Bill E $8–$25 **M** $22–$29 **D** $9–$14; 2-course lunch $25pp; degustation $55pp
Cards AE DC V MC Eftpos
Wine Good list of Iberian labels to suit most budgets; 37 by the glass
Chef Jacqui Gowan
Owner Richard Nichols
Seats 200; private rooms; bar
Child friendly Highchairs
Vegetarian Range of tapas and gluten-free options
www.subsolo.com.au
And… daily "El Desko" delivery to local offices

Sugarcane
40A Reservoir Street, Surry Hills
Tel 9281 1788   Map 3a

South-East Asian

Score 13/20

When we say this is a hidden gem, we mean it. You'll need directions to this part of Reservoir Street, so ask at any of the several backpacker hostels in this scruffy end of town. It's worth the detour just for the oysters with Sugarcane's own lime-chilli dressing, and an Indonesian-style grilled fish, with fiery tomato sambal, served in a betel leaf. The chefs/owners at this funky niche in the wall are Longrain alumni, but there seems to be more restraint and a lighter touch to many dishes and dressings. Where sourness is called for, the kitchen doesn't compromise, as in soft-shell crab with Thai eggplant, baby corn and Chinese-style pickled mustard greens. Pork hock with a Vietnamese style salad gives equal time to the freshness and fragrance of the herbs. The jury might be out on the decor here (for the record, we like the peanut-shaped light boxes) but we'll be back for the eats.

Hours Lunch Mon–Fri noon–2.30pm; Dinner Mon–Sat 6–10pm
Bill E $3–$9 **M** $15–$30 **D** $12–$14
Cards AE V MC Eftpos
Wine Small, affordable spice-friendly list; 9 by the glass
Chefs/owners Kitsana Aunarerom & Milan Strbac
Seats 50
www.sugarcanerestaurant.com.au
And… hard to find first time; it's just up from Elizabeth Street

city + suburbs

Sugaroom
Shop 2, 1 Harris Street, Pyrmont
Tel 9571 5055   Map 5b

Contemporary

Score 14/20

Pyrmont's water is flat and calm, perfect for the rowers who glide by Sugaroom's watery doorstep. Serene and smart, this is an inner-city sanctuary, with candles glowing on the tiles at dusk and the city lights reflecting off the water. The setting and attentive service are enough to please, but the food doesn't come second. Entrees are light and clean, particularly an intensely flavoured gazpacho cleverly served at room temperature to amplify flavour. An eschalot tart with beetroot, goat's curd and chervil has an appealing caramelised quality. It's a perfect introduction to a small, balanced choice of mains. Seared swordfish with Sicilian eggplant salad and anchovy fritters would benefit from a little more time over heat to marry it with the rich eggplant. A sirloin with perfect dauphinoise potatoes is refreshingly simple. Passing joggers could make you feel guilty about indulging in Eton mess with caramelised balsamic, but you're enjoying your city holiday, so take another spoonful and relax.

Hours Lunch Tues–Sun noon–3pm; Dinner Mon–Sat 6–10pm; bookings essential
Bill E $15 **M** $28–$32 **D** $15–$16; 10% surcharge on Sundays & public holidays
Cards AE (+3%) DC (+3%) V MC Eftpos
Wine Neat, food-friendly, Australian-focused list; 12 by the glass; BYO Mon–Thurs only (corkage $10 a bottle)
Chef Craig Donnelly
Owners Greg Anderson & Patricia Nunes
Seats 120; wheelchair access; outdoor seating; bar
Child friendly Kids' menu
www.sugaroom.com.au
And…a great selection of cocktails and mocktails is an after-work treat

Summit Restaurant
Level 47, Australia Square,
264 George Street, Sydney
Tel 9247 9777   Map 1

Contemporary

Score 13/20

We're slowly revolving past a spectacular view of Sydney Harbour at sunset, lamps emanate a pink glow into the very dim room and laidback tunes playing – it all feels a little bit disco up here on the 47th floor. However, there'll be no boogie for the formal, efficient staff, looking after the mainly older crowd impressed by chef Michael Moore's ambitious, theatrical cooking. Delicate smoked Petuna ocean trout becomes an indulgence with a creamy champagne broth, soft-poached quail eggs and the pop of salmon roe, although the croutons throughout proved soggy. Twice-cooked pork belly arrives with a stack of crisp raw-apple matchsticks on chunks of softly cooked apple, but the glass crackling was too leathery to sample. Desserts are a highlight. Roasted macadamia parfait on a choc-hazelnut base, not to mention the foamy vanilla custard, poached strawberries and gobstoppingly chewy spiced ginger cookies, are reasons enough to make us stay for another spin.

Hours Lunch Mon–Fri noon–3pm; Dinner daily 6–10pm; bookings essential
Bill Lunch **E** $23–$31 **M** $36–$82 **D** $18–$24; Dinner 2 courses $79pp, additional course $20; 10% surcharge on Sundays & public holidays
Cards AE DC V MC
Wine Comprehensive Australian selection with some big-name foreigners; 17 by the glass
Chefs Michael Moore & Brett Luckens
Owner Michael Moore
Seats 250; wheelchair access; bar
Child friendly Kids' menu
www.summitrestaurant.com.au
And…an imaginative cocktail list at the bar

The Good Seafood Guides.

Bank Street, Pyrmont, Sydney
Call **02 9004 1100** or visit
www.sydneyfishmarket.com.au

sushi e

Level 4, Establishment Hotel,
252 George Street, Sydney
Tel 9240 3000 Map 1

Japanese

Score 14/20

This is where the cool crowd tucks into glamorous sushi rolls, washed down with frothy sake concoctions, hidden away on the fourth floor above Establishment's pumping ground floor bar. Inside the white-marbled sushi counter that surrounds the groovy room, head chef Ura-san's confident knife skills are calming to the eye. Start with the gleaming fresh sashimi plate and move on to the expertly crafted nigiri, making sure to ask for recommendations. Quickly seared creamy salmon and sweet, milky yellowtail topped with crunchy sesame are clear winners. Refreshing ohitashi (boiled spinach) complements well-portioned sushi rolls, which may feel like mayonnaise overkill if you are trying to impress a date and order too many. The batter on fleshy Balmain bug tempura is airy and crisp, but the mayo-based chili dressing desperately needed a bit of zing. Plum wine and white chocolate tiramisu avoids the sickly sweet trap and is a joyful segue to more cocktails, downstairs or just next door.

Hours Lunch Mon–Fri noon–3pm;
Dinner Mon–Sat 6–10.30pm; bookings essential
Bill E $6–$17 **M** $28–$65 **D** $7–$10
Cards AE DC (+3%) V MC
Wine Smart list with impressive line of pricey French champagnes, plus great cocktails from adjacent Hemmesphere; 13 by the glass
Chef Nobuyuki Ura
Owner Merivale Group
Seats 38; wheelchair access; bar
Vegetarian Options available
www.merivale.com
And…don't forget your complimentary dessert

Szechuan Garden

Shop 1, 599 Pacific Highway, St Leonards
Tel 9438 2568 Map 5a

Chinese (Sichuan, Hunan & Peking)

Score 13.5/20

Newer, flashier places might have stolen their thunder but Mark and Penny Deng have been feeding us authentic Sichuan and Hunan fare for decades now. Just metres from a busy Pacific Highway corner, their mood-lit modern diner is surprisingly peaceful, although regularly populated with long-time customers – often in large work or family groups. They come in for all the signature dishes: tangy shredded lamb in Peking-style pancakes; luscious braised pork ribs Hunan-style – pulled from the bone at the table; salt and pepper calamari with fresh chilli; meltingly gooey eggplant and chilli-fried green beans. There's variety, quality and flavour in each individual dish as well as lots and lots of chilli – fresh and dried, plus the addictively unmistakeable tingle of Sichuan pepper. Service might appear aloof, however help is there for the asking, as well as advice on degrees of chilli heat. With its attractive red-splashed decor, this isn't an average suburban Chinese, nor is the food.

Hours Lunch Mon–Fri noon–3pm;
Dinner daily 6–10pm
Bill E $6.90–$16.90 **M** $13.90–$32.90
D $8–$8.80; 10% surcharge on public holidays
Cards AE DC V MC
Wine Serviceable, if small; 4 by the glass; BYO (corkage $3.80pp)
Chefs Mark Deng & John Yue
Owners Mark & Penny Deng
Seats 160; wheelchair access; outdoor seating; bar
Child friendly Highchairs
Vegetarian Plenty of options
www.szechuangardenrestaurant.com.au
And…it's around the back of a building on the Albany Street corner

city + suburbs

Tabou

527 Crown Street, Surry Hills
Tel 9319 5682   Map 3b

French
Score 14.5/20

Like a grandmother's hug, Tabou is a reassuring place to seek when your soul and faith need restoring. It's the epitome of a fine French bistro – a good-looking room of bentwood chairs, paper-topped tables, leadlights and specials on the gilded mirror. Unlike Paris, though, the waiters are happy rather than snooty, and the prices are as generous as the portions. Alisdair McKenna's clever menu offers deft classics, including a lush, twice-baked gruyere and goat's cheese souffle, as well as modern thrills such as roast and confit quail with boudin blanc (white sausage) and mushroom puree. His light touch reveals sound technique and a love for full flavours. Chou farci on mash with mushrooms offers hearty comfort – the cabbage stuffed with spice-scented offal: veal tongue, cheek and sweetbreads. Of course, there is steak frites, plus the endless pleasure of a sweet, scorched bombe alaska – if you haven't already succumbed to creme brulee.

Hours Lunch Mon–Fri noon–2.30pm; Dinner daily 6.30–10pm, Sat 6–10pm
Bill E $17–$24 **M** $27–$42 **D** $12–$15
Cards AE DC V MC
Wine Reliable, enjoyable and approachable list with French gems; 17 by the glass; BYO Sun–Thurs only (corkage $10 a bottle)
Chef Alisdair McKenna
Owners Rod & Julie McPherson
Seats 80; private room; bar
Child friendly Crayons and paper tablecloths
www.tabourestaurant.com.au
And...banquette seating in the upstairs dining room

Taiki

96 Longueville Road, Lane Cove
Tel 9428 1007   Map 7

Japanese
Score 13.5/20

Taiki, meaning "big tree", has attracted a solid local fan base since opening in 2000. Its old-school Japanese decor of smoky mirrors and subdued lighting is a simple backdrop for superb seafood and smooth service. Regulars perch on stools across from sushi master Fukunaga-san and marvel as vibrantly fresh sashimi is expertly sliced and heaped onto rolls. Follow wife Yukiko-san's words of wisdom and start with Hastings River rock oysters. Their creamy brilliance complements Taiki's sweetish milky sake, which is roughly filtered (cloudy) but smooth. Fatty o-toro nigiri of bluefin tuna is exquisitely seasoned with soy and wasabi. It's as modestly divine as braised pork belly, which is meltingly sweet with a subtle kick of Japanese mustard. Desserts, many served with homely looking cut fruit, are not where Taiki sparkles, so stick with ice-cream or relinquish your seat to other willing diners.

Hours Lunch Mon–Fri noon–2.30pm; Dinner Mon–Sat 6–10pm
Bill E $8.80–$16.80 **M** $19.80–$39.80 **D** $8.80–$13.80
Cards AE V MC, JCB
Wine Smart list of solid Australian wines plus sake; 12 by the glass; BYO (corkage $10 a bottle)
Chef/owner Yoshiki Fukunaga
Seats 70; outdoor seating
Child friendly Highchairs; kids' cutlery and bowls; drawing materials
www.taikijapaneserestaurant.com.au
And...lunch boxes from $19.80 are a hit with hungry businesspeople

city + suburbs

Taste on Sussex Lane

Unit 10, 275 Kent Street, Westpac Place, Sydney
Tel 9299 0888   Map 1

Contemporary

Score 13/20

While Taste promises casual dining, its approach is anything but, with liberal serves of good produce, personable service and attention to detail. Nestled in a courtyard at the base of an office block, it's a cheery mishmash of decorative tiles, criss-crossed beams, wrought-iron railings, screens and decorative old doors. No wonder this tasty spot bustles at lunch, for afternoon tea, and end of week dinners with cocktails. The grazing menu includes finely marbled wagyu bresaola complemented by celeriac remoulade. A marble slab bears a charcuterie selection of prosciutto, salami, rustic terrine, rich, smooth paté, pickles, grissini and bread. Delicately smoked Petuna ocean trout stars in a subtly dressed salad, with soft-boiled egg, potato salad and baby radish. Yellowfin tuna is tossed into an inventive slew of sweetcorn kernels, the odd pipi, crisp pancetta and a dab of tarragon oil. There's dessert of the day, as well as pastries, gateaux and tarts fresh from the in-house bakery.

Hours Breakfast Mon–Fri 7–11am, Lunch Mon–Fri noon–3pm; Dinner Thurs–Fri 6–9pm
Bill E $12–$18 **M** $18–$24 **D** $6–$10
Cards AE V MC Eftpos
Wine Well-balanced list, packed with good names; 17 by the glass
Chef Johnathan Mackfall
Owners Hieu Luong & Madeleine Cheah
Seats 120; wheelchair access; outdoor seating; bar
www.tastefood.net.au/sussex-lane
And...a great list of well-filled baguettes for light lunchers

Tastevin Bistro & Wine Bar

NEW ENTRY

Level 1, 292–294 Victoria Street, Darlinghurst
Tel 9356 3429   Map 2

French

Score 13.5/20

Yes, you're right. This was once Will & Toby's and more recently Ciel Rouge. We hope its latest incarnation as a well-priced French bistro lasts, in this quirky upstairs space with its rear bar and homely feel. And if the chef seems familiar, it's because French-born Alex Bourdon was a waiter (Bambini and Rocket) before returning to his natural habitat. His wife, Natasha, offers warm and chatty service. The small, versatile menu offers some dishes in entree and main sizes, including moules farcies, a luscious Provencal dish of half-shell mussels, crumbed, with garlic butter. Endive and fig salad is crunchy with candied walnuts and crowned by Roquefort mousse to deliver a harmony of taste and texture. Crisply pan-fried whole yellowbelly flounder is beautifully moist, amid brown butter, parsley and lemon, while scotch fillet in a rich red wine sauce with speck and potato is a fine take on steak and chips. Creme caramel de maman – Mum's rum-splashed take on a French classic – shows (chefs') mothers are always right.

Hours Lunch Thurs–Sun noon–5pm; Dinner Wed–Mon 5pm–midnight
Bill E $15–$17 **M** $24–$29 **D** $11–$13
Cards AE V MC Eftpos
Wine Decent, well-priced international list; 18 by the glass
Chef Alex Bourdon
Owners Alex & Natasha Bourdon
Seats 50; bar
www.tastevin.com.au
And...all-day menu, with croque monsieur and charcuterie at the bar

good food guide   137

city + suburbs

The Tea Room Gunners' Barracks

End of Suakin Drive,
off Middle Head Road, Georges Heights
Tel 8962 5900   Map 7

Contemporary

Score 13/20

This beautifully restored 19th century sandstone building has an elegantly chandeliered dining room and an expansive terrace that shows off breathtaking harbour views. Traditional silver service morning and afternoon teas tend to collide a little with lunch, so a quiet, relaxing meal can be a challenge. Scallops sit alongside blue swimmer crab-filled zucchini flowers, the plate scattered with broad beans and goat's curd. Five-spiced duck carpaccio is rich yet well balanced with a sprinkling of foie gras, raisin puree and hazelnut crumble. While it seems as though there's a lot happening on the plate, most dishes deliver. Sesame-crusted kingfish rests on an escabeche of spring vegetables and salt cod brandade. Crisp roast pigeon proves rewarding teamed with chasseur sauce, creamy polenta and radicchio. Strawberry sorbet laden with toffee, white chocolate and rocky road is irresistible.

Hours Lunch daily noon–3pm; Morning & afternoon tea Mon–Fri 11am–5pm, Sat–Sun 11am–3pm; bookings essential
Bill E $22 **M** $35 **D** $15; Morning & afternoon tea $28–$130pp; 15% surcharge on public holidays
Cards AE DC V MC
Wine Interesting, wide-ranging list; 12 by the glass
Chef Marc Philpott
Owner Manuel Spinola
Seats 130; private room; wheelchair access; outdoor seating; bar
Child friendly Highchairs; baby-changing facilities
Vegetarian Separate menu
www.thetearoom.com.au
And…a fascinating tea selection

The Tea Room QVB

Level 3, QVB (Market Street end),
455 George Street, Sydney
Tel 9283 7279   Map 1

Contemporary

Score 13/20

Walk into this magnificent former ballroom, and you'd be forgiven for thinking it's a tea time venue only. But there's more to the Tea Room than meets the eye. Impressive a la carte fare includes glossy barramundi with a salty crust, plus a single scallop ravioli parcel, broccolini and sorrel; and risotto with sweetcorn that cuts through a moat of gorgonzola foam. Service lapses – including a lack of cutlery and a long wait for drinks – suggest there's room for improvement (a little friendlier too, thanks). Bacon-wrapped prawns with couscous and mango salsa is given an unexpected floral lift by coriander, although the menu could be more descriptive. Summer berry panna cotta topped with strawberry granita is a respectable sweet note. And if tea's not your tipple, there are plenty of stronger options.

Hours Lunch daily noon–3pm; Morning & afternoon tea Mon–Fri 11am–5pm, Sat 10am–3pm, Sun 10am–5pm
Bill E $18 **M** $29 **D** $12; Morning and afternoon tea $22–$50pp; 1-course lunch plus a glass of wine $32pp, 2 courses plus a glass of wine $40pp (Mon–Fri only); 10% surcharge on weekends & public holidays
Cards AE DC V MC
Wine A solid list with plenty of lighter, lunch-friendly varieties; 13 by the glass
Chefs Mark Holmes & Keith Murray
Owner Manuel Spinola
Seats 200; wheelchair access; bar
Child friendly Highchairs; booster seats; baby-changing facilities
Vegetarian Separate menu with 3 entrees and 2 mains
www.thetearoom.com.au
And…28 types of tea (and gluten-free cakes)

city + suburbs

Temasek

The Roxy Arcade, 71 George Street, Parramatta
Tel 9633 9926   Map 6

Malaysian/Singaporean

Score 13/20

The signature Hainan chicken is only one of the drawcards at this tightly packed hawker-food haven, named for the ancient town now called Singapore. Singaporean breakfast favourite nasi lemak (literally "fat rice") is another triumph: a gleaming mound of (restrained) coconut-flavoured rice ringed with beef rendang, chicken curry, (these two with undertones of chilli), half a boiled egg topped with a slightly sweet onion sambal, ikan bilis (crisp, deep-fried anchovies) and diced cucumber. It's a mini banquet in itself. Eggplant belachan translates as long slices of squishy eggplant with shrimp paste and peanut sauce. Penang-style hor fun combines broad, flat rice noodles with capsicum, Chinese broccoli, mushrooms and snow peas, the noodles (chow fun) cooked by the heat of the sauce alone – a delicate, thickened chicken stock with egg white swirled through. Don't leave without a classic crushed ice confection of grass jelly, red beans, sweetened milk, syrup and little green cendols (pandan-flavoured drop noodles).

Hours Lunch Tues–Sun 11.30am–2.30pm; Dinner Tues–Sun 5.30–9.30pm; bookings essential
Bill E $4.80–$7.80 **M** $11.80–market price
D $4–$5; $2pp surcharge on public holidays
Cards AE DC V MC Eftpos
Wine BYO (corkage $1.50pp)
Chefs Susan Wong & Jeremy Cho
Owners Susan Wong, Jeremy Cho & Mei Ling Wong
Seats 180; private room; wheelchair access; outdoor seating
Child friendly Booster seats; lollies
Vegetarian A good range, but check the sauces
And…for a quieter dinner, book for after 8.30 on weeknights

Teppanyaki

Ivy, Level 2, 320–330 George Street, Sydney
Tel 9240 3000   Map 1

Modern Asian
Score 14/20 ♥

Ivy's upscale, Japanese-inspired eatery is themed like an oversized, highly lacquered bento box, cocooned by a hedonistic hub of bars. Find a spot, if you can, at the communal table abutting the frenzied open kitchen – the minuscule tables for two will test your juggling skills. Alternatively, head for the plushly spacious lounge chairs to enjoy tidbits from the teppan (grill) and beyond. Crisp buttons of speck add a fresh flourish to calamari salad with edamame and watercress sprigs dressed in Chinese red vinegar. A mod-Asian delicacy of stir-fried quail and pork sang choi bau is lifted with the crunch of fresh lotus root and peppery ginger. For melt-in-the-mouth decadence try twice-cooked Bangalow pork belly nestled on a salad of shaved fennel and apple with caramelised black vinegar. The only complaint is that portions barely stretch to sharing size. Dessert is either seasonal fruit or a sensational mousse-like green tea cheesecake. Japanese inspiration extends to the drinks list, too, with clever cocktails, sake and plum wine.

Hours Lunch Tues–Fri noon–3pm; Dinner Tues–Sat 6–11pm; bookings essential
Bill E $7–$39 **M** $19–$54 **D** $12–$15; banquets $40, $65, $75 & $95pp
Cards AE DC (+3%) V MC
Wine Sizeable, international and pricey; 14 by the glass; sake too
Chef Akira Urata
Owner Merivale Group
Seats 40; wheelchair access; bar
www.merivale.com
And…set menus cover everything from the grill to the wok

good food guide

city + suburbs

The Terrace on Pittwater

Newport Arms Hotel, 2 Kalinya Street (cnr Beaconsfield Street), Newport
Tel 9997 4900   Map 7

Contemporary
Score 13/20

This large, curving, corporate-looking dining room above a huge, waterfront beer garden aims high without forgetting its pub roots. The wine list bristles with heavy-hitting Aussie reds, although pouring by-the-glass wines at the table would add to the experience. The menu works hard to please all-comers, from a midweek special to a degustation, several steaks and seafood platters, as well as modern flavours and fashions on the a la carte. Quail roulade, just a little too rare in places, with lemon beurre noisette, was accompanied by seared scallops on sweetcorn puree. Like all the entrees, including mudcrab linguine with chilli, saffron butter and parmesan (an Italian faux pas for seafood), it's offered in main-course size too. Shepherd's banquet was a slightly clumsy three-way lamb-fest including a braised shank in a potato croquette. It's generous fare, so fine house-made sorbets should suffice.

Hours Lunch daily noon–3pm; Dinner Mon–Thurs 6–9pm, Fri–Sat 6–9.30pm
Bill E $14.90–$21.90 **M** $21.90–$39.90 **D** $13.90–$20.90; 2-course menu $35pp, 3 courses $45pp (midweek only); 10% surcharge on Sundays & public holidays
Cards AE DC V MC Eftpos
Wine Long list of benchmark Australian drops; 26 by the glass
Chef David Bell
Owner Bayfield family
Seats 160; wheelchair access; bar
Child friendly Kids' menu; highchairs; crayons
Vegetarian Separate menu
www.theterraceonpittwater.com.au
And… this pub will be 130 years old in 2010

Tetsuya's

529 Kent Street, Sydney
Tel 9267 2900   Map 3a

French/Japanese
Score 18/20

Only the bravest of culinary hearts attain cult status and, in that realm, Tetsuya Wakuda is king. Ditto his deft band of French-inspired kitchen ninjas, toiling mysteriously behind the scenes. Of late, however, we've wondered whether there's not a comfortable middle age to the menu. We'd certainly like a little more seasonality, diversity and innovative dazzle. Service is seamless, although it occasionally feels rote as each morsel on the 12-course expedition is delivered with a precise dissertation. At its best, nonetheless, you're left breathless. An amuse bouche of cold corn and saffron soup with vanilla ice-cream titillates. A single scampi, submerged in seawater, then lifted through lemon-scented olive oil, is a marvel, in a trio that also includes pancetta-wrapped scampi, and another with miso and passionfruit. Cape Grim lamb with rosemary and extraordinary wagyu with wasabi butter are beautifully cooked stalwarts. While gruyere with sweet lentils leaves us mystified, craftsman desserts – such as a cheeky little strawberry shortcake – are reliably superb.

Hours Lunch Sat from noon; Dinner Tues–Sat from 6pm; bookings essential
Bill Degustation menu $195pp
Cards AE DC V MC, JCB
Wine Unbelievable. A wine novella with an amazing plot. Let the sommeliers guide you; 24 by the glass
Chef/owner Tetsuya Wakuda
Seats 110; private rooms
Vegetarian Created on request
www.tetsuyas.com
And… resist filling up on bread and parmesan truffle butter

city + suburbs

Thanh Binh

52A John Street, Cabramatta
Tel 9727 9729   Map 6

Vietnamese/Chinese

Score 12/20

Here's what we love most about Vietnamese cafes: swift service, shared tables, endless hot tea poured straight from the Thermos and enough condiments on the table to pick your own adventure. The loud mix of locals, grandmas, children and food tourists adds to the low-fuss cafeteria vibe. But hidden in the menu of standard Indochinese fare are some surprises. Thick, roadside-style spring rolls, tightly packed with chunky pork, carrot and threads of clear noodles, are served with a squeeze of lemon and pickled cabbage. It's a Saigon sensation. Salty soft-shell crab has a light, crunchy batter; lime and pepper dipping sauce wets it just enough for that extra zing. While pho (beef noodle soup) was surprisingly disappointing, banh hoi chao tom (sugarcane prawns) on rice vermicelli cakes shouldn't be missed. Use the accompanying rounds of rice paper to wrap each morsel with mint and bean sprouts. For a lunchtime treat, try strong, Hanoi-style iced coffee with condensed milk.

Hours Daily 9am–9pm; weekend bookings essential
Bill E $8–$20 **M** $10–$40 **D** $4–$6
Cards V MC Eftpos
Wine BYO (corkage $2pp)
Chef Tien Dung Cao
Owner Thanh Can Huynh
Seats 90
Child friendly Highchairs
Vegetarian Numerous options
And... find more snacks and drinks at neighbouring street stalls

Tilbury Hotel

12–18 Nicholson Street, Woolloomooloo
Tel 9368 1955   Map 2

Gastro pub

Score 13.5/20

The light, bright dining room is framed by banquettes in burnt-toffee leather, looking out to the modern pub courtyard, and allowing in just enough buzz from the adjoining bar. Knowledgeable, yet somewhat casually dressed staff will take you through the Italian-accented menu. Seafood, pasta and classy riffs on trattoria/brasserie classics are presented simply yet carefully, for relaxed pub dining. Miniature zucchini flowers in super-crisp batter make up for their size with a salty brandade filling. A special of tender wagyu (marble score 5), teamed with onion puree and topped with a nest of onion rings, takes the comfort route. Even better is half a pan-roasted organic chook – forget the Colonel, this take on chicken and coleslaw is crisp-skinned, thyme-flavoured and enlivened by a cabbage and parmesan salad flecked with truffle paste. Finish with a strawberry Eton mess or a plate of French cheeses, before joining the punters on the other side of the bar.

Hours Lunch Tues–Sat noon–3pm; Dinner Tues–Sat 6–10pm, Sun 10am–8pm
Bill E $17 **M** $25–$35 **D** $10
Cards AE V MC
Wine Small, mostly Australian list; 14 by the glass
Chefs Bryan O'Gallaghan & Geoff Haines
Owner Mac Whitehouse
Seats 80; wheelchair access; outdoor seating; bar
www.tilburyhotel.com.au
And... start early with Sunday brunch

city + suburbs

Time to Vino

NEW ENTRY

66 Stanley Street, Darlinghurst
Tel 9380 4252   Map 2

Contemporary

Score 13.5/20

Casual, warm and welcoming, this accommodating little local caters for all-comers. Its eclectic wine list (including some organic and biodynamic drops) and simple, covers-all-bases menu work for drinkers, snackers and diners alike. The cutely worded menu consists of "waiting for friends" dishes such as marinated olives, crunchy parmesan-and-lemon-crumbed sardines standing in a glass of rich, tangy tomato aioli; and a serious charcuterie platter of organic salami, prosciutto, chorizo and lonzo (cured pork loin), with wedges of good brown bread and pickled vegetables. Once "friends are here", you might tuck into a rather tame but alcohol-absorbing bowl of spaghetti with garlic, chilli and parsley; or juicy and tender roast lamb chops with a generous side of excellent mash and garlicky spinach. The "who needs friends" section offers treats such as oozy, tangy, golden lemon curd inside a crisp, fragile pastry shell with decent vanilla bean ice-cream.

Hours Dinner Mon–Sat 4–11pm; no bookings
Bill E $8–$16 **M** $22–$32 **D** $10–$12
Cards AE V MC Eftpos
Wine Strong Old World focus, plus New World gems at reasonable prices, good half-bottle range; 35 by the glass
Chef Garth Bearman
Owners Nathan & Clint Hillery
Seats 60; private room; outdoor seating; bar
www.timetovino.com
And...snaffle a spot on the upstairs balcony with lounges and cushions

Toko Surry Hills

490 Crown Street, Surry Hills
Tel 9357 6100   Map 3b

Japanese

Score 13/20

Toko is all stylish good looks, with a crowd to match. A striking light sculpture beckons through the windows fronting the cocktail lounge – a smart meeting spot to sip a lychee and jasmine mojito and marvel at the cocktail and sake selection. Choose from the full menu in the bar or join a communal dining table in the warm timber, warehouse-style room. An open kitchen, sushi counter and robata grill provide plenty of theatre. (If only the somewhat unfocused waiters ensured diners had as much fun as they do.) Graze on chilli-infused edamame and more-ish soft shell crab dipped in wasabi mayo. There's super fresh sashimi and fingers of nigiri sushi with grilled eel and salmon. Juicy chicken wings with curry salt and lime; and Japanese-style lamb cutlets, marinated in hacho miso, with tangy homemade pickles, are luscious straight off the grill. Poached peach is matched with shochu jelly, raspberry sorbet and a generous splash of prosecco.

Hours Lunch Tues–Fri noon–3pm; Dinner Mon–Thurs 6–10.30pm, Fri–Sat 6–11pm; no dinner bookings
Bill E $5.80–$17.20 **M** $15.80–$54.80 **D** $11.20–$15.80; 10% surcharge on public holidays
Cards AE DC V MC
Wine Smart, concise and well-considered list; 23 by the glass; plus 32 sakes (16 by the glass)
Chef Keita Abe
Owners Daniel, Al & Matthew Yazbek
Seats 164; private room; wheelchair access; outdoor seating; bar
Child friendly Highchairs
Vegetarian Plenty of good choices
www.toko.com.au
And...bookings available for lunch and for private dining room

city + suburbs

Tran's

523 Military Road, Spit Junction, Mosman
Tel 9969 9275   Map 7

Vietnamese

Score 13/20

Known for its pungent nuoc cham (fish sauce-based dressings), punchy street fare and seamless French influence, Vietnamese food can be both exciting and refined. Lanna Tran attempts to walk a line between the two. With its turmeric-toned walls and jumbles of striking silk lanterns, this popular haunt offers a subtle take on Vietnamese cuisine, relying on top-notch produce and the flavour hit of fresh herbs to create dishes with broad appeal. Options skip from the trademark, though petite, crisp pancake (banh xeo) filled with pork and prawns, to ocean trout rice paper rolls that are fragrant with basil and a lemony hint of sorrel. And while braised oxtail and slippery rice noodles was somewhat muted in flavour, delicate banh beo (soft, silken rice cakes topped with prawns, peppery perilla and a dab of mung bean and coconut paste), show why Tran's has long been a neighbourhood fave. A classic creme caramel, given an exotic lift thanks to the addition of mango, provides a fitting end.

Hours Dinner Tues–Thurs & Sun 6–10pm, Fri–Sat 6–10.30pm
Bill E $8–$15   **M** $18–$28   **D** $8–$11
Cards AE V MC Eftpos
Wine BYO (corkage $2 pp)
Chef Lanna Tran
Owners Lanna & Tri-Tue Tran
Seats 120; private rooms; wheelchair access (downstairs only)
Vegetarian Many choices, but mind the fish sauce
www.transrestaurant.com.au
And…quotes on the menu from notable locals make for interesting reading

Uccello

Ivy, Level 4, 320–330 George Street, Sydney
Tel 9240 3000   Map 1

Italian

Score 14.5/20

We suspect the last days of the Roman Empire looked something like this sexy, extravagant, uber-chic playground, set by a cabana-rimmed swimming pool. By day it's business blokes enjoying a poolside perv; night brings the beautiful people attended by a funky, fun UN of waiters. It's a loud and lively party. Chef Massimo Bianchi offers a comprehensive Italian regional menu, with a leaning towards Rome. His take on his traditionally gutsy home cuisine is full of surprises, such as perfectly crisp crumbed baccala (salt cod) or suppli (deep-fried rice balls stuffed with mozzarella). Bianchi's bucatini all'amatriciana (pasta with tomato and cured pig's cheek) has an unexpected lightness, full of subtle flavours. Lamb chops scottadito (meaning "burnt fingers" – Romans use their hands to pick up the chops) drip with delicious, herb-infused juice. Fish is cooked in aqua pazza ("crazy" water) style with tomatoes and herbs. Desserts, such as fluffy zabaglione with buttery, house-made lingua di gatto biscuits, are beautifully executed. Hang it, go for the tasting platter.

Hours Lunch Tues–Fri noon–3pm; Dinner Tues–Sat 6–11pm, Sun 1–5pm (summer only); bookings essential
Bill E $19–$29   **M** $38–$48   **D** $15–$23
Cards AE DC (+3%) V MC
Wine A deep and comprehensive wine list with plenty of great and humble Italians, 18 by the glass; 12 grappas by the glass
Chef Massimo Bianchi
Owner Merivale Group
Seats 140; wheelchair access; outdoor seating; bar
www.merivale.com
And…stay on for the pool party

NEW TASTES TO TOUR WITH...

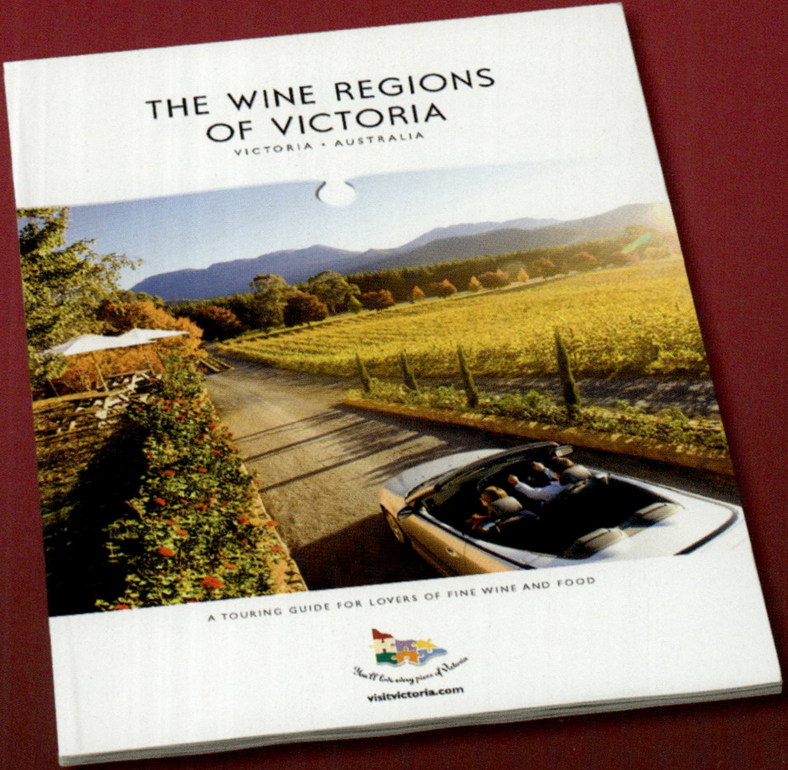

For your free copy of the new Wine Regions of Victoria guide, call **132 842** or for more information **visitvictoria.com/foodandwine**

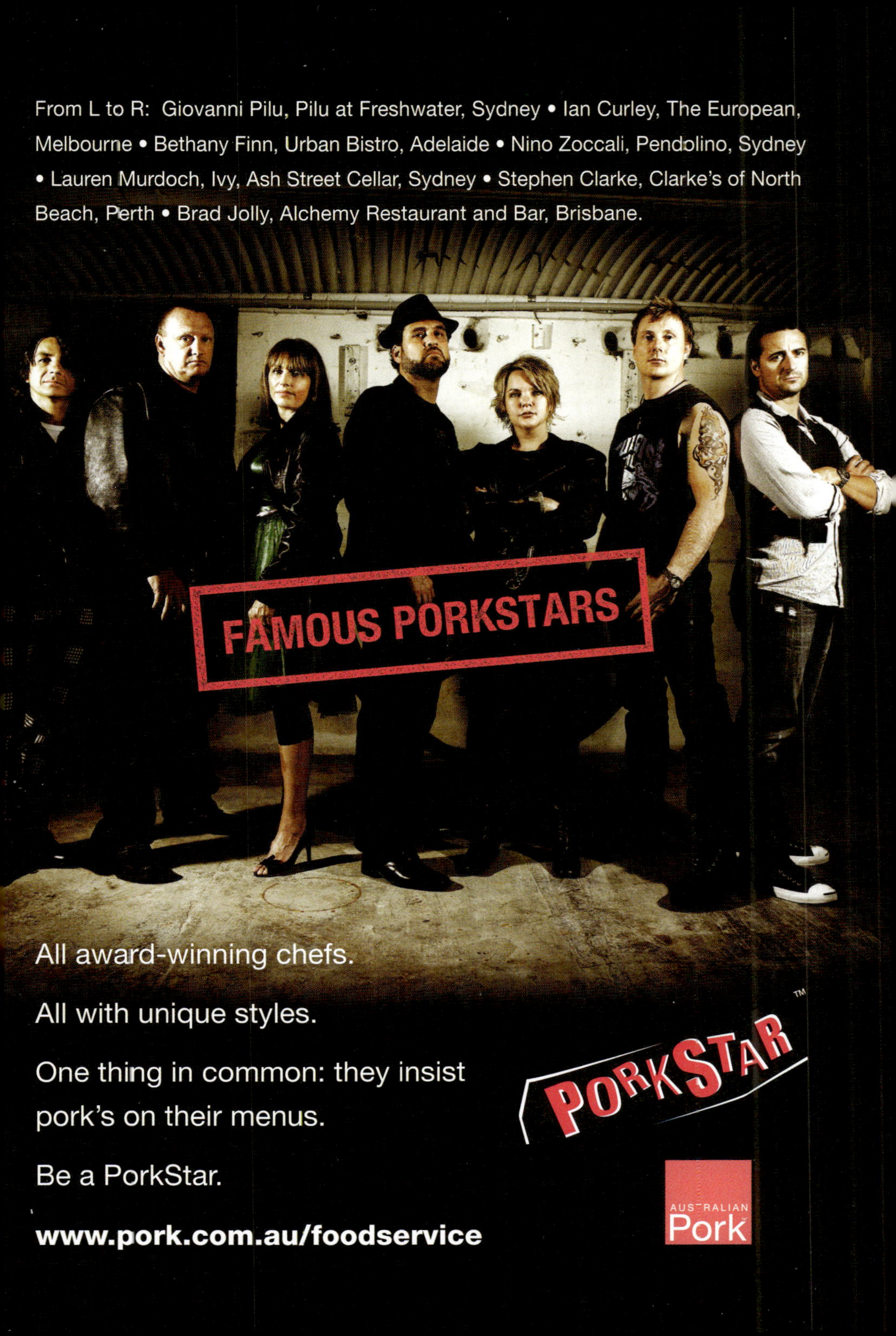

From L to R: Giovanni Pilu, Pilu at Freshwater, Sydney • Ian Curley, The European, Melbourne • Bethany Finn, Urban Bistro, Adelaide • Nino Zoccali, Pendolino, Sydney • Lauren Murdoch, Ivy, Ash Street Cellar, Sydney • Stephen Clarke, Clarke's of North Beach, Perth • Brad Jolly, Alchemy Restaurant and Bar, Brisbane.

FAMOUS PORKSTARS

All award-winning chefs.

All with unique styles.

One thing in common: they insist pork's on their menus.

Be a PorkStar.

www.pork.com.au/foodservice

Universal ★

Republic 2 Courtyard, Palmer Street,
Darlinghurst
Tel 9331 0709   Map 2

Contemporary

Score 16.5/20

FAVOURITE GLOBAL MENU

Buckle up. You're about to travel first class on a global tour of knockout flavours and masterful textural combinations. Your guide is trailblazing chef Christine Manfield. At Universal, a diverse but hip crowd enjoys the informal indoor-outdoor courtyard space. The menu is a selection of small, very sophisticated dishes – choose a series for your meal. Highlights include delicate tempura asparagus with the creamy heat of wasabi avocado puree, bright edamame and spears of salty samphire; and a soft spanner crab "pancake" luxuriating in a velvety smooth shellfish coconut soup. Miso-roasted hapuka sits alongside luscious pork belly; venison is lifted with Indian flavours – it all just works so well. While savoury courses reach new heights, Manfield has always been known for show-stopping desserts, such as her modernist take on a Splice ice-cream, and Carmen Meringay, a tall meringue cuff filled with chocolate mousse, blackberries and cherry jelly. This is one trip you won't want to miss.

Hours Lunch Fri noon–3pm;
Dinner Mon–Sat 6–10pm
Bill Tasting dishes $18–$30; sampler plate (lunch only) $35; 10% surcharge on public holidays
Cards AE V MC
Wine Truly globetrotting list; 25 by the glass (90ml out of the ordinary tastes matched to each dish)
Chefs Christine Manfield & Jessica Muir
Owner Christine Manfield
Seats 80; wheelchair access; outdoor seating; bar
www.universalrestaurant.com
And... Lunar Night dinners, last Tuesday of the month

Velero   NEW ENTRY

2/6 Cowper Wharf Road,
Woolloomooloo
Tel 9356 2222   Map 2

Spanish/Italian

Score 13/20

Is this the true face of globalisation? Take two Mediterranean nations, merge their flavours and wines, and place them in an outdoorsy, oh-so-Sydney waterside setting. Then brand it as an amalgam of tapas and cocktail bar and relaxed restaurant with paper-on-linen tables and polypropylene chairs and sunny service. There's no doubt Velero is a pleasant spot on the Woolloomooloo wharf promenade to spend the afternoon picking over olives, oysters, cured meats and Spanish cheeses. From the long Italo-Iberian tapas list, perhaps try a polite kingfish ceviche, cured tuna salad or a tortilla espanola with taleggio, pine nuts and rocket – fusion indeed. Mains tend towards Italy: perhaps house-made stracci (rag pasta) with braised lamb and pangrattato; or roast spatchcock with borlotti beans, cavolo nero and mushrooms. Fabulous desserts include a sexy marriage of coffee granita with hazelnut gelato and biscotti; and silken buttermilk pudding with cava-poached figs and candied almonds: gorgeous, in anyone's language.

Hours Lunch daily noon–3pm; Dinner daily 6–11pm
Bill Tapas $9.50–$19.50 **M** $27.50–$37.50
D $13.50–$14.50; 10% surcharge on Sundays & public holidays
Cards AE DC V MC Eftpos
Wine Long, sometimes pricey, yet appealing global list; 16 by the glass
Chef Craig McFarland
Owner George Vardis
Seats 150; private room; outdoor seating; bar
Child friendly Kids' menu
www.velero.com.au
And...simple nibbles in the bar all day

Ventuno

NEW ENTRY

7/21 Hickson Road, Walsh Bay
Tel 9247 4444   Map 1

Italian

Score 12.5/20

On the old waterfront among refurbished wharves and luxury modern apartments, Ventuno displays both real Italian style and real pizza, along with a small selection of classic dishes. The leggera di mare (seafood antipasto platter for two) shows real craft; deep-fried calamari is crisp and juicy, baby octopus is stewed in a rich tomato sauce, deep-fried harbour prawns are suitably crunchy, and there's a generous serving of decent smoked salmon. Tortiglioni al ragu, tubular pasta in a Bolognese-style sauce, demonstrates depth of flavour and complexity. If it's hot and humid, consider a refreshingly cold insalata di pasta with tuna, basil, olives, tomatoes and peas. Flavours are big and bold, occasionally too much so, with napoletana pizza suffering from too many black olives. For dessert there's Nutella pizza with hazelnuts, as well. Whether indoors or out, this is a lively little pocket of Italy with the best of Sydney views.

Hours Lunch daily noon–3pm;
Dinner daily 5.30–10pm
Bill E $6–$19 **M** $19–$28 **D** $9–$14;
10% surcharge on Sundays & public holidays
Cards AE (+2%) V MC Eftpos
Wine A smallish list of mid-range Italians and Australian/Italian styles well suited to the cuisine; 21 by the glass
Chef Roberto Taffuri
Owners Lido Russo, Vincent Aiello, Roberto Taffuri & John Verano
Seats 130; wheelchair access; outdoor seating; bar
Child friendly $15 kids' menu; highchairs
Vegetarian Good choices
www.ventuno.com.au
And…sip and snack on weekend afternoons, with hard-to-find Italian beers and complimentary snacks

Verandah

55–65 Elizabeth Street, Sydney
Tel 9239 5888   Map 1

Contemporary European

Score 13/20

There's a marked difference between lunch and dinner here. By day, the light-filled room of white linen tablecloths and more formal menu caters for executive types. By night, the cloths make way for a casual wine bar, serving tasting plates and more limited bistro fare. It's a good option after a few drinks next door at the popular Verandah Bar, although the latter's noise can be disruptive and the service patchy as the bar soaks up the attention. A generous serving of seared scallops delights, aided by sweet capsicum relish. However, lightly smoked sliced duck with beetroot and watercress salad could do with a tangy lift. Both dishes, entrees for lunch, return as tasting portions to share at night. Chargrilled scotch fillet with potato mash and forest mushrooms is pleasing, if predictable. Meltingly tender, yet crisp duck confit suits sweet potato mash and roasted cherry tomatoes. Give the rather limited dessert choice a miss and opt for the Australian and European cheese plates.

Hours Lunch Mon–Fri noon–3pm;
Dinner Wed–Fri 6–9pm; bookings essential
Bill E $18–$20 **M** $34–$46 **D** $12
Cards AE DC V MC
Wine Good Australian list, with a sprinkling of European; 25 by the glass
Chef Jonathan Ingram
Owner Haritos Hotels
Seats 100; wheelchair access; outdoor seating; bar
www.verandah.com.au
And…check out the well-priced tasting platters at night

city + suburbs

Verde Restaurant & Bar

115 Riley Street, Darlinghurst
Tel 9380 8877   Map 2

Italian (Southern)

Score 14/20

Why is Italian food so romantic? Perhaps it's the venue, in this case a beautifully restored two-storey terrace in the heart of East Sydney; warm, with candles and crisp white tablecloths. Perhaps it's the handsome waiters with their broken English and gentle solicitude. Most likely it's the glorious food. Lusciously creamy seared Queensland scallops are enlivened by a sweetly piquant beetroot puree. Baccala (salt cod) is delicately offset by calamari, fried with a touch of chilli and garlic. Confit duck is rich, dark and tender. Pan-fried gnocchi with ricotta- and spinach-stuffed zucchini flowers is wonderfully light and more-ish (so much so that it almost doesn't matter that it's also served with the duck). An outstanding tomato salad is simply tossed with olive oil and vinegar. To finish, of course, sensual tiramisu, covered in shaved Callebaut chocolate. Be still my beating heart.

Hours Lunch Tues–Fri noon–3pm; Dinner Tues–Sun 6–10pm
Bill E $6–$16 **M** $19–$34 **D** $12
Cards AE DC V MC Eftpos
Wine Thoughtful combo of Australian and Italian; 13 by the glass; BYO Tues–Thurs & Sun only (corkage $4pp)
Chef Antonio Ruggerino
Owners Antonio Ruggerino, Louie Kallas & Vince Squillace
Seats 88; private rooms; wheelchair access; outdoor seating; bar
Child friendly Kids' menu; highchairs
Vegetarian Separate menu
www.verde.net.au
And…continue the romance in the upstairs bar, complete with juliet balcony

Vini

3/118 Devonshire Street, Surry Hills
Tel 9698 5131   Map 3b

Italian

Score 14/20

The Italian enoteca is a wonderful place, home to fine wines and easy yet exciting snacks. Vini upholds the tradition with more than 50 Italian drops and liqueurs, plus food that takes centre stage. It's a small, ultra-urban space, crowded yet friendly, where you'll probably compare tasting notes with the next table. The seasonal blackboard menu offers the simple food of Tuscany and Lazio with plenty of heart. There's a hugely tempting choice of pasta and antipasto, plus just a few mains. Start with crostini, a Roman favourite: toasted bread topped with fish with capers or eggplant and mozzarella. Duck and beetroot tortellini is a lovely, bold combination with a rich and satisfying red-wine based sauce. There's pleasing, flavoursome simplicity in barramundi on a bed of lentils, as well as a big sirloin steak with roast peppers. Desserts reach beyond the usual. Spiced walnut cake with roast peach is rich and satisfying, and a ricotta and espresso panna cotta a neat little finish.

Hours Lunch Tues–Fri noon–3.30pm; Dinner Tues–Sat 6–10.30pm; no bookings (wait list over the phone from 6pm)
Bill E $3–$14 **M** $16–$29 **D** $4–$12
Cards AE DC V MC Eftpos
Wine A full Italian list from all the major regions, perfectly suited to the cuisine; 25 by the glass
Chef Andrew Cibej
Owners Andrew Cibej, Chris Walker & David King
Seats 55; private room; wheelchair access; outdoor seating; bar
Child friendly Highchairs
Vegetarian Good choices
www.vini.com.au
And…live it up and order wine from the migliori list (the best!)

city + suburbs

Waqu

308 Pacific Highway, Crows Nest
Tel 9906 7736   Map 5a

Modern Japanese

Score 14.5/20

The quiet elegance of this modern dining space with its glowing bamboo-woven lights and dark wooden furniture is a preview to Waqu's artful yet assured approach to East-West fusion. The five-course menu starts with an amuse bouche of crisp soft-shell crab sandwiched between two taco triangles and drizzled with Japanese mayonnaise and leek slivers, followed by ocean trout tartare with the kick of sharp wasabi cream dotted with salmon roe. There are three options for entrees and main courses. Salt-baked barramundi fillet with its crisp crust and grated daikon and soy sauce wins out over pan-fried calamari cake with abalone and squid ink risotto. For mains, moistly roasted quail is artfully wrapped in hoba leaf, oozing rich yuzu butter sauce. Beef tenderloin with red wine sauce, baby carrots and potatoes is meat'n'two veg, Nippon style. The dessert trio's green tea creme caramel, tiramisu and vanilla ice-cream is a fabulous fusion finish. That such an inventive meal costs so little is remarkable.

Hours Lunch Tues–Fri noon–2.30pm; Dinner Tues–Sun 6–10.30pm; bookings essential
Bill 5-course menu $55 pp
Cards AE V MC Eftpos
Wine Predominantly Australian and New Zealand; 11 by the glass; BYO (corkage $4pp); Japanese sakes and beer
Chef Tomo Usui
Owners Kana & Jumpei Nishikido
Seats 80; private room
Vegetarian 5-course menu $45 pp
www.waqu.com.au
And... try the unusual Japanese sake cocktails

Wasavie

8 Heeley Street, Paddington
Tel 9380 8838   Map 4a

Japanese

Score 13/20

The menu has decidedly shifted from fusion to old-school Japanese, but this chi-chi minimalist eatery keeps on wowing locals. The addition of a dining room alongside the existing communal table, and a new booking policy, means no more queueing, which is a bonus for this ever-crowded, value-for-money spot in one of the fancier parts of town. Start with a creamy, translucent sashimi platter and the enticingly rare beef tataki. Charcoal chicken salad is filling and refreshing with appropriately light soy dressing. The dashi jelly that accompanies the ohitashi (boiled spinach) served in an icy glass bowl, is as subtle and deferential as the waiters. But the not-so-marbled wagyu beef grilled on hot stone was too chewy and chunky to manage, and delicate saikyo miso-marinated ocean trout lacked personality. The signature "glass" desserts are gone from the revamped menu, so settle for house-made black sesame ice-cream and some soothing roasted houjicha (green tea).

Hours Lunch Fri–Sun noon–3pm; Dinner Mon–Sat 6–10pm, Sun 6–9pm
Bill E $8–$13 **M** $18–$32 **D** $4–$14
Cards AE V MC Eftpos
Wine BYO (corkage $3pp)
Chefs Naoki Hozawa & Naoki Fukazawa
Owner Saqura Investments
Seats 60; private room; outdoor seating (8 people only)
www.wasavie.com.au
And... weekend lunch set menu from $28

good food guide

city + suburbs

The Welcome Hotel
91 Evans Street, Rozelle
Tel 9810 1323   Map 5b

Modern European

Score 14/20

This Irish pub, with a 132-year history, is a hidden gem in a quiet suburban backstreet. New chef Alex Watts is back from a stint in the Mother Country, introducing a little bold Brit gastro-pub sensibility to the compact, reassuring bistro menu. The main dining room has a neat bistro look with paper-on-cloth tables, but the real fun is the tree fern-lined outdoor courtyard, with its opening roof and heaters ready to battle the elements. Lisa Wilkinson leads the efficient service, also tending a clever wine list. Roquefort, corella pear and walnut salad is a crisp contrast of sweet, bitter, piquant and creamy. Crisp-skinned quail stars on a smoky, sumac-spiced eggplant puree with a refreshing tomato, cucumber and mint salad. Gelatinous, dijon mustard-smeared beef cheeks, crunchy from a pan-fried breadcrumb coating, are lightened by pickled beetroot, frisee and an orange-scented gremolata. Desserts aren't a strong suit, although a steamed walnut and currant pudding offers plenty of comfort. And four European cheeses are perfect with another red.

Hours Lunch daily noon–3pm; Dinner Mon–Sat 6–10pm, Sun 6–9.30pm; bookings essential
Bill E $16–$19.50 **M** $26.50–$31.50 **D** $13.50–$21.50
Cards AE DC V MC Eftpos
Wine A long, classy and interesting domestic list; 15 by the glass
Chef Alex Watts
Owner Damian Silk
Seats 120; outdoor seating; bar
Child friendly Kids' meals; highchairs
www.thewelcomehotel.com
And...the great bar menu includes a cracker stout pie

The Wharf Restaurant
Pier 4, Hickson Road, Walsh Bay
Tel 9250 1761   Map 1

Contemporary

Score 14.5/20

Walk the well-trodden boards of Pier 4, where Cate and Andrew get all theatrical, to this warehouse-style dining room that's blessed with the ultimate Sydney backdrop – harbour and bridge views. Lately though, we've seen some mixed performances by this waterside star. An opening act of smooth gazpacho with ricotta fell flat, but a light, full-flavoured crab and egg soup, with a side of crunchy crab-topped toasts, is gripping drama. Simple dishes are the standouts: a generous serve of luscious roast chicken with bread sauce and watercress is comfort food at its best. Sharing centre stage is crisp-skinned salmon, its barberry sauce the perfect counterpoint, as is the accompanying salad of bitter redlof (red-leaved witlof), sweet carrot and mint. Mascarpone and pistachio ice-cream came with a lacklustre poached peach, but vanilla souffle with seville orange compote and pouring cream is a dessert worth crossing town for, and completely steals the show.

Hours Lunch Mon–Sat noon–3pm; Dinner Mon–Sat 6–10pm
Bill E $19–$22.50 **M** $26.50–$38.50 **D** $14–$15; 5% surcharge on Sundays, 10% on public holidays
Cards AE DC V MC
Wine Boutique list of Australian drops; 19 by the glass
Chefs/owners Aaron Ross & Tim Pak Poy
Seats 180; private rooms; wheelchair access; outdoor seating; bar
Child friendly Highchairs
www.thewharfrestaurant.com.au
And...dine alfresco on the deck

city + suburbs

Whitewater

35 South Steyne, Manly
Tel 9977 0322   Map 7

Contemporary

Score 13/20

This wood and wicker waterfront space – think beach shack goes black tie – gets a lot of things right. The stylishly clean decor and bifold doors keep it light, bright and casual by day, while the upper-level bar with maple floors, soft seats and open fire make it warm and sophisticated by night. The seafood-focused menu is similarly multi-purpose. Classic salt and pepper squid is at its tender best, but an eastern king prawn salad had too much fridge chill. Tempura zucchini flowers with goat's cheese was overwhelmed by powerful tomato chutney, but a Thai fishcake with smoked trout, coconut and cucumber is better balanced. Swordfish, simply grilled with a lemon olive oil, is well handled, so too sirloin steak with garlic mash. A chocolate tasting plate, including white chocolate fondant, chocolate sorbet, and chocolate brulee, might not be for those on a summer surfside diet but it's a generous finishing flourish.

Hours Breakfast Sat–Sun 8–11.30am; Lunch daily noon–3pm; Dinner Mon–Sat 6–10pm, Sun 6–9pm
Bill Lunch **E** $17–$20 **M** $19–$35 **D** $15–$25; Dinner **E** $18–$25 **M** $25–$40 **D** $15–$25; degustation menu $95 pp; 10% surcharge Sundays & public holidays
Cards AE DC V MC Eftpos
Wine Dynamic and comprehensive Australasian list, with a soupcon of France; 25 by the glass
Chef Luke Cesare
Owner Robert Hyde
Seats 110 inside; 40 outside; bar
Child friendly Kids' menu
www.whitewaterrestaurant.com.au
And… bag an outdoor table to watch the passing parade

Yellow Bistro & Food Store

57–59 Macleay Street, Potts Point
Tel 9357 3400   Map 2

Contemporary

Score 13.5/20

The light is soft under the large plane tree that shades the restaurant. Tables spill across the patio to the kerbside from this Queen Anne terrace. Opt for a meal, drop by for a ginger beer ice-cream spider, or coffee and one of Lorraine Godsmarck's splendid cakes. This was once the Yellow House, home of the dynamic '70s art movement, and the short, well-balanced menu is appropriately vibrant with well-composed dishes. A luscious tomato salad has a burst of pomegranate seeds, slivers of preserved lemon and a ping of sweetness from caramelised walnut pieces. A generous bowl of orecchiette (ear-shaped pasta shells) is doused with a rich oxtail ragout studded with twice-peeled broad beans. Diners wander through to the foodstore to choose dessert (hopefully there's date tart left) and cheese. It's all very casual, charming – especially the service – and unpretentious, just as a good neighbourhood bistro should be.

Hours Breakfast Mon–Fri 8am–noon; Brunch Sat–Sun 8am–3pm; Lunch Mon–Fri 11am–3pm; Dinner Tues–Sat 5–10pm
Bill E $18.50–$19.50 **M** $18.50–$32.50 **D** $8–$17; 10% brunch surcharge on weekends & public holidays
Cards AE V MC Eftpos
Wine A terrific, concise list, honestly priced; 9 by the glass; BYO (corkage $10 a bottle)
Chefs/owners George Sinclair & Lorraine Godsmarck
Seats 66; wheelchair access; outdoor seating
Vegetarian At least half a dozen dishes
And… is the impossibly light, intensely flavoured flourless chocolate cake the best in town? Yes

good food guide   151

Love food?

Then you'll love www.bankstownbites.com.au

Did you know that Bankstown is one of the best kept "foodie" secrets in Sydney?

Bankstown, a vibrant and colourful city in south-west Sydney, is a living showcase of cultural cooking and foods. From the incredible cuisine that locals call Bankstown-fusion to mouth-watering baklava, award-winning coffee and the largest Pho restaurant outside of Vietnam.

Visit www.bankstownbites.com.au to discover:

- **The Food Lovers' Guide to Bankstown**
  Download a guide with 5 self-guided Discovery Food Trails
- **Food tour information**
  Book a guided Discovery Food Tour
- **Business directory**
  Find a restaurant, food business or submit a review
- **Events calendar**
  What's on in Bankstown
- **Healthy lifestyle**
  Nutrition and recipes
- **Local information**
  Places to visit and local attractions to discover

BANKSTOWN
City of Progress

city + suburbs

Ying's

270 Pacific Highway, Crows Nest
Tel 9966 9182   Map 5a

Chinese (Cantonese)/Seafood

Score 13/20

Time was when this North Shore Chinese diner was trend-setting in its own right, with its brightly coloured walls and an intimate, local feel. These days though it has stiff competition from the new breed of smart Cantonese restaurants sprouting up around the city, so it may need to change a little to keep pace. The dining space is modern and elegant with its distinctive blue tables and orange walls, and service can be sleek and swift. Sometimes, though, waiters can be less than helpful, particularly when it comes to wine. The food menu has been simplified; unfortunately, so has the wine list, with many listed varieties unavailable and very few by the glass. However, our spirits are lifted when steamed whole barramundi with ginger and shallots arrives, brimming with generous soy and sesame sauce. The house-made tofu with minced prawns is silky and delicate and complements the fish well. The wok-seared beef cubes provide more excitement for the palate, with the tender and succulent beef packing a punch with wasabi sauce.

Hours Lunch daily 11am–3pm; Dinner daily 6–11pm; bookings essential
Bill E $6.60–$28.80 **M** $17.80–$38.80 **D** $5–$8.80; set price menus $45–$75; $4pp surcharge on public holidays
Cards AE DC V MC
Wine A limited Australian list; 6 by the glass; BYO (corkage $5 pp)
Chef Ken Yau
Owner Ying's Seafood Restaurant Pty Ltd
Seats 120; private rooms; wheelchair access
Child friendly Highchairs; half portions
Vegetarian Numerous tofu and vegetable dishes
And… daily yum cha is also an option

Yoshii

115 Harrington Street, Sydney
Tel 9247 2566   Map 1

Japanese

Score 15.5/20

FAVOURITE SUSHI

It's a shrine to the art of the sushi master, and to the purity of kaiseki – a series of seasonal dishes, designed for both the palate and the eye. So the arrival of Yoshii's exquisite sushi course (arguably the best in Sydney), after a cheek-puckering lemongrass sorbet, is at once jarring and revolutionary. This is just one assault on the senses chef Ryuichi Yoshii delivers during either of his two set menus (Yoshii or Saqura, changed just once a year) at his tiny lacquered bolthole at the back of the Shangri-La Hotel. Beautifully crafted ceramics arrive bearing a brittle zucchini flower filled with cuttlefish mousse, then slices of milk-fed veal adorned with jewels of forest mushrooms. Abalone, sporting a salt crust and swimming in its own juices, is a sensuous taste of the sea. Service, and communication, can be cumbersome, and the wine list needed an overhaul at the time of review (too many vintages past their use-by date, for example), but there's no faulting Yoshii-san's devotion to his craft and origins.

Hours Lunch Tues–Fri noon–2.30pm; Dinner Mon–Sat 6–10pm; bookings essential
Bill Degustation menus $110–$178pp; lunch set menu $38–$70 pp
Cards AE DC V MC
Wine International roll call of big and small labels, plus sake; 12 by the glass
Chef Ryuichi Yoshii
Owner Saqura Investment & Consulting Pty Ltd
Seats 40; private room
Vegetarian Degustation too
www.yoshii.com.au
And… shorter 5-course degustation from 8–9pm, Mon–Thurs

city + suburbs

Zaaffran

Level 2, 345 Harbourside Centre, Darling Harbour
Tel 9211 8900   Map 5b

Indian

Score 13.5/20

There are no gaudy paintings of deities (Bollywood or heavenly) in this stridently modern, decor-neutral restaurant that's taken the cliches out of Indian cuisine with great success since 1998. Soak up views of Darling Harbour lights as you explore a menu as diverse and colourful as the subcontinent itself. Spinach chaat is a crunchy play of textures crowned with the sweet-sour tang of tamarind. Juicy tandoori lamb cutlets come with a striking duo of sauces. If you're after something less familiar, "connoisseurs' favourites" include enormous (if less tender than hoped) lamb shanks in an intriguing sauce of red wine and pureed apricots, and a panoply of aromatics, served with mushroom naan. Wonderfully astringent chicken biryani (spiced pilaf rice) has a flaky pastry top that seals in moisture and adds welcome crunch. Service is a sea of smiles and politeness from waiters in head-to-toe black. This is Indian cuisine as expansive as the view, and worth seeking out.

Hours Lunch Sat–Sun noon–2.30pm; Dinner Sun–Thurs 6–9.30pm, Fri–Sat 6–10.15pm
Bill E $10.50–$19.50 **M** $19–$29.50 **D** $6.90–$11.90; banquets from $33.90; $3pp surcharge on Sundays & public holidays
Cards AE V MC Eftpos
Wine A cut above; 11 by the glass; long cocktail list
Chef Vikrant Kapoor
Owners Rush Dossa, Freddie Zulfiqar & Vikrant Kapoor
Seats 200; private room; wheelchair access; outdoor seating; bar
Child friendly Highchairs; mild dishes; drawing materials
Vegetarian Lots including separate banquet
www.zaaffran.com
And... free parking at lunch; cheap dinner deals

Zilver

Level 1, 477 Pitt Street, Haymarket
Tel 9211 2232   Map 3a

Modern Asian (Cantonese)

Score 13/20

Removed from central Chinatown's hustle and bustle, Zilver feels like quite a discovery, hidden up an escalator in a deserted (at night) office complex. But this cavernous space of reds and burgundies is a favourite for yum cha and celebratory family dinners. The extensive and easily navigated menu is divided into contemporary Asian fusion and classic dishes, with smart photography. The intriguing egg tofu mounds with scallops and roe look as pretty as baby creme caramels, with a similarly creamy texture. A more conventional snow crab, fresh from the tank, sits in chunky pieces atop fine noodles in a ginger and shallot sauce. It's outstandingly good. A steaming plate of three kinds of mushrooms is beautifully rich, melting in garlic sauce. While serenity in a Chinese restaurant is a rare treat, the service is a little too relaxed and can be absent or forgetful. Plates piled high with dumplings and barbecue dishes tempt, however a plate of fruit to finish is all that's needed.

Hours Lunch Mon–Fri 10am–3.30pm, Sat–Sun 9am–3.30pm; Dinner daily 5.30–11pm; bookings essential
Bill E $6.80–$16.80 **M** $16.80–$128 **D** $4.50–$8.80; $2.50 pp lunch surcharge ($3pp dinner surcharge) on public holidays
Cards AE DC V MC
Wine Decent list with recognisable names and reasonably priced; 8 by the glass; BYO (corkage $10 a bottle)
Chef Philip Chun
Owner Henry Tang
Seats 550; private rooms; bar
Child friendly Highchairs
Vegetarian Plenty of choice
www.zilver.com.au
And... generous portions so ask for a doggy bag

Bars
By Paul Chai

Ash St Cellar
1 Ash Street, Sydney
Tel 9240 3000
FAVOURITE WINE BAR
The imposing wine wall and equally imposing wine list — arranged by sommelier Franck Moreau into tastes and bouquets rather than varieties — show Ash Street is serious about its vino. It is also the most brooding, and charming, bar in the Ivy megaplex.

The Beresford Hotel
354 Bourke Street, Darlinghurst
Tel 9357 1111
A Sydney classic moves from seedy to savvy after a multimillion-dollar refit. The art deco front room has been given contemporary flair courtesy of a huge new island bar manned by drinks whiz Andy Penney, but it's still a great place for a beer, although you might have to dress a bit better than you did in the old days.

Hugos Lounge
33 Bayswater Road, Kings Cross
Tel 9332 1227
This low-lit, banquette-lined balcony space has allowed Sydney's dedicated party contingent to hold court for many a Cosmo-fuelled year, combining a winning mix of seasonal drinks, come-hither lighting and DJs who read the mood of the room rather than impose their own.

Kit & Kaboodle
33–37 Darlinghurst Road, Kings Cross
Tel 9368 0300
With two floors — one Asian-themed, one Doris Day meets private club — this Kings Cross newcomer has quirky takes on the classics (a Roger Ramjet Iced Tea anyone?) and is part of Sugarmill, a grand new drinking hole in a high-ceilinged former bank.

The Local Taphouse
122 Flinders Street, Darlinghurst
Tel 9360 0088
This Melbourne import (first opened in St Kilda in 2008) looks like the lovechild of a beer cafe and a laneway bar, and is housed in the angular old Palace Hotel. Preloved Chesterfields, dislocated antique tram chairs and a passion for beer (20 tap brews, 60-plus bottled and a rotating guest brewery) make this hop lovers' heaven.

Low 302
302 Crown Street, Darlinghurst
Tel 9368 1548
A pared-back, laidback Darlo addition, Low 302 has deco lady lamps, an English-pub style cosiness, interesting spirits, blackboard specials and a vibe proving that less can be more-ish.

bars + cafes

Opera Bar
Lower Concourse Level, Sydney Opera House, Sydney
Tel 9247 1666
This brash, brassy, live-jazz fuelled hotspot, at the base of the Sydney Opera House, allows you to sip a well-crafted cocktail while drinking in one of the best views in the world.

The Rum Diaries
288 Bondi Road, Bondi
Tel 9300 0440
There's so much dark wood here you could be imbibing inside an old rum barrel. More than 100 rums are put to good use in a cocktail menu that spans the drink's centuries of history.

Small Bar
48 Erskine Street, Sydney
Tel 9279 0782
Small is a bit of a misnomer for this vertiginous three-storey drinking den in a pokey CBD terrace. It refers to the fact that it's officially Sydney's first "laneway bar" under the much-heralded (but cumbersome and slothful) new liquor laws. It's less intimate than you'd expect, attracting a boisterous city crowd for after-work drinks, but it's a start.

Sticky Bar
182 Campbell Street, Surry Hills (entry via Taggerts Lane)
Tel 0416 096 916
It's like a well-organised house party, with better drinks and live music filtered through from the downstairs restaurant. The room is pipe-and-slippers cosy with funky touches, such as black-and-white photos and the ubiquitous exposed bricks; proof it didn't take new legislation to create great drinking holes.

Time to Vino
66 Stanley Street, Darlinghurst
Tel 9380 4252
The owners of this classic wine bar wanted to produce a mature watering hole, and they've hit the mark. The look is simple with wine-themed decor and mood lighting, but what draws us back is the depth of knowledge and passion – as well as the *Cheers*-style welcome.

The Vanguard
42 King Street, Newtown
Tel 9557 7992
Part ruby-red bordello, part absinthe-soaked Parisian boite with a penchant for live blues and roots, this venue recently revamped its cocktail list. Try a Voodoo (containing the Green Fairy herself) or a Billie Holiday.

Velluto
7/50 Macleay Street, Potts Point
Tel 9357 1100
An ornate little room with floor-to-ceiling black velvet curtains, medieval banquet chairs and a sandstone feature wall, this self-proclaimed champagne bar certainly takes its fizz and wine seriously with an extensive tome of wines, many by the glass.

Victoria Room
Level 1, 235 Victoria Street, Darlinghurst
Tel 9357 4488
There are shades of *A Passage to India* in this regal room tucked away off Darlo's bustling strip with afternoon high teas as well as sours, fizzes, juleps and the appropriately named Raspberry Debonair.

Zeta
Level 4, Hilton Sydney, 488 George Street, Sydney
Tel 9265 6070
Grant Collins's zeal for cocktails keeps this Hilton hangout a must-visit for lovers of the shaken and stirred. Now he's gone retro with a speakeasy-style menu of forgotten classics in antique glassware. Try a Ping Pong served Prohibition-style inside a hollowed-out book.

See also: Bambini Wine Room, Bayswater Brasserie, Foveaux Restaurant + Bar, Icebergs Dining Room and Bar, The Lord Dudley, Lotus, Madam Fling Flong and Trademark Hotel.

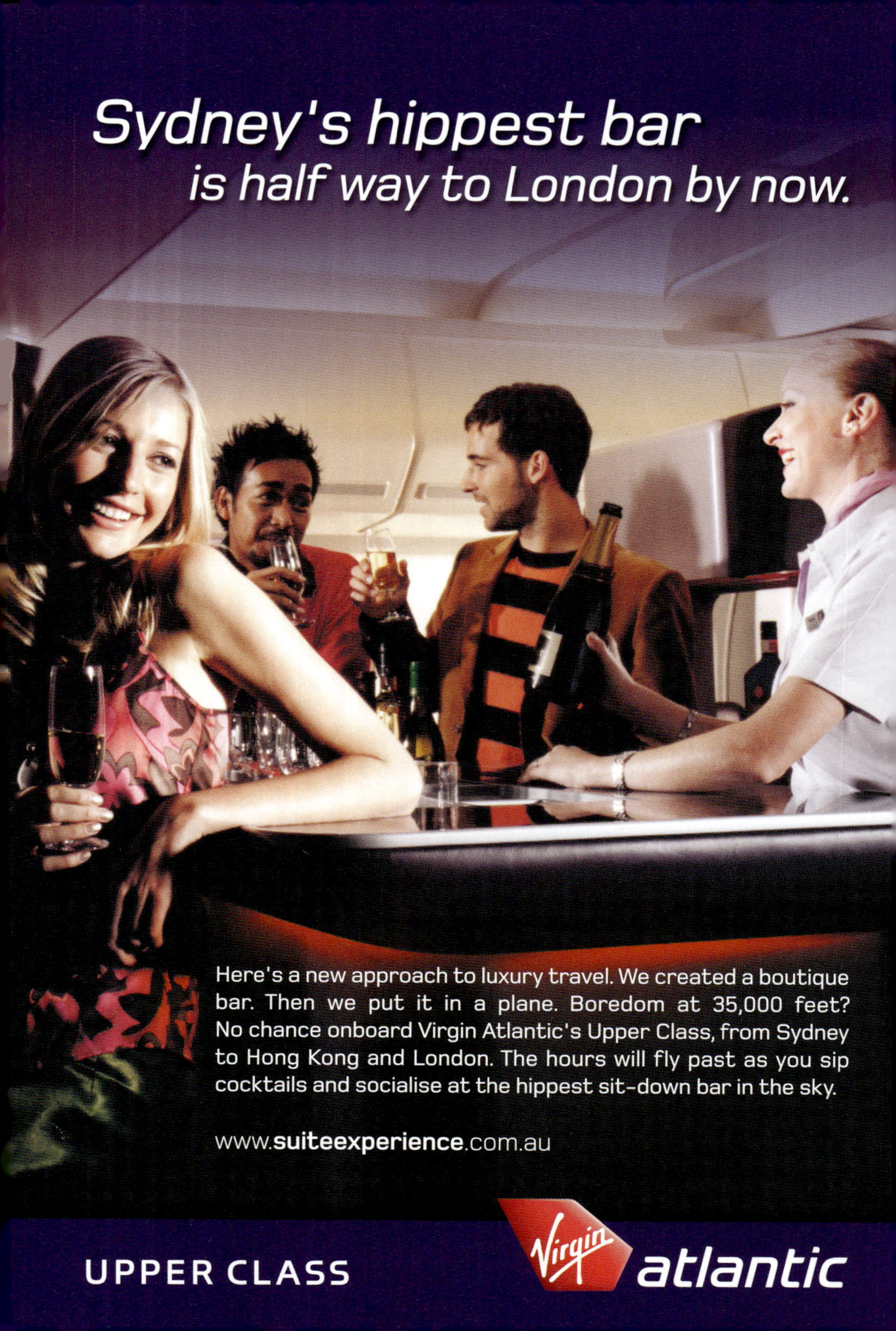
Sydney's hippest bar
is half way to London by now.
Here's a new approach to luxury travel. We created a boutique bar. Then we put it in a plane. Boredom at 35,000 feet? No chance onboard Virgin Atlantic's Upper Class, from Sydney to Hong Kong and London. The hours will fly past as you sip cocktails and socialise at the hippest sit-down bar in the sky.
www.suiteexperience.com.au
UPPER CLASS
Virgin atlantic

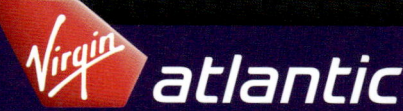

Cafes

CITY & SURRY HILLS

Bacco Wine Bar Pasticceria
Chifley Plaza, 2 Chifley Square, Sydney
Tel 9223 9552
This sleek wine bar is filled with city suits from dawn until well after dusk, but before unwinding over Marco Faraone cocktails, spuntini, cheese and great Italian dishes, swing by for coffee and something sweet.

Bar Adyar
484 Kent Street, Sydney
Tel 9283 1443
Barista Amanda Paine dispenses plenty of goodwill with a decent brew. The healthy menu is strong on organics, with tortillas, toasted turkish sandwiches, and spinach and ricotta cannelloni. There's free wireless too.

Bertoni Casalinga
262 Kent Street, Sydney
Tel 9262 5845
Also at 281 Darling Street, Balmain
Tel 9818 5845
Also at 90 Vista Street, Mosman
Tel 9969 5845
Balmain scores the most kudos, but the city spot lends the CBD's wind canyons some soul, especially after a caffe corretto (coffee with a shot of something stronger). A solid and generous Italian menu keeps everyone entertained, with seasonal specials as well as mama Maria's *sugo* on pasta.

Cafe Ish
102 Albion Street, Surry Hills
Tel 9281 1688
There's nothing else like it – a chef with a love for bush food flavours and his Japanese wife as barista. Watch them overcome any misgivings with their inventive menu of signature wattleseed "macaccino" (it has macadamia nuts in it too), kangaroo pie, soft-shell crab omelette and more. Best of all is the house-made Wagon Wheel.

Central Baking Depot
37–39 Erskine Street, Sydney
Tel 9290 2229
The Bourke Street Bakery team (Surry Hills, Alexandria and Marrickville) has a city offshoot. The sausage rolls are the stuff of legend (lamb, harissa and almond; pork and fennel; chicken, bacon and shallot). But so are the fruit brulee tarts and the changing display of creative cakes and bickies.

Colliers Sandwich Company
87/91 Cathedral Street, Woolloomooloo
Tel 9358 6233
Go the club – a fat pile of chicken, bacon, lettuce, tomato, avocado, cheddar, cranberry and mustard mayo on a toasted panino. It's the best of six toasties. Otherwise it's plump muffins, salads and wraps, and great coffee.

good food guide   159

bars + cafes

Mecca Espresso
67 King Street, Sydney **Tel 9299 8828**
Also at 1 Alfred Street, Sydney **Tel 9252 7668**
They make a stunning short black in the 1930s Grace building with its stained glass and walnut veneer, but if you're into the fad for siphon-brewing, here's your hangout. The coffee changes regularly, and you can take some home. Panini and cakes too.

Pausa
732 Harris Street, Ultimo
Tel 9212 6261
Toby's Estate fuels the airwaves – at our national public broadcaster, in any case – thanks to this very decent little outlet for excellent coffee and cafe snacks, just metres away from the ABC studios. Don't mind the wait, you might spot a famous face.

Plan B
204 Clarence Street, Sydney
Tel 9283 3450
The Becasse team also run this bolthole, baking pastries and other sweet treats to kick-start the day: muffins, pains au chocolat and croissants or mini-Becasse meals for lunch. (And watch for their baguettes at Le Grand Cafe across the road.)

Single Origin Roasters
60–64 Reservoir Street, Surry Hills
Tel 9211 0665
Boris the roaster has moved out, and this corner nook has been scrubbed up. What the team here don't know about coffee isn't worth it. Savour the dreamy and seductive crema. There's even homebrew pale ale.

Wall Cafe
80 Campbell Street, Surry Hills
Tel 9280 1980
Sure, they do soups, salads, pide and more but really this Sydney sibling to an equally stylish Melbourne haunt is all about the coffee. It's Genovese, and pumped with professional pride.

EAST

At Perry Lane
Rear 264 Oxford Street, via Perry Lane, Paddington
Tel 8354 1222
This split-level courtyard cafe-cum-bar and art studio is a bit like a tardis behind its grey wall. From eggs benny to a Moroccan-inspired mix of poached eggs, spiced lentils and relish, pressed sandwiches on a range of breads and salads such as squid and chorizo, it's got the goods.

Bar Coluzzi
322 Victoria Street, Darlinghurst
Tel 9380 5420
It was ground zero for the explosion of Sydney's cafe culture. Five decades on, Coluzzi's still cuts the mustard as you sit on tiny sidewalk stools discussing politics, the sweet science and the world game over a muscular macchiato. It's no-frills, which is just fine. *La bella vita.*

The Crabbe Hole
Poolside, Bondi Icebergs, 1 Notts Avenue, Bondi Beach
Tel 0403 074 447
Follow the Icebergs pool railing to this spectacularly positioned hole-in-the-wall serving feisty Fair Trade coffee, Adriano Zumbo's banana bread, toasted sambos or the Pat and Stick's ice-cream variety. A poolside kiosk with star quality views.

Dov at Delectica
130 Victoria Street, Potts Point
Tel 9368 0600
This affable spot trundles along with early evening meal deals, an Italian-inclined bistro standard menu priced for the times, Allpress coffee and free wireless. Chicken salad's the best seller, and there's plenty to cheer up vegetarians.

bars + cafes

Forbes & Burton
252 Forbes Street, Darlinghurst
Tel 9356 8788
Now back to being daytime only, this old sandstone bistro (it was the gaol barracks) concentrates on hearty, relaxed and mostly Italian fare. Bubble & squeak and organic eggs for brekkie; braised oxtail with gnocchi and duck ragu with fettuccine for lunch. Sunday roasts too.

Katipo
101 Bondi Road, Bondi
Tel 9389 6405
Morning sun, floppy vintage couches, free wireless and Morgan's coffee drag the Bondiscetti out in droves on weekends, or a steady stream on lazy weekday mornings. Maple and pistachio porridge in winter, bacon and egg wraps and house-baked banana bread any time of year.

Paddington Alimentari
2 Hopetoun Street, Paddington
Tel 9358 2142
An utterly chic nook in endlessly chic Paddo for good coffee, glorious panini, smallgoods, arancini and cheeses. Finding a perch is almost impossible but you can always take away.

Ruby's Diner
Shop 1, 173-179 Bronte Road, Waverley
Tel 9386 5964
After walking the headland, wander up the hill into what feels like the set of a James Dean movie, for French toast, poached eggs and fresh fruit at this retro cafe, where the burgers are truly better and the shakes simply great.

The Sweet Spot Patisserie
18 Perouse Road, Randwick
Tel 9399 3344
A pastry parthenon with indoor and outdoor tables, ancient Greek motifs and much, much more than baklava. The teensy tartas – bite-sized fruit tarts – are pop-in-the-mouth perfect. Decent coffee, morning sunshine and everything from cannoli to kourabiethes (Greek nut shortbread).

Vaucluse House Tearooms
Wentworth Road, Vaucluse
Tel 9388 8188
One of Sydney's most fascinating historic houses hosts an airy, open cafe on one side. Do the high-tea thing with excellent scones and tiny quiches, or breakfast on eggs with eggplant and harissa. Turn back time in a glorious setting.

NORTH

Belaroma
75 Kenneth Road, Manly Vale
Tel 8976 9999
This Sydney coffee roaster has added a low-key cafe with an outdoor terrace so you can try the ground beans – Paddington teas too – before taking some home. There's Italian style to the sarnies and wraps, plus sweet treats such as chocolate cannoli.

The Boathouse
Governor Phillip Park, Barrenjoey Road, Palm Beach
Tel 9974 3868
Pretend you're at your sea-breezy, designer-swish beach house as you gaze across Pittwater from this cafe-cum-florist. A menu of old faves – burgers, BLT, squid salad, steak sambos – does the trick. Remember to bring your cossie.

Cafe Splat
68a Queenscliff Road, Queenscliff
Tel 9905 0600
They warn that this cafe may contain nuts (they own it), and yes, it's fun and charming, right down to the lino floor. The view, 43 steps above the beach, is beaut. Breakfast is tops, especially huevos rancheros – poached eggs with tomatoes, beans, peppers and chorizo – with a double-shot iced coffee.

bars + cafes

Flying Fox Cafe
Winnererremy Bay Park, 2 Mona Street, Mona Vale
Tel 9986 0980
Got kids? Here's a waterside parkland setting where they can run wild, especially in a fenced playground. This modern alfresco cafe is small-fry (and pet) friendly, but if you're grown up, opt for blackboard specials over a pretty standard repertoire.

Fourth Village Providore
5a Vista Street, Mosman
Tel 9960 7162
This breakfast and lunchtime cafe turns into a smart trattoria Thursday to Sunday nights, serving fresh pasta and wood-fired pizza. La famiglia Quattroville run this bustling food market, brimming with fresh fruit, flowers, vegetables, bread, a vast gourmet deli and cheese room.

Kokoh
11 Redleaf Avenue, Wahroonga
Tel 9489 1470
A slick cafe with red streetside stools like melting marshmallows. The small menu has an organic focus, and sandwiches are made with La Tartine bread. There's Belgian hot chocolate and decent coffees and teas, but it's not cheap – muffins are $5-plus.

Montagu
Shop 2, 13 Ernest Street, Crows Nest
Tel 9438 4478
Spilling outdoors, this classy little cafe delivers super breakfasts and lunchtime Infinity and Brasserie Bread sambos. Try organic chicken, fennel, celery, mayo and watercress on levain or chunky chickpea, preserved lemon, tahini and watercress on quinoa and soya.

Pilu Kiosk
End of Moore Road, Freshwater
Tel 9938 3331
Join the queues for the Pilu restaurant's take on a beachside kiosk. That means egg, pancetta and tomato rolls and great coffee from 7am daily. Lunch on the deck with a pork, apple and fennel panino or just wander down to the beach with it. This place just goes off on a sunny day.

The Source Espresso Bar
6/914 Military Road, Mosman
Tel 9969 1368
This is caffeine geek heaven, with several single origin coffees and the roaster in the corner perfuming this slick, buzzy room of warm timbers and a convivial, communal table.

Thelma & Louise
Shop 1, Hayes Street, Neutral Bay
Tel 9953 7754
This feminine trinket-strewn harbourside cafe (prime possie is the narrow balcony over the water) bustles on weekends. Generous breakfasts and comforting lunch fare, from moroccan lamb pie to seafood linguine and antipasti.

SOUTH

Bitton Gourmet
37a Copeland Street, Alexandria
Tel 9519 5111
David Bitton's slick one-stop grocery shop, deli and cafe showcases the house-made condiments in a easygoing regional French menu so you can try before you buy, whether it's spicy tomato sauce on the corn and gruyere omelette, or chilli oil in the mussels marinieres.

Black Star Pastry
277 Australia Street, Newtown
Tel 9557 8656
This cute patisserie has a bench inside plus a few footpath seats, but its appeal is Christopher The's marvellous pastry treats, from quiche to pies and sausage rolls, plus tarts, macarons, brioche, croissants and, best of all, a dark chocolate "ginger ninja".

bars + cafes

Cafe Ella
274 Abercrombie Street, Darlington
Tel 9319 6163
We're talking Redfern shabby chic with courtyard coffee opportunities, fresh juices, house-baked bagels and a hearty Greek lentil soup with a dollop of fettal. All that makes a pretty good case for Ella's popularity with local families and students alike.

Cafe ism
187 Wilson Street, Newtown
Tel 9519 1166
It's cash only at this teensy, busy corner spot. The all-day breakfast menu is big on free-range eggs, plus fine vego options including pear and raspberry bread. Lunch is salads, sarnies, a fine burger and croque madame or monsieur.

Grind Espresso
6 Surf Road, Cronulla
Tel 0403 844 533
There are people travelling far, far from the Shire who'd rather be at Richard Calabro's grungy shrine to the perfect coffee. There's nothing to eat, but one sip of this dark, creamy, bittersweet brew and who cares.

Park Cafe on Chalmers
Redfern Oval, Chalmers Street, Redfern
Tel 8399 0661
We can't promise Russell Crowe will be here chomping on a burger, but you can get stuck into an egg and bacon roll with Vittoria coffee, a chicken and fetta pie, or fluffy apple and ricotta muffins while the Rabbitohs train out front. Dog bikkies too, but best not to bring greyhounds.

Patisse
PYD Building, 197 Young Street, Waterloo
Tel 9690 0665
Art and homewares aficionados browse the display cases here with the keen interest usually reserved for the designer stores above and beside. The cakes, pies, tarts and puddings are artworks in their own right. Savouries, all-day breakfasts and good coffee in an airy, elegant space.

Space Espresso Bar
77 Dunning Ave, Rosebery
Tel 9697 0752
This small, colourful cafe likes to keep a chilled state of mind over simple, fresh flavours in pasta, salads, soups and wraps. A decent wine list and beers certainly help.

Sideplate
664 Bourke Street, Redfern
Tel 9699 6033
A slip of a sidewalk cafe by the Plated catering team. Breakfast on buttermilk muffins, crepes with ricotta and poached fruit and eggs from the owner's farm.

St Germain Patisserie
88 Rosehill Street, cnr Gibbons Street, Redfern
Tel 9319 7161
Gorgeous patisserie and viennoiserie (croissants, pains au chocolat and more) cram the tiny counter cases. Squash in (there's barely room to sit) or carry your tarte flambee, filled baguette or tomato and brie croissant home with you. If you can wait that long, of course. Superb cakes and tarts too.

WEST

Belli Bar
80 Norton Street, Leichhardt
Tel 9564 6232
The pick of the strip for many Norton Street regulars entices them in with its beautiful baked goods, chatty vibe and the famous tramezzini – an Italian (read stylish) version of the club sandwich. Check out the combinations or settle for focaccia, panini or something sweet.

bars + cafes

Cafe Chocolat
Shop 5, 308 Darling Street, Balmain
Tel 9555 1199
FAVOURITE EXTRAVAGANCE
Adriano Zumbo is a genius patissier, creating whimsical, delicious sweet treats in this luxe little nook where chocolate, especially truffles, stars. "Hamburger" is a banoffee-pie inspired dish of chocolate macarons. There are some savoury offerings – toasted ham and cheese brioche – but why bother?

The Cove at Drummoyne
1 Henley Marine Drive, Drummoyne
Tel 9719 3022
A leafy spot loved for its pleasant Iron Cove view, long menu and generous servings. Sip on Danes coffee or a "Bay Berry" frappe while swimmers lap the pool below. Tuck into a bacon and egg panino, or vegie wrap with pea and lentil felafel.

Kelbys Cafe
293 Marrickville Road, Marrickville
Tel 9654 5165
This refreshingly community-minded corner cafe has art exhibitions, a kid-friendly lounge, good coffee and all-day brekkie. Blackboard specials run in a generous comfort-food vein, and cakes and muffins are baked daily.

Latteccino
21a Victoria Avenue, Concord West
Tel 9743 3883
Weekdays it's pram city with yummy mummies tucking into an Italian-styled menu in this outdoorsy cafe with trattoria aspirations. Weekends bring gym junkies and cyclists for bircher muesli, eggs benedict and toasted brioche from the all-day breakfast menu. Spot-on Espresso di Manfredi coffee.

Petty Cash Cafe
68 Victoria Road, Enmore
Tel 9557 2377
This little corner cafe has a retro feel with mismatched old-school furniture and an intriguing book collection. Coffee hits the mark, and the menu has lots of vego options, including roasted veg salad with haloumi. A juicy steak sandwich does meat lovers proud.

Salonbim
110 Audley Street, Petersham
Tel 9564 5737
A sunny cafe near the station for a decent Coffex coffee. The short menu proffers sandwiches on turkish or ciabatta (grilled veg with goat's cheese is good), or tuck into a bowl of organic Whisk & Pin muesli.

Sea Sweet
354 Church Street, Parramatta
Tel 1300 908 070
The closest thing to the sea is the Parramatta river. The sweet part is syrup-drenched Lebanese pastries and nutty, semolina-chewy cookies. Spoon up a tall fruit cocktail or better still, knefe – molten sweet cheese or clotted milk cream in a warm sesame-seed bun.

Sideways Deli Cafe
37 Constitution Road, Dulwich Hill
Tel 9560 1425
A great all-day brekkie and lunch spot in a sunny corner location, for "fiveways" breakfast (with bacon, chipolatas, sauteed mushies, roast tomato and woodfired toast), lamb wrap with tzatziki, and good coffee.

Sonoma Bakery Cafe
215a Glebe Point Road, Glebe
Tel 9660 2116
Also at 24/198–222 Young Street, Waterloo
Tel 8399 1310
Of course it's all about the bread, but the pastries are great too. The muesli's fine and the sandwiches extraordinary. Take a loaf or two home (don't miss the spongy, chewy marvellous miche) but be warned – parking's hard in both places.

See also: Ten of the Best Breakfasts and Favourite Cafe, Deus Cafe (page 176–7).

Global Gems

global gems

CITY

At Bangkok
Cnr George and Campbell streets, City
Tel 9211 5232   Thai

When you can't get in to Chat Thai opposite (still one of our faves and with a permanent queue) there's plenty of Bangkok-inspired cooking at this utterly casual arcade bolthole. Come for typically fast-and-furious fill-ups such as fried rice, flat rice noodles or the Chinese favourite yen ta fo – a pinkish Thai broth with rice noodles and fish balls. (The colour comes from preserved tofu.) Eat it with hot green tea, Thai style.

Cafe Kasturi
767–769 George Street, Haymarket
Tel 9288 9888   Malaysian

Muslim Malay (or Mamak) fare is all about sweet, Indian-influenced curry spices, flaky roti and murtabak – a crunchy roti parcel filled with minced beef and onion. Roti here land in a row of folded-hankie shaped pieces as good sauce-soppers for a lightly spiced chicken curry, bobbing with star anise shards and chunks of potatoes. Don't miss the gorgeously chilli-hot, dried-shrimp pungent house sambal.

Chat Thai
20 Campbell Street, Haymarket
Tel 9211 1808   Thai

Thai Town's most popular address can be a bit daunting to newcomers, lured by the window show of sizzling satays, grilling prawns or Thai ladies hand-rolling coconut and pandan sweets. Hour-long queues and self-serve waiting lists are a pretty swift deterrent. But come out of rush hour – early or late – and go for super-spicy som dtum (green papaya salad), daily northern Thai specials, and grills with bitter nam jim jeaw (dipping sauce). The dessert menu changes regularly – ask for the pick of the day.

Din Tai Fung
Level 1, World Square, 644 George Street, Sydney
Tel 9264 6010   Taiwanese
FAVOURITE GLOBAL GEM

Repeat visits to this food-is-theatre dumpling house are the only way to have something besides the house special soup dumplings (xiao lung bao) – the ones they're making in the very visible kitchen. Once you've got this must-have order out of the way, try shao mai (open-faced steamed prawn dumplings) with spicy sauce and vinegar, hot and sour or braised beef noodle soup and pork floss on tofu. Don't miss lychee and fresh mint crush either.

Emperor's Garden Barbecue
213 Thomas Street, Haymarket
Tel 9281 9899

Don't ignore the obvious. The speciality here is barbecued meat and poultry – from sweetish char siu pork to soy sauce chicken and roasted duck, hanging, awaiting the cleaver for takeaway boxes or dishes inside. A big wonton noodle soup is the standard order, with your choice of barbecue on top or on the side. A few Chinese greens and anytime-of-day cravings are sated. Remember portions are large. Take home what you can't fit in (but you'll be charged for the container).

Ichi Ban Boshi
Level 2, Galeries Victoria, 500 George Street, Sydney
Tel 9262 7677   Japanese

It's partly the atmosphere, right next to the city's most interesting bookshop chain, Kinokuniya (beware of the food books section). It's partly the permanent queues. But in the end it's about ramen – wriggly noodles, made on site, served in your choice of protein-laden soup broth (salt, soy, miso) with spring onions, kimchi, pork slices, crumbed chicken and beyond. Cold hiyashi noodles in summer come with egg, ham, cucumber and vinaigrette. Kakuni (braised pork belly) is winter heaven.

LNC Dessert House
339 Sussex Street, Sydney
Tel 9283 3823 Asian dessert

Red bean, sesame and grass jelly on a slushy Everest of shaved ice, drowning in coconut milk and palm sugar syrup? If that's your thing, you'll love this wacky red and fluoro lane-edge cafe. Check the house-made desserts such as glutinous rice and sesame dumplings in hot ginger syrup or warm red-bean porridge. Kids will love the smoothies and jellies.

Mamak
15 Goulburn Street, Haymarket
Tel 9211 1668

The Malaysian canteen of choice for roti addicts – they make them in the window – is hardly a secret. Just spot the lines outside. But crunchy, flaky, more-ish roti (eat them while hot for maximum effect) are perfect with their accompanying curry gravies and sambal or with chicken or lamb in spiced sauce. Roti even come as dessert. Have an iced dessert drink on the side, Malaysian style.

Miso
Shop 20, World Square, Pitt Street entrance, Sydney
Tel 9283 9686 Japanese

A recent addition to the hugely popular Masuya/Musashi chain, this teishoku or set-meal eatery dishes up all-inclusive Japanese lunches and dinners on lovely half-moon pottery platters, or kitsch-cute, bamboo-look plastic takeaway bentos. Unaju deluxe has sticky fingers of teriyaki eel on rice, salmon sashimi, a chicken patty, fried tofu, miso eggplant, a sweet-egg omelette roll and fruit, while miso katsu boasts a giant pork schnitzel criss-crossed with gooey, tangy miso sauce.

global gems

Ton Ton Regent
501 George Street, Sydney
Tel 9267 1313
Also Ton Ton Chifley, F1 Chifley Plaza, 2 Chifley Square, Sydney
Tel 9222 1010 Japanese

The new sibling in this noodle bar empire is opposite owner Kimitaka Azuma's posher Japanese skewers place, but you can still enjoy a beer, sake or wine here over a hearty bowl of udon or soba noodles. The setting is food-court bright, but the flavours are strong and authentic, from wagyu teriyaki with steamed rice and salad to chicken kara-age and katsu-kare, a curry of crumbed fried pork. Bento boxes are a banquet for one, while the sticky rice desserts, wagashi, are a bit of fun.

NORTH

Bangkok Betty
161 Middle Head Road, Mosman
Tel 9960 6880 Thai

You won't find Betty in the kitchen; amused staff reveal "we are all Betty". It's a tiny nook that's big on personality and fresh, easy Thai. "Betty Loves Bling" translates to steamed chicken and prawn dumplings, while "Betty's on a Roll" offers super-fresh rice-paper rolls. Eat in or take away curries, stir-fries, noodles or "Betty Beefs It Up" with a zesty Thai beef salad.

Bijolias
Shop 5/540 Sydney Road, Seaforth
Tel 9949 3641 Indian

There's a steady stream of customers popping in for takeaway in this buzzy Indian, but stay put for generous servings and regional surprises, including dhokla, a fluffy steamed semolina "bread" with a paste of ginger, mustard and coriander, plus a spicy chilli relish and nariyal beef, a tangy southern speciality in curry leaf coconut sauce. The shared $29.50 menu saves thinking and lets you try plenty.

Cibo e Vino
Shop 2, 299–301 Old Northern Road, Castle Hill
Tel 8002 0912 Italian

There's no shortage of vino (BYO and licensed) or atmosphere in this small Italian with a daily menu that may feature deep-fried salt cod balls with aioli, baby-sized gnocchi with tomato, pecorino and sage or a trio of large lamb T-bones with silverbeet, carrot, tomato and chickpea salsa, before a decent espresso made with a local roaster's blend.

Da Wan Lai
125 Rowe Street, Eastwood
Tel 0425 215 117 Chinese (northern)

Handmade noodles in a rich clear soup, fat pork-mince dumplings and crispy Shandong chicken set the tone at this family-friendly Chinese with a focus on the food of Shandong province in eastern China. The seafood, chilli, garlic and cabbage-laced menu is enhanced by fresh-from-the-tank lobster and other fishy creatures. Try Sichuan chicken, skewered and served with tofu in chilli oil. Gorgeous.

Delicado Foods
134 Blues Point Road, McMahons Point
Tel 9955 9399 Spanish

The atmosphere is pure Spain, from the wrought-iron door and the fabulous wine room (owner Ben Moechtar is a renowned wine man) to the cosy red-themed tapas bar and cafe beyond. It also doubles as a fine Spanish deli (don't miss the glorious chocolate selection) and restaurant. Come for olives, paella and a glass of Rioja or maybe a thick Spanish hot chocolate.

Joe's Pizzeria Arax
5 Tryon Place, Lindfield
Tel 9416 8452 Lebanese

Joe's pizza has plenty of loyal local devotees, but the Lebanese fare is a real drawcard at this little family-run eatery next to Lindfield train station (the Pacific Highway side). All the basics done well and at affordable prices,

global gems

including plump cabbage rolls, fresh felafel, thick flavourful hummus, and top-notch kebabs cooked to order.

Out of Africa
43–45 East Esplanade, Manly
Tel 9977 0055 Moroccan
This warm space of African artefacts and burnt orange walls is filled with the scents of a souk. Juicy king prawns rest in a yellow curry sauce that has more than a hint of Indian spice and asks to be soaked up with fluffy couscous. Kofta tagine brings minced beef balls into a satisfyingly spicy tomato sauce, while mint tea is refreshing.

Ryo's
125 Falcon Street, North Sydney
Tel 9955 0225 Japanese/Ramen
Whether in tangy soy stock or a spiced sesame-flavoured broth, with thick slices of pork or deep-fried chicken, topped with slippery nori and a crunch of daikon radish, Ryo's ramen are squiggly, chewy and eminently satisfying. Bright orange and yellow decor means you can't miss it, but the lines by the door are a giveaway too. The house special of hot and spicy pork broth arrives with the best soft-hard soy-soaked eggs.

Wakana
2A Broughton Road, Artarmon
Tel 9419 7499 Japanese barbecue
DIY barbecue (or yakiniku) is the order of the day at this cheerful, mint-green neighbourhood spot, run by bustling chef Nagasawa-san. Japanese families and the after-office crowd pop in for great-value grilling at the table: super-tender slices of harami or perhaps onion, kumera, shiitakes and zucchini slices from a mixed vegetable plate. Dip each cooked piece in your condiment of choice – barbecue sauce, citrus-sharpened soy (ponzu) or sesame-based dressing. Cash only.

Zenya Noodle Bar
217 Rowe Street, Eastwood
Tel 9874 2122 Japanese/Ramen
This funky, chocolate-hued ramen-ya (noodle shop) in Korean and Chinese dominated Eastwood is another crowd-pleaser. Noodles swim in a pretty stoneware bowl filled with soy-salty soup and topped with nori, roast pork and egg. You can also go the bento option, served in spiffy red-and-black lacquer-look trays: kabayaki eel in sweet teriyaki sauce, with seaweed salad, and baby gyoza, or maybe a classic ton-katsu (pork schnitzel). The deluxe bento comes with a tiny ramen bowl on the side. So you can have both.

SOUTH

Chez Pascal
440 Rocky Point Road, Sans Souci
Tel 9529 5444 French
Philipe Lebreux's Gallic charm is infectious. He's moved from his original can-can girl adorned premises up the road but the old-style French ambience has moved with him. Expect all the classics from onion soup to duck and his famous Normandy crepes, service that's calm and efficient, and a few well-chosen greetings bellowed out by Lebreux from the kitchen.

Concordia Club
Mackey Park, Richardsons Crescent, Tempe
Tel 9554 7388
The sleepy German hideaway is set among sprawling lawns in a spaciously neat former bowlo. Pop in for imported beers and hearty Bavarian meals of excellent German sausages, grilled kassler (smoked pork chops), meat loaf (leberkaese) and pork belly. Two kinds of potatoes, caraway-flecked sauerkraut and red cabbage come on the side, along with chewy little spaetzle (flour-and-water noodles) and gravy. Prost!

Greek Islands Taverna
Shop 2/360 Homer Street, Earlwood
Tel 9558 3334

Dips and platters territory it may be, but this blue-and-white themed diner in a very Greek part of town does the genre proud. Dip into tarama and tzatziki, nibble on dolmades and fried haloumi, then follow with grilled lamb or octopus and juicy Greek sausages. Dessert has to be galaktoboureko (a syrupy fillo and semolina custard pastry) but watch out for Greeks bearing gifts. A complimentary tsipouro (aniseed schnapps) is lethal.

Il Baretto
496 Bourke Street, Surry Hills
Tel 9361 6163   Italian

Here's the cheap local everyone wants close by. A simple trattoria where you can't book and your BYO goes in a tumbler. It's loud, lively and fun, with a simply daily menu that reads like a checklist of Italian classics, especially the house-made pasta. From carpaccio to the kick of penne arrabbiata and the signature pappardelle with duck ragu, it's a reliable stayer and the tiramisu never fails to lift spirits.

Satay Inn
430 Stoney Creek Road, Kingsgrove
Tel 9554 8889   Malaysian

The menu is staggering, covering most of south-east Asia. The key to successful ordering is the Malaysian specials posted on the walls. Rich-sauced kapitan chicken, feisty sambal tofu with soft eggplant and a classic nasi goreng make more than a meal for two, but there are also plenty of Chinese staples, such as Hakka-style fungus with pork belly.

Shanghai Yangzhou House
177 Forest Road, Hurstville
Tel 9580 9188   Chinese (Shanghai)

A bit of a stayer on the ever-changing, Chinese-accented dining scene in this part of town, this straightforward eatery (cash only) is all about great noodles, hot and sour fish

global gems

soup and an array of village-style Shanghai cold entrees on display in the window. Sichuan squid is a pick, on a bed of dried chillies, while deep-fried eggplant in duck egg yolk is a crunchy treat. Dumplings too, of course.

Sushi Bar Hiro
498A King Georges Road, Beverly Hills
Tel 9580 8219   Japanese

Locals love the value-for-money set menu ($25.80) and the endless tapas-sized entrees all under $10. Go for quirkily named "Chef's Shoes" – a sweet soy concoction of tuna, salmon and marinated nameko mushrooms. The specials include equally quirky meals such as shishamo, which is a grilled bait-like fish full of roe, a home cook's favourite in Japan.

The Smokehouse
204 Devonshire Street, Surry Hills
Tel 9699 1155   Smoked

Here's a bit of fun, with a tiny, appealing wine list to help things along. Father and son team Stephen and Adam de Launay built their own smokehouse to flavour the seafood served in this simple, charming bistro space. The simple comfort fare spans smoked garlic prawns, smoked cod fritters with fries, and a smoked salmon, cod and leek pie, all for not too many pennies.

Uchi Lounge
15 Brisbane Street, Surry Hills
Tel 9261 3524   Modern Japanese

The ground-floor bar offers a neat range of sakes, but nip upstairs to the narrow dining space lined with breezy gossamer screens and cartoon artworks for modern Japanese creations such as roasted miso and parmesan eggplant, seared beef "sashimi" with ponzu, and pan-fried barramundi with soy and rosemary butter on potato and edamame mash.

Zyka
4/176–180 Belmore Road, Riverwood
Tel 9534 1177   Pakistani/Indian

Joining the trend in upmarket South Asian dining, dropping the obvious ethnic decor touches but thankfully not the video screens for the Bollywood movies and the cricket, Zyka (meaning "taste") lives up to its name. Rich, porridgey haleem is a pureed perfection of lentils and lamb, and karahi chicken is pungent with coriander. They team well with thick, deep-green spinach-laden palak paneer; light, pull-apart naan, and thick clotted-milk kheer for dessert.

EAST

Angelo's Portugalia
262 Anzac Parade, Kensington
Tel 9662 1711   Portuguese

Angelo's is a recent addition to multi-culinary Anzac Parade. The premise is simple: straightforward Portuguese food, including a smoky chargrill sizzling with butterflied Portuguese-style chickens. Takeaway is available but eating in nets you a fierce-looking espetada (barbecued marinated beef on skewers) or a plate of salt cod with potatoes. Hearty, no-frills and tasty.

Bondi Trattoria
34B Campbell Parade, Bondi Beach
Tel 9365 4303   Italian

"The Tratt" is what it is, a well-priced neighbourhood Italian, except for views across Sydney's most famous strip of sand. Then there's the staunchly loyal following – for more than 20 years – and warm welcome for all. Better still, it's there daily for mussels in a rich chilli broth, bucatini with pork and fennel sausage, and raw tuna through lemony herb and rocket pasta.

global gems

Chairman Mao
189 Anzac Parade, Kensington
Tel 9697 9189   Chinese (Hunanese)
The vintage Mao posters are originals, the heavy wooden chairs and tables a leftover from a previous incarnation (as a hotpot restaurant). This is a rare insight into a lesser known Chinese cuisine, from the late Communist dictator's home region. The focus is on chilli and cumin, Sichuan pepper and house-smoked meats. Front-of-house is owner Andrew Bao, a charming guide to his wife's cooking. Don't miss the smoked beef and the pork meatball soup. And Mao's favourite, red-braised pork.

El Bulli del Punto
40 St Pauls Street, The Spot, Randwick
Tel 9398 2027   Spanish
There are no fine-dining pretensions at this permanently busy addition to the buzzing Spot strip. This offshoot of a Surry Hills original (501 Elizabeth Street) is all about decent sangria, lots of atmosphere and an easy tapas menu that works as a meal or a snack. Sit up at the bar for maximum effect and nibble on yummy little empanadas, toasted almonds, the very more-ish paella balls (like Hispanic arancini), chorizo in cider or tortilla espanola.

Jimbaran
129 Avoca Street, Randwick
Tel 9398 8555   Indonesian
Beyond the modest front room of this energetic Indonesian is a tropical courtyard reminiscent of a balmy Bali night. Start with fresh rice paper rolls wrapped around sweet yam bean and dried shrimp, or bite-size chicken satay sticks. The signature milkfish is lightly fried and served whole with a chilli, onion, tomato and sweet soy sambal.

Kaki Lima
3/243 Anzac Parade, Kingsford
Tel 9662 0588   Malaysian (Halal)
This miniature daytime-only eatery serves carefully cooked home-style food with a smile. Go for the breakfast staple, nasi lemak (coconut rice with curry and condiments) or generously flaky roti canai served with chilli-laced chicken gravy or sweet, thick dahl. There are daily specials plus little kueh – home-style sweets made with rice flour, shredded coconut, palm sugar and coconut cream.

Kings Lane Sandwiches
Shop 1, 28 Kings Lane, Darlinghurst
Tel 9360 8007   Sandwiches
We love the mega-stack. Sandwiches this good and this tall (8–10 cm high) are a meal in themselves. Compose your own or get a vitamin-laden vegetarian version, the mightily popular chicken schnitzel with herb mayo and lettuce, or the abundant poached chicken with celeriac coleslaw. Waiting in line is all part of the fun.

La Piadina
106 Glenayr Avenue, Bondi Beach
Tel 9300 0160   Italian
The griddle-toasted flat bread of Italy's Romagna region (the north-eastern Adriatic coast and its hinterland) is now a Bondi breakfast, brunch, lunch and dinner snack. Have it with good coffee (the owners are Italian) and a classic prosciutto filling, or perhaps ricotta and mushrooms, or spiced salami.

Snakebean
95 Oxford Street, Darlinghurst
Tel 9380 8808   Thai/Vietnamese
The teensiest shopfront and an ultra-casual tone belie the fact that this is the home kitchen of Nhut Huynh, author of the recently released *Little Vietnam* cookbook. There's no going past his excellent rice paper rolls – with prawns and pork or perhaps

global gems

coconut-poached chicken and green mango. Betel leaves, banana flower or green papaya salad are failsafe orders, or coconutty beef massaman.

Ummarin Thai
66 Perouse Road, The Spot, Randwick
Tel 9398 2153   Thai
How many Thai restaurants can you fit in one spot? This Spot has at least six. But the pick is the least obtrusive and, despite its pretty decor, most reasonably priced. From good pad thai to a rich beef massaman, a well-spiced vegetarian curry to friendly service and BYO, Ummarin definitely, er, hits the spot.

WEST

Al Aseel
Shop 4, 173 Waterloo Road, Greenacre
Tel 9758 6744   Lebanese
You'll never go home hungry from this bustling Lebanese canteen where families gather to share mixed meat platters brimming with chicken, lamb and kofta; and mop up tabbouleh, lemony hummus, dreamy babaghanoush, kibbeh nayeh and felafel in wedges of fluffy bread. With more than 60 dishes on the picture menu, including seafood, you're spoilt for choice. But remember, it's halal, so no alcohol please.

Braza Churrascaria
13 Norton Street, Leichhardt
Tel 9572 7921   Brazilian
All-you-can-eat churrasco would lure any meathead away from Little Italy's pizza and pasta joint. Sword-like skewers threaded with every cut of lamb, pork, beef and chicken arrive tableside, sliced onto your plate or proffered for plucking with your own set of mini tongs. Side dishes might be polenta, rice or the toasted cassava flour called farofa. Complete your meat feast with a caipirinha.

Cucina Viscontini
The Piazza, The Waterfront, 21 Bennelong Road, Homebush Bay
Tel 9739 8888   Italian
Here's a ristorante with its own bottle shop, deli and bakery. It's also a cafe for proper breakfasts and lunch. Gather in this bright modern piazza for platters of meat, pasta – pappardelle with hare in a tomato-based sauce – plus pizza, gelato and interesting cheeses.

Deus Cafe
98–104 Parramatta Road, Camperdown (entry via Lyons Road)
Tel 9519 3669   Italian
Cafe by day, but come evenings it's a groovy, if spartan Italian osteria with communal tables and satisfyingly sublime fare such as herb gnocchi with mixed mushroom ragout, house-made pasta, slow-cooked pork belly with braised brussels sprouts and roast parsnip, and meatballs with polenta chips.

Hai Au Lang Nuong
48 Canley Vale Road, Canley Vale
Tel 9724 9156   Vietnamese
It's a riot of colour – purple, orange and water features. And the menu is a riot of Vietnamese favourites, with some Chinese accents. But the specialities are grill-your-own and claypot dishes, including crusty claypot rice served in a little basket. Pork belly braised in young coconut juice and soy is rich and tangy, served with whole soy-braised eggs, and sweet-sour southern-style fish soup (canh chua) is a winner. Fresh juices too.

Joy Luck Shanghai's Kitchen
183C Burwood Road, Burwood
Tel 9744 5815   Chinese
This even-plainer-than-Jane BYO Shanghai canteen is cash only, but the encyclopaedic, bilingual menu is generous, and pictures of the greatest hits make the choices easier, whether it's cold, crisp, firm, salty and sweet Shanghai smoked fish, braised duck with

global gems

tea-tree mushrooms, red-braised pork belly or stir-fried mud crab with salted duck egg yolk. It's just like chowing down in the Pearl of the Orient, and just as cheap.

Kaysone Sweets
Unit 4/53 Park Road, Cabramatta
No phone   Lao
Kaysone is an easy entry into Lao cuisine, including sweet-sticky grilled dried beef or pork, sticky rice and pound-to-order green papaya salad. Try a pile of Lao snacks such as taro or sweet potato chips, plus every imaginable type of fruit smoothie – durian or avocado, anyone? There's also young coconut juice, soursop and other seasonal fruits.

Le Sarab
86 Majors Bay Road, Concord
Tel 8765 0014   Lebanese
Cafe tables and outdoor seating are deceptive, but this is not just another Majors Bay coffee spot. Le Sarab is classic Lebanese with a contemporary veneer. Try thick, chickpea-dominant hummus, freshly dressed tabbouleh, nicely balanced fattoush (crisped bread squares, onion, tomato, cucumber, parsley and iceberg lettuce) along with a few chargrilled lamb skewers. An iced limonata on granita-ish slush is gloriously good.

Shanghai Dumplings
337 Liverpool Road, Ashfield
Tel 9797 6999   Chinese
Sydney's Little Shanghai is as bursting full of eateries as a fat xiao long bao dumpling is with pork. Just watch out for the squirt of hot soup inside. They are just one of many options, but the pork and gai lan (Chinese spinach) or the mushroom-packed vegetarian version are always terrific too. Simple as they come but easy to eat with a squirt of vinegar or chilli oil.

Tan Viet
100 John Street, Cabramatta
Tel 9727 6853   Vietnamese
A bowl of noodles in soup and the legendary crunchy "criskin" (crisp-skin) chicken appear on every table. They certainly drag in the crowds. All you have to do is choose your noodle type: crinkly egg, springy hu tieu (flat, skinny rice noodles) or drop noodles – slippery white worms. Sprouts and nuoc cham (dipping sauce) are on every table plus condiments galore. Prawn and pork wontons and fish cakes are an alternative to the chicken. Better still, though, have both.

Vicini
37 Booth Street, Annandale
Tel 9660 6600   Italian
Gotta love a local where kids score free dinner (Tues–Thurs till 7pm). Downstairs at this corner terrace there's decent pizza and an antipasto bar that doubles as a cafe and weekend breakfast haunt. Upstairs is a pleasant restaurant with balcony tables for linguine with prawns, artichoke pesto and pangrattato, veal saltimbocca and a feather-light tiramisu.

10 of the Best

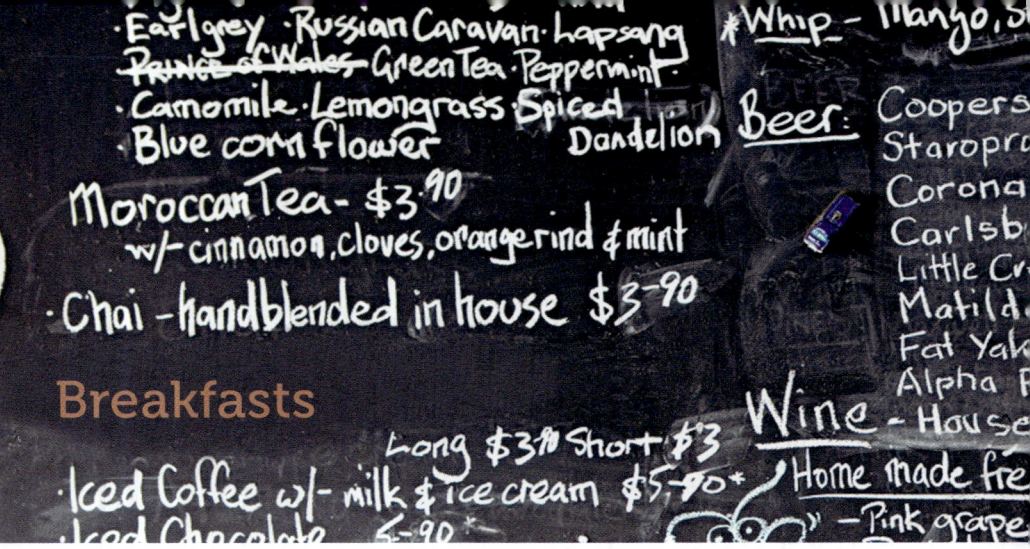

Bambini Trust Cafe
185 Elizabeth Street, Sydney
Tel 9283 7098
Kick off the working day in this European-styled setting where the classics are produced with aplomb. From a toasted ham panino to Sonoma muesli and house-made bircher, it's soulful and nourishing. The eggs are just right, but the open omelette with prosciutto, goat's curd and basil is even better, and the coffee a snappy heart-starter.

The Bathers' Pavilion Cafe
4 The Esplanade, Balmoral Beach
Tel 9969 5050
This gorgeous harbourside setting turns breakfast into a ritual. It's not cheap, yet the no-bookings approach keeps things humming. Kick off with a basket of pastries and "Balmoral sunrise" – orange and lime juice with egg and honey – before hearty baked beans with smoked-ham hock or blueberry pancakes with maple syrup.

Big Brekky
Shop 1, 316 Stanmore Road (cnr Albert Street), Petersham
Tel 9569 8588
Nim's gone but her signature poached eggs with banana chutney and pesto remain, along with new attractions, such as smoky kippers on malted sourdough. This corner-store spot feels a little like a rustic uni-student bedsit, especially when breakfast remains available until 3pm daily. Brioche french toast is divine with banana and chocolate.

bills
433 Liverpool Street, Darlinghurst
Tel 9360 9631
Also at 359 Crown Street, Surry Hills
Tel 9360 4762
Also at Queen's Court, 118 Queen Street, Woollahra
Tel 9328 7997
This is where the revolution began 17 years ago, when a smiling chap in a white T-shirt gave Sydney a better way to start the day. Bills made breakfast communal and scrambled eggs dreamy, and launched a thousand imitations of ricotta hotcakes and sweetcorn fritters. The original is still the best.

Brasserie Bread Bakery Cafe
1737 Botany Road, Banksmeadow
Tel 9666 6845
Croque monsieur or madame is a corker on bread this good, and the sourdough pancakes with banana are just fine too, along with a hollandaise-soaked florentine panino. Then there's Vegemite soldiers for your boiled egg, and fine Allpress coffee. Load up with baked goodies to see you through the day.

Cafe Giulia
92 Abercrombie Street, Chippendale
Tel 9698 4424
A blend of bustle and cool sprinkled with a European vibe gives this former butcher's shop an early groove. The rambling blackboard menu ranges from tuscan toast with ricotta and honey to kefte with scrambled eggs and mint, belgian waffles, french toast, omelettes, muffins (try poached egg, haloumi and tomato) and even boiled bagels.

Deus Cafe ★
98 Parramatta Road, Camperdown
Tel 9519 3669
FAVOURITE CAFE
After slow-cooked boston beans with AC Butchery pork sausage and poached egg, you wonder if the noise coming from the blokes on choppers is really the bikes' exhaust. Among hearty dishes in this warehouse-like space next to the boys' toys of the Deus bike shop, you'll also find the opulence of cured salmon with scrambled eggs and toasted brioche.

Jonah's
69 Bynya Road, Palm Beach
Tel 9974 5599
This luxurious eyrie overlooking the ocean is a fine place to start the day with a buffet of buttery croissants, granola with poached fruit and eggs benedict with smoked salmon. It's $45, but posh and very classy.

Kazbah on Darling
379 Darling Street, Balmain
Tel 9555 7067
This is a legendary weekend breakfast, full of Middle Eastern delight, from nut-studded sweet couscous with stewed rhubarb and cardamom milk to a spicy lamb tagine with coddled eggs and slabs of flatbread. While the spices and vibrant flavours make it exciting, there's still the calm of french toast and traditional English breakfast combos.

Spicer Street Cafe
Shop 2, 128 Queen Street, Woollahra
Tel 9328 2221
This colourfully cheerful little nook is tucked down a side street, but worth seeking out for house-made bircher muesli, organic porridge with rhubarb, organic eggs on Fuel sourdough and the decadent pleasure of vanilla-scented baked ricotta with toasted brioche and poached dried peaches. Be prepared: it's cash only.

Guilty Pleasures

Burgerman
116 Surrey Street, Darlinghurst
Tel 9361 0268
They like to joke at this no-frills burger joint, but there's also a strong sense of childhood nostalgia in chocolate milkshakes, house-made lemonade (or a beer, now you're old enough), chocolate crackles and burgers with caramelised onion and mayo, piled high enough to impress Homer Simpson.

Gelato Messina
241 Victoria Street, Darlinghurst
Tel 8354 1223
Why make dessert after dinner at home when you could pull out a tiramisu or black forest ice cream cake from Gelato Messina? We'd happily sit at home and eat it all ourselves. If you're more restrained, a few scoops from this Sicilian gelateria with its 30 fab flavours should do. Go chocolate or blood orange sorbet, or coconut and lychee or maybe apple pie gelato. Or the lot.

Glace
27 Marion Street, Leichhardt
Tel 9569 3444
Four little words: campari and grapefruit sorbet. Or perhaps three: gin and tonic. Just don't tell the kids. Or keep 'em quiet with hokey pokey ice cream in a cone, while you take home a tub of rum and raisin. There's a great mix of classic flavours as well as inventive ones. If the rose petal and pistachio is on, you've lucked in big time.

Guzman Y Gomez
175 King Street, Newtown
Tel 9517 1533
There's more to Mexican food than hallucinogenic worms, guacamole and nachos drowned in cheese. This keen-to-be-cool taqueria-style chain (now with branches in the CBD, Kings Cross and Bondi Junction), dishes up burritos, tacos and quesadillas – various forms of soft corn tortillas filled with chicken, beef, pork, fish or vegies, plus black beans, salsa, chilli and cheese – at a communal table. BYO Corona.

Harry's Cafe de Wheels
Cowper Wharf Road, Woolloomooloo
Tel 9357 3074
It's very late, you're, um, tired and emotional, with barely enough money to get home, but hungry. For 65 years this pie cart has satisfied all and sundry with decent pies filled with chunky beef, as well as pasties. Mushy peas too, and million-dollar harbourfront views, all for just a few dollars. Gravy stains on your best gear will help remind you where you were last night.

Lucio Fizzeria
Republic 2, 248 Palmer Street, Darlinghurst
Tel 9332 3766
Lucio de Falco is a passionate pizzaiolo with an excellent touch. His fluffy Napoli-style pizza is the real deal. Try a classic margherita with tomato, basil and fior di latte or a ricotta, salami and fresh mozzarella-stuffed calzone. Simple antipasti are excellent and desserts are seriously superb, including the lemony pastiera or ricotta cake and an oozy chocolate tortino.

Mongers
42 Hall St, Bondi Beach **Tel 9365 2205**
Also at 4/11 Rialto Square, Wentworth St, Manly **Tel 9977 1777**
BBQ or tempura prawns, fab skin-on chips, grilled fish with salad, kumera crisps and corn cobs, tempura vegies, chargrilled octopus, Sydney rocks opened to order: this isn't your typical fish 'n' chipper, just one of the very best. You can hang around to eat, but there's a spectacular beach nearby, so how about alfresco?

Out of the Blue
272 Clovelly Road, Clovelly
Tel 9315 8380
The chicken burgers are famous, not least because of the housemade mayo – a clue to the owners' Gallic origins. Their take on classic burgers, fish and chips or plain old fries to go is a neighbourhood treat. Just watch the lines form around dusk each day. There's barely an eat-in table and the beach is a 10-minute hike away, but you won't find better fast food in this neck of the woods.

Rockpool Bar and Grill
66 Hunter Street, Sydney
Tel 8078 1900
You don't have to spend a fortune in the main dining room to have fun here when there are burgers – beef and fish – in the bar. The $18 wagyu burger, smoky from the chargrill and piled high with house-made pickles, gruyere cheese, Schultz bacon, tomato and chilli relish, is encased in a brioche bun. Have it with onion rings and fat chips and you're set.

Rosso Pomodoro
91/24 Buchanan Street, Balmain
Tel 9555 5924
This small pizzeria is boisterous, vibrant and crowded, and shows a firm hand with a blackboard of wise rules: only Italian mozzarella, no ham and pineapple, and no corkage. The electric oven still produces thin, nicely charred, bases. The 16 different toppings range from bresaola with rocket, shaved parmesan and rosemary-scented potato with pork sausage to a salami-filled calzone.

Sushi

Fuuki
417 Pacific Highway, Crows Nest
Tel 9436 1608
A Crows Nest stayer with lots of buzz, especially on weeknights, Fuuki covers all the favourite Japanese bases with gyoza, tempura, teriyaki and udon. Specials are listed on the wall in Japanese. But ask for the sushi and sashimi of the day, or prop yourself up at the sushi counter and indulge in a series of glistening, well-crafted morsels.

Jugemu & Shimbashi
246–248 Military Rd, Neutral Bay
Tel 9904 3011
The secret's out. Housemade soba and okonomiyaki pancakes are not the only reasons Japanese expats call this place their second home. Expertly sliced, fleshy sashimi, which adorns ceramic dishes that exude zen, gets the senses ready for a series of authentic meals. Never mind that sushi is not on the lunch menu. Helpful staff ensure it appears magically at your table.

Koi
102 Woolwich Rd, Woolwich
Tel 9817 6030
Superb sushi gives this lavishly decorated northsider the edge, with its fine Japanese ceramics and top-notch sushi chefs plying their trade. Start with a few delicate nigiri sushi from master Takashi Sano – the freshest fish of the day elegantly seasoned with yuzu pepper or with citrussy ponzu for dipping.

Makoto
119 Liverpool Street, Sydney
Tel 9283 6767
Also at 336 Victoria Avenue, Chatswood
Tel 9411 1838
You can always rely on the queue, the delicately fresh sashimi and the crisp nori at these conveyor sushi hotspots. Something from Today's Fish is always a winner, as well as a la carte options such as soft shell crab karaage and hearty udon noodles. With luck there will be tuna belly (o-toro) and there is always sticky-smokey grilled eel, kabayaki style (with a sweet soy and mirin sauce).

Monkey Magic
Shop 3–4, 410 Crown Street, Surry Hills
Tel 9358 4444
Upstairs in this warehouse space with its warm timbers, exposed brick decor and dance beats, it's more like a drinking den. The Japanese menu swings both ways, with sashimi on shiso leaves in a pine box and sushi served traditionally, or drizzled with modern flavours such as yuzu cream, sesame and pesto, plus fun sushi rolls, such as soft shell crab with fried leek.

Raw Bar
136 Wairoa Avenue, Bondi Beach
Tel 9365 7200
It's moodily lit and cuddle-up cosy in winter, and beachside magical on a warm summer's night, perched discreetly at Bondi's northern end. One of the pioneering sushi spots in Sydney (since 1995) Raw Bar delivers daily seafood, sashimi, sushi, Sapporo and sake, with a steaming bowl of superbly creamy miso broth alongside. And there's a copious choice of tobiko-speckled inside-out rolls.

Sushi Choo
Ground Floor, 320–330 George Street, Sydney
Tel 9240 3000
This sushi bar is the perfect place for Thomas the Tank Engine fans. There's a cheesy-cool vibe thanks to Astro Boy, waving cats, a rock soundtrack and cheerfully eager service. The trains chug around two large white marble bars bearing decent plates of nigiri, and there's plenty to entertain from "off the rails", from hand rolls to miso cod, and the curiously appealing sashimi pizza with wasabi aioli.

Sushi Fusion
7 Belmore Road, Randwick
Tel 9399 5388
As chugging sushi trains go, this one's a real crowd-pleaser. With competent behind-the-counter staff slicing seafood and shaping hand rolls, freshness is guaranteed. Melamine plates bear everything from oysters on the shell to seared kingfish, jellyfish and sea urchin on sushi rice. Hand rolls include grilled scallops and lightly tempura-ed prawn with seriously spicy mayo.

Sushi Studio
75 Military Road, Neutral Bay
Tel 9953 7317
In this warmly lit, vibrant space, patrons marvel at the gleaming sashimi atop expertly shaped rice balls. Bonito is garnished with finely sliced garlic and grated daikon, while smooth, creamy sea urchin brims with seawater. Salads are well portioned and excellent, as is the grilled head of kingfish.

Yoshii
115 Harrington Street, Sydney
Tel 9247 2566
FAVOURITE SUSHI
Master chef Ryuichi Yoshi is a true sushi genius. Each exquisite piece is formed with utter expertise and intricate delicacy, to please both the eye and the palate. Lunchtime sets start at $38, including wonderful churashi sushi, where the toppings are "scattered" over a bowl of rice. The full omokase (chef's selection) is an extravagant but amazing $120.

See also: Azuma, Busshari, Toko, Sushi e.

Yum Cha

Dynasty
Canterbury League Club, 26 Bridge Road, Belmore
Tel 9740 6633
Weekdays may mean the order-your-own option – ticking off your choice on a flimsy paper menu – but that's one way of getting your favourite dim sum steaming fresh. The Vegas-influenced decor is something to behold, a lavish twist on the Chinese-restaurant-in-a-leagues-club tradition.

Fisherman's Wharf
1st Floor, Sydney Fish Market, Bank Street, Pyrmont
Tel 9660 9888
Nab a table near the giant windows and soak up the calming view across the still waters. It's no surprise that seafood is king here, whether on a yum cha trolley, the a la carte menu or whisked fresh from the neon-lit aquarium-like tanks. Traditional steamed dumplings are good, but deep-fried, almond-encrusted prawn balls are pure decadence.

Ho's Dim Sum Kitchen
429A Pitt Street, Sydney
Tel 9281 2725
There's nothing like having a permanent supply of char siew bao (fluffy pork buns) in the freezer. From the original hole-in-the-wall of yesteryear, Ho's now runs across two shopfronts, boasting copious fridges, freezers and a counter display for instant snacking on their takeaway and take-home buns and dumplings. A sesame-rolled sticky rice ball with sweet red bean inside is pure heaven.

Iron Chef
84 Broomfield Street, Cabramatta
Tel 9723 6228
Away from the John Street hustle and bustle (on the other side of the railway line), this Italian-owned (yes, really) Chinese seafood palace is all about smart decor and Cantonese food – from classic to creative. Yum cha is the business here, with translucent har gow (steamed prawn) or vegetable and chive dumplings, and those wacky mango pancakes to end up on.

Kam Fook
Level 6, Westfield Shopping Centre, Bondi Junction **Tel 9386 9889**
Also at Level 6, Westfield Shopping Centre, Chatswood **Tel 9413 9388**
Here's where you head for siu mai and shopping, with a 10am start so you won't miss the sales. Bondi's has views north to the harbour and ruthlessly efficient trolley matrons. Steamers always please, especially fluffy prawn or scallop and spinach dumplings, and fried rice noodles with dried shrimp, BBQ meats and, of course, pork buns.

Manly Phoenix
East Esplanade 22–23 Manly Wharf, Manly
Tel 9977 2988
Yum cha with water views? This is a relaxed treat, with a stroll along the esplanade afterwards. Decor is up on the average Cantonese too, with floor-to-ceiling windows and a from-the-tank seafood menu (don't miss chilli crab with fried "silver" buns at night time) for a la carte. Yum cha offers all the favourites, with a few creative spins.

Palace Chinese
Shop 38, Level 1, Piccadilly Tower,
133–145 Castlereagh Street, Sydney
Tel 9283 6288
One of the more relaxing city-side dim sum venues, with a less frenetic pace than its Chinatown neighbours. Dumplings, buns and desserts are nicely done and service helpful. The flaky zeppelin-shaped deep-fried dumplings known as gok (with taro or sticky rice in the pastry) are brilliant. So is the mango, sago and coconut jelly pudding.

Prince Restaurant
100 Church Street, Parramatta
Tel 9891 5888 or 9891 5777
Parramatta's yum cha palace of choice is all huge fish tanks, chandeliers and red patterned carpet. Daily specials, such as prawn on eggplant squares and rice noodle pancakes, are assembled at an open cooking station. Steamed dumplings are fat with prawns, scallops, minced pork and vegies. Look out for excellent dan tarts and red bean in bamboo leaf for dessert. Prices are excellent too.

Regal
347–353 Sussex Street, Sydney
Tel 9261 8988
Sometimes the oldies are the goodies. That's probably why Regal has stood the test of time. There are few surprises in the trolley dollies' offerings – good salt and pepper calamari, gow gee, har gow sticky-sweet soy squid, stuffed tofu and Chinese greens to order – and it's a bunfight (sorry) on weekends. Dan tarts or neon-bright jelly for the kids will send you off with a smile.

Sea Treasure
46 Willoughby Road, Crows Nest
Tel 9906 6388
The recently revamped Sea Treasure is back on form as the northside dim sum outlet of choice. Seafood specials pop on the trolleys – salt and pepper prawns, calamari and more – and while it's heaving on weekends (often on weekdays too), there's none of that barn-like Chinatown buzz.

Green Eateries

CITY

Becasse
204 Clarence Street, Sydney
Tel 9283 3440
Chef Justin North buys straight from the farm gate, forming strong bonds with farmers who share his philosophical approach to sustainability. In return, he champions those he admires, showcasing their work in regular producers' lunches. Even the wagyu is sustainable: grass-fed and organic, from Gundooee, and the kitchen's nose-to-tail approach sees various parts of each beast appear at North's offshoots, Plan B and Etch.

Billy Kwong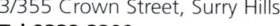
3/355 Crown Street, Surry Hills
Tel 9332 3300
SUSTAINABILITY AWARD
From the makepovertyhistory.org poster plastered across the front of her Chinese teahouse to biodynamic house wines by Vanya Cullen, Kylie Kwong was championing ethical and sustainable eating long before other kitchens caught on. She wears her passion on her sleeve and also walks the walk. She's a Fair Trade ambassador for Australia and New Zealand, her restaurant produce is organic or biodynamic and now her restaurant is carbon neutral.

Courtney's Brasserie
70 Phillip Street, Parramatta
Tel 9635 3288
We're impressed by the blackboard map, which draws a 200km radius around chef Paul Kuipers' search for local produce, and his emphasis on seasonality and organics. He proudly lists his suppliers, whether it's Sydney Basin honey, organic lamb or cheese from Bathurst.

Eurolounge
Shop 21, The Piazza, Castle Towers Shopping Centre, Castle Street, Castle Hill
Tel 8850 7077
Here's a great example of thinking globally and acting locally, with the kitchen scraps and coffee grinds going to local gardeners, shredded paper recycled by a pet store and a menu featuring local produce and organic wines. Plans for a rating system for the environmental footprint of dishes are underway.

Red Lantern
545 Crown Street, Surry Hills
Tel 9698 4355
Luke Nguyen and Mark Jensen's Vietnamese restaurant uses line-caught fish, pasture-fed, free-range pork and beef, organic fruit, vegies, coffee and poultry. They also compost, recycle and, most importantly, have installed a waterless wok burner.

Sean's Panaroma
270 Campbell Parade, Bondi Beach
Tel 9365 4924
Every week for more than a decade, Sean Moran has taken kitchen scraps to his Blue Mountains hideaway to nurture the land, returning with fruit, herbs, eggs, chickens and sometimes beef. He even uses natural cleaning products in this ocean-side restaurant. And as much as we frown on bottled water, at least Pebble Creek is sourced from the Southern Highlands.

REGIONAL

Grazing
The Royal Hotel, cnr Cork & Harp streets, Gundaroo
Tel 6236 8777
This heritage hotel has a large kitchen garden that produces the heirloom vegetables that appear on the menu. The team wastes nothing, not even the loo water, which is recycled through reed beds. The chickens do pest control, weeding, scrap disposal and soil fertilising, and also supply the eggs. Home-brewed beer sounds pretty sustainable too.

Hungry Duck
85 Queen Street, Berry
Tel 4464 2323
David Campbell has already notched up a few organic runs on the board at The Book Kitchen in Surry Hills. He takes it to another level, with an organic kitchen garden at the back of his Berry 'weekender' supplying herbs and vegies. From Fair Trade coffee to composting, organic meats and local sustainable seafood, Hungry Duck treads lightly on the land.

La Table
72 Burringbar Street, Mullumbimby
Tel 6684 2227
In the hippie hills near Byron Bay, saving the planet is a way of life and this French bistro leads the way. They are paid-up Slow Food members with a focus on local organic suppliers, including organic greens and herbs grown nearby in Newrybar. Much of the meat is organic, along with 90 per cent of the wine list, and we like the communal tables in the courtyard and the Wednesday-night set-price chef's menu.

Neila
5 Kendal Street, Cowra
Tel 6341 2188
Chef Anna Wong and her partner Jerry Mouzakis grow much of the produce used here, from Chinese dates to olives and the herbal tisanes for after dinner. The pair adheres to the "100 mile" principle, so dining at Neila is as much a showcase as a lesson in the very best of the Central West's produce.

Regional

BLUE MOUNTAINS
UPPER & LOWER MOUNTAINS, HAWKESBURY VALLEY

The eucalyptus haze giving the Mountains area its name would have to be pretty thick to hide the treats it has to offer. Outdoorsy activities draw the crowds – bushwalking and lookout hopping – while cosier indoor pastimes also get the thumbs up (particularly in the chilly winter months).

Shopaholics can choose from an abundance of antique shops scattered all around the Mountain towns, while Leura Mall boasts the terrific Megalong Books (Tel 4784 1302), the ever-popular Candy Store (Tel 4782 5210), a truly gorgeous stationery shop, Elizabeth Rosa (Tel 4784 1022) and more.

Once you've worked up an appetite, succumb to your cravings – bustling cafes, fine diners, bread fresh from the oven, fruit straight off the tree, chocolates made before your eyes – whatever your desire, the Mountains most likely can deliver, and in some wonderful settings.

At the top end of Katoomba's main street, the historic Carrington Hotel serves high tea (Sundays, Tel 4782 1111), as does The Lounge at Lilianfels, where "mystic" tea leaf readings make it all the more fun (weekends, Tel 4780 1200).

The area hosts some great festivals throughout the year (see the calendar of events at www.visitbluemountains.com.au), including the epic Winter Magic Festival in June. The Hawkesbury Valley side of the mountains, where orchards abound, also has popular annual events, including the Kurrajong Scarecrow Festival each October. Check out the Hawkesbury Harvest food trail too (www.hawkesburyharvest.com.au) to find farmgates to visit. And while Mount Tomah Gardens are beautiful at any time of the year, there's extra appeal when their Autumn Harvest Food and Wine Fair (www.mounttomahbotanicgarden.com.au).

Apple Bar

2488 Bells Line of Road, Bilpin
Tel 4567 0335 Map 12

Contemporary/Pizza

Score 13/20

When you're faint with hunger from the orchards, scenic valleys and mountain air of Bilpin, Apple Bar is the perfect place to stop and refuel. It's no fuss, friendly and reasonably priced. Sit on the verandah, at the bar or by the open fireplace to chow down on any number of hearty and happiness-inducing dishes. Chef Michael Jaggard and his team get stuck into the local produce wherever they can, but they're not afraid to venture further afield. An entree of Bilpin figs with prosciutto and blue cheese is wonderful, while delicately battered West Australian soft-shell crab is equally good. A doorstop-sized fillet of sirloin, seared on the wood-fired grill and served with cafe de paris butter is justifiably popular; locals also favour freshly made pizza with crispy-thin crusts: a prosciutto, grana padano and rocket version is flavoursome, although a towering pile of rocket was a little over-enthusiastic. A great apple cake using local fruit wraps up the locavore theme with a flourish.

Hours Thurs–Mon noon–10pm; bookings essential at weekends
Bill E $12–$19.50 **M** $19.50–$32.50
D $9–$13.50; 10% surcharge on Sundays
Cards V MC Eftpos
Wine Good value Australian-laden list with some nice higher-end choices; 16 by the glass
Chefs Michael Jaggard & Leigh Best
Owners Michael & Heidi Jaggard
Seats 130; private room; wheelchair access; outdoor seating; bar
Child friendly Up to 15 $12 kids' meals
Vegetarian Numerous dishes
www.applebar.com.au
And… fresh fruit, flowers and assorted craft at nearby roadside stalls

regional

Ashcrofts

18 Govetts Leap Road, Blackheath
Tel 4787 8297   Map 11

Contemporary

Score 14.5/20

The fresh mountain air builds an appetite for Corinne Evatt's enticing, eclectic menu. It's filled with temptations that will have you planning a return visit even before you've launched into a sizzling pot of eastern tiger prawns laced with garlic, lemongrass, ginger and lime. Lamb's brains lightly crusted with parmesan and tarragon, alongside tomato, apple and ginger relish, evokes similar feelings. This simple shopfront opens to a pristine white room, dark timber floors, walls adorned with captivating black-and-white photographs. Mary-Jane runs front of house with enthusiasm and attention to detail. Her endorsement of fricassee of New Zealand white rabbit in riesling is spot-on – it's robust, superbly flavoured and textured with cotechino (a sticky Italian pork sausage) and baby peas. A luscious daube of beef cheeks is boldly teamed with stilton yorkshire pudding, and a generous side of layered potatoes and fresh greens comes with all mains. Finally, burnt almond ice-cream with tuiles is too good to miss.

Hours Lunch Sun noon–2.30pm;
Dinner Wed–Fri 6–9pm, Sat & public holiday weekends 6–9.30pm, Sun 6–8.30pm; bookings essential
Bill 2-course menu $68pp, 3 courses $85pp
Cards AE (+3%) DC (+3%) V MC Eftpos
Wine Diverse and thoughtful list of mainly Australasian labels; 12 by the glass
Chef Corinne Evatt
Owners Corinne Evatt & Mary-Jane Craig
Seats 40
Vegetarian 3 entrees & 2 mains
www.ashcrofts.com
And…carefully marked dishes for coeliacs, as well as wheat and gluten intolerance

Darley's ★

Lilianfels Blue Mountains Resort & Spa,
Lilianfels Avenue, Katoomba
Tel 4780 1200   Map 11

Contemporary

Score 16/20

BEST REGIONAL RESTAURANT

A touch of indulgence can do wonders for the soul, and there's no better place to spoil yourself than in Darley's magnificent dining room. Set amid beautiful rambling gardens at the Lilianfels resort, this historic residence is filled with charm and impeccable service. The menu showcases the seasons: freshly shucked Sydney rock oysters with champagne vinegar sorbet are superb. A fan of yellowfin tuna sashimi partnered with mud crab, sugar-cured ocean trout, avocado and lively Vietnamese-style dressing is sensational. Junee lamb duo consists of a succulent double cutlet and slow-braised shoulder wrapped in creme fraiche pastry, paired with spiced eggplant, organic red lentils and baby herbs. A wickedly rich pressed duck confit sits alongside duck and pistachio sausage and a divine medley of chestnut mushrooms, baby onions, white turnips, pearl barley and celeriac cream. Luscious local raspberries in a vanilla cream tart with poached peaches will keep you lingering.

Hours Lunch Sun noon–1.30pm;
Dinner Tues–Sat 6–9pm; bookings essential
Bill 2-course menu $85pp, 3 courses $105pp; 6-course tasting menu $130pp; 10% surcharge on Sundays & public holidays
Cards AE DC V MC Eftpos
Wine Impressive range of regional vintages, some international notables; 12 by the glass
Chef Hugh Whitehouse
Owner Orient Express Hotels, Trains & Cruises
Seats 80; private rooms
Vegetarian Separate menu
www.lilianfels.com.au
And…look into the future and book the weekend Mystic High Tea at Lilianfels

blue mountains

Echoes

3 Lilianfels Avenue, Katoomba
Tel 4782 1966   Map 11

Contemporary

Score 13/20

Teetering dramatically on the very edge of the Blue Mountains National Park, with the spectacular panorama of the Jamison Valley unfolding below, Echoes boasts a seriously jaw-dropping setting. It's a tough ask for the kitchen to compete, but sometimes the spectacular vista comes in handy. Madeira-glazed duck liver with truffle bearnaise and poached quail eggs has all its component flavours present, but seemed slightly overcooked, while a vegetable millefeuille aims high yet landed overly oily. Mains lift the bar. The signature double-roasted Barbary duck, partnered with poached pear, marries nicely with a honey and coriander sauce. Chargrilled angus rib eye fillet is seared just right, with glorious braised oxtail providing an injection of richness. For a finale, caramelised pineapple and ginger tart is almost enough to distract you from that view, with perfect pastry and a curious yet magical combo of zingy finger lime anglaise and smooth banana sorbet.

Hours Breakfast daily 8–10am;
Lunch daily noon–2.30pm; Dinner daily 6–8.30pm
Bill Lunch dishes $7–$48; 2-course dinner menu $75pp, 3 courses $95pp
Cards AE (+3%) DC (+3%) V MC Eftpos
Wine Mainly Australasian list with a smattering of French crops; 40 by the glass
Chef Robert Stapleton
Owners George Saad & Huong Nguyen
Seats 80; private room; outdoor seating; bar
Child friendly Kids' menu; highchairs
www.echoeshotel.com.au
And... watch the sun set over the valley with pre-dinner drinks on the terrace

The Gallery

Katoomba Fine Art,
98 Lurline Street, Katoomba
Tel 4782 1220   Map 11

French/Contemporary

Score 13.5/20

As night falls in the mountains, this impressive gallery transforms into a classy bistro, dishing up heart-warming fare. It's a hugely enjoyable experience – courteous staff take your order, then invite you to take a stroll around the artworks with a glass of wine while you wait for the artists in the kitchen to do their thing. A simple shortcrust pastry tartlet of gruyere cheese, shallots and marinated artichoke hearts is a winner, while classic prawn cocktail with marie rose sauce – spruced up with a splash of cognac and a hint of tarragon – is a triumphant '80s flashback. Twice-cooked duck breast confit beds down nicely with rich, braised red cabbage ragout, studded with toasted walnuts, while a rack of Cowra lamb sports a yummy garlic, rosemary and quince paste glaze. There were a couple of fruits too many fighting for attention in the strawberry, banana, passionfruit and nectarine pavlova. But gateau nancy – flourless chocolate and almond cake – with port-poached strawberries and Yea clotted cream is a heavenly, gut-busting winner.

Hours Dinner Thurs–Sat 6–9.30pm; bookings essential
Bill 2-course menu $51pp, 3-course menu $65.50pp
Cards AE V MC Eftpos
Wine BYO (corkage $3pp)
Chef Barry O'Sullivan
Owner Geoff White
Seats 30; private room; wheelchair access
www.katoombafineart.com.au
And... complimentary seasonal veg and crisp roast potatoes accompany hearty mains

regional

Glenella

56 Govett's Leap Road, Blackheath
Tel 4787 8352   Map 11

Contemporary

Score 14/20

When your simple, elegant dining room features the world's longest Chesterfield sofa – all eight metres of it – you have to work pretty hard to get everyone back to the table. But the new team at this Blue Mountains institution does just that with a menu that's ambitious without being too tricky, aided by spot-on, understated service. The experience is full of special gestures, such as superb complimentary bread, served with hand-churned, truffle-infused butter. Start with rustic, house-made white pudding slices sitting in perfect harmony with celeriac mash, shiitake mushrooms and thyme butter. For mains, a delicate hapuka fillet luxuriates in an exquisite saffron and anise broth, with chorizo and tomato. A duo of rabbit excels – moist confit leg nestles beside divine herb-crusted fillet with rich caponata accompaniment. Desserts are top drawer too. The beautifully light, flowery aroma of lemon and lavender panna cotta was marred only by its slightly too-thick texture, while passionfruit curd tart has knockout pastry and fits hand-in-glove with toasted coconut ice-cream.

Hours Lunch Sat–Sun 11.30am–2.30pm; Dinner Thurs–Sun 6–9pm
Bill E $16 **M** $32 **D** $15
Cards AE (+3%) V MC Eftpos
Wine Nice selection of NSW drops on a well-chosen Australasian-dominated list; 13 by the glass; BYO (corkage $10 a bottle)
Chef David Smith
Owners Gareth McAuliffe & Katherine Strong
Seats 70; outdoor seating; bar
Child friendly Kids' meals; highchairs; crayons
www.glenella.com.au
And… pre-dinner drinks beside the roaring log fire

Lochiel House

1259 Bells Line of Road, Kurrajong Heights
Tel 4567 7754   Map 12

Contemporary

Score 15.5/20

Lochiel House delights on all fronts: a beautiful, convict-built house converted into a series of wood-floored, white-linen dining rooms; warm, genuinely attentive and concerned service; and fantastic food. Artichoke and mushroom soup slips down, luscious and velvety, mopped up with complimentary fresh-baked bread with Tetsuya-esque truffle oil and parmesan butter, while a superlative goat's cheese souffle with celeriac takes the notion of rich cheesiness and melt-in-the-mouth flavour to a new level. Beautifully pink duck breast is bolstered by beans and sweet baby brussels sprouts, while a thick fillet of blue-eye is sprinkled with aromatic fresh herbs and bathed in beurre blanc sauce. For dessert, white chocolate bavarois with fresh local berries, and a walnut tart with vanilla-speckled ice-cream are delights to both the soul and palate. The only downside to dining at Lochiel House is that it has to end: for city-slicker escapees and lucky locals alike, this is a spot to cherish.

Hours Lunch Thurs–Sat noon–3pm, Sun noon–4pm; Dinner Thurs–Sat 6–9pm; bookings essential
Bill E $20 **M** $32–$38 **D** $16;
12% surcharge on Sundays & public holidays
Cards DC V MC Eftpos
Wine A carefully compiled list, with food matches; 8 by the glass; BYO (corkage $10 a bottle)
Chefs/owners Monique Maul & Anthony Milroy
Seats 45; private room; outdoor seating
Child friendly Highchairs
And… in fine weather, try for an outdoor table in the pretty gardens

blue mountains

Restaurant Como
134 Great Western Highway, Blaxland
Tel 4739 8555   Map 11

Contemporary
Score 15.5/20

SILVER SERVICE AWARD

Prepare to be dazzled. Not by the location, but by memorable food and top-notch service led with charm and intelligence by Rachel McNabb. For chef Grant Farrant, food is art, and Como his gastronomic gallery, a true feast for the senses. A complimentary starter of jerusalem artichoke soup with tiny, truffled croutons is earthy and aromatic. Entrees vary from the simple delight of cherry tomato, roast capsicum and fetta bruschetta, to subtly flavoured passionfruit-cured ocean trout served with Queensland prawn and crisp-crumbed quail eggs and more; it looks too good to eat – almost. Mains also impress, especially a slow-cooked duck leg, fork-tender and more-ish, with red curry and spiced plum. A miniature celeriac "creme brulee" is an inspired addition alongside roast carrot and ginger tortellini. Desserts turn diners into food photographers, and Australia's next top model is the pretty pink rosewater meringue with passionfruit parfait.

Hours Lunch Sat noon–2pm; Dinner Wed–Sat 6–9pm; bookings essential
Bill E $13.90–$19.90 **M** $30–$38 **D** $15.90–$17.90; 8-course degustation menu $100pp
Cards AE (+2.5%) V MC Eftpos
Wine A smart list with equally intelligent advice; 13 by the glass; BYO (corkage $10 a bottle)
Chef Grant Farrant
Owners Grant Farrant & Rachel McNabb
Seats 45
Child friendly Kids' menu; highchairs; drawing materials
Vegetarian 8-course degustation, vegan also
www.restaurantcomo.com.au
And…Como is classy with finely set tables, fresh flowers and candlelight

Silk's Brasserie
128 The Mall, Leura
Tel 4784 2534   Map 11

Contemporary
Score 13.5/20

The ochre glow of Silk's classy dining room – radiating warmth into the chill air from its Federation-era shopfront on Leura's main drag – has been welcoming loyal locals and tourists alike for 15 years now. It's easy to see why diners keep coming back for more: elegant surroundings, delightful staff and well-crafted dishes are a hard-to-resist combination. A superb wafer-thin carpaccio of grain-fed beef tenderloin, paired with confit tomato and olive tapenade, is a fresh, light start to proceedings. Moist, corn-fed chicken breast with braised French green lentils, potato galette and a chorizo and sage jus is hearty and comforting. Pan-fried Tasmanian salmon fillet with grilled eggplant and kipfler potatoes is nicely offset by a winning triumvirate of gremolata, salsa verde and tonnato (tuna) sauce. Before rugging up for the homeward journey, try a fine affogato or seductive orange pudding bathed in decadent apricot, orange and Grand Marnier syrup.

Hours Lunch daily noon–3pm; Dinner daily 6–9pm
Bill E $20–$21 **M** $29–$36 **D** $12–$15; 10% surcharge on public holidays
Cards AE DC V MC Eftpos
Wine Strong Australasian list with great selection of NSW locals; 13 by the glass
Chef David Waddington
Owner Stewart Robinson
Seats 58
Child friendly Highchairs; drawing materials; simplified menu options
www.silksleura.com
And…it's a stone's throw from the railway station if you don't fancy the drive

regional

Solitary

90 Cliff Drive, Leura Falls
Tel 4782 1164   Map 11

Contemporary

Score 13/20

The union of Solitary's kiosk and restaurant might be a sign of the times but it's also a smart move. The pared-back menu is great value, offering two or three courses for dinner at an affordable set price. Now more can savour some stand-out dishes and soak up the magnificent panorama from this charming, heritage-listed cottage. It's easy to be torn between the jaw-dropping view to Mount Solitary and the splendour of a salad layered with kipfler potatoes, wild rocket and emerald asparagus, dressed with a lively lemon rouille and topped with coddled egg. House-made spaghettini tossed with chilli, garlic and pine nuts is superbly enlivened by bottarga shavings. Service is friendly but can be inattentive. Spiced chicken is generous, skilfully teamed with a salad of watercress, mint, pomegranate and orange. Grilled sirloin is mouth-watering with roast sweet potato, leek and herb butter. Adorable mini scoops of rich chocolate mousse are adorned with honeycomb.

Hours Lunch daily noon–4.30pm;
Dinner Fri–Sat 6–9.30pm
Bill Lunch E $13–$17 **M** $22–$28 **D** $7.50–$14;
Dinner 2-course menu $55pp, 3 courses $66pp; 10% surcharge on Sundays, 15% on public holidays
Cards AE (+3%) DC (+3%) V MC Eftpos
Wine Inspiring and thoughtful list of mainly Australasian labels; 12 by the glass
Chefs John Cross & David Povelsen
Owners Georgia Shepherd & John Cross
Seats 90; outdoor seating
Child friendly Highchairs; drawing materials; toys; garden
www.solitary.com.au
And...brunch, lunch and Devonshire tea for daytime mountain ramblers

Vulcans

33 Govetts Leap Road, Blackheath
Tel 4787 6899   Map 11

Contemporary/Wood-Fired

Score 15/20

You could easily miss this byword of mountain dining, squeezed among the craft shops of Blackheath, which would be a mistake for anyone seeking high-quality, innovative food. The square, red-painted room hosts two packed sittings of diners a night, all enjoying great food, calm, authoritative service and their BYO. Phillip Searle's menu is a blend of old favourites and new surprises, inspired by the massive wood-fired oven. Glazed duck sausage is consistently popular: speckled slices of flavourful sausage vividly offset by the sweetness of burgundy beetroot. Tofu – hard, soft and silken – is an unexpected success, bathed in a ginger soy reduction with nutty shiitake mushrooms and the crunch of cashews. Mains include polenta-crusted tuna topped by pungent capers and olives, and slices of velvety roasted pork with potato and green beans: both great on a cold mountain night. The outside temperature shouldn't stand in the way of dessert: the famous, oft-imitated chequerboard ice-cream is startlingly good, pineapple and star anise combining to create a sweetly triumphant note.

Hours Lunch Fri–Sun noon–2.30pm;
Dinner Fri–Sun 6–9.30pm; bookings essential
Bill E $19.50 **M** $33 **D** $14–$18
Cards V MC Eftpos
Wine BYO (corkage $5pp)
Chefs Phillip Searle & Joseph Campbell
Owners Phillip Searle & Barry Ross
Seats 38
And...make a point of ordering the warm, wonderfully fragrant bread

Last night Harriet went to bed hungry.

Tonight, Harriet has a tomato and chick pea soup with roasted vegetables and a large chocolate mousse.

It's our mission to help feed all the Tom, Dick & Harriets. Every night.

OzHarvest is Sydney's first food rescue charity, non-denominational and non-sectarian.
Since November 2004 OzHarvest has collected over 1,100 tonnes of food, from over 500 donors and has delivered 3,700,000 meals to 155 organisations feeding the hungry, needy and homeless.

Yes, you can help too.

To find out more, visit:
www.ozharvest.org
or phone 02 9516 3877

Macquarie Group Foundation
Founding Partner

BENZER

Good Cook, Good Food, Good Living.

CITY LIFE PROFESSIONAL
18/10 Stainless Steel Cookware

BOSTON CLASSIC
18/10 Stainless Steel Cookware

CALAN COPPER
18/10 Stainless Steel Copper Based Cookware
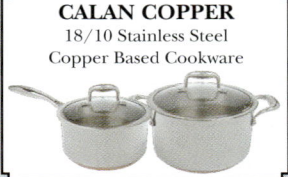

URBAN
Premium Cast Iron Cookware

FRENCH GOURMET
Cast Iron Cookware

CITY LIFE
Non Stick Frypans, Woks, Grills & Casseroles

VERNER & PISA
Professional Knife Block Sets

BAMBOO
Professional Preparation Boards

ULTAGRIP, SATOSAN, STEEL PRO & ZIEMMER
Professional Knife Collections
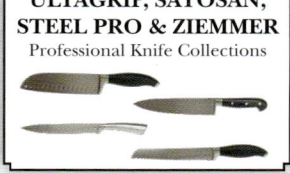

SAMBALEE & PESTA
Granite Mortar & Pestles

ITALIAN TRADITIONS
Professional Pasta Makers

SOLINGEN, ZURICH, BERLIN & OSLO
Professional Salt & Pepper Grinders

EXCLUSIVE TO
Victoria's BASEMENT
WORLD FAMOUS BRAND MERCHANTS

CITY - 9261 2674 Lower Ground Floor QVB, Sydney
AUBURN - 9748 8706 101 Parramatta Rd
ALEXANDRIA 9557 5984 1 Euston Road, (Cnr McEvoy St & Harley St)
ARTARMON - 9460 8761 89 Reserve Road, (Cnr Taylor Lane & Reserve Rd)

www.victoriasbasement.com.au

And also...

Arjuna
16 Valley Road, Katoomba
Tel 4782 4662
This is a definite local favourite for its lovely sunset-over-the-mountains view, casual vibe and good Indian fare. Crowds gather on the upstairs deck and fill up on flavourful curries – masala, kofta, vindaloo – mopped up with fresh naan.

Blue M Cafe and Food Co.
171 Lurline Street, Katoomba
Tel 4782 2650
Relax on the veranda of this cute cafe with rambling garden for a simple, tasty brekkie, lunch or dinner – and it's BYO, too. Or buy some of their own-brand chutney, elderflower cordial, and other local goodies.

Bush Rock Cafe
198 Evans Lookout Road, Blackheath
Tel 4787 7111
There are geese, gum trees and a small kitchen garden at this cafe in the bush, which serves good cake and great freshly squeezed juices.

Conservation Hut Cafe
Fletcher Street, Wentworth Falls
Tel 4757 3827
A great bacon-and-eggs spot, on the edge of the National Park, with panoramic views over the cliffs. Balcony in summer, open fire in winter, and bushwalks on all sides.

Fresh Espresso and Food Bar
Shop 5, 181 Katoomba Street, Katoomba
Tel 4782 3602
Terrific fresh-roasted coffee is just one of the attractions at this eco-friendly, carbon-neutral "cafe with a conscience". Tempting brekkie options, fresh delights from Hominy Bakery next door and plenty of choice for vegetarians also draw a loyal following.

Josophan's
12 Govetts Leap Road, Blackheath
Tel 4787 6333
Also at 132 The Mall, Leura
Tel 4784 2031
Also at 187A The Mall, Leura (cafe)
Tel 4784 3833
The Leura cafe (187A The Mall) does coffee and gourmet pies, baguettes, bagels and salads for lunch, while the shops (Blackheath and Leura) are chocaholics' heaven: artisan drops, blocks, bars and everything in between.

Hartley Valley Teahouse
Great Western Highway (cnr Baaners Lane), Little Hartley **Tel 6355 2043**
Pause here – midway between Mount Victoria and Lithgow – for lunch or an excellent Devonshire tea; purchase local preserves and art (including eccentric teapots); or take home a hellebore from the mountain nursery.

Leura Gourmet
159 The Mall, Leura
Tel 4784 1438
Breakfast or lunch in the cafe with a stunning Katoomba view or enjoy a cone of coconut and lime ice-cream while you check out the gourmet deli filled with olives, cheeses, antipasti, pies, local chutneys, jams and excellent takeaways.

Mash Cafe
19 Ross Street, Glenbrook
Tel 4739 5908
Stop in for decent Fair Trade coffee and an all-day brekkie and lunch menu – from organic free-range eggs benedict to satay chicken fillet burger. More ambitious fare for dinner Thurs–Sat (Fri–Sat during winter).

The Red Door Cafe
134 The Mall, Leura
Tel 4784 1328
This bustling indoor-outdoor cafe offers good coffee and super-fresh food. Try

regional

Spanish omelette with free-range eggs for brunch, or rare-beef Thai salad with zesty lime and chilli dressing for lunch.

Sassafras Creek Cafe
83 Old Bells Line of Road, Kurrajong
Tel 4573 0988
This picturesque weatherboard cottage houses a cafe, art gallery and gift shop: local produce features strongly in all. Browse the menu on the verandah or beside the fire; buy an artwork or perhaps a noodle bowl.

Stockmarket Cafe
179 The Mall, Leura
Tel 4784 3121
Compact in stature and big on top tucker, coffee and organic juices. Breakfasts are renowned; try vine-ripened tomato ragout and white polenta topped with poached eggs, parmesan and fresh basil. Hearty soups, salads and sambos for lunch.

Tutti Fruitti at Bilpin
1917 Bells Line of Road, Bilpin
4567 8436
A quirky green and purple cottage shop selling fruit direct from the orchard: berries, plums, passionfruit, figs, citrus and apples. There's also homemade ice-cream, snacks, and bunches of wildly perfumed field roses.

Whisk & Pin Store and Cafe
1 Railway Parade, Medlow Bath
Tel 4788 1555
The muesli mistress offers much more than cereal in this heritage-listed former PO. There are, gourmet foods and home wares but the cafe is king – try a poached egg, prosciutto, asparagus and gruyere sandwich, or dreamy corned beef hash for brekkie.

Zokoko
Unit 3/84–90 Old Bathurst Road, Emu Heights
Tel 1300 993 038
The Morgan's coffee crew are now making "bean-to-bar" artisan chocolate. Drop in for a tasting (and to see the impressive melangeur – or cocoa bean grinder), then have a first-class coffee and awesome chocolate cake. A light lunch menu is in the works.

PROVEDORES AND MARKETS
* **Bilpin Springs Orchard**, 2550 Bells Line of Road, Bilpin, **Tel 4567 1294**; pick-your-own apples, check what's in season and opening hours at www.bilpinspringsorchard.com.au.
* **Blue Mountains Food Co-op**, Shops 1 & 2, Halfpenny Lane, Katoomba, **Tel 4782 5890**; fruit, veg, bread, beans and much more – lots locally grown.
* **Hominy Bakery**, 185 Katoomba Street, Katoomba, **Tel 4782 9816**; organic sourdough, yeasted breads, cakes and pastries.
* **Kookootonga Chestnut & Walnut Farm**, 247 Mount Irvine Road, Mount Irvine, **Tel 4756 2136**; pick your own, late summer to early autumn.
* **Primavera Gourmet Deli & Cafe**, Shop 15, The Village Centre, 192 Great Western Highway, Hazelbrook, **Tel 4758 6735**; cosy deli-cafe with Italian smallgoods, cheeses, olives and pantry items, plus eat-in panini and coffee.

* **Blackheath Growers Market**, Blackheath Community Centre, cnr Gardiner Street and Great Western Highway, 2nd Sun, 8am–noon, **Tel 4572 6260**.
* **Hawkesbury Harvest**, information on farms and produce of the Hawkesbury region, www.hawkesburyharvest.com.au.

CANBERRA & SNOW REGIONS

Our nation's capital is blossoming, and not just from mid-September to mid-October when millions of flowers bloom for the Floriade festival (www.floriadeaustralia.com). The area has a lot to offer – certainly much more than politics, pyrotechnics and porn – including top-notch galleries and museums. The food scene is certainly worth exploring, from within the city to the fringes of the ACT and up and around the Snowy Mountains area.

Canberra's Slow Food movement is picking up with the Canberra Capital and Country Convivium offering about 40 events per year, including dinners and visits to food producers (www.slowfoodcanberra.com). The annual Fireside Festival in August also celebrates the area's food and wine with a month of activities and events (www.firesidefestival.com.au), while June 2009 saw the inaugural Capital Country Truffle Festival take place (www.trufflefestival.com.au).

In Murrumbateman, about 40 minutes north of Canberra, the October long weekend is reserved for the Murrumbateman Moving Feast, when a dozen-odd wineries offer a bite to eat with a matching wine (www.murrumbateman.org.au).

Collector revokes Halloween's stronghold on the pumpkin by staging its Pumpkin Festival in May (www.pumpkinfestival.com.au), while Loriendale Organic Orchard in Wallaroo holds an annual Apple Open Day. It will be extra special in March 2010, as it's the 20th time the celebration has been held (www.loriendale.com.au).

Up in the Snowy Mountains, any time when it's not snowing seems to be the right time for a festival of some sort. Thredbo has its Jazz and Country Music festivals, and about 90 minutes away in Dalgety the Snowy Mountains Regional Food Fair is held annually in October (www.snowyfoodfair.com.au).

Alto

Telstra Tower, Black Mountain Drive, Acton
Tel 6247 5518   Map 10

Contemporary
                                          Score 13/20

There's a lot going on up on Black Mountain – a smart menu, ever-changing scenery and special-occasion prices, and a new chef in the heights of Telstra Tower. A less than glamorous entrance and high-speed elevator ride give way to sleek and modern decor. Once seated, you'll pass the kitchen, cellar and bar as the restaurant revolves. A French onion and gruyere souffle is an indulgent start sitting in a puddle of rich, tasty cheese, while beautifully tender juniper venison is prepared with a light hand. Mains are ambitious, but erred on the side of over-complication; sand whiting was buried under overpowering streaky bacon pieces and pearl onions. Yet lamb cutlets are perfectly matched to stuffed eggplants and a thick potato skordalia. If you've adjusted to the motion and you'd like to see Parliament House one more time, stay for a lovely caramel semifreddo with toffee centre.

Hours Lunch Thurs–Fri & Sun noon–3pm; Dinner Tues–Sun 6–9.30pm; bookings essential
Bill E $21–$27 **M** $30–$45 **D** $18; 10% surcharge on Sundays & public holidays
Cards AE (+3%) DC (+3%) V MC Eftpos
Wine Interesting selection of wines with some import interest; 10 by the glass; BYO (corkage $15 a bottle)
Chef Noel Phear
Owners Mickey Gubas & Miriana Cavic
Seats 160; wheelchair access; bar
Child friendly Kids' menu; highchairs
www.altotower.com.au
And…a five-course tasting menu for $95

regional

Anise

20 West Row, Melbourne Building,
Canberra City
Tel 6257 0700   Map 10

Contemporary
Score 13.5/20

Anise tries hard to please with a menu that straddles the globe, zipping between Europe and Asia, with all the favourites accounted for. Check: fried zucchini flowers with fetta and balsamic reduction (and sprightly and savoury they are too). Check: poached soy quail with rice noodles, grapes and black vinegar (the bird intense with flavour). Check: duck confit with slow-roasted breast, and celery, apple and hazelnut remoulade. Inevitably, some dishes work better than others. The duck was a little dry; pan-fried ocean trout with Thai "three-flavoured" sauce was disappointingly monochromatic. But the sink-in elegance of softly padded chairs, a cushioned banquette and great swathes of tranquil tan and beige soothe frayed edges. As do complimentary Ligurian olives, house-made bread with La Barre oil, and thoughtful and extensive wine and cheese selections. Staff can be slow when busy, but are mostly affable. Finish with a spoon-crack perfect vanilla creme brulee.

Hours Lunch Tues–Fri noon–2pm;
Dinner Tues–Fri 6.30–10pm, Sat 6–10pm
Bill E $17–$21 **M** $29–$33 **D** $11–$14.50
Cards AE DC V MC Eftpos
Wine A page devoted to locals, with New Zealand and European choices thrown in; 14 by the glass; BYO (corkage $10 a bottle)
Chef Jeff Piper
Owners Jeff Piper & Justin Kavanagh
Seats 55; wheelchair access; bar
Vegetarian Separate menu
www.aniseincanberra.com.au
And…wine dinners, featuring Clonakilla and Ravensworth, every couple of months

Artespresso

31 Giles Street, Kingston
Tel 6295 8055   Map 10

Contemporary
Score 14.5/20

Once an all-day weekend option, this modern, bistro-style Canberra stalwart has switched focus. The popular brekkie is gone as Artespresso concentrates on being an elegant lunch and dinner destination. Michael Chatto's seafood-heavy menu aims high, and reaches wide as his times at Sydney's Pier and Fish Face shine through. Kingfish sashimi with traditional trimmings didn't show Chatto at his best, but silky artichoke soup does, resonant with tea-smoked cod and chive oil. We love the daring heat of spiced john dory fillets, perfect against the feather-light sweetness of a fennel and coconut emulsion. A straight-up bistro favourite such as soft, almost spongy eye fillet with eschalots, speck, and swiss brown mushrooms is equally accomplished. Artworks and a wall of windows impart hints of character to dark wooden floors and white-clothed tables, and service is competent, if occasionally a little offhand. The ingenuity of a scoop of lemon gelato alongside a savarin with poached autumn fruits adds the final sparkle to your evening.

Hours Lunch Mon–Fri noon–2pm;
Dinner Mon–Sat 6–9pm
Bill E $18–$21 **M** $30–$36 **D** $14
Cards AE DC V MC Eftpos
Wine Long, Australian-dominated, with cellar list too; 15 by the glass; BYO (corkage $9.50 a bottle)
Chef Michael Chatto
Owners Nik Gravias & Michael Chatto
Seats 120; private room; outdoor seating; bar
Vegetarian 3–4 options per course
And…it's now open on Mondays, too

good food guide

Aubergine

18 Barker Street, Griffith
Tel 6260 8666   Map 10

Modern European

Score 14/20

When Ben Willis, James Mussillon's former sous chef, bought Aubergine from his old boss in July 2008, there were no sudden changes. It looks much the same, with its cathedral ceiling, sweeping curved window and air of understated elegance, but over time, Willis has gently tweaked this Canberra favourite it's cheaper, the interior's been refreshed and made slightly less formal, and the food has relaxed too. The old clientele has taken with gusto to dishes such as fig carpaccio with quail and serrano ham, or the unexpected yet winning combination of tomato and eggplant terrine with kataifi-wrapped prawns. West Australian lamb rump had more fat and less flavour than hoped, but is affably boosted by broad beans, mint and fetta. Seafood, previously a strong point, is given a casual makeover as crisp-skinned snapper nestles next to calamari, chorizo and swirls of polenta. Desserts are as alluring as ever: pear and frangipane tart is sensational with vanilla ice-cream. The changes are subtle, but they're all for the better.

Hours Lunch Tues–Sat noon–3pm; Dinner Mon–Sat 6–10pm; bookings essential
Bill E $18 **M** $32 **D** $16; 3-course menu $58pp; 10% surcharge on Sundays for special events such as Mothers' Day
Cards AE V MC Eftpos
Wine Strong and interesting, with global reach; 16 by the glass; BYO (corkage $15 a bottle)
Chef Ben Willis
Owners Ben Willis & Andrea Collin
Seats 50; wheelchair access; outdoor seating
www.aubergine.com.au
And… the choose your own five- or seven-course tasting menu is a great option

Cape Cod

5 Duff Place, Deakin
Tel 6282 8697   Map 10

Seafood

Score 13/20

You could swear there's the smell of the sea and sound of seagulls at Cape Cod, especially due to its exclusively seafood menu. In fact, with its whimsical decor of red and white-striped wallpaper and chandeliers, and beaming waiters in striped aprons, this is one quirky restaurant in the middle of Canberra, with not a wave in sight. Classic lemon-and-pepper calamari is delicately seasoned and quite tender, however, pan-fried scallops were overwhelmed by a fennel and sweet cider dressing. There's no doubt that the favourite here is fish and chips. The golden batter and crunchy spuds are as good as any you'd find closer to the water. A fish pie with scallops comes with a crisp topping and a smear of mushy peas, nicely accompanied by scallop gravy. While burnt caramel espuma (foam) was a somewhat confused dessert, there's no confusing the fact that in landlocked Canberra, this is the place for fine marine fare.

Hours Breakfast Mon–Fri 7.30–10.30am, Sat 7.30am–noon; Lunch Mon–Fri noon–2.30pm; Dinner Mon–Sat 6–9.30pm (lunch Tues–Fri, dinner Tues–Sat during winter); bookings essential
Bill E $14–$16.50 **M** $20.50–$29.50 **D** $9.50–$12.50
Cards AE DC V MC Eftpos
Wine Thoughtfully chosen, comprehensive list of locals, imports and some back vintages; 13 by the glass; BYO (corkage $5 a bottle)
Chef Chu See Shin
Owner Chris Hansen
Seats 80; wheelchair access; outdoor seating
Child friendly Kids' fish and chips
And… grab some deluxe takeaway fish and chips earlier in the evening

regional

The Chairman and Yip

108 Bunda Street, Canberra City
Tel 6248 7109 Map 10

Modern Asian

Score 13/20

Aspiring cafes and restaurants have popped up all over the Bunda Street shopping strip, but none can match the timeless cool of The Chairman. For 16 years its decor has remained funky, with oriental motifs playing off stainless steel wall panels, and menus buried in gallery catalogues. Some evenings it works better than others, but when on form the smart pan-Asian menu is hard to beat. Calamari with rock salt, chilli and herbs is a fresh, verdant take on a ubiquitous favourite. Ditto duck pancakes, smoky and crunchy with water chestnuts, and chicken wontons in chilli oil that will blow your tastebuds away. Red chicken curry is alive with vibrant flavours, although the chicken's gelatinous texture was less appealing. Desserts such as vanilla panna cotta with passionfruit sauce avoid Asian influences entirely – and were the poorer for it. Order more savoury dishes instead. The young floor team are as jaunty and appealing as the decor.

Hours Lunch Tues–Fri noon–2.30pm; Dinner Mon–Sat 6–10.30pm
Bill E $9.50–$19.50 **M** $27.50–$33 **D** $11.50–$13.50
Cards AE DC V MC Eftpos
Wine A cut above most Asian restaurant lists, with some interesting and well-priced Australians; 11 by the glass; BYO (corkage $8.50 a bottle)
Chef William Suen
Owner Josiah Li
Seats 166; private rooms; wheelchair access
Vegetarian Diverse offerings, plus degustation menus
www.thechairmanandyip.com
And...the early-bird special of two courses for $28.50 is great value

Courgette

54 Marcus Clarke Street, Canberra City
Tel 6247 4042 Map 10

European

Score 14.5/20

It's been an even busier year than usual for restaurateur and chef James Mussillon, with the opening of Waters Edge. It might have nudged Courgette out of star billing in his cluster of three fine restaurants, but with its padded chair elegance and aura of genteel restraint, Courgette remains a favourite, especially for high-end business dinners. Each dish is complex and multifaceted. Savour the subtle interplay of basil-infused atlantic salmon with pickled ginger, soy and mustard seed dressing. Sometimes, while beautifully done, the elements seem to stand alone rather than work together, as in the muscular combination of rabbit ballotine with slowly roasted venison, and a stuffed zucchini flower. But roast duck breast interlaced with chorizo, on pickled red cabbage with prune and Armagnac sauce, comes together as smoothly as a symphony. Service, sometimes patchy, seems to be improving. When you're swooning over the last mouthful of plum and strawberry terrine with vanilla panna cotta and fine trails of chocolate, who would dream of going elsewhere?

Hours Lunch Mon–Fri noon–3pm; Dinner Mon–Sat 6–10pm
Bill E $22 **M** $38 **D** $16; 10% surcharge on public holidays
Cards AE DC V MC Eftpos
Wine Very fine list, catering for all budgets, with truly special drops from around the world; 14 by the glass; BYO (corkage $12pp)
Chef/owner James Mussillon
Seats 110; private rooms; outdoor seating; bar
www.courgette.com.au
And...choose from 12–15 superb, globally sourced cheeses

canberra & snow regions

Crackenback Cottage

902 Alpine Way, Crackenback Valley
Tel 6456 2198   Map 10

Contemporary

Score 13.5/20

This charming cottage, and its giant timber maze, is a great resting point for alpine travellers wanting something more than pit-stop fare. Start with a tasting plate, which might include rich duck paté, or a crisp croquette of local trout with horseradish aioli. Braised rabbit and wild mushroom tartlet has lovely crumbly pastry, but was overpowered by truffle oil. Smiling waiters, while occasionally forgetful, are as sweet as the single rose at each table (fragrant and freshly picked from the cottage garden). Impressive mains include golden potato and pecorino gnocchi, with spaghetti-like strips of zucchini, super juicy cherry tomatoes and goat's cheese from nearby Hobbit Farm. Beef fillet is ably accompanied by a savoury bread pudding, and horseradish and parsley mousseline. Desserts are generous, including blood plum semifreddo, prune financier and mirabelle plum sorbet: yum. The captivating horse painting above the fireplace by local artist Lucy Rose is a good reminder to order some local wildbrumby schnapps.

Hours Lunch (winter & school holidays) noon–3pm daily, Thurs–Sun noon–3pm other times; Dinner (winter & school holidays) Wed–Sun 6–8.30pm, Fri–Sun 6–8.30pm other times
Bill 2-course menu $60pp, 3 courses $70pp
Cards AE V MC Eftpos
Wine Affordable Australasian list with some familiar names; 22 by the glass; BYO (corkage $10 a bottle)
Chef Sarah Wilton
Owners Kerry Henderson & Keiran Murphy
Seats 80; private room; outdoor seating; bar
Child friendly Kids' menu; highchairs; crayons; outdoor play area
And…house-made jams to buy for home plus other knick-knacks

Credo

Diggings Terrace, Thredbo Village
Tel 6457 6844   Map 12

Contemporary

Score 13/20

The credo most Thredbo visitors follow is to ski until they drop. However, the mantra at this non-fuss, casual eatery facing Mount Kosciuszko is to serve consistently good food. Hanging on the walls are striking panoramic landscape images by local photographer Michael Scott Lees – and then there's the real thing right outside the windows. The menu is brief yet enticing with dishes such as house-made tortellini of confit rabbit (from nearby Bredbo) slick with burnt butter sage sauce. Tea-smoked rainbow trout paté is smooth and peppery, served with diced beetroot and crunchy toasted bread. Risotto is nicely cooked and flavoured with tiny cubes of preserved lemon, shaved pecorino and crisp, vibrant green asparagus and sugar snaps. Roasted capsicum-wrapped lamb was a little tough, but flavourful and enhanced by smoky eggplant puree and wilted spinach. A baked beurre bosc pear with vanilla ice-cream and sticky, sweet and tangy cognac-lime sauce would sway anyone from rushing back to the slopes.

Hours Dinner daily 6–10pm; snack menu 9.30pm–midnight (winter; summer times are variable)
Bill E $15–$17 **M** $20–$35 **D** $12–$16
Cards AE V MC Eftpos
Wine Extensive list of Australian and European drops; 15 by the glass
Chef Jason Abbott
Owners Jodie & Duane Burke
Seats 94; bar
Child friendly Kids' menu
www.credo.com.au
And…if you like the pics, the photographer has a gallery at Jindabyne

regional

Fekerte's

74/2 Cape Street, Dickson
Tel 6262 5799   Map 10

Ethiopian

Score 12.5/20

This unassuming restaurant with touches of Africa could easily remain undiscovered by a Dickson newcomer. But Canberrans know that Fekerte's is the pick in this international restaurant strip. Laid-back staff bring platters of Ethiopian specialties to families, students and regulars. To ensure you don't miss any of the house specialities, order one of the traditional platters to share. These are a popular choice – all served with kita, a more-ish Ethiopian pan bread. Many of the dishes are surprisingly spicy, so ask for some homemade cottage cheese to counter the heat. Berbere, a spicy red pepper mix, is used frequently and adds wonderfully warm heat to doro wat, chicken marinated in lemon juice until it is tender. The powerful key wat, Fekerte's speciality of spicy diced beef with onions, also uses berbere. Spiced red lentils are comforting and filling, while a strong Ethiopian coffee will send you on your way with a spring in your step.

Hours Lunch Wed–Fri noon–2pm; Dinner Tues–Sun 6–10pm; bookings essential
Bill E $6.90–$13 **M** $19–$30 **D** $5–$9.50; traditional platters $29.90pp
Cards AE DC V MC Eftpos
Wine Short list of Australian wines; 14 by the glass; BYO (corkage $6 a bottle)
Chef Fekerte Tesfaye
Owners Fekerte Tesfaye & Sendaba Gerba
Seats 100; wheelchair access; outdoor seating; bar
Vegetarian Nine dishes
www.fekertes.com.au
And…Fekerte's also has a stall at the Old Bus Depot Markets

The Ginger Room

Old Parliament House,
Queen Victoria Terrace, Canberra
Tel 6270 8262   Map 10

Contemporary

Score 12.5/20

Few dining rooms are as freighted with history as the stately, wood-panelled former dining room at Old Parliament House. The roseate glow from the ginger-decorated light box as you enter gives it just the right contemporary twist – as does the globally inspired multi-course menu. Highlights include sumptuous grilled kingfish with salsa fresca (tomato and avocado) and olive aioli, or a magnificent mix of spicy date wontons with yoghurt and pistachio parfait. But there are lowlights too. Rabbit and pistachio terrine was stolid, although nearly rescued by sweetly caramelised fig compote. Grilled scampi looked wistfully around for the promised hit of sesame, lime and orange. Service, however, is uniformly excellent – no former prime minister received better – and we love the cheese course. If, after mains, you can't manage a twice-baked souffle of Piano Hill Ironstone aged gouda, then roquefort with caramelised pear, endive and honey makes a politic finish.

Hours Lunch Thurs–Fri noon–3pm; Dinner Tues–Sat from 6–10pm
Bill 2-course menu $49pp, 3 courses $59pp, 4 courses $69pp, 5 courses $79pp; 7-course degustation $95pp
Cards AE V MC Eftpos
Wine Extensive list, organised by region, sampling gems from Canberra to France; 28 by the glass
Chef Amanda Peirce
Owner Janet Jeffs
Seats 110; private rooms; wheelchair access; bar
Child friendly Highchairs; smaller portions
Vegetarian Separate menu
www.gingercatering.com.au
And…check out the new Museum of Australian Democracy in the House on your way out

canberra & snow regions

Grazing

The Royal Hotel,
cnr Cork & Harp streets, Gundaroo
Tel 6236 8777   Map 10

Contemporary
Score 14/20

The heritage-listed Royal Hotel dates from 1865. It's a real old charmer – not grand, but genuine right down to the heirloom fruits and vegetables in the extensive gardens, which dictate much of the menu. A bowl of five different tomatoes with finely sliced heirloom beetroot and basil is offered as a side dish but makes a superb entree, worth a visit all on its own. A salad of local yabbies with prawns, sweet corn, avocado, lettuce, preserved lemon and tomato-saffron aioli is deliciously light, although a touch low on yabbies. For mains, there's succulent spatchcock with aioli and a white bean salad studded with pine nuts, raisins and grilled capsicum, with smoked tomato salsa. Spice-rubbed kangaroo on a slab of pumpkin and wilted beet greens (from the garden again) marries well with fresh mango, fenugreek and chilli chutney. Top it off with cardamom orange ice-cream crowning a disc of puff pastry with fresh figs and raspberries.

Hours Lunch Fri–Sun 11.30am–3pm; Dinner Thurs–Sat 6–10pm
Bill E $15–$16 **M** $25–$29.50 **D** $14; 10% surcharge on public holidays
Cards AE V MC Eftpos
Wine An interesting, all-local selection with many surprising finds; 17 by the glass
Chef Thomas Moore
Owners Thomas & Crystal Moore
Seats 160; private rooms; wheelchair access; outdoor seating; bar
Child friendly Kids' menu; booster seats; drawing materials; large garden
Vegetarian Separate menu with 4 options
www.grazing.com.au
And…the delicious beers on tap are brewed on the premises

Mezzalira

Melbourne Building,
cnr London Circuit & West Row, Canberra City
Tel 6230 0025   Map 10

Modern Italian
Score 13/20

Beneath the creamy Italianate colonnades of the Melbourne Building is just where you'd hope to find a restaurant that takes the authenticity of its cucina seriously. The hotel-style interior – navy and red accented by blond wood – isn't designed to stand out, but the modern Italian menu provides plenty of character, with ingredients selected from Italy (organic Ferron carnaroli rice for risotto) and around Australia (Shaw River buffalo mozzarella on pizza). Fire up things with a wood-fired crust to share, or opt for small tastes such as fried whiting "in saor" – with its addictive sweet-and-sour marinade of vinegar, pine nuts and currants. Move on to pasta such as golden tresses of tagliatelle, wound Rapunzel-style in the bowl with chunks of rabbit, spinach and lemon. Lamb shoulder wasn't quite slow-cooked enough, although flavoursome on its bed of creamy polenta and sweet roasted red peppers. Dessert is a return to form, with the tang of lemon tart amplified by light yoghurt sorbetto.

Hours Lunch Mon–Fri noon–2pm; Dinner Mon–Sat 6–10pm; bookings essential
Bill E $16–$22 **M** $29–$36 **D** $15; 5-course tasting menu $85pp
Cards AE DC V MC Eftpos
Wine Great Australasian and Italian range; 16 by the glass; BYO (corkage $1.50 a bottle)
Chefs Pasquale Trimboli & Howard Povey
Owner Trimboli Group
Seats 120; private room; wheelchair access; outdoor seating; bar
Vegetarian Several dishes
www.mezzalira.com.au
And…look out for their new pizzeria in Braddon

regional

onred

50 Red Hill Drive, Red Hill Lookout, Red Hill
Tel 6273 3517   Map 10

Contemporary

Score 14.5/20

Once more this landmark building on top of Red Hill has a restaurant befitting its panoramic view of Canberra below. Erected in 1964, it still looks like passing spacecraft might dock at the cellular-style windows. But inside the understated and comfortable semicircular dining room, it's the food that's really out of this world. Jodie Johnson (formerly of Grazing) cooks while brother Ben runs the casual (sometimes a tad slow) front of house. From an accomplished but approachable menu, try an outstanding trio of lamb: crisp cured breast with mint pea puree and cherry tomato; loin with hummus, tabbouleh and yoghurt; and crumbed brains sweetened with sauteed carrot and sultanas. Feel torn between hot and homely kingfish with fried gnocchi, harissa and asparagus, and fork-tender poached eye fillet with mash, olives, breadcrumbs, and tomato jam. Desserts are another strong point: blood plum and frangipane tart with mascarpone ice-cream and red wine syrup is galactically good. Beam me up.

Hours Lunch Wed–Fri noon–3pm; Dinner Tues–Sat 6–10pm; bookings essential
Bill E $18–$19 **M** $29–$30 **D** $14
Cards AE V MC Eftpos
Wine Plenty of local drops among a strong global list; 12 by the glass; BYO (corkage $12 a bottle)
Chef Jodie Johnson
Owners Jodie & Ben Johnson
Seats 70; private rooms
Vegetarian Separate menu
www.onred.com.au
And... book early, especially for Saturday nights

Ottoman Cuisine

9 Broughton Street, Barton
Tel 6273 6111   Map 10

Turkish

Score 15/20

High-end dining in Canberra is skewed towards men, and Ottoman makes them feel like kings. The pavilion-like restaurant has plenty of elbow room, an army of efficient staff, and confidence in spades, the formula honed over 17 years at the pinnacle of the city's dining. Many a deal has been brokered over the extensive menu of approachable and interesting food. The signature seafood dolmades are ever popular, but try specials such as mixed dolma with minced lamb and chilli, which, like most dishes, bursts with strong flavours. Or there are the subtler delights of tuna tarator, with almond meal and garlic paste, and fine herb salad, although the fish was cooked too much for our liking. Swordfish kebabs with leek and carrot are deliciously charred yet moist, while lamb kofte with white beans are worth trading in a kingdom for. This is not a place to hold back, and mastika-flavoured baked custard with pomegranate ice-cream and morello cherry sauce makes a right royal finish.

Hours Lunch Tues–Fri noon–2.30pm; Dinner Tues–Sat 6–10pm; bookings essential
Bill E $16–$21 **M** $29–$31 **D** $6–$15; 4-course degustation $70pp; 10% surcharge on public holidays
Cards AE DC V MC Eftpos
Wine Long, gutsy list with plenty of splurge options; 18 by the glass; BYO (corkage $10 a bottle)
Chef Erkin Esen
Owners Serif & Gulbahar Kaya
Seats 220; private rooms; wheelchair access; outdoor seating
Vegetarian A wide range, plus daily specials
www.ottomancuisine.com.au
And... live crayfish in a tank on site

Podfood

Pialligo Plant Farm, 12 Beltana Road, Pialligo
Tel 6257 3388   Map 10

Contemporary
Score 13.5/20

It's not quite paddock to plate; more Garden of Eden. Podfood is set in a plant nursery, and nature is close to hand in the form of pretty bouquets on the tables and a garden outside, best enjoyed from the verandah of this charming weatherboard cottage. The menu is well pitched for daytime consumption: generally light and flavoursome. Earthy, roasted beetroot, partnered with Woodside goat's curd, aged balsamic and a dusting of dukkah is a faultless rendition of a classic. Plump prawns stir-fried with mirin, sweet chilli and soy manage to hold their own in what could have been a gastronomic catastrophe in less capable hands. A tumble of mushrooms – shimeji, oyster and button – braised with candied lemon and pine nuts and served with rocket and creamy fetta mousse will even satisfy carnivores and, like the Moroccan spiced lamb salad, is packed with flavour. Head down to earth for dessert – a very rich creme brulee or mixed berry flan will do nicely.

Hours Wed–Sun 8.30am–4pm
Bill E $16–$20 **M** $22–$30 **D** $9–$12; 10% surcharge on Sundays
Cards AE V MC Eftpos
Wine List well suited to light meals; 12 by the glass; BYO (corkage $9 a bottle)
Chef Andrew Haskins
Owners Catherine & Andrew Haskins
Seats 75; wheelchair access; outdoor seating
Child friendly Kids' menu; highchairs; drawing materials; toys
www.podfood.com.au
And… pick up some plants for the garden on your way out

Rubicon

6a Barker Street, Griffith
Tel 6295 9919   Map 10

European
Score 14.5/20

As soon as you're ushered through the doors at this urbane diner on a suburban shopping strip, you feel you're in good hands. Whether seated in the spacious, cream-toned main dining room or past the impressive wine collection in the buzzy extension where groups gather, you'll receive warm attention. To start, salty-sweet pancetta-wrapped scallops are cleverly offset by a sweet plum vinaigrette, and soft-shell crab is deftly cooked, although its chilli lime caramel dressing resembled nothing so much as a standard sweet chilli sauce. Back to Europe, then, for mains, where plates are generously loaded. A nicely pink pork fillet is creatively matched with rocket gremolata, while a satisfying duck confit is accompanied by pan-fried mushrooms, caramelised eschalots and deliciously smoky Schulz bacon from the Barossa, making lyonnaise potatoes seem almost unnecessary. It's easy to see why locals keep coming back for desserts such as meringue tinged with Angostura bitters, served with passionfruit and tangy pomegranate syrup.

Hours Lunch Mon–Fri noon–2pm; Dinner Mon–Sat 6–10pm
Bill E $15.90–$21.90 **M** $27.90–$34.90 **D** $9.90–$14.90; 5-course tasting menu $75pp, 7 courses $100pp
Cards AE DC V MC Eftpos
Wine Extensive list that travels across Europe; 26 by the glass; BYO (corkage $9 a bottle)
Chefs Owen Kenyon & Evan Speed
Owners Owen & Jane Kenyon
Seats 60
Vegetarian Separate menu
www.rubiconrestaurant.com.au
And… groups are well catered for with various banquet menus and wine packages

regional

Ruby Chinese

NEW ENTRY

Ground floor, 18 Woolley Street,
Dickson
Tel 6249 8849   Map 10

Chinese (Cantonese)

Score 13/20

In a town not known for its cultural diversity, the short Woolley Street strip in Dickson is the closest Canberra gets to a Chinatown. Despite its compact size, it boasts some gems, and Ruby Chinese is the smartest, most upmarket of them all. It has all the trimmings: waistcoated waiters, a bar and regal-style decor that looks as fresh as when doors opened in 1982. Best of all, fish tanks line the back wall, an emblem of Ruby's commitment to freshness and quality. All your Cantonese favourites are here: sang choi bau, mud crab in myriad forms, live abalone in a steamboat and, yes, a deliciously light rendition of squid in spiced salt. Other treats include crab lace rolls, the moist flesh encased in a lacework batter; tea-smoked crisp-skin chicken (the smoky flavour was sadly elusive, however); and crisp lamb in a feisty, hoisin-based chef's sauce. Vegetables are served vivid and just crunchy, wafting a fresh ginger scent. Those more familiar with Sydney's Chinatown are in for another happy shock: affable, smiling service too!

Hours Tues–Mon & Thurs–Sun Lunch noon–2pm; Dinner 5–11pm
Bill E $5.50–$24.80 **M** $15.80–$49.80 **D** $5.50–$7.50
Cards AE V MC Eftpos
Wine Fairly basic list of restaurant standards; 10 by the glass; BYO wine only (corkage $7 a bottle)
Chefs Lai Kung Chan & Kam Por Chan
Owners Jimmy & Susan Chan
Seats 387
Child friendly Plenty for the kids to like
Vegetarian Plenty of options
www.rubychinese.com.au
And...try a cocktail in the bar before dinner

Sabayon

Shop 4, Melbourne Building,
West Row, Canberra City
Tel 6247 8212   Map 10

Contemporary

Score 14/20

The baby sister in James Mussillon's family of capital city restaurants aims for a more bistro casual look than his two fine diners, Waters Edge and Courgette. But here, too, you'll find Mussillon's slickly modern approach, with a menu that explores European flavours with polished zeal. The crisply white room keeps just a touch of heritage amid its smart fit-out of bare timber tables surrounded by white microsuede chairs, and the service does well to balance relaxed with attentive. While the food strives for boldness, its presentation can seem prissy, yet it's never short of flavour, as an entree of roast quail with pork and fennel sausage, grilled polenta and pear and radicchio salad amply demonstrates. The mains can be as hearty as crepinette of confit rabbit on a nest of nutty wild rice with broad beans and mustard sauce, which nonetheless finds a pleasant balance between wholesome and decadence. For dessert, the classics remain just that, especially creme brulee with elderflower-macerated berries.

Hours Lunch Mon–Fri noon–3pm; Dinner Mon–Sat 6–10pm
Bill E $18 **M** $32 **D** $15;
10% surcharge on public holidays
Cards AE DC V MC Eftpos
Wine Clever, crisp, yet pricy list of boutique Australians, plus some internationals; 8 by the glass; BYO (corkage $12pp)
Chef Chris Darragh
Owner James Mussillon
Seats 80; wheelchair access; outdoor seating; bar
www.sabayon.com.au
And...a fine cheese selection, too

canberra & snow regions

Sage

Gorman House, Batman Street, Braddon
Tel 6249 6050   Map 10

Contemporary

Score 14.5/20

There's a hidden gem in the labyrinthine Gorman House, and finding it is a lucky strike indeed. At lunch, the sun-dappled courtyard is the place to be, but at night, it's the stylish dining room, decorated with a stunning latte and white wallpapered feature wall and deer antler shades over the bar. Gems are unearthed with consummate ease. In a "study of mushroom", the clear amber jelly of a layered, jellied mushroom terrine, and clear miso broth with a mushroom tortellino are luminous. Wagyu, served with potato galette, duck liver mousse and truffle jus is an elegant play on steak and chips, plated with a precision that would impress even Euclid. A more relaxed hand is behind the baked flathead, the meaty tail equal to the hearty speck-flecked puy lentils and roasted artichoke. Desserts are pure play. DIY spider – homemade ice-cream and lemonade – generates genuine excitement, while on the cheese plate, strawberry lollipop and cherry biscotti glisten like jewels.

Hours Lunch Tues–Fri noon–2.30pm; Dinner Tues–Sat 6–9.30pm
Bill E $18 **M** $28 **D** $14
Cards AE (–2.5%) V MC Eftpos
Wine Concise list with a smattering of Canberran wines; 17 by the glass; BYO (corkage $15 a bottle)
Chef/owner Kyle Prowse
Seats 60; wheelchair access; outdoor seating
Child friendly A small selection of kids' meals
www.sagerestaurant.net.au
And…ask about the Signature Series tasting plates

Silo Bakery & Cheeseroom

36 Giles Street, Kingston
Tel 6260 6060   Map 10

European

Score 14/20

Canberra food lovers have a love–hate relationship with Silo. Unquestionably, it bakes the best bread in the city (and the best tarts – try the vanilla brulee, or the apple and almond). Unquestionably, it serves the best brekkie, with highlights including poached eggs with chilli jam, and pastries. (We love the evie with apple and raisin, the ever-popular snails, the most buttery croissants – we could go on.) Unquestionably, it offers an excellent, seasonally driven lunch menu, featuring its signature slow-cooked meats, falling apart with tenderness and steeped-in flavours, and airy, just-charred pizzas. The catch? It's so good it's often maddeningly busy, especially on Saturdays. Being jammed against the takeaway queue in this long, cool sliver of a room isn't exactly relaxing, especially as service doesn't always keep up with demand. Silo plays by its own rules: it's shut on Sundays and Mondays, by the end of which the city's foodies are getting withdrawal symptoms. And forgiving everything, yearning to come back.

Hours Breakfast Tues–Sat 7–11.30am; Lunch Tues–Fri 11.30am–2.30pm, Sat noon–3pm; no bookings for breakfast
Bill E $12 **M** $18–$24 **D** $5.50–$15
Cards AE (+2%) DC (+2%) V MC Eftpos
Wine Short but expertly chosen blackboard list; 10 by the glass
Chefs Leanne Gray & Malcolm Klose
Owners Leanne Gray & Graham Hudson
Seats 49; wheelchair access; outdoor seating
www.silobakery.com.au
And…Canberra's first cheese room is worth a visit; try the breakfast cheese plate

good food guide   207

regional

Smokehouse Cafe
431 Nanima Road, Hall
Tel 6230 2487   Map 10

Contemporary

Score 13.5/20

This pretty oasis, on a farm north of Canberra, comprises a cafe–restaurant, a winery (you can taste before ordering your wine) and fabulous offerings from the adjacent Poacher's Pantry, including products from the traditional smokehouse. The house platters for two vary each week – laying out a choice of various dips with smoked meats, seafood and vegetables, or cheeses. Any of these make for an excellent lunch, but the menu holds other treats. A roulade of chargrilled eggplant, roasted capsicum, zucchini and minted labna topped with baby spinach is deliciously light and creamy. Crisp-skinned roasted hiramasa kingfish is cooked just right, bathed in herbed caper butter, with asparagus and tiny, light-as-air spinach gnocchi. Sadly, the crisp skin promised on smoked duck breast was soft, and the salad of lychees, ginger, green papaya and crispy noodles too salty. But there are no complaints about poached local peach melba with mandarin ice-cream and hazelnut biscotti.

Hours Fri–Sun 10am–5pm (light meals after 3pm); bookings essential
Bill E $13–$14 **M** $22–$29 **D** $13–$15; 10% surcharge on public holidays
Cards V MC Eftpos
Wine A truly local list with only their own Wily Trout and the new Fingerling quaffers range; tastings encouraged; 12 by the glass
Chef Melissa Hanns
Owner Susan Bruce
Seats 160; private room; wheelchair access; outdoor seating
Child friendly Kids' menu; highchairs; lawn
Vegetarian Several choices; platters available
www.poacherspantry.com.au
And... pick up some Poachers products and wines before you leave

Terrace
The Denman Hotel,
21 Diggings Terrace, Thredbo Village
Tel 6457 6222   Map 12

Contemporary

Score 13.5/20

The Denman Hotel stands high on Diggings Terrace with a commanding mountain view, so book an early dinner to make the most of it. The ambience is a cut above, with atmospheric dim lighting and finely set tables. The occasional stumble by suave floor staff is forgotten as the aroma of basil hypnotises. The fragrance is from an entree of goat's cheese tortellini, sitting pretty on a sweet mix of red, yellow and green roasted capsicum. Seared rare tuna is a gorgeous deep red, over confit tomato, and avocado with a hint of coriander. Asparagus spears and olives add an artistic touch, but the olives overpowered the dish's subtle flavours. Anyone with a fondness for sweet flavours will love roasted duck breast with orange and endive tarte tatin, while a special of herb crusted veal with kipfler potatoes has simple, homely appeal. Chocolate self-saucing ravioli was a little dry, but that's quickly salved at the swish bar downstairs.

Hours Dinner daily 6–10.30pm (winter), Thurs–Sun 6–9.30pm (summer)
Bill E $17–$22 **M** $28–$38 **D** $18; 2-course menu $40pp (summer only); 10% surcharge on public holidays
Cards AE (+3%) DC V MC Eftpos
Wine Long list with plenty of Australian drops plus Europeans; 12 by the glass; good bar downstairs
Chef Silvana Parisi
Owners Edward & Judy Denny
Seats 120; wheelchair access; outdoor seating; bar
Child friendly Kids' menu; highchairs; drawing materials
www.thedenman.com.au
And... degustation menu with matching wines (minimum 6 people)

Waters Edge

Parkes Place, Parkes
Tel 6273 5066   Map 10

Contemporary

Score 15/20

After a few years in the doldrums, one of the capital's premier destinations is back to its best thanks to James Mussillon's ambition. While this grass-topped, glass-encased lakeside wedge is a serious fine diner, sitting on the rhumb line stretching from Parliament House to the War Memorial, the menu's 14 dishes match sharp technique with whimsical humour. To start, there's a striking, textural arrangement of seared scallops with a jelly ruler of spanner crab consomme and caramelly mascarpone, beautified by nasturtium flowers and leaves, and pumpkin seeds. Main courses include a witty mushroom and parsnip roulade with quinoa, made to look like mushies in a field. Alas john dory seemed a little overwhelmed by Asian-style braised pork belly, baby turnips and mushroom-filled tofu roulade in a ginger-scented braising liquor, and service can be slower than a Senate inquiry. Thankfully, a satiny vanilla panna cotta with strawberry and rosewater jelly terrine, sumac-spiced strawberries and glass biscuit receives a unanimous vote in favour.

Hours Lunch Wed–Sun noon–3pm; Dinner Tues–Sun 6–10pm
Bill E $18 **M** $36 **D** $16;
10% surcharge on Sundays & public holidays
Cards AE DC V MC Eftpos
Wine A modest, quirky, international list with the occasional heavy hitter; 14 by the glass; BYO (corkage $12pp)
Chefs Jason Rodwell & James Mussillon
Owner James Mussillon
Seats 100; private room; wheelchair access; outdoor seating
www.watersedgecanberra.com.au
And…cheaper lunch menu of the same dishes

And also…

CANBERRA & SURROUNDS

A Bite to Eat, A Drink as Well
Chifley Shops, Eggleston Crescent, Chifley
Tel 6260 3703
Laminex tables, mismatched chairs and carpet to bring on flashbacks – it's eclectic, all right (ignore the unwelcoming signs). Generous portions of home-style meals keep it bustling from brekkie to dinner. Hushpuppies – hash browns with fetta and parsley – are great the morning after.

Bookplate
The National Library of Australia, Parkes Place, Parkes **Tel 6262 1154**
The best cafe along this strip of national institutions offers first-rate coffee, outside tables overlooking the lake, fab house-made cakes and light meals of restaurant standard.

Dickson Asian Noodle House
29 Woolley Street, Dickson
Tel 6247 6380 or **6262 5903**
It's fast, furious and fiery. The laksa is, rightly, a Canberra legend. But almost everything on the pan-Asian menu is as good as it is cheap, especially spicy char kway teow. Thai and Lao non-noodle options are excellent, too.

The Julep Lounge
Level 1, 8 Franklin Street, Manuka
Tel 6239 5060
This little jewel box is a sedate, sophisticated meeting spot with comfy lounges, flock wallpaper and bar food to accompany a gem of a cocktail list.

Indulge in Canberra's gourmet delights!

Canberra is a great destination for food and wine lovers

Relax in modern cafes, experience first-class cuisine at stylish restaurants, dine with a view or taste award-winning wines and fresh food at a vineyard cafe. The *Gourmet guide to Canberra and the region* shares the very best in gourmet experiences on offer as well as details of local producers, providores, cooking schools and recipes from leading restaurants.

To discover more about Canberra's cuisine or to receive a FREE copy of the *Gourmet Guide* call **1300 554 114** or **visitcanberra.com.au**

visitcanberra.com.au

regional

Parlour Wine Room
16 Kendall Lane, Newacton Pavilion
Tel 6162 3656
The funkiest venue at Canberra's funkiest hotel, The Diamant, is now the best place in town for a cocktail, glass of wine, late-night dessert and tapas: from fried chillies to "Spain choi bao" – scallops, Moreton Bay bugs, chorizo and chilli.

Pulp Kitchen
Shop 1, Wakefield Gardens, Ainslie
Tel 6257 4334
An easily digestible menu picks off classic European combos: cider-glazed pork fillet with apple; octopus braised in red wine; duck confit with warm potato salad and hazelnuts. It's for quick consumption, with decent vegetarian and coeliac choices.

Rama's
Shop 6, Pearce Shopping Centre, cnr McFarland & Hodgson crescents, Pearce **Tel 6286 1964**
It's cheap, noisy and always packed, especially with groups tucking into a lush range of Indo-Fijian dishes. Specialities include yoghurty chicken dahi wala. Curries are versatile in style, just choose your heat. This 18-year stalwart is great-value fun.

Tak Kee Roast Inn
10 Woolley Street, Dickson
Tel 6257 4939
The original and best Chinese barbecue shop also specialises in gow gee soups (try the prawn). It's no frills, just fresh, excellent food, with plenty to explore. The Peking duck rocks.

Tosolini's
Baileys Corner, London Circuit (cnr East Row), Canberra City **Tel 6247 4317**
Mama Tosolini's home-style dishes are the way to go: fresh, omelette-style frittata, house-made gnocchi or chargrilled spatchcock. Alfresco dining under the pine trees is great on a sunny day.

UrbanFood Store & Cafe
Cnr Marcus Clarke Street & Edinburgh Avenue, New Acton **Tel 6162 3440**
This organic cafe and wholefoods store is where Cantrendies gather for healthy (and enormous) brekkies of house-made baked beans, scrambled silken tofu or naughtier eggs benedict. Lunch on a deluxe chargrilled chicken burger, and then pick up your 100 per cent organic supplies from the vast store.

PROVEDORES AND MARKETS
* **Blue Seas**, 5–7 Leeton Street, Fyshwick, **Tel 6239 7111**; excellent seafood, popular with chefs and home cooks alike.
* **Griffith Butcher and Bakery**, 10 Barker Street, Griffith, **Tel 6295 9781**; top quality meat including organic options.
* **Loriendale Organic Orchard**, 16 Carrington Road, Wallaroo (North of Hall), **Tel 6230 2557**; 110 varieties of apples, plus pears and smaller crops of other fruit; Saturday farmgate sales.
* **Manuka Fine Foods**, Shop 13, M Centre, Palmerston Lane, Manuka, **Tel 6162 0516**; deli, gourmet pantry items and an epic cheese room.
* **Tutto Continental**, 152 Mawson Place, Mawson, **Tel 6286 8800**; great selection of Italian deli goods plus some kitchenware.

* **Belconnen Fresh Food Markets**, Lathlain Street, Wed–Sun 8am–6pm, (some stalls open daily), see www.belconnenmarkets.com.au.
* **Capital Region Farmers' Market**, Exhibition Park in Canberra (EPIC), cnr Federal Highway & Flemington Road, Sat 8–11am, see www.capitalregionfarmersmarket.com.au.
* **Fyshwick Fresh Food Markets**, cnr Dalby & Mildura streets, Thurs–Sun, 8am–5.30pm, see www.fyshwick.info/markets.
* **Old Bus Depot Markets**, 27 Wentworth Avenue, Kingston, Sunday 10am–4pm, www.obdm.com.au.

SNOW REGION

Gourmet Forty Two
Shop 4, 100 Mowamba Place, Thredbo
Tel 6457 7500
A hole-in-the-wall cafe with a warm feel and basic menu with toasted sandwiches, big muffins and all-day brekkie. Coffee is taken seriously, with the cafe's own blend roasted in Canberra, plus T2 teas.

Iona Gardens Cafe & Nursery
Cnr Barnes & Campbell streets, Dalgety
Tel 6456 5130
Stop for coffee, a snack and to stock up on locally made pantry products. There are Cool Country Cuisine and Herb of Grace condiments, Snowy Mountains chevre, Tindery Mountain Dried Foods and more.

The Lott Food Store, Bakery & Cafe
178–180 Sharp Street, Cooma
Tel 6452 1414
Everything you need to stock a pantry (including local free-range eggs, goat's cheese from Jindabyne's Hobbit Farm) and fill your stomach. Open daily for brekkie and lunch with good coffee and an oft-changing menu of homely fare.

Thredbo Valley Distillery
Cnr Wollondibby Road and Alpine Way, Jindabyne **Tel 6457 1447**
Taste and buy terrific wildbrumby schnapps. Flavours include peach, sour cherry or pink lady apple, with most fruit used sourced from Batlow. A cafe serves hearty Austrian fare and cakes.

Canberra Wine
By Greg Duncan-Powell

This is a cool-climate wine region. The dry sheep-grazing country, with its low rainfall, warm summers, freezing winters and big diurnal differences is perfect for growing wine grapes. The only downsides are the risk of frost and the variable rainfall, but when nature is nurturing, the region can produce world-beating wines.

Canberra's 140 wineries and 30-odd cellar doors are spread over a wide range of terrain, and cabernet sauvignon, chardonnay, pinot noir, and pinot gris have been produced with success, but without doubt Canberra's best variety is riesling.

Clonakilla (Crisps Lane, Murrumbateman, **Tel 6227 5877**; open daily 11am–5pm) The shiraz-viognier remains one of Australia's top cult wines. The cellar door also has a more affordable shiraz made from Hilltops fruit.

Helm (19 Butts Road, Murrumbateman, **Tel 6227 5953** Open Thurs–Mon 10am–5pm) produces top class riesling and some very good cabernet sauvignon.

Brindabella Hills (156 Woodgrove Close via Hall, **Tel 6230 2583**; open weekends and public holidays 10am–5pm) is one of the few Canberran wineries actually inside the ACT. Winemaker Roger Harris is meticulous, the wines are modern in style, and the Rhone-like shiraz is a particular favourite.

Shaw Vineyard Estate (34 Isabel Drive Murrumbateman, **Tel 6227 5827**; open Weds–Sun & public holidays 10am–5pm) An up-and-comer producing a great riesling and a tidy range of reds.

Lark Hill (521 Bungendore Road, Bungendore, **Tel 6238 1393**; open Wed–Mon 10am–5pm) is one of the cooler sites, and viticulture is tricky, but when the season is right, Lark Hill can produce excellent riesling and pinot noir.

Mount Majura (Majura Road, Majura, **Tel 6262 3070**; open Thurs–Mon 10am–5pm) produces a wide range of quality varietals and – as is usually the case in Canberra – the riesling and the shiraz are the picks of the bunch.

regional

HUNTER VALLEY
WINE COUNTRY, MAITLAND & UPPER HUNTER

Any day is a good day for a trip to the Hunter Valley, but the best trip is a long one, since there's an ever-growing list of things to do in the region. Apart from the obvious – cellar door visits – there's plenty more to keep foodies occupied.

The annual Hunter Valley Wine and Food Month, held in June, offers wine tutorials, produce and vineyard tours, dinners, tastings and more (www.hvwineandfood.hvva.com.au).

Lovedale is where the action is on the third weekend in May, with the Lovedale Long Lunch offering a good feed (www.lovedalelonglunch.com.au), while it's all roads to Broke in early April for "a little bit of Italy in Broke" celebrating food and culture from the boot (www.brokefordwich.com.au).

November's Bitter and Twisted International Boutique Beer Festival at Maitland Gaol is proving a hit (www.bitterandtwisted.com.au). Nearby in historic Morpeth is the Honey Festival (24–25 Oct) and April's Fiery Food Festival (Tel 4933 1407 or Maitland Visitor Information 4931 2800).

When you're done eating, there are lots of outdoor concerts, film screenings, music festivals, balloon trips, aqua golfing and many other activities to fill several itineraries (Hunter Valley Wine Country Tel 4990 0900).

In the middle of it all, too, is the massive Hunter Valley Gardens – a perfect playground for families (www.hvg.com.au). There are a dozen themed gardens, and they hold various events, the most appetising of which would have to be the Chocolate Festival – yum!

With so much to do, just be sure not to forget those cellar door visits. This is after all, Australia's oldest continuous wine-producing region – which warrants a tipple.

305 Restaurant & Cafe

305 High Street, Maitland
Tel 4933 9989   Map 13

Contemporary
Score 12.5/20

With olive green walls, linen-covered tables, fine glassware and white dinnerware, now only the etched-glass fanlight hints at the pharmacy once housed in this 1867 building. Waiters glide unobtrusively between the gently buzzing dining room and open kitchen. Crab cake is a stand-out entree: crisply crusted and chock full of sweet blue swimmer meat. A main of butter-tender salmon fillet, seared then poached in extra virgin olive oil, comes with sliced kipfler potatoes, a salad of rocket, finely sliced fennel, capsicum and kalamata olives, plus dill-scented aioli and gazpacho style tomato salsa. Creme brulee disappointed with too thin caramel, while the custard and accompanying chocolate mousse was too firm. You'll nonetheless leave content with memories of well-rested prime angus fillet with oven-roasted field mushroom, potato croquettes and rich, red wine sauce, as well as silky ravioli, filled with prawn, preserved lemon and dill, floating in a seafood bisque.

Hours Lunch Tues–Sat 10am–3pm; Dinner Tues–Sat 6–9pm
Bill E $20.50 **M** $34.50 **D** $15.50; 2-course menu $53, 3 courses $67; 10% surcharge on public holidays
Cards AE (+3%) V MC Eftpos
Wine Brief, well priced list of Hunter, other Australians, plus the odd French and New Zealand drop; 7 by the glass
Chef Daniel Kibble
Owners Christine Harrison & Daniel Kibble
Seats 40; private room; wheelchair access; outdoor seating
Child friendly Kids' menu
And...a courtyard for afternoon tea

Amanda's on the Edge

Windsor's Edge Vineyard,
1039 McDonalds Road, Pokolbin
Tel 4998 7900   Map 13

Contemporary

Score 13/20

More comforting than cutting edge, Amanda's is like being at a friend's much-loved weekender. There's a touch of country chic to the dining rooms, which boast idyllic views over Windsor's Edge vineyard and a log fire in winter. Outside, lantern-topped tables for two line the curved verandah, making for a quieter, more private experience. With old-school offerings such as rustic duck liver paté and crepes with garlicky bug tails on the blackboard menu, the sense that you've stumbled into an intimate dinner party continues. More-ish labna-stuffed chicken with smashed pumpkin and macadamias offers a new twist on the classic roast, and is right at home with a crisp local semillon. The house-label sticky, meanwhile, works a treat with the cosseting range of desserts, including a toffee-spiked creme brulee with blueberry compote and crumbly shortbread. Amanda, do you mind if we crash here tonight?

Hours Lunch Fri–Mon noon–3pm; Dinner daily 6–9pm; bookings essential
Bill E $18.50–$22.50 **M** $28.50–$36.50 **D** $14.50–$15.50; 10% surcharge on Sundays & public holidays
Cards AE DC V MC Eftpos
Wine Affordable Hunter list, including Windsor's Edge's own range; 10 by the glass; BYO (corkage $4pp)
Chef Sara Connors
Owner Amanda Patton
Seats 75; private rooms; wheelchair access; outdoor seating
Child friendly Kids' menu; highchairs
Vegetarian Separate menu plus specials
www.amandas.com.au
And... just-baked bread and local olive oil

Arnott's Bakehouse

148 Swan Street, Morpeth
Tel 4934 4343   Map 13

Contemporary

Score 14/20

The biscuits might have gone offshore but the Arnott family remains in Australia, on the very site where it began with great-great-great-granddad, maintaining the bakery tradition and now adding an elegant restaurant. The three dining rooms above the bakery with their French silk curtains, Murano glass light fittings and smart, linen-covered tables are a fitting setting for some beautiful food under new chef Jose Miguel. Green-tea cured salmon, scattered with a fine julienne of pickled ginger and white radish is soft and delicate, although grilled scallops were rather overwhelmed by pancetta-spiked pumpkin risotto. Sweet parsnip puree provides an autumnal note to tender, pink lamb loin on tapenade jus, while truffled polenta is perfect for soaking up all the red wine jus around the beef eye fillet, which also comes with hand-cut potato chips. Creamy smooth yoghurt and honey panna cotta with saffron-spiced oranges proves the Arnott descendants are still on track.

Hours Lunch Fri–Sun 11.30am–3pm; Dinner Thurs–Sat 6–9pm
Bill Lunch $20–$28; Dinner 2 courses $50, 3 courses $60; 15% surcharge on Sundays & public holidays
Cards AE (+3%) DC V MC Eftpos
Wine Selection of Australian, New Zealand, German, Austrian, French and Spanish wines; 12 by the glass
Chef Jose Miguel
Owners Allison & Stephen Arnott
Seats 64; private rooms; outdoor seating; bar
Child friendly Kids' menu; highchairs; toys & books; baby-changing facilities
www.arnottsbakehouse.com.au
And... try chai or black tea from Green Tea Frog of Morpeth

regional

Bistro Molines

749 Mount View Road, Mount View
Tel 4990 9553   Map 13

French
Score 15/20

Hunter stalwart Robert Molines has moved up the hill to do what he does best: sourcing local and seasonal ingredients, using impeccable technique to produce his signature paté, gnocchi, duck and offal dishes. A vista of vines distracts diners at linen-covered tables, as they enjoy immaculately grilled scallops and asparagus with tarator; and crunchy, herb-crumbed, goat's cheese-filled zucchini flowers with olive aioli. Lamb shanks fall off the bone into a richly flavoured sauce. Well-rested beef fillet on creamy potato mousseline, caramelised onion, pencil leek with red wine jus and bearnaise sauce is all classical French. Delicate lychee, tangy lemon and intense strawberry sorbets with crumbly praline are all so good it's hard to pick a favourite. The piece de resistance is an airy meringue island adrift in a sea of creme anglaise, appropriately paired with ripe raspberries, blueberries and strawberries, while a fine, crisp almond wafer perches on top.

Hours Lunch Thurs–Mon 12–2.30pm; Dinner Fri–Sat 7–9pm; bookings essential
Bill E $22–$26 **M** $35–$39 **D** $13–$16
Cards AE V MC Eftpos
Wine A fairly extensive collection of French, Aussie and New Zealand drops with some very local options; 10 by the glass; BYO (corkage $10 a bottle)
Chef Robert Molines
Owners Robert & Sally Molines
Seats 70; wheelchair access; outdoor seating
Child friendly Kids' meals; highchairs; toys
www.bistromolines.com.au
And… what could be a lovelier setting for a wedding?

Cafe Beltree

266 Hermitage Road, Pokolbin
Tel 6574 7216   Map 13

Mediterranean
Score 13/20

Beltree is back. Original chef Mark Delandro has returned, cooking up the same understated, fresh food that made the original Margan cellar door such a popular lunch spot a few years back. Limited opening hours mean there are only a few chances to sit back and take your pick from the blackboard menu, but perhaps it means we won't take for granted designed-to-share dishes such as sugar-cured ocean trout, beautifully coloured and topped with a neat mound of pickled fennel and caper dressing. A bowl of mussels in tomato sauce with fresh parsley and just the right hint of chilli is equally delightful in its simplicity and wonderfully fresh flavours. Golden crisp whitebait fritters are great with a liberal squeeze of lemon juice, but were missing something – aioli perhaps – to provide contrast. A generous slice of crumbly and moist lemon polenta cake is as pleasing as the peaceful, green surrounds, relaxed service and rustically provincial decor.

Hours Lunch Thurs–Mon noon–3pm; cellar door open for snacks Thurs–Mon 10am–5pm; function dinners by appointment
Bill Share plates $18–$26
Cards V MC
Wine Brief, affordable list of mostly Margan wines; 16–20 by the glass; BYO (corkage $5pp)
Chef Mark Delandro
Owners The Young family
Seats 60; wheelchair access; outdoor seating
Child friendly Outdoor area; modified menu
www.huntervalleywinegrowers.com.au
And… it's a nice escape from Pokolbin's cellar door hub

Canter

109 Susan Street, Scone
Tel 6545 2286 Map 13

Contemporary

Score 13.5/20

This beautifully renovated old cottage is decorated with a touch of whimsy, evoking Scone's horsey heritage. The aptly named Canter, with its pressed-metal ceilings, old fireplaces and wraparound verandah is a relaxed country restaurant with a smart and beautifully executed menu, which changes each month to embrace seasonal produce. It trots out sophisticated sandwiches and salads for lunch and comforting produce-driven mains at dinner. A salad of figs, spinach, fetta and almonds is a summery delight, and spiced corn cakes with citrus-cured salmon is similarly light and fresh. Risotto, given a twist by using nicely fragrant wild rice, makes a fine match with pumpkin and pine nuts. There's no going past the crisp and creamy indulgence of a pavlova with mango and passionfruit – it's a true country comfort, served just as it should be. At Canter, good food, wine and service make a winning trifecta.

Hours Wed–Sat 8am–3pm & 6–10pm, Sun 9am–3pm
Bill E $12.50–$19.50 **M** $24–$34 **D** $12–$13
Cards AE DC V MC Eftpos
Wine Insightful collection of top local producers and other domestic benchmarks & affordable quality imports; 5 by the glass
Chef Angela McMurray
Owners Nicole & Tom Jordan
Seats 65; wheelchair access; outdoor seating
Child friendly Highchairs; toys; crayons
Vegetarian Many options
www.canterrestaurant.com.au
And... visit William's Workshop out the back for old-fashioned toys and home wares

The Cellar

Hunter Valley Gardens Village, Broke Road, Pokolbin
Tel 4998 7584 Map 13

Contemporary

Score 12.5/20

This 30-year stalwart is in the vast Hunter Valley Gardens Village complex amid garden walks, chopper rides and aqua golf. Walking in is like entering a glasshouse with a distinct atrium feel, where rocks and greenery encroach around the glass-panelled space. Classic old bottles of Hunter wine on the wall complete the picture, along with enthusiastic and informative service. In winter there's an open fire, while in warmer months you can dine outside. Sea-sweet seared scallops with salty crackling and mustard dressing is perfect, while a wonderfully meaty side of pork hock terrine is a hearty addition. Blue-eye fillet is delicately cooked and works well with a beetroot, asparagus and white bean puree. An excellent wagyu steak teams well with French-inspired oven potatoes but hardly needed bacon and aioli on top. To finish, house-made chocolate and raspberry mousse terrine comes with a quirky puff of fairy floss on top.

Hours Lunch Mon–Sat noon–3pm; Dinner Mon–Fri 6.30–9pm, Sat 6–9pm
Bill E $22.50 **M** $36.50 **D** $14; 2-course menu $39pp, 3 courses $49; 5-course degustation $85; 10% surcharge on public holidays
Cards AE DC V MC Eftpos
Wine Hunter-focused list; 15 by the glass; BYO Mon–Fri (corkage $10 a bottle)
Chef Andrew Wright
Owners Andrew & Janet Wright
Seats 120; private room; wheelchair access; outdoor seating; bar
Child friendly Kids' menu; highchairs; crayons
www.the-cellar-restaurant.com.au
And... note the well-priced fixed menus

regional

Esca Bimbadgen

790 McDonalds Road, Pokolbin
Tel 4998 4666   Map 13

Contemporary

Score 13/20

It's always a thrill driving up the weaving, palatial entrance to this impressive-looking winery on top of the hill. Once inside, you pass huge stainless steel wine vats on the way to this elegant restaurant with a sleek, industrial feel. Commanding views of vineyards and the nearby golf course enhance the experience, and service, while a little inexperienced, is helpful and smiling. The menu's global approach should please all-comers. Four steamed pork and scallop dumplings are packed with juicy chunks of meat and arrive with sesame soy dipping sauce. Spaghettini with fresh crab and chilli is brought to life by zucchini, preserved lemon and parsley. Delicately chargrilled lamb loins were let down by a base of chickpea, fennel, yoghurt and harissa, which lacked a subtle touch. Dessert is a highlight, especially house-made hazelnut ice-cream with side shots of Frangelico and espresso to pour over the top. It's enough to make you want to stay over, and you can: ask about Bimbadgen's accommodation options.

Hours Lunch daily noon–3pm
Bill E $22–$23 **M** $35–$36 **D** $15; 10% surcharge on public holidays
Cards AE V MC Eftpos
Wine Concise, classy Australian list; 13 by the glass
Chef Bradley Teale
Owner Bimbadgen Estate
Seats 100; private room; wheelchair access; outdoor seating; bar
Child friendly Kids' menu; highchairs; pencils
Vegetarian Vegetarian & gluten-free menu
www.bimbadgen.com.au
And…re-create at home: the estate's website features monthly recipes

Firestick Cafe

576 DeBeyers Road, Pokolbin
Tel 4998 6968   Map 13

Contemporary

Score 14/20

The venerable Rock restaurant's daytime incarnation is a casual affair, with bare tables and T-shirt clad waiters, yet it remains all class. Who can go past the irresistible thin-based pizzas: wood-fired and adorned simply with top-quality ingredients (try tomato and basil with local Binnorie labna)? Lamb shank pie is classic comfort food, with a rich and hearty filling, crisp pastry and a mixed green leaf salad on the side. For a lighter option, try salmon gravlax with poached egg balanced on crunchy brioche with a vibrant streak of salsa verde. Leek and goat's curd tart, beautifully golden on top, is served with fresh beetroot salad. As lovely as the view – big skies and shiraz vines – are desserts such as apple tarte tartin with butterscotch sauce, and a wonderfully fragrant lemon delicious pudding that lives up to its name. Move to the comfy lounges in the bar after lunch, for coffee or another glass (or two) of wine.

Hours Lunch daily 10.30am–3pm; bookings recommended
Bill E $14–$26 **M** $20–$39 **D** $12; 15% surcharge on public holidays
Cards AE V MC Eftpos
Wine Poole's Rock and Cockfighter's Ghost range; 22 by the glass
Chef Andrew Clarke
Owners Andrew & David Clarke
Seats 120; wheelchair access; outdoor seating; bar
Child friendly Kids' menu; highchairs
www.rockrestaurant.com.au
And…a side of New York fries? Why not?

Leaves & Fishes

737 Lovedale Road, Lovedale
Tel 4930 7400   Map 13

Contemporary/Seafood

Score 12.5/20

If you're after a truly relaxing lunch spot, this one's bound to please. A mix of furniture, including cushion-strewn lounges and clipboard menus, creates a casual feel, while trendy (appropriately fishy-looking) Everforge cutlery and linen-clothed tables are more serious touches. Running water trickles down the A-frame roof and into the dam over which the restaurant protrudes, providing a tranquil soundtrack and view. Settle in with Port Stephens rock oysters, served four ways including refreshing gazpacho shots with crunchy celery, and slightly battered with tangy pickled cucumber. Meanwhile, the otherwise great service can fade under pressure. Classic battered fish (ling, perhaps) and chips, is a popular choice, the large serving sure to challenge even the heartiest eaters. A fish fillet, blue-eye on our visit, is pan-fried and served with sliced king mushroom, asparagus and a light prawn cream sauce. Landlubbers will be pleased with nicely medium-rare beef medallions, while coconut tart with fresh-diced pineapple, mint and creme fraiche adds a tropical twist to the meal.

Hours Lunch Wed–Sun 11.30am–3pm; Dinner Wed–Sat 6.30–11pm
Bill E $21 **M** $32–$42 **D** $14; 10% surcharge on Sundays & public holidays
Cards AE V MC Eftpos
Wine Short, reasonably priced Hunter list; 7 by the glass
Chef Jamie Hartcher
Owner Sharon Burke
Seats 65; wheelchair access; outdoor seating
Child friendly Highchairs
www.leavesandfishes.com
And... watch the bill, these are fine-dining prices

Majors Lane

64 Majors Lane, Lovedale
Tel 4930 7832   Map 13

Contemporary

Score 14/20

When it comes to promoting the region's spoils, homegrown hero Ben Sales is leading the charge. This astute chef works wonders with local produce, turning out top-notch bacon, prosciutto, trout and more from his onsite smokehouse. Dine in the peaceful white-walled restaurant, or out on the patio where terracotta-toned water features provide a relaxing background note to a sensational meal. Miso-cured ocean trout with apple and cucumber gazpacho is a happy marriage of rich, sweet fish and zippy lime-spiked soup, while spicy handmade merguez sausages are cleverly teamed with mint yoghurt and tangy mustard fruits. Pot-roasted duck legs with a tamarind and orange glaze sit on a summer cassoulet of white beans, speck, shiitake and parsley, making for a light take on a French legend. Try Sales's tropical twist on jelly and custard – a punchy pineapple version served with a lick of creme anglaise and chewy toasted-coconut ice-cream. It's retro classic transformed into modern-day marvel.

Hours Lunch Thurs–Mon 11.30am–4pm; Dinner Thurs–Mon 6–9pm
Bill E $20 **M** $30–$39 **D** $14
Cards AE V MC Eftpos
Wine A showcase for Majors Lane wines, with a few hand-picked locals; 8 by the glass
Chef Benjamin Sales
Owners Benjamin Sales & Debbie Jenkins
Seats 120; private rooms; wheelchair access; outdoor seating
Child friendly Kids' menu; highchairs; drawing materials; meals served in lunch boxes
www.majorslane.com
And... buy some smokehouse products for home

regional

Margan

1238 Milbrodale Road, Broke
Tel 6579 1372   Map 13

Contemporary
Score 14/20

These are trying times, so go for Broke. That's where Margan lies, and it's a bargain. There are lovely house wines at cellar door prices, and food is great value by Hunter standards. Staff discuss the extensive kitchen garden, menu and wines with pride, and can tell you about Broke's other attractions, too. Ponder your itinerary while devouring garlic-and-rosemary marinated quail, with a flavourful Tuscan bread salad (finely diced red onion, tomato, basil and bread). From the specials menu, tomatoes from the garden shine with buffalo mozzarella and basil. Pan-fried john dory fillets were a little dry, yet lifted by juicy chargrilled red capsicum, eggplant and tangy gremolata. Pillowy gnocchi benefit from the flavour boost of creamy gorgonzola dolce latte sauce, while tomato jam makes a sweet match for roast veal cutlets with zucchini and pork hock. Nougatine cannoli, with its crisp shell, smooth passionfruit curd filling, pineapple salsa and yoghurt sorbet, will surely bring you back to Broke, but won't … er, send you there.

Hours Breakfast Sun 9–11am; Lunch Fri–Sun noon–3pm; Dinner Fri–Sat 6–10pm
Bill Lunch share plates $18–$24; 2-course dinner $50pp, 3 courses $60
Cards AE V MC
Wine Margan range plus good choices from further abroad; 16 by the glass
Chefs Tim Michael & Lisa Margan
Owners Andrew & Lisa Margan
Seats 60; private room; wheelchair access; outdoor seating; bar
Child friendly Highchairs; grass play area
www.margan.com.au
And…enjoy Margan's sparkling semillon as an aperitif

Mojo's on Wilderness

84 Wilderness Road, Rothbury
Tel 4930 7244   Map 13

Contemporary
Score 12.5/20

Locals have been making their way down the dirt road to this secluded cottage for 10 years now, drawn back by the hearty fare and cosy atmosphere. An eclectic mix of artworks and antiques lines the brightly painted dining room, with cushion-strewn banquettes and sturdy wooden chairs adding to the homey appeal. A platter of Mojo's own dukkah, roasted olives, caramelised balsamic and ciabatta, delivered with the menus, is a thoughtful, welcoming touch. A spinach and goat's cheese tart, crowned with watercress, pear and pecans is a good mix of buttery pastry, creamy filling and sharp salad, while a generous dish of pan-fried gnocchi with a rich mushroom braise is good rib-sticking stuff. Confit duck failed to excite, however; the delicate celeriac cream and a curious tomato and caper salad weren't enough to distract from disappointingly dry meat. Things end on a high note, thanks to a well-crafted creme brulee with raspberry sorbet.

Hours Dinner daily 6.30–8.30pm; bookings essential
Bill 2-course menu $56pp, 3 courses $70; 10% surcharge on public holidays
Cards AE V MC Eftpos
Wine Well-chosen, Australian-focused list; 10 by the glass
Chefs/owners Adam & Ros Baldwin
Seats 40; wheelchair access; outdoor seating
Child friendly Kids' menu; highchairs; toys; drawing materials
Vegetarian Separate menu
www.mojos.com.au
And…buy Mojo's own dukkah or balsamic to go

hunter valley

Muse

1 Broke Road, Pokolbin
Tel 4998 6777 Map 13

Contemporary

Score 13.5/20

The beautiful dining space and immaculate open kitchen at Hungerford Hill winery would be enough to inspire creativity in anyone. It works then, that this rebranded restaurant is called Muse. Seated at white-clothed tables on high-backed comfy seats, diners gaze appreciatively at the soaring ceilings, huge windows and enormous fireplace. Food is easy on the eyes, too, with dishes carefully composed, and pretty violets added here and there. Duck and spinach tortellini are sweetly satisfying: a trio of neat green parcels filled with shredded meat and spinach, with white bean puree and sticky balsamic reduction. For mains, baked lamb rack is served with strongly flavoured minted pea mousse, fetta and juicy baby truss tomatoes, while the highlight, roasted wild barramundi, has flaky meat and crisp skin, and comes with king brown mushroom noodles and salty anchovy and caperberry butter. A dessert of banana and macadamia crepes with honey ice-cream is the light choice next to a decadent chocolate assiette.

Hours Cafe daily 10am–5pm;
Dinner Wed–Sat 6–10pm; bookings essential
Bill E $20–$24 **M** $34–$38 **D** $16–$22; 8-course degustation $110pp
Cards AE V MC Eftpos
Wine Hunter and Hungerford drops plus prestige list; 18 by the glass; BYO (corkage $10 a bottle)
Chef Troy Rhoades-Brown
Owners Troy & Megan Rhoades-Brown
Seats 120 private room; wheelchair access; outdoor seating; bar
Child friendly Kids' menu; highchairs
Vegetarian Plenty of options
www.musedining.com.au
And...the disc on the roof represents a wine barrel lid

The Old George & Dragon

48 Melbourne Street, East Maitland
Tel 4933 7272 Map 13

Anglo–French

Score 15/20

A class act since 1982, Ian and Jenny Morphy continue to welcome French food fanciers and wine lovers to their delightfully old-school, intimate dining rooms. Tables covered with white linen, vases of fresh roses and floor-length drapes add to the feeling of anticipation. If the signature dish of sauteed kidneys in mustard sauce isn't on, perhaps try golden scallops and confit leek in a sea of bright green pea puree, or seafood chowder, a rich bisque studded with prawns, scallops and mussels. Mustard sauce makes a reappearance with a slow-cooked Macleay Valley rabbit leg, with marjoram from the garden, a frizzle of savoy cabbage providing crunch. Crisp-skinned and tender roast Redgate Farm duck twists a classic, garnished with segmented orange and braised red cabbage. Creme brulee with fresh berries is a must: the caramel crust cracking open to reveal creamy, smooth vanilla custard; sugar-macerated strawberries, blueberries and raspberries on the side are perfect partners.

Hours Dinner Wed–Sat 6.30–10pm
Bill 2-course dinner $60pp, 3 courses $75pp; 10% surcharge on public holidays
Cards AE V MC Eftpos
Wine More than 300, including many imports, plus good half-bottles; 10 by the glass
Chef Ian Morphy
Owners Ian & Jenny Morphy
Seats 56; private rooms
www.oldgeorgeanddragon.com.au
And...arrive hungry and expect to be pampered

regional

Restaurant Botanica

The Vineyards Estate,
555 Hermitage Road, Pokolbin
Tel 6574 7229   Map 13

Contemporary

Score 13.5/20

The candlelit room with terracotta tiled floor, eucalyptus green walls and double-clothed tables feels warm and comfortable. It's a pretty spot, perched on a hill overlooking the vines, with luxury accommodation a few steps away. Smiling young staff deliver sound wine advice and warm house-made bread rolls, while a kitchen garden and a menu going beyond standard offerings suggest food is taken seriously here. Subtle flavours are at work in an entree of cured ocean trout with pink grapefruit, avocado, tiny cubes of roasted beetroot, cucumber jelly and chive creme. More robust flavours are on show in a dish of harissa-marinated prawns, slightly charred and served with pearl barley, preserved lemon, and minted yoghurt. Veal osso buco makes a suitably rich and hearty main, while confit duck is mouth-wateringly good, fork-tender, with green beans and caponata (albeit with the balsamic flavour rather strong). End with lovely, light, rosewater panna cotta, or a playful take on rocky road.

Hours Dinner Wed–Sun 6–9.30pm
Bill 2-course menu $55pp, 3 courses $65pp
Cards AE V MC Eftpos
Wine Hunter wines showcased, plus a good international line-up; 10 by the glass
Chef Mark Stapleton
Owners Belinda Grant, Mark Stapleton, Graham & Jude Turner
Seats 60; wheelchair access; outdoor seating
www.thevineyardsestate.com.au
And…ask about dine-and-stay package deals

Restaurant Cuvee

Cnr Broke Road & Wine Country Drive, Pokolbin
Tel 4998 7881   Map 13

Contemporary

Score 13/20

You'd be hard-pressed to find a prettier spot for weekend dining. Housed within atmospheric Peterson Champagne House, an inviting sandstone homestead with soaring timber ceilings, the aptly named Cuvee draws crowds for sparkling-fuelled breakfasts and leisurely lunches. Outside, the sun-drenched deck is the place to be, as views of the cottage gardens and lantern-strung trees add to the charm. There's much to like about the menu, too, which spans light, snappy salads to steaks with a shiraz reduction. A fabulous duck confit salad, cut by orange, micro cress and red wine vinegar, is the perfect balance of rich, flaky meat and gentle acidic bite. Grilled flathead fillets served on a rustic panzanella salad also make fine fare. It's a shame that a moscato jelly dessert, studded with tired berries and stiff with gelatine, didn't show more finesse. Next time we'll opt for the wicked-sounding sticky banana pudding with honeycomb ice-cream.

Hours Breakfast daily 8.30–11am; Lunch daily noon–3pm
Bill E $13–$17 **M** $23–$33 **D** $14–$15
Cards AE DC V MC Eftpos
Wine Plenty of bubbles among a Hunter-heavy list; 12 by the glass
Chef Chad Pridue
Owners Colin & Judy Peterson
Seats 74; wheelchair access; outdoor seating; bar
Child friendly Kids' menu; highchairs; drawing materials
www.petersonhouse.com.au
And…the oyster bar turns out Port Stephens rocks and sparkling by the glass

Roberts

Halls Road, Pokolbin
Tel 4998 7330   Map 13

Contemporary
Score 13/20

Prepare to be charmed by this 1876 ironbark slab cottage, its rooms filled with eclectic antiques, opening to a large, lofty dining room with an A-frame ceiling and enormous fireplace. Service might lean towards impersonal yet the waiters are efficient and immaculately presented. Dishes from the European-inspired menu also look terrific, even if the prices seem very city. Start with lovely creamy Hunter Valley goat's cheese and sautéed mixed mushrooms sandwiched between flaky pastry layers, with soft-boiled quail egg and steamed asparagus. Atlantic sea scallops are served three ways; the highlight tartare style, with lime juice, capers and salmon roe. Mains include a thick, chargrilled Tassie beef fillet with a trio of slender gnocchi on top, plus baked field mushroom and black truffle butter. While savoury dishes tended towards oily, there's no faulting a cinnamon parfait pyramid, with luscious caramelised black figs and crisp icing-sugar dusted crostoli.

Hours Lunch Thurs–Sun noon–3pm; Dinner daily 6.30–9.30pm; bookings essential
Bill E $25–$28 **M** $40–$44 **D** $17; $5pp surcharge on weekends & public holidays
Cards AE DC V MC Eftpos
Wine Lots to choose from, including plenty of Hunter drops; 16 by the glass; BYO (Mon–Thurs only corkage $15 a bottle)
Chef Daniel Hunt
Owner Tower Estate Pty Ltd
Seats 120; private rooms; wheelchair access; outdoor seating
Child friendly Kids' menu; highchairs; drawing materials
www.towerestate.com
And…enjoy a long lunch with friends in one of the private rooms

Rock

576 DeBeyers Road, Pokolbin
Tel 4998 6968   Map 13

Contemporary
Score 16/20

In recent years, Australia's most-visited wine region has really stepped it up in the food stakes, and nowhere is this more apparent than at Rock, the sleek Pocle's Rock fine-diner that's fast become a destination in its own right. The restaurant's expansive windows gaze out across 90-year-old shiraz vines and a pristine dam, but inside it's all modern, clean lines, white-clothed tables and professional, yet unpretentious, service. From a menu of just nine perfectly formed dishes that assume money's no object, choose a traditional entree and main, or create your own first-rate degustation. Warm curls of jamon with sprightly cucumber jelly and tomato consomme demonstrate an assured dexterity with tastes and textures. Buttery veal tenderloin with white anchovy, capsicum, lemon and capers sings with flavour, while ocean trout roulade with an elegant beurre rouge sauce is at once robust and refined. Dessert also celebrates contrasts, as a melting, still-warm canneles bordelais is teamed with cherry ice-cream and a smooth, almond-rich blanc manger.

Hours Dinner Thurs–Sat 6.30–11pm; bookings essential
Bill E $34–$40 **M** $51–$60 **D** $9–$18; tasting dishes $17–$23
Cards AE V MC Eftpos
Wine Exceptional global list; 22 by the glass
Chef Andrew Clarke
Owners Andrew & David Clarke
Seats 72; wheelchair access; bar
Child friendly Kids' menu; highchairs
Vegetarian Separate tasting menu
www.rockrestaurant.com.au
And…gluten-free and vegan menus, too

regional

Shakey Tables

Hunter Country Lodge,
1476 Wine Country Drive, North Rothbury
Tel 4938 1744   Map 13

Contemporary

Score 13/20

The line between artist and chef is blurred for Paula Rengger. Her spacious dining room, hidden in bushland at the end of a dirt track, also acts as a gallery for her vibrant, stylised paintings, with a crayon-box collection of high-backed chairs, cushions and lanterns making for a cheerful setting. The menu reads like a who's who of comfort food faves, with sticky pork belly, braised duck and haggis (a nod to the chef's Scottish background) vying for attention. So it's a pleasant surprise to see some rather refined plates of food leaving the kitchen. To start, beef carpaccio with port jelly, figs and horseradish cream is elegant and delicious, however rock-hard pastry detracted from an otherwise lovely tomato tart. Thankfully, ale-braised beef shin delivers all the richness and warmth you could hope for. Ice-cream dominates the brief dessert menu; go all out with a rosewater, lychee and pistachio terrine, or opt for the simplicity of a deconstructed affogato.

Hours Dinner daily 6.30–10pm; bookings essential
Bill E $23 **M** $37 **D** $16
Cards AE DC V MC Eftpos
Wine Excellent selection of little-known Hunter gems and global wines of note; 12 by the glass
Chef Paula Rengger
Owners Paula & Simon Rengger
Seats 50; bar
Child friendly Highchairs
www.shakeytables.com.au
And…there's accommodation onsite

The Verandah

Calais Estate, Lot 1, Palmers Lane, Pokolbin
Tel 4998 7231   Map 13

Contemporary Tapas

Score 13/20

Billing itself as modern Australian tapas, this lively dining room above the Calais Estate cellar door holds broad appeal, thanks to a United Nations assembly of flavours. Nab a table on the expansive verandah, crowned with wrought-iron lacework and views of twisting grapevines, or within the vibrant, art-lined interior, and settle back for well-executed share plates in serves of two or four. Giant gnocchi with garlic prawns gets things off to a good start, the potato dumplings fragrant with butter, lemon and a gentle lilt of saffron. Tender tiles of seared beef, doused with ginger, soy and a smattering of black sesame, are wonderfully balanced and refined. Not all pairings are as astute, though. Crisp UFO-like snapper wontons, dusted with parmesan and served with sharp pickled cabbage, were more War of the Worlds than cross-cultural harmony. Thankfully, peace is quickly restored with the signature chocolate souffle (spiked with Grand Marnier and pistachio, perhaps), which generates appreciative nods of approval all round.

Hours Lunch Thurs–Sun noon–3pm; Dinner Thurs–Sun 6–9pm
Bill Tapas dishes $13–$48 **D** $13–$19
Cards AE DC V MC Eftpos
Wine Well-priced Hunter-focused list; 30 by the glass; BYO (corkage $9 a bottle); no BYO for groups of 10 or more
Chefs Matt Dillow & Tim Suffell
Owner Matt Dillow
Seats 100; outdoor seating
Child friendly Kids' meals; highchairs; drawing materials
Vegetarian Options on menu
www.verandahrestaurant.com.au
And…ask about the shuttle bus, so you can really explore that wine list

- Crowne Plaza
- Silo Bar
- Ristorante Il Grifone
- Baristaba Espresso
- Nagisa
- Larnna Thai
- Rocksalt
- Twist
- Isobar
- Acquazul
- The Dockyard
- Mangrove Jacks
- Source Café
- Breeze Restaurant & Bar
- Chifley Apartments
- and more

ESCAPE!

Discover something new at Honeysuckle on Newcastle's foreshore, a dining experience like no other.

Whether you're searching for casual eats, a funky wine bar or the best in fine dining, it's all here against the backdrop of Australia's most remarkable working harbour.

Just two hours north of Sydney – or less than 30 minutes by seaplane from Rose Bay.

Honeysuckle Harbour Life, the weekend escape you've been looking for.

www.honeysuckle.net

an initiative of **HDC** Hunter Development Corporation

hunter valley

The Wine House and Kitchen

NEW ENTRY

Pokolbin Village Resort,
188 Broke Road, Pokolbin
Tel 4998 7945   Map 13

Contemporary Mediterranean

Score 13.5/20

Lovely, soft, house-baked bread, pancetta cured in house, pasta and balsamic also the chef's own – the team in the open kitchen of this smart-casual eatery works hard to earn the superlatives showered on them by enamoured patrons. Young staff provide a warm welcome and readily assist with queries about the menu and extensive wine list. Plump butternut pumpkin cannelloni is a good place to start, the pasta filled with ricotta and slick with brown butter and sage, with added crunch from almonds and sweetness from muscatels. A tangle of fine pasta is tossed with pancetta and parmesan and topped with a (rather overpowering) truffle-"injected" poached egg. While the restaurant's location and view isn't one of the Hunter's best, tender, double-roasted pork belly with poached prunes, crisp kipfler potato and irresistible crackling might well be. Flourless dark choc, ginger and ricotta torte topped with soft toasted marshmallow is richly rewarding.

Hours Breakfast daily 8–11.30am; Lunch daily noon–3.30pm; Dinner Thurs–Sun 6–9pm
Bill E $18–$22 **M** $28–$36 **D** $14; 10% surcharge on Sundays & public holidays
Cards DC V MC Eftpos
Wine A thorough, informative list with a good local focus plus imported drops; 18 by the glass
Chef Mark Stapleton
Owners Belinda Grant & Mark Stapleton
Seats 120; private room; wheelchair access; outdoor seating; bar
And… pick up gourmet Hunter pantry products from the neighbouring shops

And also …

WINE COUNTRY

Australian Regional Food Store & Cafe
The Small Winemakers' Centre,
426 McDonalds Road, Pokolbin
Tel 4998 6800
An airy cafe with indoor and outdoor seating, open daily for brunch and lunch. Browse a wide range of gourmet pantry products, locally made cheeses and oils and try a few drops from boutique Hunter wineries.

Cafe Enzo
Peppers Creek, Cnr Broke & Ekerts roads, Pokolbin **Tel 4998 7233**
Lovely, casual alfresco dining plus indoor space; open daily for good coffee, brekkie and lunch (it's not cheap, but top quality). Pop into the Stone Pantry next door and David Hook wines cellar door for more palate pleasure.

Cracked Pepper
1616 Broke Road, Pokolbin
Tel 4998 7076
Next door to De Iuliis Winery, this bright little cafe–restaurant does good mushies on toast for weekend brekkie, and daily lunches of pumpkin and taleggio pizzetta or local spatchcock with Moroccan spices and couscous salad.

The Hunter Valley Smelly Cheese Shop
Tempus Two Winery, 2144 Broke Road, Pokolbin
Tel 4998 6713
This new, bigger store offers more than just cheese (although that is of course the specialty). Stop for pizza, burgers, terrific gelato and gourmet pantry products including local delights. The smaller store at Pokolbin Village gets fewer tour groups.

regional

Il Cacciatore
609 McDonalds Road, Pokolbin
Tel 4998 7639
Dedicated regulars come for the combo of pretty vineyard views, attentive floor staff and generous northern Italian fare with the odd twist, such as roast duck with rhubarb risotto. The gnocchi is great (there's gnocchi making classes, too), and you can take away pizza for a vineyard picnic lunch.

PROVEDORES

* **Binnorie Dairy**, Cnr Hermitage Road & Mistletoe Lane, Pokolbin, **Tel 4998 6660**; fetta, labna, vego-friendly mascarpone and quark (curd) and more.
* **Bliss Coffee Roasters**, Shop 2, Hunter Valley Gardens Village, Broke Road, Pokolbin, **Tel 4998 6700**; good house blends and coffee paraphernalia.
* **Hunter Valley Cheese Company**, McGuigan Wine Complex, 447 McDonalds Road, Pokolbin, **Tel 4998 7744**; terrific range of cheeses, olive oils and more, to try and buy.
* **Lovedale Smokehouse**, 64 Majors Lane, Lovedale, **Tel 4930 7832**; smoked meat and fish as served at Majors Lane Restaurant, house-made and local pantry products.
* **Pickled and Pitted**, River Flats Estate, Store 67, 530 Wollombi Road, Broke, **Tel 6579 1063**; great jams, chutneys, olives and olive oils plus olive oil soaps.

MAITLAND & UPPER HUNTER

Kerv Espresso Bar
108 Liverpool Street, Scone
Tel 6545 3111
This quirky little cafe serves "real" coffee with attitude (don't ask for it extra hot!). Antiques and home wares sit alongside a selection of deli items from brands such as Cunliffe & Waters and Toby's Estate.

The Larda
122 Kelly Street, Scone
Tel 6545 9533
Big breakfasts using local eggs, tasting plates for lunch and ready-made meals such as coq au vin are staples in this lovely stone building on the main street. Coffee is excellent Allpress, and local products include Morpeth sourdough and Hunter Valley Pasta Co pasta.

PROVEDORES AND MARKETS

* **Bacco's Bakeries**, 13 Mayne Street, Murrurundi, **Tel 6546 6822**; crispbread to enhance any cheese platter and biscotti, fresh from the source.
* **Hunter Belle Cheese**, Old Verona Winery, 75 Aberdeen Street, New England Highway, Muswellbrook, **Tel 6541 5066**; try and buy seven cheeses including soft "camembelle", plus a new range of yoghurts.
* **Morpeth Sourdough**, 148 Swan Street, Morpeth, **Tel 4934 4148**; terrific range of sourdough breads plus pantry products.
* **Organic Feast**, 10–12 William Street, East Maitland, **Tel 4934 7351**; huge range of organic products including bread, meat and dairy.
* **Paddock to Pantry**, 135 Kelly Street, Scone, **Tel 6545 9851**; mostly local, only seasonal fresh fruit and veg, plus sandwiches, local cheeses and La Tartine bread.
* **Pukara Estate**, 1440 Denman Road, Muswellbrook, **Tel 6547 1055**; olives, vinegars, and quality olive oils to try or buy, plus Toby's Estate coffee and homemade cake to eat in.

* **Kurri Kurri Farmers' Market**, Rotary Park, Kurri Kurri, 2nd Sat, 8am–1pm, **Tel 4937 2640** or **0409 153 628**.
* **Maitland Fresh Produce Markets**, Heritage Mall, High Steet, Maitland, Thursdays, 9am–5pm Jan–Sept, 9am–8.30pm Oct–Dec, **Tel 4934 1981**.
* **Maitland Markets**, Maitland Showground, Blomfield Street, Maitland, 1st Sun Feb–Sept, 1st & 3rd Sun Oct–Dec, 8am–2pm, **Tel 4962 5522**.

Hunter Valley Wine By Greg Duncan-Powell

The Hunter Valley sets a high cellar-door standard. Envied by other wine regions for its huge number of visitors, it has the customer base to provide a wide range of wine experiences. It's often criticised as a shopfront for other wine regions but that's a boon if you're looking for diversity, and there are still plenty of local Hunter products to taste. Undisputedly, the two varieties the Hunter does best are semillon and shiraz. Both produce styles in the Hunter that are unique in the wine world. The low-alcohol, cellar-worthy semillon is arguably Australia's finest white wine, and the textural, earthy shiraz is an inimitable expression of the variety.

In the heart of Pokolbin at the junction of Broke and McDonalds roads are several of the Hunter's best cellar doors.

Head for the **Small Winemakers Centre** (McDonalds Road, Pokolbin, **Tel 4998 7668**; open daily, 10am–5pm) where you can taste the wines of makers who have no cellar door, including Thomas Wines. Winemaker Andrew Thomas concentrates solely on the Hunter's strong suits and his Braemore Semillon and Kiss Shiraz are up with the best in the Valley.

Brokenwood (McDonalds Road, Pokolbin, **Tel 4998 7559**; open daily, 9.30am–5pm) is a cellar door where some fine Hunter product can be tasted alongside wines from far-flung regions such as Beechworth and Bathurst. There's even a very good chardonnay that is grown adjacent to Mountain Straight on Mount Panorama.

Tamburlaine (358 McDonalds Road, Pokolbin, **Tel 4998 7570/4210**; open daily, 9.30am–5pm) a winery that manages to sell almost all of its substantial production through the cellar door and extensive mailing list. Sourcing fruit from certified organic vineyards in the Hunter Valley and Orange, the range is large and of high quality. The merlot and chardonnay from Orange are worth looking at, along with the semillon and shiraz from the Hunter.

Lake's Folly (Broke Road, Pokolbin, **Tel 4998 7507**; open daily, 10am–4pm) is always an interesting diversion because it produces neither semillon or shiraz. Instead, Lake's Folly, the brainchild of the late Max Lake, has an enduring reputation and enviable brand recognition for cabernets and to a lesser extent, chardonnay. Both are still worthy of the hype.

The imposing **Tower Estate** (corner of Broke and Hall roads, Pokolbin, **Tel 4998 7989**; open daily, 10am–5pm) is the sort of operation that could only happen in the Hunter. It would probably be labelled pretentious if the wines weren't so good. Instead of being Hunter-centric, proven combinations of regions and varieties are matched up. So along with Hunter semillon and shiraz, there's Adelaide Hills sauvignon blanc, Yarra Valley pinot noir and Clare Valley riesling. Wine quality is exceptional, and tasting the range is an education.

A short drive up Broke Road brings you to the subregion of Broke and different terroir. **Margan Wines** (Milbrodale Road, Broke, **Tel 6579 1372**; open daily, 10am–5pm) is consistently producing some of the Hunter's best red wines and some of the most successful Italian varietals. Apart from the Limited Release Shiraz, the rosé-style shiraz saignee and barbera are particularly good.

In the same subregion is **Krinklewood** (712 Wollombi Road, Broke, **Tel 6579 1322**; open weekends & pub hols, 10am–5pm), a biodynamic vineyard on a spectacular site and home to a stylish chardonnay and shiraz.

regional

CENTRAL COAST & NEWCASTLE

First stop for foodies exploring this sand-, sun- and surf-soaked region should perhaps be Memorial Park at The Entrance. This is where, at 3.30pm, 365 days a year – regardless of the weather – pelicans gather for a good feed. You'll learn a lot about the birds and their voracious appetites, and can rest assured that whatever gastronomic activity you undertake hereafter will seem nothing but civilised by comparison.

This strip of the NSW coast is full of sleepy coastal holiday spots (where thongs and boardies are the unofficial uniform), as well as one of Australia's largest cities, Newcastle. The food scene in Newcastle is diverse: from the waterfront fine diners of the Honeysuckle precinct, to the cheerful eateries and casual cafes along Beaumont and Darby streets. In March, lookout for the Wine & Waves Festival, held in association with Surfest to showcase the culinary wares of the area, and nearby Hunter Valley (www.wine-and-waves.com).

While Port Stephens attracts visitors with whale watching in winter and beach hopping in summer – one of September's drawcards is the annual Shoal Bay Jazz Wine and Food Festival. November brings the Tastes of the Bay Food, Wine and Jazz Festival to the Nelson Bay foreshore (www.portstephens.org.au).

At Lizotte's (Kincumber and Newcastle, see "And also…" section) it's a virtual year-long food and music festival, with performances by the likes of Eric Bibb, Kasey Chambers and Renee Geyer, among many more. In the same neck of the woods each November is the Brisbane Waters Oyster Festival at Ettalong Beach, with plenty of food and wine tastings. You too can make like the pelicans and chow down (www.centralcoasttourism.com.au).

Acquazul

NEW ENTRY

E1 The Boardwalk, Honeysuckle Drive, Newcastle
Tel 4927 0800   Map 13

Italian

Score 13/20

The hybrid Spanish–Italian name means "blue water". The look is bright turquoise Mediterranean, and the outlook is pretty special, gazing out across the Newcastle waterfront, lined up among a string of buzzing bars and casual eateries. A simple, Italian-styled menu – primi, pasta, carne and more – fits right in. Crisp spinach and ricotta filled arancini, an antipasto plate and deep-fried semolina-dusted calamari with creamy lime aioli are just three of a selection of well-priced starters. Bolognese sauce, prepared from braised wagyu, is tossed through silky house-made pappardelle and sprinkled with sliced green olives. Fresh parmigiano is grated at the table. Well-rested rib-eye fillet sits on a bed of vibrant spinach with creamy potato mash ready to mop up some pleasantly sticky red wine jus. Finish with smooth, intensely flavoured gelato made from seasonal fruit, or an utterly classic tiramisu. Sit outside on a fine afternoon, soak up the atmosphere and linger over an excellent espresso.

Hours Lunch Wed–Sun noon–5pm; Dinner Tues–Sun 5pm–midnight; bookings essential
Bill E $9–$14 **M** $19–$25 **D** $8; 10% surcharge on public holidays
Cards AE DC V MC Eftpos
Wine A selection of Hunter, WA, NZ, SA, Victorian & Italian wines; 16 by the glass
Chef Ashley Reed
Owners Ashley Reed & Mark Prince
Seats 120; wheelchair access; outdoor seating; bar
Child friendly Kids' menu
www.acquazul.com.au
And…wood-fired pizza at lunch

central coast & newcastle

Bacchus

141 King Street, Newcastle
Tel 4927 1332   Map 13

Modern European

Score 15/20

Sometimes it's small things that make a difference. An amuse bouche of truffled foie gras mousse, diced pear and walnut that makes you cry out for more; a pink grapefruit sorbet palate cleanser where none was expected; crusty house-made rolls and teensy hazelnut praline petits fours are some of the small things that add up to an unforgettable whole. Bacchus is pure theatre, housed in a former playhouse with plush velvet curtains and waiters moving back and forth like actors on a stage. And the food plays more than a supporting role. There's a new chef, a new menu and new standards of service. The locally sourced rabbit is presented as an assiette of minute rack, loin, sliced kidney, liver and braised shoulder. Grapes provide a fruity foil for foie gras-topped bug tails and sliced sweetbreads. And Melba makes another last appearance. The eponymous dessert has been given a twist – the saffron-poached peach presented with raspberry sorbet and vanilla anglaise.

Hours Lunch Tues–Sat 11.30am–4pm; Dinner Tues–Sat 4–11pm; High tea Sun noon–5pm
Bill E $19–$23 **M** $36–$39 **D** $15–$16; 7-course degustation $89pp
Cards AE DC V MC Eftpos
Wine A good selection of local, Australians and a few foreigners; 22 by the glass
Chef Tim Montgomery
Owners Anthony & Alison Ventura, Matthew & Ruth Higgins
Seats 100; private room; wheelchair access; bar
Child friendly Highchairs
Vegetarian Several vegan tapas options
www.bacchusrestaurant.com.au
And… tapas served in the wings until late

Bells at Killcare

107 The Scenic Road, Killcare Heights
Tel 4360 2411   Map 12

Modern Italian

Score 15/20

Bells could be short for "bellissimo", an apt description of this gorgeous boutique resort and restaurant. Stay the night, or at least take the time to explore the lush green surrounds, manicured lawns and extensive kitchen garden. The restaurant is a breath of clean air, decked out in crisp white with bright blue and dark timber touches, and the food is just as fresh, with simple but vibrant dishes such as the irresistible salad of roast tomatoes with buffalo mozzarella and pesto. Taglierini (thin linguini) with pork cheek and mixed mushrooms had a little too much pasta, tangled in a clump, but thankfully polenta fritters please with sweet bursts of corn, topped with diced tomato and soft pieces of Moreton Bay bug. A trio of crisp-crumbed pan-fried veal and provolone cheese involtini sits on a bed of borlotti beans with slow-roasted tomato. Try baked strawberry custard tart with vanilla bean ice-cream and balsamic strawberries and you'll be back for more, with bells on.

Hours Lunch Fri–Sun noon–3pm; Dinner daily 6–9.30pm; bookings essential
Bill E $21–$24 **M** $35–$39 **D** $14.50; degustation menu $95pp; 10% surcharge on Sundays & public holidays
Cards AE DC V MC Eftpos
Wine Lengthy list of Italian and Australian, with a focus on Hunter region; 20 by the glass
Chefs Stefano Manfredi & Cameron Cansdell
Owners Karina & Brian Barry
Seats 100; private rooms; wheelchair access; outdoor seating; bar
www.bellsatkillcare.com.au
And… enjoy a pre-dinner drink in the comfy bar

good food guide   231

regional

Bistro Tartine

52 Cleary Street, Hamilton
Tel 4965 3648   Map 13

French Bistro

Score 13.5/20

Mark Hosie is still weaving his special brand of French magic at this buzzing bistro. While the menu changes seasonally, it's difficult to remove the popular house specialty of chicken liver paté and pork rillettes. Ask for a table out front and enjoy the passing parade (inside is pleasant, too, but can get quite noisy). Sit back, forget the diet and indulge in the wicked beurre blanc coating spiced scallops with crab and leek potato cake, perhaps with a glass of Scarborough chardonnay. In true French style, this place takes the marriage of food and wine seriously, with an emphasis on Hunter wines. Brokenwood cabernet sauvignon pairs well with slow-roasted lamb loin and beetroot, although confit Redgate Farm duck with spiced quince cries out for pinot noir from Geelong. The dessert list on its own would be worth a detour, and it's difficult to leave without trying more than the meringue roulade with its orange and mascarpone filling. A bientôt, not au revoir.

Hours Lunch Thurs–Fri noon–3pm; Dinner Mon–Sat 6–10pm
Bill E $19–$22 **M** $29–$38 **D** $12
Cards AE DC V MC Eftpos
Wine A well-chosen selection of reasonably priced Hunter and others; 9 by the glass; BYO Mon–Thurs only (corkage $7 a bottle)
Chef Mark Hosie
Owners Mark & Jacqui Hosie
Seats 65; wheelchair access; outdoor seating
Child friendly Kids' menu; highchairs; drawing materials
And…watch out for special wine dinners

Flair

1/488 The Entrance Road, Erina Heights
Tel 4365 2777   Map 12

Contemporary

Score 13/20

This Post-it Note-sized space in glowing lollipop red and fairy-floss pink is hidden away in a corner of a nondescript set of shops, well back from the road. It delivers on its motto of giving diners "passion with no boundaries". A trio of egg entree presents a creamy light egg custard on potato spaghetti with crisp pancetta, firm poached quail egg on a dahl of brown lentil and oregano, and a buttery, runny organic egg cocotte. Chateaubriand is served rare as requested, the sweetness of the steak cut by a zesty quenelle of mustard and green olive tapenade and the slight mustiness of tarragon jus. The accompanying sauteed Swiss browns and wilted leaves competes a little, but a better foil for this dish is a bowl of chips with rosemary salt. At dessert, a thick and crunchy toffee crust covers a creme brulee almost too huge to manage, but a shot glass of stewed rhubarb is suitably astringent as penance.

Hours Dinner Tues–Sat 6–9pm; bookings essential
Bill E $27 **M** $39 **D** $16; 2-course menu (Tues–Thurs only) $45pp; 10% surcharge on public holidays
Cards AE V MC Eftpos
Wine A short list of Australian highlights; 6 by the glass; BYO (corkage $4pp)
Chef Lawry Gordon
Owners Lawry & Wendy Gordon
Seats 50; outdoor seating; bar
Child friendly Kids' menu; highchairs
And…a choice of a la carte or a set seasonal menu

central coast & newcastle

Hobarts

Western Suburbs Leagues Club,
88 Hobart Road, New Lambton
Tel 4935 1200   Map 13

Contemporary

Score 13.5/20

NEW ENTRY

Who'd have thought you'd find fine dining in a footy club? Beyond the imposing doors of Hobarts is a carpeted oasis of white linen, cut crystal glasses, Wedgwood china and plush curtains. A gueridon produces flamed dessert crepes – an impressive performance, while diners can construct a personalised main course from a list of meat, veg and sauces, or choose from the chef's menu. Crisp-skinned, finely textured farmed kingfish with thinly shredded pan-fried red cabbage and cubes of gratin dauphinois sits on French shallot confit, its autumnal notes enhanced by an earthy mushroom glaze. Three fat prawns wrapped in fine, crisp kataifi pastry rest on steamed leek tops, a line of peanut and lime dressing and one of black bean sauce on either side. Citrus gelato balances the sweet tropical fruit macedoine accompanying a slightly bland cube of passionfruit panna cotta crowned with persian fairy floss. The service is solid silver.

Hours Dinner Fri–Sat 6–9.30pm
Bill E $18–$22 **M** $24–$92 **D** $15–$18
Cards AE DC V MC Eftpos
Wine Predictable selection of Hunter, other Australian and international wines; 7 by the glass
Chef Ben Collins
Owner Western Suburbs (Newcastle) Leagues Club
Seats 34; wheelchair access; bar
www.westsnewcastle.com.au
And... a pianist tickles the ivories in the Club's piano lounge 6–8pm, Monday to Saturday

Lamiche

80 Oceanview Drive, Wamberal
Tel 4384 2044   Map 12

Contemporary

Score 14.5/20

It's a pretty blue room, as warm and inviting as hosts Michael and Cherrill Higgins. They spoil you with attention, as if you're dining in their home, and proudly deliver some exceptional fare from a seasonal menu. Superbly presented, each dish is a work of art. Crumbed lamb's brains rests on one side of a square plate, a brush stroke of carrot puree and a smattering of baby herbs and walnuts completing the canvas and wowing the tastebuds. It all arrives with the same care. A circle of rolled ham hock with a scoop of finely slivered coleslaw and pickled nashi pear is full of flavour and texture. Ocean trout, soft and flaky under crisp skin, is paired with spring onions, baby beet and horseradish foam. Roasted pork belly has a rich depth of flavour teamed with chickpeas, baby squid and chorizo. A dessert of smashed pavlova tossed with mandarin, pineapple and passionfruit is as fabulous as the friendly farewell.

Hours Dinner Tues–Thurs 6–8.30pm, Fri–Sat 6–9pm; bookings essential
Bill E $25 **M** $35 **D** $15;
$5pp surcharge on Saturdays & public holidays
Cards AE V MC Eftpos
Wine BYO (corkage $3pp)
Chefs Jason Martin & Mel Reidl
Owners Michael & Cherrill Higgins
Seats 35; outdoor seating
Child friendly Highchairs
And... complimentary amuse bouche and petit fours are divine

good food guide   233

regional

Ocean

102 Ocean Parade, Blue Bay, The Entrance
Tel 4334 4600   Map 12

Seafood

Score 13/20

How local do you like your food? How about thumb-fat oysters from Empire Bay, just down the road, firm and unapologetic for being less famous than cousins further south? Or better still, samphire gathered off the rock shelf below your dining table, the salty bitterness of its thin needles a foil for creamy poached ocean trout left slightly rare at its centre. Dark, musky sauteed mushrooms in an ochre foam tangle with fresh soybeans and peas, spill out from under a browned cap of flaky feuillete (puff pastry) across flat squares of garlicky spinach. A shot glass of aloe vera granita intermezzo offers welcome balance, and a dessert of green apple jelly and sorbet rounds off the meal with echoes of the tang of the earlier oysters. The service is friendly and attentive in this observatory-like terrace beneath an uninspiring motel. These risky adventures beyond the fish, chips and Chiko Roll dining of beach-holiday towns deserve thanks, applause and support.

Hours Lunch Mon–Fri noon–2pm, Sat–Sun noon–2.30pm; Dinner Mon–Thurs 6–8pm, Fri–Sat 6–8.30pm
Bill E $20–$24 **M** $30–$39 **D** $16; 2-course lunch $35pp, 3 courses $45; 10% surcharge on Sundays & public holidays
Cards AE DC V MC Eftpos
Wine Moderately priced good range Australian list; 25 by the glass; BYO (corkage $5pp)
Chefs Brett Dengate & Adam Ritchie
Owners Brett Dengate & Neil Burridge
Seats 80; wheelchair access; outdoor seating; bar
Child friendly Kids' menu; highchairs
www.oceanrestaurant.com.au
And…a great place for a leisurely meal

Onda

150 Terrigal Drive, Terrigal
Tel 4384 5554   Map 12

European

Score 13.5/20

This popular Italian diner with sweeping views of the lagoon and beach through Norfolk pines is well positioned. The handsome, spacious room with white-clothed tables is warmed in winter with open fires, and spills outside for courtyard dining in summer, while the service is attentive and well informed. A starter of peppered beef and thyme carpaccio is balanced by a confit of baby beet puree, rocket and parmesan. A pretty tart filled with mustard-flavoured goat's cheese and caramelised onion is divine alongside a slow-roasted tomato salad. House-made pasta shines in ricotta and sage gnocchi, teamed with a creamy blend of four cheeses and topped with shreds of spinach and pistachio gremolata. Grilled salmon is soft and pink, textured with squares of butternut squash and creamed savoy cabbage tossed with prosciutto. Meringue topped with orange, mango, peach and saffron is a sweet note to finish, especially with a white chocolate sablé and blood orange sorbet.

Hours Lunch daily noon–2.30pm; Dinner daily 6–9pm
Bill E $22–$27 **M** $34–$38 **D** $16; $2.20pp surcharge on Saturdays, $3.30 Sundays & $6.50 public holidays
Cards AE (+2%) DC (+2%) V MC Eftpos
Wine Good Australian list with plenty of Italian labels; 15 by the glass
Chef Paul Bouwhuis
Owners Ray & Bec Fraser
Seats 100; wheelchair access; outdoor seating; bar
Child friendly Kids' menu; highchairs; drawing materials
www.onda.com.au
And…2-course meal deals with a glass of wine

central coast & newcastle

Pearls on the Beach

1 Tourmaline Avenue, Pearl Beach
Tel 4342 4400   Map 12

Contemporary

Score 13.5/20

It's a dining experience that's easy on the eye. The tranquil beach, just a few brush-turkey steps away from the white and pale green restaurant, gets all the attention at first. But as the food arrives – remarkably quickly – the beach takes a backseat. Commanding your attention might be a trio of twice-cooked pork belly pieces with small cubes of green apple jelly, alongside butter-braised leek and savoy cabbage dotted with speck. Or perhaps scallops flavoured with Middle Eastern spices, served with a fresh jumble of carrot, coriander and red onion. Generously portioned mains include grilled saltwater barramundi fillet served on warm sushi rice with edamame, bok choy, enoki and shiitake mushrooms. Middle Eastern flavours return with harissa spatchcock, served with lemon-roasted potatoes and a cherry tomato and capsicum relish. Convivial service could be more knowledgeable, but plump pear and chocolate spring rolls with cinnamon ice-cream will hold your gaze a while longer before your attention returns to that view.

Hours Lunch Thurs–Sun noon–3pm;
Dinner Thurs–Sun 6–9pm; bookings essential
Bill E $19–$22 **M** $30–$37 **D** $14;
15% surcharge on public holidays
Cards AE V MC Eftpos
Wine Affordable, extensive list of mainly Australian drops; 14 by the glass;
BYO (corkage $12 a bottle)
Chef Scott Fox
Owners Scott & Melissa Fox
Seats 75; outdoor seating
Child friendly Kids' menu for lunch and 6pm dinner sitting; highchairs
www.pearlsonthebeach.com.au
And…it's perfect for a daytrip from Sydney

Reef

The Haven, Terrigal
Tel 4385 3222   Map 12

Contemporary

Score 12.5/20

Any closer and you'll get wet feet. The magnificent ocean views from this spacious, stylish diner, perched over the southern end of picturesque Terrigal Beach, are dappled with gliding pelicans and gently lapping waves. Binoculars provided on oceanfront tables ensure you capture the full splendour. Inside, service is upbeat but can be scatty. Ocean trout cured with beetroot and tequila is matched with potato croutons and horseradish creme fraiche. Twice-cooked goat's cheese soufflé is ringed by provencale sauce, plus a micro herb and walnut salad. For main courses, the sea breeze steers mostly towards seafood. Grilled blue-eye with sea scallop foam on herb-crushed potatoes was teamed with rather superfluous, dry slipper lobster and preserved lemon cannelloni. Crisscross slices of zucchini and Binnorie fetta fritter topped with grilled asparagus are enlivened with roast capsicum, eggplant caviar and lemon pesto dressing, while coconut panna cotta sits prettily on raspberry soup laced with white rum.

Hours Lunch Tues–Sun noon–2pm;
Dinner Tues–Sat 6–9pm; bookings essential
Bill E $19–$23 **M** $29–$37 **D** $12–$13;
2-course business lunch $38.5Cpp;
$3pp surcharge on Saturdays & Sundays
& $6.50pp on public holidays
Cards AE V MC Eftpos
Wine Interesting list of solid locals; 12 by the glass; BYO (corkage $8.50 a bottle)
Chef Nathan Emerson
Owner Lynne Keeling
Seats 130; wheelchair access; bar
Child friendly Kids' menu; highchairs; drawing materials; baby-changing facilities
www.reefrestaurant.com.au
And…breakfast in the Cove cafe downstairs

regional

Restaurant II

8 Bolton Street, Newcastle
Tel 4929 1233   Map 13

Contemporary

Score 15/20

Peter Bryant and his brigade work the open kitchen's stoves in full view of the wide dining room. Linen-covered tables and sound-absorbing ceilings cope with acoustic problems from the polished timber floor as waiters add a seamless sparkle to the meal. While warm, crusty Morpeth sourdough costs extra, an anchovy-filled twist of puff pastry is a complimentary amuse bouche. Bryant's dexterity with offal and Asian flavours shines in a mahogany-skinned, boned pig's trotter, the meat meltingly tender as crisp rice balls and Asian slaw complete the theme. Slices of sparklingly fresh sashimi tuna crusted with sesame seeds are crowned with fine tresses of seaweed and fresh horseradish, a soy dipping sauce on the side. Seared duck breast is pink and well rested, and contrasts with a reconstructed confit leg, its richness cut by grilled figs. Finish with a wobbly, vanilla-flecked panna cotta, rosewater syrup-poached peach slices on the side.

Hours Lunch Fri noon–2pm; Dinner Wed–Sat 6–9pm
Bill E $18–$24 **M** $33–$37 **D** $13–$15; $5pp surcharge on public holidays
Cards AE DC V MC Eftpos
Wine Well-chosen list; 14 by the glass; BYO (corkage $5pp)
Chef Peter Bryant
Owners Therese & Peter Bryant
Seats 95; private room
Child friendly Kids' menu on request; highchairs
And…it's deceptively quiet around here at night

Ritual

Shop 1, Austral Street Shopping Village, Nelson Bay
Tel 4981 5514   Map 13

Contemporary

Score 14/20

Those in the know are making their way to a backwater shopping precinct in Nelson Bay to surrender, over some three hours, to a labyrinth of textures, flavours and combinations while a passionate team guides them. With the help of techniques and potions borrowed from modern experimental cuisine (aka molecular gastronomy), classic flavour and texture combinations are deconstructed and rebuilt to provide new but curiously familiar sensations. There is no printed menu, rather a long list of ingredients. The journey might start with garlic fairy floss on aromatic rosemary sprigs and finish with XXX-mint chocolate truffle sorbet, through a dozen stages; a crisp artichoke shell filled with artichoke sorbet; spicy-sour tom yum (Thai soup) in a sphere; tiny pink peppercorn ice-cream balls created at the table to fill dark chocolate cones. The matched wines might not suit every taste, but sit back and prepare to be guided; it's a journey worth taking.

Hours Open evenings by reservation only
Bill Taste journey $85pp
Cards V MC Eftpos
Wine A small selection of local bottles; 10 by the glass; matched wines (60ml or 125 ml) with five of the courses
Chef Carl Kenzler
Owners Carl & Kelie Kenzler
Seats 16; wheelchair access
And…go with an open mind; don't be put off by the initial sweet flavours

rocksalt

Newcastle Cruising Yacht Club,
91 Hannell Street, Wickham
Tel 4961 1676 Map 13

Seafood

Score 13/20

The marina outside Newcastle's fishermen's co-op might not be the South of France, but on a sunny day with the gulls wheeling overhead, ever on the watch for an inattentive diner, who cares? This food is worth guarding: silky lobster-mousse filled ravioli with brown butter sauce, and unbelievably tiny, lightly coated whitebait with soft-poached egg are perennial favourites. In keeping with its location, main courses continue the fishy theme. Fish of the day might be crisp-skinned barramundi fillet with mint salsa verde and tomato and red onion salsa. Meat lovers are not forgotten. Slow-cooked, melt-in-the-mouth cider beef sits on a crisp latke (potato fritter), mint and parsley flavours cutting the richness of the meat. Service can be a little patchy but all is forgiven at the sight of a pistachio-studded parfait topped with slices of orange blossom-poached nectarine, and creme brulee with poached raspberries, the smooth crust cracking open to reveal creamy custard.

Hours Lunch daily 11.45am–3.30pm; Dinner Sat 6–9pm
Bill E $17.50–$19.50 **M** $32–$69 **D** $14; 10% surcharge on Sundays & public holidays
Cards AE DC V MC Eftpos
Wine A small list with some international favourites; 12 by the glass
Chefs Justin King & Rodney Rae
Owners Jo Minett & Rick Coleman
Seats 80; wheelchair access; outdoor seating; bar
Child friendly Kids' menu; highchairs
www.rocksaltnewcastle.com.au
And... if the sun gets too much, inside is air-conditioned

Silo

1 Honeysuckle Drive, The Boardwalk, Newcastle
Tel 4926 2828 Map 13

Contemporary

Score 13/20

As one of Newcastle's coolest venues, Silo is popular for everything from a casual lunch to a wedding reception. It's not surprising, given the well-stocked bar, crowd-pleasing menu and sexy decor – with red bordello wallpaper, a sleek lounge area and harbour view. A seat outside is hard to beat on a sunny day, with a thin, crisp-base pizza to share. Margherita comes with chunky wedges of juicy tomato on top. Creamy goat's cheese and asparagus tartlet makes a light start, as does a dish of tender, salted squid with cucumber and bright green wakame. Heartier mains might include roast Berkshire pork strip-loin, or deliciously flaky confit Dutton Park duck with pea and porcini risotto and, for contrast, a small and satisfyingly tart pile of finely shredded red cabbage. Pear tarte tatin with prune and armagnac ice-cream and caramel sauce is syrupy sweet but sumptuous.

Hours Breakfast Sat 10–11.45am, Sun 9–11.30am; Lunch daily 11.45am–3pm; Dinner daily 5.30–9.30pm
Bill E $17.50–$18.50 **M** $26.50–$38.50 **D** $12.50; 3-course menu $61pp; 10% surcharge on public holidays
Cards AE (+2%) DC (+2%) V MC Eftpos
Wine A good, basic range dominated by shiraz, plus cellar selection; 24 by the glass
Chef David Cartwright
Owners Mark Seery, Paul Davies, David & Therese Cartwright
Seats 200; wheelchair access; outdoor seating; bar
Child friendly Kids' menu; highchairs; games
Vegetarian Full menu
www.silolounge.com.au
And... a daily Sydney Seaplane service

regional

Stillwaters
1 Restella Avenue, Davistown
Tel 4369 1300   Map 12

Contemporary
                                    Score 13/20

Stillwaters is the swishest spot in a sleepy waterside suburb across Brisbane Water from Woy Woy. With tranquil views of Illoura Reserve and the water, it's an understandably popular venue for special occasions. What was a general store in the 1940s now dazzles with finely set tables in a room warm with timber tones opening to a covered alfresco dining area. Floor staff look as sophisticated as the decor, and the seafood platter is a fine start with squid draped over sweet mango puree, golden tempura prawns, and melt-in-the-mouth scallops on rich cauliflower puree. Of the mains, braised lamb is as hearty as they come: the shredded meat is mixed with pine nuts and encased in crisp pastry, on a bed of potato mash with rich thyme-flavoured jus. Lighter but equally satisfying is macadamia-encrusted barramundi, served with seasonal vegies. End with a big wedge of passionfruit cheesecake.

Hours Breakfast Sat–Sun 9–11am; Lunch Wed–Sun noon–3pm; Dinner Wed–Sat 6–9pm
Bill E $16.50–$21.50 **M** $26–$36 **D** $8.50–$14
Cards AE DC V MC Eftpos
Wine All-Australian range plus a few New Zealand sauvignon blancs; 17 by the glass
Chef Michael Perrin
Owners Michael & Dominique Norris
Seats 100; wheelchair access; outdoor seating; bar
Child friendly Kids' menu; highchairs
www.stillwatersrestaurant.com.au
And…there's a boat ramp out front, and it's reportedly a very good spot to drop a line

Yum Yum Eatery
60 Araluen Drive, Hardys Bay
Tel 4360 2999   Map 12

Contemporary
                                    Score 13/20

The chirpy staff at this smartly casual eatery need little encouragement when it comes to singing the praises of chef David Featherston. Diners are quick to agree. Whether enjoying slow-cooked lamb neck or the ever popular king prawn and scallop pot stickers as the moonlight hits the water just across the road, or tucking into a huge serving of linguini with king prawns and roma tomato from the shorter lunch menu – the fantastically fresh, aromatic and artistically presented food prompts a steady flow of compliments. Distinctly Asian flavours dominate the menu, including soft salt-and-Sichuan-pepper squid with a salad of crisp green apple, bean sprouts and fragrant herbs. Some French and even the odd Indian dish make for a diverse, crowd-pleasing menu. End with a smooth Belcolade Belgian chocolate and raspberry tart. There's more than one reason this place is called Yum Yum.

Hours Breakfast Sun 9am–noon; Lunch Wed–Sun noon–3pm; Dinner Wed–Sun 6–10pm; tapas & cocktails Sun 5–10pm
Bill E $19–$29 **M** $29–$35 **D** $10–$14; (groups only) 2-course menu $50pp, 3 courses $60pp; 10% surcharge on Sundays & public holidays
Cards V MC Eftpos
Wine Appropriate list of mostly NSW whites, plus some reds; 9 by the glass; BYO (corkage $8 a bottle)
Chef David Featherston
Owners Ron & Rhonda Featherston
Seats 40; wheelchair access; outdoor seating
Child friendly Kids' menu; highchairs
www.yumyumeatery.com.au
And…ask about the yum yum trees across the road

Zest

16 Stockton Street, Nelson Bay
Tel 4984 2211 Map 13

European

Score 15/20

Weekends bring the holiday-house set and those in the know through the unimposing doors of a shopfront on busy Stockton Street, to fill the timber tables in this long, carpeted dining room. They are lured by skilfully prepared and carefully sourced seasonal produce and an eclectic, well-priced wine list. The service is competent, although perhaps not as memorable as paprika-smoky escabeche of yabby tails with Jerez vinegar and a jewel-like cucumber and watercress jelly. The perennial slow-cooked Flinders Island lamb is meltingly tender, infused with the caper, anchovy, lemon and white wine flavours of its cooking juices. A small salad of iceberg, peas, fetta and black olive crumbs continues the Mediterranean theme. We're not fans of paying for bread, however. But a 15-minute wait is well worth it for a soaring light-as-air passionfruit souffle hiding a creamy centre, the accompanying ruby sphere of berry sorbet sitting in the white bowl of a Chinese spoon.

Hours Lunch Fri 12–3pm; Dinner Tues–Sat 6.30–9.30pm; bookings essential
Bill 2-course menu $60pp, 3 courses $70pp; 10% surcharge on Sundays & public holidays
Cards AE V MC Eftpos
Wine Well-chosen list of premium labels from Australia, New Zealand, France and Italy; 15 by the glass
Chefs Glenn Thompson & Juan Hernandez
Owners Glenn & Jenny Thompson
Seats 110; private room; outdoor seating; bar
Child friendly Highchairs; booster seats
www.zestrestaurant.net.au
And…enjoy a cocktail in the courtyard in fine weather

And also…

CENTRAL COAST

Bodyfuel
Shop 1 Williams Court, Gosford
Tel 4323 6669
Also at: 2/12 Kurrawyba Avenue, Terrigal
Tel 4385 3627
Grab a seat at this cheery, light-filled pit stop offering innovative salads, juices, pasta and vegan date cakes, as well as a good cuppa.

Bellyfish Cafe
4/112 The Esplanade, Terrigal
Tel 4385 6838
Not as fishy as the name suggests. Marinated lamb wraps, well-executed pasta and breakfast fry-ups are all the rage at this breezy ocean-view cafe. Lunch specials for $10 are brilliant but modestly portioned, allowing room for white choc and macadamia cheesecake.

Caffe Jam
Shop 4, 103 Victoria Street, East Gosford
Tel 4324 8708
Eat in and escape the frenzy of the main drag, or take home antipasti, plump stuffed vegies, pasta with made-on-premises sauces and a lovely lemon polenta friand.

Coast Bistro and Lounge
3–5 Kurrawyba Avenue, Terrigal
Tel 4385 3100
It's all about the mean sangria and smart tapas at this sexy wine-red hotspot. Go straight for creamy ceviche and buttery scallops, and move on to dukkah-crusted salmon and luscious lamb tagine. Impressive desserts and great brekkie, too.

Deli Goose Cafe
Shop 3 Killcare Road, Killcare
Tel 43601888
Yeah, kill care in the banana-fringed courtyard with baked-on-premises loaves, gourmet pies, mueslis, eggs cocotte, and great coffee. Ditto pizza at night.

Lizotte's
Lot 3, Avoca Drive, Kincumber **Tel 4368 2017**
Also at: 31 Morehead Street, Lambton (Newcastle) **Tel 4956 2066**
Terrific food and a good wine list play an impressive support to a calendar jam-packed full of groovy, bluesy, rock and folk musical acts. Check what's on at www.lizottes.com.au.

Seasalt
Crowne Plaza Terrigal, Pine Tree Lane, Terrigal
Tel 4384 9133
Impeccable poached eggs, blend-your-own fruit juices, barista lattes and leafy teapots all amount to a tantalising hotel brekkie experience. Crown Plaza snags the best beach views for a crab chowder soup lunch and fancier seafood fare for dinner.

Snapper Spot
108 The Esplanade, Terrigal
Tel 4384 3780
Kick off the summer at this beachfront fish-and-chipper with sweet prawns and grilled cajun salmon, and return in winter for scrummy mussels and calamari chowder.

Zanziba
1/18 Church Street, Terrigal
Tel 4385 9144
This hip beach cafe serves up all-day brekkie from BLATs to nasi goreng and yummy bacon burritos, keeping kids happy with toasted cheese fingers. Gluten-free wraps, burgers and salads are washed down with beer or good Campos coffee.

PROVEDORES AND MARKETS
* **Caesars Coffee & Fine Food**, 222 The Entrance Road, Erina, **Tel 4365 1988**; coffee roasted on the premises, shelves of pasta and gourmet treats.
* **Taste Gourmet Grocer and Cafe**, 73 Victoria Street, East Gosford, **Tel 4324 2130**; deli goods and wide range of gourmet pantry products.
* **Sweet Solutions**, 5/42 The Esplanade, Terrigal, **Tel 4385 6722**; old-school lolly shop with nougat, liquorice and sweets paraphernalia.
* **Avoca Beach Growers' Market**, Hunters Park, cnr Avoca Drive & Vale streets, 1st Sun, 8am–noon, **Tel 4572 6260**.

NEWCASTLE & SURROUNDS

III Bean Espresso Bar
Cnr Beaumont & Tudor streets, Hamilton
Tel 4961 2020
This local hero with its strong French and Italian leanings now has a liquor licence, and serves fabulous breakfasts and lunches, using local, biodynamic and organic produce wherever possible, such as the excellent PeaBerry's coffee.

The Depot on Darby
141–143 Darby Street, Cooks Hill
Tel 4929 2666
Even if it were just tapas, this newcomer is worth the journey. But you don't want to miss out on breakfast, lunch and dinner. Attentive service and an excellent kitchen ensure this is a winner.

Estabar
61 Shortland Esplanade, Newcastle Beach
Tel 4927 1222
The vitamin D is a health bonus in this breezy cafe opposite Newcastle beach. Wicked hot chocolate, excellent coffee, arguably the best gelato in town and simple but good breakfast, lunch and dinner fare.

Heatherbrae's Pies
Cnr Pacific Highway & Masonite Road, Heatherbrae (Raymond Terrace) **Tel 4987 5561**
This great road-trip pit stop has a range of 13 savoury pies, including top-notch chunky steak and onion; single serve or family size, plus sweet pastries and Zentveld's coffee.

Kyrenia
Ground Floor, Landmark Apartments, 115–117 Pacific Highway, Charlestown
Tel 4943 1531
This bright, fresh space in a new apartment development is popular with local socialites and office workers for its good Allpress coffee and thoughtfully presented meals (generous seafood risotto is a real highlight). Open B, L & D.

The Lakehouse Cafe
11 Shoreside Row, Murrays Beach
Tel 4971 1745
Take in the bush and water views over perfectly poached eggs on sourdough, fresh fruit plate or buttermilk pancakes. Coffee is good, and lunch options include angus sirloin or barbecued king prawns. Also dinner Fri–Sat.

Roladoor
1 Beaumont Street, Hamilton
Tel 4969 1786
It's out of the Beaumont cafe strip but worth seeking for great Di Bella coffee, healthy berry muesli at breakfast and Turkish bread sandwiches or salads for lunch. Order takeaways at the side roll-a-door.

Snows Patisserie
144 Union Street, The Junction
Tel 4962 4733
The original Snows (now with a sibling at Kotara Westfield) still delivers fresh cakes, pies and sandwiches as well as hearty breakfast fare and excellent coffee at its popular patisserie.

Source
Shop 1, 74–76 The Lane, Maryville
Tel 4940 8023
This smart cafe on Newcastle's foreshore walk attracts joggers, cyclists, local mums and the babycino set for excellent coffee, generous breakfasts and innovative lunches, as well as dinner on Fridays and Saturdays. Hope for fine nights at the monthly full-moon dinner.

PROVEDORES AND MARKETS
* **Chocolate Bliss**, 140 Pacific Highway, Charlestown, **Tel 4943 0688**; novelty chocolates and terrific truffles made on site.
* **Commercial Fishermen's Co-operative**, 97 Hannell Street, Wickham, **Tel 4965 4221**; large waterfront premises selling huge variety of fresh and frozen, wild and farmed, fish and shellfish.
* **Feast Catering**, 84 Bull Street, Cooks Hill, **Tel 4929 1939**, also Feast Deli 34 Ridge Street, Merewether, **Tel 4963 1810**; great catering, sandwiches, pastries and take-home meals; excellent cheese counter.
* **Fishermen's Wharf Seafoods at the Co-op**, 1 Teramby Street, Nelson Bay, **Tel 4984 3330**; local prawns and oysters, fresh fish (have it cooked to order next door).
* **PeaBerry's Gourmet Coffee**, 4/12 Alma Road, New Lambton, **Tel 4952 3366**; coffee roaster with about eight blends.
* **Wicked Chocolates**, 3/305 Hillsborough Road, Warners Bay, **Tel 4956 6300**; Callebaut couverture is used to create great chocolates, and other sweet treats.
* **Newcastle City Farmers' Market**, Newcastle Showground, Griffiths Road, Broadmeadow, most Sundays, 8am–1pm, **Tel 4930 5156**, www.newcastlecityfarmersmarket.com.au.

regional

SOUTH COAST
ILLAWARRA REGION, SHOALHAVEN, EUROBODALLA COAST & SAPPHIRE COAST

From rolling green hills and charming historic towns such as Braidwood and Central Tilba (both classified by the National Trust) to gorgeous white-sand beaches around Jervis Bay, the South Coast is holiday heaven. But it's not just a pretty place – there are also plenty of opportunities for a good feed in this region.

Heading down to Wollongong, take the slow road if you can. That way you won't miss out on the pretty cliffside villages from Stanwell Park to Bulli, through Coalcliff, Coledale, Austinmer, Thirroul and more. The views along the Grand Pacific Drive give Victoria's Great Ocean Road a run for its money, and there are plenty of cafes for panoramic pit stops.

In Eurobodalla, the local Slow Food convivium offers information about sustainable agriculture and gardening and runs various events, including a Slow Food Celebration, held for the first time in June 2009 (www.eurobodallaslowfood.com.au).

Meanwhile, oysters are king in the Eurobodalla area. Get in touch with Moonlight Flat Oysters in Batemans Bay, to ask how you can get your hands on some of their renowned Clair de Lune oysters (www.moonlightflatoysters.com.au). Time your visit well and you'll be close by for Narooma's annual Oyster Festival in May (www.narooma.org.au).

The festivities continue on the June long weekend each year, when the Shoalhaven Coast Winter Wine Festival takes place (www.shoalhavencoast.com.au). On the Sapphire Coast, in Bermagui, April is party time, with the Four Winds Festival (www.fourwinds.com.au), and the annual Eden Whale Festival takes place from October 30 to November 1 this year with a variety of activities on offer, including the chance to go whale-watching (www.edenwhalefestival.com).

55 on Collins
Shop 1, 55 Collins Street, Kiama
Tel 4232 2811   Map 11

Contemporary

Score 14/20

You'll never tire of this cheerful, bright, warm and generous local bistro. Collins Street is perfectly situated to allow full appreciation of the lovely sea hamlet of Kiama; pine trees lit up at night, and beyond that the sea. Front of house is well served by Christobel, wife of chef Jason Hughes who honed his skills in French cooking at Sydney's Galileo. The menu is a tempting list of classic bistro fare. A tapas plate sticks to Spanish tradition with warm olives, frittata and skewered beef, while blue swimmer crab and coconut soup with lemongrass is light and fragrant. Mains take their time when 55 is buzzing with happy locals, but they arrive, generous in both size and flavour. Cheese souffle is as light as they come, and roasted salmon on a bed of luscious risotto is a textually perfect match. Although you won't be screaming that you need dessert, be seduced by the utterly decadent chocolate trio.

Hours Breakfast & lunch Mon–Tues & Thurs–Sun 9am–4pm; Dinner Mon–Sat 6–9pm
Bill E $9.50–$21 **M** $18.90–$33 **D** $12.50–15.50; 10% surcharge on Sundays & public holidays
Cards AE (+2%) V MC Eftpos
Wine Solid list with decent regional selections, including a few good locals; 9 by the glass; BYO wine only (corkage $3 a bottle)
Chef Jason Hughes
Owners Jason & Christobel Hughes
Seats 55; wheelchair access; outdoor seating
Child friendly Kids' menu; highchairs
And…leave some time to visit the pelicans in the bay

south coast

The Albion
119 Wallace Street, Braidwood
Tel 4842 1422   Map 12

European

Score 13/20

The National Trust classifies Braidwood as a historic town. This includes the old Albion Hotel (circa 1872), where the day now begins with great coffee and quality breakfasts. Progressing to lunch means more substantial fare, such as succulent smoked trout with roasted baby beetroot, kipfler potatoes, asparagus and a citrus dressing. At night, candles add ambience, but not enough light to appreciate properly the prettiness of an entree of roasted red and yellow capsicums doused in olive oil and sprinkled with salted capers. If your luck's in, exceptionally creamy Clyde River oysters might be on offer. Attention to quality ingredients also shines in roasted lamb cutlets (from nearby Bungendore) teamed with shaved fennel, chunks of potato, garden-fresh green beans and minted yoghurt. Salmon rests on a blue lentil salad with dill and a simple, clean-cut tomato salsa. An old-fashioned blackberry and apple crumble is as timelessly comforting as the Albion itself.

Hours Breakfast daily 8am–noon; Lunch daily noon–3pm; Dinner Fri–Sun 6–9pm
Bill Dishes $6–$26
Cards V MC Eftpos
Wine Small list of reasonably priced local wines; 3 by the glass; BYO (corkage $4 a bottle)
Chef Warwick Noble
Owner Melissa Smith
Seats 80; outdoor seating
Child friendly Highchairs
Vegetarian Several dishes
And... fig and orange jam for brekkie with excellent sourdough toast from the nearby Dojo bakery

Bannisters
191 Mitchell Parade, Mollymook
Tel 4454 1933   Map 12

Contemporary

Score 14/20

A lodge, restaurant, bar and day spa: Bannisters is Mollymook's pamper central. Its headland position allows for spectacular ocean views (glimpsed through gum trees from the restaurant), but there's still plenty to impress once the sun retires and the view disappears. Leek and potato soup is smooth, creamy comfort, poured steaming from a jug over poached free-range egg and tiny potato discs. Flavours and textures mingle and compete with sashimi and tartare of yellowfin tuna served with mud crab salad, fennel puree and refreshing gazpacho sorbet. Lovely herb-crusted jewfish fillet is moist and flaky, the accompanying pillowy saffron gnocchi and crisp squid tentacles providing an appealing contrast. Mouth-wateringly good medium–rare lamb loin sits alongside richly flavoured "pressed" lamb shank and shoulder, thick eggplant puree and crisp parmesan croquettes. The green apple sorbet with apple parfait and mini doughnuts is so good you'll be tempted to ask the polite floor staff for more.

Hours Breakfast daily 7.30–10.30am; Dinner Wed–Sun 6.30–9.30pm; bookings essential
Bill E $18–$21 **M** $35–$39 **D** $16; 10% surcharge on Sundays & public holidays
Cards AE V MC Eftpos
Wine An extensive Australasian and European list with too few NSW drops, plus helpful advice; 15 by the glass
Chef Russell Chinn
Owner Conbrae Pty Ltd
Seats 110; private room; outdoor seating; bar
Child friendly Kids' menu; highchairs
www.bannisters.com.au
And... head to the (infinity) poolside bar for a pre-dinner drink

good food guide

regional

Bellachara

1 Fern Street, Gerringong
Tel 4234 1359   Map 11

Contemporary

Score 13.5/20

A boutique restaurant attached to a boutique motel makes this a very attractive South Coast destination, especially when it's backed up by knowledgeable and efficient service. Singles can enjoy the elegant dining room while parents allow toddlers to frolic in the nearby (supervised) play club. In the restaurant, presentation is a classy tour de force with rectangular plates allowing for spacious elegance. Dukkah-crusted salmon (albeit cooked too much for our liking) takes centre stage, while shredded saffron-scented kipfler potatoes and superb squares of snow peas and roasted capsicum remoulade sit at the sides on a tasty base of Australian green lentils. Equally impressive is roasted lamb backstrap with a delicious rocket and pear salsa, sweet potato galette and pan-fried haloumi perched around as though admiring the lamb. The interplay of flavours and textures in a dessert of vanilla bean and lime creme brulee with lychee slices and blueberry salsa, along with hospitable, helpful service, ensure this is a memorable experience.

Hours Dinner Tues–Sat 6–10pm
Bill E $10–$25 **M** $25–$40 **D** $8–$15
Cards AE V MC Eftpos
Wine Well-priced, small but interesting list; 25 by the glass
Chef Martin Widjaja
Owner Gregg Currie
Seats 150; private room; wheelchair access; outdoor seating; bar
Child friendly Kids' meals; kids' club; highchairs; baby-changing facilities; outdoor play area
www.bellachara.com.au
And…on a balmy southern night, the garden tables are a tempting option

Berry Woodfired Sourdough Bakery

23 Prince Alfred Street, Berry
Tel 4464 1617   Map 11

Contemporary

Score 14/20

What did Berry do before Jelle and Joost came to town? Not only is their range of sourdough bread, pastries and tarts the best in the region by a country mile, their breakfast and lunch are a must for any passer-by. This reinvigorated silo space, complete with an open loft where flour is now stored, has been revamped with new leather banquettes and plenty of seating inside and out. The warm, yeasty smell of baking sourdough makes it impossible to leave without sitting down for a satisfying meal. Try rich scrambled eggs with chorizo, or a light goat's cheese omelette with cherry tomatoes, served with the signature bread. The ever-changing lunch menu features local produce, and can be as fresh and light as gnocchi with tomatoes, ricotta and peas, or substantial bistro fare such as sirloin with cafe de paris butter and fries. To finish, or indeed for afternoon tea, nothing compares to the glorious chocolate espresso cake.

Hours Breakfast Wed–Sun 8–11.30am; Lunch Wed–Sun 11.30am–3pm
Bill Breakfast $5–$14.50, Lunch $15–$22 **D** $9; 10% surcharge on Sundays & public holidays
Cards V MC Eftpos
Wine BYO (corkage $5 a bottle)
Chefs Glenn Parkes & Simon Edwards
Owners Jelle & Joost Hilkemeijer
Seats 52; wheelchair access; outdoor seating
Child friendly Kids' meals; highchairs; toys
And…check the fridge for house-made dips to spread on your sourdough

Bistro 345

345 Lawrence Hargrave Drive, Thirroul
Tel 4268 3345   Map 11

Contemporary

Score 13/20

The setting is remarkable. Enter from Lawrence Hargrave Drive (the highway) and you step into Pantry 345 serving coffee, light meals and take-home products such as chef Nick's jams and biscuits. From the Thirroul station side, you walk through a park on to a large, open-air patio next to the railway line and into the bistro side of things. Run by a bunch of Sydney seachangers, the menu is consistently interesting, and dishes show the occasional hint of Central European saltiness (the chef is Russian). Start with butter-smooth duck liver paté set against a sharp, sweet nectarine salsa; or the subtle interplay of flavours and textures in egg yolk ravioli on crisp asparagus spears with white truffle hollandaise. For mains, slow-cooked Thirlmere duck is presented on a bed of roasted red and green peppers, complemented by crisp polenta and a grape vinaigrette. Dessert includes a clever green apple bavarois set against a sharp, tangy pineapple sherbet and crunchy apple chips, finished with cinnamon syrup.

Hours Breakfast Sat–Sun 9am–noon; Lunch Tues–Thurs & Sat–Sun noon–3pm; Dinner Tues–Thurs 5–9pm, Sat–Sun 6–9pm (in winter, lunch (noon–3pm) and dinner (6–9.30pm) are Fri–Sun only)
Bill E $12–$17 **M** $16–$34 **D** $12–$14
Cards AE V MC Eftpos
Wine Small, predominantly Australian list; 12 by the glass; BYO wine only (corkage $7 a bottle)
Chefs Nick Alexeeff & Thomas Gripton
Owners Joady Weatherup & Nick Alexeeff
Seats 90; private room; outdoor seating
Child friendly Kids' menu; highchairs; crayons; toybox; ride-ons for use in adjacent park
Vegetarian Several lunch and dinner options
www.bistro345.com.au
And…on weeknights enjoy the passing parade of Sydney commuters

Caveau

122–124 Keira Street, Wollongong
Tel 4226 4855   Map 11

Modern French

Score 15/20

Slatted blinds, painted boards and witty corro-lined walls (this is the Steel City after all) set this "cave" apart from the rest of Wollongong's chief restaurant beat. The food does too. Caveau is a plain shopfront room where the cooking is anything but. From a sip of carrot and cumin soup with polenta-dusted house rolls, serious but savvy staff bear beautiful gifts: flounder with blue swimmer crab mousse, a lovely bisque-like foam and beurre blanc, scallops crunchy with pork crackling on a slightly doughy duxelle and pea veloute. Each elegant assemblage shows thought and effort, including a between-course green apple jelly and sorbet palate cleanser. Gamey venison is utter winter pleasure with chocolatey, crumbly boudin noir and tiny roast veg. Blue-eye pairs with a sticky oxtail rotolo, tiny turnips and confit cabbage. A fine cheese choice is almost enough to distract you from a butterscotchy honeycomb and pear parfait with honeycomb sauce. But of course, you could do both.

Hours Lunch Thurs–Fri noon–2pm; Dinner Tues–Sat 6–10pm; bookings essential
Bill 2-course menu $58pp, 3 courses $72pp; 7-course degustation $90pp
Cards AE (+2%) V MC Eftpos
Wine An ambitious France-inspired list: 15 by the glass; BYO Wed only (no corkage)
Chef Peter Sheppard
Owners Peter & Nicola Sheppard
Seats 62; private room
Child friendly Highchairs
www.caveau.com.au
And…an oft-intriguing wine match suggested with each dish

regional

The Gunyah

Paperbark Camp,
571 Woollamia Road, Woollamia
Tel 4441 7299   Map 11

Contemporary

Unscored

When you book, just remember one extra will join you for dinner – a possum strutting along the balcony rail to check out the meal. The Gunyah's softly lit setting, part of a tented eco-resort, is something special amid the treetops. In summer, it unfurls to become part of the natural surrounds, while cooler nights see diners lounging around the fire. Get closer to the wildlife on the balcony, or settle at paper-on-cloth tables in the airy, candlelit timber room to contemplate a concise blackboard menu that of late has focussed on Asian and European influences. Unlike the sugar gliders flying from tree to tree, the food hasn't always soared in recent years, but that's set to change with the arrival, in late August 2009, of the talented John Evans and his sophisticated European bistro food. It's too early to unveil a menu, but we hope to see dishes such as his delightful brioche-crumbed Meredith goat cheese and lamb rump on crushed Nicola potatoes with ratatouille. Fingers crossed.

Hours Dinner daily 6.30–8pm; bookings essential
Bill E $16–$21 **M** $28–$34 **D** $15–$21; 10% surcharge on Sundays & public holidays
Cards AE V MC Eftpos
Wine Small & reasonable, with some locals; 8 by the glass
Chef John Evans
Owners Irena & Jeremy Hutchings
Seats 50; wheelchair access; outdoor seating; bar
Child friendly Kids' menu; highchairs
www.paperbarkcamp.com.au
And…make a weekend of it by staying on site

Hungry Duck

85 Queen Street, Berry
Tel 4464 2323   Map 11

Modern Asian

Score 14/20

All manner of Asian tastes have come to Berry since The Book Kitchen's David Campbell made a tree-change. Campbell, a former Billy Kwong wok star, has brought tastes of Thailand and China with the odd Western influence to this smart little cottage complete with its own organic vegie patch. Sharing plates of pan-Asian flavours stream out of the kitchen, each with a slight twist. Stand-outs include snapper and chorizo gyoza, tender and nicely salty, and a succulent main of fried local snapper with chilli salt and lime. It's impossible to resist the eponymous bird, and rich red duck curry has a wonderful heat and density. While the use of garden produce makes most vegie dishes sing, a salad of heirloom tomatoes and tofu didn't work; the pairing proving unnatural. Although the famous neighbouring Berry doughnut van might be calling, try the more exotic and refined Chinese five-spiced doughnuts with butterscotch sauce – you won't be disappointed.

Hours Dinner Wed–Sun 6–10pm
Bill Share plates $9–$32 **D** $12; 5-course banquet $45pp, 9 courses $75
Cards V MC Eftpos
Wine Neat list of Australian boutiques, plus interesting foreign additions including Asian wines; 14 by the glass; BYO (corkage $5pp)
Chef David Campbell
Owners David & Nicole Campbell
Seats 45; wheelchair access; outdoor seating
Child friendly Highchairs
www.hungryduck.com.au
And…the banquet menu changes daily, $45 for 5 courses or $75 for 9 courses

south coast

Hyams Beach Cafe

NEW ENTRY

76 Cyrus Street, Hyams Beach
Tel 4443 3874   Map 11

Contemporary

Score 12.5/20

This is no-frills, flavoursome summer fun. Check out the bistro-style blackboard menu, head to the counter and order and pay up front. It's part of a general store now filled with gourmet goodies thanks to Brad Seymour, who Swans fans might remember as a decade-long defender up until 2003. The rear dining area has a freshly scrubbed beachy feel, with glimpses across the rooftops to Jervis Bay. It's popular, so if all else fails, you can always grab takeaway for the white-sand beach below. Start the day with French toast or Mittagong mushies on sourdough after your swim. The coffee's good, too. Lunch includes vivid chilli-salt soft shell crab with green papaya salad and nam jim, and braised lamb shank and peas on pappardelle. Over summer, the boldly satisfying dinner menu features quail breast confit on potato galette; and chargrilled rib-eye with herb butter. Rhubarb jelly seems like a childhood reminiscence. What a great day at the beach.

Hours Breakfast daily 8–11am; Lunch daily 11am–3pm; Dinner daily (Dec–Easter only) 6–10pm

Bill E $14.50–$17 **M** $22–$33 **D** $15; breakfast & lunch $7–$17

Cards V MC Eftpos

Wine BYC (no corkage)

Chefs Doug Innes-Will, Louise Korelin & Drew Fisher

Owners Brad & Melissa Seymour

Seats 44; wheelchair access; outdoor seating

Child friendly Kids' menu; drawing materials; ice-cream & sweets from general store

And…yes, the fantastic burgers and chips are still on the takeaway menu

Lorenzo's Diner

119 Keira Street, Wollongong
Tel 4229 5633   Map 11

Modern Italian

Score 13/20

Lorenzo Pagnan is quite the local identity, feeding Wollongong for more than a decade in this location alone – a plain-lined modern restaurant behind a somewhat aloof frosted-glass streetfront. Like the enclosed dining space with its large abstract art works, his Italianate menu (a flirtation with Asian flavours appears to have cooled) is agreeable and appealing, with the occasional clanger. Grilled sardines from a blackboard menu arrive as described. But a "Milanese" risotto was thick with braised veal and too light on the advertised saffron and lemon notes, let alone grainy, stock-braised rice. Get up close to a main course of pancetta-stuffed quails (those bones are made for gnawing) or a fine chargrilled sirloin, rare as ordered, with a classic veal and eschalot jus. Never mind the seeming inexperience of black-clad waitresses, torta di verona is a gorgeously creamy combination of almond and brioche-like pandoro pieces, and just the way to wrap up another evening with Lorenzo.

Hours Lunch Thurs–Fri noon–2.30pm; Dinner Tues–Sat 6–9.30pm

Bill E $18–$23 **M** $27–$34 **D** $13–$15

Cards AE DC (+5% for groups of 20 or more) V MC

Wine 8 by the glass; BYO lunch & Tues–Wed dinner only (corkage $7 a bottle)

Chefs Graeme Thornton & Daniel Sherley

Owner Lorenzo Pagnan

Seats 50

www.lorenzosdiner.com.au

And…check the website for Lorenzo's classic recipes

regional

Michael's Ristorante

1/50 Crown Street, Wollongong
Tel 4225 9542   Map 11

Italian

Score 12.5/20

Michael's is another proud flag waver for Aussie-Italian dining. Fervent fans pack out the open, rectangular room, its white walls broken up by a large, wrought-iron wine rack and menu boards covered with the evening's antipasto, cheese, gelato and recommended wine choices. There's a bouncy, affable ease to the place, boosted by relaxed, casual yet confident service. Stuffed, crumbed, deep-fried olives, and eggplant rolls oozing melted fontina (a soft Italian cheese), make a nice opening nibble. Chilli octopus, on the other hand, was admirably soft, although light on tomato punch. Good quality dried pasta and a dense, meaty sauce make pappardelle with oxtail ragu a no-brainer entree pick. Kingfish on "smashed" jerusalem artichokes and a large rib-eye with clever sweet and sour beetroot notes are reliable mains. A lick of tangy strawberry sorbetto, or smooth pistachio gelato folded around a few nutty chunks, will get you waving the flag too, in surrender.

Hours Lunch Tues–Fri noon–2.45pm; Dinner Tues–Sat 6–9.45pm
Bill E $16.50–$21.50 **M** $26.50–$35 **D** $12.50; 3-course chef's selection $59pp
Cards AE V MC
Wine 11 by the glass; BYO wine only (corkage $7.50 a bottle)
Chef Michael Ciot
Owners Michael Ciot & Jennifer Rowles
Seats 55
Child friendly Highchairs; small portions
Vegetarian Options on main menu
www.michaelsristorante.com.au
And...BYO is big but changes to wine list promised

The Posthouse

137 Queen Street, Berry
Tel 4464 2444   Map 11

Contemporary

Score 13/20

The telltale facade, if not the name, gives it away. This used to be a typical country post office. Now stripped back to timber and solid walls, it's inevitably a little noisy, but the impact of the din is softened by truly friendly staff, no-fuss fresh food, and not the slightest hint of pretension. At dinner time, start with blue swimmer crab tart and salad greens, and admire its artless simplicity. Then move on effortlessly to a lamb backstrap with a suitably rustic, mild mustard mash and snappy green beans; or spiced snapper fillets with baby spinach, cream and kipfler potatoes. Desserts are basic but oh so delicious. Try apple and rhubarb crumble, caramelised citrus tart with raspberry coulis, or perhaps a straight-up-and-down sticky date pudding with butterscotch sauce. The Toby's Estate coffee and T2 teas are fine for the next morning with eggs served every which way. How better to start or end the day?

Hours Breakfast Sat–Sun 9am–noon; Lunch Thurs–Mon 11am–2.30pm; Dinner Thurs–Sun 6–8.30pm
Bill E $12.95–$16.95 **M** $18.95–$28.95 **D** $8; 10% surcharge on Sundays
Cards AE V MC Eftpos
Wine A modest list of Australian varietals; 6 by the glass
Chef Horst Bleuel
Owners Horst & Patricia Bleuel
Seats 104; private room; outdoor seating
Child friendly Highchairs
Vegetarian A range of options
www.berryposthouse.com.au
And...there's an "overnight postal service" (that is, rooms for hire)

The River Moruya

16B Church Street, Moruya
Tel 4474 5505 Map 12

European

Score 14.5/20

The view of Moruya River, with barely a ripple disturbing its surface and a backdrop of rolling hills, is as calming and uplifting as a breath of fresh air. Conversation is minimal for couples seated closest to the view (they're too busy taking it in) while further inside, small groups chatter enthusiastically, looked after by keen young staff. Flavours tend towards sweet on a menu boasting local produce. Yellowfin tuna from Bermagui is tremendously fresh, served in olive-tapenade rimmed slices with thin zucchini ribbons, parmesan crisps and bright dollops of sweet red pepper mousse. Mains include roasted lamb loin with seared sage gnocchi, onion fondant, creamy shallot puree and super sweet madeira jus. While house-made farfalline (little pasta bows) are nicely al dente, served with tomato sugo, zucchini, and ricotta, the dish failed to excite. House-made strawberry sorbet was the highlight in a dessert of soft yoghurt and vanilla panna cotta with a thin shortbread disc and fresh strawberries.

Hours Lunch Wed–Sun noon–3pm; Dinner Wed–Sat 6–9pm; bookings essential

Bill E $16–$19 **M** $27–$34 **D** $16–$18; 2-course lunch with glass of wine $33pp, 3 courses $38pp; 15% surcharge public holidays

Cards V MC Eftpos

Wine Appealing local options plus some from further afield; 15 by the glass; BYO (Fri only) (corkage $5pp)

Chefs/owners Tobie Patrick, Tim Saffery & Peter Compton

Seats 65; wheelchair access

Child friendly Kids' menu

www.therivermoruya.com.au

And…sample the local products on the menu and wine list

regional

Samuels

382 Lawrence Hargrave Drive, Thirroul
Tel 4268 2244   Map 11

Contemporary

Score 13.5/20

There's nothing subtle about Samuels. But that's not the idea. It's a big, white space with a cheery, happy, hospitable air, lots of happy customers (and good acoustics) and hearty, happy food. There's an outside area for balmy evenings, lovingly worn wooden floors, straw-covered chairs and a long banquette. And then there's host Cameron Davis with his nothing-is-too-much-trouble approach. Chef's Yorkshire roots show in a whimsical mini-roast entree – sliced roast beef, onions and gravy, draped on a puffy, cooked-as-it-should-be yorkshire pud. Main courses are piles of protein: chicken in creamy claypot miso, a Moroccan-esque tagine of sweet-spiced mutton. They come with your choice (two each) of creative side dishes, in little white bowls on a long wooden tray. Try a braised fennel "salad" with almonds and seeded mustard, spiced chickpeas with harissa or perhaps lightly battered ("tempura") cauli florets. Apple brioche with poached apples, caramel sauce and cream is easy to share – unless you want a great big wodge of gooey banoffee pie.

Hours Lunch Sat–Sun noon–2.30pm; Dinner Tues–Sun 6–10pm
Bill E $15–$17 **M** $25–$28 **D** $10; 2-course dinner (Tues–Thurs only) $35pp, 2-course roast dinner (Sun only) $25pp
Cards AE DC V MC Eftpos
Wine An eclectic, no-frills collection; 14 by the glass; BYO (corkage $5 a bottle)
Chef Peter Walker
Owners Cameron Davis & Paula Callanan
Seats 75; outdoor seating; bar
Child friendly Kids' menu; highchairs
And...don't miss the boutique beer selection, it's great fun

Seagrass Brasserie

13 Currambene Street, Huskisson
Tel 4441 6124   Map 11

Contemporary

Score 12.5/20

Seagrass does a solid job of being all things to all comers who invade this bustling holiday town. The relaxed service is happier than the dolphins entertaining tourists in the bay, and keeps things ticking along. This breezy, shuttered cottage offers more casual dining on the awning-covered deck, which glitters with fairy lights, or slightly smarter and closer to the open kitchen action inside. Chef Kierrin McKnight's ambition is in evidence on an elaborate Eurasian menu that doesn't always achieve its goals, yet scores points for generosity, despite ambitious prices. With good local oysters available, we can't help wondering why Tassie pacifics feature. Asian-style roast pork belly with black vinegar was unfortunately dry and tough, but a main of Barossa chicken confit relishes the company of sweetcorn puree, truffled cabbage and a veal jus. Braised beef cheek curry with bamboo, wing beans and cashews offers both sweet and heat, while the tangy citrus tart with vanilla ice-cream gives a warm glow like a day in the sun.

Hours Lunch Sat–Sun 11.30am–3pm; Dinner daily 5.30–8.30pm
Bill E $19.50 **M** $29.50–$33 **D** $9.50–$14.50; 10% surcharge on Sundays, 15% on public holidays
Cards AE V MC Eftpos
Wine Modest list of boutique Australians; 12 by the glass; BYO (corkage $8 a bottle)
Chef Kierrin McKnight
Owners Kierrin McKnight & Nathan Fay
Seats 85; private rooms; wheelchair access; outdoor seating; bar
Child friendly Kids' meals; highchairs; crayons
Vegetarian Separate menu
www.seagrass.net.au
And...five-course tasting menu for $75

south coast

The Vineyard Kitchen

NEW ENTRY

Cupitt's Winery, 58 Washburton Road, Ulladulla
Tel 4455 7888   Map 11

Italian/French

Score 12.5/20

Cupitt's or Cupid's, diners might well fall in love here. It's not hard to become enamoured of this rustic space with its casual feel, vineyard location and rolling green Budawang Ranges views. Start your flirtation with a tartlet; crumbly buttery pastry holding fresh figs, caramelised onion, mascarpone and not-quite-enough gorgonzola with rocket leaves on top. Take it to the next step with a generous special of linguine served with chilli, garlic, coriander and dozens of clams; it comes together nicely with a squeeze of lemon juice. Spatchcock, skin crisp and slightly charred, is appealing in its provincial simplicity, served with smashed peas, Lyonnaise potatoes and a creamy tarragon sauce. No love affair is complete without something sweet, and there are plenty of sugary treats here, including a generous wedge of yummy, old-fashioned blueberry pie with a scoop of vanilla bean ice-cream. Once bitten, you'll be smitten.

Hours Lunch Wed–Sun noon–3pm; Dinner Fri–Sat 6–10pm; extended hours during holidays
Bill E $13–$16 **M** $20–$30 **D** $12.50; 12% surcharge on public holidays
Cards V MC Eftpos
Wine Affordable Australian list including Cupitt's own; 14 by the glass
Chef Simon Brazill
Owner Griff & Rosie Cupitt
Seats 100; private room; wheelchair access; outdoor seating
Child friendly Kids' menu
www.cupittwines.com.au
And...the cellar door is just a few steps from the restaurant

Zanzibar Cafe

Cnr Main & Market streets, Merimbula
Tel 6495 3636   Map 12

Contemporary

Score 13.5/20

Merimbula's culinary scene has ebbed and flowed as often as the oyster-filled Merimbula bay over the years but Zanzibar has outlasted most. It won't win points on location (above Target and next to Best & Less) or decor (all blond wood, paper napkins and faux flora) but its heart is certainly in the right place. It has attentive owner-host-wine-waiter Alby Sedaitis, who sources as much produce locally as he can (mussels, tuna, blueberries) and the mod-Oz menu has something for everyone. Occasionally, dishes are less than impressive, such as a rather tough fillet of beef, or a heavy-handed sesame-crusted duck confit. But there would be a mutiny if the red-braised pork belly with scallops and chilli jam, or seared tuna and soba noodle salad went missing. A Hobbit Farm goat's cheese tart with leeks is as fine an entree as you'll find, and vanilla bean panna cotta with blueberries is worth climbing out of the sapphire sea for.

Hours Dinner Tues–Sat 6–9pm
Bill E $16–$17.50 **M** $25–$37 **D** $12.50
Cards DC V MC Eftpos
Wine Small, well-priced list of classic Australian wines with a few French thrown in for interest; 9 by the glass
Chefs John O'Brien & Damian Schaeffer
Owners Pam & Alby Sedaitis
Seats 42; wheelchair access
And...go crazy and order the four-course degustation for $50

regional

And also...
ILLAWARRA REGION

AustiBeach Cafe
104 Lawrence Hargrave Drive, Austinmer
Tel 4268 5680
With pole position for beach views, this large, modern cafe is known for fresh juices, smoothies, coffee and ricotta pancakes.

Bombora
Fishermans Co-op, Endeavour Drive, Wollongong
Tel 4229 7011
It's touristy but great for a fisherman's basket (order at the counter) on the waterfront with fishing charter boats bobbing beneath.

Diggies
1 Cliff Road, North Beach, Wollongong
Tel 4226 2688
Permanently packed and right on the beach, Diggies is big brekkie, decent coffee, friendly service and lingering over the papers territory.

Leeandme
87 Crown Street, Wollongong
Tel 4244 0695
A heritage-style terrace with a book-lined back room, lovely cakes and an upstairs verandah – and funky clothes shop.

Mylan
193 Keira Street, Wollongong
Tel 4228 1588
Mylan is the more modern, cover-all-Asian-bases version of Trang's down the road. Stick to its Vietnamese heart: ricepaper rolls, pho with all the trimmings, house-made lemon soda, Vietnamese iced coffee.

The Palms Cafe
111 Lawrence Hargrave Drive, Stanwell Park
Tel 4294 3371
Cock-a-leekie soup, baguettes, boston beans, blueberry and banana bread, decent Allpress coffee and attractive shops next door.

Seahaven Cafe
19 Riverleigh Avenue, Gerroa
Tel 4234 3796
Glimpses across the lagoon to Seven Mile Beach are matched by an excellent cafe serving light meals, top-notch seafood and burgers, good coffee and homemade cakes.

PROVEDORES AND MARKETS
* **Harleys and Johns Seafoods**, 7 Daisy Street, Fairy Meadow **Tel 4284 7177**; old-style fishmongers, a brilliant range including catch-of-the-day specials.
* **Swell Coffee,** rear of 135 Crown Street, Wollongong, **Tel 4229 5579**; own-brand, house-roasted coffee, Fair Trade, organic etc with a small cafe area, too.
* **Zweefers Divine Cakes**, 43–45 Princes Highway, Fairy Meadow. **Tel 4285 4155**; famous cakes and pies in the Gong's food-shopping hub.

* **Gerringong Markets**, Gerringong Town Hall and Old School Park, Fern Street, 3rd Sat, 8.30am–1.30pm, **Tel 4234 1672**.
* **Kiama Produce Market**, Black Beach, Kiama, 4th Sat, 8am–1pm, **Tel 4232 3322**.
* **Wollongong Produce and Creative Traders Market**, Crown Street Mall, Wollongong, Fri, 9am–3pm, **Tel 0422 781 920**.

SHOALHAVEN

Brill on the Green
107 Princes Highway, Milton **Tel 4454 0640**
Also at Cafe Brill
117 Princes Highway, Burrill Lake **Tel 4455 3344**
Stop in for a strong Allpress coffee and range of house-made cakes. Service can be slow, but a seat outside on a sunny day is hard to beat.

The Emporium Food Company
127b Queen Street, Berry
Tel 4464 1570
Stay for a fresh wrap or sandwich, or choose some tempting takeaway at this popular

south coast

provedore and cafe. The front counter is filled with cheeses, olives and cakes and the walls lined with top-shelf products, including loose-leaf teas.

Hayden's Pies
166 Princes Highway, Ulladulla
Tel 4455 7798
Bypass Ulladulla's shopping strip (and lone traffic lights) for these seriously good pies. Traditional meat pies, vegie options and gourmet rarities, all with irresistible flaky pastry. Eat in, with a Princes "Pieway" view.

Husky Bakery
11 Currambene Street, Huskisson
Tel 4441 5015
Gotta love a bakery with a back verandah and fenced kid's play area. The chunky meat pie and cornish pastie, and the old-fashioned pastries (vanilla slice, custard tart, cheesecake), will thrill both lips and hips.

Locavore
2/66 Owen Street, Huskisson
Tel 4441 5464
This cafe's philosophy is in the name: local produce, preferably organic, and food with a slow food bent. Try smoked lamb burger and pizzetta with local fetta. Take home the local goodies, especially Black Cockatoo relishes.

Pilgrims Wholefoods Cafe
The Settlement, Princes Highway, Milton
Tel 4455 3421
Want a yummy, wholesome, filling vegetarian meal? This is the place for you. The burgers are huge and hugely popular, and the coffee is good. Seating inside and out.

River Deli Cafe
84 Kinghorne Street, Nowra
Tel 4423 1344
The communal tables in Nowra's best cafe bustle with fans of fine coffee and fresh juices, snacking on wholesome, simple, familiar fare. The "deli" range of boutique sausages, quiches and pies and fresh meat is for stocking up the holiday house.

Supply
1/54 Owen Street, Huskisson
Tel 4441 5815
Part stylish gourmet provedore, part deli and part fresh-faced cafe. Pay up front for a treat from a long breakfast list, fine fluids, then harissa chicken burger, BLAT, and even prawn and chestnut ravioli for lunch.

PROVEDORES AND MARKETS

* **Jasper Peel Breads,** Shop 1/16 Wason Street, Ulladulla, **Tel 4455 7969**; great bread, plus pizza to eat in at lunch.

* **The Olive Farm,** 1106 Princes Highway (cnr Peterson Road), Falls Creek, **Tel 4447 8791**; an Italian market garden shed for olives and oil, honey, preserves, fruit and veg.

* **Berry Country Fair,** Berry Showground, 1st Sun (except Feb), 8am–2.30pm, **Tel 4464 1476.**

* **Shoalhaven Heads Seafood and Produce Markets,** Shoalhaven Heads Hotel, River Road, every Sat 7.30–11.30am, **Tel 4448 7125.**

EUROBODALLA COAST

The Dairy Shed
52 Princes Highway, Bodalla
Tel 4473 5555
A lovely new lunch spot serving old-fashioned milkshakes – the milk is from a local dairy – and beef burgers. Bodalla Bakery, just up the road, isn't bad either.

North Street Cafe & Bar
5 North Street, Batemans Bay
Tel 4472 5710
A funky cafe with homemade cakes and muffins, plus lovely sandwiches, salads and plenty of gluten-free options. Open daily for brekkie and lunch, Fri–Sat for dinner.

regional

Red Box Pizza
93b Trafalgar Road, Tuross Heads
Tel 4473 8537
When we say "right on the water" we mean it. Next door to two popular seafood eateries, Red Box offers something different, with more-ish wood-fired pizza and Pure Gelato. A heavenly spot, just don't fall in!

Rose & Sparrow
4 Bate Street, Central Tilba
Tel 4473 7229
This historic village boasts a top pie shop, the ABC cheese factory (for cheese and honey tastings), plus this homely cafe and produce shop. Try a honey latte or refreshing homemade cordial and lovely warm scones.

Sydney Street Cafe
34 Sydney Street (cnr Princes Highway), Mogo
Tel 4474 5572
Cakes, jams, local, "almost" organic free-range eggs and honey are just a few reasons to love this cafe with its big wooden tables. Coffee under the gorgeous weeping willow makes a great road trip reviver.

PROVEDORES AND MARKETS
* **Bay Marlin Seafoods**, Shop 8–9, Bridge Plaza, Clyde Street, Batemans Bay, **Tel 4472 3244**; top seafood including Clyde River oysters, local fish and lobsters.
* **Braidwood Bakery**, 99 Wallace Street, Braidwood, **Tel 4842 2541**; great old-fashioned high-top bread and good cakes.
* **Dojo Bread**, Rear Lane, 91 Wallace Street, Braidwood, **Tel 0438 648 468**; terrific sourdough breads Tues–Sat 9am–1pm, or until sold out (be quick!).
* **The Pearly Oyster Bar**, 6 North Street, Batemans Bay, **Tel 4472 4233**; Clyde River oysters "direct from our farm".

* **Tilba Growers' Market**, Big Hall, Central Tilba, every Sat 8am–noon, **Tel 4473 7284**.

SAPPHIRE COAST

Saltwater
75 Lamont Street, Bermagui
Tel 6493 4328
This glass-enclosed restaurant overlooks fishing boats bobbing in the water. Dine in or order and takeaway local oysters and fish from the kiosk window. Battered juicy flathead with chips is a simple joy.

Valley Edge Cafe
59 Princes Highway, Cobargo
Tel 6493 6007
House-roasted coffee and smart, amiable staff with a passion for it. Have a top-notch ristretto with cakes, biscuits and panini for lunch. Service is smart and amiable, with seating inside and out. Catering also available.

PROVEDORES AND MARKETS
* **Maryvale Lavender Farm**, 821 Bermagui Road, Cobargo, **Tel 6493 6211**; lavender jams, mustard, honey, tea, lollies. Phone first.

* **Bega Farmers' Market**, Littleton Gardens, Zingel Place, Bega, 1st and 3rd Fri, 8am–1pm, **Tel 6492 0161**, www.scpa.org.au.
* **Candelo Market**, Candelo Sportsground, Loftus Park and Candelo Town Hall, 1st Sun, 6am–1pm, **Tel 6493 2636** after 7.30pm.
* **Nethercote Market**, Old Nethercote Hall, cnr Nethercote and Back Creek roads, dates vary, **Tel 6495 7102**.

South Coast Wine
By Greg Duncan-Powell

Like the Hunter Valley, the South Coast often gets its rain in January, February and March, which is the wrong time for both vignerons and holidaymakers. Like the Hunter, that hasn't stopped it producing some brilliant semillon. Because of the rain and humidity, the disease-resistant red variety chambourcin is also widely planted.

The white variety that has recently caused the most excitement is the Spanish varietal albarino, which is being grown at Rusty Fig near Bermagui and made by Roger Harris at Brindabella Hills in Canberra. Rusty Fig doesn't have a cellar door, and the cellar doors in the region are rather far flung.

Coolangatta Estate (1335 Bolong Road, Shoalhaven Heads, **Tel 4448 7131**; open daily, 10am–5pm), is one of the more established and consistently successful wineries, especially for its semillon, which regularly picks up medals in the big wine shows. Have a look around the historic, convict-built estate, which is the site of the South Coast's first European settlement. A decent lunch spot too.

Cambewarra Estate (520 Illaroo Road, Cambewarra, **Tel 4446 0170**; open Thur–Sun & school & public holidays, 10am–5pm) produces a good range of wines made by Tamburlaine in the Hunter Valley. The semillon is a stand-out.

Kladis Estate (Princes Highway, Wandandian, **Tel 4443 5606**; open daily, 10am–5pm) is large in South Coast terms. It's a 10,000-case winery producing wine from the vineyards at Wandandian as well as fruit purchased from elsewhere. The Kladis Dion Reserve Cabernet Sauvignon 2005 from a small block of old vines in the Hunter Valley is particularly special.

regional

SOUTHERN HIGHLANDS

First, work up an appetite. It's not hard to do, with the crisp Highlands air, lots of great bushwalking options (Carrington, Fitzroy or Belmore Falls, to name a few), golfing at one of several local courses, and canoeing on the Kangaroo River in picturesque Kangaroo Valley. Add (or substitute) a good chunk of time browsing various antique stores and bookshops around the traps, including the Berkelouw Book Barn at Berrima (Tel 4877 1370). And of course, be a good Australian citizen and visit Bowral's Bradman Museum of Cricket (Tel 4862 1247) and Bradman Oval, where you might even catch a game.

Now it's time to eat. From hatted fine diners to cosy cafes, the Highlands ticks all the boxes. You can even book in for a gourmet cooking class at Blue Bowl Brown Sugar cooking school (www.bluebowl.com.au). With a wide range of local produce available and a Slow Food Convivium (www.slowfoodsouthernhighlands.com) running epicurean events and appetising activities, the only way is up for Highlands foodies.

When you're dining out, check the menu for dishes featuring Mittagong Tunnel mushrooms. These amazing exotic mushies are grown in a disused railway tunnel, built in 1866 between Bowral and Mittagong (www.li-sunexoticmushrooms.com.au) and are sold at farmers' markets.

A visit to Sutton Forest's Montrose Berry Farm – growers of raspberries, blueberries, loganberries, currants (red and black) and hazelnuts – is also worthwhile. You can pick your own, but call ahead as seasons vary (www.montroseberryfarm.com.au, Tel 4868 1544).

The Black Swan

11 Old Hume Highway, Berrima
Tel 4877 2222   Map 11

Contemporary

Score 13.5/20

New owners have revolutionised the interior here (the Journeyman's former home), restoring the massive fireplace in the original 1840s Crown Inn, adding another warming fire and linking the restaurant's two rooms to a more casual cafe that extends graciously over a couple of upper levels. Extra casual tables extend into the excavated old cellar, which will intrigue history buffs. Start with a crisp pastry disc topped with caramelised eschallots, baby beetroot and goat's curd, or tuck into a healthy pile of well-dressed chopped tomatoes, green olives and pomegranate crowned with grilled haloumi. For mains, seafood lovers will enjoy strongly crab-flavoured risotto, topped with a thick slab of succulent barramundi and a thatch of shaved fennel salad. It gets serious competition from confit duck on a citrussy pumpkin puree, spinach and fig jus. Top off a satisfying meal with strawberry buttermilk panna cotta strewn with shards of coconut and fresh coriander.

Hours Morning tea 10am–noon; Lunch 11am–noon; Dinner 6–10pm
Bill E $16.95–$19.95 **M** $24.95–$36.95 **D** $13.95–$15.95
Cards AE DC V MC Eftpos
Wine An eclectic list with some unusual drops; 7 by the glass
Chef Michael Weir
Owners Jan and Trevor Weekes
Seats 50
And...the same owners run the popular Magpie Cafe, just up the road

southern highlands

Centennial Vineyards
Woodside, Centennial Road, Bowral
Tel 4861 8701   Map 11

Contemporary

Score 13/20

The huge wooden beams and big welcoming fireplace in the baronial dining room are reminiscent of a Spanish vineyard. The verandah is more informal, with wooden tables and views over the vines, which produce the restaurant's wines. French doors keep out the cold. Start with a tasting plate featuring a morsel of pork terrine with beetroot, light-as-air semolina gnocchi with mushrooms and crisp sage, prosciutto-wrapped melon, a more-ish tomato shot with prosciutto and pesto, and a tiny barramundi cake topped with aioli. A main of twin souffles stars local Mittagong mushrooms teamed with fetta, and a crisp rocket salad balances an abundance of rich parmesan cream. Or go for a simple, satisfying dukkah-crusted barramundi fillet perched on a fennel and orange salad. A sparkling wine and hibiscus jelly with kiwi fruit granita and fresh mango slices was overly solid, so indulge instead in a trifle featuring local Cuttaway Creek raspberries in season.

Hours High tea Mon & Wed–Fri 11am–4pm; Lunch Wed–Mon noon–3pm
Bill E $14.50–$19.50 **M** $28.50–$36 **D** $14.50; 10% surcharge on Sundays & public holidays
Cards AE V MC Eftpos
Wine All 31 wines from Centennial's own vineyard, matched to each dish; 13 by the glass
Chefs Warrick Brook & Robin Murray
Owners Robin & Mandy Murray
Seats 140; private rooms; wheelchair access; outdoor seating; bar
Child friendly Kids' menu; highchairs
Vegetarian Several options
www.centennial.net.au
And... house-made bread with excellent local Glenlee olive oil

Eschalot
24 Old Hume Highway, Berrima
Tel 4877 1977   Map 11

Contemporary   ♇

Score 14.5/20

This Highlands favourite, in a lovely sandstone heritage home, has lost its footing slightly due to staffing changes. But there's still so much to spoil diners, with refined decor and a pleasingly uncomplicated menu featuring many ingredients sourced from the extensive garden behind the kitchen. Big flavours combine for maximum impact in a punchy, meat-free entree of grilled radicchio with mushrooms, hazelnuts and melting taleggio, all kept in check by a cabernet vinegar dressing. Chargrilled lamb rump and poached ocean trout are nicely medium-rare, the former served on a bed of garlicky cannelini beans, the latter with a creamy sauce given added zing by fresh sorrel. End on a high with a dessert platter for two, including pavlova, brulee and strawbs. He might be a little stretched but consummate restaurateur Richard Kemp is on a winner here.

Hours Lunch Fri–Sun noon–2.30pm; Dinner Wed–Sat 6–8.30pm; open outside of set hours for group bookings
Bill E $16–$22 **M** $32–$42 **D** $14–$16; 10% surcharge on Sundays & public holidays
Cards AE V MC Eftpos
Wine Top locals and plenty from further afield; 20 by the glass; BYO Wed–Fri (corkage $10 a bottle)
Chef/owner Richard Kemp
Seats 72; private rooms; outdoor seating; bar
Child friendly Highchairs
Vegetarian Seasonal selection of 6–8 items
www.eschalot.com.au
And... ask about packages for functions, corporate events and weddings

regional

Esco Pazzo

84 Main Street, Mittagong
Tel 4872 2400   Map 11

Italian (Roman)

Score 13/20

Esco Pazzo is housed in three rooms in an old 1890s building on the corner of Mittagong's main street. It's always buzzing with happy diners, and the friendly, competent service accommodates large groups without fuss. Many come for thin-crust pizza from the wood-fired oven. The menu's fairly predictable list of bruschetta, pizza, pasta and Italian staples offers rich, generous portions, but check out the daily specials for some real finds. Fine tuna carpaccio, dusted with parmesan and doused with a lemon-infused olive oil and a heap of well-dressed rocket makes a memorable start. Or go for quail risotto, topped with a deboned bird, but be warned: it's a generous serve. Three skewers of plump scallops and flavoursome mushrooms served on a rich porcini sauce will also ensure you leave happy and more than satisfied. Desserts might be a tough ask after the big helpings, but gelato slides down effortlessly.

Hours Lunch Tues–Sun noon–3pm; Dinner Tues–Sun 5.30–9pm
Bill E $18.50–$22.50 **M** $27.50–$34 **D** $7.50–$13.50; 10% surcharge on public holidays
Cards DC V MC Eftpos
Wine A moderately priced list featuring some local offerings; 14 by the glass; BYO (corkage $3pp)
Chef Emilio Picchio
Owners Emilio Picchio & Kurt Schmid
Seats 150; private room; wheelchair access; outdoor seating; bar
Child friendly Kids' menu including small-sized pizzas; highchairs; drawing materials
Vegetarian Pizza, pasta & entrees
And... enjoy the outside area under umbrellas during the day, especially with kids

Josh's Cafe

Shop 2, 9 Old Hume Highway, Berrima
Tel 4877 2200   Map 11

Mediterranean

Score 13/20

The food in this colourful cottage is far more refined than the cafe appellation implies. Sit out front to soak up the highland sunshine. Inside offers classic bistro paper-topped tables, although the bright orange and lime green walls might induce migraines. Cheerfully helpful service keeps the pace snappy, and the menu remains hearty yet sophisticated by day and night. Dill-sprinkled chargrilled quail relishes the tang of tzatziki with the sweet perfume of honey and cinnamon roasted pumpkin. Four pancetta- and sage-wrapped scallops enjoy the company of pea puree and peppery watercress. For mains, a filling blackboard special of deftly cooked, just-chalky mushroom risotto hits the spot, while chilli-spiced chargrilled veal, smothered in creamy lemon mustard sauce, is stacked amid chargrilled eggplant and sauteed spinach, surrounded by scrummy skin-on rosemary-infused chips. Croissant and butter pudding with jam and creme anglaise keeps out winter chills, and apple tarte tatin with vanilla ice-cream simply thrills.

Hours Breakfast Sun 9am–noon; Lunch Wed–Sun noon–3pm; Dinner Thurs–Sat 6–9pm
Bill E $10–$21 **M** $19.50–$35 **D** $11.50; 10% surcharge on Sundays & public holidays
Cards AE V MC Eftpos
Wine BYO (corkage $3pp)
Chefs Joshua Levings & Benn Troy
Owners Erika & Victoria Smith, & Joshua Levings
Seats 60; outdoor seating
Child friendly Highchairs; drawing materials
Vegetarian Numerous options
And... house-made lemonade and organic coffee

southern highlands

Journeyman
5 Boolway Street, Bowral
Tel 4861 2442   Map 11

Contemporary

Score 15/20

Husband and wife team Tim Pratt and Deb Pearce – he produces sassy, reassuring food, she's the wine-buff host – make an exciting return after relocating from Berrima. Their large, elegant, modern dining room of long drapes, double-clothed tables and banquettes is a smart stage for Pratt's shrewdly flamboyant approach. His playful contrasts of texture and flavour include an astringent tomato gazpacho with a refreshing island of sweet cucumber sorbet, ringed by blue swimmer crab and toasted almonds. Warm octopus salad with salsa verde is a pretty conga line of soft, lemony tentacles interspersed with potato crisps, asparagus and mushrooms. Twelve-hour roasted lamb shoulder with braised French green lentils, cavolo nero and kohlrabi puree is better than a fireside cuddle, while luscious star-anise scented Thirlmere duck with confit parsnip, beetroot and caramelised orange sauce is cracker quacker. After strawberry shortcake ice-cream as pre-dessert, pan-fried bread and butter pudding with port caramel sauce and port ripple ice-cream is equally sublime.

Hours Lunch daily noon–3pm; Dinner daily 5.30–9pm
Bill E $17–$20 **M** $29–$36 **D** $14.50; 15% surcharge on public holidays
Cards AE √ MC Eftpos
Wine Impressive international range, with some absolute corkers; 20 by the glass; BYO (corkage $3.50pp)
Chef/owner Tim Pratt
Seats 60; wheelchair access; bar
Child friendly Highchairs
www.highlandsnsw.com.au/journeyman
And… you can just drop by to try the wines in the bar

Katers
Peppers Manor House, Kater Road, Sutton Forest
Tel 4860 3111   Map 11

Contemporary/French

Score 15/20

Chef Francois Razavet cooks with adventurous aplomb while paying homage to the history of this classy country manor restaurant as well as his own heritage. The recently renovated dining room boasts picturesque views of a quaint courtyard and garden. Service is sincere and welcoming, with staff taking time to explain the menu and the sometimes unusual presentation; for example, an entree of seared scallops served on what was reportedly once a manor roof tile. They come with a crisp apple and micro herb salad and the extra crunch of pork crackling. Another entree features a quirky yet ultimately successful combination of crabmeat rillettes with marshmallows coated in superfine carrot shavings, crunchy squid ink-soaked breadcrumbs, avocado puree and popcorn. Mains are more straightforward; try lamb with bean cassoulet, or flamiche – crisp pastry filled with sweet buttery leek and balanced by rhubarb puree. Lemon and polenta pudding with eucalyptus sorbet and berry compote is fragrant and delightful.

Hours Breakfast daily 7–10.30am; Lunch daily noon–2.30pm; Dinner daily 6.30–9pm; bookings essential
Bill E $15–$20 **M** $32–$37 **D** $18
Cards AE DC V MC Eftpos
Wine Good range including lots of local drops; 20 by the glass
Chefs Francois Razavet, John Shelly & Pat Cavenagh
Owner Peppers Leisure Ltd
Seats 120; private rooms; wheelchair access; outdoor seating
Child friendly Kids' menu; highchairs
www.peppers.com.au/manor-house
And… the Peppers website has bargain last-minute accommodation deals

good food guide   259

regional

Onesta Cucina
Penders Corner, Wingecarribee Street, Bowral
Tel 4861 6620   Map 11

Italian

Score 13.5/20

They promise "honest fare" within the walls of this charming art deco building. And while noise levels can rise, the package includes a comfortable and intimate atmosphere, much loved by locals. Service is friendly and efficient. Luke Latimer did time at Sydney's Cafe Sopra, and brings his love of fresh, carefully sourced ingredients to the Highlands. This shines through in an entree of pan-fried mirror dory nestled into baby cos lettuce with ribbons of baby leek, asparagus, the freshest herbs and a zingy lemon dressing tang. For a richer offering, there's crisply coated polenta with a lip-smacking gorgonzola and mushroom ragout. Full-flavoured rare Junee lamb rump is delicious on peperonata, with rocket and herby cherry tomatoes on the side. Or try cannelloni stuffed with Macleay Valley rabbit and topped with porcini. Thankfully, there's a brief lull before the dark, oozy sweetness of a rich chocolate tortino.

Hours Lunch Thurs–Sat noon–3pm; Dinner Mon–Sat 6–9pm
Bill E $14–$21 **M** $27–$33 **D** $12.50
Cards AE V MC Eftpos
Wine A well-chosen list with some interesting selections, including six local offerings; 22 by the glass; BYO (corkage $7 a bottle)
Chef/owner Luke Latimer
Seats 100; outdoor seating
Child friendly Highchairs; smaller portions
And…enjoy lunch outside if the sun is shining then browse in the top-rating adjoining bookshop

Post Cafe and Bar

1/249 Argyle Street, Moss Vale
Tel 4868 3878   Map 11

Contemporary

Score 13/20

Post has modernised the interior of the charming old 1895 Moss Vale Post Office, yet it retains the warmth of yesteryear with friendly service, a simple, short menu and reasonable prices. It's open daily as a popular cafe but, by night, tables don a white paper covering, and blackboard specials swell the usual lunch menu. Whet your appetite with roasted baby beetroot and a pile of finely sliced, crunchy green beans layered with a scattering of lentils and quinoa, then topped with a splodge of persian fetta. For something a little naughtier, there's lightly battered soft-shell crab and prawns with chilli aioli. Mains move from a warming dish of braised lamb shanks with a caramelised glaze, spinach and a big chunk of baked pumpkin, to a perfectly cooked ocean trout fillet crowned with anchovy butter and perched on kipfler potatoes, roman and white beans. Treat yourself (and a friend) to a delectably rich chocolate pot served with espresso ice-cream.

Hours Breakfast daily 8am–noon; Lunch Wed–Sun noon–3pm; Dinner Fri–Sat 6–9pm
Bill Dishes from $9–$27.50 **D** $7.50; 10% surcharge on Sundays & public holidays
Cards AE V MC Eftpos ($1 surcharge on card transactions)
Wine An interesting list with some local offerings; 12 by the glass; BYO (corkage $5 a bottle)
Chef Gregory Pickup
Owners Gregory Pickup & Chris Alleyn
Seats 78; private room; outdoor seating; bar
Vegetarian Several choices
And…enjoy breakfast, lunch or just a good coffee outside in comfy chairs

southern highlands

Red Olive

3/185 Old Hume Highway, Mittagong
Tel 4871 2298   Map 11

Contemporary

Score 12.5/20

This 1860s heritage-listed stone cottage sits incongruously next to a big shopping centre, but offers respite with casual dining in two cosy rooms and on a larger decked area. At lunch, there's a choice of more than a dozen tapas-style dishes, including zucchini and sweet corn fritters, lamb cutlets with salsa verde or duck-filled rice paper rolls. Cloths and candles create a more sultry evening atmosphere, when the focus on tapas remains. Servings are generous, and a bowl of tender chilli squid has the lightest, crispest batter. Just-seared scallops, wrapped in prosciutto, are flavoured with a white wine marinade. Lamb racks, doused in rosemary jus, perch on pearl couscous with red capsicum, tiny olives and green beans, and would easily serve two. Duck with a spicy plum jus tops roasted baby beetroot, fat asparagus spears and silverbeet is equally generous. Dessert is superfluous but a shared macadamia and peach brulee is irresistible.

Hours Lunch Fri–Sun noon–3pm; Dinner Tues–Sat 6–9pm; bookings essential
Bill Tapas menu $8–$16; **M** $24–$34 **D** $15
Cards V MC Eftpos
Wine A small list with quite a few imports and local drops: 11 by the glass; good beer selection
Chef Melinda Christensen
Owner Tim Drummond
Seats 60; private rooms; wheelchair access; outdoor seating; bar
Vegetarian plenty of choices
And… be thankful for the heritage listing that saved this cottage from demolition

Stones

Eling Forest Winery,
Hume Highway, Sutton Forest
Tel 4878 9449   Map 11
Contemporary

Score 13/20

The bread is delicious, but that's no surprise. Sydneysiders might remember afternoon teas at the Sofitel Wentworth where co-owner Mark Stone showcased his training at Lenotre, the renowned Parisian patisserie school and gourmet outlet. Stone's treechange south with wife Megan, who runs front of house with good-natured aplomb, gives reason to pause between Canberra and Sydney, not least for superb desserts such as a martini glass of "deconstructed" tiramisu with chocolate custard and amaretto jelly. While set in a rustic brick homestead on an 1840s heritage-listed property, the menu is thoroughly modern. Timeless, however, is a textbook duck liver paté with Cumberland sauce and toasted sourdough. Soft-shell crab adrift in sweetcorn and basil soup gives fresh verve to a familiar Chinese match. While pine-nut laced pumpkin and goat's cheese lasagne was dense and flat-footed, the only complaint about herb-crusted lamb rack with roast tomatoes and spiced eggplant relish is the generous portion. Meanwhile, parents (and kids) love the $10 spag bol with broccoli.

Hours Breakfast Sat–Sun 8.30–10.30am; Lunch Thurs–Sun noon–3pm; Dinner Thurs–Sat 6–10pm
Bill E $16–$18.50 **M** $25.50–$29 **D** $16; 10% surcharge on public holidays
Cards AE V MC Eftpos
Wine Concise, affordable, interesting mix of local, Australian & French; 19 by the glass
Chefs/owners Mark & Megan Stone
Seats 90; private room; outdoor seating; bar
Child friendly Kids' menu; highchairs; toys; books
www.elingforest.com.au
And… weekend afternoon teas

good food guide   261

regional

Vida

17 Links Road, Bowral
Tel 4861 1977   Map 11

Contemporary

Score 13/20

Set in the elegant boutique Links House Hotel, this small restaurant is an oasis of calm (you can stay the night, too). Enjoy a quiet drink in the lounge before dining in the carpeted dining room, where the service is both affable and capable. The menu is arranged into price categories, making it ideal for grazing through to guzzling. Share a tapas plate featuring great garlic bruschetta, tempura prawn, tiny potato balls with tomato, chorizo, a couple of delicate meatballs, olives and a salty–sweet chunk of Valdeon (a feisty Spanish blue cheese). Larger plates include a succulent slice of salmon swimming prettily in a lemony broth studded with teensy chopped vegies and a dice of red, green and yellow capsicum. Slices of lamb backstrap sit happily beside pea and potato mash, grilled haloumi, roasted tomato and a drizzle of balsamic reduction. Spoon up apple, lychee and walnut crumble with ginger ice-cream and contemplate a round on the golf links tomorrow to work it off.

Hours Breakfast daily 8–9.30am; Dinner Wed–Sat 6.30–10pm
Bill E $12–$18 **M** $26–$30 **D** $12
Cards AE (+3%) V MC Eftpos
Wine A small, well-chosen list with selected local wines; 13 by the glass; BYO (Wed–Thurs only; corkage $8 a bottle)
Chef Jim McClelland
Owners Robyn Laverack & Judith Fletcher
Seats 64; private room; bar
Child friendly Kids' menu; highchairs; drawing materials; games
Vegetarian Nine dishes plus seven sides for vegans & vegetarians, plus 11 for coeliacs
www.linkshouse.com.au
And…the golf course is just across the road

Willow Vale Mill

Mill Road, Laggan
Tel 4837 3319   Map 12

European

Score 13/20

It's a brave, perhaps foolhardy, restaurateur who won't put pepper and salt on his tables, certain he has seasoned his dishes sufficiently. But then, it's a brave, perhaps foolhardy, person who rebuilds a 19th-century flour mill to house a one-man farmhouse/traveller's-inn styled eatery where what is served on the day – laid out buffet style on the long bar – is based on what's best on the day in the kitchen garden, or from the local farmers and herders. That might mean hearty chickpea and lamb soup for starters, followed by a well-done boiled leg of lamb with baked baby beetroot, sliced, baked charlotte potatoes and pink rounds of corned beef on the side. Next comes rhubarb and apple pie, and poached pears with sultanas in syrup, followed by plunger coffee with homemade chestnut and almond biscuits. Put your trust in Graham Liney, though, and you'll have a meal of thoughtful simplicity, abundant generosity and true conviviality.

Hours Dinner Wed–Sat 7–10pm; bookings essential
Bill 4-course set menu $63pp
Cards Cash or cheque only
Wine There's no list, just an idiosyncratic, rewarding selection including local pressings; 3 by the glass
Cook/owner Graham Liney
Seats 150; private room; outdoor seating
Vegetarian Plenty of choice
And…take your coffee and bickie out under the massive Gethsemane olive trees

southern highlands

And also...

Burrawang General Store Cafe
11 Hoddle Street, Burrawang
Tel 4886 4496
A decade year ago, Burrawang's general store closed after 132 years. It's been charmingly restored to life as a delightful cafe. Go for a brekkie, a scrumptious light lunch or just drop in for coffee and cake.

Cafe Bella
151 Moss Vale Road, Kangaroo Valley
Tel 4465 1660
The valley's most popular meeting and eating spot. Go for a hearty breakfast, yummy muffins with your morning coffee, lunch or weekend dinners. Unpretentious food, generous servings and friendly atmosphere.

Exeter General Store
Cnr Exeter & Middle roads, Exeter
Tel 4883 4289
If only there were more of these wonderful old general stores – welcoming atmosphere, second-hand books, food (including some locally grown produce) plus decent coffee and tea, hearty breakfasts and lunches.

Gastronome
23A Boolway Street, Bowral
Tel 4861 3614
This simple cafe is the latest "find" in Bowral. It's not big on atmosphere but who needs it when the coffee is good and the food comes from a kitchen where someone is so obviously passionate about good produce?

The Magpie Cafe
Old Hume Highway, Berrima
Tel 4877 2008
This crowd-pleasing cafe open daily for B, L and D, offers eclectic decor and an oft-changing menu (try the signature steak sandwich with caramelised onion, beetroot chutney and lime aioli). Loose-leaf teas and good looking cakes, too.

The Milk Factory Gallery Cafe
31 Station Street, Bowral
Tel 4862 1077
There are several floors of quality art exhibits and Bowral's best cup of coffee. The great breakfast-menu choices extend to noon, when light or full lunch options take over. Details of exhibits and cafe at www.milkfactorygallery.com.au.

Paragon Cafe
174–176 Auburn Street, Goulburn
Tel 4821 3566
An original art deco country cafe in Goulburn's main drag still offers the foods of yesteryear: mixed grills, a roast of the day, old-fashioned hamburgers and milkshakes as well as pasta and pizza.

Pizzas in the Mist
42 Hoddle Street, Robertson
Tel 4885 1799
Come in from the bracing Highlands air for some friendly country service. Toppings on the pizza from the big wood-fired oven range from simple to sumptuous. The blackboard menu also offers a selection of seasonal dishes.

Robertson Cheese Factory Cafe
1 Illawarra Highway, Robertson
Tel 4885 1133
As well as the excellent range of cheeses (some local) and other deli goodies, the old factory has had a makeover and now incorporates a great little cafe with delicious lunches, snacks and quality ice-cream.

The Royal Brasserie and Steakhouse
The Royal Hotel, 255 Bong Bong Street, Bowral
Tel 4862 5588
At the back of this popular Bowral watering hole, a casual restaurant offers pizza, pasta and nachos. More notable are their prized steaks: choose from pasture- or grain-fed beef, either locally grown or from the Riverina.

regional

PROVEDORES AND MARKETS

* **The Cheese Store**, Shop 6B Corbett Plaza, Bowral, **Tel 4862 3749**; great range of cheeses plus deli items – many local.
* **Gumnut Patisserie**, 7 Bong Bong Street Bowral, **Tel 4862 2819**; also at Post Office Corner, Berrima, **Tel 4877 2177**; also at 16 Dalton Street, Mittagong, **Tel 4872 2172**; great pies, cakes and sourdough bread.
* **Il Topolino Alimentari Delicatessen**, 281 Bong Bong Street Bowral, **Tel 4861 4957**; top deli with quality sausages.
* **The Little Hand Stirred Jam Shop**, 1/9 Old Hume Highway, Berrima, **Tel 4877 1404**; jams, chutneys, mustards and honeys.
* **A Little Piece of Scotland**, cnr Illawarra Highway & Exeter Road, Sutton Forest, **Tel 4868 3492**; great shortbread, Dundee cakes, whisky-flavoured muckle plus tartans and Scottish knick-knacks.
* **Mauger's Meats**, 21 Hoddle Street, Burrawang, **Tel 4886 4327**; paddock to plate perfection with aged grass-fed meat, sausages and their own smoked chicken.
* **Montrose Berry Farm**, Cnr Exeter Road & Ormond Street, Sutton Forest, **Tel 4868 1544**; charming old farm with berries and asparagus in season, plus jams, jellies, chutneys, vinegars and berry pies.
* **Old Goulburn Brewery**, 23 Bungonia Road, Goulburn, **Tel 4821 6071**; continuously brewing since the 1830s – take a tour and enjoy!
* **Wild Food**, 250A Bong Bong Street, Bowral, **Tel 4861 2838**; organic fresh and packaged foods plus a cafe for healthy tucker.

* **Berrima Food Market**, Berrima Courthouse, Cnr Wilshire & Argyle streets, and in winter at Anglican Church hall and grounds, Argyle Street, 4th Sat, 9am–1pm, **Tel 4877 1164**.
* **Bowral Farmers' Market**, Bowral Public School, Bowral, 2nd Sat, 8am–noon, **Tel 0437 136 693**.
* **Mittagong Markets**, cnr Albert & Alice streets, Mittagong, 3rd & 5th Sat, 8am–3pm, **Tel 4684 1261**.

Southern Highlands Wine
By Greg Duncan-Powell

It's surprising it has taken so long for the Southern Highlands to become a wine region. With its proximity to Sydney, cool climate and beautiful scenery, it seems that all it was lacking was vines.

It did have a wine industry in the 1800s but that was before cattle and horses became more profitable. The rebirth occurred this millennium, and with only a handful of vintages under its belt, the greatness or otherwise of Southern Highlands wines is yet to be proven. Chardonnay is the hero, and pinot noir in the right site has a future too. Classy cabernet sauvignon and spicy shiraz are also produced.

Centennial Vineyards (Centennial Road, Bowral, **Tel 4861 8700**; open daily, 10am–5pm) is an impressive operation producing a range of stylish wines and a very good sparkling.

Blue Metal Vineyard and Cafe (Compton Park Rd, Berrima, **Tel 4877 1877**; open Thur–Mon 10am–5pm) produces a particularly tasty cabernet sauvignon. Now has a cafe open weekends and public holidays 11am–4pm.

NORTH COAST

RICHMOND & CLARENCE VALLEYS, BYRON SHIRE, COFFS COAST, GREAT LAKES & MANNING VALLEY, PORT MACQUARIE, THE TWEED

This beautiful, varied region is by no means a small one, covering 600 kilometres of coastline between the Great Lakes and Tweed Heads. The mere thought is enough to stoke the appetite. Thankfully, there's plenty to delight ravenous food lovers, with beachside restaurants, trendy main street cafes and terrific fine dining.

Keep your eyes peeled, too, for roadside stalls and some of the state's best farmers' markets, where you can pick up fresh local produce and seafood, especially around the Coffs Coast. Speaking of seafood, oyster lovers take note – the Oyster Farm in Wooli sells Sydney Rocks by the plot, a season ahead, and will let you know when they're in their prime (meanwhile, you can visit your brood at the farm or online; www.theoysterfarm.com.au).

There's a bite to be bit at every turn, and plenty of food-themed events, too. In May, Kingscliff hosts its annual Art, Food and All That Jazz festival, while in nearby Tweed Valley, August is time for the Banana Festival and Harvest Week celebrations (www.bananafestival.org). Sawtell, just south of Coffs Harbour, spices things up good and proper with their annual Chilli Festival, in July (www.sawtellchillifestival.com.au). And Port Macquarie treats visitors to Tastings of the Hastings in October, with more than 50 local food producers showing off their wares (Tel 0414 376 868). Showcasing the best in food and wine from the Camden Haven region (just south of Port Macquarie) is Taste of Haven, an annual festival held in May (www.camdenhaveninfo.org.au).

Keep the tastebuds tantalised during non-festival times with the region's abundance of lovely restaurants and casual cafes, many of which focus their menus on good local produce (though perhaps not often enough on NSW wines). And when you're well and truly fed and watered, grab some food for thought at the Byron Bay Writers Festival, held every year in August (www.byronbaywritersfestival.com).

Bamboo

Santai Resort, 9 Dianella Drive, Casuarina Beach
Tel 6670 5555   Map 13

Contemporary

Score 15/20

This low-lit, moody, sleek-boutique eatery overlooks a courtyard "lagoon", festooned with stone bowls, Buddhas and frangipani trees. You might think this is where Balinese leviathans cavort, such is the scale of the grand pavilions with soaring ceilings, gargantuan timber beams and cavernous foyers. Then you're met with infectiously casual, yet professionally astute, service and at once the playfulness amid the decadence makes sense. There's a degustation menu, various tapas-style options for sharing and a la carte. They all feature the briny, shimmering delights of freshly shucked oysters with semillon and eschalot dressing. The kitchen really hits its straps with mains; a wagyu eye-fillet with mash and smashed peas is deluxe perfection, although it's the sweet pork cheeks with seared scallops, herbed gnocchi and shaved fennel that steal the show. Pistachio "snow egg" with toffee and blood orange granita provides a glimmer of restraint among the calorific culinary pickings.

Hours Breakfast Sat–Sun 7–11.30am; Lunch Tues–Sun noon–3.30pm; Dinner Tues–Sat 6–9.30pm; bookings essential
Bill E $19–$21 **M** $29–$39 **D** $13; 2-course lunch $35pp; 10% surcharge on Sundays & public holidays
Cards AE DC V MC
Wine Balanced, predominantly local list with the odd inflated foreign gatecrasher; 14 by the glass
Chefs Greg Pieper & Marc Petersen
Owner Greg Pieper
Seats 90; private room; wheelchair access; outdoor seating; bar
Child friendly Kids' menu; highchairs
Vegetarian Degustation menu
www.bamboorestaurant.com.au
And…dinner is best for special occasions

regional

Byron Beach Cafe

Clarkes Beach, Lawson Street, Byron Bay
Tel 6685 8400   Map 13

Contemporary

Score 14/20

Like a cool summer breeze, the upbeat staff and surf club vibe of this blond wood and polished concrete cafe invite all comers to chill out and tuck in – whether in salt-crusted togs or an open-neck business shirt. The unique location nudging the sand dunes of Byron's iconic beach, 180-degree views up and down the coast, indoor-outdoor seating and a takeaway kiosk: there's so much on offer, likewise the plethora of menus covering breakfast, brunch, lunch, tapas and dinner. Herein lies the strength and weakness – you can find something to tempt, no matter the time or mood, however occasionally the ambition is stretched. Yet who can begrudge when the service is this switched on and most dishes deliver in spades? Salt-and-Sichuan-pepper calamari is lifted by a Vietnamese pickled carrot salad. Earthy confit duck salad is paired with fetta, rocket, kipfler potato and truffle oil. Orange and cumin-marinated lamb cutlets have a smoky chipotle and corn salsa. Casual, funky and flavoursome – the evolution of Byron continues.

Hours Breakfast daily 7.30–11.30am; Lunch daily noon–6pm; Dinner Thurs–Sun 6–10pm
Bill E $15–$18 **M** $26–$32 **D** $15; 10% surcharge on Sundays, 15% on public holidays
Cards V MC Eftpos
Wine Short, summery, snappy list; 11 by the glass
Chef Nathaniel Marshall
Owners Ben & Belinda Kirkwood
Seats 110; wheelchair access; outdoor seating; bar
Vegetarian Several options
www.byronbeachcafe.com.au
And…can't wait for an outside table? Grab a takeaway and nest among the dunes

Ça Marche

Cassegrain Winery, 764 Fernbank Creek Road (cnr Pacific Highway), Port Macquarie
Tel 6582 8320   Map 13

French/Contemporary

Score 14.5/20

The approach to Cassegrain is like stepping through the looking glass: one minute you're playing cat and mouse with semitrailers plying the highway, the next you're inching along a narrow, winding road lined with exuberant rose bushes to a beautifully positioned restaurant and cellar door. Like Alice, you might as well enter into the spirit of things. With the help of Julia Hickey, who manages the room with the poise of a veteran, that shouldn't be hard. Vitello tonnato – paper-thin slices of rare veal, tuna mayo, capers and parmesan crisps – delivers big flavour. More delicate is prawn and scallop ravioli in a crystal clear tomato consomme, so melodious it's a wake-up call to the senses. Where to next? Deboned, barbecued spatchcock makes an earthy match with artichoke, peas and wilted witlof while rabbit ballotine, served with nuggety, buttery sweetbreads and braised red cabbage, demonstrates yet again the talent in the kitchen. In the end, it's the traditional tiramisu that says, "Eat me."

Hours Morning tea daily 10–11.30am; Lunch daily noon–3pm; Afternoon tea daily 2.30–4pm; Dinner Fri 6–9pm; bookings essential
Bill E $17–$22 **M** $27.80–$37 **D** $10–$14
Cards V MC Eftpos
Wine The fruits of Cassegrain's cellar (try the chambourcin); 12 by the glass
Chef Patrick Bowen
Owners Michael Kelly & Julia Hickey
Seats 100; wheelchair access; outdoor seating
Child friendly Kids' menu; outdoor areas
Vegetarian Great vegetarian alternatives
www.camarche.com.au
And…take time out to sit back and smell the roses

north coast

Dish

85–87 Jonson Street, Byron Bay
Tel 6685 7320   Map 13

Contemporary
Score 14/20

They get the lighting right here, adding ambience to a room that bends from bar to restaurant around a corner site, all angled roof, Doctor Who lights, moody nooks, white walls, dark woods, banquettes and beams. While we wish there were more NSW representatives on the long wine list, the easy finesse of the food is at one with the relaxed atmosphere. The stack is back, in a salad of gently house-smoked quail, seasonal peach slices, lardons and pine nuts in piquant burnt orange vinaigrette. Fish of the day, perhaps mulloway perked by crisp pea tendrils, comes with nicely yielding potato gnocchi. A neat round of slow-cooked pork belly is bathed in apple puree, capped by a slice of apple and puffs of crackling. To end, a platter featuring a trio of lemon desserts appeals, but traditional rice pudding wins hands down. A cosmopolitan crowd in high heels (the girls) or thongs (the blokes) bathe in balmy breezes wafting through big foldaway windows.

Hours Lunch Thurs–Sun 11am–3pm; Dinner daily 6–10pm; bookings essential
Bill E $22–$26 **M** $29–$38 **D** $16
Cards AE DC V MC Eftpos
Wine A long, interesting list, with some Spanish; 20 by the glass
Chef Bret Cameron
Owners Ross Skinner & Michael de Laurence
Seats 50; wheelchair access; bar
Child friendly Kids' menu; highchairs
www.dishbyronbay.com
And... the bar menu is a meal in itself

fatbellykat

26 Tweed Street, Brunswick Heads
Tel 6685 1100   Map 13

Modern Greek
Score 14.5/20

Consider moussaka that's not gluggy, sauce nutmeg-fragrant, cuddling chunks of chicken, squishy eggplant and sliced potato, and served in the restaurant's signature ovenware. Savour a sweet beetroot salad judiciously scattered with cold-smoked fetta. Plump local prawns sit in a reduction of red wine, raisins, pine nuts and English spinach, the sweet–sour flavours intensely concentrated. A splodge of rice "pud" with poached pear is sparked by a clever, crunchy pinch of basil-infused sugar. Indulge in just one chocolate truffle of the day, say, champagne and pomegranate. The menu is wonderfully varied, from shared mezze to main courses or banquets, plus a full dessert list. Olives from Adelaide and Lismore, house-made bread and haloumi, spiced local cuttlefish and more-ish lamb meatballs are enthusiastically served in a clean, fresh, sparsely furnished room of light colours and blond wooden tables. Six years and three children later, Katerina and Damian have a true family restaurant. Like "Bruns" itself, we hope it never changes.

Hours Dinner Wed–Fri 6–9pm, Sat–Sun 6–10pm
Bill Mezze $3.90–$16.90; Banquet $23.90–$29.90; **D** $2.20–$12.90; 10% surcharge on public holidays
Cards V MC Eftpos
Wine BYO (corkage $2pp)
Chef Katerina Williams
Owners Katerina & Damian Williams
Seats 70; wheelchair access; outdoor seating
Child friendly Highchairs
Vegetarian Several options
www.fatbellykat.com
And... oysters are still on the menu in all their inventive guises

regional

Fiasco Ristorante

22 Orlando Street, Coffs Harbour
Tel 6651 2006   Map 13

Italian (Northern)

Score 14/20

Who would know it was here? Fiasco is a genuine regional treasure, complete with incongruous location (by the railway line, under an apartment block). A name change, from Caffe Fiasco, reflects its very Italian focus on dining rather than snacking. With a leafy herb garden and lots of outdoor areas around a central kitchen, the ambience is firmly family-oriented, with wood-fired pizza and good house gelato – almondy cassata with fruit pieces, dark chocolate and hazelnut-flecked bacio – to tempt all ages and stages. There's a serious adult menu, too, with seafood, intelligent pasta combinations and meaty mains, such as excellent duck with chickpea puree and a sweet–sour caponata. Flavours are uncompromisingly Italian, with a few frills: a balsamic-dressed frisee salad zings with the textural contrasts of prosciutto, peach, mozzarella and pistachio. Spaghetti alle vongole is sea-salty with bottarga, cherry tomatoes and diced zucchini. A tomatoey cacciuco (fish soup) comes, as it should, with toasty bruschetta. Service sparkles with proficiency and charm.

Hours Dinner Tues–Sun 6–9pm
Bill E $16.50–$18.50 **M** $21–$37 **D** $11.70–$21; 10% surcharge on Sundays & public holidays
Cards AE (+2.5%) DC (+2.5%) V MC Eftpos
Wine A simple but effective Australian–Italian list; 24 by the glass
Chef Stefano Mazzina
Owners Mark, Alex & Skye Hawkins, & Stefano Mazzina
Seats 75; wheelchair access; outdoor seating; bar
Child friendly Kids' menu; highchairs; kids' cutlery
www.caffefiasco.com.au
And… a fiasco is a straw-covered wine bottle

Fins

5/6 Bells Boulevard, Salt Village, South Kingscliff
Tel 6674 4833   Map 13

Seafood

Score 15.5/20

The familiar hospitality of Steven Snow's casual fine diner provides relief from the labyrinth surrounding it. ("Truman, wake up!") Amid the glass and concrete of Salt Village, its rustic, recycled floorboards, comfy chairs and ceiling fans paint a faux plantation patina. Service is exceptional with sommelier Ben Richards sure-footed across a pescatarian-friendly list. The food is innovative albeit occasionally hit and miss, with chef Shunichi Tanabe weaving a Japanese aesthetic among the evolving classics of cataplana (a Portuguese-style bouillabaisse) and Moroccan tagine. Chilli tempura soft-shell crab, fish spatzle and edamame rests on a painterly flourish of yuzu sauce for a triumph of elusive fusion. Less inspiring was "Fins fish" – slightly overdone – on a heavy slab of crisp sushi rice with white miso truffle sauce, and prawn and lotus root roll. "Snowy's fish" is simple perfection: line-caught fillet (perhaps kingfish) with stock-braised onions, riesling, lemon and parsley. Ethereal panna cotta with lemon myrtle foam and finger lime syrup is a refined, dreamy finale.

Hours Lunch Fri–Sun noon–3pm; Dinner daily 5.30–10pm; bookings essential
Bill E $18–$26 **M** $34.90–$49 **D** $15–$18; 6-course degustation $95pp; 10% surcharge on Sundays, 15% on public holidays
Cards AE DC V MC Eftpos
Wine Seafood specialists with interesting Spanish & Portuguese options; 17 by the glass
Chefs Steven Snow, Tiffany Richards & Shunichi Tanabe
Owner Steven Snow
Seats 100; wheelchair access; outdoor seating; bar
Child friendly Kids' menu; highchairs
www.fins.com.au
And… sit in the bar for tapas and champagne

Flooded Gums

Bonville Golf Resort, North Bonville Road, Bonville
Tel 6653 4002 Map 13

Contemporary

Score 13/20

The setting is superb: pencil-straight silver gums, velvet lawns and manicured hedges. Tones of heritage green and bullnose verandahs add a timeless note to a modern clubhouse building. A smart wine list (a little more in-house knowledge of it would help) and intriguing menu, utterly pleasant outdoor tables and amiable staff are a promise of fine moments to come. So is an agreeably summery entree of Thai sausage and apple, mint and chilli salad. Ambition, however, often overshadows quality produce – local Sydney rocks kilpatrick were drowned in worcestershire and bacon; delicious eastern king prawns were, strangely, offset by potato puree and a crisp pasta nest, and a rather too-cooked steak was curiously paired with peas and potatoes in a vine-leaf parcel. Crepes suzette from the gueridon add a touch of old-fashioned charm, however, and lemon meringue pie with local lemons and anglaise ice-cream is utterly divine, unless of course you follow with a chocoholic's dream: a decadent chocolate trio.

Hours Breakfast daily 6.30–10am; Lunch daily 10.30am–5.30pm; Dinner daily 6.30–9.30pm; bookings essential
Bill E $16.50–$19.50 **M** $29.50–$39 **D** $13–$18; 10% surcharge on public holidays
Cards AE (+2.5%) DC (+2.5%) V MC Eftpos
Wine Lots of big hitters: 15 by the glass
Chefs George Francisco & Lee O'Caroll
Owner Ironhill Management Pty Ltd
Seats 150; private rooms; wheelchair access; outdoor seating; bar
Child friendly Kids' menu; highchairs; drawing materials
www.bonvillegolf.com.au
And… chef Francisco is at Jonah's, Sydney

Frangipan

11–13 The Crescent, Angourie
Tel 6646 2553 Map 13

Contemporary

Score 13.5/20

Fresh frangipanis on the beautifully set tables are just part of the sweet welcome and attention to detail at this coastal treasure. You can hear the ocean, it's so close. Settle into a starter of snapper croquettes – three fat, crumbed parcels drizzled with lemon and dill aioli – or a superb, creamy, crab salad tumbled with apple wafers and crunchy caramelised walnuts, texturally sublime. Feathery light gnocchi are enveloped in a luxurious puddle of mascarpone and gorgonzola. Fatly sliced pink lamb is stacked alongside a rich, tomatoey ratatouille. Service is faultless and seamless – your dropped napkin replaced in a neat roll in your absence. The atmosphere is languid and moody, and the generously proportioned desserts, especially a fig and ginger pudding in a swirl of molten toffee syrup, simply gorgeous. Comfy couches in this lofty interior, along with surfing memorabilia, make lingering over coffee a tempting option.

Hours Breakfast & lunch Sat–Sun 9am–2pm; Dinner Tues–Sat 6.30–8.30pm; bookings essential
Bill E $16–$19 **M** $19–$33 **D** $11; 15% surcharge on public holidays
Cards AE DC V MC Eftpos
Wine Intelligent list featuring some Italians; 11 by the glass
BYO (corkage $8 a bottle)
Chef Lindsay McDonald
Owners Lindsay & Stewart McDonald, Tracey Hunt
Seats 55; outdoor seating; bar
Child friendly Kids' menu; highchairs
Vegetarian Well catered for
www.frangipan.com.au
And… ask about the limousine service for groups

regional

Fresca

Bangalow Hotel, 1 Byron Street, Bangalow
Tel 6687 1711 Map 13

Contemporary/Mediterranean

Score 13/20

This sleek, casual eatery attached to the art deco local watering hole welcomes all with attentive service and an open, airy atmosphere. The main dining area features a hardwood deck, backed by an enormous frangipani tree and clear plastic blinds for when the weather turns feral. An entree of Pedro Ximenez-glazed local king prawns and pork neck confit with sweet pumpkin puree delights the palate (if not the wallet at $29), but shows there's talent and confidence behind a global "greatest hits" menu. Not so assured was fish of the day, which somehow failed to unite the supporting ingredients of green beans, spuds and beurre blanc. However, grilled, spiced lamb rump lolling atop a Greek salad with persian feta, cumin, mint and citrus yoghurt is simple, light, assured fare. Home cooking returns with apple and rhubarb crumble with cinnamon ice-cream, as well as raspberry and vanilla bean creme fraiche trifle.

Hours Lunch daily noon–3pm; Dinner daily 6–9pm
Bill E $18–$25 **M** $21–$34 **D** $12.90–$13.90; 2-course lunch $28pp, 3-course dinner $40pp; 10% surcharge on Sundays, 15% on public holidays
Cards AE V MC Eftpos
Wine Predictable but decent-value Australian pub list from the bar; 12 by the glass
Chefs/owners Patrick & Kathy Hobbs
Seats 120; private rooms; wheelchair access; outdoor seating; bar
Child friendly Kids' menu; highchairs; books; drawing materials
Vegetarian Several entrees
www.fresca.net.au
And…a simplified bar menu can be had on the back deck beneath the swaying Bangalow palms

Fusion 7

6/124 Horton Street, Port Macquarie
Tel 6584 1171 Map 13

Contemporary

Score 13/20

You'd be advised to read the menu in conjunction with the photographs and postcards taped to the wall. As owner and inveterate traveller Lindsey Schwab's travelogue, it provides vital clues to his food influences, many of them appearing together – not just on the menu, but on the plate. Continents collide when kangaroo fillet joins potato rosti, beetroot pesto and tahini but, like the Indian potato cakes on buttered spinach and field mushrooms with baba ghanoush and cumin labna, it seems to work, albeit in an earthy, peace-and-love kind of way. Goat's cheese and sorrel tart with caramelised onion stays well within French borders, while barramundi in tomato and saffron broth wanders towards Italy with the addition of vongole, white beans and radicchio. The fit-out is no-fuss, a collection of functional pine furniture in a nondescript shopfront on the main street, but it has a certain charm, as evidenced by the crowd.

Hours Dinner Tues–Sat 6–9pm; bookings essential
Bill E $18–$20 **M** $26–$34 **D** $3.50–$12; 10% surcharge on public holidays
Cards AE (+2.5%) V MC Eftpos
Wine BYO (corkage $3pp)
Chef/owner Lindsey Schwab
Seats 50; outdoor seating
Child friendly Kids' menu; highchairs
www.fusion7.com.au
And…save room for the vodka, passionfruit and shiso shaved ice

north coast

Georgie's at the Gallery

Grafton Regional Gallery,
158 Fitzroy Street, Grafton
Tel 6642 6996   Map 13

Contemporary

Score 13.5/20

The quadrangular space – simply set tables and spectacular raintree – makes for outdoor dining at its most stylishly relaxed. Casual and buzzy by day, Georgie's attains a warm intimacy at night when you might be blown away by a special of fried silken tofu sticky with caramelised black vinegar, sherry and rich jammy eggplant. Spanning Asia and the Mediterranean, the menu offers expertly cooked dishes which occasionally soar, with homely touches such as "Geoff's secret recipe sausages". Duck confit with bacon arrives on mash in a syrupy lake of pine-nutty jus, while blue-eye in saffron beurre blanc, topped with scallop and prawns, is all clean, clear flavours. Service is unfailingly devoted. A citrus tart with thickish pastry was not quite a match for the signature warm apple hazelnut "pud" – but whichever way you go, Grafton is worth a visit for Georgie's alone.

Hours Brunch/lunch Tues–Sun 9am–2pm; Dinner Wed–Sat 6–9pm
Bill E $10.50–$16 **M** $20–$30 **D** $9.50; 10% surcharge on Sundays, 15% on public holidays
Cards AE V MC Eftpos
Wine Small list of known labels, and some local varieties; 10 by the glass; BYO (corkage $4pp)
Chefs Mark Hackett & Geoff Platt
Owners Mark & Judy Hackett
Seats 150; private rooms; wheelchair access; outdoor seating
Child friendly Kids' menu; highchairs; toys; lucky dip; baby-changing facilities
Vegetarian Several interesting options
www.georgiescafe.com.au
And...the sunny courtyard, mellow jazz filtering through, makes this a perfect breakfast venue

La Table

72 Burringbar Street, Mullumbimby
Tel 6684 2227   Map 13

NEW ENTRY

Modern French (Provence)

Score 13/20

The babble of French accents and appetite-whetting aromas filling the air place this welcoming bistro firmly in France. The slim room, with its simple banquette-lined tables, open kitchen and convivial communal seating in the courtyard beyond, return you resoundingly to country Australia. It's back to France again, however, when warm, yeasty bread rolls appear to stave off hunger. It's just as well they do, as the deftly crafted dishes take a while to arrive whisked to you by utterly charming, if occasionally elusive, staff. A light touch defines every dish, from a brilliant pairing of earthy jerusalem artichokes with a luscious ricotta and olive tartlet; to the mint-green pea puree and delicate shellfish sauce that make a snowy snapper fillet shine; and the warmth and depth that honey and five spice add to extraordinarily succulent duck confit with softly sweet pumpkin tart tatin. Dessert, warm almond pithivier, needed a little more almond oomph but is deliciously crisp and light.

Hours Dinner Wed–Sat 6–9pm
Bill E $16 **M** $29 **D** $14; 2-course chef's table menu (Wed only) $35pp, 3 courses $45pp; 15% surcharge on public holidays
Cards V MC Eftpos
Wine Concise, moderately priced list with some interesting organic wines; 7 by the glass
Chef Bruno Pouget
Owners Bruno Pouget & Louise Riviere-Pouget
Seats 45; private room; outdoor seating; bar
Child friendly Highchairs; courtyard; smaller portions
www.latable.com.au
And...for breakfast, lunch or terrific house-made cakes, visit its sister cafe next door

regional

No. 2 Oak Street
2 Oak Street, Bellingen
Tel 6655 9000   Map 13

Contemporary
Score 15.5/20

Inside is cosy, but the outside verandah is equally homely, an extension of the warm hospitality for which this restaurant is renowned. As legendary is the cooking here: restrained, carefully composed creations of impeccable technique and wondrous flavours. To start, lovely house-made bread arrives puffing out of little pots, with tomato relish, quality butter, olive oil and balsamic. A hillock of the most tender black Kinkawooka mussels in a delicate tomato broth arrives laced with pesto and crunchy chargrilled toast; another amber broth, saffron-scented, yields both wild spinach and rare ocean trout crested with perfect aioli. Fried polenta cake, gold in its ringlet of tomato oil, is more like a cloud-light souffle beneath a herbaceous melange of meaty mushrooms. Don't be misled by the smallish serves: this food is rich and complex, so that even the chocolate and espresso assiette – granita, bavarois, ice-cream and flourless chocolate cake – might require that extra stomach. Laughing staff ensure, above all, that you'll have fun.

Hours Dinner Wed–Sat 6.30–9pm; bookings essential
Bill E $17–$18 **M** $37–$41 **D** $16; 15% surcharge on Sundays & public holidays
Cards AE V MC Eftpos
Wine Superlative list of mostly boutique wines; 12 by the glass; BYO (corkage $7 a bottle)
Chefs Ray & Michael Urquhart
Owners Ray & Toni Urquhart
Seats 50; wheelchair access; outdoor seating
www.no2oakst.com.au
And... "Bello" has had a rough trot with wild weather and floods, but No. 2 powers on

Ocean Chill
58 Ridge Street, Nambucca Heads
Tel 6568 8877   Map 13

Contemporary
Score 13/20

Several rungs up the ladder of typical coastal dining, this minimalist eatery stands out – not, mind you, due to its location, an unobtrusive shopfront away from Nambucca's hub. Operating for less than two years, its spare, contemporary space offers amazing value – if occasionally heavy food. A fish soup starter crams salmon, prawns and mussels into a thick red broth, while bruschetta supports a tower of ephemerally tender squid on softened onions and chorizo discs – ample, big-flavoured beginnings which could well suffice. Except then there's soft, buttery chicken on sweetcorn mash, or a pillar of slow-cooked, fall-apart, red-winey blade steak rearing up over meaty mushrooms and green peas. Here is a chef unafraid to use less fashionable ingredients – cabbage, chicken wings – but whose dessert of choc mousse dome with an oozy caramel heart and toffee sculpture will fill you with joy. Moody jazz and friendly waiters deflect the uncomfortable fact that somehow you have managed to lick every plate clean.

Hours Dinner Wed–Sat 6–9pm; bookings essential
Bill E $15–$18 **M** $29–$33 **D** $12
Cards V MC Eftpos
Wine BYO (corkage $2.50pp)
Chef Matthew Knight
Owners Matthew & Heidi Knight
Seats 50
Child friendly Kids' menu; highchairs
Vegetarian Imaginative offerings
And... heavenly house-baked sourdough can be purchased by the loaf

north coast

Olivo

34 Jonson Street, Byron Bay
Tel 6685 7950   Map 13

Contemporary

Score 13/20

Locals and visitors continue to be drawn to this lively restaurant in the heart of Byron, as much as anything for owner James Lancaster's unfailingly courteous and expert service, as well as for consistently well-cooked food. The restaurant is simple – two narrow rows of banquette-lined tables running the length of the distressed brick walls, a few interesting paintings and flattering lighting. It doesn't need much else as Byron's fascinating pedestrian parade provides a constant source of entertainment, as does the food. A pretty trio of jammy seared scallops are all the more voluptuous for their crisp pancetta, avocado, tomato and saffron accompaniments. Unusual grains feature in textbook crisp-skin salmon where addictively chewy barley is laced with celery and an earthy tahini sauce; and in the brilliant pistachio-studded wild rice that partners succulent, if somewhat overly cinnamony, orange duck confit. Finish off with a surprisingly light chocolate semifreddo capped with crunchy roasted hazelnuts and beguiling fresh cherry compote.

Hours Dinner daily 6.30–10pm; bookings essential
Bill E $14–$16 **M** $26–$32 **D** $12–$14; 15% surcharge on public holidays
Cards AE V MC Eftpos
Wine They do a roaring trade in cocktails; 10 wines by the glass plus some good Aussie drops; BYO (corkage $4pp)
Chef David Prowse
Owner James Lancaster
Seats 55
Child friendly Kids' menu
And... James makes a mean mojito

O-pes

90–92 Ballina Street, Lennox Head
Tel 6687 7388   Map 13

Contemporary

Score 12.5/20

The wide smiles of the staff are enough to draw you into this comfortably stylish, bar-cum-restaurant, let alone the inviting lounges and quirky artworks that generate a warm, welcoming vibe perfect for the casually clad diners who frequent O-pes. Although you can settle for tapas only, the brisk breeze off the adjacent ocean tends to whet the appetite for rustic dishes. Crisp-skinned pork belly's succulence is offset by the metallic tang of green olive tapenade and fennel seeds. A Persian-style lamb shank needed just a smidgen of salt to sharpen its honey-sweet cargo of pumpkin, dates and olives. Closer to home, a generous bowl of lip-tingling panang-style duck curry is awash with herbs and greens although the duck was a tad chewy. This is more than made up for by an intensely chocolatey parfait, where the crunch of fig seeds and a delicate spun-sugar lattice add just the right contrast to each silken spoonful.

Hours Breakfast Sat–Sun 9-11.30am; Lunch daily noon–3pm; Dinner daily 5.30–9pm
Bill E $10–$15.90 **M** $24.90–$32 **D** $12.90; 10% surcharge on Sundays, 15% on public holidays
Cards AE V MC Eftpos
Wine Moderately priced, predominantly Australasian list with a good mix of well-known and boutique wines; 14 by the glass
Chef Nou Nou Phothirath
Owners Wayne & Chelle Slater
Seats 80; wheelchair access; outdoor seating; bar
Child friendly Kids' menu; highchairs
And... it's *the* place in Lennox to go for breakfast on the weekend

good food guide   273

regional

Orient Express Eatery
1/2 Fletcher Street, Byron Bay
Tel 6680 8808   Map 13

Modern Asian

Score 14/20

Smiles are all the go here from the benevolent Buddha surveying his domain of two rooms and a terrace, old mah-jong tables, lucky red lacquered wooden chairs and antiques. There's smiling service too, as well as patrons' grins as they sight the generous servings, albeit carefully balanced and composed. These are exuberant, varied and compelling, yet not confronting tastes. Sang choi bau in its crisp lettuce wrapper is a delightful, watch-those-runny-juices mouthful. A salad built around finely sliced fish cakes, with mint, coriander, peanuts, bean sprouts and carrots is heady with fish sauce, palm sugar and rice vinegar. Duck noodles, festooned with flavours, come from an obviously well-seasoned wok; delicious fillets of sweetlip are touched with mere wisps of batter and a zing of chilli. Coconut custard is set on a thin base of black sticky rice in a limpid pool of coconut creme, yet sweetness is restrained. Take the Orient Express to Thailand, Taiwan, Sichuan province, Malaysia and Singapore via downtown Byron Bay.

Hours Lunch Fri–Sun 11.30am–3pm; Dinner daily 5.30–9pm; no bookings
Bill E $8.90–$16.90 **M** $19.90–$29.90 **D** $11.90; 15% surcharge on Sundays & public holidays
Cards AE V MC Eftpos
Wine Food-friendly list, fairly priced; 12 by the glass; BYO (corkage $10 a bottle)
Chefs Tippy Heng & Nicholas Lazzaroni
Owner Tippy Heng
Seats 60; wheelchair access; outdoor seating; bar
Child friendly Kid-friendly menu; highchairs; toys
Vegetarian Over a dozen options in the vegetarian menu, plus extensive weekend yum cha
And...hand-thrown clay caddies of fine Chinese tea to take home

Pacific Dining Room
Bay Street, Byron Bay
Tel 6680 7055   Map 13

Contemporary

Score 15/20

With salt spray on the air, palms swaying in the courtyard and its super-relaxed Bahamas-meets-Bali beach house feel, Pacific Dining Room captures Byron's laid-back beach culture to a T. Don't be fooled by the deceptively simple menu and casually dressed (read straight off the beach) look of staff and guests – there is some seriously good food and wine to be had here. It begins with a rustic dish of baked salt cod – deliciously mellow, lush with potatoes and olives, its richness cut by the bright freshness of parsley. A platter of heirloom tomatoes disappointed, but a peppery ingot of baked ricotta swathed in fine pastry and offset by broad beans and toasted hazelnuts is a winner. So is luscious, crisped, lamb confit, salted and slow-cooked for eight hours, which brilliantly partners roast saddle with sweet tomatoes and an airy fennel puree. Desserts – intensely flavoured licorice parfait and Madagascan chocolate popsicles – are sophisticated yet delicious takes on childhood sweetshop favourites.

Hours Dinner daily 6–10pm
Bill Small plates $4–$20 Large plates $25–$70 (meals for 2) **D** $8–16; feasting menus from $50pp; 10% surcharge on Sundays, 15% on public holidays
Cards AE DC V MC Eftpos
Wine Extensive 19-page list full of terrific Australian and international wines; 17 by the glass
Chef David Moyle
Owners John & Lisa van Haandel
Seats 140; private room; outdoor seating; bar
Child friendly Kid-friendly menu; highchairs
Vegetarian 5 imaginative dishes
www.pacificdiningroom.com.au
And...share to your heart's content from the menu's big and small plates

north coast

Paupiettes
56 Ballina Road, Lismore
Tel 6621 6135   Map 13

Contemporary
Score 13.5/20

Lismore locals should be so lucky to have an affordable gem such as Paupiettes to call their own. Red terra walls are adorned with artwork above warm dark slate floors, and while the ambience can be a touch subdued, the value is unmistakeable. The sizeable blackboard menu is lugged around to each table by beneficent and knowledgeable floor staff. Chef David Forster knows his strengths, and plays to them admirably with a simple entree of gently warmed, ripe prosciutto-wrapped figs filled with goat's cheese. Slightly more daring is spice-crusted scallops with parsnip puree. Staples such as twice-cooked cheese souffle, duck confit and chargrilled rib-eye are textbook bistro, although bombe alaska was more competent than consummate. The standout main is local sweet Bangalow pork belly, the fall-apart flesh topped with immaculate crackling and matched with a jumble of finely sliced apple and fennel. Consistent, approachable food and friendly, attentive service are a sound recipe for local devotion.

Hours Dinner Tues–Sat 6.30–9pm; bookings preferred
Bill E $12.50–$18 **M** $27–$29.50 **D** $12–$16
Cards AE DC V MC Eftpos
Wine Compact, affordable, predominantly Australian list with some regional intrigue; 5 by the glass; BYO (corkage $5 a bottle)
Chef David Forster
Owners David & Shirley Forster
Seats 50
And…parking at rear

Pippi's Cafe & Bar

Yamba Beach Motel,
cnr Clarence & Queen streets, Yamba
Tel 6646 1425   Map 13

Contemporary

Score 12/20

It's a bustling cafe by day, but Pippi's smartens up come evening with white tablecloths and a huge blackboard menu of modern, occasionally busy choices. The room is so airy and spacious, it feels alfresco, and with the beach just down the road, a holiday mood is ensured. A camisard, or pancetta-wrapped goat's cheese, is lushly creamy with hints of smoked paprika in its circlet of dainty artichoke wedges. It's a worthy preface to spatchcock with broad beans, fetta and semi-dried tomato, flesh so more-ishly good you'll gnaw it to the bone. A well-rested eye fillet alongside a gratin-topped buttery mash was somewhat let down by an over-dressed salad. Servings are big to compensate for slightly high prices, often absent (though friendly) service – and the inescapable fact that you're in a cafe. Crooner Michael Buble is the soundtrack, and excellent desserts – honeycomb ice-cream napping a superior, marsala-laced tiramisu, for example – guarantee you won't leave disappointed.

Hours Daily, Breakfast 7–11.30am; Lunch noon–2.30pm; Dinner 6–8.15pm
Bill E $9–$18 **M** $29–$30 **D** $9.50–$12.50; 10% surcharge on public holidays
Cards AE V MC Eftpos
Wine Mostly familiar affordable Australian brands plus separate list of regional wines; 21 by the glass; BYO (corkage $6 a bottle)
Chef Sebastian Molloy
Owners Michael & Ann George
Seats 70; wheelchair access; outdoor seating; bar
Child friendly Kids' menu; highchairs; books
And…an extra list of New England wines from three vineyards

regional

The Point
2 Martin Street, Ballina
Tel 6618 1188   Map 13

Contemporary

Score 13/20

Dining in country hotel restaurants generally holds as much appeal as staying with Norman Bates. Thankfully, this glorious riverside setting under the Ramada Hotel is an exception. Despite the anodyne decor – it's also a bar and cafe – this breezy, glass-encased space takes full advantage of the subtropical setting and soothing water views, with plenty of outdoor seating. Enthusiastic service adds to the appeal. The menu spans Asia and the Mediterranean with an understandable seafood focus, yet French-trained Thierry Belloir proves a dab hand. Delightful salt-and-pepper cuttlefish is given a twist with Japanese ponzu dipping sauce, while fisherman's soup with rouille and garlic bread shows you can take the chef out of Gaul, but ... Mains turn European and country hearty with herb-crusted lamb rack on ratatouille and the slightly overwhelming duck confit on mash with wilted spinach and orange sauce. Flourless pineapple and coconut cake with rockmelon sorbet seems in keeping with the balmy summer surrounds, but the fine apple tart is no slouch either.

Hours Breakfast 7–11am; Lunch 11am–2.30pm; Dinner 2.30–10.30pm
Bill E $10–$15 **M** $19–$32 **D** $9.50–$13
Cards AE DC V MC Eftpos
Wine 20 by the glass
Chef Thierry Belloir
Seats 150; private rooms; wheelchair access; outdoor seating
Child friendly Kids' menu; highchairs
www.thepointballina.com.au
And...good buffet breakfasts

The Restaurant at The Byron at Byron
The Byron at Byron Resort,
77–97 Broken Head Road, Byron Bay
Tel 6639 2111   Map 13

Contemporary

Score 14/20

Dusk here marks the changing of the guard, when the thrum of cicadas fades, only to be replaced with the joyful croaks of a frog orchestra. Rainforest forms the backdrop to this serene resort restaurant, which brings together elements of earth, timber, fire and water in a casually elegant alfresco space that draws locals as well as stylish, beach-chic clad resort guests. And the food fits the setting. Gavin Hughes's restrained, confident cooking, highlighting local produce, is reflected in everything the attentive service whisks to the table. Plump calamari tubes burst with chilli-tinged kumara and cashew stuffing; succulent Hervey Bay scallops pair with a subtly smoky eggplant puree, and five-spice duck breast paddles in an intense duck consomme anchored with earthy Asian greens. Dessert – creamy coconut parfait paired with a tingling fresh pineapple sorbet and salsa, with hints of mint and chilli – is as refreshing as a dip in the nearby pool.

Hours Breakfast daily 7–10.45am; Lunch daily noon–3pm; Dinner daily 6–10pm
Bill E $15–$24 **M** $25–$38 **D** $16–$17; 10% surcharge on Sundays & public holidays
Cards AE (+2.5%) DC V MC (+1.8%) Eftpos
Wine A well-selected list with some high-end names; 15 by the glass
Chef Gavin Hughes
Owners Gerry Harvey & Katie Page
Seats 150; private rooms; wheelchair access; outdoor seating; bar
Child friendly Kids' menu; highchairs; drawing materials
www.thebyronatbyron.com.au
And...chill out with a cocktail on the tropical verandahs (and cosy fire bar in winter)

north coast

Restaurant Two Forty

4 Red Gum Road, Boomerang Beach
Tel 6554 0766   Map 13

Contemporary

Score 13.5/20

The Great Lakes got greater still with the arrival of this bright and breezy restaurant within the BreakFree Mobys resort. As if people really needed another reason to visit stunning Boomerang Beach – an aptly named surf spot where holidaymakers return again and again. Yet here it is, a coolly casual space with white bare tables, touches of colour from local artwork and the warmth of candlelight. Food is simple and well executed, with produce sourced locally where possible, as is an entree of Wallis Lake prawns – fantastically fresh and perfectly matched with sweet mango slices, prosciutto and cucumber. Mains include scrumptious pumpkin gnocchi slick with burnt butter and sage, with goat's cheese and crushed walnuts scattered on top. Seared duck breast seemed a little overcooked, but makes good comfort food teamed with five-spice couscous, confit baby onions, balsamic and pomegranate glaze. Raspberry semifreddo with sweet, minty pineapple salsa is a dessert from holiday heaven.

Hours Holidays & high season Breakfast daily 7–11.30am, Lunch daily 11.30am–5.30pm; Dinner daily 6–10pm; Low season Dinner Wed–Sun 6–10pm
Bill E $16–$18 **M** $24–$30 **D** $13; 15% surcharge on public holidays
Cards V MC Eftpos
Wine Affordable Australians the order of the day; 10 by the glass
Chefs/owners David Speck & Peter Agnew
Seats 120; wheelchair access; outdoor seating; bar
Child friendly Kids' menu
www.masticate.com.au
And…an extensive list of T2 teas available

Saltwater

104 Fiddaman Road, Emerald Beach
Tel 6656 1888   Map 13

Contemporary

Score 12.5/20

This is undeniably a hot spot. By day the slow pace is comfortable and cordial, but as darkness descends, so does a crowd of regulars, speeding things up and removing some of the sense of warmth. Aim for a table under the terrace sailcloth with the glimmering splendour of the ocean over the road, and explore the smart Asian-accented menu. A lovely starter of soft wontons enfolding kingfish was too strongly flavoured with kaffir lime leaf, while the same could be said of a dish of soft-shell crab, the meat barely discernable under its honey cinnamony coating. Elsewhere, as in the star-anise broth for a puck of sweet salmon wrapped in pancetta on a ropy coil of noodles, restraint is more evident. Creamy walls, glamorous bar, water feature and a cruisy soundtrack create a relaxed and stylish vibe, which on a busy night might turn party-ish. While a little more warmth alongside the slick efficiency would be welcome, desserts are a delight, including heavenly pistachio and rosewater cake dense with syrup.

Hours Breakfast Wed–Fri 9–11am, Sat–Sun 8–11am; Lunch Wed–Sun noon–2.30pm; Dinner Wed–Sat 6–10pm
Bill E $19–$23 **M** $29–$33 **D** $10–$15; 10% surcharge on Sundays & public holidays
Cards AE V MC
Wine Large, thoughtful list with vintages and ratings; 11 by the glass; BYO (corkage $7 a bottle)
Chef Donna Lee
Owner Carol Walsh
Seats 55; wheelchair access; outdoor seating
Child friendly Kids' menu; highchairs; drawing materials
Vegetarian Several options
www.saltwateronthebeach.com
And…they do tapas and wine every Friday evening from 4.30–6.30 for $15 a head

regional

Satiate

33 Byron Street, Bangalow
Tel 6687 1010   Map 13

Modern European

Score 15/20

In Bangalow's boho-chic main street, a young couple dares to fly where angels fear to tread. Welcome to fine dining hinterland style. Climb the stairs above the slumbering cafe to discover a serenely elegant, if a tad solemn room, then nestle in for a time-consuming, circuitous culinary journey. Like a thespian with a thousand soliloquies, chef Shannon Debreceny (formerly of Tetsuya's) isn't going to let you go until you experience every one of his exquisite morsels, such as scallop ceviche interlaced with garlic chives and finger lime. The occasional miss is forgivable, so high is the aim, and so great the rewards. Succumb to a gelatinous cube of Bangalow Sweet Pork belly, a deboned lamb rack with shimeji mushrooms and date sauce, or pistachio marshmallow with flourless chocolate cake and pain perdu ice-cream. Small portions and overstretched if knowledgeable service might not be to everyone's liking, but for innovation and spontaneity with market fare, this is one of the goldmines of regional dining.

Hours Dinner Tues–Sat 6.30–9pm; bookings essential
Bill 5-course degustation menu $65pp
Cards AE V MC Eftpos
Wine Neat, predominantly Australasian list, with southern European cameos; 13 by the glass
Chef Shannon Debreceny
Owners Seana, Greg & Angela Ryan & Shannon Debreceny
Seats 40; private room; outdoor seating; bar
Child friendly Kids' menu; highchairs
Vegetarian Separate 5-course degustation
www.ate.net.au
And…nab a balcony table on a balmy night

The Stunned Mullet

Shop 1, 12 William Street, The Sandcastle, Port Macquarie
Tel 6584 7757   Map 13

Contemporary

13/20

It's just what you want in a holiday town – a laidback, marine-coloured casual setting of bare tables with a candy-striped banquette running along one wall and impressive views along the coast. Bifold doors peel back to add to the alfresco feel. While the name sounds like an '80s AFL player's nickname, The Stunned Mullet aspires to greater heights with a menu of Mediterranean and Asian flavours. Service is chirpy, but could be more attentive, especially if the kitchen's pace flags. Salt-and-pepper squid with garlic chips gets a little lost in so much rocket it's almost a nature strip. Crumbed eggplant with layers of tomato, basil, buffalo mozzarella and rocket is a reasonable take on a parmigiana of eggplant, while grilled sirloin with kipflers and a tizz of crisp leek gets an Asian twist from wasabi and shiitake butter. An impressive looking caramelised banana split turnover is given a modern makeover by strawberry ice-cream with shiso leaf, dark chocolate and pistachio pashmak.

Hours Breakfast Sat–Sun 9–11.30am; Lunch daily noon–3pm; Dinner daily 6–9pm winter, 6–10.30pm summer
Bill E $17–$24 **M** $26–$36 **D** $13–$15; 10% surcharge on Sundays, 15% public on holidays
Cards AE V MC Eftpos
Wine 5 by the glass; BYO wine only (corkage $8 a bottle)
Chefs David Henry & Eric Robinson
Owners Lou Perri & David Henry
Seats 87; wheelchair access; outdoor seating
Child friendly Kids' menu; highchairs
www.thestunnedmullet.com.au
And…great weekend breakfast include bacon and potato hash and Belgian waffles

north coast

And also...

RICHMOND & CLARENCE VALLEYS

Beachwood
22 High Street, Yamba
Tel 6646 9781
You'll be lucky to get a table at this popular little cafe. Lush, golden scrambled eggs chunked with fetta alongside puffy Turkish toast and heavenly coffee are highlights.

Blackboard at the Beach
50 Pacific Parade, Lennox Head
Tel 6687 4333
Two nights a week, this cruisy, beachside cafe flexes its muscles to turn out mod-Oz fare such as confit duck with blood oranges, succulent salmon with celeriac puree, and dreamy orange blossom bavarois.

Eltham Valley Pantry
713 Boatharbour Road, Eltham
Tel 6629 1418
Detour to this tranquil cafe in a lush pecan and coffee farm to savour home produce or local smoked ham, salami and cheese.

Gorman's
Yamba Bay, Yamba
Tel 6646 2025
This family-run institution poised above the river oozes old-fashioned atmosphere and charm. Go for simpler options such as grilled red emperor, unless you're in the mood for the full-blown, endearingly retro platters.

Melba's Verandah
Cnr Fischer Street & Pacific Highway, Broadwater
Tel 6682 8099
Slip off the highway and step back in time. This gracious Federation homestead surrounded by a serene and coiffured garden is the perfect pit stop for Devonshire tea or a cane cutters' platter.

PROVEDORES AND MARKETS

* **Goanna Bakery and Cafe**, 171 Keen Street, Lismore, **Tel 6622 2629**; organic sourdough, spelt and gluten-free breads and pastries vie for attention with wood-fired pizza and scrummy salads.

* **Northern Rivers Seafood**, Pacific Highway, West Ballina, **Tel 6686 2187**; local prawn specialists, cracking fresh seafood with excellent seasonal variety.

* **Grafton Market Square**, Pound Street, every Thurs, 7am–noon, **Tel 6642 3336**.
* **North Coast Lismore Showground**, Alexandra Parade, every Sat, 8–11am, **Tel 6629 3229**.
* **Rainbow Region Organic Market**, Lismore Showground, every Tues, 7.30–11am, **Tel 6628 1084**.

BYRON SHIRE

Ate
33 Byron Street, Bangalow
Tel 6687 2555
The gorgeous shopfront with stained-glass windows is in fact a snappy uber-cafe with great coffee and breakfast treats such as pancetta, mushroom and provolone omelette.

Bay Leaf Cafe
Shop 8/87 Jonson Street, Byron Bay
Tel 6685 8900
This funky local favourite is always buzzing, and pumps out great coffee, music and food in equal measure. Everything is fresh, and served with a smile. Breakfast is a must.

Bolo Bistro
Mullumbimby Bowling Club, Jubilee Avenue, Mullumbimby
Tel 6684 2209
Scottish-born chef James Coakley cooks bistro classics and imaginative mod-Oz fare with great flair. Try crisp-skin salmon with mashed peas and light-as-air seafood wontons. It's one of the most popular, and top value, places in town.

regional

Fishmongers
Shop 1, Bay Lane, Byron Bay
Tel 6680 8080
It's hard to go past fat, hand-cut chips and super-fresh battered fish but this is also the place for sensational oysters, fish of the day grilled to perfection and preternaturally tender barbecued octopus, plus a great line in tempura vegies.

one one one
1/111 Jonson Street, Byron Bay
Tel 6680 7388
The chilled-out vibe of this bohemian cafe belies the fact that they turn out some seriously good food. Share plates of rustic Mediterranean dishes such as succulent braised squid and slow-cooked lamb.

St Elmo
Cnr Lawson Lane & Fletcher Street, Byron Bay
Tel 66807426
Noisy, buzzy and bustling, this great new venue from the team behind the Bay Leaf Cafe boasts a superb wine list, great cocktails and a smallish menu of favourites, tapas included. No bookings though.

Spice It Up Thai
Mullumbimby Golf Club, Jubilee Avenue, Mullumbimby
Tel 6684 2273
Some authentic flavours can be found among the specials, with plenty of toned-down options for the kiddies, generous portions and (of course!) cheap drinks.

Utopia
13 Byron Street, Bangalow
Tel 6687 2088
Darlinghurst comes to Bangalow albeit with a strong local emphasis. A bright space serving decadent desserts, an ever-changing tapas plate and good coffee (their own blend using local organic beans). Brekkie and lunch daily, dinner Fri–Sat.

PROVEDORES AND MARKETS
* **Bangalow Cheese Co.**, available weekly at Byron Bay and Bangalow Farmers' Markets (see below), Tel 6629 1888; handmade farmhouse cheeses and dairy products.
* **Green Garage**, 63 Tennyson Street, Byron Bay, Tel 6680 8577; food emporium specialising in local products.
* **L'Ultime Patisserie**, 5 Lawson Street, Byron Bay, Tel 6685 8383; fabulous French bread, pastries and chocolates.
* **Red Ginger**, 2/111 Jonson Street, Byron Bay, Tel 6680 9779; fabulous Asian foods, snacks and home wares.
* **Wholly Smoked Organic Foods**, Shop 7, 130 Jonson Street, Byron Bay, Tel 6685 6261; top-quality organic meat and products.

* **Bangalow Farmers' Market**, Byron Street (behind the Bangalow Hotel), every Sat, 8–11am, Tel 6687 1137, www.byronfarmersmarket.com.au.
* **Byron Bay Farmers' Market**, Butler Street Reserve, Byron Bay, every Thurs, 8–11am, Tel 6687 1137, www.byronfarmersmarket.com.au.
* **New Brighton Farmer's Market**, River Street, New Brighton, every Tues, 8–11am, Tel 6684 5390.

COFFS COAST

Hearth Fire Organic Wood-Fired Bakery
73–75 Hyde Street, Bellingen
Tel 6655 0088
A lofty, narrow space with a warehouse feel, this fabulous bakery–cafe serves a range of sturdy yeast-free breads (olive provincial, ciabatta, spelt, macadamia fruit) as well as cakes and flaky savoury tartlets. Try a yeast-free croissant with good coffee.

north coast

Lake Russell Gallery
12 Smiths Road, Emerald Beach
Tel 6656 1092
An oasis of calm just off the highway, this airy modern art gallery is annexed to a light-flooded gazebo dispensing good Merlo coffee, scones and yummy cakes. A small lunch menu and live music on Sunday afternoons.

Lick the Spoon/ Waterfall Way Winery
51–53 Hickory Street, Dorrigo
Tel 6657 1373
Deli-cum-cafe, this glamorous boutique is also home to the owners' fruit wines, aperitifs and vodkas – the Dorrigo Potato is especially lovely. Gluten-free cakes, house-made chutneys, jellies and pickles as well as kitchenware are all there too.

Lodge 241 Gallery Cafe
117–121 Hyde Street, Bellingen
Tel 6655 2470
There's verandah seating or an inside communal table at this friendly spot by the river. Fortify yourself with tangy house-made lemonade and a divine Portuguese tart or more substantial fare. Segafredo coffee is excellent.

Ruby's Cafe and Books
18–20 Cudgery Street, Dorrigo
Tel 6657 2356
Sit out the back of this long space, combining a cafe with a well-organised second-hand bookstore. Ruby's offers light meals (try the fantastic tortilla stack) as well as homemade cakes and scones.

Taste
11 First Avenue, Sawtell
Tel 6658 3583
The newer kid in town is giving the popular Sawtell Hotel (fish, seafood and steaks) a serious run for its money as well as the stylish strip of First Avenue cafes opposite. This is a pleasant fine diner with smart mod-Oz fare and reasonable prices.

PROVEDORES AND MARKETS

* **Dangerous Dan's Butchery**, 3 Princess Street, Macksville, **Tel 6568 1036**; fantastic, ever-changing range of house-made sausages, superb smoky house-cured bacon.
* **It's Wild Seafood**, 12 Gateway Place, 23 Hurley Drive, Coffs Harbour, **Tel 6652 3000**; wild-caught prawns, ocean fish and more, snap-frozen on the boat. Also at the excellent Coffs markets (see below).
* **Ranae's Choclatique**, 78 High Street, Bowraville, **Tel 6564 7133**; exquisite, handmade chocolates in a tempting array of shapes and flavours.

* **Bellingen Growers' Market**, Bellingen Showground, Black Street, 2nd & 4th Sat, 8am–1pm, **Tel 6653 5288**.
* **Coffs Coast Growers' Market**, City Square, Harbour Drive, every Thurs, 8am–4pm, **Tel 6648 4084**.

GREAT LAKES & MANNING VALLEY

Bent on Food
95 Isabella Street, Wingham
Tel 6557 0727
A perennial favourite for fresh hearty brekkies (love the bacon and egg roll) and an always interesting lunch menu. A focus on local produce and supply of gourmet pantry products and kitchenware are drawcards.

Perenti
69 Church Street, Gloucester
Tel 6558 9219
Stop in for yummy pies, frittata and salads for lunch, or a good coffee or tea with scones, and stock up on house-made jams, chutneys, meat rubs and salad dressings.

regional

Twenty by Twelve
Shop 7A, 207 Boomerang Drive, Blueys Beach
Tel 6554 0452
A bustling little cafe serving Danes coffee, free-range Manning Valley eggs and Morpeth sourdough, plus lunch specials, cakes and a range of gourmet pantry products.

MARKETS
* Great Lakes, Great Produce Market, Little Street, Forster (Visitors' Centre grounds), 3rd Sat, 8am–noon, **Tel 6555 4351** or **0408 306 222**.
* Nabiac, Nabiac Showground Hall, Nabiac Street, last Sat, 8am–noon, **Tel 6554 1906**.
* Wingham Showground, Wingham Showground, Gloucester Road, 1st Sat, 8am–noon, **Tel 6550 5761**.

PORT MACQUARIE

Cafe Red
221 Blackmans Point Road, Port Macquarie
Tel 6585 0663
Fresh from the packing shed come tomatoes and strawberries, made into strawberry jam for Devonshire tea, tomato relish for the steak sandwich, and tomato on bruschetta. Pick your own strawbs in season.

Cedro
70 Clarence Street, Port Macquarie
Tel 6583 5529
Hearty breakfasts are the calling card, from French toast to Persian eggs with spiced mince lamb and pomegranate roasted onions, but lunch shouldn't be overlooked. The leaning is Italian, but all bases are covered.

Crema Espresso Bar
Cnr Horton and Clarence streets,
Port Macquarie
Tel 6583 9858
A slick, energetic operation. Locally roasted Peak coffee is the main attraction, as well as complimentary babycinos, hummingbird cake, mini carrot cakes, caramel tarts and rocky road slice baked by local ladies.

Netherby House Cafe
5 Little Rudder Street, Kempsey
Tel 6563 1777
A delightful riverside setting for pizza, sandwiches (gluten-free bread available), good cakes and coffee. From Sydney turn left at the Riverside Cafe sign just south of the bridge.

MARKETS
* Port Macquarie, Historic Maritime Museum, William Street, 2nd Sat, 8am–noon, **Tel 0414 376 868**.
* Wauchope, Wauchope Showground, High Street, 4th Sat, 8am–noon, **Tel 0414 376 868**.

TWEED

Cafe Sbiza
2/86 Marine Parade, Kingscliff
Tel 6674 4140
A safe bet for consistently satisfying fare made from top quality (often local) ingredients, Sbiza seems the local favourite – just across the road from Kingscliff Beach.

Flutterbies Cottage Cafe
23–25 Coolman Street, Tyalgum
Tel 6679 3221
A rather girly cafe and gift shop (floral and fairy-filled) serving very good Jaspers fair trade coffee and a basic menu (homemade pot pies, tarts and big salads). The 100-year-old building – with indoor and outdoor dining – isn't far from the magnificent Mount Warning.

Mavis's Kitchen & Cabins
64 Mt Warning Road, Uki via Murwillumbah
Tel 6679 5664
Simple, organic home-cooked food with soul includes Mavis's mixed grill with homemade tomato relish, served with the omniscient Mt Warning as a backdrop.

New Leaf Cafe
Shop 10/47 Main Street Murwillumbah
Tel 6672 4073
Excellent vego fare – from Middle Eastern mezze to a daily thali plate – primarily sourced from their adjoining organic grocery next door.

Salt Bean Espresso Bar
Shop 12, Salt Village, Kingscliff
Tel 6674 1922
Just a skip towards the beach from Fins, this counter-cafe punches out a mean coffee and cryptic wraps such as the "flying pig", (i.e. chicken and bacon).

PROVEDORES AND MARKETS
* Chillingham Banana Cabana and Bush Tucker Garden, Murwillumbah–Nerang Road, Chillingham, **Tel 6679 1022**; hard-to-find tropical fruits and bush tucker.
* Tropical Fruit World, Duranbah Road, Duranbah, **Tel 6677 7222**; abundance of fruit, fruit trees and information, farm tours and a cafe, too.

* Kingscliff Farmers & Friends Markets, Beachfront, Marine Parade, 2nd & 4th Sat, **Tel 6674 0827** or **0406 724 323**.

regional

THE WEST
NORTHERN TABLELANDS, CENTRAL WEST, CENTRAL TABLELANDS & THE RIVERINA

Love a sunburnt country, a land of sweeping plains? Reportedly the inspiration for poet Dorothea MacKellar's immortal poem (Gunnedah, specifically), the vast western region, up to Armidale in New England, out to Griffith and down to Albury is also an inspiration for food-lovers.

Time your trip well, and you'll encounter some of the most passionate farmers, winemakers and chefs in the state, showing off their stuff at a food festival or farmers' market (not to mention restaurants and cafes).

Orange Food week is one of the biggest food fests, held annually in April (www.orangefoodweek.com.au), with activities including farm tours, cooking classes, lunches and dinners. Also in April, and not too far off, is Bathurst's Harvest Festival (www.bathurstharvestfestival.com).

The Northern Tablelands is also getting in on the act, with the resumption of the annual Tamworth Taste festival in early May (www.visittamworth.com). Meanwhile, nearby Armidale proudly proclaims itself as the newest wine-growing region, so envision an annual food and wine festival starting up in the near future.

In the Central West, the Mudgee Wine and Food Festival takes place throughout September, and includes the popular "Go Grazing" food and wine-matching event (www.mudgeewine.com.au).

December is cherry season, and in Young – cherry capital of Australia – the National Cherry Festival takes place (www.visityoung.com.au). Some orchards allow visitors to pick their own, including Allambie (Tel 6384 3243) and Cherryhaven (Tel 6382 4023).

9inety 2wo
92 Bentinck Street, Bathurst
Tel 6332 1757  Map 12

Contemporary

Score 13/20

The unassuming, cottage-like exterior hides a contemporary, elegant space. Like the restaurant's idiosyncratically spelt name, it certainly puts a new spin on an old number. The open kitchen and well-dressed yet casual staff serve a concise menu containing some classics pepped up with an unexpected ingredient or two. Some newer creations border on over-adventurous: confit quail, poached chicken sausage, emu pancetta and thyme jus anyone? No doubt some thought has been put into creamy golden lamb's brains and herb nut salsa, but a Thai-influenced seared ocean trout fillet with coconut rice and palm sugar caramel needed more searing, as well as crunch for textural balance. Better is the rare, marinated kangaroo fillet, well matched with earthy barley, leek, and a sweet beetroot puree. Desserts are in hearty abundance, including good sticky date and beer pudding with a treacly caramel sauce and ice-cream, in a ready-to-share portion.

Hours Lunch Tues–Fri 11.30am–2.30pm; Dinner Mon–Sat 6–9pm; bookings essential
Bill E $16 **M** $32 **D** $12
Cards AE (+3%) DC (+3%) V MC Eftpos
Wine Concise, adequate and mainly NSW wines; 8 by the glass
Chef Brett Melhuish
Owners Brett Melhuish & Robert Salana
Seats 72; wheelchair access; outdoor seating; bar
And...best views of the room are in front of, not behind, the central fireplace

the west

Clock

239–243 Banna Avenue, Griffith
Tel 6962 7111   Map 12

Contemporary
                                              Score 13.5/20

The contrast between Clock's interior and the main street on which it's located couldn't be more dramatic, with the latter all bustle, shopfronts and bleaching sun. Inside, Clock is a cool, renovated former bank with a high ceiling and chocolate, grey and white tones. The food, like the decor, is smart-casual with good pizza and pasta options, plus more sophisticated fare. Fat, firm king prawns and black mussels bathe in a saffron broth with just a touch of paprika heat, the perfumed broth nicely cut by the smokiness of a chargrilled slice of bruschetta alongside. A thick porterhouse, blue as requested, sits on a chunky, thyme-infused potato cake studded with sliced black olive. Even the ubiquitous rocket and parmesan salad is treated with care and restraint; the dressing light, the parmesan spare, the rocket wild and peppery. To cap it off, there's a great big affogato for dessert: coffee, vanilla gelato and almond biscotti served in a martini glass.

Hours Lunch Tues–Sat noon–2.30pm; Dinner Mon–Sat 6–9.30pm
Bill E $16–$22 **M** $27–$34 **D** $10–$14; 10% surcharge on public holidays and Sundays
Cards AE DC V MC Eftpos
Wine A welcome focus on local wines, plus respectable mid-range and classic Aussies; 9 by the glass; BYO (corkage $6pp)
Chef Michelle Armstrong
Owners Michelle Armstrong & Janelle Mannes
Seats 90; wheelchair access; bar
Child friendly Highchairs
www.theclockgriffith.com.au
And... pre- or post-dinner drinks in the bar, open from 5.30pm

Cobblestone Lane

2/173–179 George Street, Bathurst
Tel 6331 2202   Map 12

Contemporary
                                              Score 14/20

The historic Webb Chambers building housed Bathurst's first and finest department store, which sold high-quality imports and regional produce. Today, under the same gloriously high ceilings, Cobblestone Lane follows suit with chef–owner Heath Smith dishing out fantastic fare with a focus on fresh, local produce. The buzzing open kitchen and smart, enthusiastic staff serve a cleverly concise menu. Try a rather dainty rabbit remoulade, the meat infused with thyme and bound with the sauce, its sweetness complemented by rhubarb, and creaminess offset by shaved fennel. A hazelnut and chive souffle was less impressive, with a dense consistency more akin to quiche. Flaky, moist, braised Cowra lamb comes to the rescue, well matched with figs, a nutty chickpea puree and Israeli couscous. Slow-roasted capretto (young milk-fed goat) raises the bar again; its earthiness the right match for warm pears and muscatels in sweet cider. Finish with locally roasted coffee and creme brulee, choc fondant or both.

Hours Lunch Tues–Sat noon–2pm; Dinner Tues–Sat 6–9pm
Bill E $15 **M** $35 **D** $15; 2-course brisk lunch $20pp, 3 courses $25
Cards AE DC V MC Eftpos
Wine Small, interesting list with mostly well-priced Australians; 10 by the glass; BYO (corkage $5 a bottle)
Chef Heath Smith
Owners Heath & Elissa Smith
Seats 70; private room; wheelchair access; outdoor seating
www.cobblestonelane.com.au
And... be sure to peer down the deep, convict-built well

regional

Eltons Brasserie
81 Market Street, Mudgee
Tel 6372 0772   Map 13

Contemporary
Score 12.5/20

This quiet shopfront eatery is tucked away behind the main street in Mudgee's town centre. It's a popular breakfast spot and good for weekend lunches when town offerings are limited. At dinnertime, a wood-fired oven turns out 10 different pizzas. Service can be complacent but once ordered, meals arrive swiftly, starting with deep-fried rings of salt-and-pepper squid with a light chilli dipping sauce. A steaming bowl of garlic prawn fettuccine was too creamy and rather bland, but it's hard to beat an authentic steak sandwich complete with grated beetroot, caramelised onions and slivers of pickled gherkin, plus thick-cut chips. Sorbets of rosewater and glace cherry were a bit hit and miss but nougat-studded ice-cream with a sweet, red-wine poached pear is a definite stand-out. The nougat is top notch, and happily, it's available by the bar to take home in three flavours: hazelnut, almond and pistachio–cranberry.

Hours Breakfast Tues–Sun from 9am; Lunch Tues–Sun from noon; Dinner Tues–Sat 6–9pm
Bill E $15.50–$16.50 **M** $22.50–$33.50 **D** $10.50–$16.50; 10% surcharge public holidays
Cards AE DC V MC Eftpos
Wine Changeable blackboard list of local drops; 6 by the glass; BYO wine only (corkage $3pp)
Chef/owner David Cox
Seats 40; wheelchair access; outdoor seating; bar
Child friendly Kids' menu; highchairs; baby-changing facilities; toy cup
www.eltons.com.au
And…ask about Eltons' special event dinners

Green Papaya
NEW ENTRY
Shop 1, Girraween Shopping Centre, Queen Elizabeth Drive, Armidale
Tel 6771 3611   Map 13

Thai (North-eastern)
Score 13/20

Given the name of this unassuming little restaurant, it's lucky Thai-born owner Am Braun has found a place in nearby Bellingen to get organic papaya for her fresh and fiery green papaya salad. Like other dishes on offer, it's authentic and bursting with flavour. Am and her husband Leon declare their love for Thai cuisine on the first page of the menu, and this enthusiasm comes to life as she chats with diners in the modestly decorated room, before getting busy in the kitchen. Start with ubiquitous yet more-ish spring rolls, curry puffs and moneybags, or open the airways with warming tom yum goong, a spicy–sour soup with prawns and button mushrooms bobbing on top. Crying tiger scotch fillet comes highly recommended, the gently charred, flavourful meat sliced and served with chilli–lime sauce. Steamed rice soaks up the sweet red curry sauce in a choo chee goong (prawn curry), while house-made durian ice-cream is wonderfully sweet and subtle.

Hours Dinner Tues–Thurs from 5.30–10pm, Fri–Sat 5.30–11pm
Bill E $6.90–$9 **M** $14.90–$29.90 **D** $7.90–$10
Cards V MC Eftpos
Wine BYO (corkage $1.50pp)
Chef Am Braun
Owners Am & Leon Braun
Seats 40–48
Child friendly Highchairs; toys; drawing materials
Vegetarian Separate menu
And…next door to a pizza chain but there's nothing fast and franchised here

the west

Lolli Redini

48 Sale Street, Orange
Tel 6361 7748   Map 12

Contemporary

Score 15/20

Simonn Hawke has created a feast for all the senses. The room is a visual delight – an interplay of mad exhibitionism and cool restraint. The impressive art on the walls includes a very fine Martin Coyte painting, while jazz filters through the air. The menu is a celebration all things Orange, yet the scope has broadened to touch lightly on influences from around the planet. Sweet and tender Belubula pork belly stars in a salad of green papaya, cucumber, avocado and mayonnaise. A braised Bumbaldry rabbit pie, the pastry crisp-edged and feather-light, the filling sticky and fall-apart, is ably matched with roasted organic tomato, celeriac mash and caramelised eschalots. Even the simplest things are beautifully done, such as beef fillet with potato boulangere and buttered English spinach, lifted with a light, piquant horseradish mustard cream. Service may wane as the night wears on, but after one mouthful of beurre noisette ice-cream on a warm fig, almond and quince tart, all is forgiven.

Hours Lunch Fri noon–2.30pm; Dinner Tues–Sat 6–9pm
Bill 2-course menu $60pp, 3 courses $75pp; 10% surcharge on Sundays, 15% on public holidays
Cards AE (+3%) DC V MC Eftpos
Wine Delicious list features lesser-known varieties and locals; 8 by the glass
Chef Simonn Hawke
Owners Simonn Hawke & Leah Morphett
Seats 60; wheelchair access; outdoor seating
Child friendly Kids' menu
www.lolliredini.com.au
And... try the 100-mile terrine, made using local ingredients to save on food miles

The Monastery Brasserie

18 Church Street, Wagga Wagga
Tel 6931 8288   Map 12

Contemporary

Score 12.5/20

Want a taste of the monk's life? This welcome addition to regional dining is tucked away on the banks of the Murrumbidgee in the ground-floor rooms of a sympathetically converted monastery. The main room has photographs of the old monastery and school life on the walls, and retains some of the austerity of its former days, while outside seating is along the verandah and on a deck built into the old garden. Munificent fare – each dish available in entree or main size – includes oven-baked roast capsicum risotto cake, fat and moist with a golden, crumbed crust, and topped with garlic-fried field mushrooms, sharp goat's cheese, salad greens and a drizzle of black truffle-infused mayonnaise. Bite-size skinned roast chicken pieces are highlighted by a light basil and buttermilk dressing, shaved parmesan, crisp pancetta wafers and tortilla croutons. While chocolate brulee isn't as sweet as the eager-to-please floor staff, that's no great sin.

Hours Tues–Wed 10am–3pm, Thurs–Sat 10am–9pm, Sun 9am–3pm
Bill E $16.50–$19.50 **M** $26.50–$31.50 **D** $12.50
Cards V MC Eftpos
Wine A modest list over a good range of styles with some locals; 14 by the glass and 10 beers
Chef Sam Longden
Owners Gregory & Christine Bannon
Seats 70; wheelchair access; outdoor seating
www.themonastery.com.au
And... aromas of lavender and thyme in the garden are another reason to nab a verandah seat

regional

Neila

5 Kendal Street, Cowra
Tel 6341 2188   Map 12

Contemporary

Score 15.5/20

Warmth prevails in this long narrow restaurant, its dark wooden tables set simply with white napery and glassware. Colourful artworks by a local artist, Ngari, adorn stone-hued walls, and a comfortable banquette stretches the length of one wall. The service, led by the gently affable Jerry Mouzakis, is efficient and wonderfully hospitable. In the kitchen his partner, Anna Wong, works wonders with produce from Neila's farm paddocks and the local area. Bumbaldry rabbit tortellini, tender meat encased in fine pasta, is accompanied by sweet carrot puree and coconut foam, which complements and adds another dimension to the dish. Confit duck with tender saltwater duck breast is served with both a salad and a puree of apple and cauliflower. Also enjoyable is lamb sirloin with splinantero (spleen and heart sausage) with fresh pea puree and wilted lettuce. Chocolate mousse, salted peanuts and spiced caramel ice-cream is just one of the desserts not to be missed.

Hours Dinner Thurs–Sat 6.30–9pm; bookings essential
Bill E $18–$20 **M** $32–$35 **D** $16
Cards AE V MC
Wine BYO (corkage $3pp)
Chef Anna Wong
Owners Jerry & Ari Mouzakis & Anna Wong
Seats 48; wheelchair access; outdoor seating
www.neila.com.au
And...order a couple of weeks in advance for suckling pig or stir-fried mud crab

Pagès on Pine

119b Pine Avenue, Leeton
Tel 6953 7300   Map 12

Steakhouse (Southern French)

Score 12.5/20

British food writer Elizabeth David believed strongly in the sufficiency of an omelette and a glass of wine. Pagès on Pine brings David's words to mind, not only because they serve a creamy yet light omelette, as well as nicely chilled local whites. It's also the yellow-ochre walls and pale blue ceiling with sun filtering through a small skylight, and bare board floor, which prompt dreams of drifting along the canals of Provence. While the Riverina's irrigation canals aren't quite as navigable, you can indulge in Provencalism with Eric Pagès' food. Strips of just-seared beef tenderloin surround a risotto, flecked with a ratatouille of capsicum, eggplant and tomato, diced as finely as the rice itself and all coated in a silky sauce with hints of saffron. It's a positively sunny dish that's apt for Leeton, home of SunRice. Meanwhile, lemon sorbet on citrus curd with rouge coulis and petite meringue is a gloriously tart dessert.

Hours Breakfast Sun 10am–noon; Lunch Wed–Sat 11.45am–2pm; Dinner Wed–Sat (& Sin – long weekends only) 6–9pm
Bill E $10–$18 **M** $18–$34 **D** $5.50–$11
Cards AE V MC Eftpos
Wine A small list with an accent on local wines; 4 by the glass; BYO (corkage $6 a bottle)
Chef Eric Pagès
Owners Eric & Vanessa Pagès
Seats 50
Child friendly Kids' menu; highchairs; toys; books
And...do yourself and the region a favour and drink the local wines

the west

Racine at La Colline

NEW ENTRY

42 Lake Canobolas Road, Orange
Tel 6365 3275   Map 12

Contemporary

Score 13.5/20

It takes a while to see whether a transplanted tree will take root in its new home, and that's the case here. After a much-feted debut at The School House, husband-and-wife team Shaun and Willa Arantz – he's in the kitchen, she runs the cheerful floor – have relocated to the other side of town, putting out shoots in a glorified shed at La Colline vineyard. It's a light, airy space that holds promise but is screaming out for some personality. Arantz hits the ground running with quail pithivier: whole quail encased in a dome of golden pastry, served with parsnip puree and clear quail consomme for a confident mix of country comfort and showy technique. Alas, his step faltered with rather clunky pork belly on curried dauphinoise potatoes and a tortured roast snapper bouillabaisse. Mushroom tart, redolent of the French countryside, hits the mark beautifully, however. A sublime coffee and cardamom ice-cream is further proof that these shoots will blossom with time.

Hours Lunch Fri–Sun (& Mon on long weekends only) & Mon noon–2.30pm; Dinner Thurs–Sat (& Sun on long weekends only) 6–9.30pm
Bill E $18 **M** $35 **D** $16; 2-course menu $60pp, 3 courses $70pp; 10% surcharge on public holidays
Cards AE (+3%) V MC Eftpos; surcharges
Wine The pick of the Orange crop; 12 by the glass
Chefs Shaun Arantz & Tom Grasso
Owners Shaun & Willa Arantz
Seats 65; wheelchair access; outdoor seating; bar
Vegetarian Several options
www.racinerestaurant.com.au
And...the paintings on the wall are for sale

Rajarani

75 Church Street, Mudgee
Tel 6372 3968   Map 13
Also at 124 Wentworth Street, Blackheath
Tel 4787 6968   Map 11

Indian

Score 12.5/20

Mudgee's only Indian restaurant is what you'd expect: a pink room at the quiet end of the street, flat-screen televisions playing Bollywood classics, and a knowing waitress in a flowing sari. Locals arrive for an early dinner with kids and wine-cooler bags in tow. Crisp samosas are filled with spicy potato and peas, deep-fried to a light crunch and served with yoghurt. Vegetable bhaji of green vegetables and onions combined with chickpea batter was a tad bland, but kolinada maachi, marinated white fish fried in spices, goes down nicely with a cold beer. Safedi murgh – chicken fillet cooked in a curry of cashew nut puree – might be an acquired taste. Be warned: Goan prawn curry of red-hot chilli and coconut is seriously fiery (make sure you ask for mild if you can't take the heat). From the tandoor, aloo paratha stuffed with potato is tasty and handy for mopping up curry gravy.

Hours Lunch Thurs–Fri noon–2pm; Dinner Tues–Sun 6–9pm
Bill E $6.80–$13.20 **M** $13.40–$20.20 **D** $5.90
Cards AE DC V MC Eftpos
Wine BYO (no corkage)
Chef Harjinder Singh
Owner Mohan Singh
Seats 90; wheelchair access; outdoor seating
Child friendly Kids' menu; highchairs
Vegetarian Many options
And...try the excellent mango lassi

regional

Rose Garden Thai
208 Brisbane Street, Dubbo
Tel 6882 8322   Map 12

Thai

Score 13.5/20

This white house surrounded by rose bushes is a godsend for anyone wishing to escape the fast-food chains dominating Dubbo's culinary scene. Step inside and you'll hear the reassuring sound of mortar being pounded by pestle; in true Thai style, the pastes are made from scratch. Owner Tish Pintusen smiles as she moves gently between the kitchen and diners seated at unclothed dark wooden tables in a room decorated with Thai ornaments. Goong nang fah, succulent battered prawns with shredded coconut, are perfect dipped in homemade sweet chilli sauce. Pad met ma-muang, tender chicken and vegetables stir-fried in a mild chilli sauce, would improve from the addition of fresh herbs, while a massaman curry of flaky beef has depth of flavour thanks in part to sweet spices. To finish, Thai custard with sticky rice is guaranteed comfort food, and comes highly recommended.

Hours Lunch daily noon–2.30pm; Dinner daily 5.30–10pm
Bill E $8.90–$10.90 **M** $16.80–$18.90 **D** $6–$7.50
Cards AE V MC Eftpos
Wine Familiar names, 5 by the glass
Chefs Pornpun Changkept & Tish Pintusen
Owner Tish Pintusen
Seats 60; bar
Child friendly Highchairs
Vegetarian A good portion of the menu
And…come with friends, the food here is perfect for sharing

Selkirks
179 Anson Street, Orange
Tel 6361 1179   Map 12

Contemporary

Score 14.5/20

This Orange stalwart is finding its feet again after a change of guard two years ago, thanks to fine, sound food from chef Euan Macpherson. There's a cordial reception on opening the door of this converted Federation bungalow where the rooms are set with linen-clothed tables and accented with red. Quail with soba noodles and spiced cherries is an unlikely combination, yet the flavours warm to each other. Macpherson's tutelage under Selkirks' predecessor, Michael Manners, shines in the coarse pork and pistachio sausage accompanying roast pork and pumpkin. Kingfish with smoky Trunkey speck, leek and vongole, sweet saffron and vanilla sauce is surprising, but again it works. A perfect palate cleanser of apricot and orange sorbet is exquisite, while white chocolate and honey bavarois with dark chocolate mousse and caramel crackle is an indulgent finish. The restaurant gets its name from poet Robert Burns's pre-meal thanksgiving, The Selkirk Grace, and there's a lot to give thanks for here.

Hours Lunch Fri noon–3pm; Dinner Tues–Sat 6.30–9pm; bookings essential
Bill 2-course menu $55pp, 3 courses $68pp
Cards AE V MC Eftpos
Wine Regional and interstate choices, with matching suggestions; 15 by the glass
Chefs Euan Macpherson & Ben Vaughan
Owners Euan Macpherson & Tara Pentecost
Seats 70; private room; wheelchair access
www.selkirksrestaurant.com.au
And…indulge in the degustation (on request) for $75pp

Sister's Rock

Borrodell Vineyard,
298 Lake Canobolas Road, Orange
Tel 6365 3128   Map 12

Contemporary

Score 12/20

A steep, winding drive makes its way between rows of cherry trees and vines to a restaurant where virtually every table has magnificent views. Diners gaze over Borrodell's pinot vines, to the picturesque Towac Valley and Orange, further afield. An entree of scampi with salmoriglio is a good dish, but ricotta- and parmesan-filled tortellini impresses more, with lovely house-made pastas, a simple drizzle of olive oil and a scattering of pine nuts and baby rocket. Oven-baked kingfish is nicely cooked, with chardonnay beurre blanc, but the accompanying fennel salad was more rocket and spinach than fennel. A promised espresso ice-cream with light, flourless chocolate cake and chocolate sauce was absent without explanation. Service is pleasant, but can gradually fall by the wayside. Fortunately, it is easy to while away the time taking in the view over a glass of Borrodell wine. With a little extra attention to detail, Sister's Rock could certainly take a place at the top of the Mount.

Hours Lunch Fri–Sun noon–3pm; Dinner Fri–Sat 6–9.30pm
Bill E $18 **M** $34 **D** $12; 2-course menu $50pp, 3 courses $60; 10% surcharge Sundays & public holidays
Cards V MC Eftpos
Wine Borrodell Vineyard wines; 8 by the glass
Chef Andrew Marr
Owners Gaye Stuart-Nairne & Borry Gartrell
Seats 65; private room; wheelchair access; outdoor seating; bar
Child friendly Kids' menu; highchairs; play area
www.borrodell.com.au
And... the underground cellar door is close by

sourcedining

664 Dean Street, Albury
Tel 6041 1288   Map 12

Contemporary

Score 15/20

Baroque gold-framed mirrors line the wall of this narrow, sage-and-umber venue, serving as an apt metaphor for Jodie Jones' intelligently molecular gastronomy-infused food. Each dish comes to the table as an eye-catching, palate-piquing ensemble of bold, frequently curvaceous forms, elaborately ornamented but finely balanced. Gazpacho terrine has layers of capsicum, zucchini and roasted tomato in a tomato jelly, tiny dice of cucumber and spiced capsicum jelly, minuscule croutons and a sphere of translucent tomato juice. Wild rabbit boudin, rack and saddle, is an assiette of sublime delicacy, each element distinct in flavour. The tiny-boned rack is elegantly skinned, its earthiness matched by a skinless sausage of roasted tomato and chorizo. Dessert is a grin-inducing take on two Aussie favourites, lamington ice-cream (a small ball of sponge encased in a big ball of chocolate rolled in coconut) sitting on a sandwich of chocolate sablés and white marshmallow.

Hours Lunch Thurs–Fri noon–2.30pm; Dinner Tues–Sat 6–9.30pm; bookings essential
Bill E $17–$21 **M** $29–$36 **D** $14
Cards AE DC V MC Eftpos
Wine Justly reputed list of fortifieds and an equally small but focused selection of local and European varietals; 10 by the glass
Chef Jodie Jones
Owners Steve Carne & Jodie Jones
Seats 100; wheelchair access; outdoor seating
Child friendly Highchairs; books; drawing materials
www.sourcedining.com
And... wines by the glass on Steve's recommendation is the way to go

regional

Tonic

Cnr Pym & Victoria streets, Millthorpe
Tel 6366 3811   Map 12

Contemporary
Score 15/20

Gazing through large casement windows to an expansive streetscape, it's easy to imagine it's the late 19th century. Inside, high ripple-iron ceilings, hung with large drum lights, span a room with spaciously arranged, linen-clothed tables. An amuse bouche of potato and leek soup with a hint of truffle is a welcome start. Chef Tony Worland is true to his ingredients, especially regionally sourced meats, including tender, thinly sliced Mandagery Creek venison layered in a millefeuille of crisply flaky pastry, silken duck liver parfait and figs. Roulade of Bumbaldry rabbit, spinach and pancetta with creamy risotto, studded with freshly shelled peas, is a triumph. Blayney pork is pink and succulent accompanied by sautéed cabbage and parsnip puree. Plump, just-cooked cherries with a hint of almond are encased in buttery pie pastry and served with coconut sorbet. Service is friendly and enthusiastic, if occasionally inconsistent, but this shouldn't discourage, as you will certainly find remedy in Worland's cooking.

Hours Brunch Sat–Sun 10am–noon; Lunch Sat–Sun 12.30–2pm; Dinner Thurs–Sat 6.30–8.30pm; bookings essential
Bill 2-course menu $55pp, 3 courses $65pp
Cards AE DC V MC Eftpos
Wine Many locals and a few from further afield; 16 by the glass; BYO (corkage $8 a bottle)
Chef Tony Worland
Owners Tony & Nicole Worland
Seats 180; private room; wheelchair access
www.tonicmillthorpe.com.au
And... watch out for truffle lunches in season, which include a truffle hunt

Union Bank Wine Store ★

Cnr Sale & Byng streets, Orange
Tel 6360 0495   Map 12

Contemporary
Score 13/20

REGIONAL WINE LIST OF THE YEAR
This understated restaurant and wine bar is a favourite with locals, who are greeted by name and feel welcome to drop in and linger over a glass of wine, a coffee or meal, any day of the week. This former schoolhouse has a relaxed atmosphere, with whitewashed walls, dark wood finishes, a communal bench inside and shady courtyard area. Service is warm and eager, although you have to order at the counter. Choose from a menu that aligns itself with the season; perhaps a light salad of salt-and-pepper squid with soy, crisp noodles and cabbage, or a hearty wagyu rump with cafe de paris butter and creamy mash. Risotto with sweet, perfectly cooked prawns and lovely flakes of cod fell short due to too-crunchy rice. The distinct flavours in a dessert of passionfruit, pineapple and raspberry ice-cream vacherin capture the essence of summer. Weekends hum with the sound of happy patrons; it's popular, so arrive early to beat the rush.

Hours Lunch daily noon–2.30pm; Dinner Mon–Sat 6–9pm; limited bookings Fri–Sat dinner
Bill E $12–$17 **M** $15–$27 **D** $10
Cards AE V MC Eftpos
Wine A long list with Belgravia house wines, plenty of local drops and a few from further abroad; 25 by the glass
Chef Scott Want
Owners RGH Investments
Seats 100; private rooms; outdoor seating; bar
Child friendly Kids' portions; drawing materials
www.unionbank.com.au
And... ask about wine events and cottage accommodation at the vineyard

Wineglass Bar & Grill

NEW ENTRY

Cobb & Co Court Boutique Hotel,
97 Market Street, Mudgee
Tel 6372 7245   Map 13

Contemporary

Score 13.5/20

The setting is part of the charm at Wineglass. The historic Cobb & Co Court Boutique Hotel feels like a cosy, wine-stocked shed, complete with friendly waiters. The wine list is an extensive selection of local and regional offerings. Owner and chef Scott Tracey uses seasonal, regional produce to compose a menu of hearty country staples. To start, pork belly with roasted potatoes and red wine jus is perfect on a cold winter's evening and as delicious as it sounds. So too is pan-fried trout served on a bed of avocado, parmesan and lettuce with a side of steaming sweet dutch carrots. A generous portion of duck confit was unfortunately a touch dry, however the popular parmesan-crumbed lamb cutlet with smashed peas and baby potatoes is a reminder of how very good Aussie lamb can be. Chocolate fondant wraps up a heavy meal nicely, and there's also that dessert wine.

Hours Breakfast daily 7–11am; Lunch daily 11.30am–2.30pm; Dinner Mon–Sat 6–9pm, Sun 6–8.30pm
Bill E $11–$21 **M** $30–$34 **D** $11–$15; 10% surcharge on Sundays, 15% on public holidays
Cards AE (+2%) DC (+2%) V MC Eftpos
Wine Extensive list of local and regional wines, reasonably priced; 16 by the glass
Chef/owner Scott Tracey
Seats 75; private room; wheelchair access; outdoor seating; bar
Child friendly Kids' menu; space for prams
www.cobbandcocourt.com.au
And…ask about the special dine-and-stay deals

And also…

NORTHERN TABLELANDS

Bistro on Cinders
14 Cinders Lane, Armidale
Tel 6772 4273
This classy little joint serves local Altitude coffee as well as muffins and cakes. Breakfast on brilliant eggs benedict, or test out the enticing lunch and dinner menus.

Bottega Caffe and Deli
Shop 2/14 Moore Street, Armidale
Tel 6772 6262
A deli–cafe with a strong Italian bent: lunch options include frittata, risotto, polenta wedges and linguini. There's also Incas coffee and a top range of products, including Amedei chocolate, Morpeth sourdough and Black Mountain ham and bacon.

Cafe Graze
21n Derby Street, Walcha
Tel 6777 2409
Open for brekkie and lunch, this modern cafe with a big, open kitchen serves Allpress coffee, sandwiches and more hearty blackboard specials. Gourmet pantry products and a kids' playroom are bonuses.

Goldfish Bowl Espresso Bar
Shop 10/206 Beardy Street, Armidale
Tel 6771 3271
If you like coffee and like it strong, this is the place. This trendy, friendly little spot with a handful of seats, also serves gourmet sandwiches, house-baked bread and pastries.

regional

Monty's
Quality Hotel Powerhouse, Armidale Road, Tamworth
Tel 6766 7000
This formal diner has all the posh trimmings, with competant service and rather high prices. British chef Ben Davies isn't afraid to experiment (bacon ice-cream, anyone?), although tempura Moreton bay bug with chunky polenta fries is satisfyingly simple.

The Sleepy Monkey
403 Peel Street, Tamworth
Tel 6766 6539
Toby's Estate Coffee plus local and house-made cakes make this bright, modern cafe worth a visit. It's licensed and open for brekkie and lunch most days, and dinner Friday and Saturday nights.

PROVEDORE
* **Altitude Coffee Roastery**, Shop 14, 112 Dangar Street, Armidale, **Tel 6772 3020**; various blends roasted in house.

CENTRAL WEST

Bizzy Bird's Cafe
Cnr Louee Street & Cudgegong Road, Rylstone
Tel 6379 1189
For a coffee fix and home-baked bread-and-butter puddings, banana and walnut cakes, and carrot cake with yummy yoghurt icing as well as lunchtime sandwiches and salads.

Butcher Shop Cafe
49 Church Street, Mudgee
Tel 6372 7373
Also at 113 Mayne Street, Gulgong
Tel 6374 2322
Join the communal long table for an easy brekkie or lunch with eggs any style, crisp bacon, fresh juices and coffee. Be tempted by home-style treats such as gooey chocolate, carrot and banana cakes.

Foxwood Farm Fine Food Cafe
Castlereagh Highway, Running Stream
Tel 6358 8251
On the way home from Mudgee, drop in for a country hamper of home-baked pies and a cuppa. Sweet and savoury are covered at this roadside stall: steak, chicken and mushroom, apple and rhubarb and even lemon meringue.

High Valley Wine & Cheese Co
137 Cassilis Road, Mudgee
Tel 6372 1011
Head here for a posh brekkie with fresh sourdough, organic eggs and strong Toby's Estate coffee. For lunch, it's cheese platters and olives with wines by the glass. Enjoy a tasting while you're there, and take a peek into the cheese workshop.

Lazy River Estate
29r Old Dubbo Road, Dubbo
Tel 6882 2111
Enjoy views of the vines and Macquarie River while feasting on beer-battered dory fillets with chips, or sirloin steak sandwich. There's also brunch, light lunches and kids' meals. Phone ahead for a picnic hamper.

The Quaff Shop Gallery Cafe
13 Lewis Street, Mudgee
Tel 6372 4940
For crafty knick-knacks, chai tea and addictively warm caramel fudge brownies, look no further. This cute cottage also serves a full breakfast complete with organic eggs and gluten-free options.

Roth's Wine Bar
30 Market Street, Mudgee
Tel 6372 1222
Visit this historic venue and relax with mezze plates and bar food to share. There might even be live music depending on the evening. Enjoy an extensive list of Mudgee and regional wines, plus locally brewed beer.

the west

Two Doors Tapas and Wine Bar
215b Macquarie Street, Dubbo
Tel 6885 2333
On a balmy summer evening, enjoy a glass of wine or beer in the shady courtyard. In winter, opt for a comfy sofa in the cosy, cellar-like rooms inside, with a range of share plates to nibble on.

PROVEDORES AND MARKETS
* **Hodges Butchery**, Shops 8–9 Town Centre, 19 Church Street, Mudgee, **Tel 6372 1599**; stock up for a picnic in the vineyards with crackers, smallgoods, olives, patés and pastes.
* **Jannei Goat Dairy**, 8 View Street, Lidsdale, **Tel 6355 1107**; the best milky goat's cheese in the region: Buche Blanc triple cream, aged cheddar and chevre. By appointment only.
* **Mudgee Gourmet @ The Railway**, Railway Station, Inglis Street, Mudgee, **Tel 6372 0030**; jams, honeys, pickles, sauces, simmers, pastes, and chutneys to try and buy.
* **Newtown Providores**, 62 Wingewarra Street, Dubbo, **Tel 6882 0055**; a great range of gourmet ingredients, a selection of charcuterie, cheese, and coffee and light meals.

* **Dubbo Farmers' Market**, Visitors Centre, cnr Newell Highway & Macquarie Street, 1st & 3rd Sat, 8am–noon. **Tel 0488 685 006**.
* **Mudgee Organic Market**, St Mary's Church grounds, cnr Market & Church streets, 3rd Sat, 8.30am–12.30pm, **Tel 6372 6594** or **0407 288 797**.

CENTRAL TABLELANDS

Beekeepers Inn
2319 Mitchell Highway, Vittoria
Tel 6368 7382
The historic Cobb & Co building between Bathurst and Orange has been sating appetites since 1859. The 21st-century menu includes all-day brekkie, spinach and fetta tart and steak with cajun chips, plus good Vittoria coffee, gelato and a huge selection of regional deli goods.

Bills Beans
148 McLachlan Street, East Orange
Tel 6361 1611
A corner store transformed into a comfy, modern cafe for frittata, quiche and Turkish sandwiches, but it's mostly all about the coffee. Roaster Bill Parianos is always trying new blends, with about 10 on offer.

Bodhi Garden
341 Summer Street, Orange
Tel 6360 4478
A well-worn vegetarian teahouse with a menu revealing the owner's Taiwanese heritage: gow gee, steamed buns, racish cake and taro triangles to start, and mains such as braised eggplant hotpot and hot-and-spicy tofu.

The Hub Espresso Bar & Eatery
52 Keppel Street, Bathurst
Tel 6332 1565
Personable, friendly service, local Fish River Roasters coffee, fantastic desserts from nearby Le Gall Patisserie, live jazz nights and guest chefs for global culinary exploration in a beautiful leafy courtyard.

Le Gall Patisserie
56 Keppel Street, Bathurst
Tel 6331 5800
Intensely popular for its sweet and savoury goodies, so come early before they're all gone. Experience a slice of the good life with bon vivant, a masterpiece of chocclatey goodness, or a wonderfully aromatic mini orange cake.

regional

O'Connell Cafe
2431 O'Connell Road, O'Connell
Tel 6329 4880
The vegies are grown in the garden, the coffee and loose-leaf tea are from Fish River Roasters, and the sweets are made from scratch, such as crumbly medieval honey cake or buttery apple walnut danish.

The Old Convent
307 Convent Road, Borenore
Tel 6365 2420
An extremely popular cafe in a fresh, modern extension of the convent, fittingly only open on Sunday. Enjoy muesli with yoghurt and poached local fruits or eggs benedict (with sinfully buttery hollandaise). For lunch it's simple combinations such as rabbit pie with kipfler potatoes, snow peas and tomato relish.

taste Canowindra
42 Ferguson Street, Canowindra
Tel 6344 2332
Stop here on the way between Orange and Cowra to try more than 50 local wines, view local arts and crafts or buy local produce. The cafe makes a good coffee with cake, plus more substantial meals.

PROVEDORES AND MARKETS
* **The Borenore Store**; 595 Borenore Road, Borenore, **Tel 6365 2261**; more than 50 local drops, local produce, pantry staples, and Saturday arvo wine tastings.
* **Country Fruit**, 165 George Street, Bathurst, **Tel 6331 1742**; fresh produce and a good range of cheeses, antipasti, pasta and olive oils.
* **M & J's Butchery**, 30 Moulder Street, Orange, **Tel 6362 2037**; a smart butcher selling prime rib, minced, stuffed "magic-mushroom" pumpkins and more.
* **Manners & Borg**, Woolworths carpark, behind 166 Summer Street, Orange, **Tel 6362 2792**; take-home meals by former Selkirks chef Michael Manners, from classic beef cheeks in red wine to lasagne.

* **Totally Local**, 426 Mitchell Highway, Orange, **Tel 6360 4604**; local olive oils, meat (venison, goat and beef), cheese, fruit and veg, nuts, and a wine store.
* **Union Bank Wine Store**, cnr Sale & Byng streets, Orange, **Tel 6360 0495**; a selection of local drops and good advice, too.

* **Bathurst Region Farmers' Market**, Bathurst Showgrounds, 4th Sat, 8am–noon, inquire about extra dates Nov–March, **Tel 6368 1104**.
* **Cowra Farmers' Market**, Cowra Showground, 3rd Sat, 8am–noon, **Tel 6342 9225**.
* **Orange Farmers' Market**, 2nd Sat, 8.30am–noon, May–Oct Orange Showground, Nov–April Orange Regional Gallery Northcourt, **Tel 0425 259 350**.
* **Young & Region Farmer's Market**, Anderson Park Railway Station, 1st & 3rd Sat, 8–11am and 7–11am during daylight saving, **Tel 0407 990 711**.

RIVERINA

Baan Sabai Jai
459 Smollett Street, Albury
Tel 6021 2250
Is that really a gleaming steel Thai hawker trolley on a footpath in side-street Albury? Are they really cooking Thai noodle soups, stir fries and pad thai? Make way for tangy, spicy, fresh Asian, and don't hold the chilli!

Border Wine Room
Upstairs, 492 Dean Street, Albury
Tel 6021 0900
David Sutherland has put his years of wine-industry experience to excellent use in creating this upper-floor wine room boasting an enviable collection of international, Australian and local wines accompanied by a menu ranging from tapas to contemporary light dishes.

Bullocky Bills
Dog on the Tucker Box Road, Gundagai
Tel 6944 4500
The location and decor are uninviting, but if you haven't the time to traipse the byways, this one-stop shop has an extensive range of regional wares; olive and mustard oils, jams, pickles, ocal pies and cakes, too.

Dolce Dolce Pasticceria
449 Banna Avenue, Griffith
Tel 6962 1888
"Sweets must be gratifying to the eye, the palate and the spirit," philosophises this deco-fronted gem, and their deliriously yellow lemon tart and humble biscotti are all that and more. There's spongy focaccia, good coffee and homemade pasta.

Green Zebra
484 Dear Street, Albury
Tel 6023 1100
This crazy green-and-white striped site has an excellent range of house-made pasta (golden egg fettuccine, pepper-flecked tagliatelle) and sauces (rich chunky arrabbiata, bright green pesto), Italian cakes, good coffee; all good to eat in or take home.

La Scala Restaurant
455 Banna Avenue, Griffith
Tel 6962 4322
Nostalgic for the bare bones Italian trattoria serving, as they do here, good home-style Italian meals? There's enough variety and steps into the less familiar to offer choices beyond pizza and pasta. This'll bring the memories back.

Long Track Pantry
Riverside Drive, Jugiong
Tel 6945 4144
A cleverly rustic-look old timber store, with breakfast and lunch menu making the best of local product, and a range of flavourful jams, preserves, and old-fashioned citrus cordial to take away, attractively boxed or bagged.

Premium Coffee Roasters
34 Trail Street, Wagga Wagga
Tel 6921 4155
Local caffeine addicts flock to this tiny shopfront eager for takeaways of freshly roasted daily blends, and locally baked treats such as wholegrain raisin bread. Seats outside overlook the tree-lined street.

Zest BYO
168 Hoskins Street, Temora
Tel 6978 0332
Peppermint green walls, Tchaikovsky tunes, Jasper coffee, pancakes with maple syrup and crisp bacon, the quiet buzz of conversation – go on, grab a house-made muffin and a lightly spiced chicken and salad roll for the road.

PROVEDORES AND MARKETS

* **Butt's Gourmet Smokehouse**, 417 Tribune Street, Albury, Tel 6021 3987; excellent locally sourced smoked trout and meats.
* **Quinty Cake and Bakehouse**, 42 Morgan Street (Olympic Highway), Uranquinty, Tel 6922 9119; also at **Quinty on the Run**, cnr Best and Forsyth streets, Wagga Wagga; ciabatta, olive and parmesan, sun-dried tomato, and organic sourdough loaves and rolls.
* **The Red Pomegranate**, 14/15 Neslo Arcade, 117 Baylis Street, Wagga Wagga, Tel 6931 0223; excellent range of local organic and conventional products, fruit and veg.
* **Riverina Cheese**, 470–482 Hovell Street, Albury, Tel 6023 5325; factory shopfront cheeses and a good sampling of other regional products.
* **Riverina Grove**, 4 Whybrow Street, Griffith, Tel 6962 7988; a shed full of sauces and tapenade made on the premises and the best of other regional goods.

* **Wagga Wagga Farmers Market**, Civic Centre Gardens, Tarcutta Street, 2nd Sat, 8am–1pm, Tel 6922 9221.

regional

Western Wine By Greg Duncan-Powell

Orange
The Orange wine region is unique in that it is defined by altitude. Everything above 600 metres is Orange, everything below falls into the Central Ranges category.

The region climbs up to 900 metres at the base of Mount Canobolas (the highest western point in Australia before you get to South Africa), and some sites are much cooler than others. This means that it's difficult to choose a hero grape variety for Orange.

A reputation is growing for sauvignon blanc, particularly after the impressive Logan Sauvignon Blanc from 2008, but the truth is that Orange is an all-rounder. That might be bad for marketing but is a boon for the cellar-door traveller.

Philip Shaw Wines' Koomooloo Vineyard (Caldwell Lane, Borenore via Orange, **Tel 6365 2334**; open weekends noon–5pm) is a unique experience: the cellar door is actually Philip Shaw's house – the tasting bench is the kitchen bench. His deft winemaking touch and attention to detail in the vineyard ensure that the entire Philip Shaw range of wines is top notch. **Canobolas-Smith** (Boree Lane, Orange, **Tel 6365 6113**; open Sat, long weekends & public holidays, 11am–5pm; and by appointment) is one of the typical boutique operations in Orange, and has a well-deserved reputation for very stylish chardonnay. There's also an interesting sparkling red made from quality pinot noir that's worth a taste.

Union Bank Wine Bar and Wine Store (Cnr Byng & Sale streets, Orange, **Tel 6361 4441**; open Mon–Thurs 9am–6pm, Fri–Sat 9am–7.30pm, Sun 10am–5pm) is where Mudgee duo David Lowe (whites) and Jane Wilson (reds) of Lowe Family Wines make the Belgravia wines headlining this store, and wine guru Peter Bourne also offers some of the region's finest.

Hilltops
This region surrounding the cherry town of Young would probably be a much bigger wine region were it not for the lack of irrigation water. The dry climate produces big, bold reds that have style and varietal panache. It's mostly shiraz and cabernet sauvignon but that's not all. There's some semillon and chardonnay, and Brian Freeman at Freeman Vineyards is making excellent Italian-styled wines from rondinella and corvina with the use of a prune dehydrator. Unfortunately, Freeman has no cellar door, but there are a couple of worthy cellar doors a short distance from Young.

Grove Estate (Murringo Road, Young, **Tel 6382 6999**; open Sat–Sun, 10am–5pm) was once a cherry orchard, and the emphasis is very much still on fruit. As if to underline this, Grove Estate sells grapes to Clonakilla in exchange for winemaking services, and the Tim Kirk-made Grove Estate shiraz-viognier is one worth investigating.

On the other side of Young is a big fruit shed which houses the **Chalkers Crossing** (285 Henry Lawson Way, Young, **Tel 6382 6900**; open Mon–Thurs, 10am–4pm) winery and cellar door. French winemaker Celine Rousseau is making stylish wine sourced from fruit from Hilltops and farther afield. The Hilltops cabernet sauvignon and Tumbarumba chardonnay are particularly good.

Mudgee
The Aboriginal people who named Mudgee – which means "nest in the Hills" – could not have chosen better. It's a scenic sanctuary and always a favourite of cellar door travellers. The warm climate means that elegance isn't a strong point but big, honest flavours are, especially for shiraz and cabernet sauvignon.

Botobolar (89 Botobolar Rd, Mudgee, **Tel 6373 3840**; open Mon–Sat 10am–5pm; Sun & pub hols 10am–3pm) was one of the pioneers of organic and biodynamic viticulture, and is well worth a visit. The Preservative Free Dry Red is still one of the best of its type.

Logan Wines (Castlereagh Highway, Apple Tree Flat, **Tel 6373 1333**; open daily, 10am–5pm) has a large array of high-quality wines made from fruit sourced from both Orange and Mudgee.

Robert Stein Vineyard (Pipeclay Lane, Mudgee, **Tel 6373 3991**; open daily, 10am–4.30pm) has a great verandah for sipping and admiring the view, and produces the occasional stunning wine. Last year, it was the 2008 riesling. The motorcycle museum is a bonus.

Riverina

With vineyards the size of suburbs and dams the size of lakes, the wine region surrounding Leeton and Griffith is not what you would call "boutique". But that doesn't mean it doesn't hold some interest for the cellar door traveller.

Without doubt the wine for which the region is famous is the sticky – or as it is less colloquially known, botrytis-affected semillon. The Griffith-Leeton area produces such luscious examples of this fungus-affected wine with such regularity it's uncanny. But it's no one-trick pony, and just about every grape variety in Australia is planted. Favourites are durif and petit verdot, which produce robust, tactile wines in the warm climate. Elegance is not a word normally associated with the whites but the odd one can surprise, and they're always at a good price point.

In Leeton, the cellar door of choice is **Lillypilly Estate** (Lillypilly Road, Leeton, **Tel 6953 4069**; open Mon–Sat, 10am–5.30pm & Sun by appointment). Winemaker Robert Fiumara makes a solid range of wines but the stars are his stickies, particularly the Noble Blend. He also produces worthy tawny and vintage ports.

Westend Estate Wines (Brayne Road, Griffith, **Tel 6969 0800**; open Mon–Fri, 9am–5pm) are made by teetotal winemaker, Bill Calabria, but that doesn't seem to affect quality. Some of his whites challenge warm climate preconceptions. The Richland pinot grigio and sauvignon blanc are both excellent value, but the two wines worth the trip are the 3 Bridges Winemaker's Selection durif and 3 Bridges Reserve botrytis.

Nugan Estate (72 Banna Avenue, Griffith, **Tel 6962 1822**; open Mon–Fri, 9am–5pm) has quickly risen to the top in the Riverina, and the large range is consistently good. The cellar door is in the winery restaurant, and is one of few in the Griffith region offering wines made from other regions, including Coonawarra and the King Valley.

New England

This is another "new" NSW region with a long history. It goes back to 1841 but most of the modern vineyards were planted in late 1990s. Given the height of the Great Dividing Range around Armidale and Tenterfield, the region has similarities to Queensland's Granite Belt, and with one vineyard at 1150 metres it is winemaking at the top of Australia. Chardonnay tends to shine at these altitudes as do riesling and sauvignon blanc. If ripening isn't an issue, shiraz and cabernet sauvignon exhibit typical cool climate qualities.

Blickling Estate (Green Valley Road, Bendemeer, **Tel 6769 6786**; open daily, 9am–5pm) north of Tamworth produces a range of the above varietals, with the riesling and chardonnay the standouts.

Whyworry Wines (Kingston Road, Uralla, **Tel 6778 4147**; open Sat–Sun, 10am–4pm) is a 14-hectare vineyard with a fruit salad of grape varieties. It's a high-altitude vineyard, and the whites are the most consistent.

Interstate

MELBOURNE & REGIONAL VICTORIA

BY MICHAEL HARDEN

Attica
74 Glen Eira Road, Ripponlea
Tel (03) 9530 0111
Attica's menu can seem slightly deranged (smoked trout broth, crackling, basil seeds, fresh smoke) but chef Ben Shewry's immense skill in combining odd and familiar ingredients ensures there is order rather than chaos at this very original restaurant.

Bar Lourinha
37 Little Collins Street, Melbourne
Tel (03) 9663 7890
Communal tables, stools and a waiting list rule at this popular, often noisy but always buzzing Spanish-style bar. An Iberian-dominated wine list plus brilliantly conceived small dishes (kingfish carpaccio with lemon oil has cu t status) make it worth the wait.

City Wine Shop
159 Spring Street, Melbourne
Tel (03) 9654 6657
A prime example of the hybrid businesses Melbourne does so well. The bottle shop/bar/bistro components are helped along by simple bistro food – think salumi platters or pork belly with lentils – and the sturdy wine knowledge and barista skills of its personable staff.

The Commoner
122 Johnston Street, Fitzroy
Tel (03) 9415 6876
The Commoner's slightly eccentric but exceptionally hospitable nature makes it one of the city's more individual experiences. It's "modern British" approach has as many influences from the Middle East and southern Europe as from the UK, and a wood-fired oven out the back is used to great effect – particularly with weekly Sunday roasts.

Cumulus Inc
45 Flinders Lane, Melbourne
Tel (03) 9650 1445
Andrew McConnell's city outpost is an "eating house and bar" located in a slickly renovated former gallery space. Fashionable and often crowded, this no-bookings restaurant usually entails a wait but McConnell's brilliantly flavoured food (tuna tartare with crushed pea salad, Moonlight Flat oysters) makes up for any delays in getting a seat.

Cutler & Co Dining Room & Bar
55–57 Gertrude Street, Fitzroy
Tel (03) 9419 4888
This latest venture from Andrew McConnell is a sexily renovated, dark-hued restaurant in a former factory space. Its dramatic mix of rough and luxe is perfectly mirrored in a menu of inventive, beautiful food that mixes foie gras with barbecued quail, smoked tongue with confit gizzards and tapioca pearls with ginger granita.

Gerald's Bar
386 Rathdowne Street, North Carlton
Tel (03) 9349 4748
Consciously relaxed and studiously low key, yet Gerald's Bar doesn't stint on quality, with excellent ingredients in a small, daily-changing range of meals, or on its interesting and geographically democratic wine list. It doesn't hold back on the hospitality either, making it more clubhouse than bar.

Gigibaba
102 Smith Street, Collingwood
Tel (03) 9486 0345
Combine superb modern Turkish food with a no-bookings, tapas bar approach, a stylish, slightly bohemian location and an eccentric, mood-enhancing fit-out and you'll end up with Gigibaba. Always crowded, noisy, casual and exciting, it's a place that lives up to its considerable hype.

interstate

Giuseppe Arnaldo & Sons
Crown Complex, 8 Whiteman Street, Southbank
Tel (03) 9694 7400
The supremely theatrical fit-out and flashy casino location can sometimes mask the fact that Giuseppe Arnaldo & Sons – think North Bondi Italian Food sans beach – is a truly fine Italian restaurant with a commitment to sharp service, excellent ingredients (the spotlit bread and salumi displays give some indication) and classically good, deceptively simple, trattoria-style cooking.

Hellenic Republic
434 Lygon Street, Brunswick East
Tel (03) 9381 1222
George Calombaris's Press Club is all about modern Greek food, but here he opts for the tradition, style and attitude of a taverna in an updated, quality-conscious form. Large and noisy with a lengthy menu of grilled meats, superb salads and simply, respectfully treated seafood, this glossy restaurant shows how good trad Greek can be.

Jacques Reymond
78 Williams Road, Windsor
Tel (03) 9525 2178
Jacques Reymond's eponymous fine diner combines all the traditional trappings – luxurious room, crack service, impressively voluminous wine list – with some of the most modern, intricate and interesting food in town. The artful plating and intuitive combinations of Asian and European flavours are a consistent source of surprise and delight. No wonder it's *The Age Good Food Guide*'s Restaurant of the Year once again

Journal Canteen
1st Floor, 253 Flinders Lane, Melbourne
Tel (03) 9650 4399
Also known as Rosa's Kitchen, after co-owner and chef Rosa Mitchell, this lunch-only joint specialises in Sicilian dishes, many based on Rosa's family recipes. An open kitchen, communal tables and an abundance of natural light make this one of the city's most personable small diners.

MoMo
Lower Plaza Level, 123 Collins Street, Melbourne
Tel (03) 9650 0660
The new version of Greg Malouf's acclaimed modern Middle Eastern restaurant in the Grand Hyatt's revamped basement is an unashamedly upmarket affair, all snowy linen, highly skilled floor staff and luxuriously carpeted hush. Masterful, dreamy and costly, it still shouldn't be missed.

MoVida
1 Hosier Lane, Melbourne
Tel (03) 9663 3038
The opening of the smaller, more bar-like MoVida Next Door has done little to alleviate the crush at the MoVida mothership. To experience Frank Camorra's robust, meaty take on tapas and raciones while sampling a truly fine selection of sherry, you still need to book well ahead to join this ever-popular Spanish party.

Pearl
631–633 Church Street, Richmond
Tel (03) 9421 4599
Now that the bar and cafe have their own space a few blocks away, Pearl is fully focused on being a restaurant. It is obviously enjoying the attention – Geoff Lindsay's always impressive modern take on Asian, Middle Eastern and European flavours seems particularly well-balanced and playful with the shimmery, still-sexy dining room providing the perfect backdrop.

Rumi
116 Lygon Street, Brunswick East
Tel (03) 9388 8255
Rumi's modern take on Lebanese and Persian flavours has a wonderful lightness of touch. Aromatic spices, the tang of yoghurt and lemon juice, orange blossom cocktails and sour barberries abound, while a recent relocation from corner shop to former bank has meant more room to move.

interstate

Regional Victoria

Lake House
King Street, Daylesford
Tel (03) 5348 3329
This guesthouse restaurant pays more than lip service to regionality, with a menu that reads like a snapshot of what the local area is capable of producing. High levels of service, a lengthy wine list and impressive service help keep this stayer on the radar.

Provenance
86 Ford Street, Beechworth
Tel (03) 5728 1786
This gold rush-era bank building is home to contemporary, regionally obsessed cooking. Dishes such as house-made black pudding with pickled cherries or local beef with miso butter are easy on the eye and the palate, and feel right at home in these grand surrounds

Royal Mail Hotel
Parker Street, Glenelg Highway, Dunkeld
Tel (03) 5577 2241
Dan Hunter's time at Spain's Mugaritz is an obvious influence at the Royal Mail but a bigger inspiration is local produce, particularly the stuff pulled from the restaurant's own gardens. Subtle, pretty and sometimes amazing, the food here – and an exemplary wine list – rewards those who make the journey.

Sunnybrae Restaurant
Cape Otway Road, Birregurra
Tel (03) 5236 2176
This weekend lunch-only restaurant has an almost cult following thanks to owner–chef George Biron's skills in the kitchen, the vegie patch and his reputation as a passionate teacher. The "restaurant in the middle of a paddock" serves a degustation-type menu that reflects his commitment to regional, seasonal produce.

BRISBANE

Anise Bistro & Wine Bar
697 Brunswick Street, New Farm
Tel (07) 3358 1558
Ignore the daggy entrance and tiny space, which is really just a skinny bar counter for 21 lucky imbibers revelling in Guy Edensor's feisty French fare, which adds quirky twists to classics, such as rabbit cassoulet with truffled Berkshire pork sausage. If the game bird degustation's on, go for it.

Bar Alto
Level 1, Powerhouse Arts Centre,
119 Lamington Street, New Farm
Tel (07) 3358 1063
This is Italian with soul and heart, in a funky, loud and lively industrial space. The gutsy Mediterranean approach ranges from cotechino and ox tongue with fennel, rocket and salsa verde, to the signature pappardelle with goat ragu.

The Buffalo Club
Level 1, cnr Wickham & Brunswick streets, Fortitude Valley
Tel (07) 3216 1323
Missed out again on Spain's El Bulli? Thomas Keller's Per Se too far away in the USA? Ryan Squires cooked at both legendary restaurants, and now cuts loose with a daily degustation of 10 or 17 courses of boundary-riding culinary wizardry. It's from the team behind hot drinking spot The Bowery, so the booze is cool, too, and there's a fab bar.

Confit Bistro
Shop 4, 9 Doggett Street, Fortitude Valley
Tel (07) 3254 4001
Former Isis Brasserie chef Jason Peppler has downsized to a casual French bistro with Italian inclinations, such as orecchiette with spanner crab and osso buco with polenta. Calf's liver with champ is no lesser for it, and crepes suzette with campari ice-cream shows the flair's still there.

good food guide

interstate

The Crosstown Eating House
23 Logan Road, Woolloongabba
Tel (07) 3162 3839
The Gabba's latest culinary hotspot is a former antiques store (opposite Pearl and 1889 Enoteca) with a whitewashed retro-'50s feel and no-nonsense fare to share. Think cheese and crackers, slow-braised lamb with pasta, mini ice-cream cones and jam drops.

Era Bistro
102 Melbourne Street, South Brisbane
Tel (07) 3832 4722
This bold, contemporary bistro is headline act in a sprawling, spartan complex that also houses a cafe, bottle shop, cocktail lounge and bar. Clever Mediterranean-styled dishes – the prices defy the bistro tag – are packed with passionately bold, intriguing flavours, such as smoked trout, salmon tartare, campari jelly and olives.

Pearl Cafe
28 Logan Road, Woolloongabba
Tel (07) 3392 3300
This 19th-century terrace tucked away in a previously rundown corner of the 'Gabba is now a groovy bistro with retro panache and the nostalgic comfort of fish finger (crumbed salmon) sandwich with tartare and cos. Homely roast chicken breast on dreamy gnocchi is just fine, too.

Restaurant Two
2 Edward Street, Brisbane
Tel (07) 3210 0600
After 16 years and three restaurants, chef David Pugh and host Michael Conrad have parted ways, yet under Pugh, this CBD fine diner remains the benchmark for lush, contemporary Queensland flavours, such as soft-shell mud crab tempura with tomato and avocado salad and seaweed.

Sono
Level 1, Building 7, Portside Wharf, Hamilton
Tel (07) 3268 6655
There's a city sibling in Queen Street Mall, but take the trip east to where the cruise liners dock for this serenely elegant riverside Japanese. From fine tempura to the $75 platter of greatest hits and wagyu shabu shabu, it's all good.

Urbane
179 Mary Street, Brisbane
Tel (07) 3229 2271
This CBD bolthole is where you'll find some of Brisbane's finest cooking. Chef Kym Machin balances wit with precision in carefully composed, modern dishes, such as tea-smoked salmon with apple and vermouth sorbet, and the quirky fun of a rocky road bombe alaska.

QUEENSLAND RESORTS

Berardo's
52 Hastings Street, Noosa
Tel (07) 5447 5666
Also Berardo's on the Beach
49 Hastings Street, Noosa
Tel (07) 5448 0888
Chef Shane Bailey's switch from the beachside bistro to the mothership is a perfect match for this fresh, breezy setting. His light and lively Mediterranean and Asian flavours favour local produce, such as gorgeous Noosa red tomatoes with Gympie goat's curd. Lower prices reflect the times, too.

Ristorante Fellini
Level 1, Marina Mirage, Seaworld Drive, Main Beach
Tel (07) 5531 0300
Armando Percuoco's sibling, Tony, runs this elegant Italian ristorante overlooking Broadwater's bobbing gin palaces. Fellini's focus on the classics has old-school panache. They make the pasta, including poppyseed-freckled duck ravioli.

interstate

Fish & Wine
Reflections Tower Two, 110 Marine Parade, Greenmount (Coolangatta)
Tel (07) 5536 7775
Enjoy the sea breeze from this casual seafood bistro's alfresco tables. Chill out over well-priced Asian- and Mediterranean-influenced fare, including soft-shell crab on fennel and rocket salad, a seafood platter for two and even steak.

Muse
8 Hastings Street, Noosa Heads
Tel (07) 5447 2433
This hip, stylish diner on the main drag cheerfully tackles a mix of pan-Asian and Mediterranean flavours, such as gnocchi with braised lamb; and salmon with soba noodles and a pungent nam jim. The upstairs alfresco setting is perfect for balmy Noosa nights.

Nu Nu
123 Williams Esplanade, Palm Cove
Tel (07) 4059 1880
Can life get any better than sand between your toes and a smoked red emperor miang (betel leaf) in your mouth? You could happily spend all day dropping by this sea-breezy, sleek, chiffon-wrapped setting for vibrant breakfasts (mud crab omelette), cheerful lunches (Vietnamese pork ribs) and vivid dinners (red curry of fried barramundi).

Reef House
Sebel Reef House, 99 Williams Esplanade, Palm Cove
Tel (07) 4080 2662
From barramundi with fried egg rice for breakfast (or local biodynamic yoghurts) to an ambitiously diverse dinner menu of Asian, Middle Eastern and Mediterranean influences, the real star of this show is a setting under centuries-old tea trees, with views from the teak deck through the palms to the ocean.

Sassi at Balé
1 Bale Drive, Port Douglas
Tel (07) 4084 3000
Sassi is this resort town's byword for modern Italian, and this third incarnation, at Peppers Balé Resort, of Tony and Di Sassi's ristorante, with its unfussed coastal classics from Europe's boot, is given the occasional Japanese inflection.

Spirit House
20 Ninderry Road, Yandina
Tel (07) 5446 8994
It's the Queensland setting of your southern city fantasies: a magical, alfresco space of rainforest, croaking frogs, wind chimes, babbling water and burning torches. The fragrant Asian menu of shared dishes, from duck miang to salmon with black beans and jungle curries, lingers mostly in Thailand.

Vanitas
Palazzo Versace, 94 Sea World Drive, Main Beach
Tel 1800 098 000
Need a waiter? Just rattle your jewellery. Luxuriate in this opulent fine diner at Palazzo Versace. Caviar? No probs, perhaps with a drop from a 5000-bin wine list. The French-influenced food is modern and deft, so pinch yourself and enjoy the surrounds.

Wasabi
2 Quamby Place, Noosa Heads
Tel (07) 5449 2443
The move from Sunshine Beach to a riverside setting (opposite Ricky's) has lifted this smart Japanese. Yes it's loud, but then everyone's enthusiastic about spanner crab with edamame soup, silken tuna tartare and aburi wagyu with sesame dressing. Chef Shinichi Maeda's shimmering, light-handed skills make Wasabi one of Australia's finest Japanese restaurants.

interstate

SOUTH AUSTRALIA
BY MARINA GOLDSWORTHY

Appellation
The Louise, cnr Seppeltsfield & Stonewell roads, Marananga
Tel (08) 8562 4144
Chef Mark McNamara uses the best produce from Barossa's traditional purveyors. Barossa corn-fed chicken and lachsschinken with garlic and sage glaze is rich and comforting. His son Mat is the sommelier. Elegant surrounds, excellent wine list. Stay the night.

Chianti Classico
160 Hutt Street, Adelaide
Tel (08) 8232 7955
If you're looking to team a barolo from the stellar '99 vintage with braised rabbit, pancetta and sage then the stylish Chianti is the place for you. All wines available by the glass are Italian, and the gnocchi and pasta are house-made. An institution in Adelaide for breakfast and pavement dining.

d'Arry's Verandah
Osborne Road, McLaren Vale
Tel (08) 8329 4848
With bucolic views over the vines to the ranges, d'Arry's Verandah adjoins d'Arenberg's popular tasting room. The seasonal menu matches the wine offerings – boldly flavoured and well crafted. Signature dishes are lobster medallion with blue swimmer crab, prawn ravioli and lobster bisque.

Flying Fish Cafe
No 1 The Foreshore, Horseshoe Bay, Port Elliot
Tel (08) 8554 3504
South Australia's iconic gastronomic experience is the marriage of King George whiting and Clare Valley riesling. At Flying Fish Cafe, an hour south of Adelaide and as close to the beach as you can be without getting your feet wet, the fish is in crisp Coopers Ale batter, with hand-cut chips, while the wine list is full of cult locals.

Jasmin Indian Restaurant
31 Hindmarsh Square, Adelaide
Tel (08) 8223 7837
This South Australian culinary treasure is an oasis of calm and elegance mid city. Chef and family matriarch Anant Singh Sandhu's legendary beef vindaloo is richly dark and intense with a measured amount of heat. The Premier says it's his choice for a last meal, political or otherwise.

The Lane Vineyard
Ravenswood Lane, Hahndorf
Tel (08) 8388 1250
At the Lane Vineyard's slick new cellar door and bistro, you can be settled on the deck with a cold pinot gris and a plate of duck rillettes 30 minutes from the city. With glorious 180-degree views over distant hills and vineyards, this is the Adelaide Hills' most popular restaurant, so be sure to book.

The Manse
142 Tynte Street, North Adelaide
Tel (08) 8267 4636
Pink Jasper Conran crockery, black flock wallpaper and stark white Louis XIII dining chairs create a mod French-salon feel. Chef Ayhan Erkoc serves up a few molecular tricks, enhancing his butter-poached white asparagus and parmesan custard with mini egg yolk pearls. Adelaide's finest diner oozes elegance and style.

The Pot Food & Wine
160 King William Road, Hyde Park
Tel (08) 8373 2044
This tiny, dark, sexy and chic restaurant offers sensational bistro-styled food in tapas-sized servings. Wedges of iceberg with aioli, egg and anchovies are a revelation, and the sticky six-hour braised lamb with macaroni cheese is the stuff dreams are made of.

Sparrow Kitchen and Bar
10 O'Connell Street, North Adelaide
Tel (08) 8267 2444
Fancy a duck, cotechino and baked bean toasty for breakfast? This chic newcomer's large, Mediterranean-influenced menu is based on the wood oven and antique red Berkel meat slicer. Begin with tapas of duck doughnuts and porcini salt or gorgonzola arancini. Larger courses include braises such as pork tail with Pedro Ximenez, as well as grills and pizza.

T-Chow
68 Moonta Street, Adelaide
Tel (08) 8410 1413
This barn-sized Chinese cheapie in the Central Market precinct is an Adelaide institution. Everyone in town has a T-Chow favourite dish – oyster omelette, prawn-stuffed cabbage rolls, crispy taro duck or quail with pine nuts. Popular with wine-istas for their friendly BYO policy.

WESTERN AUSTRALIA
BY MEGAN ANDERSON

Bar One
250 St Georges Terrace, Perth
Tel (08) 9481 8400
This inner-city comfort zone oozes European chic with its black banquettes and formidable timber bar. The calibre of the fare – from early-morning coffee to post-work charcuterie and grown-up drinks – sustains the effect. Revel in love-infused Italian staples, such as veal meatballs and spinach pappardelle with wild mushrooms.

Divido
170 Scarborough Beach Road, Mount Hawthorn
Tel (08) 9443 7373
Nothing in the chocolate-toned, moody dining room suggests it's on a main thoroughfare, but this classy space heralds some of Perth's best Italian food. Weekend degustation dinners take the headache out of choosing.

Otherwise, plump for smoked buffalo mozzarella, cauliflower tagliatelle or wood roasted duck, and trust in the sommelier.

Harvest
1 Harvest Road, North Fremantle
Tel (08) 9336 1831
An arty charm pervades this converted house. Everyone comes to get amongst the ever-expanding repertoire, from cocktail lounge (Pimm's in jugs is big) to bustling breakfast hangout to scene of degustation dinners. There are worse ways to launch Saturday than with the Freo Scramble.

Il Lido Italian Canteen
88 Marine Parade, Cottesloe
Tel (08) 9286 1111
Long, communal tables and a boldly carpeted back wall are part of the milieu at this Italian cantina – the indoor yin to Cottesloe Beach's outdoor yang. Rustic dishes are persuasive regardless of weather – try the osso buco or pappardelle with duck ragu and marsala. A long list of antipasti sates sea-breeze induced appetites.

Little Creatures Brewing
40 Mews Road, Fremantle
Tel (08) 9430 5555
There's no wanting for atmosphere in this buzzing micro-brewery on Fremantle harbour. Rogers ale on tap flows from breakfast to late, and a cheerful brigade tends to the communal tables and booths in the cavernous, industrial space. Go for drinking food, such as wood-fired pizzas and spiced lentils.

Moore & Moore
46 Henry Street, Fremantle
Tel (08) 9335 8825
Part funky closed-in alley, part gorgeous limestone-clad courtyard, this nook-laden cafe abuts an art gallery in Fremantle's historic West End. Its laidback vibe is matched with top-notch cafe grub – colourful salads, chunky frittatas, devilish toasted muffins and excellent coffee.

interstate

Must Winebar
107 Bussell Highway, Margaret River
Tel (08) 9758 8877
Also at 519 Beaufort Street, Highgate
Tel (08) 9328 8255
The gene pool was uncompromised when Perth's celebrated bistro spawned a Margaret River offshoot. Must's trademark charcuterie, dry aged beef (see it hanging dramatically from the mood-lit main floor) and chunky wine list continue the class act down south, where regional fare adds a point of difference. Must try: gnocchi with braised duck.

Nahm Thai
223 Bulwer Street, Perth
Tel (08) 9328 7500
Perth's food scene sat up straight when this modern Thai diner claimed instant star status. Chef Kevin Pham is Vietnamese but his grasp on authentic Thai with a fresh twist is assured. Wow moments are everywhere, especially exquisite ma hor and duck curry with lychees and quail eggs.

Star Anise
225 Onslow Road, Shenton Park
Tel (08) 9381 9811
A decade of accolades hasn't dimmed the shine on David Coomer's fine diner. Defiantly non-fad in its elegant suburban locale, its take on Asian-influenced modern fare remains unsurpassed in Perth. Coomer's sublime alchemy includes Vietnamese-stye wagyu, crispy duck, and Manjimup marron in spiced coconut broth.

Wild Duck
112 York Street, Albany
Tel (08) 9842 2554
Something of a beacon on the regional dining landscape, this French-influenced mod-Oz establishment brings finesse (and foam) to the south coast. Beef cheeks quiver at Andrew Holmes's instruction, and his deboned spatchcock with king prawn, chorizo and chicken and saffron broth is a menu stayer.

HOBART & REGIONAL TASMANIA
BY GRAEME PHILLIPS

Black Cow Bistro
70 George Street, Launceston
Tel (03) 6331 9333
Formerly a famous butcher shop, this art deco corner building is now appropriately a steakhouse, specialising in free-range, grass-fed dry-aged Tasmanian beef for seriously good steaks with great Aussie wine to match.

Cargo Bar Pizza Lounge
47–51 Salamanca Place, Hobart
Tel (03) 6223 7788
Hip Cargo is hugely popular for wood-fired pizzas. There's a traditional margherita, and wackier toppings such as hoisin duck or tandoori chicken, plus sweet pizzas (apple crumble, chocolate truffle or pinot-poached pears) and cool gelati.

The Lotus Eaters Cafe
10 Mary Street, Cygnet
Tel (03) 6295 1996
A small space and terrific food mean seating at the Lotus is usually cheek-by-jowl. The food is nothing fancy – just simple, intelligent and beautifully flavoured seasonal offerings, from the bread to garden-fresh salads, the daily blackboard specials, luscious cakes, desserts and coffee.

Margot
15 Pendrigh Place, St Helens
Tel (03) 6376 2594
From slow-simmered, deeply flavoured braises to the house-made charcuterie, voluptuous souffles, shiny copper pots and Gallic accents, this is provincial France charmingly transported and translated into seaside St Helens.

Meadowbank Estate
699 Richmond Road, Cambridge
Tel (03) 6248 4484
Vines, views, art, impressive estate wines and contemporary, seasonal menus offering beautifully composed, small-plate dishes of fresh, balanced ingredients – that's Meadowbank Estate.

Me Wah
16 Magnet Court, Sandy Bay, Hobart
Tel (03) 6223 3688
Also at 39/41 Invermay Road, Invermay
Tel (03) 6331 1308
Head here for classic Cantonese, sumptuous Chinoiserie and great yum cha. Waiters can bone a snapper or fold a duck pancake with a few deft twists of the wrist, and the impressive wine list leads a few credit cards astray.

Piccolo Restaurant & Wine Bar
323a Elizabeth Street, North Hobart
Tel (03) 6234 4844
A very busy, very good modern Italian of dishes full of character and real flavour, running from silky pasta with sea urchin roe, sublime autumnal chestnut and mushroom ravioli and, at the more rustic end, braised Sardinian-style lamb with olives and garlic-rosemary crumbs.

Piermont Restaurant
Piermont Retreat, Swansea
Tel (03) 6257 8131
The menu includes views across Great Oyster Bay to the famed pink-granite Hazards of Freycinet Peninsula. On the plate, the modern, Mediterranean-inspired food is delicious and creative. A well-stocked walk-in cellar and excellent service are further highlights.

Pierres
88 George Street, Launceston
Tel (03) 6331 6835
More Parisian backstreet than downtown Lonny, this stylish spot has boudoir-red and lace-black decor, banquettes and timeless French bistro fare. The atmosphere is brasserie by day, white-linen by night for escargot, steak tartare and entrecote with cafe de paris butter.

Raincheck Lounge
394 Elizabeth Street, North Hobart
Tel (03) 6234 5975
Join the eclectic, laidback crowd for great coffee, Coco Pops, or eggs with smoky Raincheck beans. Lunch might be provencale fish soup and a glass of local bubbles; and later, tapas or hearty braised wallaby shanks.

Index

index

Alphabetical

III Bean Espresso Bar (Hamilton) 240
55 on Collins (Kiama) 242
9inety 2wo (Bathurst) 284
305 Restaurant & Cafe (Maitland) 214
A Bite to Eat, A Drink as Well (Chifley) 209
A Little Piece of Scotland (Sutton Forest) 264
a tavola 2
Abhi's 2
Acquazul (Newcastle) 230
Aki's 3
Al Aseel 173
The Albion (Braidwood) 243
Alio 3
Almond Bar 4
Altitude 4
Altitude Coffee Roastery (Armidale) 294
Alto (Acton) 197
Amanda's on the Edge (Pokolbin) 215
a'Mews 7
Amici 7
Angelo's Portugalia 171
Anise (Canberra) 198
Anise Bistro & Wine Bar (New Farm) 303
Aperitif 8
Appellation (Marananga) 306
Apple Bar (Bilpin) 187
Aqua Dining 8
Aria 9
Arjuna (Katoomba) 195
Arnott's Bakehouse (Morpeth) 215
Artespresso (Kingston) 198
Arun Thai 9
As Nature Intended (New Acton) 209
Ash St Cellar 10, 156
Ashcrofts (Blackheath) 188
Assiette 10
Astral 11
At Bangkok 166
At Perry Lane 160
Ate (Bangalow) 279
Attica (Ripponlea) 301
Aubergine (Griffith) 199
Austi Beach Cafe (Austinmer) 252
Australian Regional Food Store & Cafe (Pokolbin) 227
Avoca Beach Growers' Market (Avoca Beach) 240
Azuma 11
Azuma Kushiyaki 12
Baan Sabai Ja (Albury) 296
Bacchus (Newcastle) 231
Bacco Wine Bar Pasticceria 159
Bacco's Bakeries (Murrurundi) 228
Bai Yok 12
Bambini Trust Cafe 13, 176
Bamboo (Casuarina Beach) 265
Banana Blossom 13
Bangalow Cheese Co. (Byron

Bay, Bangalow) 280
Bangalow Farmers' Market (Bangalow) 280
Bangkok Betty 168
Bannisters (Mollymook) 243
Bar Adyar 159
Bar Alto (New Farm) 303
Bar Coluzzi 160
Bar Lourinha (Melbourne) 301
Bar One (Perth) 307
Barrenjoey House 14
The Bathers' Pavilion Cafe 176
The Bathers' Pavilion Restaurant 14
Bathurst Region Farmers' Market (Bathurst) 296
Bay Leaf Cafe (Byron Bay) 279
Bay Marlin Seafoods (Batemans Bay) 254
Bayleaf Brasserie 15
Bayswater Brasserie 15
Beachwood (Yamba) 279
Becasse 16, 184
Beekeepers Inn (Vittoria) 295
Bega Farmers' Market (Bega) 254
bel mondo 16
Belaroma 161
Belconnen Fresh Food Markets (Belconnen) 212
Bellachara (Gerringong) 244
Bellevue Hotel Dining Room 17
Belli Bar 163
Bellingen Growers' Market (Bellingen) 281
Bells at Killcare (Killcare Heights) 231
Bellyfish Cafe (Terrigal) 239
Bent on Food (Wingham) 281
Bentley Restaurant & Bar 17
Beppi's 18
Berardo's (Noosa) 304
The Beresford Hotel 18, 156
Berowra Waters Inn 19
Berrima Food Market (Berrima) 264
Berry Country Fair (Berry) 253
Berry Woodfired Sourdough Bakery (Berry) 244
Bertoni Casalinga 159
Big Brekky 176
Big Mama's 19
Bijolias 168
bills 176
Bills Beans (East Orange) 295
Billy Kwong 20, 184
Bilpin Springs Orchard (Bilpin) 196
Bilson's 20
Bin24 Wine Bar & Wood Fire Eatery 21
Binnorie Dairy (Pokolbin) 228
Bird Cow Fish 23
Bistro 345 (Thirroul) 245
Bistro CBD 24
Bistro Molines (Mount View) 216
Bistro Moncur 25
Bistro on Cinders (Armidale) 293

Bistro Ortolan 25
Bistro Tartine (Hamilton) 232
Bistrode 26
Bistro-Fax 24
Bitton Gourmet 162
Bizzy Bird's Cafe (Rylstone) 294
Black Cow (Launceston) 308
Black Star Pastry 162
The Black Swan (Berrima) 256
Blackboard at the Beach (Lennox Head) 279
Blackheath Growers' Market (Blackheath) 196
Blackwater 26
Blancharu 27
Blancmange 27
Blickling Estate Winery (Bendemeer) 299
Bliss Coffee Roasters (Pokolbin) 228
Blue Eye Dragon 28
Blue M Cafe and Food Co. (Katoomba) 195
Blue Metal Vineyard (Berrima) 264
Blue Mountains Food Co-op (Katoomba) 196
Blue Seas (Fyshwick) 212
The Boathouse 161
The Boathouse on Blackwattle Bay 28
Bodega 29
Bodhi Garden (Orange) 295
Bodyfuel (Gosford) 239
Bolo Bistro (Mullumbimby) 279
Bombora (Wollongong) 252
Bondi Trattoria 171
The Book Kitchen 29
Bookplate (Parkes) 209
Border Wine Room (Albury) 296
The Borenore Store (Borenore) 296
Botanic Gardens Restaurant 30
Botobolar Winery (Mudgee) 298
Bottega Caffe and Deli (Armidale) 293
Bowral Farmers' Market (Bowral) 264
Braidwood Bakery (Braidwood) 254
Brasserie Bread Bakery Cafe 176
Braza Churrascaria 173
Brill on the Green (Milton) 252
Brindabella Hills (Close via Hall) 213
Brokenwood (Pokolbin) 229
Bronte Road Bistro 30
Brown Sugar 31
The Buffalo Club (Fortitude Valley) 303
Bullocky Bills (Gundagai) 296
Buon Ricordo 31
Burgerman 178
The Burlington Bar and Dining 32
Burrawang General Store Cafe (Burrawang) 263

Bush Rock Cafe (Blackheath) 195
Busshari 32
Butcher Shop Cafe (Mudgee, Gulgong) 294
Butt's Gourmet Smokehouse (Albury) 297
buzo trattoria 33
Byron Bay Farmers' Market (Eyron Bay) 280
Byron Beach Cafe (Byron Bay) 266
Ça Marche (Port Macquarie) 266
Caesars Coffee & Fine Food (Erina) 240
Cafe Bella (Kangaroo Valley) 263
Cafe Beltree (Pokolbin) 216
Cafe Chocolat 163
Cafe Ella 163
Cafe Enzo (Pokolbin) 227
Cafe Giulia 177
Cafe Graze (Walcha) 293
Cafe Ish 159
Cafe ism 162
Cafe Kasturi 166
Cafe Red (Port Macquarie) 282
Cafe Sbiza (Kingscliff) 282
Cafe Sopra 33
Cafe Splat 161
Cafe Sydney 34
Caffe Jam (East Gosford) 239
Camoewarra Estate (Cambewarra) 255
Candelo Market (Candelo) 254
Canobolas-Smith Wine (Orange) 298
Canter (Scone) 217
Cape Cod (Deakin) 199
Capital Region Farmers' Market (Canberra) 212
Cargo Bar Pizza Lounge (Hobart) 308
Catalina 34
Catalonia 35
Caveau (Wollongong) 245
Cedro (Port Macquarie) 282
The Cellar (Pokolbin) 217
Centennial Parklands Restaurant 35
Centennial Vineyards (Bowral) 264
Centennial Vineyards Restaurant (Bowral) 257
Central Baking Depot 159
The Chairman and Yip (Canberra) 200
Chairman Mao 172
Chalkers Crossing Winery (Young) 298
Chat Thai 166
The Cheese Store (Bowral) 264
Chequers 36
Chez Pascal 169
Chianti Classico (Adelaide) 306
Chillingham Banana Cabana and Bush Tucker Garden (Chillingham) 283

good food guide 311

index

Chinta Ria ... Temple of Love 36
Chocolate Bliss (Charlestown) 241
Cibo e Vino 168
City Wine Shop (Melbourne) 301
Civic Dining 39
Clareville Kiosk 39
Claude's 40
Clock (Griffith) 285
Clonakilla (Murrumbateman) 213
Coast 40
Coast Bistro and Lounge (Terrigal) 239
Cobblestone Lane (Bathurst) 285
The Codfather 41
Coffs Coast Growers' Market (Coffs Harbour) 281
Colliers Sandwich Company 159
Commercial Fishermen's Co-operative (Wickham) 241
The Commoner (Fitzroy) 301
Concordia Club 169
Confit Bistro (Fortitude Valley) 303
Conservation Hut Cafe (Blackheath) 195
Coolangatta Estate (Shoalhaven Heads) 255
Cottage Point Inn 41
Country Fruit (Bathurst) 296
Courgette (Canberra) 200
Courtney's Brasserie 42, 184
The Cove 163
Cowra Farmers' Market (Cowra) 296
The Crabbe Hole 160
Cracked Pepper (Pokolbin) 227
Crackenback Cottage (Crackenback) 201
Credo (Thredbo Village) 201
Crema Espresso Bar (Port Macquarie) 282
The Crosstown Eating House (Woolloongabba) 304
Cucina Viscontini 173
Cumulus Inc (Melbourne) 301
Cutler & Co (Fitzroy) 301
d'Arry's Verandah (McLaren Vale) 306
da Gianni trattoria 42
Da Wan Ido 168
The Dairy Shed (Bodalla) 253
Dangerous Dan's Butchery (Macksville) 281
Danks Street Depot 43
Darley's (Katoomba) 188
Deli Goose Cafe (Killcare) 240
Delicado Foods 168
The Depot on Darby (Cooks Hill) 240
Deus Cafe 173, 177
Dickson Asian Noodle House (Dickson) 209
Diggies (Wollongong) 252
Din Tai Fung 166
Dish (Byron Bay) 267

Divido (Mount Hawthorn) 307
Dojo Bread (Braidwood) 254
Dolce Dolce Pasticceria (Griffith) 297
Dome 43
Dov at Delectica 160
Dubbo Farmers' Market (Dubbo) 295
Dukes Lane 44
Dynasty 182
Echoes (Katoomba) 189
Efendy 44
El Bulli del Punto 172
Element Bistro 45
Elio 45
Eltham Valley Pantry (Eltham) 279
Eltons Brasserie (Mudgee) 286
Elysium 46
Emma's On Liberty 46
Emperor's Garden Barbecue 166
The Emporium Food Company (Berry) 252
Era Bistro (South Brisbane) 304
Esca Bimbadgen (Pokolbin) 218
Eschalot (Berrima) 257
Esco Pazzo (Mittagong) 258
est. 47
Estabar (Newcastle) 240
Etch 47
Eurolounge 48, 184
Exeter General Store (Exeter) 263
Fare Nosh 48
fatbellykat (Brunswick Heads) 267
Feast Catering (Cooks Hill) 241
Fekerte's (Dickson) 202
Fellini (Main Beach) 304
Fiasco Ristorante (Coffs Harbour) 268
Fico Ristorante 49
finefish 49
Fins (South Kingscliff) 268
Fiorenzoni 50
Firestick Cafe (Pokolbin) 218
Fish & Wine (Coolangatta) 305
Fish Face 50
Fisherman's Wharf 182
Fishermen's Wharf Seafoods at the Co-op (Nelson Bay) 241
Fishmongers (Byron Bay) 280
Fix St James 51
Flair (Erina Heights) 232
Flavour of India 51
Flavours of Peking 52
Flinders Inn 52
Flooded Gums (Bonville) 269
Flutterbies Cottage Cafe (Tyalgum) 282
Flying Fish 55
Flying Fish Cafe (Port Elliot) 306
Flying Fox Cafe 161
Fook Yuen 55
Forbes & Burton 161

Forty One 56
Four in Hand Dining Room 56
Fourth Village Providore 162
Foveaux Restaurant + Bar 57
Foxwood Farm Fine Food Cafe (Running Stream) 294
Frangipan (Angourie) 269
Fratelli Paradiso 57
Fresca (Bangalow) 270
Fresh Espresso and Food Bar (Katoomba) 195
Fuuki 180
Fusion 7 (Port Macquarie) 270
fu manchu 58
Fyshwick Fresh Food Markets (Fyshwick) 212
Galileo 58
The Gallery (Katoomba) 189
Garfish 59
Gastronome (Bowral) 263
Gelato Messina 178
Georgie's at the Gallery (Grafton) 271
Gerald's Bar (North Carlton) 301
Gerringong Markets (Gerringong) 252
Gigibaba (Collingwood) 301
Ginger & Spice 59
The Ginger Room (Canberra) 202
Giuseppe, Arnaldo & Sons (Southbank) 302
Glace 178
Glass Brasserie 60
Glebe Point Diner 60
Glenella (Blackheath) 190
Goanna Bakery and Cafe (Lismore) 279
Golden Century 61
Golden Sichuan 61
Goldfish Bowl Espresso Bar (Armidale) 293
Gorman's (Yamba) 279
Gourmet Forty Two (Thredbo) 213
Grafton Market Square (Grafton) 279
Grappa 62
Grazing (Gundaroo) 185, 203
Great Lakes Market (Forster) 282
Greek Islands Taverna 170
Green Garage (Byron Bay) 280
Green Gourmet 62
Green Papaya (Armidale) 286
Green Zebra (Albury) 297
Griffith Butcher and Bakery (Griffith) 212
Grind Espresso Bar 163
Grove Estate Winery (Young) 298
Guillaume at Bennelong 63
Gumnut Patisserie (Bowral) 264
The Gunyah (Woollamia) 246
Guzman Y Gomez 178
Hai Au Lang Nuong 173
harbourkitchen&bar 63
Harley and John Seafoods (Fairy Meadow) 252
Harry's Cafe de Wheels 178
Hartley Valley Teahouse (Little

Hartley) 195
Harvest (North Fremantle) 307
Hayden's Pies (Ulladulla) 253
Hearth Fire Organic Wood-Fired Bakery (Bellingen) 280
Heatherbrae's Pies (Heatherbrae) 241
Hellenic Republic (Brunswick East) 302
Helm (Murrumbateman) 213
High Valley Wine & Cheese Co (Mudgee) 294
Ho's Dim Sum Kitchen 182
Hobarts (New Lambton) 233
Hodges Butchery (Mudgee) 295
Hominy Bakery (Katoomba) 196
Hotel Saravana Bhavan 64
The Hub Espresso Bar & Eatery (Bathurst) 295
Hugo's Bar Pizza 64
Hugos Lounge 156
Hugo's Manly 65
Hungry Duck (Berry) 185, 247
Hunter Belle Cheese (Muswellbrook) 228
Hunter Valley Cheese Company (Pokolbin) 228
Husky Bakery (Huskisson) 253
Hyams Beach Cafe (Hyams Beach) 247
Icebergs Dining Room and Bar 65
Ichi Ban Boshi 166
Il Baretto 170
Il Cacciatore (Pokolbin) 228
Il Lido Canteen (Cottesloe) 307
Il Perugino 66
il piave 66
Il Punto 67
Il Topolino Alimentari Delicatessen (Bowral) 264
Infusion @ 333 67
Intermezzo Ristorante 68
Iona Gardens Cafe & Nursery (Dalgety) 213
Iron Chef 68, 182
It's Wild Seafood (Coffs Harbour) 281
Jannei Goat Dairy (Lidsdale) 295
Japaz 71
Jasmin Indian Restaurant (Adelaide) 306
Jasper Peel Breads (Ulladulla) 253
Jaspers 71
Jimbaran 172
jimmy liks 72
Joe's Pizzeria Arax 168
Jonah's 72, 177
Josh's Cafe (Berrima) 258
Josophan's (Blackheath and Leura) 195
Journal Canteen (Melbourne) 302
Journeyman (Bowral) 259
Joy Luck Shanghai's Kitchen 173

312 good food guide

index

Jugemu & Shimbashi 73, 180
The Julep Lounge (Manuka) 212
Ju-Rin 73
Kable's 74
Kaki Lima 172
Kam Fook 74, 182
Katers (Sutton Forest) 259
Katipo 161
Kaysone Sweets 174
Kazbah on Darling 75, 177
Kelby's Cafe 164
Kensington Peking 75
Kerv Espresso Bar (Scone) 228
Kiama Produce Market (Kiama) 252
Kings Lane Sandwiches 172
Kingscliff Farmers & Friends Markets (Kingscliff) 283
Kit & Kaboodle 156
Kladis Estate (Wandandian) 255
Koi 180
Koi 76
Kokoh 162
Kookootonga Chestnut & Walnut Farm (Mount Irvine) 196
Krinkelwood (Broke) 229
Kuali 76
Kurri Kurri Farmers' Market (Kurri Kurri) 228
Kyrenia Cafe (Charlestown) 241
L'étoile 80
L'Ultime patisserie (Byron Bay) 280
La Grande Bouffe 77
La Grillade 77
La Locanda 78
La Perla 78
La Piadina 172
La Scala Restaurant (Griffith) 297
La Table (Mullumbimby) 185, 271
La Tratt 79
Lake House (Daylesford) 303
Lake Russell Gallery (Emerald Beach) 231
Lake's Folly (Pokolbin) 229
The Lakehouse Cafe (Murrays Beach) 241
Lamiche (Wamberal) 233
The Lane (Hahndorf) 306
The Larda (Scone) 228
Lark Hill (Bungendore) 213
Lattecino 164
Lazy River Estate (Dubbo) 294
Le Bukhara 79
Le Gall Patisserie (Bathurst) 295
Le Pelican 80
Le Sarab 174
Leaves & Fishes (Lovedale) 219
Leeandme (Wollongong) 252
Leura Gourmet (Leura) 195
Libertine 81
Lick the Spoon/ Waterfall Way Winery (Dorrigo) 281
The Light Brigade Bistro 81

Lillypilly Estate Winery (Leeton) 299
Little Creatures (Fremantle) 307
The Little Hand Stirred Jam Shop (Berrima) 264
Lizotte's (Kincumber, Lambton) 240
LNC Dessert House 167
The Local Taphouse 156
Locavore (Huskisson) 253
Lochiel House (Kurrajong Heights) 190
Lodge 241 Gallery Cafe (Bellingen) 281
Logan Wines (Mudgee) 298
Lolli Redini (Orange) 287
Long Track Pantry (Jugiong) 297
Longrain 82
Lorenzo's Diner (Wollongong) 248
Loriendale Organic Orchard (Wallaroo) 212
The Lott Food Store, Bakery & Cafe (Cooma) 213
Lotus 82
The Lotus Eaters Cafe (Cygnet) 308
Lovedale Smokehouse (Lovedale) 228
Low 302 157
Lucio Pizzeria 179
Lucio's 83
M & J's Butchery (Orange) 296
Machiavelli 83
Macleay Street Bistro 84
Mad Cow 84
The Magpie Cafe (Berrima) 263
Mahjong Room 87
Maitland Fresh Produce Markets (Maitland) 228
Maitland Markets (Maitland) 228
Maitre Karl 87
Majors Lane (Lovedale) 219
Makoto 180
Malabar 88
The Malaya 88
Mamak 167
Manly Phoenix 183
Manners & Borg (Orange) 296
The Manse (North Adelaide) 306
Manta 89
Manuka Fine Foods (Manuka) 212
Margan (Broke) 220
Margan Wines (Broke) 229
Margot (St Helens) 308
Marigold 89
Marque 90
Maryvale Lavender Farm (Cobargo) 254
Mash Cafe (Glenbrook) 195
Mauger's Meats (Burrawang) 264
Mavis's Kitchen & Cabins (Uki via Murwillumbah) 283
MCA Cafe 90
Me Wah (Hobart) 309

Meadowbank Estate (Cambridge) 309
Mecca Espresso 160
Medusa Greek Taverna 91
Melba's Verandah (Broadwater) 279
Mezzalira (Canberra) 203
Mezzaluna 91
Michael's Ristorante (Wollongong) 248
The Milk Factory Gallery Cafe (Bowral) 263
Milsons 92
Mino 92
Miso 167
Mission 93
Mittagong Markets (Mittagong) 264
Mojo's on Wilderness (Rothbury) 220
Momo (Melbourne) 302
The Monastery Brasserie (Wagga Wagga) 287
Moncur Terrace 93
Mongers 179
Monkey Magic 180
Montagu 91
Montrose Berry Farm (Sutton Forest) 264
Monty's (Tamworth) 294
Moore & Moore (Fremantle) 307
Morpeth Sourdough (Morpeth) 228
MoS Cafe 94
Mount Majura (Majura) 213
MoVida (Melbourne) 302
Mudgee Gourmet @ The Railway (Mudgee) 295
Mudgee Organic Market (Mudgee) 295
Mumu Grill 94
Muse (Noosa Heads) 305
Muse (Pokolbin) 221
Must Winebar (Margaret River) 308
Mylan (Wollongong) 252
Nabiac Market (Nabiac) 282
Nahm Thai (Perth) 308
Neila (Cowra) 185, 288
Nelson's Brasserie 95
Neptune Palace 95
Netherby House Cafe (Kempsey) 282
Nethercote Market (Nethercote) 254
New Brighton Farmer's Market (New Brighton) 280
New Leaf Cafe (Murwillumbah) 283
Newcastle City Farmers' Market (Broadmeadow) 241
Newtown Providores (Dubbo) 295
Nilgiri's 96
No. 2 Oak Street (Bellingen) 272
North Bondi Italian Food 96
North Coast Lismore Showground (Lismore) 279

North Street Cafe (Batemans Bay) 254
Northern Rivers Seafood (West Ballina) 279
Nostos 97
Nu Nu (Palm Cove) 305
Nu5 98
Nugan Estate Winery (Griffith) 299
Number One Wine Bar 97
O'Connell Cafe (O'Connell) 295
Ocean Chill (Nambucca Heads) 272
Ocean (The Entrance) 234
Ocean Room 98
Oceanic Thai 99
Old Bus Depot Markets (Kingston) 212
The Old Convent (Borenore) 296
The Old George & Dragon (East Maitland) 221
Old Goulburn Brewery (Goulburn) 264
The Olive Farm (Falls Creek) 253
Oliveto 99
Olivo (Byron Bay) 273
Onda (Terrigal) 234
Onde 100
one one one (Byron Bay) 280
Onesta Cucina (Bowral) 260
onred (Red Hill) 204
Opera Bar 157
O-pes (Lennox Head) 273
Orange Farmers' Market (Orange) 296
Organic Feast (East Maitland) 228
Orient Express Eatery (Byron Bay) 274
Oscillate Wildly 100
Osvaldo Polletti 103
Otto Ristorante 103
Ottoman Cuisine 104
Ottoman Cuisine (Barton) 204
Out of Africa 169
Out of the Blue 179
Pacific Dining Room (Byron Bay) 274
Paddington Alimentari 161
Paddock to Pantry (Scone) 228
Pages on Pine (Leeton) 288
Palace Chinese 104, 183
The Palms Cafe (Stanwell Park) 252
Paragon Cafe (Goulburn) 263
Park Cafe on Chalmers 163
Parlour Wine Room (Canberra) 212
Patisse 163
Paupiettes (Lismore) 275
Pausa 160
PeaBerry's Gourmet Coffee (New Lambton) 241
Pearl (Richmond) 302
Pearl Cafe (Woolloongabba) 304
Pearls on the Beach (Pearl Beach) 235
The Pearly Oyster Bar (Eatemans Bay) 254

good food guide 313

index

Pendolino 105
Perama 105
Perenti (Gloucester) 281
Petty Cash Cafe 164
Philip Shaw Wines' Koomooloo Vineyard (Orange) 298
Piccolo Restaurant & Wine Bar (North Hobart) 309
Pickled and Pitted (Broke) 228
Pier 106
Piermont Restaurant (Swansea) 309
Pierres on George (Launceston) 309
Pilgrims Wholefoods Cafe (Milton) 253
Pilu at Freshwater 106
Pilu Kiosk 162
Pippi's Cafe & Bar (Yamba) 275
Pizza e Birra 107
Pizzas in the Mist (Robertson) 263
Plan B 160
Podfood (Pialligo) 205
The Point (Ballina) 276
Pomegranate Thai 107
Pompei's (Bondi Beach) 108
Pony Lounge & Dining 108
Port Macquarie Market (Port Macquarie) 282
Post Cafe and Bar (Moss Vale) 260
Postales Restaurante & Tapas Bar 109
The Posthouse (Berry) 249
The Pot Food & Wine (Hyde Park) 306
Premium Coffee Roasters (Wagga Wagga) 297
Primavera Gourmet Deli & Cafe (Hazelbrook) 196
Prime 109
Prince Restaurant 183
Provenance (Beechworth) 303
Pukara Estate (Muswellbrook) 228
Pulp Kitchen (Ainslie) 212
Qmin 110
The Quaff Shop Gallery Cafe (Mudgee) 294
Quay 110
Quinty Cake and Bakehouse (Uranquinty) 297
Quinty on the Run (Wagga Wagga) 297
Racine at La Colline (Orange) 289
Rainbow Region Organic Market (Lismore) 279
Raincheck (North Hobart) 309
Rajarani (Mudgee) 289
Rama's (Pearce) 212
Rambutan 111
Ranae's Choclatique (Bowraville) 281
Ratu Sari 111
Raw Bar 181
Red Box Pizza (Tuross Heads) 254
Red Chilli 112
The Red Door Cafe (Leura) 195
Red Ginger (Byron Bay) 280
Red Lantern 112, 184

Red Olive (Mittagong) 261
The Red Pomegranate (Wagga Wagga) 297
Reef House (Palm Cove) 305
Reef (Terrigal) 235
Regal 183
Rengaya 113
Republic Dining 113
The Restaurant @ Art Gallery of NSW 114
Restaurant Arras 114
The Restaurant at 3 Weeds 115
The Restaurant at The Byron at Byron (Byron Bay) 276
Restaurant Atelier 115
Restaurant Balzac 116
Restaurant Botanica (Pokolbin) 222
Restaurant Como (Blaxland) 191
Restaurant Cuvee (Pokolbin) 222
Restaurant II (Newcastle) 236
Restaurant Two (Brisbane) 304
Restaurant Two Forty (Boomerang Beach) 277
Ripples at Chowder Bay 116
Ritual (Nelson Bay) 236
River Deli Cafe (Nowra) 253
The River Moruya (Moruya) 250
Riverina Cheese (Albury) 297
Riverina Grove (Griffith) 297
Riverview Hotel & Dining 119
Robert Stein Vineyard (Mudgee) 299
Roberts (Pokolbin) 223
Robertson Cheese Store Cafe (Robertson) 263
Rock (Pokolbin) 223
Rocket 119
Rockpool 120
Rockpool Bar and Grill 120, 179
rocksalt (Wickham) 237
Roladoor (Hamilton) 241
Rose & Sparrow (Central Tilba) 254
Rose Garden Thai (Dubbo) 290
Rosso Pomodoro 179
Roth's Wine Bar (Mudgee) 294
Royal Bar & Grill 121
The Royal Brasserie and Steakhouse (Bowral) 263
Royal Mail Hotel (Dunkeld) 303
Rubicon (Griffith) 205
Ruby Chinese (Dickson) 206
Ruby's Cafe and Books (Dorrigo) 281
Ruby's Diner 161
The Rum Diaries 157
Rumi (Brunswick East) 302
Ryo's 169
Sabayon (Canberra) 206
Safi 121
Sage (Braddon) 207
Sahra by the River 122
Sailors Thai 122
Sailors Thai Canteen 123

Sailors Thai Potts Point 123
Sails on Lavender Bay 123
Sakana-Ya 124
Salonbim 184
Salt Bean Espresso Bar (Kingscliff) 283
Saltwater (Bermagui) 254
Saltwater (Emerald Beach) 277
Samuels (Thirroul) 250
Sanders Waterfront 124
Sassafras Creek Cafe (Kurrajong) 196
Sassi at Bale (Port Douglas) 305
Satay Inn 170
Satiate (Bangalow) 278
Sea Sweet 164
Sea Treasure 125, 183
Seagrass Brasserie (Huskisson) 251
Seahaven Cafe (Gerroa) 252
Sean's Kitchen 125
Sean's Panaroma 126, 185
Seasalt (Terrigal) 240
Selah 126
Selkirks (Orange) 290
Sepia 127
Sevardi Cucina Italiana 127
Shakey Tables (North Rothbury) 224
Shanghai Dumplings 174
Shanghai Yangzhou House 170
Shaw Vineyard Estate (Murrumbateman) 213
Shoalhaven Heads Seafood and Produce Markets (Shoalhaven Heads) 253
Sideplate 163
Sideways Deli Cafe 164
Silk's Brasserie (Leura) 191
Silo Bakery & Cheeseroom (Kingston) 207
Silo Restaurant & Lounge (Newcastle) 237
Silvas 128
Single Origin Roasters 160
Sister's Rock (Orange) 291
The Sleepy Monkey (Tamworth) 294
Small Bar 157
Small Winemakers Centre (Pokolbin) 229
The Smelly Cheese Shop (Pokolbin) 228
The Smokehouse 171
Smokehouse Cafe (Hall) 208
Snakebean 172
Snapper Spot (Terrigal) 240
Snows Patisserie, the Junction (The Junction) 241
Solitary (Leura Falls) 192
Sono (Hamilton) 304
Sonoma Bakery Cafe 164
Source Cafe (Maryville) 241
The Source Espresso Bar 162
sourcedining (Albury) 291
Space Espresso Bar 163
Sparrow kitchen and bar (North Adelaide) 307
Spice I Am 128
Spice It Up Thai (Mullumbimby) 280

Spice Temple 129
Spicer Street Cafe 177
Spirit House (Yandina) 305
St Elmo (Byron Bay) 280
St Germain Patisserie 163
Star Anise (Shenton Park) 308
Starfish Avalon 129
Steel Bar and Grill 130
Sticky Bar 157
Stillwaters (Davistown) 238
Stockmarket Cafe (Leura) 196
Stones (Sutton Forest) 261
Strangers with Candy 130
The Stunned Mullet (Port Macquarie) 278
Subsolo 131
Sugarcane 131
Sugaroom 132
Summit 132
Sunnybrae Restaurant (Birregurra) 303
Supply (Huskisson) 253
Sushi Bar Hiro 171
Sushi Choo 181
sushi e 135
Sushi Fusion 181
Sushi Studio 181
Sweet Solutions (Terrigal) 240
The Sweet Spot Patisserie 161
Swell Coffee (Wollongong) 252
Sydney Street Cafe (Mogo) 254
Szechuan Garden 135
Tabou 136
Taiki 136
Tak Kee Roast Inn (Dickson) 212
Tamburlaine (Pokolbin) 229
Tan Viet 174
Taste (Sawtell) 281
taste Canowindra (Canowindra) 296
Taste Gourmet Grocer and Cafe (East Gosford) 240
Taste on Sussex Lane 137
Tastevin Bistro & Wine Bar 137
T-Chow (Adelaide) 307
The Tea Room Gunners' Barracks 138
The Tea Room QVB 138
Temasek 139
Teppanyaki 139
Terrace (Thredbo Village) 208
The Terrace On Pittwater 140
Tetsuya's 140
Thanh Binh 141
Thelma & Louise 162
Thredbo Valley Distillery (Jindabyne) 213
Tilba Growers' Market (Central Tilba) 254
Tilbury Hotel 141
Time to Vino 142, 157
Toko Surry Hills 142
Ton Ton Regent 168
Tonic (Millthorpe) 292
Tosolini's (Canberra) 212
Totally Local (Orange) 296
Tower Estate (Pokolbin) 229
Tran's 143
Tropical Fruit World (Duranbah) 283

index

Tutti Fruitti at Bilpin (Bilpin) 196
Tutto Continental (Mawson) 212
Twenty by Twelve (Blueys Beach) 282
Two Doors Tapas and Wine Bar (Dubbo) 294
Uccello 143
Uchi Lounge 171
Ummarin Thai 173
Union Bank Wine Store (Orange) 292
Union Bank Wine Shop (Orange) 296
Universal 146
Urbane (Brisbane) 304
Utopia (Bangalow) 280
Valley Edge Cafe (Cobargo) 254
The Vanguard 157
Vanitas (Main Beach) 305
Vaucluse House Tearooms 161
Velero 146
Velluto 157
Ventuno 147
Verandah 147
The Verandah (Pokolbin) 224
Verde Restaurant & Bar 148
Vicini 174
Victoria Room 157
Vida (Bondi) 262
The Vineyard Kitchen (Ulladulla) 251
Vini 148
Vue de Monde (Melbourne) 302
Vulcans (Blackheath) 192
Wagga Wagga Farmers Market (Wagga Wagga) 297
Wakana 159
Wall Cafe 160
Waqu 149
Wasabi (Noosa Heads) 305
Wasavie 149
Waters Edge (Parkes) 209
Wauchope Market (Wauchope) 282
The Welcome Hotel 150
Westend Estate Wines (Griffith) 299
The Wharf 150
Whisk & Pin Store and Cafe (Medlow Bath) 196
Whitewater 151
Wholly Smoked Organic Foods (Byron Bay) 280
Whyworry Wines (Uralla) 299
Wicked Chocolates (Warners Bay) 24
Wild Duck (Albany) 308
Wild Food (Bowral) 264
Willow Vale Mill (Laggan) 262
The Wine House and Kitchen (Pokolbin) 227
Wineglass Bar & Grill (Mudgee) 293
Wingham Showground Market (Wingham) 282
Wollongong Produce and Creative Traders Market (Wollongong) 252

Yellow Bistro & Food Store 151
Ying's 153
Yoshii 153, 181
Young & Region Farmer's Market (Young) 296
Yum Yum Eatery (Hardys Bay) 238
Zaaffran 154
Zanziba (Terrigal) 240
Zanzibar (Merimbula) 251
Zenya 169
Zest BYO (Temora) 297
Zest (Nelson Bay) 239
Zeta 157
Zilver 154
Zokoko (Emu Heights) 196
Zweefers Divine Cakes (Fairy Meadow) 252
Zyka 171

Cuisine

Asian
Ashcrofts (Blackheath) 188
Banana Blossom (Cremorne) 13
The Chairman and Yip (Canberra) 200
fu manchu (Darlinghurst) 58
Green Gourmet (St Leonards, Newtown) 62
Hungry Duck (Berry) 185, 247
Infusion @ 333 (Sydney) 67
jimmy liks (Potts Point) 72
Orient Express Eatery (Byron Bay) 274
Spice Temple (Sydney) 129
Sugarcane (Surry Hills) 131
Teppanyaki (Sydney) 139
Zilver (Haymarket) 154

British
a'Mews (Glebe) 7
The Old George & Dragon (East Maitland) 221
Restaurant Arras (Walsh Bay) 114
Restaurant Balzac (Randwick) 116
Riverview Hotel & Dining (Balmain) 119

Chinese
Billy Kwong (Surry Hills) 20, 184
Chequers (Chatswood) 36
Flavours of Peking (Castlecrag) 52
Fook Yuen (Chatswood) 55
fu manchu (Darlinghurst) 58
Golden Century (Sydney) 61
Golden Sichuan (Sydney) 61
Iron Chef (Cabramatta) 68, 182
Kam Fook (Bondi Junction, Chatswood) 74
Kensington Peking (Kensington) 75
Mahjong Room (Surry Hills) 87
Marigold (Sydney) 89
Neptune Palace (Circular Quay) 95

Palace Chinese (Sydney) 104, 183
Red Chilli (Haymarket) 112
Ruby Chinese (Dickson) 206
Sea Treasure (Crows Nest) 125, 183
Szechuan Garden (St Leonards) 135
Ying's (Crows Nest) 153

Contemporary
305 Restaurant & Cafe (Maitland) 214
55 on Collins (Kiama) 242
9inety 2wo (Bathurst) 284
Altitude (The Rocks) 4
Alto (Acton) 197
Amanda's on the Edge (Pokolbin) 215
Anise (Canberra) 198
Aqua Dining (Milsons Point) 8
Aria (East Circular Quay) 9
Arnott's Bakehouse (Morpeth) 215
Artespresso (Kingston) 198
Assiette (Surry Hills) 10
Bamboo (Casuarina Beach) 265
Bannisters (Mollymook) 243
The Bathers' Pavilion Restaurant (Balmoral) 14
Bayswater Brasserie (Kings Cross) 15
Bellachara (Gerringong) 244
Bellevue Hotel Dining Room (Paddington) 17
Bentley Restaurant & Bar (Surry Hills) 17
Berry Woodfired Sourdough Bakery (Berry) 244
Bird Cow Fish (Surry Hills) 23
Bistro 345 (Thirroul) 245
Bistro CBD (Sydney) 24
Bistro-Fax (Sydney) 24
The Black Swan (Berrima) 256
The Book Kitchen (Surry Hills) 29
Botanic Gardens Restaurant (Sydney) 30
Byron Beach Cafe (Byron Bay) 266
Cafe Sydney (Circular Quay) 34
Canter (Scone) 217
Catalina (Rose Bay) 34
The Cellar (Pokolbin) 217
Centennial Parklands Restaurant (Centennial Park) 35
Centennial Vineyards Restaurant (Bowral) 257
Clareville Kiosk (Clareville Beach) 39
Clock (Griffith) 285
Cobblestone Lane (Bathurst) 285
Cottage Point Inn (Cottage Point) 41
Crackenback Cottage (Crackenback) 201
Credo (Thredbo Village) 201
Danks Street Depot (Waterloo) 43

Darley's (Katoomba) 188
Dish (Byron Bay) 267
Dome (Sydney) 43
Echoes (Katoomba) 189
Eltons Brasserie (Mudgee) 286
Elysium (Randwick) 46
Esca Bimbadgen (Pokolbin) 218
Eschalot (Berrima) 257
est. (Sydney) 47
Fare Nosh (Summer Hill) 48
Firestick Cafe (Pokolbin) 218
Flair (Erina Heights) 232
Flooded Gums (Bonville) 269
Forty One (Sydney) 56
Frangipan (Angourie) 269
Fusion 7 (Port Macquarie) 270
Georgie's at the Gallery (Grafton) 271
The Ginger Room (Canberra) 202
Glebe Point Diner (Glebe) 60
Glenella (Blackheath) 190
Grazing (Gundaroo) 185, 203
The Gunyah (Woollamia) 246
Hooarts (New Lambton) 233
Hyams Beach Cafe (Hyams Beach) 247
Jaspers (Hunters Hill) 71
Jonah's (Whale Beach) 72, 177
Journeyman (Bowral) 259
Kable's (Sydney) 74
Lamiche (Wamberal) 233
Lochiel House (Kurrajong Heights) 190
Lolli Redini (Orange) 287
Lotus (Potts Point) 82
Macleay Street Bistro (Potts Point) 84
Majors Lane (Lovedale) 219
Manta (Woolloomooloo) 89
MCA Cafe (The Rocks) 90
Misons (Kirribilli) 92
Mission (Chippendale) 93
Mojo's on Wilderness (Rothbury) 220
The Monastery Brasserie (Wagga Wagga) 287
MoS Cafe (MoS Cafe) 94
Muse (Pokolbin) 221
Nela (Cowra) 185, 288
Nelson's Brasserie (The Rocks) 95
No. 2 Oak Street (Bellingen) 272
Ocean Chill (Nambucca Heads) 272
Olivo (Byron Bay) 273
oned (Red Hill) 204
O-pes (Lennox Head) 273
Oscillate Wildly (Newtown) 100
Pacific Dining Room (Byron Bay) 274
Paupiettes (Lismore) 275
Pearls on the Beach (Pearl Beach) 275
Pippi's Cafe & Bar (Yamba) 275
Podfood (Pialligo) 205
The Point (Ballina) 276

good food guide 315

index

Pony Lounge & Dining (The Rocks) 108
Post Cafe and Bar (Moss Vale) 260
The Posthouse (Berry) 249
Quay (The Rocks) 110
Racine at La Colline (Orange) 289
Red Olive (Mittagong) 261
Reef (Terrigal) 235
The Restaurant @ Art Gallery of NSW (Sydney) 114
The Restaurant at The Byron at Byron (Byron Bay) 276
Restaurant Botanica (Pokolbin) 222
Restaurant Como (Blaxland) 191
Restaurant Cuvee (Pokolbin) 222
Restaurant II (Newcastle) 236
Restaurant Two Forty (Boomerang Beach) 277
Ripples at Chowder Bay (Mosman) 116
Ritual (Nelson Bay) 236
Roberts (Pokolbin) 223
Rock (Pokolbin) 223
Rocket (Chatswood) 119
Rockpool (The Rocks) 120
Royal Bar & Grill (Paddington) 121
Sabayon (Canberra) 206
Sage (Braddon) 207
Sails on Lavender Bay (McMahons Point) 123
Saltwater (Emerald Beach) 277
Samuels (Thirroul) 250
Sanders Waterfront (Cabarita) 124
Seagrass Brasserie (Huskisson) 251
Sean's Panaroma (Bondi Beach) 126, 185
Selah (Circular Quay) 126
Selkirks (Orange) 290
Sepia (Sydney) 127
Shakey Tables (North Rothbury) 224
Silk's Brasserie (Leura) 191
Silo Bakery & Lounge (Newcastle) 237
Sister's Rock (Orange) 291
Smokehouse Cafe (Hall) 208
Solitary (Leura Falls) 192
sourcedining (Albury) 291
Starfish Avalon (Avalon) 129
Stillwaters (Davistown) 238
Stones (Sutton Forest) 261
Strangers with Candy (East Redfern) 130
The Stunned Mullet (Port Macquarie) 278
Sugaroom (Pyrmont) 132
Summit (Sydney) 132
Taste on Sussex Lane (Sydney) 137
The Tea Room Gunners' Barracks (Georges Heights) 138
The Tea Room QVB (Sydney) 138

Terrace (Thredbo Village) 208
The Terrace On Pittwater (Newport) 140
Tilbury Hotel (Woolloomooloo) 141
Time to Vino (Darlinghurst) 142, 157
Tonic (Millthorpe) 292
Union Bank Wine Bar/Wine Store (Orange) 292
Universal (Darlinghurst) 146
Vida (Bowral) 262
Waters Edge (Parkes) 209
The Wharf (Walsh Bay) 150
Whitewater (Manly) 151
Wineglass Bar & Grill (Mudgee) 293
Yellow Bistro & Food Store (Potts Point) 151
Yum Yum Eatery (Hardys Bay) 238
Zanzibar (Merimbula) 251

Ethiopian
Fekerte's (Dickson) 202

European
The Albion (Braidwood) 243
Astral (Pyrmont) 11
Aubergine (Griffith) 199
Bacchus (Newcastle) 231
Bambini Trust Cafe (Sydney) 13, 176
Becasse (Sydney) 16, 184
Bistrode (Surry Hills) 26
Blancmange (Petersham) 27
Bronte Road Bistro (Waverley) 30
The Burlington Bar and Dining (Crows Nest) 32
Ça Marche (Port Macquarie) 266
Courgette (Canberra) 200
Courtney's Brasserie (Parramatta) 42
Dukes Lane (East Balmain) 44
Etch (Sydney) 47
Eurolounge (Castle Hill) 48
Foveaux Restaurant + Bar (Surry Hills) 57
Onda (Terrigal) 234
Republic Dining (Sydney) 113
The Restaurant at 3 Weeds (Rozelle) 115
Restaurant Atelier (Glebe) 115
The River Moruya (Moruya) 250
Rubicon (Griffith) 205
Satiate (Bangalow) 278
Silo Bakery & Cheeseroom (Kingston) 207
Verandah (Sydney) 147
The Welcome Hotel (Rozelle) 150
Willow Vale Mill (Laggan) 262
Zest (Nelson Bay) 239

French
a'Mews (Glebe) 7
Aperitif (Potts Point) 8
Berowra Waters Inn (Berowra Waters) 19
Bilson's (Sydney) 20

Bistro Molines (Mount View) 216
Bistro Moncur (Woollahra) 25
Bistro Ortolan (Leichhardt) 25
Bistro Tartine (Hamilton) 232
Blancharu (Elizabeth Bay) 27
Caveau (Wollongong) 245
Claude's (Woollahra) 40
Element Bistro (Sydney) 45
Four in Hand Dining Room (Paddington) 56
Galileo (Sydney) 58
The Gallery (Katoomba) 189
Glass Brasserie (Sydney) 60
Guillaume at Bennelong (Sydney) 63
Katers (Sutton Forest) 259
L'étoile (Paddington) 80
La Grande Bouffe (Rozelle) 77
La Grillade (Crows Nest) 77
La Table (Mullumbimby) 185, 271
Le Pelican (Darlinghurst) 80
Libertine (Kings Cross) 81
The Light Brigade Bistro (Woollahra) 81
Marque (Surry Hills) 90
The Old George & Dragon (East Maitland) 221
Onde (Darlinghurst) 100
Pagès on Pine (Leeton) 288
Prime (Sydney) 109
Restaurant Balzac (Randwick) 116
Tabou (Surry Hills) 136
Tastevin Bistro & Wine Bar (Darlinghurst) 137
Tetsuya's (Sydney) 140

Greek
Civic Dining (Sydney) 39
fatbellykat (Brunswick Heads) 267
Medusa Greek Taverna (Sydney) 91
Nostos (Leichhardt) 97
Perama (Petersham) 105

Indian
Abhi's (North Strathfield) 2
Aki's (Woolloomooloo) 3
Bayleaf Brasserie (Crows Nest) 15
Flavour of India (Edgecliff) 51
Hotel Saravana Bhavan (Croydon) 64
Le Bukhara (Double Bay) 79
Malabar (Darlinghurst, Crows Nest) 88
Nilgiri's (St Leonards) 96
Qmin (St Leonards) 110
Rajarani (Mudgee) 289
Zaaffran (Darling Harbour) 154

Indonesian
Ratu Sari (Kingsford) 111

Italian
a tavola (Darlinghurst) 2
Acquazul (Newcastle) 230
Alio (Redfern) 3
Amici (Cammeray) 7
Barrenjoey House (Palm Beach) 14

bel mondo (The Rocks) 16
Bells at Killcare (Killcare Heights) 231
Beppi's (East Sydney) 18
The Beresford Hotel (Darlinghurst) 18
Big Mama's (Woollahra) 19
Blackwater (Sans Souci) 26
Buon Ricordo (Paddington) 31
buzo trattoria (Woollahra) 33
Cafe Sopra (Potts Point) 33
Coast (Sydney) 40
da Gianni trattoria (Annandale) 42
Elio (Leichhardt) 45
Esco Pazzo (Mittagong) 258
Fiasco Ristorante (Coffs Harbour) 268
Fico Ristorante (Balmain) 49
Fiorenzoni (Chatswood) 50
Fratelli Paradiso (Potts Point) 57
Grappa (Leichhardt) 62
harbourkitchen&bar (The Rocks) 63
Hugo's Bar Pizza (Kings Cross) 64
Hugo's Manly (Manly) 65
Il Perugino (Mosman) 66
il piave (Rozelle) 66
Il Punto (Liverpool) 67
Intermezzo Ristorante (Sydney) 68
La Locanda (Bronte) 78
La Perla (Gladesville) 78
La Tratt (Fairfield) 79
Lorenzo's Diner (Wollongong) 248
Lucio's (Paddington) 83
Machiavelli (Sydney) 83
Margan (Broke) 220
Mezzalira (Canberra) 203
Mezzaluna (Potts Point) 91
Michael's Ristorante (Wollongong) 248
North Bondi Italian Food (North Bondi) 96
Oliveto (Rhodes) 99
Onesta Cucina (Bowral) 260
Osvaldo Polletti (Leichhardt) 103
Otto Ristorante (Woolloomooloo) 103
Pendolino (Sydney) 105
Pilu at Freshwater (Freshwater) 106
Pizza e Birra (Surry Hills) 107
Sevardi Cucina Italiana (Beecroft) 127
Uccello (Sydney) 143
Velero (Woolloomooloo) 146
Ventuno (Millers Point) 147
Verde Restaurant & Bar (Darlinghurst) 148
Vini (Surry Hills) 148

Japanese
Azuma (Sydney) 11
Azuma Kushiyaki (Sydney) 12
Blancharu (Elizabeth Bay) 27
Busshari (Potts Point) 32
Jugemu & Shimbashi (Neutral Bay) 73, 180

316 good food guide

index

Ju-Rin (Crows Nest) 73
Koi (Woolwich) 76
Mino (Mosman) 92
Ocean Room (The Rocks) 98
Prime (Sydney) 109
Rengaya (North Sydney) 113
Sakana-Ya (Crows Nest) 124
sushi e (Sydney) 135
Taiki (Lane Cove) 136
Tetsuya's (Sydney) 140
Toko Surry Hills (Surry Hills) 142
Waqu (Crows Nest) 149
Wasavie (Paddington) 149
Yoshii (Sydney) 153, 181

Lebanese
Emma's On Liberty (Enmore) 46
Safi (North Sydney) 121
Sahra by the River (Parramatta) 122

Malaysian
Chinta Ria ... Temple of Love (Sydney) 36
Ginger & Spice (Neutral Bay) 59
Kuali (Lane Cove) 76
The Malaya (Sydney) 88
Neptune Palace (Circular Quay) 93
Temasek (Parramatta) 139

Mauritian
Le Bukhara (Double Bay) 79

Mediterranean
Aperitif (Potts Point) 8
Ash St Cellar (Sydney) 10, 156
Barrenjoey House (Palm Beach) 14
Bin24 Wine Bar & Wood Fire Eatery (North Strathfield) 23
Brown Sugar (Bondi) 31
Cafe Beltree (Pokolbin) 216
Fix St James (Sydney) 51
Fresca (Bangalow) 270
Icebergs Dining Room and Bar (Bondi Beach) 65
Josh's Cafe (Berrima) 258
Number One Wine Bar (Sydney) 97
Tetsuya's (Sydney) 140
The Vineyard Kitchen (Ulladulla) 251
The Wine House and Kitchen (Pokolbin) 227

Middle Eastern
Almond Bar (Darlinghurst) 4
Kazbah on Darling (Balmain) 75, 177
Safi (North Sydney) 121

Pizza
Apple Bar (Bilpin) 187
Cargo Bar Pizza Lounge (Hobart) 308
Hugo's Bar Pizza (Kings Cross) 64
Hugo's Manly (Manly) 65
Moncur Terrace (Woollahra) 93
Pompei's (Bondi Beach) 108
Pizza e Birra (Surry Hills) 107

Pizzas in the Mist (Robertson) 263
Red Box Pizza (Tuross Heads) 254

Portuguese
Silvas (Petersham) 128
Subsolo (Sydney) 131

Seafood
The Boathouse on Blackwattle Bay (Glebe) 28
Cape Cod (Deakin) 199
The Codfather (Stanmore) 41
finefish (Neutral Bay) 49
Fins (South Kingscliff) 268
Fish Face (Darlinghurst) 50
Flying Fish (Pyrmont) 55
Garfish (Manly, Kirribilli, Crows Nest) 59
Iron Chef (Cabramatta) 68, 182
La Perla (Gladesville) 78
Leaves & Fishes (Lovedale) 219
Ocean (The Entrance) 234
Ocean Room (The Rocks) 98
Pier (Rose Bay) 106
rocksalt (Wickham) 237
Ying's (Crows Nest) 153

Singaporean
Ginger & Spice (Neutral Bay) 59
Temasek (Parramatta) 139

Spanish
Bodega (Surry Hills) 29
Catalonia (Kirribilli) 35
Postales Restaurante & Tapas Bar (Sydney) 109
Subsolo (Sydney) 131
Velero (Woolloomooloo) 146

Sri Lankan
Hotel Saravana Bhavan (Croydon) 64

Steakhouse
La Grillade (Crows Nest) 77
Mad Cow (Sydney) 84
Mumu Grill (Crows Nest) 94
Pagès on Pine (Leeton) 288
Prime (Sydney) 109
Rockpool Bar and Grill (Sydney) 120, 179
The Royal Brasserie and Steakhouse (Bowral) 263
Steel Bar and Grill (Sydney) 130

Taiwanese
Blue Eye Dragon (Pyrmont) 28

Tapas
Japaz (Neutral Bay) 71
Postales Restaurante & Tapas Bar (Sydney) 109
Two Doors Tapas and Wine Bar (Dubbo) 294

Thai
Arun Thai (Potts Point) 9
Bai Yok (Castlecrag) 12
Green Papaya (Armidale) 286
Longrain (Surry Hills) 82
Nu's (McMahons Point) 98
Oceanic Thai (Clovelly) 99
Pomegranate Thai (Balmain) 107

Rambutan (Darlinghurst) 111
Rose Garden Thai (Dubbo) 290
Sailors Thai (The Rocks, Potts Point) 122
Sailors Thai Canteen (The Rocks, Potts Point) 123
Spice I Am (Surry Hills) 128

Turkish
Efendy (Balmain) 44
Ottoman Cuisine (Walsh Bay) 104
Ottoman Cuisine (Barton) 204

Vietnamese
Libertine (Kings Cross) 81
Red Lantern (Surry Hills) 112, 184
Thanh Binh (Cabramatta) 141
Tran's (Mosman) 143

BYO

City
Abhi's (North Strathfield) 2
Alio (Redfern) 3
Amici (Cammeray) 7
Bai Yok (Castlecrag) 12
Banana Blossom (Cremorne) 13
The Bathers' Pavilion Restaurant (Balmoral) 14
Bayleaf Brasserie (Crows Nest) 15
Billy Kwong (Surry Hills) 20, 184
Bistro-Fax (Sydney) 24
Blanchard (Elizabeth Bay) 27
Blue Eye Dragon (Pyrmont) 28
The Book Kitchen (Surry Hills) 29
Brown Sugar (Bondi) 31
Busshari (Potts Point) 32
Cafe Sopra (Potts Point) 33
Chinta Ria ... Temple of Love (Sydney) 36
Claude's (Woollahra) 40
The Codfather (Stanmore) 41
da Gianni trattoria (Annandale) 42
Element Bistro (Sydney) 45
Elio (Leichhardt) 45
Emma's On Liberty (Enmore) 46
Fiorenzoni (Chatswood) 50
Fish Face (Darlinghurst) 50
Fix St James (Sydney) 51
Flavour of India (Edgecliff) 51
Flavours of Peking (Castlecrag) 52
fu manchu (Darlinghurst) 58
Garfish (Manly, Kirribilli, Crows Nest) 59
Ginger & Spice (Neutral Bay) 59
Glebe Point Diner (Glebe) 60
Golden Century (Sydney) 61
Golden Sichuan (Sydney) 61
Grappa (Leichhardt) 62
Hotel Saravana Bhavan (Croydon) 64
Il Perugino (Mosman) 66

Il Punto (Liverpool) 67
Iron Chef (Cabramatta) 68, 182
Jaspers (Hunters Hill) 71
Kazbah on Darling (Balmain) 75, 177
Kensington Peking (Kensington) 75
Kuali (Lane Cove) 76
La Perla (Gladesville) 78
Le Bukhara (Double Bay) 79
Macleay Street Bistro (Potts Point) 84
Maitre Karl (Willoughby) 87
Malabar (Darlinghurst, Crows Nest) 88
Milsons (Kirribilli) 92
Mino (Mosman) 92
Mission (Chippendale) 93
Mumu Grill (Crows Nest) 94
Nilgiri's (St Leonards) 96
Nu's (McMahons Point) 98
Oliveto (Rhodes) 99
Oscillate Wildly (Newtown) 100
Osvaldo Polletti (Leichhardt) 103
Perama (Petersham) 105
Pomegranate Thai (Balmain) 107
Pompei's (Bondi Beach) 108
Qmin (St Leonards) 110
Ratu Sari (Kingsford) 111
Red Chilli (Haymarket) 112
Rengaya (North Sydney) 113
Ripples at Chowder Bay (Mosman) 116
Rocket (Chatswood) 119
Safi (North Sydney) 121
Sahra by the River (Parramatta) 122
Sakana-Ya (Crows Nest) 124
Sea Treasure (Crows Nest) 125, 183
Sean's Panaroma (Bondi Beach) 126, 185
Sevardi Cucina Italiana (Beecroft) 127
Silvas (Petersham) 128
Spice I Am (Surry Hills) 128
Starfish Avalon (Avalon) 129
Strangers with Candy (East Redfern) 130
Szechuan Garden (St Leonards) 135
Taiki (Lane Cove) 136
Temasek (Parramatta) 139
Thanh Binh (Cabramatta) 141
Tran's (Mosman) 143
Waqu (Crows Nest) 149
Wasavie (Paddington) 149
Yellow Bistro & Food Store (Potts Point) 151
Ying's (Crows Nest) 153
Zilver (Haymarket) 154

Regional
The Albion (Braidwood) 243
Alto (Acton) 197
Amanda's on the Edge (Pokolbin) 215
Anise (Canberra) 198
Aubergine (Griffith) 199

good food guide 317

index

Berry Woodfired Sourdough Bakery (Berry) 244
Bistro 345 (Thirroul) 245
Bistro Molines (Mount View) 216
Cafe Beltree (Pokolbin) 216
Cape Cod (Deakin) 199
The Chairman and Yip (Canberra) 200
Clock (Griffith) 285
Cobblestone Lane (Bathurst) 285
Courgette (Canberra) 200
Crackenback Cottage (Crackenback) 201
Eltons Brasserie (Mudgee) 286
Esco Pazzo (Mittagong) 258
fatbellykat (Brunswick Heads) 267
Fekerte's (Dickson) 202
Flair (Erina Heights) 232
Frangipan (Angourie) 269
Fusion 7 (Port Macquarie) 270
The Gallery (Katoomba) 189
Georgie's at the Gallery (Grafton) 271
Glenella (Blackheath) 190
Green Papaya (Armidale) 286
Hungry Duck (Berry) 185, 247
Hyams Beach Cafe (Hyams Beach) 247
Josh's Cafe (Berrima) 258
Journeyman (Bowral) 259
Lamiche (Wamberal) 233
Lochiel House (Kurrajong Heights) 190
Mezzalira (Canberra) 203
Michael's Ristorante (Wollongong) 248
Muse (Pokolbin) 221
Neila (Cowra) 185, 288
No. 2 Oak Street (Bellingen) 272
Ocean Chill (Nambucca Heads) 272
Ocean (The Entrance) 234
Olivo (Byron Bay) 273
Onesta Cucina (Bowral) 260
onred (Red Hill) 204
Orient Express Eatery (Byron Bay) 274
Ottoman Cuisine (Barton) 204
Pagès on Pine (Leeton) 288
Paupiettes (Lismore) 275
Pearls on the Beach (Pearl Beach) 235
Pippi's Cafe & Bar (Yamba) 275
Podfood (Pialligo) 205
Post Cafe and Bar (Moss Vale) 260
Rajarani (Mudgee) 289
Reef (Terrigal) 235
Restaurant Como (Blaxland) 191
Restaurant II (Newcastle) 236
Rubicon (Griffith) 205
Sabayon (Canberra) 206
Sage (Braddon) 207
Saltwater (Emerald Beach) 277
Samuels (Thirroul) 250

Seagrass Brasserie (Huskisson) 251
The Stunned Mullet (Port Macquarie) 278
Tonic (Millthorpe) 292
The Verandah (Pokolbin) 224
Vulcans (Blackheath) 192
Waters Edge (Parkes) 209
Yum Yum Eatery (Hardys Bay) 238

Dine and Stay

Amanda's on the Edge (Pokolbin) 215
Bamboo (Casuarina Beach) 265
Bannisters (Mollymook) 243
Bellachara (Gerringong) 244
Bells at Killcare (Killcare Heights) 231
Canter (Scone) 217
Darley's (Katoomba) 188
Echoes (Katoomba) 189
Esca Bimbadgen (Pokolbin) 218
Flooded Gums (Bonville) 269
Glenella (Blackheath) 190
The Gunyah (Woollamia) 246
Katers (Sutton Forest) 259
Mojo's on Wilderness (Broke) 220
The Old George & Dragon (East Maitland) 221
Pacific Dining Room (Byron Bay) 274
Pippi's Cafe & Bar (Yamba) 275
The Point (Ballina) 276
The Posthouse (Berry) 248
Restaurant Botanica (Pokolbin) 222
The Restaurant at The Byron at Byron (Byron Bay) 276
Restaurant Two Forty (Boomerang Beach) 277
Saltwater (Emerald Beach) 277
Shakey Tables (North Rothbury) 224
Sister's Rock (Orange) 291
Terrace (Thredbo Village) 208
Vida (Bowral) 262
The Vineyard Kitchen (Ulladulla) 251
Willow Vale Mill (Laggan) 262
Wineglass Bar & Grill (Mudgee) 293

Late-night Dining

a tavola (Darlinghurst) 2
Acquazul (Newcastle) 230
Aperitif (Potts Point) 8
Bacchus (Newcastle) 231
Bentley Restaurant & Bar (Surry Hills) 17
Beppi's (East Sydney) 18
Bin24 Wine Bar & Wood Fire Eatery (North Strathfield) 23
The Book Kitchen (Surry Hills) 29

buzo trattoria (Woollahra) 33
Cafe Sydney (Circular Quay) 34
Chequers (Chatswood) 36
Efendy (Balmain) 44
Etch (Sydney) 47
Flavour of India (Edgecliff) 51
Fook Yuen (Chatswood) 55
Fratelli Paradiso (Potts Point) 57
Golden Sichuan (Sydney) 61
jimmy liks (Potts Point) 72
Kable's (Sydney) 74
L'étoile (Paddington) 80
Leaves & Fishes (Lovedale) 219
Longrain (Surry Hills) 82
Lotus (Potts Point) 82
Macleay Street Bistro (Potts Point) 84
Mad Cow (Sydney) 84
Marigold (Sydney) 89
Mezzaluna (Potts Point) 91
Number One Wine Bar (Sydney) 97
Nu's (McMahons Point) 98
Ocean Room (The Rocks) 98
Pizza e Birra (Surry Hills) 107
Pompei's (Bondi Beach) 108
Rambutan (Darlinghurst) 111
Rockpool (The Rocks) 120
Rockpool Bar and Grill (Sydney) 120, 179
Sea Treasure (Crows Nest) 125, 183
Subsolo (Sydney) 131
Tastevin Bistro & Wine Bar (Darlinghurst) 137
Teppanyaki (Sydney) 139
Time to Vino (Darlinghurst) 142, 157
Uccello (Sydney) 143
Velero (Woolloomooloo) 146
Ying's (Crows Nest) 153
Zilver (Haymarket) 154

New Entries

City

Ash St Cellar (Sydney) 10, 156
Azuma Kushiyaki (Sydney) 12
The Beresford Hotel (Darlinghurst) 18
Blancharu (Elizabeth Bay) 27
Bronte Road Bistro (Waverley) 30
Centennial Parklands Restaurant (Centennial Park) 35
Dukes Lane (East Balmain) 44
Elysium (Randwick) 46
Etch (Sydney) 47
Fico Ristorante (Balmain) 49
finefish (Neutral Bay) 49
Flinders Inn (Paddington) 52
Ginger & Spice (Neutral Bay) 59
Golden Sichuan (Sydney) 61
Hotel Saravana Bhavan (Croydon) 64
Hugo's Manly (Manly) 65

Iron Chef (Cabramatta) 68, 182
Japaz (Neutral Bay) 71
Ju-Rin (Crows Nest) 73
Koi (Woolwich) 76
Nostos (Leichhardt) 97
Postales Restaurante & Tapas Bar (Sydney) 109
Sahra by the River (Parramatta) 122
Sean's Kitchen (Pyrmont) 125
Sepia (Sydney) 127
Spice Temple (Sydney) 129
Steel Bar and Grill (Sydney) 130
Sugarcane (Surry Hills) 131
Tastevin Bistro & Wine Bar (Darlinghurst) 137
Time to Vino (Darlinghurst) 142, 157
Uccello (Sydney) 143
Velero (Woolloomooloo) 146
Ventuno (Millers Point) 147
Waqu (Crows Nest) 149

Regional

9inety 2wo (Bathurst) 284
305 Restaurant & Cafe (Maitland) 214
Acquazul (Newcastle) 230
The Albion (Braidwood) 243
Bistro 345 (Thirroul) 245
Bistro Molines (Mount View) 216
The Black Swan (Berrima) 256
Canter (Scone) 217
Fusion 7 (Port Macquarie) 270
Green Papaya (Armidale) 286
Hobarts (New Lambton) 233
Hyams Beach Cafe (Hyams Beach) 247
La Table (Mullumbimby) 185, 271
The Monastery Brasserie (Wagga Wagga) 287
Muse (Pokolbin) 221
Ocean Chill (Nambucca Heads) 272
onred (Red Hill) 204
Pagès on Pine (Leeton) 288
Pippi's Cafe & Bar (Yamba) 275
The Point (Ballina) 276
Post Cafe and Bar (Moss Vale) 260
Racine at La Colline (Orange) 289
Red Olive (Mittagong) 261
Restaurant Botanica (Pokolbin) 222
Restaurant Cuvee (Pokolbin) 222
Restaurant Two Forty (Boomerang Beach) 277
Ruby Chinese (Dickson) 206
Sister's Rock (Orange) 291
Stones (Sutton Forest) 261
The Albion (Braidwood) 243
The Black Swan (Berrima) 256
The Monastery Brasserie (Wagga Wagga) 287
The Vineyard Kitchen (Ulladulla) 251

index

Vida (Bowral) 262
The Wine House and Kitchen (Pokolbin) 227
Wineglass Bar & Grill (Mudgee) 293

Private Rooms

City
305 Restaurant & Cafe (Maitland) 214
a tavola (Darlinghurst) 2
a'Mews (Glebe) 7
Abhi's (North Strathfield) 2
Alio (Redfern) 3
Altitude (The Rocks) 4
Amici (Cammeray) 7
Aqua Dining (Milsons Point) 8
Aria (East Circular Quay) 9
Arun Thai (Potts Point) 9
Astral (Pyrmont) 11
Azuma (Sydney) 11
Bambini Trust Cafe (Sydney) 13, 176
Barrenjoey House (Palm Beach) 14
The Bathers' Pavilion Restaurant (Balmoral) 14
Bayleaf Brasserie (Crows Nest) 15
Bayswater Brasserie (Kings Cross) 15
bel mondo (The Rocks) 16
Bellevue Hotel Dining Room (Paddington) 17
Beppi's (East Sydney) 18
Berowra Waters Inn (Berowra Waters) 19
Big Mama's (Woollahra) 19
Bilson's (Sydney) 20
Bistro Ortolan (Leichhardt) 25
Blancmange (Petersham) 27
Botanic Gardens Restaurant (Sydney) 30
Buon Ricordo (Paddington) 31
Cafe Sopra (Potts Point) 33
Cafe Sydney (Circular Quay) 34
Catalonia (Kirribilli) 35
Chequers (Chatswood) 36
Claude's (Woollahra) 40
Coast (Sydney) 40
Courtney's Brasserie (Parramatta) 42
da Gianni Trattoria (Annandale) 42
Dukes Lane (East Balmain) 44
Efendy (Balmain) 44
Elio (Leichhardt) 45
Elysium (Randwick) 46
est. (Sydney) 47
Etch (Sydney) 47
Eurolounge (Castle Hill) 48
Flavours of Peking (Castlecrag) 52
Flying Fish (Pyrmont) 55
Fook Yuen (Chatswood) 55
Forty One (Sydney) 56
Four in Hand Dining Room (Paddington) 56
Fratelli Paradiso (Potts Point) 57

fu manchu (Darlinghurst) 58
Galileo (Sydney) 58
Garfish (Manly, Kirribilli, Crows Nest) 59
Glass Brasserie (Sydney) 60
Golden Century (Sydney) 61
Golden Sichuan (Sydney) 61
Green Gourmet (St Leonards, Newtown) 62
Guillaume at Bennelong (Sydney) 63
harbourkitchen&bar (The Rocks) 63
Hotel Saravana Bhavan (Croydon) 64
Il Perugino (Mosman) 66
Iron Chef (Cabramatta) 68, 182
Jaspers (Hunters Hill) 71
Jonah's (Whale Beach) 72, 177
Jugemu & Shimbashi (Neutral Bay) 73, 180
Kable's (Sydney) 74
Kensington Peking (Kensington) 75
Koi (Woolwich) 76
La Grillade (Crows Nest) 77
La Perla (Gladesville) 78
Le Pelican (Darlinghurst) 80
Libertine (Kings Cross) 81
Longrain (Surry Hills) 82
Lucio's (Paddington) 83
Mahjong Room (Surry Hills) 87
Manta (Woolloomooloo) 89
Marigold (Sydney) 89
Marque (Surry Hills) 90
Mezzaluna (Potts Point) 91
Milsons (Kirribilli) 92
Mission (Chippendale) 93
Neptune Palace (Circular Quay) 95
Nilgiri's (St Leonards) 96
Nu's (McMahons Point) 98
Ocean Room (The Rocks) 98
Otto Ristorante (Woolloomooloo) 103
Ottoman Cuisine (Walsh Bay) 104
Palace Chinese (Sydney) 104, 183
Pendolino (Sydney) 105
Perama (Petersham) 105
Pier (Rose Bay) 106
Pilu at Freshwater (Freshwater) 106
Prime (Sydney) 109
Quay (The Rocks) 110
Rambutan (Darlinghurst) 111
Red Chilli (Haymarket) 112
Rengaya (North Sydney) 113
Republic Dining (Sydney) 113
Restaurant Arras (Walsh Bay) 114
Restaurant Atelier (Glebe) 115
Restaurant Balzac (Randwick) 116
Ripples at Chowder Bay (Mosman) 116
Riverview Hotel & Dining (Balmain) 119
Rocket (Chatswood) 119
Rockpool (The Rocks) 120

Rockpool Bar and Grill (Sydney) 120, 179
Safi (North Sydney) 121
Sails on Lavender Bay (McMahons Point) 123
Sakana-Ya (Crows Nest) 124
Sanders Waterfront (Cabarita) 124
Sea Treasure (Crows Nest) 125, 183
Sean's Kitchen (Pyrmont) 125
Sepia (Sydney) 127
Spice Temple (Sydney) 129
Steel Bar and Grill (Sydney) 130
Strangers with Candy (East Redfern) 130
Subsolo (Sydney) 131
Tabou (Surry Hills) 136
The Tea Room Gunners' Barracks (Georges Heights) 138
Temasek (Parramatta) 139
Tetsuya's (Sydney) 140
The Burlington Bar and Dining (Crows Nest) 32
The Codfather (Stanmore) 41
The Malaya (Sydney) 88
The Restaurant @ Art Gallery of NSW (Sydney) 114
The Wharf (Walsh Bay) 150
Time to Vino (Darlinghurst) 142, 157
Toko Surry Hills (Surry Hills) 142
Tran's (Mosman) 143
Velero (Woolloomooloo) 146
Verde Restaurant & Bar (Darlinghurst) 148
Vini (Surry Hills) 148
Waqu (Crows Nest) 149
Wasavie (Paddington) 149
Ying's (Crows Nest) 153
Yoshii (Sydney) 153, 181
Zaaffran (Darling Harbour) 154
Zilver (Haymarket) 154

Regional
Amanda's on the Edge (Pokolbin) 215
Arnott's Bakehouse (Morpeth) 215
Artespresso (Kingston) 198
Bacchus (Newcastle) 231
Bamboo (Casuarina Beach) 265
Bannisters (Mollymook) 243
Bellachara (Gerringong) 244
Bells at Killcare (Killcare Heights) 231
Caveau (Wollongong) 245
The Cellar (Pokolbin) 217
Centennial Vineyards Restaurant (Bowral) 257
The Chairman and Yip (Canberra) 200
Cobblestone Lane (Bathurst) 285
Courgette (Canberra) 200
Crackenback Cottage (Crackenback) 201
Darley's (Katoomba) 188

Echoes (Katoomba) 189
Eltons Brasserie (Mudgee) 286
Esca Bimbadgen (Pokolbin) 218
Eschalot (Berrima) 257
Esco Pazzo (Mittagong) 258
Flooded Gums (Bonville) 269
Fresca (Bangalow) 270
The Gallery (Katoomba) 189
Georgie's at the Gallery (Grafton) 271
The Ginger Room (Canberra) 202
Grazing (Gundaroo) 185, 203
Katers (Sutton Forest) 259
La Table (Mullumbimby) 185, 271
Lochiel House (Kurrajong Heights) 190
Loli Redini (Orange) 287
Majors Lane (Lovedale) 219
Margan (Broke) 220
Mezzalira (Canberra) 203
Muse (Pokolbin) 221
The Old George & Dragon (East Maitland) 221
onred (Red Hill) 204
Ottoman Cuisine (Barton) 204
Pacific Dining Room (Byron Bay) 274
The Point (Ballina) 276
Post Cafe and Bar (Moss Vale) 260
The Posthouse (Berry) 249
Red Olive (Mittagong) 261
The Restaurant at The Byron at Byron (Byron Bay) 276
Restaurant II (Newcastle) 236
Rooerts (Pokolbin) 223
Samuels (Thirroul) 250
Satiate (Bangalow) 278
Seagrass Brasserie (Huskisson) 251
Selkirks (Orange) 290
Sister's Rock (Orange) 291
Smokehouse Cafe (Hall) 208
sourcedining (Albury) 291
Stones (Sutton Forest) 261
Union Bank Wine Bar/Wine Store (Orange) 292
Vida (Bowral) 262
The Vineyard Kitchen (Ulladulla) 251
Willow Vale Mill (Laggan) 262
The Wine House and Kitchen (Pokolbin) 227
Wineglass Bar & Grill (Mudgee) 293
Zest (Nelson Bay) 239

Vegetarian

City
Abhi's (North Strathfield) 2
Aki's (Woolloomooloo) 3
Alio (Redfern) 3
Almond Bar (Darlinghurst) 4
Altitude (The Rocks) 4
Amici (Cammeray) 7
Arun Thai (Potts Point) 9
Azuma (Sydney) 11

good food guide 319

index

Bai Yok (Castlecrag) 12
Banana Blossom (Cremorne) 13
The Bathers' Pavilion Restaurant (Balmoral) 14
Bayleaf Brasserie (Crows Nest) 15
Becasse (Sydney) 16, 184
Bentley Restaurant & Bar (Surry Hills) 17
Beppi's (East Sydney) 18
Berowra Waters Inn (Berowra Waters) 19
Billy Kwong (Surry Hills) 20, 184
Bodega (Surry Hills) 29
Brown Sugar (Bondi) 31
Buon Ricordo (Paddington) 31
buzo trattoria (Woollahra) 33
Cafe Sydney (Circular Quay) 34
Catalonia (Kirribilli) 35
Chequers (Chatswood) 36
Coast (Sydney) 40
Cottage Point Inn (Cottage Point) 41
Courtney's Brasserie (Parramatta) 42
da Gianni trattoria (Annandale) 42
Efendy (Balmain) 44
Emma's On Liberty (Enmore) 46
est. (Sydney) 47
Flavour of India (Edgecliff) 51
Flavours of Peking (Castlecrag) 52
Flying Fish (Pyrmont) 55
Fook Yuen (Chatswood) 55
Forty One (Sydney) 56
Foveaux Restaurant + Bar (Surry Hills) 57
fu manchu (Darlinghurst) 58
Garfish (Manly, Kirribilli, Crows Nest) 59
Golden Century (Sydney) 61
Grappa (Leichhardt) 62
Green Gourmet (St Leonards, Newtown) 62
harbourkitchen&bar (The Rocks) 63
Hotel Saravana Bhavan (Croydon) 64
il piave (Rozelle) 66
Il Punto (Liverpool) 67
Iron Chef (Cabramatta) 68, 182
Japaz (Neutral Bay) 71
Ju-Rin (Crows Nest) 73
Kable's (Sydney) 74
Kam Fook (Bondi Junction, Chatswood) 74
Kensington Peking (Kensington) 75
Kuali (Lane Cove) 76
Le Bukhara (Double Bay) 79
Libertine (Kings Cross) 81
Longrain (Surry Hills) 82
Machiavelli (Sydney) 83
Mahjong Room (Surry Hills) 87
Malabar (Darlinghurst, Crows Nest) 88

The Malaya (Sydney) 88
Manta (Woolloomooloo) 89
Marigold (Sydney) 89
Medusa Greek Taverna (Sydney) 91
Mission (Chippendale) 93
Mumu Grill (Crows Nest) 94
Neptune Palace (Circular Quay) 95
Nilgiri's (St Leonards) 96
Nostos (Leichhardt) 97
Nu's (McMahons Point) 98
Oliveto (Rhodes) 99
Oscillate Wildly (Newtown) 100
Osvaldo Polletti (Leichhardt) 103
Otto Ristorante (Woolloomooloo) 103
Ottoman Cuisine (Walsh Bay) 104
Palace Chinese (Sydney) 104, 183
Pendolino (Sydney) 105
Pier (Rose Bay) 106
Pizza e Birra (Surry Hills) 107
Pony Lounge & Dining (The Rocks) 108
Qmin (St Leonards) 110
Rambutan (Darlinghurst) 111
Red Chilli (Haymarket) 112
Red Lantern (Surry Hills) 112, 184
Restaurant Arras (Walsh Bay) 114
Safi (North Sydney) 121
Sahra by the River (Parramatta) 122
Sakana-Ya (Crows Nest) 124
Sea Treasure (Crows Nest) 125, 183
Sean's Panaroma (Bondi Beach) 126, 185
Sevardi Cucina Italiana (Beecroft) 127
Spice Temple (Sydney) 129
Steel Bar and Grill (Sydney) 130
Strangers with Candy (East Redfern) 130
Szechuan Garden (St Leonards) 135
The Tea Room Gunners' Barracks (Georges Heights) 138
The Tea Room QVB (Sydney) 138
The Terrace On Pittwater (Newport) 140
Thanh Binh (Cabramatta) 141
Toko Surry Hills (Surry Hills) 142
Ventuno (Millers Point) 147
Verde Restaurant & Bar (Darlinghurst) 148
Vini (Surry Hills) 148
Waqu (Crows Nest) 149
Yellow Bistro & Food Store (Potts Point) 151
Ying's (Crows Nest) 153
Yoshii (Sydney) 153, 181
Zaaffran (Darling Harbour) 154
Zilver (Haymarket) 154

Regional
Amanda's on the Edge (Pokolbin) 215
Anise (Canberra) 198
Artespresso (Kingston) 198
Ashcrofts (Blackheath) 188
Bamboo (Casuarina Beach) 265
Ça Marche (Port Macquarie) 266
Canter (Scone) 217
Centennial Vineyards Restaurant (Bowral) 257
Darley's (Katoomba) 188
Esca Bimbadgen (Pokolbin) 218
Eschalot (Berrima) 257
Fekerte's (Dickson) 202
Frangipan (Angourie) 269
Fresca (Bangalow) 270
Georgie's at the Gallery (Grafton) 271
Grazing (Gundaroo) 185, 203
Green Papaya (Armidale) 286
Josh's Cafe (Berrima) 258
Mezzalira (Canberra) 203
Michael's Ristorante (Wollongong) 248
Mojo's on Wilderness (Rothbury) 220
Muse (Pokolbin) 221
Ocean Chill (Nambucca Heads) 272
onred (Red Hill) 204
Orient Express Eatery (Byron Bay) 274
Ottoman Cuisine (Barton) 204
Pacific Dining Room (Byron Bay) 274
Post Cafe and Bar (Moss Vale) 260
Racine at La Colline (Orange) 289
Rajarani (Mudgee) 289
Red Olive (Mittagong) 261
Restaurant Como (Blaxland) 191
Rock (Pokolbin) 223
Rose Garden Thai (Dubbo) 290
Rubicon (Griffith) 205
Ruby Chinese (Dickson) 206
Saltwater (Emerald Beach) 277
Satiate (Bangalow) 278
Seagrass Brasserie (Huskisson) 251
Silo Restaurant & Lounge (Newcastle) 237
Smokehouse Cafe (Hall) 208
The Chairman and Yip (Canberra) 200
The Ginger Room (Canberra) 202
The Posthouse (Berry) 249
The Verandah (Pokolbin) 224
Vida (Bowral) 262
Zanzibar (Merimbula) 251

Wheelchair Access
City
Abhi's (North Strathfield) 2
Alio (Redfern) 3

Altitude (The Rocks) 4
Amici (Cammeray) 7
Aperitif (Potts Point) 8
Aqua Dining (Milsons Point) 8
Aria (East Circular Quay) 9
Ash St Cellar (Sydney) 10, 156
Astral (Pyrmont) 11
Azuma Kushiyaki (Sydney) 12
Bai Yok (Castlecrag) 12
Bambini Trust Cafe (Sydney) 13, 176
Bathers' Pavilion RestaurantThe (Balmoral) 14
Bayleaf Brasserie (Crows Nest) 15
bel mondo (The Rocks) 16
Beresford HotelThe (Darlinghurst) 18
Bilson's (Sydney) 20
Bin24 Wine Bar & Wood Fire Eatery (North Strathfield) 23
Bird Cow Fish (Surry Hills) 23
Bistro CBD (Sydney) 24
Bistro Moncur (Woollahra) 25
Bistro Ortolan (Leichhardt) 25
Bistro-Fax (Sydney) 24
Blackwater (Sans Souci) 26
Blancharu (Elizabeth Bay) 27
Blancmange (Petersham) 27
The Boathouse on Blackwattle Bay (Glebe) 28
Bodega (Surry Hills) 29
The Book Kitchen (Surry Hills) 29
Botanic Gardens Restaurant (Sydney) 30
Brown Sugar (Bondi) 31
Busshari (Potts Point) 32
Cafe Sydney (Circular Quay) 34
Catalonia (Kirribilli) 35
Centennial Parklands Restaurant (Centennial Park) 35
Chequers (Chatswood) 36
Chinta Ria ... Temple of Love (Sydney) 36
Coast (Sydney) 40
Dome (Sydney) 43
Dukes Lane (East Balmain) 44
est. (Sydney) 47
Etch (Sydney) 47
Eurolounge (Castle Hill) 48
Fare Nosh (Summer Hill) 48
finefish (Neutral Bay) 49
Fiorenzoni (Chatswood) 50
Flying Fish (Pyrmont) 55
Forty One (Sydney) 56
Foveaux Restaurant + Bar (Surry Hills) 57
Fratelli Paradiso (Potts Point) 57
Galileo (Sydney) 58
Garfish (Manly, Kirribilli, Crows Nest) 59
Glass Brasserie (Sydney) 60
Glebe Point Diner (Glebe) 60
Golden Sichuan (Sydney) 61

320 good food guide

index

Grappa (Leichhardt) 62
Guillaume at Bennelong (Sydney) 63
harbourkitchen&bar (The Rocks) 63
Hotel Saravana Bhavan (Croydon) 64
Hugo's Bar Pizza (Kings Cross) 64
Hugo's Manly (Manly) 65
Icebergs Dining Room and Bar (Bondi Beach) 65
Infusion @ 333 (Sydney) 67
Intermezzo Ristorante (Sydney) 68
Iron Chef (Cabramatta) 68, 182
Jonah's (Whale Beach) 72, 177
Jugemu & Shimbashi (Neutral Bay) 73 180
Kable's (Sydney) 74
Kam Fook (Bondi Junction, Chatswood) 74
Kazbah on Darling (Balmain) 75, 177
Kensingtor Peking (Kensington) 75
La Grande Bouffe (Rozelle) 77
La Perla (Gladesville) 78
La Tratt (Fairfield) 79
Longrain (Surry Hills) 82
Lotus (Potts Point) 82
Mad Cow (Sydney) 84
Maitre Karl (Willoughby) 87
Malabar (Darlinghurst, Crows Nest) 88
The Malaya (Sydney) 88
Marque (Surry Hills) 90
Medusa Greek Taverna (Sydney) 91
Mission (Chippendale) 93
Moncur Terrace (Woollahra) 93
MoS Cafe (MoS Cafe) 94
North Bondi Italian Food (North Bondi) 96
Number One Wine Bar (Sydney) 97
Ocean Room (The Rocks) 98
Oceanic Thai (Clovelly) 99
Oliveto (Rhodes) 99
Ottoman Cuisine (Walsh Bay) 104
Palace Chinese (Sydney) 104, 183
Pizza e Birra (Surry Hills) 107
Pomegranate Thai (Balmain) 107
Pony Lounge & Dining (The Rocks) 103
Postales Restaurante & Tapas Bar (Sydney) 109
Prime (Sydney) 109
Qmin (St Leonards) 110
Quay (The Rocks) 110
Ratu Sari (Kingsford) 111
Republic Dining (Sydney) 113
The Restaurant @ Art Gallery of NSW (Sydney) 114
Restaurant Arras (Walsh Bay) 114

The Restaurant at 3 Weeds (Rozelle) 115
Restaurant Atelier (Glebe) 115
Restaurant Balzac (Randwick) 116
Rocket (Chatswood) 119
Rockpool (The Rocks) 120
Rockpool Bar and Grill (Sydney) 120, 179
Sahra by the River (Parramatta) 122
Sails on Lavender Bay (McMahons Point) 123
Sanders Waterfront (Cabarita) 124
Sea Treasure (Crows Nest) 125, 183
Sean's Kitchen (Pyrmont) 125
Sepia (Sydney) 127
Sevardi Cucina Italiana (Beecroft) 127
Silvas (Petersham) 128
Spice Temple (Sydney) 129
Steel Bar and Grill (Sydney) 130
Sugaroom (Pyrmont) 132
Summit (Sydney) 132
sushi e (Sydney) 135
Szechuan Garden (St Leonards) 135
Taste on Sussex Lane (Sydney) 137
The Tea Room Gunners' Barracks (Georges Heights) 138
Tea Room QVBThe (Sydney) 138
Temasek (Parramatta) 139
Teppanyaki (Sydney) 139
The Terrace On Pittwater (Newport) 140
Tilbury Hotel (Woolloomooloo) 141
Toko Surry Hills (Surry Hills) 142
Tran's (Mosman) 143
Uccello (Sydney) 143
Universal (Darlinghurst) 146
Ventuno (Millers Point) 147
Verandah (Sydney) 147
Verde Restaurant & Bar (Darlinghurst) 148
Vini (Surry Hills) 148
The Wharf (Walsh Bay) 150
Yellow Bistro & Food Store (Potts Point) 151
Ying's (Crows Nest) 153
Zaaffran (Darling Harbour) 154

Regional
305 Restaurant & Cafe (Maitland) 214
55 on Collins (Kiama) 242
9inety 2wo (Bathurst) 284
Acquazul (Newcastle) 230
Alto (Acton) 197
Amanda's on the Edge (Pokolbin) 215
Anise (Canberra) 198
Aubergine (Griffith) 199

Bacchus (Newcastle) 231
Bamboo (Casuarina Beach) 265
Bellachara (Gerringong) 244
Bells at Killcare (Killcare Heights) 231
Berry Woodfired Sourdough Bakery (Berry) 244
Bistro Molines (Mount View) 216
Bistro Tartine (Hamilton) 232
Byron Beach Cafe (Byron Bay) 266
Ça Marche (Port Macquarie) 266
Cafe Beltree (Pokolbin) 216
Canter (Scone) 217
Cape Cod (Deakin) 199
The Cellar (Pokolbin) 217
Centennial Vineyards Restaurant (Bowral) 257
The Chairman and Yip (Canberra) 200
Clock (Griffith) 285
Cobblestone Lane (Bathurst) 285
Dish (Byron Bay) 267
Eltons Brasserie (Mudgee) 286
Esca Bimbadgen (Pokolbin) 218
Esco Pazzo (Mittagong) 258
fatbellykat (Brunswick Heads) 267
Fekerte's (Dickson) 202
Fiasco Ristorante (Coffs Harbour) 268
Fins (South Kingscliff) 268
Firestick Cafe (Pokolbin) 218
Flooded Gums (Bonville) 269
Fresca (Bangalow) 270
The Gallery (Katoomba) 189
Georgie's at the Gallery (Grafton) 271
The Ginger Room (Canberra) 202
Grazing (Gundaroo) 185, 203
The Gunyah (Woollamia) 246
Hobarts (New Lambton) 233
Hungry Duck (Berry) 185, 247
Hyams Beach Cafe (Hyams Beach) 247
Journeyman (Bowral) 259
Katers (Sutton Forest) 259
Leaves & Fishes (Lovedale) 219
Lolli Redini (Orange) 287
Majors Lane (Lovedale) 219
Margan (Broke) 220
Mezzalira (Canberra) 203
Mojo's on Wilderness (Rothbury) 220
The Monastery Brasserie (Wagga Wagga) 287
Muse (Pokolbin) 221
Neila (Cowra) 185, 288
No. 2 Oak Street (Bellingen) 272
Ocean (The Entrance) 234
Onda (Terrigal) 234
O-pes (Lennox Head) 273
Orient Express Eatery (Byron Bay) 274
Ottoman Cuisine (Barton) 204

Pippi's Cafe & Bar (Yamba) 275
Podfood (Pialligo) 205
The Point (Ballina) 276
Racine at La Colline (Orange) 289
Rajarani (Mudgee) 289
Red Olive (Mittagong) 261
Reef (Terrigal) 235
The Restaurant at The Byron at Byron (Byron Bay) 276
Restaurant Botanica (Pokolbin) 222
Restaurant Cuvee (Pokolbin) 222
Restaurant Two Forty Boomerang Beach) 277
Ritual (Nelson Bay) 236
The River Moruya (Moruya) 250
Roberts (Pokolbin) 223
Rock (Pokolbin) 223
rocksalt (Wickham) 237
Sabayon (Canberra) 206
Sage (Braddon) 207
Saltwater (Emerald Beach) 277
Seagrass Brasserie (Huskisson) 251
Selkirks (Orange) 290
Silo Bakery & Cheeseroom (Kingston) 207
Silo Restaurant & Lounge (Newcastle) 237
Sister's Rock (Orange) 291
Smokehouse Cafe (Hall) 208
sourcedining (Albury) 291
Stillwaters (Davistown) 238
The Stunned Mullet (Port Macquarie) 278
Terrace (Thredbo Village) 208
Tonic (Millthorpe) 292
The Vineyard Kitchen (Ulladulla) 251
Waters Edge (Parkes) 209
The Wine House and Kitchen (Pokolbin) 227
Wineglass Bar & Grill (Mudgee) 293
Yum Yum Eatery (Hardys Bay) 238
Zanzibar (Merimbula) 251

good food guide 321

The best luxury escapes

Featuring independent reviews of the country's best short-holiday destinations, *Good Weekends Away* has something for everyone and every budget.

This book will take the hassle out of planning for that long weekend and will help you make the most of your downtime.

Each review lists the features of the property and describes the sights and amenities in the surrounding area.

Available from all good bookstores or buy direct from the *Herald* RRP $29.95

To order direct go to smhshop.com.au or call 1300 656 052

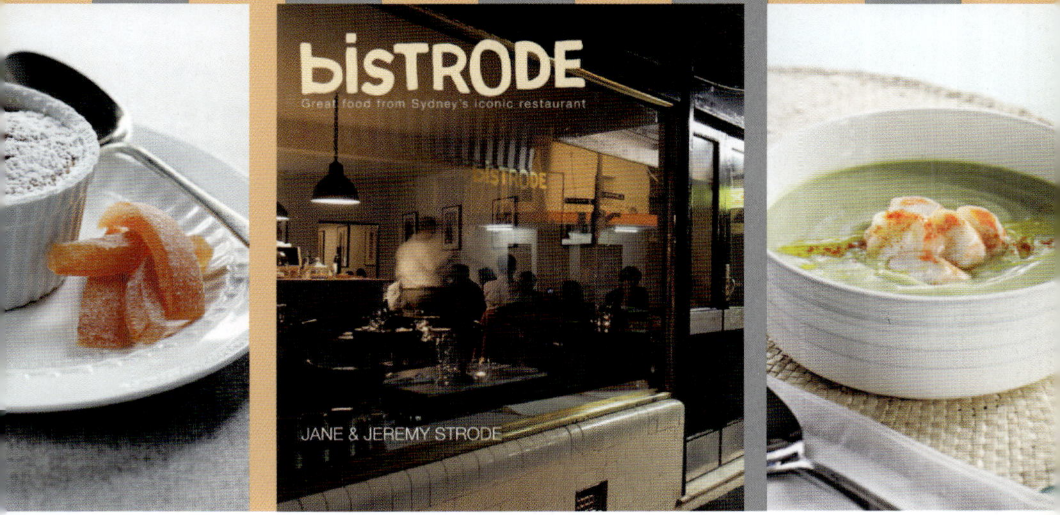

Create your own restaurant experience at home

The book includes diverse recipes that have appeared on menus throughout the many seasons of Jane and Jeremy Strode's international restaurant careers and, more recently, in Bistrode and the pages of Good Living.

Available from all good bookstores or buy direct from the *Herald* RRP $34.95.

To order direct go to smhshop.com.au or call 1300 656 059.

maps

• main reviews   □ other recommendations

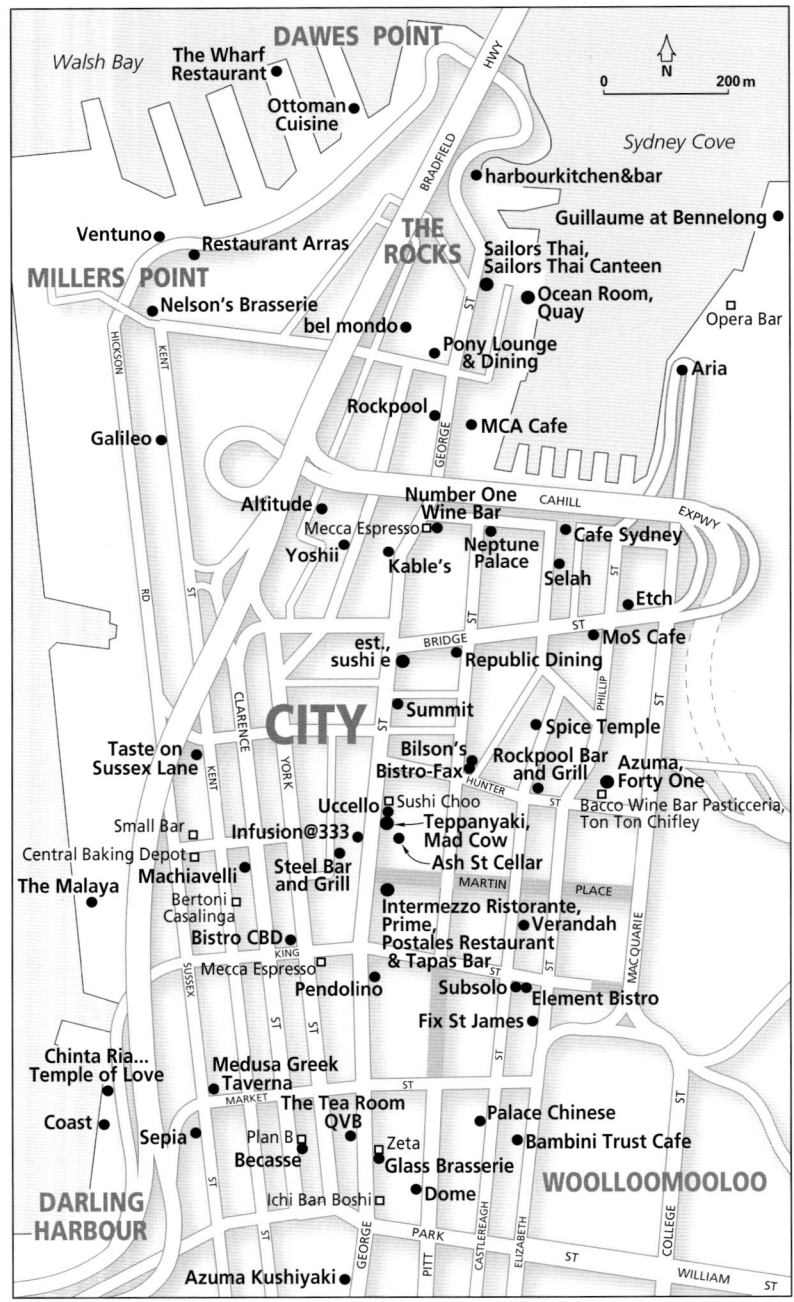

1 CENTRAL SYDNEY

maps

• main reviews   ▫ other recommendations

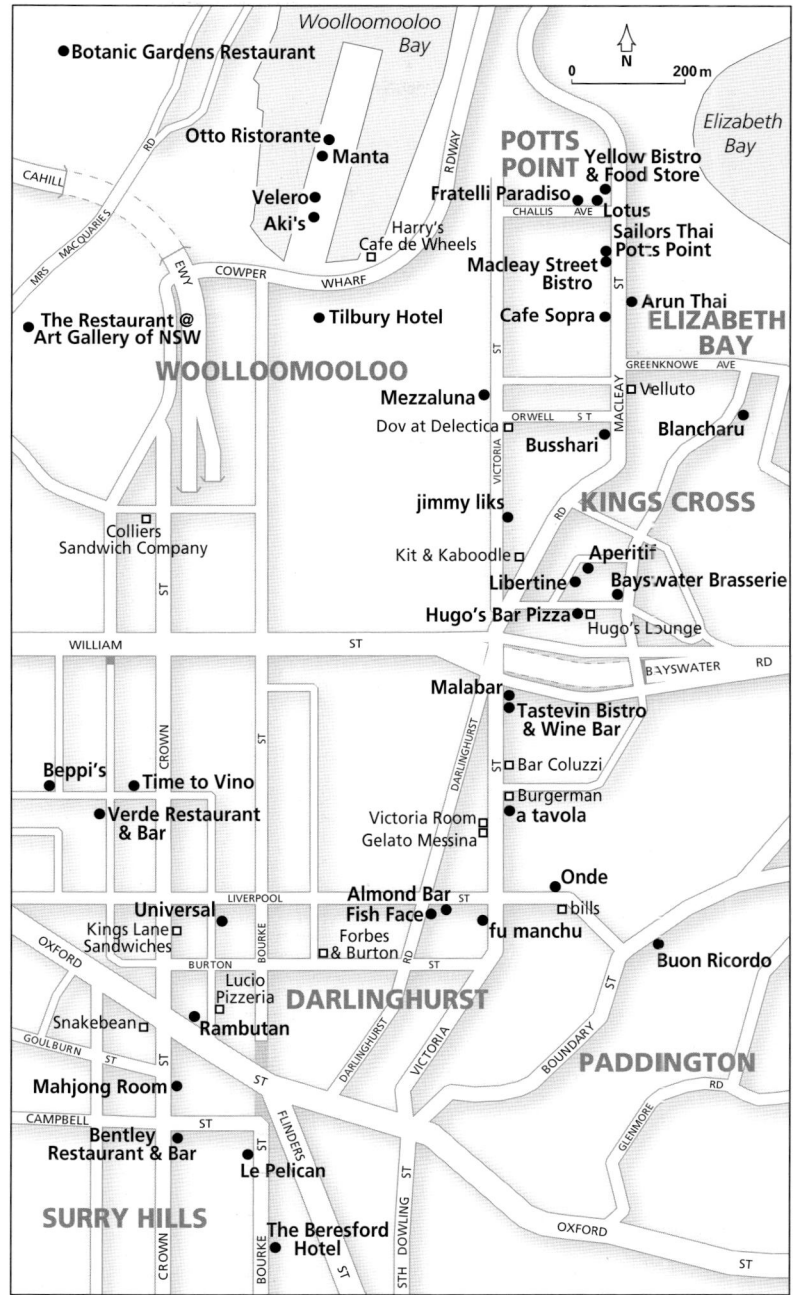

maps

- main reviews   □ other recommendations

3a

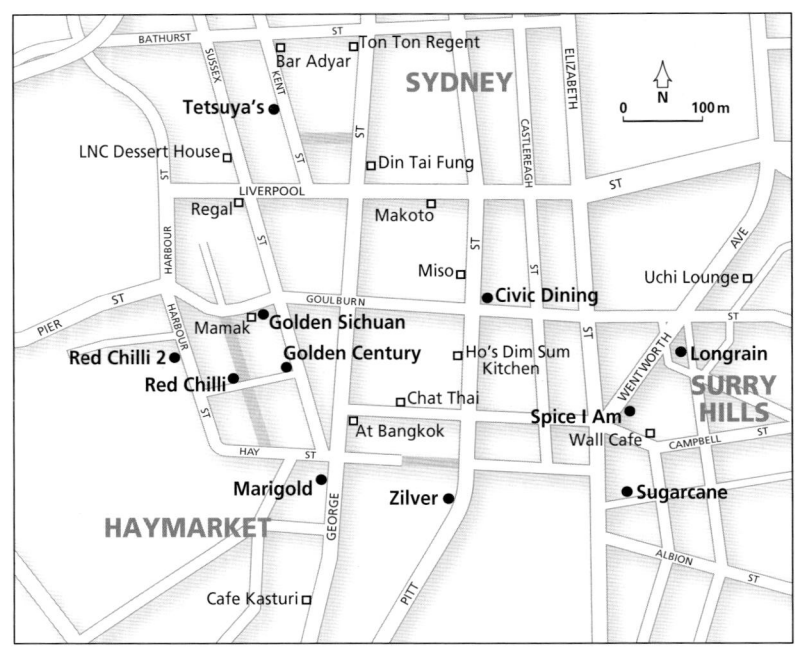

3b

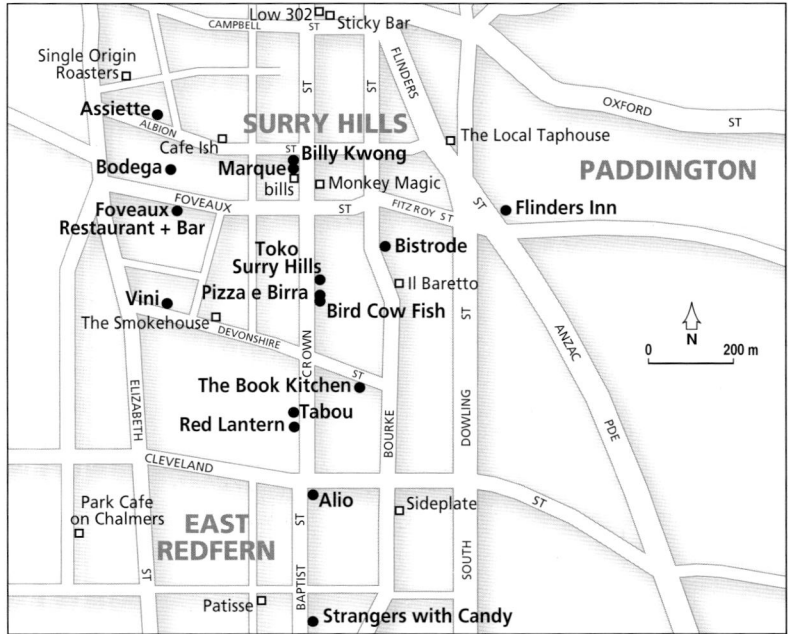

maps

• main reviews   □ other recommendations

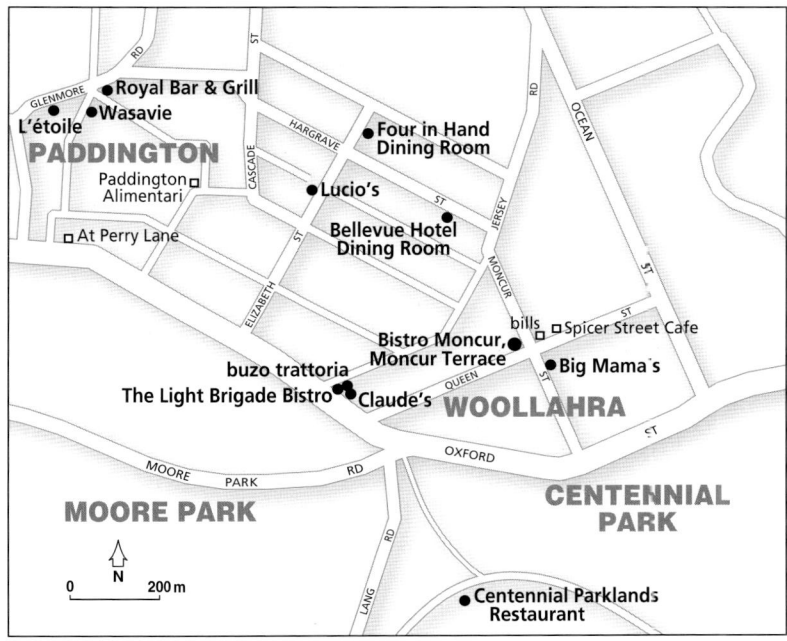

4a WOOLLAHRA

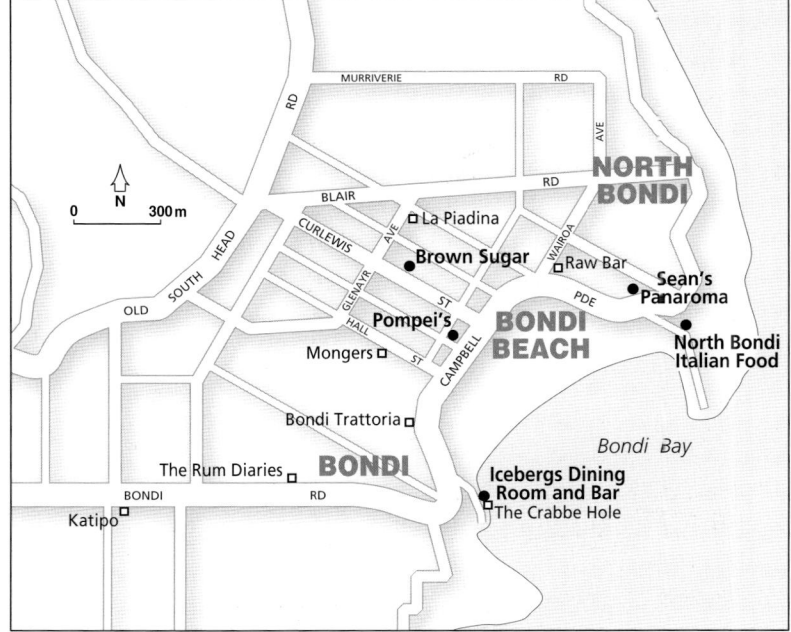

4b BONDI

maps

- main reviews   □ other recommendations

5a ST LEONARDS TO MILSONS POINT

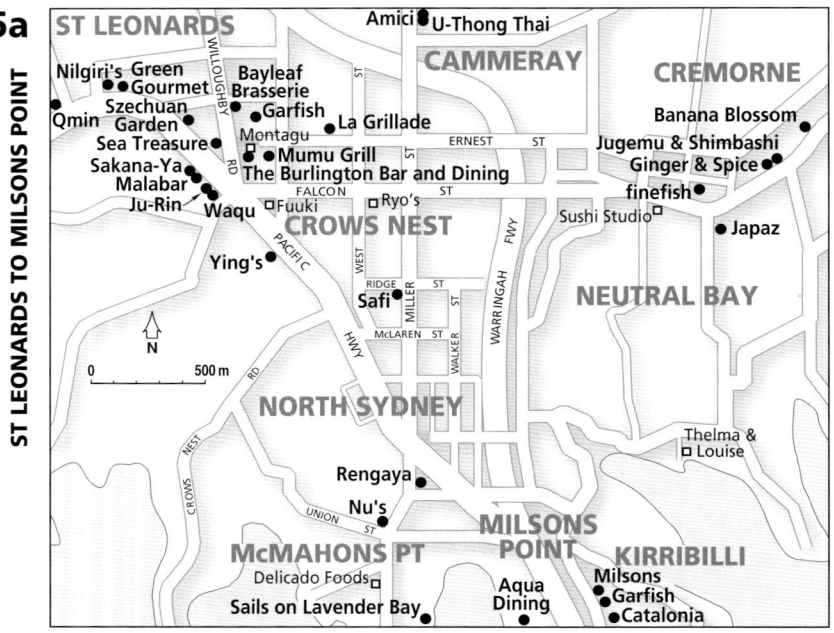

5b DRUMMOYNE TO GLEBE

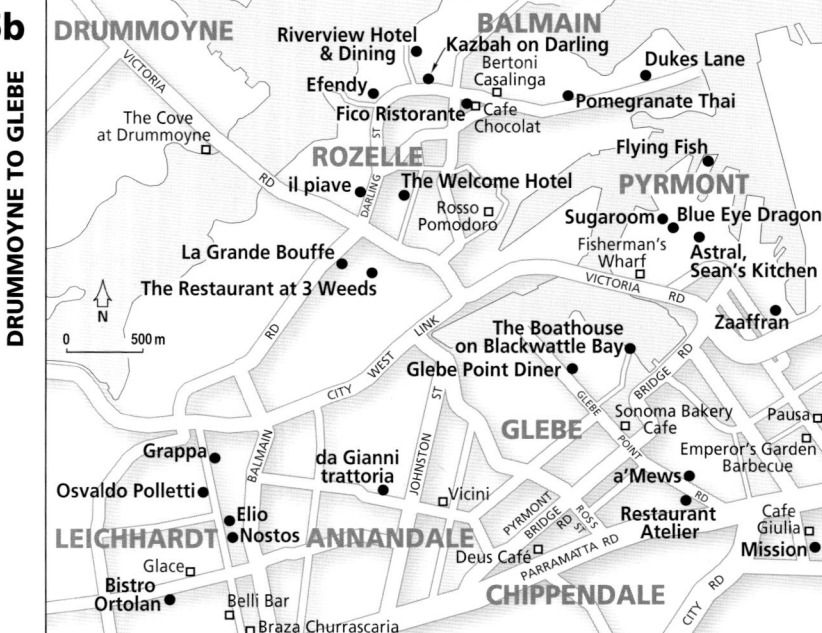

maps

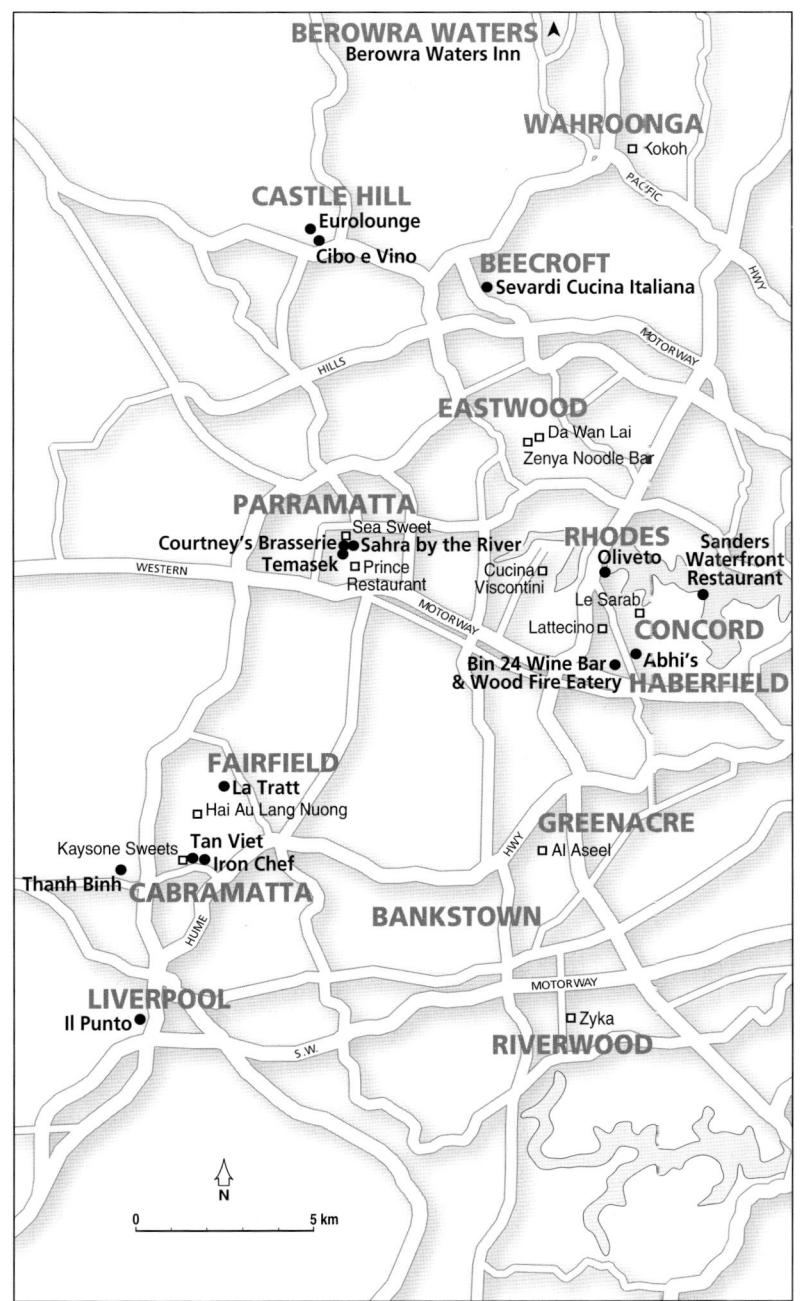

maps

- main reviews   □ other recommendations

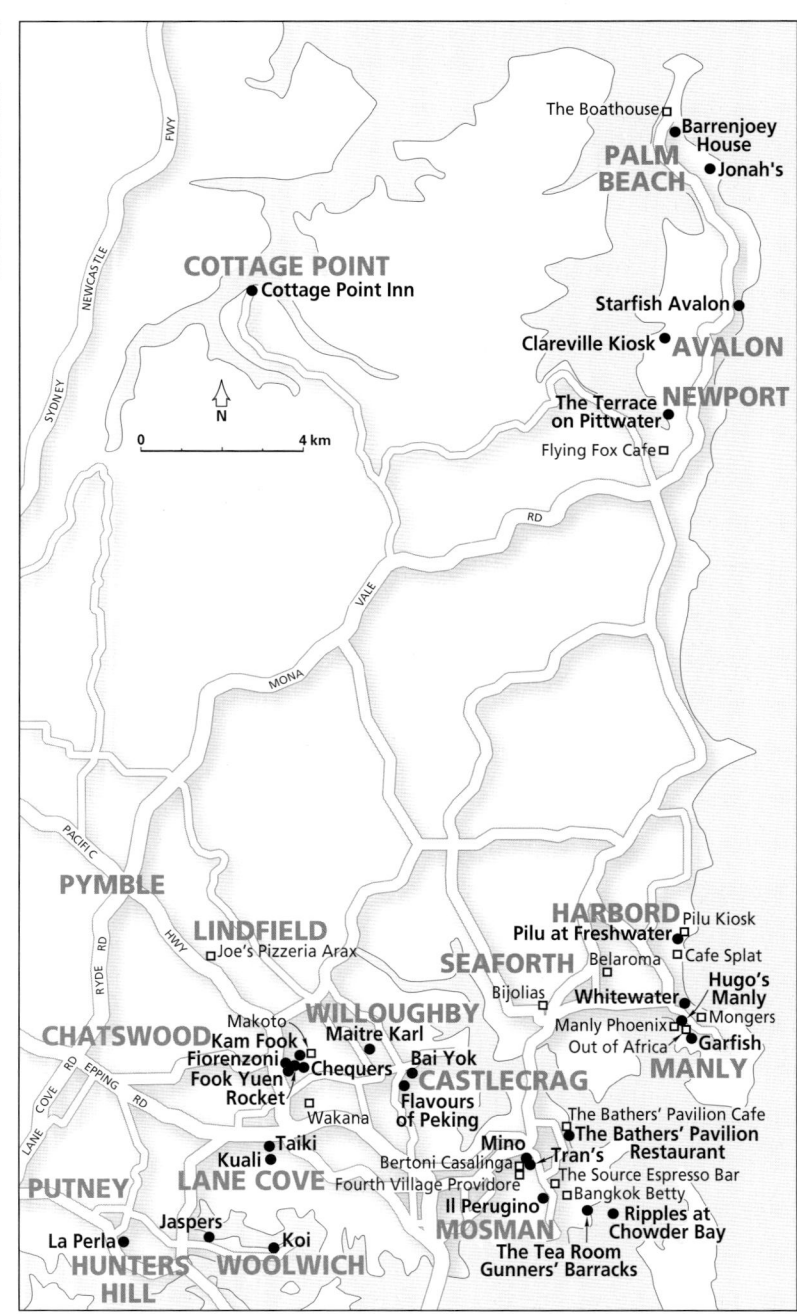

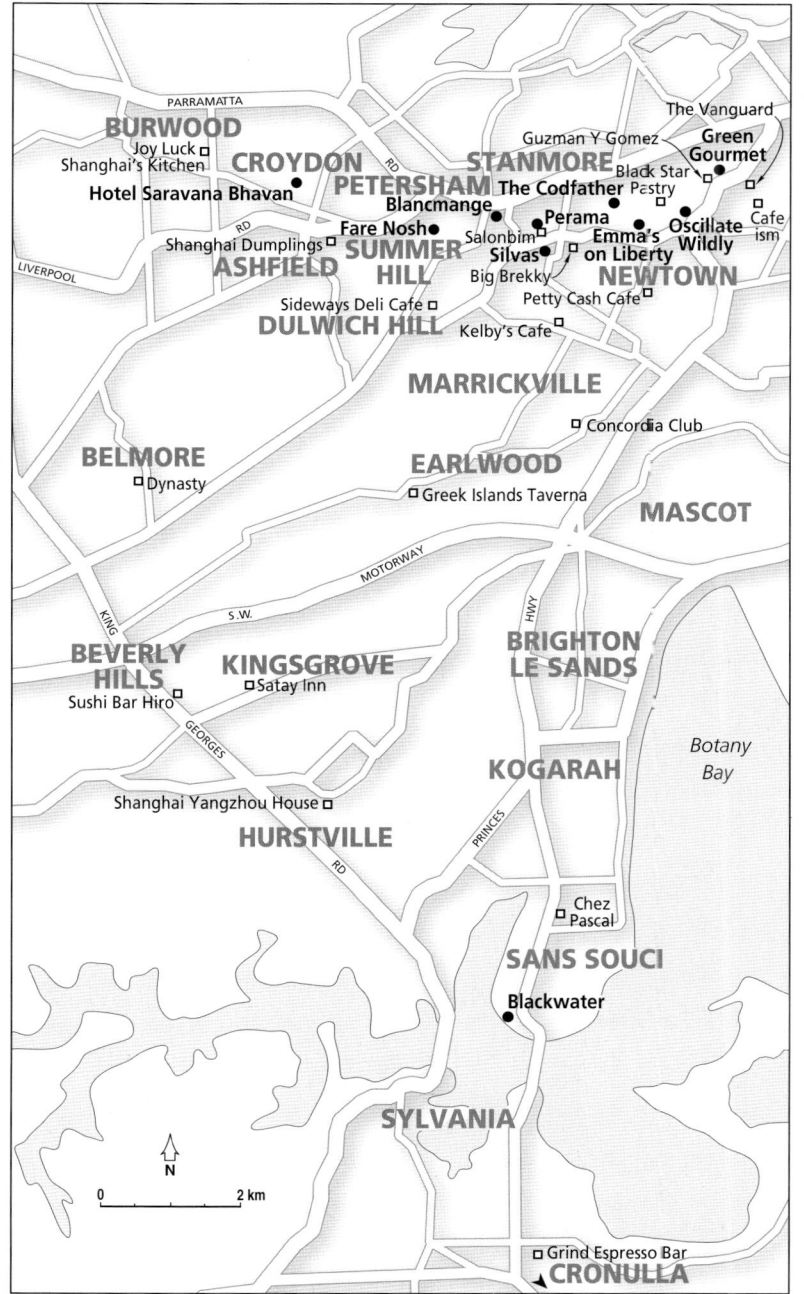

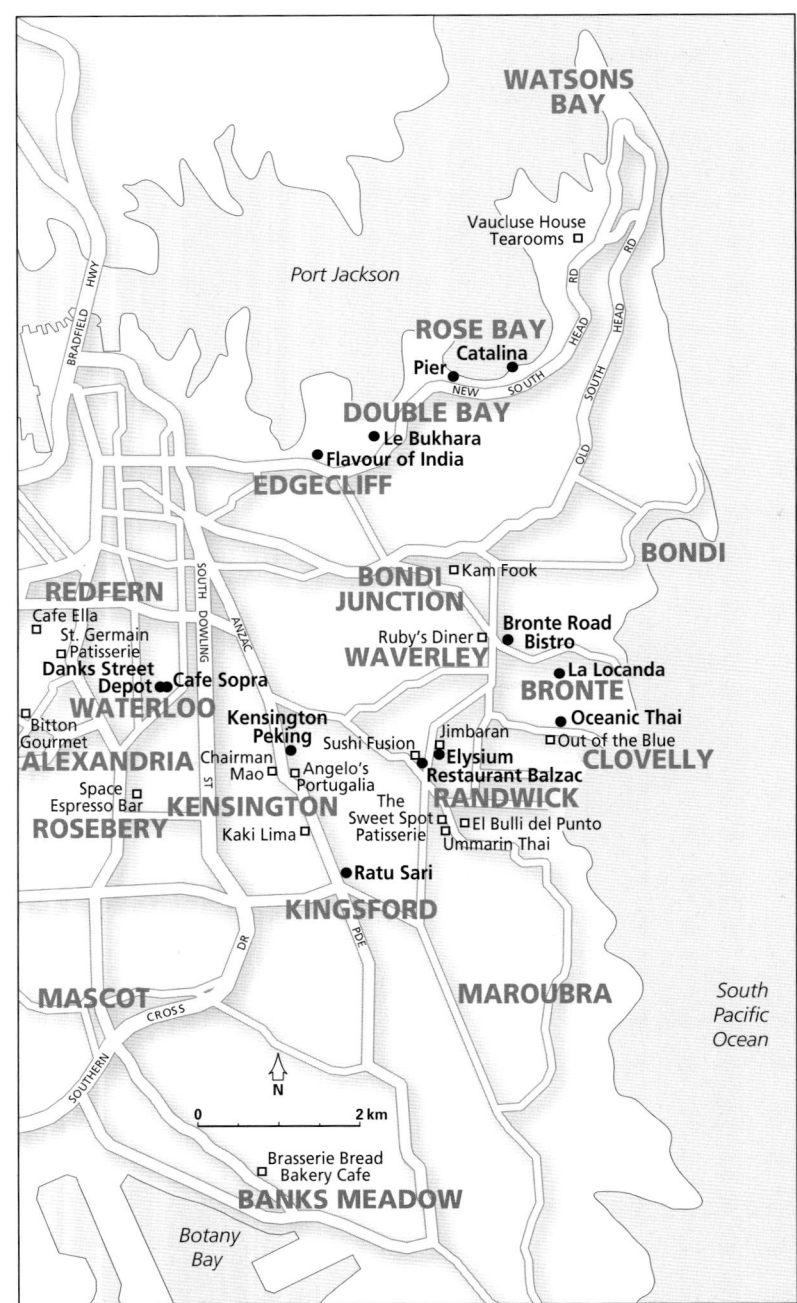

maps

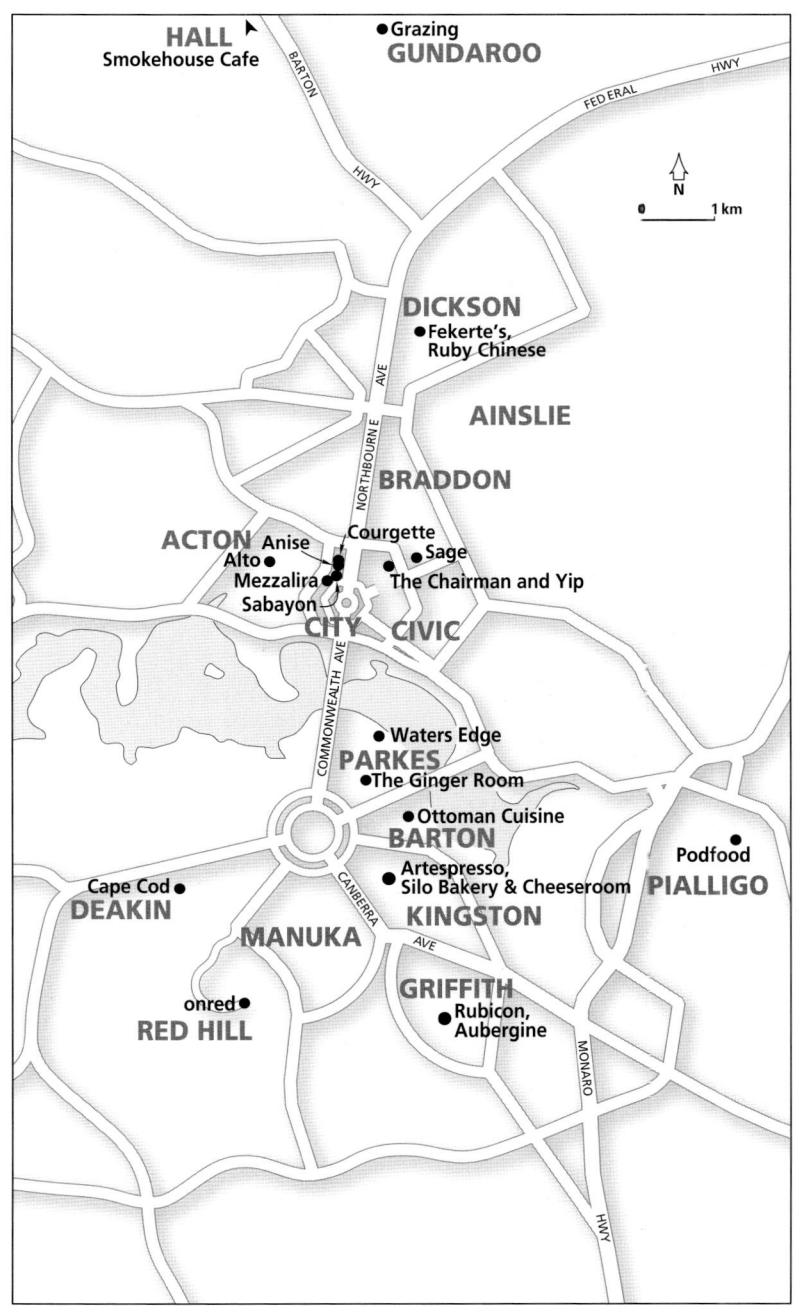

10 CANBERRA

- main reviews
- □ other recommendations

maps

- main reviews   □ other recommendations

11 SOUTHERN HIGHLANDS & BLUE MOUNTAINS

BLACKHEATH
Ashcrofts, Glenella, Rajarani, Vulcans

LEURA
Solitary
Silk's Brasserie

BLAXLAND
Restaurant Como

KATOOMBA
Arjuna, Darley's, Echoes, The Gallery

BLUE MOUNTAINS

SYDNEY

THIRROUL
Bistro 345, Samuels

MITTAGONG
Esco Pazzo, Red Olive

WOLLONGONG
Caveau, Lorenzo's Diner, Michael's Ristorante

BERRIMA
The Black Swan, Eschalot, Josh's Cafe

BOWRAL
Centennial Vineyards, Hordern's, Journeyman, Onesta Cucina, Vida

SUTTON FOREST
Katers, Stones

SHELLHARBOUR
Relish on Addison

KIAMA
55 on Collins

MOSS VALE
Post Café and Bar

GERRINGONG
Bellachara

BERRY
Berry Woodfired Sourdough Bakery, Hungry Duck, The Posthouse

SOUTHERN HIGHLANDS

HUSKISSON
The Gunyah, Seagrass Brasserie

HYAMS BEACH
Hyams Beach Cafe

0 — 20 km

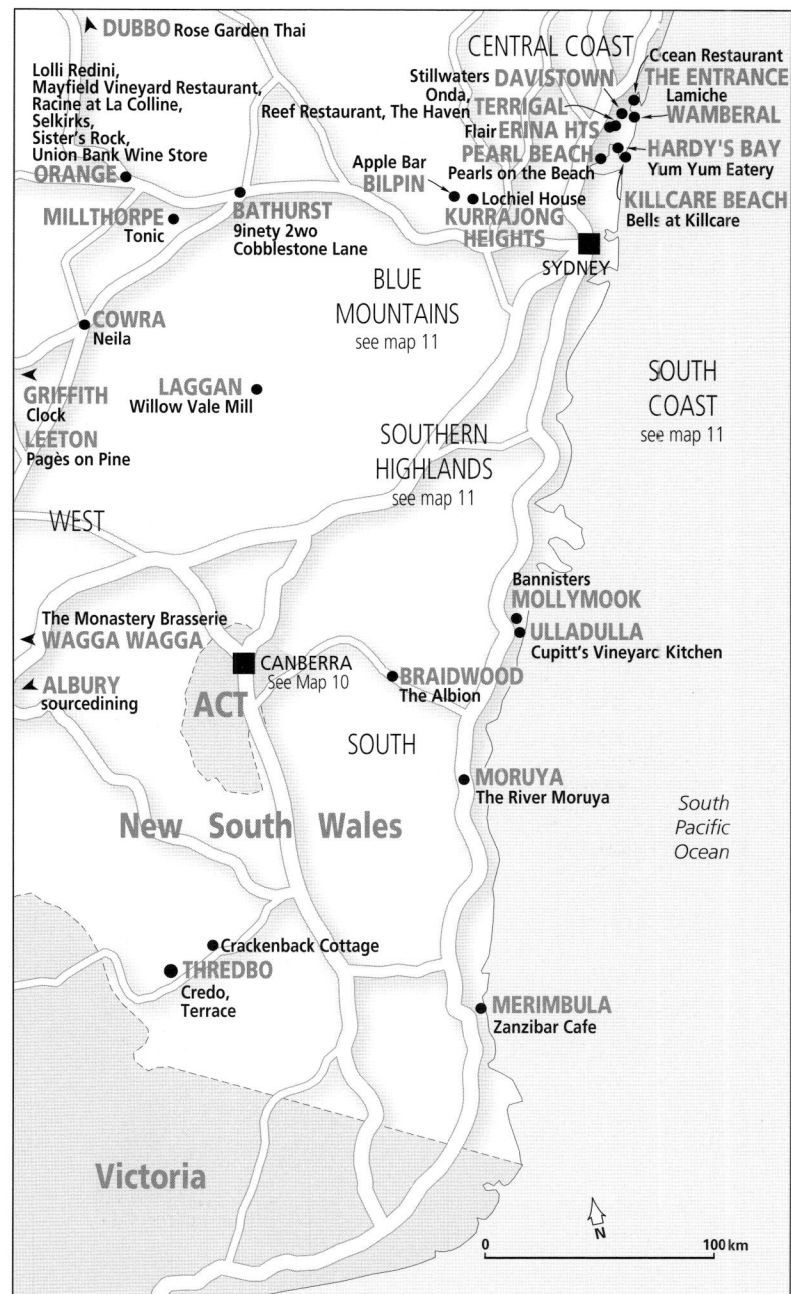

maps

- main reviews
- other recommendations

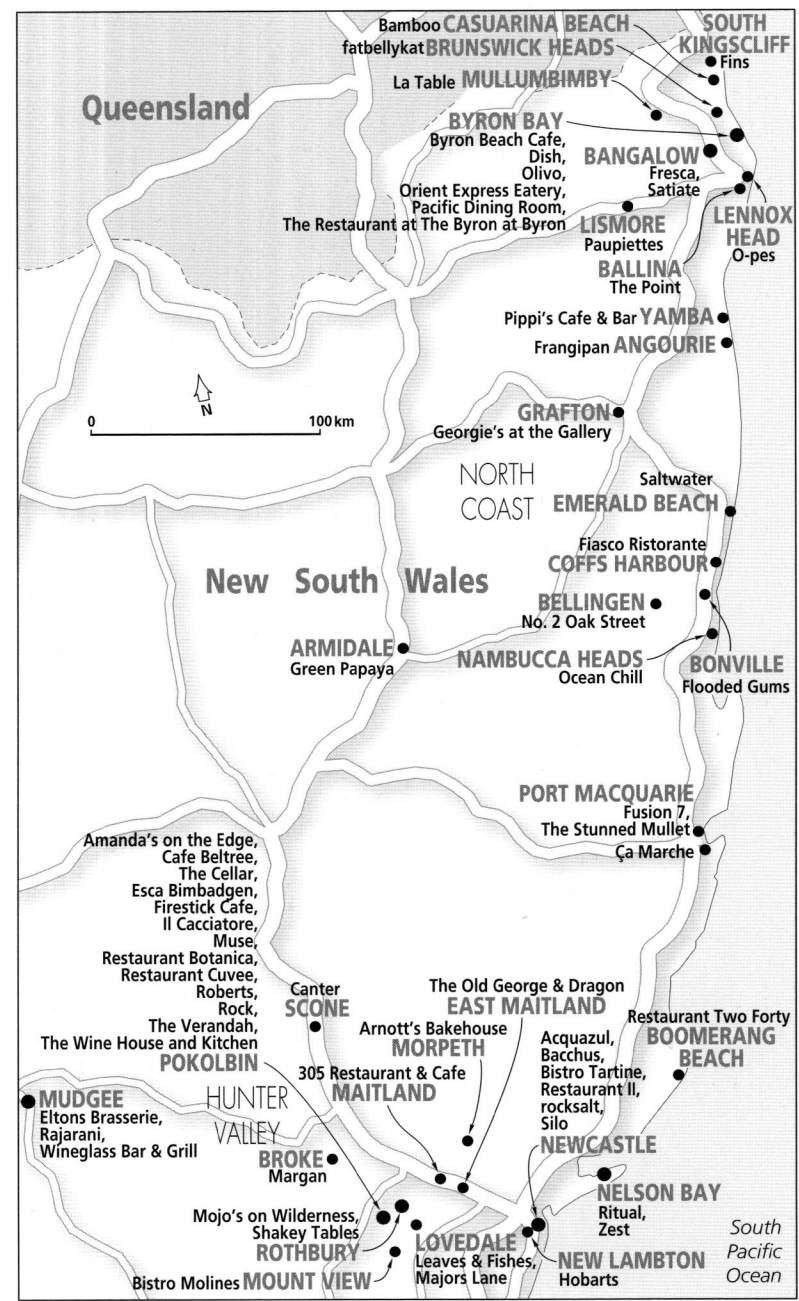

13 NORTHERN NSW COUNTRY & COAST